OFFICIAL
(ISC)² GUIDE TO THE
CISSP® EXAM

OTHER AUERBACH PUBLICATIONS

The ABCs of IP Addressing
Gilbert Held
ISBN: 0-8493-1144-6

The ABCs of LDAP: How to Install, Run, and Administer LDAP Services
Reinhard Voglmaier
ISBN: 0-8493-1346-5

The ABCs of TCP/IP
Gilbert Held
ISBN: 0-8493-1463-1

Building an Information Security Awareness Program
Mark B. Desman
ISBN: 0-8493-0116-5

Building a Wireless Office
Gilbert Held
ISBN: 0-8493-1271-X

The Complete Book of Middleware
Judith Myerson
ISBN: 0-8493-1272-8

Computer Telephony Integration, 2nd Edition
William A. Yarberry, Jr.
ISBN: 0-8493-1438-0

Electronic Bill Presentment and Payment
Kornel Terplan
ISBN: 0-8493-1452-6

Information Security Architecture
Jan Killmeyer Tudor
ISBN: 0-8493-9988-2

Information Security Management Handbook, 4th Edition, Volume 1
Harold F. Tipton and Micki Krause, Editors
ISBN: 0-8493-9829-0

Information Security Management Handbook, 4th Edition, Volume 2
Harold F. Tipton and Micki Krause, Editors
ISBN: 0-8493-0800-3

Information Security Management Handbook, 4th Edition, Volume 3
Harold F. Tipton and Micki Krause, Editors
ISBN: 0-8493-1127-6

Information Security Management Handbook, 4th Edition, Volume 4
Harold F. Tipton and Micki Krause, Editors
ISBN: 0-8493-1518-2

Information Security Policies, Procedures, and Standards: Guidelines for Effective Information Security Management
Thomas R. Peltier
ISBN: 0-8493-1137-3

Information Security Risk Analysis
Thomas R. Peltier
ISBN: 0-8493-0880-1

Interpreting the CMMI: A Process Improvement Approach
Margaret Kulpa and Kurt Johnson
ISBN: 0-8493-1654-5

IS Management Handbook, 8th Edition
Carol V. Brown and Heikki Topi
ISBN: 0-8493-1595-6

Managing a Network Vulnerability Assessment
Thomas R. Peltier and Justin Peltier
ISBN: 0-8493-1270-1

A Practical Guide to Security Engineering and Information Assurance
Debra Herrmann
ISBN: 0-8493-1163-2

The Privacy Papers: Managing Technology and Consumers, Employee, and Legislative Action
Rebecca Herold
ISBN: 0-8493-1248-5

Securing and Controlling Cisco Routers
Peter T. Davis
ISBN: 0-8493-1290-6

Six Sigma Software Development
Christine B. Tayntor
ISBN: 0-8493-1193-4

Software Engineering Measurement
John Munson
ISBN: 0-8493-1502-6

A Technical Guide to IPSec Virtual Private Networks
James S. Tiller
ISBN: 0-8493-0876-3

Telecommunications Cost Management
Brian DiMarsico, Thomas Phelps IV, and William A. Yarberry, Jr.
ISBN: 0-8493-1101-2

AUERBACH PUBLICATIONS

www.auerbach-publications.com
To Order Call: 1-800-272-7737 • Fax: 1-800-374-3401
E-mail: orders@crcpress.com

OFFICIAL
(ISC)² GUIDE TO THE
CISSP® EXAM

Susan Hansche, CISSP
John Berti, CISSP
Chris Hare, CISSP

SECURITY TRANSCENDS TECHNOLOGY℠

AUERBACH PUBLICATIONS

A CRC Press Company
Boca Raton   London   New York   Washington, D.C.

Grateful acknowledgment is made to reprint the following from *The Information Security Management Handbook,* Volumes 1–4, Harold F. Tipton and Micki Krause, Eds.; *Data Security Management;* and *Data Communication Management.* Copyright 1999–2003, CRC Press LLC.

Excerpts from Michael H. Agranoff, *Policies for Secure Personal Data*; Jim Appleyard, *Information Classification: A Corporate Implementation Guide*; John Berti and Marcus Rogers, *Social Engineering: The Forgotten Risk*; Christina Bird, *An Introduction to Secure Remote Access*; Steven F. Blanding, *An Introduction to LAN/WAN Security*; Patricia A.P. Fisher, *Operations Security and Controls*; Thomas DeFelice, *Designing and Implementing Firewalls*; Frederick Gallegos, *Wireless LANs: Technology and Security*; Susan D. Hansche, *Making Security Awareness Happen*; Gilbert Held, *Overcoming Wireless LAN Security Vulnerabilities*; Donna Kidder, *Enabling the Future with Quality of Service*; Joe Kovara and Ray Kaplan, *Implementing Kerberos in Distributed Systems*; Nathan Muller, *Protecting Information in Distributed Environments*; Nathan Muller, *Network Disaster Recovery Planning*; William Hugh Murray, *Principles and Applications of Key Management*; Duncan Napier, *Security of Virtual Private Networks*; Will Ozier, *Risk Analysis and Assessment*; Ed Skoudis, *A Primer on Hacking*; Bill Stackpole, *Centralized Authentication Services (RADIUS, TACACS, and DIAMETER)*; Peter S. Tippett, *Computer Ethics*; Harold F. Tipton, *Purposes of Information Security Management*; Thomas Welch, *Computer Crime Investigation and Computer Forensics.* Reprinted by permission.

Library of Congress Cataloging-in-Publication Data

Hansche, Susan.
    Official (ISC)²® guide to the CISSP® exam / Susan Hansche, John Berti, Chris Hare.
      p. cm.
    ISBN 0-8493-1707-X (alk. paper)
      1. Electronic data processing personnel—Certification. 2. Computer networks—Security measures—Examinations—Study guides. I. Berti, John. II. Hare, Chris, 1962- III. Title.

QA76.3.H363 2003
005.8—dc22

2003059504

Visit the Auerbach Publications Web site at www.auerbach-publications.com

© 2004 by Susan Hansche, John Berti, and the International Systems
Security Certification Consortium (ISC)²®
Auerbach is an imprint of CRC Press LLC

No claim to original U.S. Government works
International Standard Book Number 0-8493-1707-X
Library of Congress Card Number 2003059504
Printed in the United States of America 3 4 5 6 7 8 9 0
Printed on acid-free paper

Table of Contents

1   **Information Security Management. 1**
        Introduction 3
        1.1   Purposes of Information Security Management 3
                Concepts: Availability, Integrity, Confidentiality. 3
        1.2   Risk Analysis and Assessment. 8
                Information Protection Requirements 8
                Information Protection Environment 15
                Security Technology and Tools 20
                Assurance, Trust, and Confidence Mechanisms 29
                Information Protection and Management Services 30
        1.3   Information Classification 31
                Information Protection Requirements 31
                Information Protection Environment 32
                Security Technology and Tools 33
                Assurance, Trust, and Confidence Mechanisms 38
                Information Protection and Management Services 40
        1.4   Policies, Procedures, Standards, Baselines, Guidelines. 46
                Information Protection Requirements 46
                Information Protection Environment 47
                Security Technology and Tools 48
                Information Protection Requirements 54
        1.5   Setting the Goal 55
                Information Protection Environment 56
        1.6   Social Engineering. 57
        1.7   Implementation (Delivery) Options 68
                Security Technology and Tools 68
                Assurance, Trust, and Confidence Mechanisms 69
                Information Protection and Management Services 70
        1.8   Common Body of Knowledge (CBK) 72
                Components. 72
                Examples 73
        1.9   Sample Questions for the CISSP Exam 75

2   **Security Architecture and Models** **79**
    Introduction 80
    2.1   Information Protection Requirements 81
          The A-I-C Triad 81
    2.2   Information Protection Environment 81
          Platform Architecture 82
          Network Environment 97
          Enterprise Architecture 101
          Security Models 103
    2.3   Security Technology and Tools 114
          Network Protection 125
    2.4   Assurance, Trust, and Confidence Mechanisms 127
          Trusted Computer Security Evaluation Criteria (TCSEC) . . . 129
          The Trusted Network Interpretation (TNI) 131
          Information Technology Security Evaluation Criteria
            (ITSEC) 131
          The Common Criteria (CC) 134
          Certification and Accreditation 136
    2.5   Information Protection and Management Services 137
          Summary 138
    2.6   Common Body of Knowledge (CBK) 139
    2.7   Sample Questions for the CISSP Exam 142

3   **Access Control Systems and Methodology** **147**
    Introduction 147
    3.1   Information Protection Requirements 148
    3.2   Information Protection Environment 150
    3.3   Security Technology and Tools 164
          Centralized Access Control Methodologies 184
          Decentralized/Distributed Access Control Methodologies . . 190
          Access to Data 199
    3.4   Assurance, Trust, and Confidence Mechanisms 205
          Intrusion Detection 205
          Analysis Engine Methods 207
    3.5   Information Protection and Management Services 214
          Summary 216
    3.6   Common Body of Knowledge (CBK) 216
    3.7   Sample Questions for the CISSP Exam 219

4   **Applications and Systems Development** **225**
    Introduction 225
    4.1   Information Protection Requirements 227
          The A-I-C Triad 227
    4.2   Information Protection Environment 228
          Open Source Code and Closed Source Code 229
          Software Environment 230

The Database and Data Warehousing Environment 239
DBMS Architecture 239
Database Interface Languages 247
Security Assertion Markup Language (SAML) 251
Data Warehousing 251
Database Vulnerabilities and Threats 255
4.3   Security Technology and Tools 257
System Life Cycle and Systems Development 257
System (Software) Development Methods 258
Including Security in a Systems Development Method 265
Programming Languages 273
Assemblers, Compilers, and Interpreters 274
Programming Language and Security 289
Software Protection Mechanisms 290
DBMS Controls 304
4.4   Assurance, Trust, and Confidence Mechanisms 312
Information Integrity 313
Information Accuracy 313
Information Auditing 313
Evaluation/Certification and Accreditation 314
4.5   Information Protection and Management Services 314
Configuration Management 314
Summary 315
4.6   Common Body of Knowledge (CBK) 315
4.7   Sample Questions for the CISSP Exam 318

5   **Operations Security** **325**
Introduction 325
5.1   Information Protection Requirements 326
5.2   Information Protection Environment 329
5.3   Security Technology and Tools 340
5.4   Assurance, Trust, and Confidence Mechanisms 357
5.5   Information Protection and Management Services 363
Summary 366
5.6   Common Body of Knowledge (CBK) 366
5.7   Sample Questions for the CISSP Exam 372

6   **Cryptography** **377**
Introduction 377
6.1   Information Protection Requirements 378
The A-I-C Triad 378
6.2   Information Protection Environment 379
Introduction 379
Definitions 379
Cryptanalysis and Attacks 389
Import/Export Issues 393

6.3   Security Technology and Tools 396
Basic Concepts of Cryptography. 396
Encryption Systems 403
Symmetric Key Cryptography Algorithms 408
Asymmetric Key Cryptography Algorithms. 414
Message Integrity Controls. 423
6.4   Assurance, Trust, and Confidence Mechanisms 426
Digital Signatures and Certificate Authorities 426
Public Key Infrastructure (PKI) 431
6.5   Information Protection and Management Services. 434
Key Management 434
Key Management Functions 435
Key Generation 435
Distribution 435
Installation 436
Storage 436
Change 436
Control 437
Disposal 437
Modern Key Management. 437
Principles of Key Management 439
Summary. 441
6.6   Common Body of Knowledge (CBK) 441
Components 441
Examples. 442
6.7   Sample Questions for the CISSP Exam 444

7   Physical Security 449
Introduction 451
7.1   Information Protection Requirements 452
The A-I-C Triad. 452
7.2   Information Protection Environment 454
Crime Prevention through Environmental Design
(CPTED) 455
7.3   Security Technology and Tools 464
Perimeter and Building Grounds Boundary Protection 466
Building Entry Points 481
Inside the Building: Building Floors, Office Suites,
Offices 489
Penetration (Intrusion) Detection Systems 496
7.4   Assurance, Trust, and Confidence Mechanisms 505
Drills/Exercises/Testing 505
Vulnerability/Penetration Tests. 505
Creating a Checklist. 505
Maintenance and Service 505

7.5 Information Protection and Management Services 506
    Awareness and Training 506
    Summary 507
7.6 Common Body of Knowledge (CBK) 507
    Components 508
    Examples 508
7.7 Sample Questions for the CISSP Exam 509

8 Telecommunications, Network, and Internet Security 515
8.1 Information Protection Requirements 516
8.2 Information Protection Environment 516
    Data Networks 516
    Remote Access Services 550
    Network Protocols 551
    Network Threats and Attacks 578
8.3 Security Technology and Tools 593
    Content Filtering and Inspection 626
    Intrusion Detection 627
8.4 Assurance, Trust, and Confidence Mechanisms 650
8.5 Information Protection and Management Services 654
    Summary 655
8.6 Common Body of Knowledge (CBK) 655
8.7 Sample Questions for the CISSP Exam 658

9 Business Continuity Planning 663
Introduction 663
Defining a Disaster 666
9.1 Information Protection Requirements 667
9.2 Information Protection Environment 668
9.3 Security Technology and Tools 669
    Phase I: Project Management and Initiation 670
    Phase II: Business Impact Analysis (BIA) 672
    Phase III: Recovery Strategies 679
    Phase IV: Plan Development and Implementation 691
    Phase V: Testing, Maintenance, Awareness, and Training 698
9.4 Assurance, Trust, and Confidence Mechanisms 698
9.5 Information Protection and Management Services 701
    Summary 702
9.6 Common Body of Knowledge (CBK) 703
9.7 Sample Questions for the CISSP Exam 705

10 Law, Investigations, and Ethics 709
10.1 Law 711
    Information Protection Requirements 711
    Information Protection Environment 713
    Privacy 725

Recommended Course of Action......................... 730
Security Technology and Tools 731
Assurance, Trust, and Confidence Mechanisms 732
Information Protection and Management Services......... 732
10.2 Investigation.. 732
Information Protection Requirements 732
Information Protection Environment 733
Security Technology and Tools 734
Assurance, Trust, and Confidence Mechanisms 754
Information Protection and Management Services......... 754
10.3 Ethics... 755
Information Protection Requirements 755
Computer Ethics 756
Information Protection Environment 757
Security Technology and Tools 765
Assurance, Trust, and Confidence Mechanisms 766
Information Protection and Management Services......... 766
Summary.. 766
10.4 Common Body of Knowledge (CBK)..................... 767
10.5 Sample Questions for the CISSP Exam 769

Appendix A   Glossary 773

Appendix B   Annotated Bibliography 823

Appendix C   Answers to Sample Test Questions................831

Index...875

Foreword

As the networked world continues to shape and impact every aspect of life, threats to the global network infrastructure have continued to rise in parallel. That is why there has never been greater urgency for a global standard of excellence for those in the information security profession who protect the networked world.

That has been the mission of the International Information Systems Security Certification Consortium (ISC)²® from its inception. Formed in 1989 by multiple professional associations to develop an accepted industry standard for the practice of information security, (ISC)² created the information security industry's first and only Common Body of Knowledge (CBK). Continually updated to stay current with rapidly changing information technologies, the CBK continues to serve as the basis for (ISC)² training and certification programs. To date, (ISC)² has certified thousands of security professionals and practitioners in over 85 countries and continues to meet the growing demand for information security accreditation.

Just as technology and its impact have dramatically changed since (ISC)² was first envisioned, so has the role of information security professionals. The need for highly qualified information security professionals to protect information assets has now been accepted by organizations worldwide, both private and public. In recent years, the rise of the Chief Information Security Officer position has been a watershed event in the influence and significance of the information security professional in maintaining effective IT governance and risk management. The specter of international cyber terrorism has hastened the speed of information security implementation and, correspondingly, the demand for information security professionals throughout the world.

What has remained constant, however, is (ISC)²'s commitment to ensuring that the highest standards of information security are maintained by certified professionals worldwide. Its Certified Information Systems Security Professional (CISSP) certification, considered the Gold Standard in the information security industry, continues to be an invaluable tool in independently validating a candidate's expertise in developing information security policies, standards, and procedures, as well as managing implementation across the enterprise.

In addition to passing the six-hour CISSP exam, applicants must sub-scribe to the (ISC)² Code of Ethics and have four years of professional experience (or three years of experience plus a bachelor's degree) in one or more of the CBK domains. The Code of Ethics describes the professional behavior expected of the CISSP.

A major point that sets the CISSP apart from other security certifications is the breadth of knowledge and the experience necessary to pass the exam. CISSP candidates cannot be overly specialized in just one domain; they must know and understand the full spectrum of the CBK to become certified. To maintain their certification, holders of the CISSP are required to earn 120 Continuing Professional Education (CPE) credits every three years. Re-certification is required in order for information security profes-sionals to maintain their CISSP title.

The official (ISC)² Study Guide is the only document that addresses all the topics and sub-topics contained in the CBK. The authors of this new, comprehensive CBK Study Guide edition have provided an extensive sup-plement to the CBK review seminars that are designed to help candidates prepare for CISSP certification.

More than 800 pages are devoted to discussing the details included in the ten domains of the CBK. The details include historical and background information that contributes to the ability to understand current informa-tion security technologies and management issues. Each domain is broken down into the areas of security requirements, the environment most related to the domain, the various tools available to address the require-ments in the environment, and the means of assuring that the require-ments are being successfully met. The final section addresses the work appropriate for the security management function to perform in imple-menting the tools to meet the requirements or provide the necessary assurances.

(ISC)² highly recommends the latest edition of the CBK Study Guide not only for information security professionals attempting to achieve CISSP certification, but also for those practitioners who are trying to decide which, if any, certification to pursue. Executives and organizational manag-ers who want a more complete understanding of all the elements required to effectively protect their enterprise will also find this document extremely useful.

Sincerely,

JAMES E. DUFFY, CISSP
Executive Director
(ISC)²

Acknowledgments

This book was greatly improved by the involvement of several CISSPs who took their time to review the chapters. Of course, any errors and omissions in each chapter are the fault of each respective author. Because the chapters were divided among the authors, we have each chosen to write our specific chapter acknowledgments. However, one person who served as the project manager, project supporter, editor, subject matter expert, and a multitude of other roles was Harold (Hal) Tipton.

(ISC)^2 has supported us through this endeavor and most remarkably suggested Hal Tipton as our overall editor and reviewer. It must be said that without Hal Tipton providing his guidance and knowledge, this book may never have made it to its final form. We all think of Hal as our mentor and personal expert on information system security and we thank him for his perseverance, guidance, support, and expertise on this book project. We want to thank Jim Duffy, Managing Director of (ISC)^2, and the (ISC)^2 Board of Directors for their support and confidence in our ability to author this book.

We also want to thank all the fine people at Auerbach Publishing, especially Rich O'Hanley, who kept up the faith and provided gentle prodding, and Managing Editor Claire Miller and Project Editor Gerry Jaffe, who helped us through the final production.

Susan's Acknowledgments

After each chapter was written, it went through a review cycle by several CISSPs to make sure the content was accurate. Several individuals reviewed all chapters and others just a specialized area. As mentioned, Hal was my cornerstone for support, making sure we had the right information in the right place. Hal reviewed all the chapters several times and even found a few typos. I would like to especially acknowledge Rob Slade (Scholar and Computer Security Consultant), who really went out of his way to provide guidance. He reviewed all of my chapters and in the Applications Program chapter was a valuable resource for technical concepts and ideas to be included. Thanks Rob! Chris Hare, CISSP (Information Security and Control Advisor, Nortel Networks), also reviewed my chapters and provided guidance, especially on the Security Architecture chapter. In the early reviews, all of my chapters were reviewed by Ben Rothke, CISSP (Senior Security Consultant, ThruPoint, Inc.) — Ben, thanks for the guidance. In addition, due credit belongs to the following people for taking the time to provide guidance and input:

- *Access Control Systems and Methodology:* John Glover, CISSP, President, MayneStay Consulting Group, Ltd.
- *Applications and Systems Development:* Kevin Henry, CISSP, CISA, Trainer and Program Development Manager, (ISC)²
- *Business Continuity Planning:* Rick Bellwood, CISSP, CBCP, Team Leader, Infrastructure Security, Natural Resources Canada
- *Security Architecture and Models:* Chris Hare, CISSP, CISA, Information Security and Control Advisor, Nortel Networks; and Ed Fleschute, CISSP, Computer Security Consultant, Secured Online Solutions
- *Physical Security:* Michael Corbett, CISSP, Security Engineering Officer, U.S. Department of State; and Bruce Matthews, CISSP, Security Engineering Officer, U.S. Department of State

Also, thanks to John Berti for thinking this was a great idea and agreeing to do so much of the work. Through the countless telephone calls and emails, we reached our goal.

As always, thanks to my family and friends for their continued love and encouragement. And a special thank you to JB for listening attentively and supporting my crazy ideas. Even when I was working on these chapters and did not have time to give to them, they gave me strength to keep going and also forgiveness for not always being there.

John's Acknowledgments

As with Susan's chapters, once each chapter was written, it went through a review cycle by several Subject Matter Experts to make sure the content was accurate and technically sound. A special thanks to Rob Slade, Chris Hare, and Ben Rothke, who spent considerable time reviewing all the chapters.

Many people contributed to this process, as outlined below, but I would specifically like to acknowledge Hal Tipton's contribution. Although we have described the immeasurable contribution that he has made to this book in a paragraph above, it must be said once more. This man is the most wonderful person you could ever meet. His knowledge of this entire field is unmatched by anyone, and his professionalism and character have allowed me, and many others I'm sure, the ability to learn and become very knowledgeable and successful in this field. Thanks, Hal, you're the greatest!

In addition, I owe a great debt of gratitude to the contributors to the *Information Security Management Handbook* and other Auerbach publications for their work, which is too numerous to cite in every instance: Michael H. Agranoff, Christina Bird, Steven Blanding, Thomas DeFelice, Patricia A.P. Fisher, Frederick Gallegos, Gilbert Held, Ray Kaplan, Donna Kidder, Joe Kovara, Nathan Muller, William H. Murray, Duncan Napier, Ed Skoudis, Bill Stackpole, Peter S. Tippett, and Thomas Welch.

Due credit belongs to the following people for taking the time to provide guidance and input for the Law, Investigations and Ethics chapter: Marcus Rogers, CISSP [(ISC)^2 Instructor and Computer Security Consultant], and Sanford Sherizen, CISSP [(ISC)^2 Instructor and Computer Security Consultant].

A great thanks to Susan Hansche for sharing this experience with me. Through the countless communications, she provided endless support and a constant reminder that there was light at the end of the tunnel. Her dedication to and belief in this endeavor are tremendous.

A big thanks to my employer, Deloitte & Touche, a wonderful organization, full of very energetic and skillful people. The knowledge base and support provided by Deloitte & Touche were more than anyone could ever ask for.

And, of course, I want to thank my family and friends for their tremendous love and support. A great big thanks to my daughters, Cassandra and Janessa, and to my special love, Darlene, for allowing me the time to pursue this opportunity.

Chris's Acknowledgments

First, I thank God for giving me the intelligence and talents to achieve all I have done. It is His Divine influence, love, and guidance that make us successful. Second, I give a special thank you to my best friend, colleague, and boss, Mignona Coté. She motivates me to accomplish tasks above and beyond the average person, challenges me with intriguing security concepts, and coaches me through complex situations. It was her daily probing that enabled me to conclude my work on this book and innumerable articles. Thank you, Mignona.

Finally, I must thank one of the most dynamic leaders in the industry, Marwan Shishakly. He let me be me! He listened and provided insight to me, which taught me how to reach the majority while also acknowledging the few. He has been my personal Confucius! Thank you, Marwan.

Introduction

This book came into existence as an effort to help candidates studying for the Certified Information Systems Security Professional (CISSP) exam understand the CISSP Common Body of Knowledge (CBK) so they could prepare for the exam. The idea behind the book stems from my own experience of studying for the exam. Like most CISSP candidates, I had strengths and weaknesses within the ten domain areas. Those domains where I needed further information, I wanted to have one source that would provide enough details so I could understand and make sense of the material, but not so much detail that I would need to read an entire book. This book is an attempt to provide other CISSP candidates with that resource — just enough to help explain the major concepts and also limiting enough to be able to read the material within the time allocated for studying for the exam.

To meet this goal, my co-authors — John Berti, Chris Hare — and I have provided a little more information on the background and basic concepts of each domain so that the material can be understood in the broad perspective of the information system security field. For example, in the Application Program Security chapter, there is background information on several Software Development Methods. Although the CISSP exam is not going to ask for a comparison of the Waterfall method and the Prototyping method, a brief summary of each type of method is provided so that candidates can have some perspective on the entire range of Software Development Methods.

After receiving my CISSP certification, I proposed to (ISC)² the idea of distributing a comprehensive guide to the CISSP CBK. So, in addition to my full-time job as Director of Training for Information Assurance at PEC Solutions, I agreed to work on a comprehensive guide to the CISSP CBK. From this proposal, I met John Berti, a Senior Manager for Deloitte & Touche's Security Services Practice and also one of the Senior Lead Instructors for (ISC)². John was also excited about the project and together we decided that we could produce a better book with both of us concentrating on the chapters that were our strengths. Due to the magnitude of the Telecommunications chapter, we also sought guidance from Chris Hare, who collaborated with

John on this chapter. Chris is a Senior Information Security Analyst for Nortel Networks and an Assistant Instructor for (ISC)². Chris specializes in Information System Auditing, system and application assessments, incident response, networking, communications, and Unix. The combined efforts of John, Chris, and I are this book. John has written the chapters on Information Security Management; Operations Security; Cryptography; Telecommunications, Network, and Internet Security (with assistance from Chris Hare); and Law, Investigation and Ethics. I have written the chapters on Access Control Systems and Methodology; Application Program Security; Business Continuity Planning; Computer, Systems, and Security Architecture; and Physical Security. Although our writing styles may differ, it is our belief as authors that the material contained in this book can help the CISSP candidate successfully prepare for the CISSP exam.

This book is also intended as a reference guide for anyone interested or involved in information system security. The CISSP Certification was designed to recognize mastery of an international standard for information security, as reflected in a thorough understanding of the CBK.

What Is the CISSP CBK?

The CISSP CBK is the compilation and distillation of all security information, collected internationally, of relevance to Information Security professionals. The CISSP CBK was developed in 1989 in anticipation of the creation of the CISSP exam. At that time, a select group of professionals in the field, representing both the private and public sectors, worked together to identify the key topics required of information system security professionals. These topics were identified as those that a professional in the field of information security should know enough about to be able to discuss them intelligently with peers. Throughout the past decade, the CBK has been updated and reorganized several times, but the main concepts of the field have prevailed. Today, "ten domains" define the CBK, which correlates to how this book is organized. They are:

- Information Security Management
- Security Architecture and Models
- Access Control Systems and Methodology
- Applications and System Development
- Operations Security
- Cryptography
- Physical Security
- Telecommunications, Network, and Internet Security
- Business Continuity Planning
- Law, Investigations, and Ethics

In 1999, the (ISC)² CBK Committee further defined the CBK domains into five functional areas:

- *Information Protection Requirements:* describes what information security professionals are expected to know about security requirements and their origins or authority.
- *Information Protection Environment:* identifies what information security professionals must know about the information technology, networks, systems, and applications that make up the context in which the requirements must be met.
- *Security Technology and Tools:* describes what information system security professionals must know about the security technology, mechanisms, and tools they may employ to meet requirements.
- *Assurance, Trust, and Confidence Mechanisms:* identifies what the information system security professional must know about those tools and mechanisms that enable them to know that controls are reliable and functioning as intended.
- *Information Protection and Management Services:* provides information about the business functions and services that are under the direct control of information security managers or management.

Organization of the Book

The organization of this book follows the CISSP CBK model. The domains are represented as the ten chapters, and within each chapter the material is divided into the five functional areas. In some chapters, the material is divided into sections, which are then separated into the five functional areas because more than one major topic is covered in the domain. For example, in the Law, Investigations and Ethics chapter (Chapter 10), the topics are divided into three sections and those sections are further divided into the five functional areas. The material also follows the organization of the Official (ISC)² CBK Review Seminar. For those CISSP candidates who attend the CBK Review Seminar, this book should be used as a companion to the seminar material. In addition, at the end of each chapter is a list of objectives from the CISSP CBK that outlines what candidates should know about the domain in order to fully understand the material.

The CISSP Exam

The CISSP exam is composed of 250 well-researched, multiple-choice questions. Once you have passed the CISSP exam, you can volunteer to write exam questions to obtain required continuing professional education (CPE) credits and learn of the complexity and knowledge required for each question. For example, each question requires at least two references from the body of recognized literature and is field-tested before becoming part of the official bank of test questions. Candidates have six hours to complete the exam.

Using This Book to Prepare for the CISSP Exam

Regardless of whether or not you take a review course, you must spend time preparing for the exam. If you take the time to prepare for the exam — that is, review the ten domains and study those you have identified as your weak spots — you can succeed in passing the exam.

Although I have heard of CISSPs who were able to walk into an exam room without studying for the exam, those are rare cases. When beginning the review of the CBK domains, most candidates will discover that they know some of the domains very well, some a little, and some not at all. Because the CISSP candidate must have four years of experience to sit for the exam, it is expected that most will know several of the domains based on their practical experience. Based on this real-life (practical) experience, CISSP candidates should begin by narrowing down their study needs into three categories: (1) domains they know, (2) domains they have some familiarity with but need to review, and (3) domains they need to learn.

As of the completion of writing, this book covers the entire CBK material, as it is currently defined. Although technologies will change and cause the CBK to be updated, the basic concepts of the security involved within each technology will remain the same. Keep in mind that the CISSP exam is written to evaluate the security professional's broad knowledge of the field — not whether he or she knows the name of the current wireless protocol being tested in a specific country. Remember to stay focused on understanding the implications of information system security within each of the domains.

Preparing a Study Strategy

The most important part of preparing to study is to consciously agree to study. Many CISSP candidates fail because they do not take the time to study the material. Most have great ideas on how they will study and use their time; however, when exam day arrives, they feel they did not give themselves enough time to study.

Step Number One. Identify how much time you have available to study. Take a typical two-week time period and write down how you currently spend your time. Do you work 10 to 12 hours a day? Have responsibilities to relationships and/or family? Belong to organizations, clubs, associations that require a commitment of time? Essentially, you need to realistically identify how much time you have available each week to devote to studying. One of my most productive study times was sitting in a hotel room in Frankfurt, Germany. Six weeks prior to my exam date, I had to travel on business for three weeks to Frankfurt. Although I would rather have spent my weekends touring the sites of southern Germany, instead I read books and articles on Information System Security. Although my travel companions thought I was very boring, I knew that my weekends at home would never allow me to spend six to seven hours each day reviewing the material.

Step Number Two. Identify your strengths and weaknesses of the CISSP CBK. As mentioned, within each domain identify the specific topics in three categories: (1) topics within the domain that you know, (2) topics within the domain with which you have some familiarity but need to review, and (3) topics you need to learn.

Michael Arant, CISSP (in an unpublished article, 2002), wrote some good advice:

> *Don't get yourself wound around the axle of thinking you need to know everything about everything, like elliptic curves or derivation of the factors of the product of large prime numbers. Just learn the words and be able to associate them with concepts, like (in this case) keystream generation. As you look over the "sample" exam questions, you'll see what we're getting at.*

Once you have identified your weak areas, do the research to teach yourself the topic. In addition to this book, some of the best resources for the entire ten domains are the H. Tipton and M. Krause *Information System Security Handbooks*. Published each year, the handbooks provide edited articles about specific topics within the ten domains. Recently, a colleague of mine was preparing for the CISSP exam and wanted me to explain the different methods of cryptanalysis. After a futile attempt, I loaned my colleague all of the handbooks along with directions to read the in-depth articles provided. As a side note, the handbooks are an excellent resource to help keep current on many of the subjects that you may not deal with in your day-to-day practical experience.

Step Number Three. Once you have identified what you need to review (or learn) and how much time you have available to study, prepare a study plan. Be specific about when you will study — for example, during your lunch hour at work, from 8:00 p.m. to 10:00 p.m. (after work and dinner, you have two hours available), or a few hours on Sunday afternoons. Be realistic! If you have a lot of distractions at home, then plan to study at a local library or another location where it is quiet.

Give yourself plenty of time to prepare for the exam. Remember that 30% of all candidates fail on their first attempt! For most CISSP candidates, studying for the exam and taking the exam can be stressful. One method of decreasing that stress level is to feel confident about your knowledge of the material. One of the most common mistakes unsuccessful CISSP candidates make is to believe that attending a CISSP Exam Prep course can prepare them for taking the exam. Many candidates take a prep course for three to five days, and then sit for the exam on the day following the prep course. Most of the prep courses I have read about are designed to review the material — not to teach the material. The courses are excellent methods of highlighting the key topics you will need to know to pass the exam. They are also an opportunity to ask a CISSP about questions you may have related to the topics. As a final reason for taking the time to study and prepare for the exam, think of the CISSP exam as not the type of event you want to repeat, so make sure you are ready and can be successful on your first attempt.

Step Number Four. Use sample questions to test your knowledge and remember how to answer a multiple-choice question. Some CISSP candidates may not have taken a multiple-choice exam in many years, while others may have taken some technical certification exams. For those who have taken a technical certification exam, keep in mind that the CISSP exam questions are, for the most part, more complex than those in some technical exams. Also, there are more of them — 250 questions to answer can be a grueling experience.

In addition to the questions at the end of each chapter in this book, there are several other resources that provide sample exam questions. Released in 2002, *The Total CISSP Exam Prep Book: Practice Questions, Answers, and Test Taking Tips and Techniques* (Thomas Peltier and Patrick Howard) is a great resource for sample test questions. The (ISC)² CBK Review Seminar also conducts a sample exam by offering 100 questions in a timed format. There are also several Web sites where CISSPs have written sample questions to help CISSP candidates. All said, let me also offer a word of caution about sample questions: they are good practice for taking multiple-choice exams by helping the candidate get into the test-taking mode. However, some of the sample questions I have seen do not reflect the complexity of those on the exam.

On the Day of the Exam. Each candidate has six hours to complete the exam. Some key things to remember about exam day are:

- Pay attention to your time — at the three-hour mark, you should have completed at least 50% of the exam or 125 questions.
- Use all the time you have.
- Read each question at least twice. Comments such as "the questions are worded to be tricky" are not really true; the questions are not worded to try and fool the candidates. However, the questions are written to guarantee that the candidates understand the true element of the question.
- There are no absolutes on what will work best for each candidate taking the exam. Some candidates prefer to answer all the "easy" questions first and then answer the "hard" questions. Some like to highlight those they are unsure of and return to those questions

later; others just persevere slowly through each question, finish, close the book, and turn in the exam. Whatever is your most comfortable mode for taking the exam, follow it — just keep your time restrictions in mind.

- Bring something to snack on. If you think you will need sugar to get through, bring a candy bar; if you need something more in the healthy range, bring fruit, a granola bar, etc. Most exam times begin in the morning and continue through the lunch hour into the afternoon. Thus, you should plan to bring something with you to help keep your energy at a high level into the afternoon.
- Take a stretch break — it may help more oxygen flow to the brain. Most exam proctors will allow you to take a stretch break at the back of the room; inquire at the beginning of the exam on the rules of where and how to take a stretch break.
- Do not plan anything for after the exam, except rest and relaxation.

As a final thought, all the authors wish you a successful career in the information system security field. It is an exciting time to be involved in this emerging discipline, and we welcome your expertise and enthusiasm into the CISSP fold.

Chapter 1
Information Security Management

Information Security Management entails the identification of an organization's information assets and the development, documentation, and implementation of policies, standards, procedures, and guidelines, which ensure their availability, integrity, and confidentiality. Management tools such as data classification, security awareness training, risk assessment, and risk analysis are used to identify the threats, classify assets, and rate their vulnerabilities so that effective security controls can be implemented.

Risk management is the identification, measurement, control, and minimization of loss associated with uncertain events or risks. It includes overall security reviews, risk analysis, evaluation and selection of safeguards, cost/benefit analysis, management decisions, safeguard implementation, and effectiveness reviews.

The CISSP should understand:

- The planning, organization, and roles of individuals in identifying and securing an organization's information assets
- The development of effective employment agreements; employee hiring practices, including background checks and job descriptions; security clearances; separation of duties and responsibilities; job rotation; and termination practices
- The development and use of policies stating management's views and position on particular topics and the use of guidelines, standards, baselines, and procedures to support those policies
- The differences between policies, guidelines, standards, baselines, and procedures in terms of their application to information security management
- The importance of security awareness training to make employees aware of the need for information security, its significance, and the specific security-related requirements relative to the employees' positions
- The importance of data classification, including sensitive, confidential, proprietary, private, and critical information

- The importance of risk management practices and tools to identify, rate, and reduce the risk to specific information assets, such as:
  - Asset identification and evaluation
  - Threat identification and assessment
  - Vulnerability and exposures identification and assessment
  - Calculation of single occurrence loss and annual loss expectancy
  - Safeguards and countermeasure identification and evaluation, including risk management practices and tools to identify, rate, and reduce the risk to specific information assets
  - Calculation of the resulting annual loss expectancy and residual risk
  - Communication of the residual risk to be assigned (i.e., insured against) or accepted by management
- The regulatory and ethical requirements to protect individuals from substantial harm, embarrassment, or inconvenience, due to the inappropriate collection, storage, or dissemination of personal information
- The principles and controls that protect data against compromise or inadvertent disclosure
- The principles and controls that ensure the logical correctness of an information system; the consistency of data structures; and the accuracy, precision, and completeness of the data stored
- The principles and controls that ensure that a computer resource will be available to authorized users when they need it
- The purpose of and process used for reviewing system records, event logs, and activities
- The importance of managing change and the change control process
- The application of commonly accepted best practices for system security administration, including the concepts of least privilege, separation of duties, job rotation, monitoring, and incident response
- The internal control standards reduce that risk; they are required to satisfy obligations with respect to the law, safeguard the organization's assets, and account for the accurate revenue and expense tracking; there are three categories of internal control standards— general standards, specific standards, and audit resolution standards:
  - General standards must provide reasonable assurance, support the internal controls, provide for competent personnel, and assist in establishing control objectives and techniques
  - Specific standards must be documented, clear, and available to personnel; they allow for the prompt recording of transactions, and the prompt execution of authorized transactions; specific standards establish separation of duties, qualified supervision, and accountability
  - Audit resolution standards require that managers promptly resolve audit findings; they must evaluate the finding, determine the corrective action required, and take that action

Introduction

The purpose of Information Security is to protect an organization's valuable resources, such as information, hardware, and software. Through the selection and application of appropriate safeguards, Information Security helps the organization's mission by protecting its physical and financial resources, reputation, legal position, employees, and other tangible and intangible assets. Unfortunately, Information Security is sometimes viewed as hindering the mission of the organization by imposing poorly selected, bothersome rules and procedures on users, managers, and systems. On the contrary, well-chosen Information Security rules and procedures should not exist for their own sake — they are put in place to protect important assets and thereby support the overall organizational mission.

Information Security, then, should be designed to increase the organization's ability to be successful. It achieves this through protecting the organization's resources from damage, loss, or waste. One aspect of Information Security is that it ensures that all resources are protected, and available to an organization, at all times, when needed.

Information systems are often critical assets that support the mission of an organization. Protecting them can be as critical as protecting other organizational resources, such as money, tangible assets, and employees. However, including Information Security considerations in the management of information systems does not completely eliminate the possibility that these assets will be harmed. Ultimately, management has to decide what level of risk it is willing to accept. This needs to be balanced with the cost of security safeguards. This whole area of Information Security is referred to as Risk Management. One key aspect of Risk Management is the realization that, regardless of the controls that are put in place, there will always be some residual risk.

ⓘ 1.1 Purposes of Information Security Management

Concepts: Availability, Integrity, Confidentiality

Information Security Managers must establish and maintain a security program that ensures three requirements: the availability, integrity, and confidentiality of the organization's information resources. These are the three basic requirements of security management programs.

Availability

Availability is the assurance that a computer system is accessible by authorized users whenever needed. Two facets of availability are typically discussed:

- Denial-of-service
- Loss of data processing capabilities as a result of natural disasters (e.g., fires, floods, storms, or earthquakes) or human actions (e.g., bombs or strikes)

Denial-of-service usually refers to user or intruder actions that tie up computing services in a way that renders the system unusable by authorized users. The loss of data processing capabilities as a result of natural disasters or human actions is perhaps more common. Such losses are countered by contingency planning, which helps minimize the time that a critical data processing capability remains unavailable. Contingency planning — which may involve business resumption planning, alternative-site processing, or simply disaster recovery planning — provides an alternative means of processing, thereby ensuring availability. Physical, technical, and administrative controls are important aspects of security initiatives that address availability.

The physical controls include those that prevent unauthorized persons from coming into contact with computing resources, various fire and water control mechanisms, hot and cold sites for use in alternative-site processing, and off-site backup storage facilities.

The technical controls include fault-tolerance mechanisms (e.g., hardware redundancy, disk mirroring, and application checkpoint restart), electronic vaulting (i.e., automatic backup to a secure, off-site location), and access control software to prevent unauthorized users from disrupting services.

The administrative controls include access control policies, operating procedures, contingency planning, and user training. Although not obviously an important initiative, adequate training of operators, programmers, and security personnel can help avoid many computing errors that result in the loss of availability. For example, availability can be disrupted if a security office accidentally locks up a user database during routine maintenance, thus preventing authorized users access for an extended period of time.

Considerable effort is being devoted to addressing various aspects of availability. For example, significant research has focused on achieving more fault-tolerant computing. Another sign that availability is a primary concern is that increasing investments are being made in disaster recovery planning combined with alternate-site processing facilities. Investments in anti-viral products continue to escalate. Denial-of-service associated with computer viruses, Trojan horses, and logic bombs continues to be a major security problem. Known threats to availability can be expected to continue. New threats such as distributed denial-of-service attacks will continue to emerge as technology evolves, making it quicker and easier for users to share information resources with other users, often at remote locations.

The combination of integrity, availability, and confidentiality in appropriate proportions to support the organization's goals can provide users with a trustworthy system — that is, users can trust it will consistently perform according to their expectations. Trustworthiness has a broader definition than simply security, in that it combines security with assurance, safety, and reliability, as well as the protection of privacy (which is already considered a part of security). In addition, many of the mechanisms that provide security also make systems more trustworthy in general. These multipurpose safeguards should be exploited to the extent practicable.

Integrity

Integrity is the protection of system information or processes from intentional or accidental unauthorized changes. The challenge of the security program is to ensure that information and processes are maintained in the state that users expect. Although the security program cannot improve the accuracy of data that is put into the system by users, it can help ensure that any changes are intended and correctly applied. An additional element of integrity is the need to protect the process or program used to manipulate the data from unauthorized modification. A critical requirement of both commercial and government data processing is to ensure the integrity of data to prevent fraud and errors. It is imperative, therefore, that no user be able to modify data in a way that might corrupt or cause the loss of assets, the loss of financial information, or render decision-making information unreliable. Examples of government systems in which integrity is crucial include air traffic control systems, military fire control systems (which control the firing of automated weapons), and Social Security and welfare systems. Examples of commercial systems that require a high level of integrity include medical and health information systems, credit reporting systems, production control systems, and payroll systems. As with the confidentiality policy, identification, authentication, and authorization of users are key elements of the information integrity policy. Integrity depends on access controls; therefore, it is necessary to positively and uniquely identify and authenticate all persons who attempt access.

Protecting against Threats to Integrity. Like confidentiality, integrity can be compromised by hackers, masqueraders, unauthorized user activity, unprotected downloaded files, networks, and unauthorized programs (e.g., Trojan horses and viruses) because each of these threats can lead to unauthorized changes to data or programs. For example, authorized users can corrupt data and programs accidentally or intentionally if their activities on the system are not properly controlled.

5

Three basic principles are used to establish integrity controls:

- Granting access on a need-to-know (least privilege) basis
- Separation of duties
- Rotation of duties

Need-to-Know Access (Least Privilege). Users should be granted access only to those files and programs that they absolutely need to perform their assigned job functions. User access to production data or programs should be further restricted through use of well-formed transactions, which ensure that users can change data or programs only in controlled ways that maintain integrity. A common element of well-formed transactions is the recording of data/program modifications in a log that can be reviewed later to ensure that only authorized and correct changes were made. To be effective, well-formed transactions must be implemented through a specific set of programs. These programs must be inspected for proper construction, installation, and controls to prevent unauthorized modification. Because users must be able to work efficiently, access privileges should be judiciously granted to allow sufficient operational flexibility, and need-to-know access should enable maximum control with minimum restrictions on users. The security program must employ a careful balance between ideal security and practical productivity.

Separation of Duties. To ensure that no single employee has control of a transaction from beginning to end, two or more people should be responsible for performing it — for example, anyone allowed to create or certify a well-formed transaction should not be allowed to execute it. Thus, a transaction cannot be manipulated for personal gain unless all persons responsible for it participate.

Rotation of Duties. Job assignments should be changed periodically so that it is more difficult for users to collaborate to exercise complete control of a transaction and subvert it for fraudulent purposes. This principle is effective when used in conjunction with a separation of duties. Problems in effectively rotating duties usually appear in organizations with limited staff resources and inadequate training programs. However, there are several other advantages to the organization as a result of a regular rotation of duties process. These include succession planning, minimizing loss of knowledge after losing a key employee, and the availability of backup personnel.

Confidentiality

Confidentiality is the protection of information within systems so that unauthorized people, resources, and processes cannot access that information. That is, confidentiality means the system does not allow information to be disclosed to anyone who is not authorized to access it. Privacy issues, which have received a great deal of attention over the past number of years, emphasize the importance of confidentiality on protecting personal information maintained in automated information systems by both government agencies and private-sector organizations.

Confidentiality must be well defined, and procedures for maintaining confidentiality must be carefully implemented. Crucial aspects of confidentiality are user identification, authentication, and authorization.

Threats to Confidentiality

Confidentiality can be compromised in several ways. The following are some of the most commonly encountered threats to information confidentiality:

- *Hackers.* A hacker or cracker is someone who bypasses the system's access controls by taking advantage of security weaknesses that the system's developers have left in the system. In addition, many hackers are adept at discovering the passwords of authorized users who choose passwords that are easy to guess or appear in dictionaries. The activities of hackers represent serious threats to the confidentiality of information in computer systems. Many hackers have created copies of inadequately protected files and placed them in areas of the system where they can be accessed by unauthorized persons.
- *Masqueraders.* A masquerader is an authorized, or unauthorized, user of the system who has obtained the password of another user and thus gains access to files available to the other user by pretending to be the authorized user. Masqueraders are often able to read and copy confidential files. Masquerading, therefore, can be defined as an attempt to gain access to a system by posing as an authorized user.
- *Unauthorized user activity.* This type of activity occurs when authorized, or unauthorized, system users gain access to files they are not authorized to access. Weak access controls often enable such unauthorized access, which can compromise confidential files.
- *Unprotected downloaded files.* Downloading can compromise confidential information if, in the process, files are moved from the secure environment of a host computer to an unprotected microcomputer for local processing. While on the microcomputer, unprotected confidential information could be accessed by unauthorized users.
- *Networks.* Networks present a special confidentiality threat because data flowing through networks can be viewed at any node of the network, whether or not the data is addressed to that node. This is particularly significant because the unencrypted user IDs and secret passwords of users logging on to the host are subject to compromise

7

by the use of "sniffers" as this data travels from the user's workstation to the host. Any confidential information not intended for viewing at every node should be protected by encryption techniques.

- *Trojan horses.* Trojan horses can be programmed to copy confidential files to unprotected areas of the system when they are unknowingly executed by users who have authorized access to those files. Once executed, the Trojan horse can become resident on the user's system and can routinely copy confidential files to unprotected resources.

- *Social engineering.* Social engineering is a term that describes a nontechnical kind of intrusion that relies heavily on human interaction and often involves tricking other people to break normal security procedures. For example, a person using social engineering to break into a computer network would try to gain the confidence of someone who is authorized to access the network in order to get him to reveal information that compromises the network's security.

The following sections discuss Security Management as a whole, which includes the following topics:

- Risk Analysis
- Information Classification
- Policies, Procedures, Standards, Baselines, and Guidelines
- Information Security Awareness

1.2 Risk Analysis and Assessment

Information Protection Requirements

While there are a number of ways to identify, analyze, and assess risk and considerable discussion of "risk" in the media and among information security professionals continues, there is little real understanding of the process and metrics of analyzing and assessing risk. Certainly everyone understands that "taking a risk" means "taking a chance," but a risk or chance of what is often not so clear. When one passes on a curve or bets on a horse, one is taking a chance of suffering injury or financial loss — undesirable outcomes. We usually give more or less serious consideration to such an action before taking the chance, so to speak. Perhaps we would even go so far as to calculate the odds (chance) of experiencing the undesirable outcome and, further, take steps to reduce the chance of experiencing the undesirable outcome.

To effectively calculate the chance of experiencing the undesirable outcome, as well as its magnitude, one must have an awareness of the elements of risk and their relationship to each other. This, in a nutshell, is the process of risk analysis and assessment. Knowing more about the risk, one is better prepared to decide what to do about it — accept the risk as now assessed (go ahead and pass on the blind curve or make that bet on the horses), or do something to reduce the risk to an acceptable level (wait for a safe opportunity to pass or put the bet money in a savings account with guaranteed interest). This is the process of risk mitigation or risk reduction. There is a third choice: to transfer the risk; that is, buy insurance. However prudent good insurance may be, all things considered, having insurance will not prevent the undesirable outcome; it will only serve to make some compensation — almost always less than complete — for the loss. Further, some risks such as betting on a horse are uninsurable.

The processes of identifying, analyzing and assessing, mitigating, or transferring risk are generally characterized as Risk Management. There are thus a few key questions that are at the core of the Risk Management process:

- What could happen (threat event)?
- If it happened, how bad could it be (threat impact)?
- How often could it happen (threat frequency, annualized)?
- How certain are the answers to the first three questions (recognition of uncertainty)?

These questions are answered by analyzing and assessing risk. Uncertainty is the central issue of risk. Sure, one might pass successfully on the curve or win big at the races, but does the gain warrant taking the risk? Do the few seconds saved with the unsafe pass warrant the possible head-on collision? Are you betting this month's paycheck on a long shot to win? Cost/benefit analysis would most likely indicate that both of these examples are unacceptable risks.

Prudent management, having analyzed and assessed the risks by securing credible answers to these four questions, will almost certainly find there to be some unacceptable risks as a result. Now what? Three questions remain to be answered:

- What can be done (risk mitigation)?
- How much will it cost (annualized)?
- Is it cost-effective (cost/benefit analysis)?

Answers to these questions, decisions to budget and execute recommended activities, and the subsequent and ongoing management of all risk mitigation measures — including periodic reassessment — comprise the balance of the Risk Management paradigm. Information Risk Management (IRM) is an increasingly complex and dynamic task. In the budding Information Age, the technology of information storage, processing, transfer, and access has exploded, leaving efforts to secure that information effectively in a never-ending catch-up mode. For the risks potentially associated with information and information technology (IT) to be identified and managed cost-effectively, it is essential that the process of analyzing and assessing risk is well understood by all parties and executed on a timely basis.

Terms and Definitions

To discuss information risk analysis and assessment, several terms need to be defined:

Annualized Loss Expectancy (ALE). This discrete value is derived, classically, from the following algorithm (see also the definitions for single loss expectancy [SLE] and annualized rate of occurrence [ARO] below):

Annualized Loss Expectancy = Single Loss Expectancy × Annualized Rate of Occurrence

To effectively identify risk and to plan budgets for information risk management and related risk reduction activity, it is helpful to express loss expectancy in annualized terms. For example, the preceding algorithm will show that the ALE for a threat (with an SLE of $1,000,000) that is expected to occur only about once in 10,000 years is $1,000,000 divided by 10,000, or only $100.00. When the expected threat frequency of 1/10,000 (ARO) was factored into the equation, the significance of this risk factor was addressed and integrated into the information risk management process. Thus, risk was more accurately portrayed, and the basis for meaningful cost/benefit analysis of risk reduction measures was established.

Annualized Rate of Occurrence (ARO). This term characterizes, on an annualized basis, the frequency with which a threat is expected to occur. For example, a threat occurring once in ten years has an ARO of 1/10 or 0.1; a threat occurring 50 times in a given year has an ARO of 50.0. The possible range of frequency values is from 0.0 (the threat is not expected to occur) to some whole number whose magnitude depends on the type and population of threat sources. For example, the upper value could exceed 100,000 events per year for minor, frequently experienced threats such as misuse of resources. For an example of how quickly the number of threat events can mount, imagine a small organization — about 100 staff members, having logical access to an information processing system. If each of those 100 persons misused the system only once a month, misuse events would be occurring at the rate of 1200 events per year. It is useful to note here that many confuse ARO or frequency with the term and concept of probability (defined below). While the statistical and mathematical significance of these metrics tend to converge at about 1/100 and become essentially indistinguishable below that level of frequency or probability, they become increasingly divergent above 1/100, to the point where probability stops — at 1.0 or certainty — and frequency continues to mount undeterred, by definition.

Exposure Factor (EF). This factor represents a measure of the magnitude of loss or impact on the value of an asset. It is expressed as a percent, ranging from 0 to 100%, of asset value loss arising from a threat event. This factor is used in the calculation of single loss expectancy (SLE), which is defined below.

Information Asset. This term, in general, represents the body of information an organization must have to conduct its mission or business. A specific information asset may consist of any subset of the complete body of information (i.e., accounts payable, inventory control, payroll, etc.). Information is regarded as an intangible asset separate from the media on which it resides. There are several elements of value to be considered: first is the simple cost of replacing the information, second is the cost of replacing supporting software, and the third through the fifth elements constitute a series of values that reflect the costs associated with loss of the information's confidentiality, availability, and integrity. Some consider the supporting hardware and netware to be information assets as well. However, these are distinctly tangible assets. Therefore, using tangibility as the distinguishing characteristic, it is logical to characterize hardware differently than the information itself. Software, on the other hand, is often regarded as information. These five elements of the value of an information asset often dwarf all other values relevant to an assessment of risk. It should be noted as well that these elements of value are not necessarily additive for the purpose of assessing risk. In both assessing risk and establishing cost justification for risk-reducing safeguards, it is useful to be able to isolate safeguard effects among these elements. Clearly, for an organization to conduct its mission or business, the necessary information must be present where it is supposed to be, when it is supposed to be there, and in the expected form. Further, if desired confidentiality is lost, results could range from no financial loss if confidentiality is not an issue, to loss of market share in the private sector, to compromise of national security in the public sector.

Qualitative/Quantitative. There are two methods for performing risk analysis: quantitative and qualitative. Quantitative risk analysis attempts to assign independently objective numeric numbers (i.e., monetary values) to all elements of the risk analysis. Qualitative risk analysis, on the other hand, does not attempt to assign numeric values at all, but rather is scenario oriented.

The terms "qualitative" and "quantitative" indicate the (oversimplified) binary categorization of risk metrics and information risk management techniques. In reality, there is a spectrum, across which these terms apply, virtually always in combination. This spectrum can be described as the degree to which the risk management process is quantified.

If all elements — asset value, impact, threat frequency, safeguard effectiveness, safeguard costs, uncertainty, and probability — are quantified, the process may be characterized as fully quantitative. It is virtually impossible to conduct a purely quantitative risk analysis project, because the quantitative measurements must be applied to some qualitative properties, that is, characterizations of vulnerability of the target environment. For example, "failure to impose logical access control" is a qualitative statement of vulnerability. However, it is possible to conduct a purely qualitative risk analysis project.

A vulnerability analysis, for example, might identify only the absence of risk-reducing countermeasures, such as logical access controls (although even this simple qualitative process has an implicit quantitative element in its binary yes/no method of evaluation). In summary, risk assessment techniques should be described not as either qualitative or quantitative but in terms of the degree to which such elementary factors as asset value, exposure factor, and threat frequency are assigned quantitative values.

Probability. This term characterizes the chance or likelihood that an event will occur. For example, the probability of getting a 6 on a single roll of a die is 1/6, or 0.16667. The possible range of probability values is 0.0 to 1.0. A probability of 1.0 expresses certainty that the subject event will occur within the finite interval. Conversely, a probability of 0.0 expresses certainty that the subject event will not occur within a finite interval.

Risk. The potential for harm or loss is best expressed as the answers to these four previously mentioned questions:

- What could happen? (What is the threat?)
- How bad could it be? (What is the impact or consequence?)
- How often might it happen? (What is the frequency?)
- How certain are the answers to the first three questions? (What is the degree of confidence?)

Risk Analysis. This term represents the process of analyzing a target environment and the relationships of its risk-related attributes. The analysis should identify threat vulnerabilities, associate these vulnerabilities with affected assets, identify the potential for and nature of an undesirable result, and identify and evaluate risk-reducing countermeasures.

Risk Assessment. This term represents the assignment of value to assets, threat frequency (annualized), consequence (i.e., exposure factors), and other elements of chance. The reported results of risk analysis can be said to provide an assessment or measurement of risk, regardless of the degree to which quantitative techniques are applied. For consistency in this chapter, the term "risk assessment" hereafter is used to characterize both the process and the result of analyzing and assessing risk.

Risk Management. This term characterizes the overall process. The first, or risk assessment, phase includes identifying risks, risk-reducing measures, and the budgetary impact of implementing decisions related to the acceptance, avoidance, or transfer of risk. The second phase of risk management includes the process of assigning priority to, budgeting, implementing, and maintaining appropriate risk-reducing measures. Risk management is a continuous process of ever-increasing complexity. It is how we evaluate the impact of exposures and respond to them.

Safeguard. This term represents a risk-reducing measure that acts to detect, prevent, or minimize loss associated with the occurrence of a specified threat or category of threats. Safeguards are also often described as controls or countermeasures.

Safeguard Effectiveness. This term represents the degree, expressed as a percent, from 0 to 100%, to which a safeguard can be characterized as effectively mitigating a vulnerability (defined below) and reducing associated loss risks.

Single Loss Expectancy or Exposure (SLE). This value is classically derived from the following algorithm to determine the monetary loss (impact) for each occurrence of a threatened event:

$$\text{Single Loss Expectancy} = \text{Asset Value} \times \text{Exposure Factor}$$

Threat. This term defines an event (e.g., a tornado, theft, or computer virus infection), the occurrence of which could have an undesirable impact on the well-being of an asset.

Uncertainty. This term characterizes the degree, expressed as a percent, from 0.0% to 100%, to which there is less than complete confidence in the value of any element of the risk assessment. Uncertainty is typically measured inversely with respect to confidence; that is, if confidence is low, uncertainty is high.

Exposure. This term refers to an instance of being exposed to losses from a specific threat.

Vulnerability. This term characterizes the absence or weakness of a risk-reducing safeguard. It is a condition that has the potential to allow a threat to occur with greater frequency, greater impact, or both. For example, not having a fire suppression system could allow an otherwise minor, easily quenched fire to become a catastrophic fire. Both the expected frequency (ARO) and the exposure factor (EF) for fire are increased as a consequence of not having a fire suppression system.

Central Tasks of Information Risk Management

The following sections describe the tasks central to the comprehensive information risk management process. These tasks provide concerned management with the identification and assessment of risk as well as cost-justified recommendations for risk reduction, thus allowing the execution of well-informed management decisions on whether to avoid, accept, or transfer risk cost-effectively. The degree of quantitative orientation determines how the results are characterized and, to some extent, how they are used.

Establish Information Risk Management Policy. A sound IRM program is founded on a well-thought-out IRM policy infrastructure that effectively addresses all elements of information security. IRM policy should begin with a high-level policy statement and supporting objectives, scope, constraints, responsibilities, and approach. This high-level policy statement should drive subordinate controls policy, from logical access control, to facilities security, to contingency planning.

Finally, IRM policy should be effectively communicated and enforced to all parties. Note that this is important both for internal control and, with EDI, the Internet, and other external exposures, for secure interface with the rest of the world.

Establish and Fund an IRM Team. Much of IRM functionality should already be in place — logical access control, contingency planning, etc. However, it is likely that the central task of IRM, risk assessment, has not been built into the established approach to IRM or has, at best, been given only marginal support. At the most senior management level possible, the tasks and responsibilities of IRM should be coordinated and IRM-related budgets cost-justified based on a sound integration and implementation of risk assessment. At the outset, the IRM team can be drawn from existing IRM-related staffing. The person charged with responsibility for executing risk assessment tasks should be an experienced Information Technology generalist with a sound understanding of the broad issues of information security. This person will need the incidental support of one who can assist at key points of the risk assessment task, that is, scribing a Modified Delphi information valuation. In the first year of an IRM program, the lead person could be expected to devote 50 to 75% of his or her time to the process of establishing and executing the balance of the IRM tasks, the first of which follows immediately below. Funds should be allocated according (1) to the above minimum staffing and (2) to acquire and be trained in the use of a suitable automated risk assessment tool.

Establish IRM Methodology and Tools. There are two fundamental applications of risk assessment to be addressed: (1) determining the current status of information security in the target environment(s) and ensuring that associated risk is managed (accepted, mitigated, or transferred) according to policy, and (2) assessing risk strategically. Strategic assessment assures that risk is effectively considered before funds are expended on a specific change in the information technology environment: a change that could have been shown to be "too risky." Strategic assessment allows management to effectively consider the risks in its decision-making process.

With the availability of good automated risk assessment tools, the methodology is, to a large extent, determined by the approach and procedures associated with the tool of choice. Increasingly, management is looking for quantitative results that support cost/benefit analysis and budgetary planning.

Identify and Measure Risk. Once IRM policy, team, and risk assessment methodology and tools are established and acquired, the first risk assessment will be executed. This first risk assessment should be as broadly scoped as possible, so that (1) management gets a good sense of the current status of information security, and (2) management has a sound basis for establishing initial risk acceptance criteria and risk mitigation priorities.

Project Sizing. This task includes the identification of background, scope, constraints, objectives, responsibilities, approach, and management support. Clear project-sizing statements are essential to a well-defined and well-executed risk assessment project. It should also be noted that a clear articulation of project constraints (what is not included in the project) is very important to the success of a risk assessment.

Information Protection Environment

Threat Analysis

This task includes the identification of threats that may adversely impact the target environment.

Asset Identification and Valuation

This task includes the identification of assets, both tangible and intangible, their replacement costs, and the further valuing of information asset availability, integrity, and confidentiality. These values can be expressed in monetary (for quantitative) or non-monetary (for qualitative) terms.

Vulnerability Analysis

This task includes the identification of vulnerabilities that could increase the frequency or impact of threat event(s) affecting the target environment.

Risk Evaluation

This task includes the evaluation of all collected information regarding threats, vulnerabilities, assets, and asset values in order to measure the associated chance of loss and the expected magnitude of loss for each of an array of threats that could occur. Results are usually expressed in monetary terms on an annualized basis (ALE) or graphically as a probabilistic "risk curve" for a quantitative risk assessment. For a qualitative risk assessment, results are usually expressed through a matrix of qualitative metrics such as ordinal ranking (low, medium, high, or 1, 2, 3) and a scenario description of the threat and potential consequences.

Interim Reports and Recommendations

These key reports are often issued during this process to document significant activity, decisions, and agreements related to the project.

- *Project sizing.* This report presents the results of the project sizing task. The report is issued to senior management for their review and concurrence. This report, when accepted, assures that all parties understand and concur in the nature of the project before it is launched.
- *Asset identification and valuation.* This report may detail (or summarize) the results of the asset valuation task, as desired. It is issued to management for their review and concurrence. Such review helps prevent conflict about value later in the process. This report often provides management with its first insight into the value of the availability, confidentiality, or integrity of the information assets.
- *Risk evaluation.* This report presents management with a documented assessment of risk in the current environment. Management may choose to accept that level of risk (a legitimate management decision) with no further action or proceed with risk mitigation analysis.

Establish Risk Acceptance Criteria

With the results of the first risk assessment determined through the risk evaluation task and associated reports (see above), management, with the interpretive help from the IRM leader, should establish the maximum acceptable financial risk. For example, "do not accept more than a 1 in 100 chance of losing $1,000,000" in a given year. With that, and possibly additional risk acceptance criteria, such as "do not accept an ALE greater than $500,000," proceed with the task of risk mitigation.

Mitigate Risk

The first step in this task is to complete the risk assessment with the risk mitigation, costing, and cost/benefit analysis. This task provides management with the decision support information necessary to plan for, budget, and execute actual risk mitigation measures; that is, fix the financially unacceptable vulnerabilities. The following risk assessment tasks are discussed in further detail in the section entitled "Tasks of Risk Assessment" later in this chapter.

Safeguard Selection and Risk Mitigation Analysis

This task includes the identification of risk-reducing safeguards that mitigate vulnerabilities and the degree to which selected safeguards can be expected to reduce threat frequency or impact. That is, this task comprises the evaluation of risk regarding assets and threats before and after selected safeguards are applied.

Cost/Benefit Analysis

This task includes the valuation of the degree of risk reduction that is expected to be achieved by implementing the selected risk-reducing safeguards. The gross benefit, less the annualized cost for safeguards selected to achieve a reduced level of risk, yields the net benefit. Tools such as present value and return on investment are often applied to further analyze safeguard cost-effectiveness.

Final Report

This report includes the interim report results as well as details and recommendations from the safeguard selection and risk mitigation analysis, and supporting cost/benefit analysis tasks. This report, with approved recommendations, provides responsible management with a sound basis for subsequent risk management action and administration.

Monitor Information Risk Management Performance

Having established the IRM program, and gone this far — recommended risk mitigation measures have been acquired or developed and implemented — it is time to begin and maintain a process of monitoring IRM performance. This can be done by periodically reassessing risks to ensure that there is sustained adherence to good control or that failure to do so is revealed, consequences considered, and improvement, as appropriate, duly implemented.

Strategic risk assessment plays a significant role in the risk mitigation process by helping to avoid uninformed risk acceptance and having, later, to retrofit necessary information security measures.

There are numerous variations on this risk management process, based on the degree to which the technique applied is quantitative and how thoroughly all steps are executed. For example, the asset identification

17

and valuation analysis could be performed independently. The vulnerability analysis could also be executed independently. It is commonly but incorrectly assumed that information risk management is concerned only with catastrophic threats, and that it is useful only to support contingency planning and related activities. A well-conceived and well-executed risk assessment can and should be used effectively to identify and quantify the consequences of a wide array of threats that can and do occur, often with significant frequency as a result of ineffectively implemented or nonexistent information technology management, administrative, and operational controls.

A well-run information risk management program — an integrated risk management program — can help management to significantly improve the cost-effective performance of its information systems environment whether it is network, mainframe, client/server, Internet, or any combination — and to ensure cost-effective compliance with regulatory requirements. The integrated risk management concept recognizes that many, often uncoordinated, units within an organization play an active role in managing the risks associated with the failure to assure the confidentiality, availability, and integrity of information. Security concerns should be an integral part of the entire planning, development, and operation of an information system. Much of what needs to be done to improve security is not clearly separable from what is needed to improve the usefulness, reliability, effectiveness, and efficiency of the information system. A risk analysis is essential to the determination of the controls necessary to securely operate a system that contains valuable/sensitive/critical information in a specific environment.

Resistance and Benefits

"Why should I bother with doing risk assessment?" "I already know what the risks are!" "I've got enough to worry about already!" "It hasn't happened yet...." Sound familiar? Most resistance to risk assessment boils down to one of three conditions:

- Ignorance
- Arrogance
- Fear

Management often is ignorant, except in the most superficial context, of the risk assessment process, the real nature of the risks, and the benefits of risk assessment. Risk assessment is not yet a broadly accepted element of the management toolkit, yet virtually every large consultancy firm and other major providers of information security services offer risk assessment in some form.

The importance of the bottom line often drives an organization's attitude about information security and, therefore, makes it arrogant about risk assessment. "Damn the torpedoes, full speed ahead!" becomes the marching order. If it cannot readily be shown to improve profitability, do not do it. It is commendable that information technology has become so reliable that management could maintain that attitude for more than a few giddy seconds. Despite the fact that a well-secured information environment is also a well-controlled, efficient information environment, management often has difficulty seeing how sound information security can and does affect the bottom line in a positive way. This arrogance is often described euphemistically as an "entrepreneurial culture."

There is also the fear of discovering that the environment is not as well managed as it could be and having to take responsibility for that; the fear of discovering, and having to address, risks not already known; and the fear of being shown to be ignorant or arrogant. While good information security may seem expensive, inadequate information security will be not just expensive, but — sooner or later — catastrophic. Risk assessment, although still a young science with a certain amount of craft involved, has proven itself to be very useful in helping management understand and cost-effectively address the risks to their information environments.

Finally, with regard to resistance, when risk assessment had to be done manually or could be done only quantitatively, the fact that the process could take many months to execute and that it was not amenable to revision or "what-if" assessment was a credible obstacle to its successful use. But that is no longer the case. Some specific benefits are described below:

- Risk assessment helps management understand:
  - What is at risk?
  - The value at risk, as associated with the identity of information assets and with the confidentiality, availability, and integrity of information assets.
  - The kinds of threats that could occur and their annualized financial consequences.
  - Risk mitigation analysis: what can be done to reduce risk to an acceptable level.
  - Risk mitigation costs (annualized) and associated cost/benefit analysis: whether suggested risk mitigation activity is cost-effective.
- Risk assessment enables a strategic approach to risk management. That is, possible changes being considered for the information technology environment can be assessed to identify the least risk alternative before funds are committed to any alternative. This information complements the standard business case for change and may produce critical decision support information that could otherwise be overlooked.

- "What-if" analysis is supported using automated risk analysis systems. This is a variation on the strategic approach to risk management. Alternative approaches can be considered and their associated level of risk compared in a matter of minutes.
- Results are timely; a risk assessment can be completed in a matter of a few days to a few weeks using qualitative risk analysis techniques. Risk assessment no longer has to take many months to execute.
- Information security professionals can present their recommendations with credible statistical and financial support.
- Management can make well-informed risk management decisions.
- Management can justify, with quantitative tools, information security budgets or expenditures that are based on a reasonably objective risk assessment.
- Good information security supported by risk assessment will ensure an efficient, cost-effective information technology environment.
- Management can avoid spending that is based solely on an inadequate perception of risk.
- A risk management program based on the sound application of quantitative/qualitative risk assessment can be expected to reduce liability exposure and insurance costs.

Security Technology and Tools

Qualitative versus Quantitative Approaches

As characterized briefly above, there are two fundamentally different metric schemes applied to the measurement of risk elements: qualitative and quantitative.

Early efforts to conduct quantitative risk assessments ran into considerable difficulty. First, because no initiative was executed to establish and maintain an independently verifiable and reliable set of risk metrics and statistics, everyone came up with his own approach; second, the process, while simple in concept, was complex in execution; third, large amounts of data were collected that required substantial and complex mapping, pairing, and calculation to build representative risk models; and fourth, with no software and desktop computers, the work was done manually — a very tedious and time-consuming process. Results varied significantly. As a consequence, while some developers launched and continued efforts to develop credible and efficient automated quantitative risk assessment tools, others developed more expedient qualitative approaches that did not require independently objective metrics.

These qualitative approaches enabled a much more subjective approach to the valuation of information assets and the scaling of risk. Take the example where the value of the availability of information and the associated risk are described as "low," "medium," or "high" in the opinion of knowledgeable management, as gained through interviews or question-naires. Often, when this approach is taken, a strategy is defined wherein the highest risk exposures require prompt attention, the moderate risk exposures require plans for corrective attention, and the lowest risk exposures can be accepted.

Elements of Risk Metrics

There are six primitive elements of risk modeling to which some form of metric can be applied:

- Asset Value
- Threat Frequency
- Threat Exposure Factor
- Safeguard Effectiveness
- Safeguard Cost
- Uncertainty

To the extent that each of these elements is quantified in independently objective metrics such as the monetary replacement value for Asset Value or the Annualized Rate of Occurrence for Threat Frequency, the risk assessment is increasingly quantitative. If all six elements are quantified with independently objective metrics, the risk assessment is said to be fully quantified, and the full range of statistical analyses is supported.

The classic quantitative algorithm that lays out the foundation for infor-mation security risk assessment is simple:

(Asset Value × Exposure Factor = Single Loss Exposure)
× Annualized Rate of Occurrence
= Annualized Loss Expectancy

For example, take a look at the risk of fire. Assume the asset value is $1M, the exposure factor is 50%, and the annualized rate of occurrence is 1/10 (once in ten years). Plugging these values into the algorithm yields the following:

($1M × 50% = $500K) × 1/10 = $50K

Using conventional cost/benefit assessment, the $50K ALE represents the cost/benefit break-even point for risk mitigation measures. That is, the organization could justify spending up to $50K per year to prevent the occurrence or reduce the impact of a fire.

This effort to simplify fundamental statistical analysis processes so that everyone can readily understand the algorithms developed for quantita-tive risk analysis sometimes goes too far. The consequences are sometimes results that have little credibility for several reasons, three of which follow:

- The classic algorithm addresses all but two of the elements recommended: safeguard effectiveness and uncertainty. Both of these must be addressed in some way; and uncertainty, the key risk factor, must be addressed explicitly.
- The algorithm cannot distinguish effectively between low-frequency/high-impact threats (such as "fire") and high-frequency/low-impact threats (such as "misuse of resources"). Therefore, associated risks can be significantly misrepresented.
- Each element is addressed as a discrete value, which, when considered with the failure to address uncertainty explicitly, makes it difficult to actually model risk and illustrate probabilistically the range of potential undesirable outcomes.

In other words, this primitive algorithm did have shortcomings, but advances in quantitative risk assessment technology and methodology to explicitly address uncertainty and support technically correct risk modeling have largely done away with those problems.

Pros and Cons of Qualitative and Quantitative Approaches

In this brief analysis, the features of specific tools and approaches will not be discussed. Rather, the pros and cons associated in general with qualitative and quantitative methodologies will be addressed.

- Qualitative pros:
  - Calculations, if any, are simple and readily understood and executed.
  - It is usually not necessary to determine the monetary value of information (its availability, confidentiality, and integrity).
  - It is not necessary to determine quantitative threat frequency and impact data.
  - It is not necessary to estimate the cost of recommended risk mitigation measures and calculate cost/benefit because the process is not quantitative.
  - A general indication of significant areas of risk that should be addressed is provided.
- Qualitative cons:
  - The risk assessment and results are essentially subjective in both process and metrics. The use of independently objective metrics is eliminated.
  - No effort is made to develop an objective monetary basis for the value of targeted information assets. Hence, the perception of value may not realistically reflect actual value at risk.
  - No basis is provided for cost/benefit analysis of risk mitigation measures, only subjective indication of a problem.

- It is not possible to track risk management performance objectively when all measures are subjective.
- Quantitative pros:
  - The assessment and results are based substantially on independently objective processes and metrics. Thus, meaningful statistical analysis is supported.
  - The value of information (availability, confidentiality, and integrity), as expressed in monetary terms with supporting rationale, is better understood. Thus, the basis for expected loss is better understood.
  - A credible basis for cost/benefit assessment of risk mitigation measures is provided. Thus, information security budget decision making is supported.
  - Risk management performance can be tracked and evaluated.
  - Risk assessment results are derived and expressed in management's language, monetary value, percentages, and probability annualized. Thus, risk is better understood.
- Quantitative cons:
  - Calculations are complex. If they are not understood or effectively explained, management may mistrust the results of "black-box" calculations.
  - It is not practical to attempt to execute a quantitative risk assessment without using a recognized automated tool and associated knowledge bases. A manual effort, even with the support of spreadsheet and generic statistical software, can easily take ten to twenty times the work effort required with the support of a good automated risk assessment tool.
  - A substantial amount of information about the target information and its IT environment must be gathered.
  - As of this writing, there is not yet a standard, independently developed and maintained threat population and threat frequency knowledge base. Thus, users must rely on the credibility of the vendors that develop and support the automated tools or do threat research on their own.

Tasks of Risk Assessment

In this section, we explore the classic tasks of risk assessment and the key issues associated with each task, regardless of the specific approach to be employed. The focus is, in general, primarily on quantitative methodologies. However, wherever possible, related issues in qualitative methodologies are discussed.

Project Sizing. In virtually all project methodologies, there are a number of elements to be addressed to ensure that all participants, and the target audience, understand and are in agreement about the project. These elements include:

- Background
- Purpose
- Scope
- Constraints
- Objective
- Responsibilities
- Approach

In most cases, it is not necessary to discuss these individually, as most are well-understood elements of project methodology in general. In fact, they are mentioned here for the exclusive purpose of pointing out the importance of (1) ensuring that there is agreement between the target audience and those responsible for executing the risk assessment, and (2) describing the constraints on a risk assessment project. While a description of the scope (i.e., what is included) of a risk assessment project is important, it is equally important to describe specifically, and in appropriate terms, what is not included.

Typically, a risk assessment is focused on a subset of the organization's information assets and control functions. If what is not to be included is not identified, confusion and misunderstanding about the risk assessment's ramifications can result. Again, the most important point about the project sizing task is to ensure that the project is clearly defined and that a clear understanding of the project by all parties is achieved.

Threat Analysis. In manual approaches and some automated tools, the analyst must determine what threats to consider in a particular risk assessment. Because there is not, at present, a standard threat population and readily available threat statistics, this task can require a considerable research effort. Of even greater concern is the possibility that a significant local threat could be overlooked and associated risks inadvertently accepted. Worse, it is possible that a significant threat is intentionally disregarded.

The best automated tools currently available include a well-researched threat population and associated statistics. Using one of these tools virtually ensures that no relevant threat is overlooked, and associated risks are accepted as a consequence.

If, however, a determination has been made not to use one of these leading automated tools and instead to do the threat analysis independently, there are good sources for a number of threats, particularly for all natural disasters, fire, and crime (oddly enough, not so much for computer crime), and even falling aircraft. Also, the console log is an excellent source of in-house experience of system development, maintenance, operations, and other events that can be converted into useful threat event statistics with a little tedious review. Finally, in-house physical and logical access logs (assuming such are maintained) can be a good source of related threat event data.

However, gathering this information independently, even for the experienced risk analyst, is no trivial task. Weeks, if not months, of research and calculation will be required, and, without validation, results may be less than credible.

Asset Identification and Valuation. While all assets can be valued qualitatively, such an approach is useless if there is a need to make well-founded budgetary decisions. Therefore, this discussion of asset identification and valuation will assume a need for the application of monetary valuation.

There are two general categories of assets relevant to the assessment of risk in the IT environment:

- Tangible assets
- Intangible assets

Tangible Assets. The tangible assets include the IT facilities, hardware, media, supplies, documentation, and IT staff budgets that support the storage, processing, and delivery of information to the user community. The value of these assets is readily determined, typically, in terms of the cost of replacing them. If any of these are leased, of course, the replacement cost may be nil, depending on the terms of the lease.

Sources for establishing these values are readily found in the associated asset management groups, that is, facilities management for replacement value of the facilities, hardware management for the replacement value for the hardware — from CPUs to controllers, routers and cabling, annual IT staff budgets for IT staff, etc.

Intangible Assets. The intangible assets, which might be better characterized as information assets, are comprised of two basic categories:

- Replacement costs for data and software
- The value of the confidentiality, integrity, and availability of information

Replacement Costs. Developing replacement costs for data is not usually a complicated task unless source documents do not exist or are not backed up, reliably, at a secure off-site location. The bottom line is that "x" amount of data represents "y" keystrokes — a time-consuming but readily measurable manual key entry process.

Conceivably, source documents can now be electronically "scanned" to recover lost, electronically stored data. Clearly, scanning is a more efficient process, but it is still time-consuming. However, if neither source documents nor off-site backups exist, actual replacement may become virtually impossible and the organization faces the question of whether such a condition can be tolerated. If, in the course of the assessment, this condition is found, the real issue is that the information is no longer available, and a determination must be made as to whether such a condition can be overcome without bankrupting the private-sector organization or irrevocably compromising a government mission.

Value of Confidentiality, Integrity, and Availability

In recent years, a better understanding of the values of confidentiality, integrity, and availability and how to establish these values on a monetary basis with reasonable credibility has been achieved. That understanding is best reflected in the ISSA-published "Guideline for Information Valuation" (GIV). These values often represent the most significant "at-risk" asset in IT environments. When an organization is deprived of one or more of these with regard to its business or mission information, depending on the nature of that business or mission, there is a very real chance that unacceptable loss will be incurred within a relatively short time.

For example, it is well accepted that a bank that loses access to its business information (loss of availability) for more than a few days is very likely to go bankrupt. A brief explanation of each of these three critical values for information is presented below.

Confidentiality. Confidentiality is lost or compromised when information is disclosed to parties other than those authorized to have access to the information. In today's complex world of IT, there are many ways a person can access information without proper authorization if appropriate controls are not in place. Without appropriate controls, that access or theft of information could be accomplished without a trace. Of course, it still remains possible to simply pick up and walk away with confidential documents carelessly left lying about or displayed on an unattended, unsecured PC.

Integrity. Integrity is the condition that information in or produced by the IT environment accurately reflects the source or process it represents. Integrity can be compromised in many ways, from data entry errors to software errors to intentional modification. Integrity can be thoroughly compromised, for example, by simply contaminating the account numbers of a bank's demand deposit records. Because the account numbers are a primary reference for all associated data, the information is effectively no longer available. There has been a great deal of discussion about the nature of integrity. Technically, if a single character is wrong in a file with millions of records, the file's integrity has been compromised. Realistically, however, some expected degree of integrity must be established. In an address file, 99% accuracy (only 1 out of 100 is wrong) may be acceptable. However, in the same file, if each record of 100 characters had only one character wrong — in the account number — the records would meet the poorly articulated 99% accuracy standard, but be completely compromised. That is, the loss of integrity can have consequences that range from trivial to catastrophic.

Of course, in a bank with one million clients, 99% accuracy means, at best, that the records of 10,000 clients are in error. In a hospital, even one such error could lead to loss of life.

Availability. Availability — the condition that electronically stored information is where it needs to be, when it needs to be there, and in the form necessary — is closely related to the availability of the information processing technology. Whether because the process is unavailable, or the information itself is somehow unavailable, makes no difference to the organization dependent on the information to conduct its business or mission. The value of the information's availability is reflected in the costs incurred, over time, by the organization, because the information was not available, regardless of cause.

Vulnerability Analysis

This task consists of the identification of vulnerabilities that would allow threats to occur with greater frequency, greater impact, or both. For maximum utility, this task is best conducted as a series of one-on-one interviews with individual staff members responsible for developing or implementing organizational policy through the management and administration of controls. To maximize consistency and thoroughness, and to minimize subjectivity, the vulnerability analysis should be conducted by an interviewer who guides each interviewee through a well-researched series of questions designed to ferret out all potentially significant vulnerabilities.

Threat/Vulnerability/Asset Mapping. Without connecting — mapping — threats to vulnerabilities and vulnerabilities to assets and establishing a consistent way of measuring the consequences of their interrelationships, it becomes nearly impossible to establish the ramifications of vulnerabilities in a useful manner. Of course, intuition and common sense are useful, but how does one measure the risk and support good budgetary management and cost/benefit analysis when the rationale is so abstract?

For example, it is only good common sense to have logical access control, but how does one justify the expense? Take an example of a major bank whose management, in a cost-cutting frenzy, comes very close to terminating its entire logical access control program! With risk assessment, one can show the expected risk and annualized asset loss/probability coordinates that reflect the ramifications of a wide array of vulnerabilities.

By mapping vulnerabilities to threats to assets, we can see the interplay among them and understand a fundamental concept of risk assessment:

Vulnerabilities allow threats to occur with greater frequency or greater impact. Intuitively, it can be seen that the more vulnerabilities there are, the greater the risk of loss.

Risk Metrics/Modeling. There are a number of ways to portray risk, some qualitative, some quantitative, and some more effective than others. In general, the objective of risk modeling is to convey to decision makers a credible, usable portrayal of the risks associated with the IT environment, answering (again) these questions:

- What could happen (threat event)?
- How bad would it be (impact)?
- How often might it occur (frequency)?
- How certain are the answers to the first three questions (uncertainty)?

With such risk modeling, decision makers are on their way to making well-informed decisions — either to accept, mitigate, or transfer associated risk.

Risk Mitigation Analysis. With the completion of the risk modeling and associated report on the observed status of information security and related issues, management will almost certainly find some areas of risk that they are unwilling to accept and for which they wish to see a proposed risk mitigation analysis. That is, they will want answers to the previous three questions for those unacceptable risks:

- What can be done?
- How much will it cost?
- Is it cost-effective?

There are three steps in this process:

- Safeguard Analysis and Expected Risk Mitigation
- Safeguard Costing
- Safeguard Cost/Benefit Analysis

Safeguard Analysis and Expected Risk Mitigation. With guidance from the results of the risk evaluation, including modeling and associated data collection tasks, and reflecting management concerns, the analyst will seek to identify and apply safeguards that could be expected to mitigate the vulnerabilities of greatest concern to management. Management will, of course, be most concerned about those vulnerabilities that could allow the greatest loss expectancies for one or more threats, or those subject to regulatory or contractual compliance. The analyst, to do this step manually, must first select appropriate safeguards for each targeted vulnerability; second, map or confirm mapping, safeguard/vulnerability pairs to all related threats; and third, determine, for each threat, the extent of asset risk mitigation to be achieved by applying the safeguard. In other words, for each affected threat, determine whether the selected safeguard(s) will reduce threat frequency, reduce threat exposure factors, or both, and to what degree.

Done manually, this step will consume many days or weeks of tedious work effort. Any "What-If" assessment will be very time-consuming as well. When this step is executed with the support of a knowledge-based expert automated tool, however, only a few hours to a couple of days are expended, at most.

Safeguard Costing. To perform a useful cost/benefit analysis, estimated costs for all suggested safeguards must be developed. While these cost estimates should be reasonably accurate, it is not necessary that they be precise. However, if one is to err at this point, it is better to overstate costs. Then, as bids or detailed cost proposals come in, it is more likely that cost/benefit analysis results, as shown below, will not overstate the benefit.

There are two basic categories of costing for safeguards:

- Cost per square foot, installed
- Time and materials

In both cases, the expected life and annual maintenance costs must be included to get the average annual cost over the life of the safeguard. These average annual costs represent the break-even point for safeguard cost/benefit assessment for each safeguard. Most of the leading automated risk assessment tools allow the analyst to input bounded distributions with associated confidence factors to articulate explicitly the uncertainty of the values for these preliminary cost estimates. These bounded distributions with confidence factors facilitate the best use of optimal probabilistic analysis algorithms.

Assurance, Trust, and Confidence Mechanisms

Safeguard Cost/Benefit Analysis

The risk assessment is now almost complete, although this final set of calculations is, once again, not trivial. In previous steps, the expected value of risk mitigation — the annualized loss expectancy (ALE) before safeguards are applied, less the ALE after safeguards are applied, less the average annual costs of the applied safeguards — is conservatively represented individually, safeguard by safeguard, and collectively. The collective safeguard cost/benefit is represented first, threat by threat with applicable selected safeguards; and, second, showing the overall integrated risk for all threats with all selected safeguards applied. This can be illustrated as follows:

$$\text{Safeguard } 1 \rightarrow \text{Vulnerability } 1 \rightarrow n \rightarrow \text{Threat } 1 \rightarrow n$$

One safeguard can mitigate one or more vulnerabilities to one or more threats. A generalization of each of the three levels of calculation is represented below.

For the Single Safeguard. A single safeguard can act to mitigate risk for a number of threats. For example, a contingency plan will contain the loss for disasters by facilitating a timely recovery. The necessary calculation includes the integration of all affected threats' risk models before the safeguard is applied, less their integration after the safeguard is applied to define the gross risk reduction benefit. Finally, subtract the safeguard's average annual cost to derive the net annual benefit.

This information is useful in determining whether individual safeguards are cost-effective. If the net risk reduction (mitigation) benefit is negative, the benefit is negative (i.e., not cost-effective).

For the Single Threat. Any number of safeguards can act to mitigate risk for any number of threats. It is useful to determine, for each threat, how much the risk for that threat was mitigated by the collective population of safeguards selected that act to mitigate the risk for the threat. Recognize at the same time that one or more of these safeguards can also act to mitigate the risk for one or more other threats.

For All Threats. The integration of all individual threat risk models for before selected safeguards are applied and for after selected safeguards are applied shows the gross risk reduction benefit for the collective population of selected safeguards as a whole. Subtract the average annual cost of the selected safeguards, and the net risk reduction benefit as a whole is established.

This calculation will generate a single risk model that accurately represents the combined effect of all selected safeguards in mitigating risk for the array of affected threats. In other words, an executive summary of the expected results of proposed risk-mitigating measures is generated.

Information Protection and Management Services

Final Recommendations

After the risk assessment is complete, final recommendations should be prepared on two levels: (1) a categorical set of recommendations in an executive summary, and (2) detailed recommendations in the body of the risk assessment report. The executive summary recommendations are supported by the integrated risk model reflecting all threats' risks before and after selected safeguards are applied, the average annual cost of the selected safeguards, and their expected risk mitigation benefit.

The detailed recommendations should include a description of each selected safeguard and its supporting cost/benefit analysis. Detailed recommendations might also include an implementation plan. However, in most cases, implementation plans are not developed as part of the risk assessment report. Implementation plans are typically developed upon executive endorsement of specific recommendations.

1.3 Information Classification

We will now discuss Information Classification, which gives organizations a way to address their most significant risks, by affording them the appropriate level of security.

Information Protection Requirements

Classifying corporate information based on business risk, data value, or other criteria (as discussed later in this chapter) makes good business sense. Not all information has the same value or use, or is subject to the same risks. Therefore, protection mechanisms, recovery processes, etc., are — or should be — different, with differing costs associated with them. Data classification is intended to lower the cost of overprotecting all data, and improve the overall quality of corporate decision making by helping to ensure a higher level of trust in critical data upon which the decision makers depend.

The benefits of an enterprisewide data classification program are realized at the corporate level, not the individual application or even departmental level. Some of the benefits to the organization are:

- Data confidentiality, integrity, and availability are improved because appropriate controls are used for all data across the enterprise.
- The organization gets the most for its information protection dollar because protection mechanisms are designed and implemented where they are needed most, and less costly controls can be put in place for noncritical information.
- The quality of decisions is improved because the data upon which the decisions are made can be trusted.
- The company is provided with a process to review all business functions and informational requirements on a periodic basis to determine appropriate data classifications.

Information Protection Environment

This section discusses the processes and techniques required to establish and maintain a corporate data classification program. There are costs associated with this process; however, most of these costs are front-end start-up costs. Once the program has been successfully implemented, the cost savings derived from the new security schemes, as well as the improved decision making, should more than offset the initial costs over the long haul, and certainly the benefits of the ongoing program outweigh the small administrative costs associated with maintaining the data classification program.

Although many methodologies exist for developing and implementing a data classification program, the one described here is very effective. The following topics will be addressed:

- Getting started: questions to ask
- Policy
- Business impact analysis
- Establishing classifications
- Defining roles and responsibilities
- Identifying owners
- Classifying information and applications
- Ongoing monitoring

Getting Started: Questions to Ask

Before the actual implementation of the data classification program can begin, the Information Security Officer — who, for the purposes of this discussion, is the assumed project manager — must get the answers to some very important questions.

Is there an executive sponsor for this project? Although not absolutely essential, obtaining an executive sponsor and champion for the project could be a critical success factor. Executive backing by someone well respected in the organization who can articulate the Information Security Officer's position to other executives and department heads will help remove barriers, and obtain much needed funding and buy-in from others across the corporation. Without an executive sponsor, the Information Security Officer will have a difficult time gaining access to executives or other influential people who can help sell the concept of data ownership and classification.

What are you trying to protect, and from what? The Information Security Officer should develop a threat and risk analysis matrix to determine the threats to corporate information, the relative risks associated with those threats, and what data or information is subject to those threats. This matrix provides input to the business impact analysis and forms the beginning of the plans for determining the actual classifications of data, as will be discussed later in this chapter.

Are there any regulatory requirements to consider? Regulatory requirements will have an impact on any data classification scheme, if not on the classifications themselves, at least on the controls used to protect or provide access to regulated information. The Information Security Officer should be familiar with these laws and regulations, and use them as input to the business case justification for data classification.

Has the business accepted ownership responsibilities for the data? The business, not IT (information technology), owns the data. Decisions regarding who has what access, what classification the data should be assigned, etc., are decisions that rest solely with the business data owner and are based on organization policy. IT provides the technology and processes to implement the decisions of the data owners, but should not be involved in the decision-making process. The executive sponsor can be a tremendous help in selling this concept to the organization. Too many organizations still rely on IT for these types of decisions. The business manager must realize that the data is his data, not IT's; IT is merely the custodian of the data. Decisions regarding access, classification, ownership, etc., reside in the business units. This concept must be sold first if data classification is to be successful.

Are adequate resources available to do the initial project? Establishing the data classification processes and procedures, performing the business impact analysis, conducting training, etc., require an up-front commitment of a team of people from across the organization if the project is to be successful. The Information Security Officer cannot and should not do it alone. Again, the executive sponsor can be of tremendous value in obtaining resources, such as people and funding for this project, that the Information Security Officer could not do alone. Establishing the processes, procedures, and tools to implement good, well-defined data classification processes takes time and dedicated people. First you have to create and implement the policy.

Security Technology and Tools

Policy

An essential tool in establishing a data classification scheme is to have a corporate policy implemented stating that the data is an asset of the corporation and must be protected. Within that same document, the policy should state that information will be classified based on data value, sensitivity, risk of loss or compromise, and legal and retention requirements. This provides the Information Security Officer with the necessary authority

Exhibit 1. Sample Information Security Policy

All information, regardless of the form or format, that is created or used in support of company business activity is corporate information. Corporate sensitive and critical information is a company asset and must be protected from its creation, through its useful life and authorized disposal. It should be maintained in a secure, accurate, and reliable manner and be readily available for authorized use. Information will be classified based on its sensitivity, criticality, legal and retention requirements, and type of access required by employees and other authorized personnel.

Information security is the protection of data against accidental or malicious disclosure, modification, or destruction. Information will be protected based on its value or sensitivity or criticality to the company, and the risk of loss or compromise. At a minimum, information will be update-protected so that only authorized individuals can modify or erase the information.

---

to start the project, seek executive sponsorship, and obtain funding and other support for the effort. If there is an Information Security Policy, these statements should be added if they are not already there. If no Information Security Policy exists, then the Information Security Officer should put the data classification project on hold and develop an Information Security Policy for the organization. Without this policy, the Information Security Officer has no real authority or reason to pursue data classification. Information must first be recognized and treated as an asset of the company before efforts can be expended protecting it.

Assuming there is an Information Security Policy that mentions or states that data will be classified according to certain criteria, another policy — Data Management Policy — should be developed that establishes data classification as a process to protect information and defines:

- The definitions for each of the classifications
- The security criteria for each classification for both data and software
- The roles and responsibilities of each group of individuals charged with implementing the policy or using the data

Exhibit 1 shows a sample Information Security Policy. Note that the policy is written at a very high level and is intended to describe the "whats" of information security. Procedures, baselines, standards, and guidelines are the "hows" for implementation of the policy. The policy in Exhibit 1 is the minimum requirement to proceed with developing and implementing a data classification program. Additional policies may be required, such as an Information Management Policy, which supports the Information Security Policy. The Information Security Officer should consider developing this policy, and integrating it with the Information Security Policy. This policy would:

- Define information as an asset of the business unit
- Declare local business managers as the owners of information
- Establish IT as the custodians of corporate information
- Clearly define roles and responsibilities of those involved in the ownership and classification of information
- Define the classifications and criteria that must be met for each
- Determine the minimum range of controls to be established for each classification

By defining these elements in a separate Information Management Policy, the groundwork is established for defining a corporate information architecture, the purpose of which is to build a framework for integrating all the strategic information in the company. This architecture can be used later in the support of larger, more strategic corporate applications. The supporting policies, procedures, and standards required to implement the Information Security and Information Management policies must be defined at an operational level and be as seamless as possible. These are the "mechanical" portions of the policies and represent the day-to-day activities that must take place to implement the policies. These include but are not limited to:

- The procedure for conducting a Business Impact Analysis (BIA) for critical system outages or a Risk Analysis (RA) for sensitive system compromise
- Procedures to classify the information, both initially after the RA/BIA has been completed, and to change the classification later, based on business need
- The process to communicate the classification to IT in a timely manner so the controls can be applied to the data and software for that classification
- The procedure to periodically review:
  - Current classifications to determine if they are still valid
  - Current access rights of individuals and groups who have access to a particular resource
  - Controls in effect for classifications to determine their effectiveness
  - Training requirements for new data owners
- The procedure to notify custodians of any change in the classification of data/software or access privileges of individuals or groups

The appropriate policies are required as a first step in the development of a Data Classification program. The policies provide the Information Security Officer with the necessary authority and mandate to develop and implement the program. Without it, the Information Security Officer will have an extremely difficult time obtaining the funding and necessary support to move forward. In addition to the policies, the Information Security Officer should solicit the assistance and support of both the Legal Department and Internal Audit. If a particular end-user department has some particularly sensitive data, its support would also provide some credibility to the effort.

Risk Analysis

The next step in this process is to conduct a high-level risk analysis on the major business functions within the company. Eventually, this process should be carried out on all business functions, but initially it must be done on the business functions deemed most important to the organization.

A critical success factor in this effort is to obtain corporate sponsorship. An executive who supports the project, and may be willing to be the first whose area is analyzed, could help persuade others to participate, especially if the initial effort is highly successful and there is perceived value in the process.

A Study Team comprised of individuals from Information Security, Information Systems (application development and support), Business Continuity Planning, and business unit representatives should be formed to conduct the initial impact analysis. Others that may want to participate could include Internal Audit and Legal. The Risk Analysis process is used by the team to:

- Identify major functional areas of information (i.e., human resources, financial, engineering, research and development, marketing, etc.).
- Analyze the classification requirements associated with each major functional area. This is simply identifying the risk to data/processes associated with loss of confidentiality, integrity, or availability.
- Determine the risk associated with the classification requirement (i.e., the classification requirement could be to avoid disclosure of sensitive information, but the risk could be low because of the number of people who have access and the controls that are imposed on the data).
- Determine the effect of loss of the information asset on the business (this could be financial, regulatory impacts, safety, etc.) for specific periods of unavailability — one hour, one day, two days, one week, a month.
- Build a table detailing the impact of loss of the information.
- Prepare a list of applications that directly support the business function (i.e., human resources could have personnel, medical, payroll files, skills inventory, employee stock purchase programs, etc.).

From the information gathered, the team can determine classification requirements that cut across all business functional boundaries. This exercise can help place the applications in specific categories or classifications with a common set of controls to mitigate the common risks. The sensitivity of the information, ease of recovery, and criticality must be considered when determining the classification of the information.

Establish Classifications

Once all the risk and classification criteria have been gathered and analyzed, the team must determine how many classifications are necessary and create the classification definitions, determine the controls necessary for each classification for the information and software, and begin to develop the roles and responsibilities for those who will be involved in the process. Relevant factors, including regulatory requirements, must be considered when establishing the classifications.

Too many classifications will be impractical to implement and most certainly will be confusing to the data owners and meet with resistance. The team must resist the urge for special cases to have their own data classifications. The danger is that too much granularity will cause the process to collapse under its own weight. It will be difficult to administer and costly to maintain. On the other hand, too few classes could be perceived as not worth the administrative trouble to develop, implement, and maintain. A perception might be created that there is no value in the process, and indeed the critics may be right.

Each classification must have easily identifiable characteristics. There should be little or no overlap between the classes. The classifications should address how information and software are handled from their creation, through authorized disposal. Following is a sample of classification definitions that have been used in many organizations:

- *Public:* information that, if disclosed outside the company, would not harm the organization, its employees, customers, or business partners.
- *Internal Use Only:* information that is not sensitive to disclosure within the organization, but could harm the company if disclosed externally.
- *Company Confidential:* sensitive information that requires "need-to-know" before access is given.

It is important to note that controls must be designed and implemented for both the information and the software. It is not sufficient to classify and control the information alone. The software, and possibly the hardware on which the information or software reside, must also have proportionate controls for each classification the software processes.

Assurance, Trust, and Confidence Mechanisms

The following lists a set of minimum controls for both classified information and software that should be considered.

Classified Information: Minimum Controls

- *Encryption.* Data is encrypted with an encryption algorithm so that the data is "unreadable" to those who are unauthorized to view it. When the data is processed or viewed, it must be decrypted with the same key used to encrypt it. The encryption key must be kept secure and known only to those who are authorized to have access to the data. Public/private key algorithms could be considered for maximum security and ease of use.
- *Review and approve.* A procedural control, the intent of which is to ensure that any change to the data is reviewed by someone technically knowledgeable to perform the task. An authorized individual other than the person who developed the change should do the review and approval.
- *Backup and recovery.* Depending on the criticality of the data and ease of recovery, plans should be developed and periodically tested to ensure that the data is backed up properly and can be fully recovered.
- *Separation of duties.* The intent of this control is to help ensure that no single person has total control over the data entry and validation process, which would enable someone to enter or conceal an error that is intended to defraud the organization or commit other harmful acts. An example would be not allowing the same individual to establish vendors to an Authorized Vendor File, and then also be capable of authorizing payments to a vendor.
- *Universal access: none.* No one has access to the data unless given specific authority to read, update, etc. This type of control is generally provided by access control software.
- *Universal access: read.* Everyone with access to the system can read data with the control applied; however, update authority must be granted to specific individuals, programs, or transactions. This type of control is provided by access control software.
- *Universal access: update.* Anyone with access to the system can update the data, but specific authority must be granted to delete the data. This control is provided by access control software.
- *Universal access: alter* — Anyone with access to the system can view, update, or delete the data. This provides virtually no security.
- *Security access control software.* This software allows the administrator to establish security rules as to who has access rights to protected resources. Resources can include data, programs, transactions, individual computer IDs, and terminal IDs. Access

control software can be set up to allow access by classes of users to classes of resources, or at any level of granularity required by any particular resource or group of resources.

Software: Minimum Controls

- *Review and approve.* The intent of this control is that any change to the software should be reviewed by someone technically knowledgeable to perform this task. The review and approval should be an authorized individual other than the person who developed the change.
- *Review and approve test plan and results.* A program change test plan would be prepared, approved, documented, and followed.
- *Backup and recovery.* Procedures should be developed and periodically tested to ensure that backups of the software are performed in such a manner that the most recent production version is recoverable within a reasonable amount of time.
- *Audit/history.* Information documenting the software change such as the work request detailing the work to be performed, test plans, test results, corrective actions, approvals, who performed the work, and other pertinent documentation required by the business.
- *Version and configuration control.* Refers to maintaining control over the versions of software checked out for update, being loaded to staging or production libraries, etc. This would include the monitoring of error reports associated with this activity and taking appropriate corrective action.
- *Periodic testing.* Involves taking a test case and periodically running the system with known data that have predictable results. The intent is to ensure the system still performs as expected and does not produce results that are inconsistent with the test case data. These tests could be conducted at random or on a regular schedule.
- *Random checking.* Production checking of defined data and results, such as making sure that output totals match input totals, check digits are correct, etc.
- *Separation of duties.* This procedural control is intended to meet certain regulatory and audit system requirements by helping ensure that one single individual does not have total control over a programming process without appropriate review points or requiring other individuals to perform certain tasks within the process prior to final user acceptance. For example, someone other than the original developer would be responsible for loading the program to the production environment from a staging library.
- *Access control of software.* In some applications, the coding techniques and other information contained within the program are

sensitive to disclosure. Therefore, the source code must be protected from unauthorized access.

- *Virus checking.* All software destined for any type of platform, regardless of source, should be scanned by an authorized virus-scanning program for computer viruses before it is loaded into the network. Some applications would have periodic testing as part of a software quality assurance plan.

Information Protection and Management Services

Defining Roles and Responsibilities

To have an effective Information Classification program, the roles and responsibilities of all participants must be clearly defined. An appropriate training program, developed and implemented, is an essential part of the program. The Study Team identified to conduct the Risk Analysis is a good starting point to develop these roles and responsibilities and identify training requirements. However, it should be noted that some members of the original team such as Legal, Internal Audit, or Business Continuity Planning most likely will not be interested in this phase. They should be replaced with representatives from the corporate organizational effectiveness group, training, and possibly corporate communications.

Not all the roles defined in the following sections are applicable for all information classification schemes, and many of the roles can be performed by the same individual. The key to this exercise is to identify which of the roles defined is appropriate for your particular organization, while keeping in mind that an individual might perform more than one of these when the process is fully functional.

- *Information owner.* A business executive or business manager who is responsible for a company business information asset. Responsibilities include, but are not limited to:
  - Assign initial information classification and periodically review the classification to ensure it still meets the business needs.
  - Ensure security controls are in place commensurate with the classification.
  - Review and ensure currency of the access rights associated with the information assets they own.
  - Determine security requirements, access criteria, and backup requirements for the information assets they own.
  - Perform, or delegate if desired, the following:
    - Approval authority for access requests from other business units or assign a delegate in the same business unit as the executive or manager owner
    - Backup and recovery duties or assign to the custodian
    - Approval of the disclosure of information

- Act on notifications received concerning security violations against their information assets
- *Information custodian.* The information custodian, usually an information technology or operations person, is the system administrator or operator for the Information Owner, with primary responsibilities dealing with running the program for the owner and backup and recovery of the business information. Responsibilities include:
  - Perform backups according to the backup requirements established by the Information Owner.
  - When necessary, restore lost or corrupted information from backup media to return the application to production status.
  - Perform related management functions as required to ensure availability of the information to the business.
  - Ensure record retention requirements are met based on the Information Owner's analysis.
- *Application owner.* Manager of the business unit who is fully accountable for the performance of the business function served by the application. Responsibilities include:
  - Establish user access criteria and availability requirements for their applications.
  - Ensure the security controls associated with the application are "commensurate to support the highest level of information classification used by the application.
  - Perform or delegate the following:
    - Day-to-day security administration in conjunction with the organization's security policy
    - Approval of exception access requests
    - Appropriate actions on security violations when notified by security administration
    - The review and approval of all changes to the application prior to being placed into the production environment
    - Verification of the currency of user access rights to the application
- *User manager.* The immediate manager or supervisor of an employee. They have ultimate responsibility for all user IDs and information assets owned by company employees. In the case of non-employee individuals such as contractors, consultants, etc., this manager is responsible for the activity and for the company assets used by these individuals. This is usually the manager responsible for hiring the outside party. Responsibilities include:
  - Inform security administration of the termination of any employee so that the user ID owned by that individual can be revoked, suspended, or made inaccessible in a timely manner.

- Inform security administration of the transfer of any employee if the transfer involves the change of access rights or privileges.
- Report any security incident or suspected incident to Information Security.
- Ensure the currency of user ID information such as the employee identification number and account information of the user ID owner.
- Receive and distribute initial passwords for newly created user IDs based on the manager's discretionary approval of the user having the user ID.
- Educate employees with regard to security policies, procedures, and standards for which they are accountable.

- *Security administrator.* Any company employee who owns an "administrative" user ID that has been assigned attributes or privileges that are associated with any type of access control system. This user ID allows them to set systemwide security controls or administer user IDs and information resource access rights. These security administrators may report to either a business division or Information Security within the organization. Responsibilities include:
  - Understanding the different data environments and the impact of granting access to them
  - Ensuring access requests are consistent with the policies and security guidelines
  - Administering access rights according to criteria established by the Information Owners
  - Creating and removing user IDs as directed by the User Manager
  - Administering the system security within the scope of their job description and functional responsibilities
  - Distributing and following up on security violation reports
- *Security analyst.* Person responsible for determining the data security directions (strategies, procedures, guidelines) to ensure information is controlled and secured based on its value, risk of loss or compromise, and ease of recoverability. Duties include:
  - Provide data security guidelines to the information management process.
  - Develop a basic understanding of the information to ensure that proper controls are implemented.
  - Provide data security design input, consulting, and review.
- *Change control analyst.* Person responsible for analyzing requested changes to the Information Technology infrastructure and determining the impact on applications. This function also analyzes the impact of changes to the databases, data-related tools, application code, etc.
- *Data analyst.* This person analyzes the business requirements to design the data structures and recommends data definition

standards and physical platforms, and is responsible for applying certain data management standards. Responsibilities include:
- Designing data structures to meet business needs
- Designing physical database structure
- Creating and maintaining logical data models based on business requirements
- Providing technical assistance to data owner in developing data architectures
- Recording metadata in the data library
- Creating, maintaining, and using metadata to effectively manage database deployment

- *Solution provider.* Person who participates in the solution (application) development and delivery processes in deploying business solutions; also referred to as an integrator, application provider/programmer, Information Technology provider. Duties include:
  - Working with the data analyst to ensure that the application and data will work together to meet the business requirements
  - Giving technical requirements to the data analyst to ensure performance and reporting requirements are met

- *End user.* Any employee, contractor, or vendor of the company who uses information systems resources as part of their job. Responsibilities include:
  - Maintaining the confidentiality of logon password(s)
  - Ensuring security of information entrusted to their care
  - Using company business assets and information resources for management-approved purposes only
  - Adhering to all information security policies, procedures, standards, and guidelines
  - Promptly reporting security incidents to management

- *Process owner.* This person is responsible for the management, implementation, and continuous improvement of a process that has been defined to meet a business need. This person:
  - Ensures that data requirements are defined to support the business process
  - Understands how the quality and availability affect the overall effectiveness of the process
  - Works with the data owners to define and champion the data quality program for data within the process
  - Resolves data-related issues that span applications within the business processes

- *Product line manager.* Person responsible for understanding business requirements and translating them into product requirements, working with the vendor/user area to ensure the product meets requirements, monitoring new releases, and working with the stakeholders when movement to a new release is required. This person:

- Ensures that new releases of software are evaluated and upgrades are planned for and properly implemented
- Ensures compliance with software license agreements
- Monitors performance of production against business expectations
- Analyzes product usage, trends, options, and competitive sourcing, etc., to identify actions needed to meet project demands of the product

Identifying Owners

The steps previously defined are required to establish the information classification infrastructure. With the classifications and their definitions defined, and roles and responsibilities of the participants articulated, it is time to execute the plan and begin the process of identifying the information owners. As stated previously, the information owners must be from the business units. It is the business unit that will be most affected if the information becomes lost or corrupted; the data exists solely to satisfy a business requirement. The following criteria must be considered when identifying the proper owner for business data:

- The proper owner must be from the business; information ownership is not an Information Technology responsibility.
- Senior management support is a key success factor.
- Information owners must be given (through policy) the necessary authority commensurate with their responsibilities and accountabilities.
- For some business functions, a multi-level approach may be necessary. A phased approach will most likely meet with less resistance than trying to identify all owners and classify all information at the same time.

A training program must also be developed and be ready to implement as the information owners and their delegates are named. Any tools such as spreadsheets for recording application and information ownership and classification and reporting mechanisms should be developed ahead of time for use by the information owners. Once the owners have been identified, training should commence immediately so that it is delivered at the time it is needed.

Classify Information and Applications

The information owners, after completing their training, should begin collecting the metadata about their business functions and applications. A formal data collection process should be used to ensure consistency in the methods and types of information gathered. This information should be stored in a central repository for future reference and analysis.

Once the information has been collected, the information owners should review the definitions for the information classifications and classify their data according to those criteria.

The owners can use the following information in determining the appropriate controls for the classification:

- Audit information maintained; how much and where it is, and what controls are imposed on the audit data
- Separation of duties required? If yes, how is it performed?
- Encryption requirements
- Data protection mechanisms and access controls defined based on classification, sensitivity, etc.
- Universal access control assigned
- Backup and recovery processes documented
- Change control and review processes documented
- Confidence level in data accuracy
- Data retention requirements defined
- Location of documentation

The following application controls are required to complement the data controls, but care should be taken to ensure that all controls (both data and software) are commensurate with the information classification and the value of the information:

- Audit controls in place
- Develop and approve test plans
- Separation of duties practiced
- Change management processes in place
- Code tested, verified for accuracy
- Access control for code in place
- Version controls for code implemented
- Backup and recovery processes in place

Ongoing Monitoring

Once the information processes have been implemented and the data has been classified, the ongoing monitoring processes should be implemented. The Internal Audit Department should lead this effort to ensure compliance with policy and established procedures. Information Security, working with selected information owners, Legal, and other interested parties, should periodically review the information classifications themselves to ensure they still meet business requirements.

The information owners should periodically review the data to ensure they are still appropriately classified. Also, the access rights of individuals should be periodically reviewed to ensure that these rights are still appropriate for the job requirements. The controls associated with each classification should also be reviewed to ensure that they are still appropriate for the classification they define.

Summary

Information and software classification is necessary to better manage information. If implemented correctly, classification can reduce the cost of protecting information because in today's environment, the "one-size-fits-all" idea will no longer work within the complexity of most corporation's heterogeneous platforms that make up the Information Technology infrastructure. Information classification enhances the probability that controls will be placed on the data where they are needed the most, and not applied where they are not needed.

Classification security schemes enhance the usability of data by ensuring the confidentiality, integrity, and availability of information. By implementing a corporatewide information classification program, good business practices are enhanced by providing a secure, cost-effective data platform that supports the company's business objectives. The key to the successful implementation of the information classification process is senior management support. The corporate information security policy should lay the groundwork for the classification process and be the first step in obtaining management support and buy-in.

No Information Security program is effective unless it is built on a foundation of appropriate policies, procedures, standards, baselines, and guidelines. We will now discuss these in more detail.

1.4 Policies, Procedures, Standards, Baselines, Guidelines

Information Protection Requirements

The overall objective of an information security program is to protect the integrity, confidentiality, and availability of information. The primary threats that keep an organization from attaining this goal are unauthorized access, modification, destruction, and disclosure. These threats can be either accidental or deliberate. An information protection program should be part of any organization's overall asset protection program. The goals and objectives that make up the information security program must be understandable by all employees.

As long as there have been Information Security Officers, there has been a need to create and implement information security policies, procedures, guidelines, baselines, and standards. The Information Security Officer was usually brought in from one of the various groups within Information Technology and charged with the responsibility to create these documents. The background in Information Technology often helped the Information Security Officer in understanding technical issues, but it was sometimes a hindrance in grasping the business strategies and objectives. With this very vaguely defined charter, the Information Security Officer would usually try to find a book on the subject and often look to attend a seminar or workshop. The information gathered from these resources often provided the "how-to," but usually failed in the "why-for."

Corporations have legal and business requirements to have policies and procedures in place. In addition to these requirements, there are also laws and acts that define who is responsible and what they must do to meet corporate obligations. Generally, directors and officers of a corporation are required to perform specific duties: a duty of loyalty and a duty of due care.

Information Protection Environment

By assuming office, senior management commits allegiance to the enterprise and acknowledges that interests of the enterprise must prevail over any personal or individual interests. The basic principle here is that senior management should not use its position to make a personal profit or gain other personal advantage. The duty of loyalty is evident in certain legal concepts:

- *Conflict of interest.* Individuals must divulge any interest in outside relationships that might conflict with the enterprise's interests.
- *Duty of fairness.* When presented with a conflict of interest, the individual has an obligation to act in the best interest of all parties.
- *Corporate opportunity.* When presented with "material inside information" (advanced notice on mergers, acquisitions, patents, etc.), the individual will not use this information for personal gain.
- *Confidentiality.* All matters involving the corporation shall be kept in confidence until they are made public.

In addition to owing a duty of loyalty to the enterprise, the officers and directors also assume a duty to act carefully in fulfilling the important tasks of monitoring and directing the activities of corporate management and all employees. Generally, officers and directors need to act:

- In good faith
- With the care an ordinarily prudent person in a like position would exercise under similar circumstances
- In a manner he or she reasonably believes is in the best interest of the enterprise

The requirement here is for management to show "due diligence" in establishing an effective compliance, or security, program. There are seven elements that capture the basic functions inherent in most compliance programs:

- Establish policies, standards, baselines, guidelines, and procedures to guide the workforce.
- Appoint a high-level manager to oversee compliance with the policies, standards, baselines, guidelines, and procedures.
- Exercise due care when granting discretionary authority to employees.
- Ensure that compliance policies are being carried out.
- Communicate the policies, standards, baselines, guidelines, and procedures to all employees and others.
- Enforce the policies, standards, baselines, and procedures consistently through appropriate disciplinary measures.
- Implement procedures for corrections in case of violations.

It is a well-accepted fact that it is important to protect the information essential to an organization, in the same way that it is important to protect the financial assets of the organization. To protect the sensitive assets of a corporation, it is important to understand the requirements for protecting the information. However, identifying these requirements is not good enough; to enforce controls, it is necessary to have a formal written policy that can be used as the basis for all standards, baselines, and procedures.

Although there are legal and regulatory reasons why policies, standards, baselines, and procedures should be implemented, the bottom line is that good controls make good business sense. Failing to implement controls can lead to financial penalties in the form of fines. Such activities can lead to loss of customer confidence, competitive advantage, and, ultimately, jobs.

The avoidance of public criticism, and saving time on the investigation and subsequent disciplinary process, are very effective benefits to the organization that can be obtained by the implementation of proper controls. Every organization is required to provide its services or products to its customers, legally and/or contractually. To ensure that the business objectives are met in a timely and efficient manner, effective policies and standards must be in place. Protecting shareholder interests is a key component in the need to implement effective controls.

Security Technology and Tools

Objectives of Policies, Procedures, Standards, Baselines

Policies, standards, baselines, and procedures are key elements in ensuring that personnel understand how to handle specific job tasks. The policy lays out the general requirements, the standard specifies the tools required, the baseline designates the parameters to be used, and the procedures provide the step-by-step process required in routine activities. They can also be used when employees are required to make decisions.

Well-written procedures will never take the place of supervision, but they can take some of the more mundane tasks and move them out to the employees. These documents are basically management resources that focus performance for the organization. The objectives of policies, standards, baselines, and procedures are to:

- *State and clarify goals.* Employees have a resource to which they can refer to assist them in making correct decisions.
- *Define duties, responsibilities, and authority.* The policy can identify who is responsible for which activity and the procedure can provide the step-by-step process needed to complete the task at hand.
- *Formalize duties.* An effective set of desk procedures can assist the organization in meeting two key security requirements: separation of duties and rotation of assignments.
  - *Separation of duties.* No single individual should have complete control of a business process or transaction from inception to completion. This control concept limits the error, opportunity, and temptation of personnel and can best be defined as segregating incompatible functions (accounts payable activities with disbursement). The activities of a process are split among several people. Mistakes made by one person tend to be caught by the next person in the chain, thereby increasing information integrity. Unauthorized activities will be limited because no one person can complete a process without the knowledge and support of someone else.
  - *Rotation of assignments.* Individuals should periodically alternate various essential tasks involving business activities or transactions. There are always some assignments that can cause an organization to be at risk unless proper controls are in place. To ensure that desk procedures are being followed as well as provide for staff backup on essential functions, individuals should be assigned to different tasks at regular intervals. One of the often-heard knocks against rotation of assignments is that it reduces job efficiency. However, it has been proven that an employee's interest declines over time when doing the same job for extended periods. Additionally, employees sometimes develop shortcuts when they have been in a job too long. By rotating assignments, the organization can compare how the task was being done and where changes should be made.
- *Establish standards.* Once a policy has been implemented, it will be necessary to create the standards that can be used to support the policy. This can be, for example, what anti-virus software is to be used and what remote access protocol is to be implemented.
- *Provide information to employees, customers, etc.* The ability to communicate management directions is what policies, standards,

baselines, and procedures are all about. Management does not have the luxury of sitting down with each employee, customer, client, vendor, supplier, etc., and telling them what is expected, how they are to perform their assignments, and what tools are to be used. A well-crafted set of policies, standards, baselines, and procedures act as the voice for management when working with personnel.

- *Educate users*. Some organizations have thousands of users accessing various systems and applications. The ability to provide them with the information they need to correctly perform this task is an essential element in well-written policies, standards, baselines, and procedures.

Definitions

Policy. An information security policy contains senior management's directives to create an information security program, establish its goals, measures, and target and assign responsibilities (see Exhibit 2). This policy defines an organization's high-level information security philosophy. Policies are brief, technology- and solution-independent documents. They provide the necessary authority to establish and implement technology- and solution-specific standards. In general, policies remain relevant and applicable for a substantial period of time, and only require revisions when there is a fundamental change to an organization's business or operational objectives and environment. Functional policies implement the high-level policy and further define the information security objectives in topical areas. Standards, in contrast, provide more measurable guidance in each policy area. Further, procedures describe how to implement the standards.

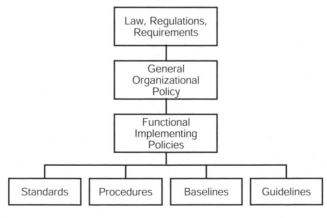

Exhibit 2. Policy Chart

Exhibit 3. Sample Email Policy

The Company maintains a voice-mail system and an electronic-mail (email) system to assist in the conduct of business within the Company. These systems, including the equipment and the data stored in the system, are and remain at all times the property of the Company. As such, all messages created, sent, received, or stored in the system are and remain the property of the Company.

Messages should be limited to the conduct of business at the Company. Voice mail and electronic mail may not be used for the conduct of personal business.

The Company reserves the right to retrieve and review any message composed, sent, or received. Messages may be reviewed by someone other than the intended recipient.

Messages may not contain content that may reasonably be considered offensive or disruptive to any employee. Offensive content would include, but would not be limited to, sexual comments or images, racial slurs, gender-specific comments, or any comments that would offend someone on the basis of his or her age, sexual orientation, religious or political beliefs, national origin, or disability.

Employees learning of any misuse of the voice-mail or electronic-mail system or violations of this policy shall notify the Director of Human Resources immediately.

A policy (see Exhibit 3), then, is defined as a high-level statement of enterprise beliefs, goals, and objectives and the general means for their attainment for a specified subject area. A policy is brief and set at a high level. Because a policy is written at a broad level, organizations must also develop standards, guidelines, baselines, and procedures that offer employees, managers, and others a consistent method of implementing the policy and meeting the organization's business objectives or mission.

Standards. Standards are mandatory activities, actions, rules, or regulations designed to provide policies with the support structure and specific direction they require to be meaningful and effective. A standard is defined as a specific product or mechanism that is selected for universal use throughout the organization in order to support the policy.

Example: Computer Virus Protection.

- *Policy.* Information custodians are responsible for providing a safe and secure processing environment in which information can be maintained with integrity.
- *Standard.* Custodians of information processing systems must use "XXXXXX" anti-viral software to ensure that the system is free from destructive software elements (such as viruses) that would impair the normal and expected operation of the system.

Baselines. Baselines are mandatory descriptions of how to implement security packages to ensure that implementations result in a consistent level of security throughout the organization. Different systems (platforms) have different methods of handling security issues. Baselines are created to inform user groups about how to set up the security for each platform so that the desired level of security is achieved consistently.

- *Policy.* Information custodians are responsible for providing a safe and secure processing environment in which information can be maintained with integrity.
- *Standard.* Custodians of information processing systems must use "XXXXXX" access control software to ensure that the system is accessed only by authorized users.
- *Baseline.* The values of the parameters available in the "XXXXXX" access control software will be established as follows to ensure that all elements of the organization maintain a consistent level of security.

Procedures. Procedures spell out the step-by-step specifics of how the policy and the supporting standards and guidelines will actually be implemented in an operating environment.

- *Policy.* Information custodians are responsible for providing a safe and secure processing environment in which information can be maintained with integrity.
- *Standard.* Custodians of information processing systems must use "XXXXXX" anti-viral software to ensure that the system is free from destructive software elements (such as viruses) that would impair the normal and expected operation of the system.
- *Procedure.* All users utilizing "XXXXXX" anti-viral software will have anti-viral signature files updated weekly. Employees are to turn off and lock up desktop systems at the end of the workday to prevent unauthorized access and possible virus contamination.
  - Employees are to use the "write protection" tabs on diskettes whenever possible.
  - The following procedure is to be followed when updating your anti-virus signature files every week (followed by the actual procedure).
  - Employees are to report any type of unauthorized access, theft, and virus infection to the Information Protection group or the Help Desk upon discovery, and the following is the procedure to do it (followed by the actual procedure).

Guidelines. Guidelines are more general statements designed to achieve the policy's objectives by providing a framework within which to implement controls not covered by procedures. While standards are mandatory, guidelines are discretionary recommendations.

- *Policy.* Information custodians are responsible for providing a safe and secure processing environment in which information can be maintained with integrity.
- *Standard.* Custodians of information processing systems must use "XXXXXX" anti-viral software to ensure that the system is free from destructive software elements (such as viruses) that would impair the normal and expected operation of the system.
- *Procedure.* All users utilizing "XXXXXX" anti-viral software will have anti-viral signature files updated weekly.
- *Guidelines.* Employees having access to computer systems should attend a training session on the virus threat to understand the damage a virus infection can inflict and understand their personal responsibility for protecting their own systems.

Summary

The policy is the cornerstone of an organization's information security architecture. A policy is important to establish both internally and externally what an organization's position on a particular topic might be. Policies are supported by standards, baselines, procedures, and guidelines.

An effective information security policy within a comprehensive and practical framework has the following characteristics:

- Both senior management and users must accept the policy as the official reference document on security.
- The policy should firmly integrate security within the overall business and technical strategies, and within risk management practices.
- The business should drive the policy and policy enforcement — not the other way around.
- The policy must be consistent with existing corporate directives and guidelines, and with applicable government legislation and regulations.
- The scope of the policy should define what resources are affected and to whom the policy applies (e.g., all employees, full-time employees only, contractors, consultants, or customers).
- The policy should be limited to stating the organization's security objectives, priorities, and high-level strategies, thus serving as a framework for the various business areas.
- The policy should be concise and written in clear, unambiguous language that speaks directly to a broad audience. It should be carefully structured to allow easy reference to particular sections.
- As a living document, the policy should be reviewed and updated at regular intervals, or as significant events, such as a merger or an acquisition, require.

- The policy should focus exclusively on broad principles and objectives.
- The policy document must be carefully worded and ensure that all terms are accurately and precisely defined, and used exactly as intended.
- The policy should clearly delineate responsibility, accountability, and lines of authority across the organization.
- The policy must be technically and organizationally feasible.
- The various constituents governed by the policy should have access to relevant policy material, rather than being required to read and understand all of the policy information.
- Each policy should clearly describe how exceptions to the policy are to be considered and adjudicated.
- The initial policy document, and subsequent updates, should have a version number and a date.
- Policies should not exist that the organization is either unwilling or unable to enforce.

Just as policy is the cornerstone of an organization's information security architecture, Information Security awareness makes sure that all employees are aware of the importance of policies and other Information Security programs. We will now discuss this topic in more detail.

Information Security Awareness

The goal of a security awareness program is to heighten the importance and understanding of information systems security and the possible negative effects of a security breach or failure. During an awareness campaign, the end user simply receives information. It is designed to reach a broad audience using various promotional techniques. In a training environment, the student is expected to be an active participant in the process of acquiring new insights, knowledge, and skills.

Information Protection Requirements

To protect the confidentiality, integrity, and availability of information, organizations must ensure that all individuals involved understand their responsibilities. To achieve this, employees must be adequately informed of the policies and procedures necessary to protect the organization's information systems. As such, all end users of information systems must understand the basics of Information Security and be able to apply good security habits in the daily work environment. After receiving commitment from senior management, one of the initial steps is to clearly define the objective of the security awareness program. Once the goal has been established, the content must be decided, including the type of implementation (delivery) options available. During this process, key factors to consider include how to overcome obstacles and face resistance. The final step is evaluating success.

1.5 Setting the Goal

Before beginning to develop the content of a security awareness program, it is essential to establish the objective or goal. It may be as simple as "all employees must understand their basic security responsibilities" or "develop in all employees an awareness of the information security threats the organization faces and motivate the employees to develop the necessary habits to counteract the threats and protect the information systems." Some may find it necessary to develop something more detailed, such as formalizing awareness program objectives as follows.

Awareness Program Objectives

Employees must be aware of:

- Security policies, standards, procedures, baselines, and guidelines
- Threats to physical assets and stored information
- Threats to open network environments
- Laws and regulations they are required to follow
- Specific organization or department policies they are required to follow
- How to identify and protect sensitive (or classified) information
- How to store, label, and transport information
- Who they should report security incidents to, regardless of whether it is just a suspected or an actual incident
- Email/Internet policies and procedures
- Social engineering

When establishing the goals for the security awareness program, keep in mind that these goals should reflect and support the overall mission and goals of the organization. At this point in the process, it may be the right (or necessary) time to provide a status report to the Chief Information Officer (CIO) or other executive and senior management members.

Deciding on the Content

An information security awareness program should create sensitivity to the threats and vulnerabilities of information systems and also remind employees of the need to protect the information they create, process, transmit, and store. Basically, the focus of an information security awareness program is to raise the security consciousness of all employees.

The level and type of content depends on the needs of the organization. Essentially, employees need to be told what they need to protect, how they should protect it, and how important information systems security is to the organization.

Information Protection Environment

When designing and developing an information security training program, there is a wide range of options that are based on specific job requirements and the daily management, operation, and protection of information systems. Information Technology (IT) is apparent in every aspect of our daily life — so much so that in many instances, it seems completely natural. Can you imagine conducting business without email or voice mail? How about handwriting a report that is later typed using an electric typewriter? As one is well aware, computer technology and open-connected networks are the core components of all organizations, regardless of the industry or the specific business needs.

IT has enabled organizations in the government and private sectors to create, process, store, and transmit an unprecedented amount of information. The IT infrastructure created to handle this information flow has become an integral part of how business is conducted. In fact, most organizations consider themselves dependent on their information systems. This dependency on information systems has created the need to ensure that the physical assets (e.g., the hardware and software) and the information they process are protected from actions that could jeopardize the ability of the organization to effectively service their clients and reach their business objectives.

While advances in IT have increased exponentially, very little has been done to inform users of the vulnerabilities and threats of the new technologies. Not only must information systems security professionals receive training, but all employees who have access to information systems must be made aware of the vulnerabilities and threats to the information system they use and what they can do to help protect their information. Employees — especially end users of the information system — are typically not aware of the security consequences caused by certain actions. For most employees, the information system is a tool to perform their job responsibilities as quickly and efficiently as possible; security is viewed as a hindrance rather than a necessity. Thus, it is imperative for every organization to provide employees with information security information that points out the threats and ramifications of not actively participating in the protection of their information.

Employees are one of the most important factors in ensuring the security of information systems and the information they process. In many instances, information security incidents are the result of employee actions that originate from inattention and not being aware of information security policies and procedures. Therefore, informed and trained employees can be a crucial factor in the effective functioning and protection of information systems. If employees are aware of information security issues, they can be the first line of defense in the prevention and early detection of problems. In addition, when everyone is concerned and focused on information security, the protection of assets and information can be much easier and more efficient.

Often, the weakest link in information security is the individual employee who can be susceptible to being conned out of sensitive information by clever manipulators. The process the con artists use is called social engineering. Every security awareness program should include some social engineering countermeasure training to assist employees in resisting this attack.

1.6 Social Engineering

Information Security practitioners are keenly aware of the major goals of information technology: availability, integrity, and confidentiality (the AIC triad). Yet, none of these goals is attainable if there is a weak link in the defense or security "chain." It has often been said that with information security, you are only as strong as your weakest link. When we think of Information Security, we tend to focus our collective attention on certain technical areas of this security chain. There are numerous reference sources available to Information Security practitioners that describe the latest operating system, application, or hardware vulnerabilities. Many companies have built their business plans and are able to survive based on being the first to discover these vulnerabilities and then provide solutions to the public and to the vendors themselves. It is quite obvious that the focus of the security industry has been primarily on the hardware, software, firmware, and the technical aspects of Information Security.

The security industry seems to have forgotten that computers and technology are merely tools, and that it is the human that is using, configuring, installing, implementing, and abusing these tools. Information Security is more than just implementing a variety of technologically complex controls. It also encompasses dealing with the behavior or, more appropriately, the misbehavior of people. To be effective, Information Security must also address vulnerabilities within the "wetware," a term used to describe "people." We can spend all the money and effort we want on technical controls and producing better, more secure code, but all of this is moot if our people give away the "keys to the kingdom." Recent research on network attacks clearly indicates that this is exactly what people are doing, albeit unintentionally. We seem to have done a good job instilling the notions of teamwork and cooperation in our workplace — so much so that in our eagerness to help out, we are falling prey to unscrupulous people who gain unauthorized access to systems through attacks categorized as Social Engineering.

We will attempt to shed some light on Social Engineering by examining how this attack works, what are the common methods used, and how we can mitigate the risk of Social Engineering by proper education, awareness training, and other controls. This is not intended to be a "how-to" explanation, but rather a discussion of some of the details of this type of attack and how to prevent becoming a victim of Social Engineering. None of this information is secret, and is already well known to certain sectors of society. Therefore, it is also important for Information Security professionals to be aware of Social Engineering and the security controls to mitigate the risk.

Defining Social Engineering

To understand what Social Engineering is, it is first important to clearly define what we are discussing. The term "Social Engineering" is not a new term. It comes from the field of social control. Social Engineering can refer to the process of redefining a society, or more correctly, engineering society, to achieve some desired outcome. The term can also refer to the process of attempting to change people's behavior in a predictable manner, usually in order to have them comply with some new system. It is the latter social psychological definition of Social Engineering that is germane to our discussion. For our purposes, Social Engineering will refer to:

> *Successful or unsuccessful attempts to influence a person(s) into either revealing information or acting in a manner that would result in unauthorized access to, unauthorized use of, or unauthorized disclosure of an information system, a network, or data.*

As we can see by our definition, Social Engineering is somewhat synonymous with conning or deceiving someone. Using deception or conning a person is nothing new in the field of criminal activity; yet despite its longevity, this kind of behavior is still surprisingly effective.

It would be very interesting at this point to include some information on the apparent size of the Social Engineering problem. Unfortunately, there is very little data to use for this purpose. Despite the frequent references to Social Engineering in the Information Security field, there has not been much direct discussion of this type of attack. The reasons for this vary; some within the field have suggested that Social Engineering attacks the intelligence of the victim and, as such, there is a reluctance to admit that it has occurred. Yet despite this reluctance, some of the most infamous computer criminals have relied more on Social Engineering to perpetrate their crimes than on any real technical ability. Why spend time researching and scanning systems looking for vulnerabilities and risk being detected when one can simply ask someone for a password to gain access? Most computer criminals, or any criminal for that matter, are opportunists. They look for the easy way into a system, and what could be easier than asking someone to let them in?

Why Does Social Engineering Work?

The success of Social Engineering attacks is primarily due to two factors: basic human nature and the business environment.

Human Nature. Falling victim to a Social Engineering attack has nothing to do with intelligence, and everything to do with being human, being somewhat naïve, and not having the proper mindset and training to deal with this type of attack. People, for the most part, are trusting and cooperative by nature. The field of social psychology has studied human interactions both in groups and individually. These studies have concluded that almost anyone who is put in the right situation and who is dealing with a skilled person can be influenced to behave in a specific manner or divulge information he usually would not in other circumstances. These studies have also found that people who are in authority, or have the air of being in authority, easily intimidate other people.

For the most part, Social Engineering deals with individual dynamics as opposed to group dynamics, as the primary targets are help desks or administrative or technical support people, and the interactions are usually one-on-one but not necessarily face-to-face (i.e., the relationship is usually virtual in nature, either by phone or online). As we will discuss in the following sections, attackers tend to seek out individuals who display signs of being susceptible to this psychological attack.

Business Environment. Combined with human nature, the current business trend of mergers and acquisitions, rapid advances in technology, and the proliferation of wide area networking has made the business environment conducive to Social Engineering. In today's business world, it is not uncommon to have never met the people we deal with on a regular basis, including those from our own organizations, let alone suppliers, vendors, and customers. Face-to-face human interaction is becoming even more rare with the widespread adoption of telecommuting technologies for employees. In today's marketplace, we can work for an organization and, apart from a few exceptions, rarely set foot in the office. Despite this layer of abstraction we have with people in our working environment, our basic trust in people, including those we have never actually met, has pretty much remained intact.

Businesses and organizations today have also become more service oriented than ever before. Employees are often rated on how well they contribute to a "team" environment, and on the level of service they provide to customers and other departments. It is rare to see a category on an evaluation that measures the degree to which someone used common sense, or whether employees are conscious of security when performing their duties. This is a paradigm that needs to change in order to deal effectively with the threat of Social Engineering.

Social Engineering Attacks. Social Engineering attacks tend to follow a phased approach and, in most cases, the attacks are very similar to how intelligence agencies infiltrate their targets.

For the purposes of simplicity, the phases can be categorized as:

- Intelligence gathering
- Target selection
- The attack

Intelligence Gathering. One of the keys to a successful Social Engineering attack is information. It is surprisingly easy to gather sufficient information on an organization and its staff in order to sound like an employee of the company, a vendor representative, or in some cases a member of a regulatory or law enforcement body. Organizations tend to put far too much information on their Web sites as part of their marketing strategies. This information often describes or gives clues as to the vendors they may be dealing with; lists phone and email directories; and indicates whether there are branch offices and, if so, where they are located. Some organizations even go as far as listing their entire organizational charts on their Web pages. All this information may be nice for potential investors, but it also can be used to lay the foundation for a Social Engineering attack.

Poorly thought-out Web sites are not the only sources of open intelligence. What organizations throw away can also be a source of important information. Going through an organization's trash (also known as dumpster diving) can reveal invoices, correspondence, manuals, etc., that can assist an attacker in gaining important information. Several convicted computer criminals confessed to dumpster diving to gather information on their targets.

The attacker's goal at this phase is to learn as much information as possible in order to sound like a legitimate employee, contractor, vendor, strategic partner, and in some cases, a law enforcement official.

Target Selection. Once the appropriate amount of information is collected, the attacker looks for noticeable weaknesses in the organization's personnel. The most common target is help desk personnel, as these professionals are trained to give assistance and can usually change passwords, create accounts, reactivate accounts, etc. In some organizations, the help desk function is contracted out to a third party with no real connection to the actual organization. This increases the chances of success, as the contracted third party would usually not know any of the organization's employees. The goal of most attackers is to either gather sensitive information or get a foothold into a system. Attackers realize that once they have access, even at a guest level, it is relatively easy to increase their privileges, launch more destructive attacks, and hide their tracks.

Administrative assistants are the next most common victims. This is largely due to the fact that these individuals are privy to a large amount of sensitive information that normally flows between senior management members. Administrative assistants can be used either as an attack point or to gather additional information regarding names of influential people in the organization. Knowing the names of the "movers and shakers" in an organization is valuable if there is a need to "name drop." It is also amazing how many administrative assistants know their executive managers' passwords. A number of these assistants routinely perform tasks for their managers that require their managers' account privileges (e.g., updating a spreadsheet, booking appointments in electronic calendars, etc.).

The Attack. The actual attack is usually based on what we would most commonly call a "con." These are broken down into three categories: (1) attacks that appeal to the vanity or ego of the victim, (2) attacks that take advantage of the feelings of sympathy or empathy, and (3) attacks that are based on intimidation.

Ego Attacks. In the first type of attack, ego or vanity attacks, the attacker appeals to some of the most basic human characteristics. We all like to be told how intelligent we are and that we really know what we are doing or how to "fix" the company. Attackers will use this to extract information from their victims, as the attacker is a receptive audience for the victims to display how much knowledge they have. The attacker usually picks victims who feel they are underappreciated and are working in a position that is beneath their talents. Attackers can usually sense this after only a brief conversation with such individuals. Attackers using this type of an attack will often call several different employees until they find the right one. Unfortunately, in most cases, the victims have no idea that they have done anything wrong.

Sympathy Attacks. In the second category of attacks, the attacker usually pretends to be a fellow employee (usually a new-hire), a contractor, or a new employee of a vendor or strategic partner, who just happens to be in a real jam and needs assistance to get some tasks done immediately. The importance of the intelligence phase becomes obvious here, as the attacker will have to create some level of trust with the victim that he is who he says he is. This is done by name dropping, using the appropriate jargon, or displaying knowledge of the organization. The attacker pretends that he is in a rush and must complete some task that requires access, but he cannot remember his account name or password, or he inadvertently locked himself out, etc. A sense of urgency is usually part of the scenario because this provides an excuse for circumventing the required procedures that may be in place to regain access if he was truly who he was pretending to be. It is human nature to sympathize or empathize with who the attacker is pretending to be; so in the majority of cases, the requests are granted. If the attacker fails to get the access or the information from one employee, he will just keep trying until he finds a sympathetic ear, or until he realizes that the organization is getting suspicious.

Intimidation Attacks. In the third category, the attacker pretends to be an authority figure, either an influential person in the organization or, in some documented cases, law enforcement. The attacker will target a victim several levels within the organization below the level of the individual he is pretending to be. The attacker creates a plausible reason for making some type of request for a password reset, account change, access to systems, or sensitive information (in cases where the attacker is pretending to be a law enforcement official, the scenario usually revolves around some "hush-hush" investigation, or national security issue, and the employee is not to discuss the incident). Again, the attacker will have done his homework and pretends to be someone with just enough power to intimidate the victim, but not enough to be either well known to the victim, or implausible for the scenario. The attacker uses a scenario in which time is of the essence and that he needs to circumvent whatever the standard procedure is. If faced with resistance, the attacker will try to intimidate the victim into cooperation by threatening sanctions against them.

Mitigating the Risk. Regardless of the type of Social Engineering attack, the success rate is alarmingly high. Many convicted computer criminals joke about the ease with which they were able to fool their victims into letting them literally walk into systems. The risk and impact of Social Engineering attacks are high. These attacks are often difficult to trace and, in some cases, difficult to identify. If the attacker has gained access via a legitimate account, in most cases the controls and alarms will never be activated, as they have done nothing wrong as far as the system is concerned.

If Social Engineering is so easy to do, then how do organizations protect themselves against the risks of these attacks? The answer to this question is relatively simple, but it entails a change in thinking on behalf of the entire organization. To mitigate the risk of Social Engineering, organizations need to effectively educate and train their staff on Information Security threats and how to recognize potential attacks. The controls for these attacks can be found in education, awareness training, and other controls, which we will now discuss.

Social Engineering concentrates on the weakest link of the information security chain — people. The fact that someone could persuade an employee to provide sensitive information means that the most secure systems become vulnerable. The human part of any information security solution is the most essential. In fact, almost all information security solutions rely on the human element to a large degree. This means that this weakness, the human element, is universal, and independent of hardware, software, platform, network, age of equipment, etc.

Many companies spend hundreds of thousands of dollars to ensure effective information security. This security is used to protect what the company regards as its most important assets, including information. Unfortunately, even the best security mechanisms can be bypassed when Social Engineering techniques are used. Social Engineering uses very low-cost and low-technology means to overcome impediments imposed by information security measures.

Protection against Social Engineering

To protect ourselves from the threat of Social Engineering, we need to have a basic understanding of Information Security. In simple terms, Information Security can be defined as the protection of information against unauthorized disclosure, transfer, modification, or destruction, whether accidental or intentional. In general terms, Information Security denotes a state that a company reaches when its data and information, systems and services, are adequately protected from any type of threat. Information Security protects information from a wide range of threats in order to ensure business continuity, minimize business damage, and maximize return on investment and business opportunities. Information Security is about safeguarding your business's money, image, and reputation — and perhaps its very existence.

Protection mechanisms usually fall into three categories (previously defined in this chapter but further discussed below) and it is important to note that to adequately protect your Information Security assets, regardless of the type of threat, including those from Social Engineering attacks, a combination of all three is required:

- Physical security
- Logical (technical) security
- Administrative security

Information Security practitioners have long understood that a balanced approach to Information Security is required. That "balance" differs from company to company and is based on the system's vulnerabilities, threats, and information sensitivity, but in most instances will require a combination of all three elements mentioned above. Information Security initiatives must be customized to meet the unique needs of the business. That is why it is very important to have an Information Security program that understands the needs of the corporation and can relate its Information Security needs to the goals and missions of the organization. Achieving the correct balance means implementing a variety of Information Security measures that fit into our three categories, but implementing the correct balance in order to meet your security requirements as efficiently and cost-effectively as possible. Effective Information Security is the result of a process of identifying an organization's valued information assets, considering the range of potential risks to those assets, implementing effective policies addressing those specific conditions, and ensuring that those policies are developed, implemented, and communicated properly.

Physical Security. The physical security components are the easiest to understand and, arguably, the easiest to implement. Most people will think of keys, locks, alarms, and guards when they think of physical security. While these are by no means the only security precautions that need to be considered when securing information, they are a logical place to begin. Physical security, along with the other two (logical and administrative), is a vital component and is fundamental to most Information Security solutions. Physical security refers to the protection of assets from theft, vandalism, catastrophes, natural disasters, deliberate or accidental damage, and from unstable environmental conditions such as electrical, temperature, humidity, and other such related problems. Good physical security requires efficient building and facility construction, emergency preparedness, reliable electrical power supplies, reliable and adequate climate control, and effective protection from both internal and external intruders.

Logical (Technical) Security. Logical security measures are those that employ a technical solution to protect the information asset. Examples include firewall systems, access control systems, password systems, and intrusion detection systems. These controls can be very effective but usually they rely on a human element or interaction to work successfully. As mentioned, it is this human element that can be exploited rather easily.

Administrative Security. Administrative security controls are those that usually involve policies, procedures, guidelines, etc. Administrative security examples include Information Security policies, awareness programs, and background checks for new employees, etc. All of these examples are administrative in nature, do not require a logical or technical solution to implement, but all address the issue of Information Security.

Coverage

To be effective, Information Security must include the whole organization, from the top to the bottom, from the managers to the end users. Most importantly, the highest level of management present in any organization must endorse and support the idea and principles of Information Security. Everyone from top to bottom must understand the security principles involved and act accordingly. This means that high-level management must define, support, and issue the Information Security policy of the organization, which every person in the organization must then abide by. It also means that upper management must provide appropriate support, in the way of funding and resources, for Information Security. To summarize, a successful Information Security policy requires the leadership, commitment, and active participation of top-level management.

Critical Information Security strategies rely primarily on the appropriate and expected conduct on the part of personnel, and secondly on the use of technological solutions. This is why it is critical, for all Information Security programs, to address the threat of Social Engineering.

Securing against Social Engineering Attacks

Policies, Awareness, and Education. Social Engineering attacks are very difficult to counter. The problem with countering Social Engineering attacks is that most logical security controls are ineffective as protection mechanisms. Because the Social Engineering attacks target the human element, protective measures need to concentrate on the administrative portion of Information Security. An effective countermeasure is to have very good, established Information Security policies that are communicated across your organization. Policies are instrumental in forming "rules of behavior" for employees. The second effective countermeasure is an effective user awareness program. When you combine these two administrative Information Security countermeasure controls effectively, the result is an integrated security program that everyone understands and believes is part of his or her own required job duties. From a corporate perspective, it is critical to convey this message to all employees, from top to bottom. The result will be an organization that is more vigilant at all levels, and an organization comprised of individuals who believe they are "contributing" to the well-being of the overall corporation. This is an important perception that contributes greatly to employee satisfaction level. It also protects from the threat of disgruntled employees, another major concern to Information Security programs. It can be these disgruntled employees who willingly give sensitive information to unauthorized users, regardless of the Social Engineering methods.

Most people learn best from firsthand experience. Once it has been demonstrated that each individual is susceptible to Social Engineering attacks, these individuals tend to be more wary and aware. It is possible to make your organizations more immune to Social Engineering attacks by providing a forum for discussions of other organizations' experiences.

Continued awareness is also very important. Your awareness programs need to be repeated on a regular basis in order to reaffirm your policies regarding Social Engineering. With today's technology it is very easy to set up effective ways to communicate with your employees on a regular basis. A good way to provide this type of forum is to use an intranet Web site that will contain not only your policies, but also safety tips and information regarding amusing Social Engineering stories. Amusing stories tend to get the point across better, especially if you take into account that people love to hear about other people's misfortunes.

Recognition of Good "Catches"

Sometimes, the positive approach to recognition is the most effective one. If an employee has done the appropriate thing when it comes to a Social Engineering incident, acknowledge the good action and reward that person appropriately. But do not stop there. Let everyone else in your organization know; and as a result, your entire organization's preparedness will be improved.

Preparedness of Incident Response Teams

All companies should have the capability to deal effectively with what they may consider an incident. An incident can be defined as any event that threatens the company's livelihood. From an Information Security perspective, dealing with any outside threat, including Social Engineering, would be considered an incident. The goals of a well-prepared incident response team are to detect potential Information Security breaches and provide an effective and efficient means of dealing with the situation in a manner that reduces the potential impact to the corporation. A secondary but very important goal would be to provide management with sufficient information to decide on an appropriate course of action. Having a team in place comprised of knowledgeable individuals from key areas of the corporation that would be educated and prepared to respond to Social Engineering attacks is a key aspect of an effective Information Security program.

Testing Your Readiness

Penetration testing is a method of examining the security controls of an organization from an outsider's point of view. To be effective, it involves testing all controls that prevent, track, and warn of internal and external intrusions. Companies that want to test their readiness against Social Engineering attacks can use this approach to reveal weaknesses that may not have been previously evident. You must remember, however, that although penetration testing is one of the best ways to evaluate an organization's controls, it is only as effective as the efforts of the individuals who are performing the test.

Immediate Notification to "Targeted Groups"

If someone reports or discovers a Social Engineering attempt, you need to notify personnel in similar areas. It is very important at this point to have a standard process and a quick procedure to do this. This is where a well-prepared incident response team can help. Assuming that a procedure is already in place, the incident response team can quickly deal with the problem and effectively remove it before any damage is done.

Apply Technology Where Possible. Other than making employees aware of the threat and providing guidance on how to handle both co-workers and others asking for information, there are no true solid methods for protecting information and employees from Social Engineering. However, a few options to consider might include:

- *Trace calls if possible.* Tracing calls may be an option, but only if you have the capability and are prepared for it. What you do not want in the midst of an attack is having to ask yourself, "How do we trace a call?" Again, be prepared. Have some incident response procedures in place that will allow you to react accordingly in a very efficient manner.
- *Ensure good physical security.* As mentioned, good physical security is a must in order to provide efficient protection. There are many ways to protect your resources effectively using the latest technology. This may mean using methods that employ biometrics or smart cards.
- *Mark sensitive documents according to data classification scheme.* If you have a well-established information classification scheme in place, it may protect you from revealing sensitive information in the event of a Social Engineering attack. For example, if someone is falling for an attack and he pulls out a document that is marked "Confidential," this may prevent him from releasing that information. Similarly, if a file is electronically marked according to your classification schemes, the same would apply.

Social Engineering methods, when employed by an attacker, pose a serious threat to the security of information in any organization. There are far too many real-life examples of the success of this type of attack. However, following some of the basic principles of information systems security can mitigate the risk of Social Engineering. Policies need to be created to provide guidelines for the correct handling and release of information that is considered critical and sensitive within your organization. Information

Security awareness also plays a very critical role. People need to be aware of the threats and, most importantly, they need to know exactly how to react to such an event. Explaining to employees the importance of Information Security and that there are people who are prepared to try and manipulate them to gain access to sensitive information is a wise first step in your defense plan. Simply forewarning people of possible attacks is often enough to make them alert enough to be able to spot them, and react accordingly. The old saying is true: "knowledge is power;" or in this case, it increases security.

It is far easier to hack people than to hack some technically sound security device such as a firewall system. However, it is also takes much less effort to educate and prepare employees so that they can prevent and detect attempts at Social Engineering than it takes to properly secure that same firewall system. Organizations can no longer afford to have people as the weakest link in the Information Security chain.

1.7 Implementation (Delivery) Options

Security Technology and Tools

The methods and options available for delivering security awareness information are very similar to those used for delivering other employee awareness information (e.g., sexual harassment or business ethics). And although this is true, it may be time to break with tradition and step out of the box — in other words, it may be time to try something new. Think of positive, fun, exciting, and motivating methods that will give employees the message and encourage them to practice good computer security habits. Keep in mind that the success of an awareness program is its ability to reach a large audience through several attractive and engaging materials and techniques. Examples of Information Technology security awareness materials and techniques include:

- Posters
- Posting motivational and catchy slogans
- Videotapes
- Classroom instruction
- Computer-based delivery, such as CD-ROM, DVD, intranet access, Web-based access, etc.
- Brochures/flyers
- Pens/pencils/keychains (any type of trinket) with motivational slogans
- Post-it notes with a message on protecting the Information Technology system
- Stickers for doors and bulletin boards

- Cartoons/articles published monthly or quarterly in an in-house newsletter or specific department notices
- Special topical bulletins (security alerts in this instance)
- Monthly email notices related to security issues or email broadcasts of security advisories
- Security banners or pre-logon messages that appear on the computer monitor
- Distribution of items as an incentive. (For example, distribute packages of the gummy-bear-type candy that is shaped into little snakes. Attach a card to the package, with the heading "Gummy Virus Attack at XYZ." Add a clever message, such as "Destroy all viruses wiggling through the network — make sure your anti-virus software is turned on.")

Assurance, Trust, and Confidence Mechanisms

Evaluation

All management programs, including the security awareness program, must be periodically reviewed and evaluated. In most organizations there will be no need to conduct a formal quantitative or qualitative analysis. It should be sufficient to informally review and monitor whether behaviors or attitudes have changed. The following provides a few simple options to consider:

- Distribute a survey or questionnaire seeking input from employees. If an awareness briefing is conducted during the new-employee orientation, follow up with the employee (after a specified time period of three to six months) and ask how the briefing was perceived (e.g., what do they remember, on what would they have liked more information, etc.).
- While pouring a cup of coffee in the morning, ask others in the room about the awareness campaign. How did they like the new poster? How about the cake and ice cream during the meeting? Remember: the objective is to heighten the employee's awareness and responsibilities of Information Security. Thus, even if the response is, "That poster is silly," do not fret; it was noticed and that is what is important.
- Track the number and type of security incidents that occur before and after the awareness campaign. Most likely, it is a positive sign if there is an increase in the number of reported incidents. This is an indication that users know what to do and who to contact if they suspect a computer security breach or incident.
- Conduct "spot checks" of user behavior. This may include walking through the office, checking to see if workstations are logged on while unattended, or if sensitive media are not adequately protected.

- If delivering awareness material via computer-based delivery (e.g., loading it on the organization's intranet), record usernames and completion status. On a periodic basis, check to see who has reviewed the material. One could also send a targeted questionnaire to those who have completed the online material.
- Have the system manager run a password-cracking program against the employees' passwords. If this is done, consider running the program on a stand-alone computer and not installing it on the network.

Usually, it is not necessary or desirable to install this type of software on a network server. Beware of some free password-cracking programs available from the Internet because they may contain malicious code that will export a password list to a waiting hacker.

Keep in mind that the evaluation process should reflect and answer whether or not the original objectives of the security awareness program have been achieved. Sometimes, evaluations focus on the wrong item. For example, when evaluating an awareness program, it would not be appropriate to ask each employee how many incidents have occurred over the past year. However, it would be appropriate to ask each employee if he or she knows whom to contact if a security incident is suspected.

Information Protection and Management Services

Another key success factor in an awareness program is remembering that it never ends — the awareness campaign must repeat its message. If the message is very important, then it should be repeated more often, and in a different manner each time. Because Information Security awareness must be an ongoing activity, it requires creativity and enthusiasm to maintain the interest of all audience members. The awareness materials should create an atmosphere in which Information Security is important not only to the organization, but also to each employee. It should ignite an interest in following the Information Security policies and rules of behavior.

An awareness program must remain current. If Information Security policies are changing, the employees must be notified. It may be necessary and helpful to set up technical means to deliver immediate information. For example, if the latest virus has been circulating overnight, the system manager could post a pre-logon message to all workstations. In this manner, the first item the users see when turning on their workstations is information on how to protect the system, such as what to look for and what not to open.

Finally, the security awareness campaign should be simple. For most organizations, the awareness campaign does not need to be expensive, complicated, or overly technical in its delivery. Make it easy for employees to get the information and make it easy to understand.

Security awareness programs should (be):

- Supported and led by example from management
- Simple and straightforward
- Positive and motivating
- A continuous effort
- Repeat the most important messages
- Entertaining
- Humorous where appropriate — make slogans easy to remember
- Tell employees what the threats are and their responsibilities for protecting the system

In some organizations, it may be a necessary (or viable) option to outsource the design and development of the awareness program to a qualified vendor. To find the best vendor to meet an organization's needs, one can review products and services on the Internet, contact others and discuss their experiences, and seek proposals from vendors that list previous experiences and outline their solutions for your goals.

Overcoming Obstacles

As with any employeewide program, the security awareness campaign must have support from senior management. This includes the financial means to develop the program. For example, each year, management must allocate dollars that will support the awareness materials and efforts. Create a project plan that includes the objectives, cost estimates for labor and other materials, time schedules, and outline any specific deliverables (i.e., 15-minute video, pens, pencils, etc.). Have management approve the plan and set aside specific funds to create and develop the security awareness materials. Keep in mind that some employees will display passive resistance. These are the employees who will not attend briefings, and who will create a negative atmosphere by ignoring procedures and violating security policies. For this reason, it is important to gain management support before beginning any type of security procedures associated with the awareness campaign. Although there might be resistance, most employees want to perform well in their jobs, do the right thing, and abide by the rules.

Summary

Employees are the single, most important aspect of an information system security program, and management support is the key to ensuring a successful awareness program. The security awareness program needs to be a line item in the information system security plan. In addition to the operational and technical countermeasures needed to protect the system, awareness (and training) must also be an essential item.

Various computer crime statistics show that the threat from insiders ranges from 65 to 90%. This is not an indication that 60% of the employees in an organization are trying to hack into the system; it does mean that employees, whether intentionally or accidentally, may allow some form of harm to the system. This includes loading illegal copies of screensaver software, downloading shareware from the Internet, creating weak passwords, or sharing their passwords with others. Thus, employees need to be made aware of the information system "rules of behavior" and how to practice good computer security skills.

The security awareness program should be structured to meet the organization's specific needs. The first step is to decide on the goals of the program — what it should achieve — and then to develop a program plan. This plan should then be professionally presented to management. Hopefully, the program will receive the necessary resources for success, such as personnel, monetary, and moral support. In the beginning, even if there are not enough resources available, start with the simple and no-cost methods of distributing information. Keep in mind that it is important just to begin; and along the way, seek more resources and ask for assistance from key Information Technology team members.

The benefit of beginning with an awareness campaign is to set the stage for the next level of Information Security information distribution, which is Information Security training. Following the awareness program, all employees should receive site-specific training on the basics of Information Security. Remember that awareness does not end when training begins; it is a continuous and important feature of the information system security awareness and training program.

1.8 Common Body of Knowledge (CBK)

The current CBK for the Security Management Domain is listed below to assist in determining topics for further review. Although this Study Guide is very detailed in many areas, it is not possible to thoroughly discuss every CBK topic in a single book; therefore, additional study of items from the bibliography may be advisable.

Components

The professional can meet the expectations defined at the beginning of this chapter by understanding such Security Management Practices, Topics, and Methodologies as:

- Change Control/Management
- Hardware Configuration
- System and Application Software
- Change Control Process
- Data Classification
- Objectives of a Classification Scheme
- Criteria by which Data Is Classified
- Commercial Data Classification
- Government Data Classification
- Employment Policies and Practices
- Background Checks/Security Clearances
- Employment Agreements
- Hiring and Termination Practices
- Job Descriptions
- Roles and Responsibilities
- Separation of Duties and Responsibilities
- Job Rotations
- Policies, Standards, Guidelines, and Procedures
- Risk Management
- Principles of Risk Management
- Threats and Vulnerabilities
- Probability Determination
- Asset Valuation
- Risk Assessment Tools and Techniques
- Qualitative versus Quantitative Risk Assessment Methodologies
- Single Occurrence Loss
- Annual Loss Expectancy (ALE) Calculations
- Countermeasure Selection
- Countermeasure Evaluation
- Risk Reduction/Assignment/Acceptance
- Roles and Responsibilities
- Individuals/Data Owners and Custodians
- Security Awareness Training
- Security Management Planning

Examples

Examples of Knowledge/Ability

- Describe Internal Control Standards
- Define Configuration Auditing
- Describe Management Responsibilities toward Security Policies
- Distinguish between Policies, Standards, and Procedures
- Compare and contrast International Security Evaluation Criteria
- Describe Trusted Computer System Evaluation Criteria (TCSEC)

- Describe Information Technology Security Evaluation Criteria (ITSEC)
- Describe the "Common Criteria" effort
- Compare and contrast Classified versus Sensitive Data/Information
- Describe Data/Information Classification Schemes
- Describe the Risk and Countermeasures of Data Aggregation
- Describe the Roles and Responsibilities of IS/IT Security Function
- Compare and contrast Various Organizational Placement of the IT/IS Security Function
- Compare and contrast Data Owner, Custodian, and User Responsibilities
- Define Standard Activities of Security Management Personnel
- Define Separation of Duties
- Compare and contrast Aspects of Technological and Non-Technological Security
- Define requirements for, and objectives of, a Security Awareness Program
- Identify the appropriate topics for Security Awareness Training
- Describe Military-Oriented War Threats to Information Security
- Compare and contrast the Vulnerabilities, Threats, and Risks of Economic Espionage
- Describe Potential Terrorist Actions
- Compare and contrast Types of Malicious Code Threats
- Compare and contrast Types of Viruses
- Describe how good computing practices reduce exposure to Viruses
- Distinguish between and define assets, threats, vulnerabilities, and risks
- Describe the valuation rationale for data/information worth
- Compare and contrast data/information collection and analysis techniques
- Describe typical threats
- Describe threat classification
- Describe typical vulnerabilities
- Describe the calculation of risks
- Distinguish between and define risk reduction, countermeasures, assignment, and acceptance
- Identify typical countermeasures
- Describe the selection criteria for countermeasures
- Define Principle of Due Care in regard to risk analysis
- Define quantitative risk analysis
- Define qualitative risk analysis
- Define risk analysis evaluation functions
- Identify risk analysis steps
- Compare and contrast strengths and weaknesses of various Anti-virus Programs

- Define Security Principles of Least Privilege, Separation of Duties/Functions, Assignment/Control of System Privileges, and Accountability
- Distinguish between Separation of Duties and Rotation of Duties

1.9 Sample Questions for the CISSP Exam

1. In addition to protecting important assets, security rules and procedures should:
   a. Be cost-effective
   b. Justified by risk analysis
   c. Support the organizational mission
   d. Apply to everyone in the organization
2. Masquerading is:
   a. Attempting to hack a system through backdoors to an operating system or application
   b. Pretending to be an authorized user
   c. Always done through IP spoofing
   d. Applying a subnet mask to an internal IP range
3. Integrity is protection of data from all of the following EXCEPT:
   a. Unauthorized changes
   b. Accidental changes
   c. Data analysis
   d. Intentional manipulation
4. A security program cannot address which of the following business goals:
   a. Accuracy of information
   b. Change control
   c. User expectations
   d. Prevention of fraud
5. In most cases, integrity is enforced through:
   a. Physical security
   b. Logical security
   c. Confidentiality
   d. Access controls
6. A "well-formed transaction" is one that:
   a. Has all the necessary paperwork to substantiate the transaction
   b. Is based on clear business objectives
   c. Ensures that data can be manipulated only in authorized ways
   d. Is subject to duplicate processing
7. In an accounting department, several people are required to complete a financial process. This is most likely an example of:
   a. Segregation of duties
   b. Rotation of duties

    c. Need-to-know

    d. Collusion

8. Risk Management is commonly understood as all of the following EXCEPT:

    a. Analyzing and assessing risk

    b. Identifying risk

    c. Accepting or mitigation of risk

    d. Likelihood of a risk occurring

9. The percentage or degree of damage inflicted on an asset used in the calculation of single loss expectancy can be referred to as:

    a. Exposure Factor (EF)

    b. Annualized Rate of Occurrence (ARO)

    c. Vulnerability

    d. Likelihood

10. The absence of a fire-suppression system would be best characterized as a(n):

    a. Exposure

    b. Threat

    c. Vulnerability

    d. Risk

11. Risk Assessment includes all of the following EXCEPT:

    a. Implementation of effective countermeasures

    b. Ensuring that risk is managed

    c. Analysis of the current state of security in the target environment

    d. Strategic analysis of risk

12. A Risk Management project may be subject to overlooking certain types of threats. What can assist the Risk Management team to prevent that?

    a. Automated tools

    b. Adoption of qualitative risk assessment processes

    c. Increased reliance on internal experts for risk assessment

    d. Recalculation of the work factor

13. Data classification can assist an organization in:

    a. Eliminating regulatory mandates

    b. Lowering of accountability of data classifiers

    c. Reducing costs for protecting data

    d. Normalization of databases

14. Who "owns" an organization's data?

    a. Information Technology group

    b. Users

    c. Data custodians

    b. Business units

15. An information security policy does not usually include:

    a. Authority for Information Security department

    b. Guidelines for how to implement policy

   c. Basis for data classification

   d. Recognition of information as an asset of the organization

16. The role of an information custodian should NOT include:

   a. Restoration of lost or corrupted data

   b. Regular backups of data

   c. Establishing retention periods for data

   d. Ensuring the availability of data

17. A main objective of awareness training is:

   a. Provide understanding of responsibilities

   b. Entertaining the users through creative programs

   c. Overcoming all resistance to security procedures

   d. To be repetitive to ensure accountability

18. What is a primary target of a person employing Social Engineering?

   a. An individual

   b. A policy

   c. Government agencies

   d. An information system

19. Social engineering can take many forms EXCEPT

   a. Dumpster diving

   b. Coercion or intimidation

   c. Sympathy

   d. Eavesdropping

20. Incident response planning can be instrumental in:

   a. Meeting regulatory requirements

   b. Creating customer loyalty

   c. Reducing the impact of an adverse event on the organization

   d. Ensuring management makes the correct decisions in a crisis

References

Jim Appleyard, "Information Classification: A Corporate Implementation Guide," in *Handbook of Information Security Management, 3rd ed.*, Boca Raton, FL: Auerbach Publications, 1999.

John Berti and Marcus Rogers, "Social Engineering: The Forgotten Risk," in *Information Security Management Handbook, 4th ed., Vol. 3*, Harold F. Tipton and Micki Krause, Eds., Boca Raton, FL: Auerbach Publications, 2002.

Susan Hansche, "Making Security Awareness Happen," in *Information Security Management Handbook, 4th ed., vol. 3*, Boca Raton, FL: Auerbach Publications, 2002.

Will Ozier, "Risk Assessment and Management," *EDP Auditing*, February 1998.

Thomas Peltier, *Information Security Policies and Procedures: A Practitioner's Reference*, Boca Raton, FL: Auerbach Publications, 1999.

Chapter 2
Security Architecture and Models

The Security Architecture and Models Domain contains the concepts, principles, structures, and standards used to design, implement, monitor, and secure operating systems, equipment, networks, applications, and those controls used to enforce various levels of availability, integrity, and confidentiality.

One of the key aspects of being an information system security professional is to design and build a security infrastructure that meets current and future business needs. This chapter explains the key principles and concepts central to the security architecture of any organization. When coupled with the concepts covered in the other chapters (with particular emphasis on the telecommunications, cryptography, and access control modules), this chapter gives the CISSP the necessary breadth to address the challenges of developing a security architecture and the insight to evaluate the existing or legacy architecture of an organization.

The CISSP candidate should be able to:

- Identify the security issues and controls associated with architectures and designs.
- Describe the principles of common computer and network organization, architectures, and designs.
- Define security models in terms of confidentiality, integrity, and information flow.

This chapter is divided into five topic areas. The first section begins by defining the concept of a secure architecture. The Information Protection Environment section identifies the system architecture environment and outlines some of the factors associated with designing a secure architecture. The third section, Security Technology and Tools, provides an explanation of the types of controls available to designers developing a secure architecture. In addition, the concepts of security models are introduced to provide an overview of various security theories for designing a secure system. The final topics outline what organizations can do to ensure that security is a part of the architectural design and several management controls are mentioned.

Introduction

Defining Security Architecture

Building an information system requires a balance among various requirements, such as capability, flexibility, performance, ease of use, cost, business requirements, and security. Security should be considered a requirement from the beginning — it is simply another feature that needs to be included. Attempting to retrofit the required and desired security controls after the fact can lead to user frustration, a lowered security posture, and significantly increased implementation costs. Based on the importance of each requirement, various trade-offs may be necessary during the design of the system. Thus, it is important to identify what security features must be included. Then if a performance or flexibility requirement means downgrading or not including a security feature, the architecture designers can keep the primary goals of the system in check and make compromises on the nonessential points.

Security architecture is simply a view of an overall system architecture from a security perspective. It provides some insight into the security services, mechanisms, technologies, and features that can be used to satisfy system security requirements. It provides recommendations on where, within the context of the overall system architecture, security mechanisms should be placed. The security view of a system architecture focuses on the system security services and high-level mechanisms, allocation of security-related functionality, and identified interdependencies among security related components, services, mechanisms, and technologies, and at the same time reconciling any conflict among them. The security architecture is only one aspect of the enterprise or system architecture, which may also include network architecture or physical connectivity architecture.

Security architecture describes how the system is put together to satisfy the security requirements. It is not a description of the functions of the system; it is more of a design overview, describing at an abstract level the relationships between key elements of the hardware, operating systems, applications, network, and other required components to protect the organization's interests. It should also describe how the functions in the system development process follow the security requirements. For example, if the security requirements specify that the system must have a given level of assurance as to the correctness of the security controls, the security architecture must prescribe these specifications in the development process.

Security requirements are not added steps to the development process; instead, the specifications or guidelines of the security architecture provide an influence during all development processes. During the beginning stages, the security architecture should outline high-level security issues, such as the system security policy, the level of assurance required, and any potential impacts security could have on the design process. As the system is developed, the security architecture should evolve in parallel, and may even need to be slightly ahead of the development process so that the security requirements will guide the development process.

2.1 Information Protection Requirements

The A-I-C Triad

The security architecture is designed so that the A-I-C goals of information security can meet the business and security needs of the organization.

The goal is to think about security in the beginning stages and how it will affect the availability, integrity, and confidentiality requirements. The security architecture can guide the early decisions and avoid needing to correct or retrofit the system after development has been completed. Adding security after a system has been developed can significantly increase the costs, making it an essential part of the system functionality. Thus, if security is to be included in the system, it should be considered in the beginning.

2.2 Information Protection Environment

It is important to think of the security architecture as including several underlying architectures. For example, there is the platform architecture of the computer hardware, and the software architecture that defines how an operating system will interact with the hardware components. Exhibit 1 represents the computer system layers. It begins with the end user at the top. The user interacts with data and the network resources through applications. The applications sit on top of the utilities and operating system. The operating system provides management of the computer hardware resources.

This section is divided according to these underlying architectures and provides a brief overview of how these individual architectures operate and how security can be affected by these elements. While the impact of the network is discussed in this chapter as it relates to the security architecture, the chapter on Telecommunications, Network, and Internet Security (Chapter 8) covers the elements related to controls and specific network threats. The approach in all the sections, except Security Models, is based on practical terms. Because the Security Models section explains the theory of some of the most common security models, the approach

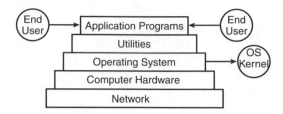

Exhibit 1. Layered Approach

used is more formal. The underlying architectures explained in this section include:

- Platform Architecture
- Network Environment
- Enterprise Architecture
- Security Models
- Protection Mechanisms

Before discussing the elements of the architecture, it is essential to point out how the architecture is related to overall organization security policy. At the point of developing the components in the architecture or the specific elements within a given system, the overall security policy provides the framework the architecture will implement. Without an existing security policy, it is virtually impossible for personnel to address the organization's specific security goals. Consequently, if there is no organizational security policy, the system will not achieve the organizational security goals.

> ## Security Policy
>
> *A security policy is a high-level statement of enterprise beliefs, goals, and objectives and the general means for their attainment for a specified subject area.*

Platform Architecture

The platform topic encompasses the computer and how it manages various system resources or system utilities. To explain this, the platform architecture section is separated into:

- Operating System Software and Utilities
- Central Processing Unit (CPU) States
- Memory Management Overview
- Input/Output Devices
- Storage Devices

Operating System Software and Utilities

The operating system (OS) software is the heart and soul of any computing platform. It is initially loaded into the computer by a boot program, which is the process of loading the operating system into the computer's main memory or random access memory (RAM). Note that on larger computer systems, such as mainframes, the boot sequence is referred to as the Initial Program Load (IPL). During the boot sequence, a small program is loaded into the memory that can, in turn, control the loading of the full operating system. Once the operating system is loaded, it controls various subsystems, such as software utilities, software applications, file systems, and access controls for users or other subsystems.

There are two primary objectives of the operating system; the first is to control the use of the system's resources. The operating system must share the computer's resources among a number of simultaneous users, or if the computer only has one user, it must share resources between multiple tasks. The second is to provide a convenient and easy-to-understand view or interface of the computer to its users (whether the users are people or programs), which is usually done through a graphical user interface (GUI).

The fundamental components of the computer operate based on the installed software. The first layer of software is the operating system (OS). The applications run on top of the OS software. The concept of layering is not unique to secure operating systems. Layering promotes a structured design assisting in the achievement of some assurance goals. A layered OS has an internal structure resembling a stack of systems, each having an interface for use by the layers above and below.

Layers are hierarchical in nature. That is, the lower layers provide primitive functions while the higher layers use the primitive functions to provide more complex functions. The software and data in each layer know only their own data and the set of functions available for them to use. Layering constrains the functions in each layer, preventing any single layer from providing sufficient capabilities to be an operating system in itself.

Having a single security layer is difficult because each layer has its own set of objects requiring secure management. For security purposes, each layer should provide security features or implement access to a common set of security functions. Additionally, the security primitives should be placed in one of the lower levels, with additional security elements implemented at all layers.

For example, if unauthorized users were able to gain system privileges in the operating system layer they might be able to change programs or files containing the control data for security mechanisms in the services and applications layers. Thus, when evaluating the security of the system, it is necessary to verify that the security mechanisms in any layer cannot be bypassed. The more complex the system becomes, the more difficult it is to perform the security check. A clear understanding of the security requirements at each level during the design phases assists in the development of tests to evaluate the resulting implementation.

Ideally, the inner core of the system is structured reasonably simple as to allow for a complete check that the security mechanisms cannot be circumvented. Another reason for putting security mechanisms in a lower layer is to increase the performance of the system. The performance is increased by putting the execution of the security elements lower in the operating system, with lower overhead within the operating system.

Three security technologies used by operating systems are the reference monitor, the security kernel, and the trusted computing base. More information on these tools is given in the Security Technology and Tools section.

Operating system services include items such as program creation, program execution, access to input/output devices, controlled access to files, system access, error detection and response, and accounting. As shown in Exhibit 2, the hardware resources controlled by the operating system

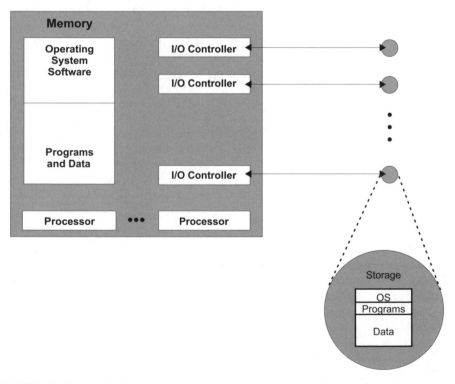

Exhibit 2. Operating System

include the CPU, memory, input/output (I/O) requests/devices, and storage devices.

In the early days, software programmers had to include information on how the hardware resources would handle resource usage requests. This left the resources in an idle state while waiting for the next input. To enhance the computer's capabilities, programmers began to write routines for handling the hardware and spooling systems for buffering input and output to the processor (via memory).

> *The earliest programming system made available to the general user was the UNIVAC generalized programming (GP) for the UNIVAC I and UNIVAC II computers. It was an assembly language and in its early development it served as a pseudo operating system.*

A development of this is the concept of multitasking — several programs can coexist within the computer, each taking turns to use the processor. Because I/O devices are relatively slow, the requests can be stacked, which provides a more efficient use of the processor.

As part of the spooling system, input requests waiting for the processor are stored in some type of memory storage, usually Random Access Memory (RAM). RAM is considered volatile. That is, all data stored in RAM is not permanently stored and is gone when the computer is turned off. The contents of RAM are necessary for the computer to process any data. The CPU receives instructions from RAM, uses the data in RAM for processing, and temporarily keeps the results of processing in RAM until they are needed again. Exhibit 3 provides an example.

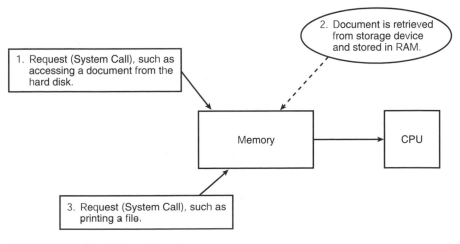

Exhibit 3. Memory Example

1. The user (or process on behalf of the user) inputs a request to open a file that is stored on a permanent storage device.
2. The file is brought from the storage device and held in random access memory.
3. If the user wants to print the file, the computer saves time by having the document readily available in memory, instead of retrieving it again from the storage device.

An operating system is also responsible for performing services for applications, such as:

- If the operating system has multitasking, the operating system determines which applications should run in what order and how much time should be allowed for each application before giving another application a turn.
- Managing the sharing of internal memory among multiple applications.
- Handling input and output to and from attached hardware devices, such as hard disks.
- Sending messages to each application, interactive user, or system operator about the status of operation and any errors that may have occurred.
- Freeing the management of batch jobs (i.e., printing) so that the initiating application is freed from this work.

In addition, the operating system software may provide for additional operations, such as multitasking, multithreading, multiprocessing, and multiprogramming. Although the terms may seem somewhat similar, each has different concepts. A brief description of several of these terms follows:

- *Multitasking* systems allow a user to perform more than one computer task (such as the operation of an application program) at the same time. The operating system keeps track of where the user is in these tasks and switches from one to the other without losing information. Examples of operating systems that provide multitasking are Microsoft Windows 2000, IBM's OS/390, and Linux — almost all operating systems today can provide multitasking. The operating system handles multitasking in either a preemptive or cooperative fashion. A preemptive system relies on the operating system to manage the time intervals, or slices, an application or task is allocated within the CPU. In cooperative mode, the application manages the resources of the CPU. As long as an application requires the CPU, it maintains control. If the application is waiting, it can allow other programs to use the CPU.
- *Multithreading* is the ability of a program (or an operating system process) to manage its use by more than one user at a time and to even manage multiple requests by the same user without having to have multiple copies of the programming running in the computer.

When a user requests a program, it is kept track of as a thread with a separate identity. While the program is working on behalf of the initial request for that thread and is interrupted by other requests, the status of work on behalf of that thread is kept track of until the work is completed.

- A *multiprogramming system* is one that allows for the interleaved execution of two or more programs by a processor. This term is rarely used because all but the most specialized computer operating systems support multiprogramming.

- *Multiprocessing* is the coordinated processing of two or more programs by a processor that contains parallel processors. A multiprocessor system uses parallel processors to execute the same application faster on multiple processors or can execute different processes on different processors, allowing for the simultaneous execution of more than one program. Essentially, it can mean either (1) the dynamic assignment of a program to one of two or more processors working in tandem or (2) multiple computers working on the same program at the same time (parallel processing). Parallel processing is divided into symmetric multiprocessing and massively parallel processing. In symmetric processing, the processors share memory and the I/O bus or data path. A single copy of the operating system is in charge of all the processors. In massively parallel processing, up to 200 or more processors can work on the same application. Each processor has its own operating system and memory, but an interconnect arrangement of data paths allows messages to be sent between the processors.

A vulnerability associated with multiprogramming systems is object reuse. In a single-processor multiprogramming system, several processes may be loaded and ready to execute at the same time; however, only one can own the processor at any instance in time. When the operating system deactivates the running process to activate the next process, a context switch must be performed. Any information necessary for the subsequent continuation of the execution must be saved and any new information for the new process has to be set up. For security reasons, it is important to avoid storage residues. Storage residues occur when data is left behind in the memory area that could be allocated to new processes. A process returning RAM to the operating system can "scrub" the RAM prior to releasing it. However, in the context switch, the operating system itself must scrub the RAM to prevent storage residue.

Another vulnerability associated with multiprogramming and multiple processors is time of check/time of use (TOC/TOU), which is a form of asynchronous attack. It can occur when one process passes pointers to parameters residing in its virtual memory to the operating system. At the same time, another process, with access to the same memory containing the parameters, modifies the parameters between the time the operating system validates them and the time they are used. The first process making the call is suspended during the call so that it cannot modify the parameters, but any other process or processor may be able to run during the call. This is difficult to achieve in practice and also difficult to check for.

Another OS Vulnerability is maintenance hooks. *Maintenance hooks* are instructions in software code allowing easy maintenance and additional feature development; they are commonly referred to as trapdoors or backdoors. They are not typically defined during access or design specifications and are generally intended to be removed prior to the completion of the code, which does not always occur. Because hooks can provide entry into the software code at unusual points or without the usual checks, they pose a serious security risk. Essentially, an unauthorized user who knows that the entry point exists could gain access to information or insert malicious code into the software. Ideally, maintenance hooks should never be inserted into the program during development. At a minimum, maintenance hooks should be removed prior to live implementation.

Central Processing Unit (CPU) States

The core components of the hardware platform are the CPU, memory, and the bus connections. All program instructions are executed in the CPU. The CPU is responsible for instruction execution, registers, memory address, memory buffer, I/O address, I/O buffer, and program counter. Registers are used to control and track the progress of a program execution. For example, the program counter always contains the address in memory of the next instruction to be executed. For more information on the fundamental concepts of computer architecture, refer to books such as *Computer Architecture* by M. De Blasi (1990) or *Building a Secure Computer System* by M. Gasser (1988).

The main components of the CPU include:

- Arithmetic Logic Unit (ALU). An ALU executes instructions given in a machine language. While executing an instruction, it may also set bits in the status register.
- Registers. There are two different types of registers: general-purpose registers and dedicated registers. One dedicated register is the program counter that points to the memory location that contains the next instruction to be executed. Another example is the status register, which allows the CPU to keep essential state information.

A CPU has two principle states: user and supervisor or privileged. There in fact may be more states, depending on the system architecture, implemented through protection rings or layers. The specific hardware defines the layers at the chip level. Only non-privileged instructions can be executed while the CPU is in user state, while any privileged and non-privileged instruction can be executed while the CPU is in supervisor state.

While some hardware defines the outer layer as supervisor state, most operating systems use the outer layer to represent user state. Each inner layer represents additional instructions, which can be executed by the CPU to the inner layer representing the supervisor or privileged state. This can be confusing and lead to implementation and design difficulties for the application and system programmers.

Using this state model, the application can request that its operating state be increased or decreased by the operating system, as required. This allows for data hiding, to protect information that should only be available in the higher layers.

Process states are not the same as CPU states. While the CPU state defines the operating mode of the CPU, the process state refers to the mode or level the application or process is running in. Process states are defined by the particular operating system and can include the following:

- *Run.* In the run state, the CPU is executing instructions for the current process.
- *Wait.* The process is waiting for a defined event to occur, such as retrieving data from a hard disk.
- *Sleep.* The process is suspended and waiting for its next time slice in the CPU, or a given event to occur such as an alarm.
- *Masked/interruptible state.* Interrupts are implemented to allow system events to be synchronized. For example, if the masked bit is not set, the interruption is disabled (masked off).

A vulnerability of a system state could occur when a system crashes. During the crash, the system creates a core dump of its internal state, including RAM and program stacks and CPU registers, allowing for investigation and identification of the cause leading to the crash. If the internal state contains sensitive information and the core dump data is stored in a file potentially accessed and read by everyone, inadvertent release of the sensitive information could occur.

Memory Management Overview

Many people commonly use the term "memory" to refer to Random Access Memory (RAM). RAM is used by the computer to hold temporary instructions and data needed to complete tasks. This process enables the computer's CPU to access instructions and data stored in memory very quickly and thus speed up processing time for the user.

One of the most fundamental hardware requirements for a secure system is memory protection. Memory protection is needed to prevent a user's programs from affecting the operating system or the processes of other users, which is typically a function performed by the operating system. The security features of memory protection are parallel to those in memory management that are designed for efficient use of memory. An overview of memory management will be provided; however, if more detail is desired, refer to other resources for a more thorough explanation.

To begin, the types of memory available are:

- *Random Access Memory (RAM)* is read/write memory. It is the computer's primary working memory. It stores program instructions and data, and is accessible directly by the CPU.
  - *Dynamic Random Access Memory (DRAM)* is the most common form of RAM in a personal computer or workstation. "Dynamic" refers to the ability to hold data for a short period of time; thus, its storage cells must be refreshed periodically or given a new electronic charge every few milliseconds. DRAM stores each bit in a storage cell consisting of a capacitor and a transistor. Because capacitors tend to lose their charge rather quickly, they need to be recharged.
  - *Extended Data Output RAM (EDO RAM)* is a type of RAM chip that improves the time to read from memory on faster microprocessors such as the Intel Pentium. SDRAM is recommended for faster computers.
  - *Synchronous DRAM (SDRAM)* is a generic name for various kinds of DRAM that are synchronized with the clock speed for which the microprocessor is optimized. This enables the memory controller to know the exact clock cycle when the requested data will be read; thus, the CPU does not need to wait between memory accesses. This increases the number of instructions that the processor can perform in a given time interval.
  - *Double Data Rate SDRAM (DDR SDRAM)* is the next-generation SDRAM technology. It allows the memory chip to activate output (operate transactions) on both the rising and falling edges of the clock cycle rather than on just the rising edge. This could potentially double the output or transactions.
  - *Burst Extended Data Output DRAM (BEDO DRAM)* is a type of DRAM that can send data back to the computer from one read operation at the same time that it is reading in the address of the next data to be sent. It works well in high-speed processors.
- *Read-Only Memory (ROM)* is built-in memory that contains data that can only be read (not written to). ROM is usually used for storing parts of the operating system that allows the computer to be booted. It is different from RAM in that the data it contains is not lost when the computer power is turned off — the data is sustained by a small long-life battery in the computer.

- *Programmable Read-Only Memory (PROM)* is ROM that can be modified once by a user. It allows a user to tailor a microcode program using a special machine called a PROM programmer. The PROM programmer supplies an electrical current to specific cells in the ROM that effectively blows a fuse in them. The process is known as "burning the PROM." Because this process leaves no margin for error, most ROM chips designed to be modified by users use EPROM or EEPROM.
- *Erasable and Programmable Read-Only Memory (EPROM)* is PROM that can be erased and reused.
- *Electrically Erasable Programmable Read-Only Memory (EEPROM)* is user-modifiable ROM that can be erased and reprogrammed (written to) repeatedly through the application of higher-than-normal electrical voltage.

- *Flash Memory* is a rewritable memory that functions like RAM and a hard disk drive combined. It stores bits of electronic data in memory cells like RAM; but when it is turned off, the data remains, like ROM. It is used primarily in applications that need high speed and durability, such as digital cellular phones, digital cameras, PC cards for notebook computers, and pagers.

To use memory efficiently, operating systems provide "memory management." The method of memory management used is system dependent and typically cannot be changed by the user or system administrator because it is optimized for the specific operating system.

The objective of memory management is to separate programs into different parts of memory and still have them work properly. To accomplish this, memory space is divided into an addressing scheme. I/O requests are then assigned to an addressable location within the memory's space. Addressing controls ensure that the addresses used internally are independent of physical hardware addresses. Early memory management techniques were developed to handle this. To prevent errors in one program from corrupting other programs, it was necessary to provide some way of isolating the addresses used by one program from those of another.

An example of memory management is to have certain applications, upon execution, reserve space in memory. As necessary, the application will write "pages" (the size of the page depends on the system) of information to that reserved address space. Alternatively, applications can reserve and commit pages during the same request call. The term "locked memory" is when pages are locked in the memory space (or reserved by an application), thus taking up memory capabilities until they are explicitly unlocked. Locked memory is specifically prevented from being written to virtual memory, and the memory pages cannot be used by another program until released.

In most cases, adding more memory to a computer system can increase its performance. Operating systems provide the ability to expand memory space by using space on the hard disk as an extension of RAM. The ability to use the storage disk to simulate RAM is called *virtual memory*. This process, also referred to as *swapping or paging*, can slow down the system. In an average computer, it takes the CPU approximately 200 ns (nanoseconds) to access RAM compared to 12,000,000 ns to access the hard drive (Kingston Technology, 2002).

Swapping involves moving the entire memory region associated with the process or application. When swapping is used:

- Processes are stored on disk in some type of queue.
- Processes are swapped into memory as space becomes available.
- As a process completes, it is moved out of main memory.

Alternatively, *paging* works with the defined memory page size for the system regardless of the actual amount of memory used by the application. When paging is used:

- Memory is split into equal-sized, small chunks called page frames.
- Programs (processes) are also split into equal-sized, small chunks called pages.
- The system allocates the required number of page frames to a process.
- The operating system maintains a list of free frames using a page table (a page table keeps track of pages and available frames).
- Each page table entry contains the frame number of the corresponding page in main memory.
- A bit is needed to indicate whether or not the page is in main memory.

Most systems use virtual memory to allow physical locations to vary to particular virtual addresses. Virtual addresses are usually implemented through pointers that relate virtual addresses to physical locations. There is, however, a security risk with virtual storage versus RAM. The contents of RAM disappear when the computer is turned off, while the data stored in virtual memory remains on the hard drive when the computer is turned off and may be recovered from these temporary files. An attacker would be able to retrieve data from these locations with little difficulty if access is gained. Some operating systems include the ability to erase the virtual memory file when the system is shut down, thus reducing this risk. Another countermeasure is that several operating system vendors offer the ability to encrypt or separate the swap partition. For example, Open-BSD supports an encrypted swap partition. In Windows NT and 2000, it is possible to force the swap file(s) to be held on certain partitions. Creating a small drive and placing the swap file there will reduce the risk of it getting fragmented and will also make it easier to control access to it, especially because controlling access to the main drive on a Windows machine too tightly might break many applications. In Linux, it is possible to encrypt partitions using a number of methods.

Another security consideration is for Flash Memory security that is used in devices like personal digital assistants (PDAs), where data is being transferred wirelessly, or if the device containing sensitive data could be stolen. One of the initiatives to protect flash memory is the Mobile Commerce Extension Specification (MC-ES). In a cooperative project, Toshiba, Hitachi, SanDisk, Matsushita Electric Industrial, and Ingentix (known collectively as 5C) have said that the new MC-ES for flash memory cards would add increased security to the standard memory features already supported by existing flash cards.

One of the newest challenges for memory has to do with encryption. For example, an encryption program can read data in an encrypted file, decrypt it, and work on the data while it is in memory. As a result of paging, the data can be transferred onto the hard drive, where it might be available. To counter this, the system administrator can implement a memory lock, which keeps the data in memory and prevents paging or swapping the data to the hard drive.

Another example of a threat to memory was in Microsoft Security Bulletin #MS01-024, "Malformed Request to Domain Controller Can Cause Memory Exhaustion":

Technical Description

A core service running on all Windows 2000 domain controllers (but not on any other machines) contains a memory leak, which can be triggered when it attempts to process a certain type of invalid service request. By repeatedly sending such a request, an attacker could deplete the available memory on the server. If memory were sufficiently depleted, the domain controller could become unresponsive, which would prevent it from processing logon requests or issuing new Kerberos tickets. An affected machine could be put back into service by rebooting.

Mitigating factors:

- *Users who were already logged on and using previously issued Kerberos tickets would not be affected by domain controller unavailability.*
- *If there were multiple domain controllers on the domain, the unaffected machines could pick up the other machine's load.*
- *If normal security practices have been followed, Internet users would be prevented by firewalls and other measures from levying requests directly to domain controllers.*

www.microsoft.com.technet
© 2002 Microsoft Corporation

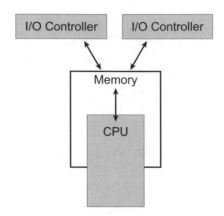

Exhibit 4. Input/Output Device

Input/Output Devices

I/O (see Exhibit 4) is a privileged operation carried out only by the operating system and tends to be one of the most complex. The I/O device usually sends information to memory, but it can send information directly to the CPU. Once the data is copied to memory, an interrupt is generated signaling the CPU that the requested data is now available for processing.

A process is a program in execution. It is an important unit of control for the operating system and security. A process consists of executable code, data, and any relevant execution information. A process works in its own address space and can communicate with other processes only through primitives provided by the operating system. Threads are strands of execution within a process.

Processors are designed to deal with interruptions in program execution caused by the program itself, by user requests, or hardware failure. Depending on the type of event, the mechanisms interrupting program execution can be called exceptions, interrupts, or traps. For an example of how security can be affected, we can look at a type of interrupt, as shown in Exhibit 5.

The hardware interrupt is a special input to the CPU specifying an address in the interrupt vector table. The interrupt table provides the location of the program addressing the condition specified in the interrupt, called the interrupt handler. When an interrupt occurs, the system saves its current state on the stack and then executes the interrupt handler. During this event, control is taken from the user program. The interrupt handler has to make sure the system is restored to a proper state, such as clearing the supervisor status bit, before returning control to the user program.

Additionally, another security flaw could exist if other interrupts arrived while the processor was dealing with a current interrupt. If the new interrupt

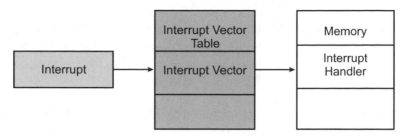

Exhibit 5. Interrupt

has a higher priority than the current interrupt being handled, the processor would then have to transfer execution to the interrupt handler with the higher priority. Once the higher-priority interrupt has been processed, execution returns to the previous interrupt. If the interrupt is of a lower priority, it is cached and handled when the current processing is completed. If interrupt handling is not handled securely, a breach may occur, allowing a previous process to gain the supervisor status of an operating system call.

Exceptions and traps are typically the software equivalent of a hardware interrupt. When a program attempts to execute a privileged instruction while in user mode, an exception occurs, generally causing the failure of the program. Exceptions can also occur due to code errors created when the program was written.

Another vulnerability is the possibility of *redirection of interrupts*. Malicious code is most damaging when it is executing in a privileged mode. To get into the privileged mode of a microprocessor, an interrupt must be generated. During the interrupt, the operating system finds the address of the interrupt handler from the interrupt table. The interrupt table, and other similar structures, is a target of attack. Manipulating or changing the address of the interrupt handler could redirect the operating system to execute the malicious code (virus). The malicious code could then make itself memory resident as a terminate-and-stay-resident program and could be executed whenever the corresponding interrupt occurs.

At the operating system level, a table similar to the interrupt vector table is created to store the memory locations of the system calls or functions. This includes functions such as opening or closing a file, reading information, or requesting additional memory. Should the address of the system call be changed by the malicious code, the operating system would then execute the malicious code and then execute the legitimate function. The same process of altering the location of system calls is used by some external security management software.

The redirection of an interrupt attack is difficult to detect because it does not change the original interrupt handler. Second, without prior knowledge of where the interrupt handlers are located in memory and what the contents of the interrupt vector table should be, it is almost impossible to detect these changes. Additionally, operating systems do not currently provide an integrity check or control mechanism to prevent interrupt or system call redirection.

Storage Devices

A computer requires several different types of storage devices to hold information for short and long periods of time. The various storage devices offer different access times and information volatility, both of which affect the operation of the application and system.

The types of storage devices include:

- *Primary.* Computer's main memory directly accessible to the CPU. Systems can access primary storage much faster than secondary storage. This is typically Random Access Memory (RAM).
- *Secondary.* Nonvolatile storage medium (e.g., disk drive). Stored program instructions and data are retained even when the power is off.
- *Real.* A program is given a definite storage location in memory and direct access to peripheral devices (the ability to move memory among resources is available).
- *Virtual.* The ability to extend the apparent size of RAM using parts of the hard disk. Extend memory using secondary storage for program pages not being executed. It is composed of independent numbered segments.
- *Volatile.* RAM — a complete loss of stored information results if power is interrupted.
- *Nonvolatile* storage includes:
  - *Sequential.* Computer moves through a sequence of stored data items to reach the desired one (items are stored in blocks).
  - *Real Space.* Main storage — used to hold instructions and data during computing.
  - *Virtual Space.* Virtual storage — virtual address space is used by the computer system. It can be mapped into a combination of real main and auxiliary storage.
- *Write-Once Read Memory — WORM.* It is a data storage technology that allows information to be written to a disk a single time and prevents the drive from erasing the data. The disks are intentionally not rewritable. These types of disks are traditionally used to store data so that the information cannot accidentally be erased.

The array of storage devices increases continuously. Examples of common storage devices include:

- Floppy disks or diskettes
- Hard disks
- Removable media such as Zip and Jaz disks

- CD-ROM
- Rewritable CD
- Mini-disk
- Optical disk
- DVD
- Compact Flash, Smart Media, and similar devices
- Magnetic tape

Each device has its own specific advantages and disadvantages. For example, with removable media and CD formats, the media can be easily transported and read on other computers. This can increase the organization's risk of data loss if appropriate controls are not established on where and when these devices are utilized.

Network Environment

A network is defined as a data communication system allowing a number of devices to communicate with each other. It allows the users of the network to share common resources and to send and receive information.

The network provides an interface for the users of the network resources, just as an operating system provides an interface consisting of system calls. The functions of the network interface allow the users (entities) to send and receive data, to obtain status information, etc. For two entities to communicate with each other, they must agree on common protocols, or a set of rules.

The transfer of data across the network is controlled and managed by these various protocols. Just as in the platform environment, it is also good practice to use a layered architecture approach in the network environment. An important element of network security is to determine the most appropriate network layer for specific security services.

The typical network layer models are the ISO Open Systems Interconnection (OSI) model and the Transmission Control Protocol/Internet Protocol (TCP/IP) suite, which are described in the Telecommunications, Network, and Internet Security chapter (Chapter 8).

From the overall systems security and architecture viewpoint, we must be concerned with network connectivity as it presents an avenue for both authorized users to perform unauthorized tasks and unauthorized users to attempt to gain access. Failing to consider the network in today's computing environment means ignoring some of the enterprise's greatest risks.

Shared Environment

Computer networks are the communications infrastructure for transmitting data between nodes in a distributed system. One of the most common types of distributed (shared) network systems is the client/server environment. Client/server means different things to different people and in different situations. It might refer to the design implementing the roles, the programming tools to write the related processes, or to describe the implemented applications — it depends on the audience. However, the two main components are the client and the server. The *client* engages services of another. Client machines are generally single-user PCs or workstations that provide a highly user-friendly interface to the end user. The *server* provides a set of shared user services to the clients.

Client/server is defined here as a style of computer use or application — the mode or manner in which the computer or computers are used to achieve a result. The client/server environment is designed so that front-end processing — the interface, data input, etc. — is done on the client workstation and back-end processing — such as databases, etc. — is done on the central server system. The security goal is to provide a consistent level of security for both clients and servers.

Some of the threats to shared environments include:

- Unconfigured or misconfigured file protection controls
- Database corruption
- Unsecured remote access
- Unsecured locations and physical accessibility
- Lack of built-in security controls
- Multiple control points
- Inconsistent user identification and authentication across shared environments and networks
- Multiple administrative processes and appearances
- Multiple administrators
- Malicious code
- Hidden escape mechanisms
- Lack of multiple-log and journal synchronization
- Lack of audit trail data control
- Lack of alarm notifications

When examining the security of shared systems, we must consider who and how users will access them. For example, client workstations with storage devices and external drives are at a higher security risk than those with dumb terminals (i.e., thin clients).

Regardless of the exact nature of our implementation, the protection of data can be either easier or more difficult, depending on the openness of our systems. *Closed systems* are proprietary to the vendor. The vendor does not share information about their design, construction, or operation. The only way to get software and support is typically through the manufacturer. Consequently, they generally lack the interfaces and mechanisms to connect to other systems.

On the other hand, *open systems* are just that — open. Anyone can obtain the specifications for system operation, design, etc. That means more people will build hardware and software for these systems. Furthermore, open systems allow for interoperability and data exchange between systems from different vendors.

"Open system" does not mean the same as "open application." Application vendors will work very hard to protect their own intellectual property regarding their application design. Refer to the Application Program Security chapter (Chapter 4) for the difference between open source systems and closed source systems, which refer to having open source code for the applications.

Types of Security Environments

From a historical perspective, security requirements were satisfied through the use of physical, personnel, and information security countermeasures. With the advances in technical capabilities, it was possible to put the countermeasures in the computer system itself. The U.S. Department of Defense Trusted Computer System Evaluation Criteria (TCSEC) document was developed to establish the levels of trust achievable by vendor products after undergoing rigorous testing. They also identified certain types of security features needed to achieve each level of trust. The criteria were used by vendors to describe the level of trust their products could provide and by users to select those products that enable them to comply with the security policy of their organizations.

Several security operating modes have been identified as (taken from "Technical Rationale Behind CSC-STD-003-85: Computer Security Requirements," June 1985):

- *Dedicated security mode*: the mode of operation in which the system is specifically and exclusively dedicated to and controlled for the processing of one particular type or classification of information, either for full-time operation or for a specified period of time. A system is operating in the dedicated mode when each user with direct or indirect individual access to the system, its peripherals, remote terminals, or remote hosts has all of the following: (1) a valid personal clearance for all information on the system; (2) formal access approval for, and has signed nondisclosure agreements for all the information stored and/or processed; and (3) a valid need-to-know for all information contained within the system.
- *System high-security mode*: the mode of operation in which system hardware/software is only trusted to provide need-to-know protection between users. In this mode, the entire system, to include all components electrically and/or physically connected, must operate with security measures commensurate with the highest classification

and sensitivity of the information being processed and/or stored. All system users in the environment must possess a valid personal clearance, formal access approval for, and have signed nondisclosure agreements for all the information stored and/or processed, and a valid need-to-know for some of the information contained in the system. All system output must be clearly marked with the highest classification and all system caveats, until the information has been reviewed manually by an authorized individual to ensure appropriate classifications and caveats have been affixed.

- *Multi-level security mode*: the mode of operation that allows two or more classification levels of information to be processed simultaneously within the same system when some users are not cleared for all levels of information present. All users must have proper clearance and the formal access approval for the information they will have access to and a valid need-to-know for the information.

- *Controlled mode*: the mode of operation that is a type of multi-level security in which a more limited amount of trust is placed in the hardware/software base of the system, with resultant restrictions on the classification levels and clearance levels that can be supported.

- *Compartmentalized security mode*: the mode of operation that allows the system to process two or more types of compartmented information (information requiring a special authorization) or any one type of compartmented information with other than compartmented information. In this mode, system access is secured to the highest level of information in the system, but all system users need not necessarily be formally authorized access to all types of compartmented information being processed and/or stored in the systems. All system users must have a valid personal clearance for the most restricted information processed by the system, formal access approval for, and have signed nondisclosure agreements for that information to which they will have access and a valid need-to-know for that information to which they will have access.

The level of computer security required in a system depends on both the risk assessment and the nature of the environment.

Environment: the aggregate of external circumstances, conditions, and objects that affect the development, operation, and maintenance of a system.

Application: the portion of a system, including portions of the operating system, that is not responsible for enforcing the system's security policy.

Malicious code: hardware, software, or firmware that is intentionally included for the purpose of causing loss or harm.

Enterprise Architecture

Before beginning this topic, first think about your answer to these questions: Who designed the enterprise architecture for your current network system? Do you have an enterprise architecture? Did an enterprise architect design it? Is there such a thing as an enterprise architect?

There has been a recent understanding within the IT industry that when current information systems are being designed and developed they lack some type of design framework or an architect who designs the system. In fact, some have viewed this insight as the next evolution within the information system field — the need for an architectural framework or engineer.

Although the concept of enterprise architecture may seem recent, it is actually a few decades old. In the 1980s, the concept of an architecture to describe an enterprise first emerged. Since then various frameworks for defining an enterprise architecture have been published.

An enterprise can be defined as any purposeful activity, while an architecture can be characterized as the structure of any activity. An *enterprise architecture* can then be viewed as systematically derived and captured structural descriptions (such as useful models, diagrams, and narratives) of the mode of operation for any given enterprise.

In its simplest definition, it is an attempt to provide to people of all organizational levels an explicit, common, and meaningful structural frame of reference that allows an understanding of (1) what the enterprise does; (2) when, where, how, and why it does it; and (3) what it uses to do it. It provides a clear and comprehensive picture of the structure of an entity, whether an organization or a functional or mission area. It is an essential tool for effectively and efficiently engineering business processes and for implementing and evolving supporting systems (GAO-03-584G, April 2003).

In the mid-1980s, John Zachman, widely recognized as a leader in the field of enterprise architecture, identified the need to use an architecture for defining and controlling the integration of systems and their components. Accordingly, Zachman developed a framework for defining and capturing an architecture, now known simply as the *"Zachman Framework."* His framework identified the kinds of work products needed for people to understand and thus build a given system or entity.

The Zachman framework provides for six perspectives (or windows) from which to view the enterprise or how a given entity operates. Zachman also proposed six abstractions or models associated with each of these perspectives.

Six Perspectives	Six Models
Strategic planner	How the Entity Operates
System user	What the Entity Uses to Operate
System designer	Where the Entity Operates
System developer	Who Operates the Entity
Subcontractor	When Entity Operations Occur
System itself	Why the Entity Operates

The Zachman framework provides a way to identify and describe an entity's existing and planned component parts and the parts' relationships before one begins the costly and time-consuming efforts associated with developing or transforming the entity.

Since Zachman introduced his framework, a number of other frameworks have been proposed. In September 1999, the U.S. federal CIO Council published the Federal Enterprise Architecture Framework (FEAF), which describes an entity's business, data necessary to conduct the business, applications to manage the data, and technology to support the applications. More recently, the U.S. Office of Management and Budget established the Federal Enterprise Architecture Program Management Office to develop a federated enterprise architecture according to a collection of five reference models that are intended to facilitate a governmentwide improvement of IT systems. The five models are:

- The *Business Reference Model* is intended to describe the business operations of the federal government independent of the agencies that perform them, including defining the services provided to state and local governments.
- The *Performance Reference Model* is to provide a common set of general performance outputs and measures for agencies to use to achieve business goals and objectives.
- The *Data and Information Reference Model* is to describe, at an aggregate level, the type of data and information that support program and business line operations, and the relationships among these types.
- The *Service Component Reference Model* is to identify and classify IT service (i.e., application) components that support federal agencies and promote the reuse of components across agencies.
- The *Technical Reference Model* is to describe how technology is supporting the delivery of service components, including relevant standards for implementing the technology. (GAO-03-584G, April 2003).

Although post-Zachman frameworks differ in their approach, the frameworks consistently provide for defining an enterprise's operations in both *logical terms*, such as interrelated business processes and business rules, information needs and flows, and work locations and users, and *technical terms*, such as hardware, software, data, communications, and security attributes and performance standards. The frameworks also provide for defining these perspectives both for the enterprise's current (or as-is) environment and for its target (or to-be) environment, as well as a transition plan for moving from the current to the target environment.

If managed appropriately and effectively, an enterprise architecture can clarify and help optimize the interdependencies and relationships among an organization's business operations and the underlying IT infrastructure and applications that support these operations. Employed in concert with other important management controls, enterprise architectures can greatly increase the chances that organizations' operational and IT environments will be configured so as to optimize mission performance.

The next section provides some theoretical background for the architecture design of platforms and how the operating systems will control access to resources and data.

Security Models

Security models are an important concept in the design and analysis of secure computer systems. They take into account the security policy that should be enforced in the system. The first security models were designed to meet the needs of *multi-level security*. Multi-level security is defined as a class of system-containing information with different sensitivities that simultaneously permits access by users with different security clearances and needs-to-know, but prevents users from obtaining access to information for which they lack authorization (DoD TCSEC 1985). This first originated in the late 1960s when the U.S. Department of Defense wanted to develop a method of protecting classified information stored on computers. Prior to this time, the regulations did not allow classified information on a system that also allowed uncleared users. Consequently, no computer system was trusted to protect the classified data. Although the situation today has not changed much, systems have been, and continue to be, developed to provide the security controls for multi-level security uses.

The underlying security policy for the U.S. Department of Defense is commonly referred to as a *military security policy*. In this policy, information, also referred to as the "object," possesses a classification; and people, also referred to as the "subject," possess a clearance. When determining whether a person is allowed to read a document, the person's clearance is compared to the document's classification.

The purpose of a multi-level security system is to prevent compromise where users are able to read information classified at a level for which they are not cleared. The military security policy also has parallels in industry. For examples, industry information may be considered

103

commercially sensitive or have privacy considerations, such as personnel or medical information.

In the military security policy, the security levels are considered hierarchical, such as unclassified > confidential > secret > top secret. To access information, a person must possess an access class whose level is greater than or equal to the level of the access class of the information. Multi-level security is a mathematical description of the military security policy. The first mathematical model of a multi-level security system, and probably the most famous, is the Bell-LaPadula model (Bell and LaPadula, 1973). The model defined a number of terms and concepts that have since been adopted by most other models of multi-level security.

Bell-LaPadula Model

The Bell-LaPadula model is a state machine model capturing the *confidentiality* aspects of access control. Access permissions are defined both through an access control matrix and through security levels. Security policies prevent information flowing downward from a high security level to a low security level. This is referred to as an unauthorized downgrading of information, where that access class of a file has not been changed. However, the actual compromise of the information would not take place until an unclassified process or user read the downgraded information. Consequently, the specific act permitting the eventual compromise is the writing of information.

> The state machine model involves the concept of a state and of state changes occurring at discrete points in time. A state is a representation of the system at one moment in time. The possible state transitions can be specified by a state transition that defines the next state, depending on the present state and input. When looking at the security state of a machine, the first step is to identify all the states possible. Then it is necessary to check whether all state transitions preserve this property. If this occurs, and if the system starts in an initial state having a specific property, then through a process of induction that property will always hold. Thus, if all state transitions in a system are secure and if the initial state of the system is secure, then every subsequent state will also be secure, regardless of the inputs. (More information on state machine models is discussed in the Information Flow Model section.)

When a process can write information into a file whose access class is less than its own, it is called a *write-down*. Multi-level security requires that the capability to write-down be prohibited. The vulnerability of write-down on a computer system involves malicious code on the higher level being able to write information down to the lower level. The controlling of write-down is called the **property* ("star property") in the Bell-LaPadula model.

> *Simple security property. A subject can only read an object if the access class of the subject dominates the access class of the object. Thus, a subject can read down but cannot read up.*
>
> *Star property. A subject can only write to an object if the access class of the object dominates the access class of the subject. Thus, a subject can write up, but cannot write down.*

In multi-level security, access classes are represented in the computer and appropriate checks can be made when a user tries to access a file. Enforcing multi-level security must be done in a mandatory manner so neither users nor their programs can change a user's clearances or a file's classification. This enforcement of multi-level security is commonly called *simple security* in the Bell-LaPadula model.

The *property and simple security property are shown in Exhibit 6. In addition, in order for a subject to both read and write an object, the access classes of the subject and object must be equal (strong star property).

The capability to write to a higher level where the writer is not allowed to read creates a type of covert channel because if the writer tries to read what was written and is denied access, it is possible to infer that a more secret level of information exists on the system. The existence of this secret information is not intended to be divulged to those not authorized to access it. The countermeasure is to put the information that is written to

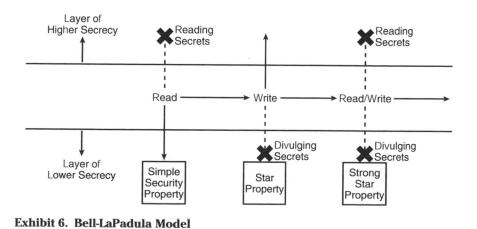

Exhibit 6. Bell-LaPadula Model

the higher level also at the level available to the writer. This action of putting information in more than one place is called polyinstantiation.

The Bell-LaPadula model has played an important role in the design of secure operating systems, and almost all models are compared to it. One of the reasons for its popularity and holding power is because it defines security in terms of access control.

Because the goal of the Bell-LaPadula model is to prevent unauthorized disclosure, it deals only with the confidentiality of information. As such, it does not address the issue of integrity.

To address integrity, Biba released a technical report in 1977, entitled "Integrity Considerations for Secure Computer Operations." The Biba integrity model expanded on the Bell-LaPadula model by providing controls for unauthorized modification of information.

Biba Security Model

The Biba integrity model mathematically describes read and write restrictions based on integrity access classes of subjects and objects (Biba used the terms "integrity level" and "integrity compartments"). Integrity levels and compartments are based on corruption potential, and a lattice model applies to the protection conditions. The integrity model looks similar to the multi-level security model; however, the major difference is that the read-and-write condition must be reversed. Thus:

- A subject can write to an object only if the integrity access class of the subject dominates the integrity class of the object (integrity *property).
- A subject can read an object only if the integrity access class of the object dominates the integrity class of the subject (simple integrity property).

In the Biba model (see Exhibit 7), there is a lattice of integrity levels. These levels form the basis of expressing integrity policies that refer to the corruption of "clean" high-level entities by "dirty" low-level entities. In the integrity lattice, information can only flow downward. The simple integrity property and the *integrity property prevent clean subjects and objects from being contaminated by dirty information.

Gasser (1988) states that it may be easier to think of integrity by not thinking about multi-level security. A high-integrity file is one whose contents are created by high-integrity processes. The two rules just identified guarantee that the high-integrity file cannot be contaminated by information from low-integrity processes. In addition, the high-integrity process writing the files cannot be subverted by low-integrity processes or data.

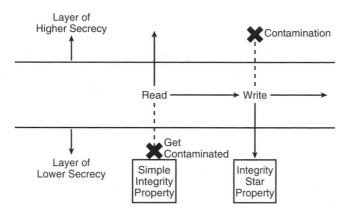

Exhibit 7. Biba Model

The integrity class label on a file thus guarantees that the contents came only from sources of at least that equivalent degree of integrity.

The Biba model can be extended to include an access operation, called *invoke*. A subject can invoke another subject, such as a software utility, to access an object. The *invocation property* states that the subject cannot send messages (logical request for service) to subjects of higher integrity. Subjects are only allowed to invoke utilities or tools at the same or lower level. Otherwise, a dirty subject could use a clean tool to access or contaminate a clean object.

Clark-Wilson Model

The Clark-Wilson model addresses the integrity requirements of applications. They believe that these requirements are about process and data *integrity*. The Clark-Wilson model identified three rules of integrity:

- Unauthorized users should make no changes.
- The system should maintain internal and external consistency.
- Authorized users should make no unauthorized changes.

In addition to the three rules of integrity are the concepts of internal and external consistency:

- *Internal consistency:* the properties of the internal state of a system that can be enforced by the computing system. This ensures that the process does what it is expected to do every time it is run.
- *External consistency:* the relation of the internal state of a system to the real world that must be enforced by means outside the computing system. This ensures that the data in the system is consistent with the value of similar data in the real world.

The mechanisms for enforcing integrity are through:

- *Well-formed transaction*. The process and data items can be changed only by a specific set of trusted programs. Users have access to programs rather than to data items. This establishes the access tuple: users access the program, which in turn accesses the system. Binding is established between the user and the program and between the program and the system. The well-formed transaction preserves and ensures internal consistency because users can change the process and data only in ways that ensure internal consistency. It also addresses the third rule of integrity by ensuring authorized users can only make authorized changes.
- *Separation of duties*. Without separation of duties, users need to collaborate to manipulate data and to connive to penetrate the security system. During the operation of the system, different persons would need to collaborate to enable a transaction. Having separation of duties ensures external consistency.

A subject's access is controlled by the authorization to execute the program (well-formed transaction). Therefore, unauthorized users cannot execute the program (first integrity rule) and authorized users could each access different programs, thus allowing each to make specific, unique changes (separation of duties).

The Clark-Wilson model considers the following points (Gollman, 1999):

- Subjects have to be identified and authenticated.
- Objects can be manipulated only by a restricted set of programs.
- Subjects can execute only a restricted set of programs.
- A proper audit log must be maintained.
- The system must be certified to work properly.

In a formalization of the model, the data items governed by the security policy are called Constrained Data Items (CDIs). Inputs to the system are referred to as Unconstrained Data Items (UDIs). The conversion of UDIs to CDIs is an important part of the system that cannot be controlled solely by the security mechanisms in the system. CDIs can be manipulated only by Transformation Procedures (TPs). The integrity of a state is checked by Integrity Verification Procedures (IVPs).

Security properties are on one side defined through five certification rules, suggesting that checks should be conducted so the security policy is consistent with the application requirements. These are:

- Integrity Verification Procedures must ensure that all Constrained Data Items are in a valid state when the procedure is run.
- Transformation Procedures must be certified to be valid. That is, valid Constrained Data Items must always be transformed into valid

items. Each Transformation Procedure is certified to access a specific set of Contrained Data Items.

- The access rules must satisfy any separation of duties requirements.
- All Transformation Procedures must write to an append-only log.
- Any Transformation Procedure taking an Unconstrained Data Item as input must either convert the unconstrained item into a Constrained Data Item or reject the unconstrained item and perform no transaction at all (Gollman, 1999, pp. 57–58).

Following these procedures, the Clark-Wilson model addresses all three integrity goals:

- Preventing unauthorized users from making modifications
- Preventing authorized users from making improper modifications
- Maintaining internal and external consistency

Access Control Matrix

This is a general model of access control that is based on the concept of subjects and objects. The subject is an entity capable of accessing objects, such as users, applications, or the processes that represent those users and applications. An object is anything that is controlled, such as files, databases, and programs. There is an access right or capability that defines how a subject can access an object, such as read, write, execute, or delete.

This information can be outlined in an access control matrix consisting of rows (users) and columns (objects). Each entry in the matrix represents the access type held by that user to that object. A sample access control matrix is shown in Exhibit 8.

One axis of the matrix consists of the identified subjects, the other axis lists the objects that may be accessed. Each entry in the matrix identifies the access rights of that subject for that object.

An access control matrix (see Exhibit 9) is usually implemented by either an Access Control List (ACL) or a Capability List. An Access Control

Exhibit 8. Sample Access Control Matrix

	UserMary Directory	UserBob Directory	UserBruce Directory	Printer001
Mary	Full Control	Write	Write	Execute
Bob	Read	Full Control	Write	Execute
Bruce	No Access	Write	Full Control	Execute
Sally	No Access	No Access	No Access	No Access

Exhibit 9. ACL Example

Access Control List
   Object: UserMary Directory
   Bruce: No Access
   Sally: No Access
   Bob: Read
   Mary: Full Control

Capability List
   Subject: Mary
   UserMary Directory: Full Control
   UserBob Directory: Write
   UserBruce Directory: Write
   Printer001: Execute

List provides a list of all subjects (users or processes) and their access permissions. A Capability List specifies authorized objects and operations for a user.

Information Flow Model

To understand the information flow model, it is important to recognize the basic theories of the state model. In the state machine model, a system is an abstract mathematical state machine. State variables represent the state of the machine, and transition functions describe how the variables change.

State machine models were originally favored because they represented a computer system in a manner that imitated the execution of an operating system and hardware. A state variable is an abstraction for each of the bits and bytes in the system that change as the system is running. For example, every word in memory or in registers is a state variable.

The steps involved in developing a state machine model include:

1. Define the security-relevant *state variables*. Typically, the state variables represent the subjects and objects of the system, their security attributes, and the access rights between subjects and objects.
2. Define the conditions for a *secure state*. This definition is an invariant expressing the relationships between values of the state variables that must always be maintained during state transitions.
3. Define *state transition functions*. These functions describe permissible changes to the state variables. They are also called *rules of operation* because their purpose is to constrain the types of changes the system can make, rather than to specify all possible changes.
4. Prove that the functions maintain the secure state. To make sure the model is consistent with the definition of the secure state, you must

prove that the system state is preserved and restored after the operation.

5. Define the *initial state*. Pick a value for each of the state variables that model how the system starts out in an initially secure state.

6. Prove that the initial state is secure in terms of the definition of the secure state (step 2) (Gasser, 1988, p. 138).

Gasser (1988) gives an example of a state machine model as follows:

> The security policy states: "A person may read a document only if the person's clearance is greater than or equal to the classification of the document."

> To transfer this into the computer world, the items are classified as:

Real-World Item	Computer-World Abstraction
Person	Subject
Document	Object
Clearance	Access Class
Classification	Access Class

> "The translation of the policy can now be: (1) a subject may read an object only if the access class of the subject is greater than or equal to the access class of the object; or (2) a subject may write an object only if the access class of the object is greater than or equal to the access class of the subject."

These policies are then transferred into mathematical equations following six steps — defining the state variables, defining the secure state, defining the transition functions, proving the transition functions, and defining and proving the initial state.

In the state model, a transition function can be viewed as a procedure call to a system service routine requested by the subject, and the desired service is a specific change to the state variables. The parameters to the function are specified by the subject and must be checked by the system for validity before the system carries out any state change. This is a simplistic view because not all state changes are initiated by any subject, such as interrupts or asynchronous events. A state transition will cause an information flow from one object (x) to another object (y), if we can learn more about one object (x) by observing another object (y).

The *information flow model* is a variant of the access control model. The access control model describes the security state of the system in terms of the security attributes of subjects and objects. The access modes a subject has to an object are determined by comparing their security attributes, rather than by looking them up in a matrix. The information flow model attempts to control the transfer of information from one object into another object, constrained according to the two objects' security attributes. The major difference between access models and information flow models is that an information flow model can help you find covert channels. A covert channel is an information flow that is not controlled by a security mechanism.

The access control model can be used for both confidentiality and integrity — confidentiality by controlling "read" operations and integrity by controlling "write" operations. The information flow model is based on object security levels — information can flow to the same or higher level. In the Bell-LaPadula model, information can flow from a high-security level to a low-security level through a covert channel.

For example, a low-level subject creates an object at its own level. Its high-level accomplice can either upgrade the security level of the object or leave it unchanged. At a later point, the low-level subject tries to read the object. Success or failure of this request discloses the action of the high-level subject. One bit of information has migrated from high to low. Simply telling a subject that a certain operation is not permitted creates an information flow.

In addition to the information flow through access operations, information flow models consider any type of information flow. A system is considered secure if it does not allow any unauthorized or illegal information flows. Currently, information flow models are areas of research and not used for the basis of a practical methodology for the design of secure systems.

Chinese Wall Model

Brewer and Nash proposed the Chinese Wall model in 1989. It provides a model for access rules in a consultancy business where analysts have to make sure that no conflicts of interest arise when they are dealing with different clients. Conflicts could arise when clients are direct competitors in the same market or because of the ownership of companies. For example, an investment firm might contain the accounts of two companies, x and y. Two separate analysts (a) and (b) represent each company. If the first analyst (a) makes a change that includes sensitive information into the account of x, it must be guaranteed that the second analyst (b) cannot view that information and thus, by being able to analyze the competitor's information, be able to affect the status of company y. Thus, in the Chinese Wall model, the rule is that there must be no information flow potentially causing a conflict of interest. The system must ensure that the appropriate access controls are implemented to restrict access to only authorized individuals.

Lattice Model

The Bell-LaPadula model defines a structure of an access class and establishes the partial ordering relationship between classes that are called *dominates*. To obtain access to information, a person must possess an access class (clearance, i.e., top secret) whose category set includes all of the categories of the access class of the information (i.e., top secret and secret). When the categories and levels are combined, several relationships are possible between two access classes — this is called *partial ordering*. When used to express a partial ordering relationship, the word *dominate* means "greater than or equal to." The partial ordering relationships are as follows:

1. The first access class dominates the second — it is greater than or equal to the level of the second, and the category set of the first contains all the categories of the second.
2. The second access class dominates the first.
3. The access classes are equal, which is a special case where both 1 and 2 are true.
4. None of the above is true — the access classes are disjointed and cannot be compared. The first contains a category not in the second, and the second contains a category not in the first.

Looking at the example in Exhibit 10 and following the partial ordering rules, consider whether both users can read the document. User 1 with its access class (Top Secret, DoD, NATO, and Nuclear) can read the document because the user possesses a higher level and all the categories of the document. User 2 with its access class (Top Secret and NATO) cannot read the document because the user is missing the DoD category.

In addition to defining a partial ordering, the dominant relationship has two properties that make it a *lattice*. If given any two access classes (A) and (B):

- In the set of all access classes dominated by both (A) and (B), there is a unique *greatest lower bound* dominating all the others. The greatest lower bound is the highest level dominated by the element.
- In the set of all access classes that dominate both (A) and (B), there is a unique *least upper bound* dominated by all the others. The least upper bound is the lowest level dominated by the element.

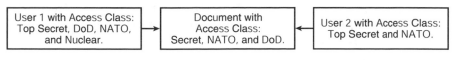

Exhibit 10. Partial Ordering Rules

In the lattice model, the higher up in secrecy, the more constraints on the data; the lower in secrecy, the less constraints on the data. For example, it is possible to use the lattice model to define two unique access classes: system high and system low. System high would dominate all other access classes and would contain the highest possible security level and all possible categories. System low would be dominated by all other access classes and would not contain security levels or categories.

2.3 Security Technology and Tools

In this section, we look at the security technology and tools available to design security architectures. It follows a similar format to the Information Protection Environment section by separating the tools into three major protection categories: platform, mainframe, and network.

Protection mechanisms are used to ensure the separation between objects in a system. Two categories of protection mechanisms are active or passive. An active protection mechanism prevents access to an object if, according to the protection mechanism, the access is not authorized. For example, an active protection mechanism is when memory protection is provided by the hardware architecture, where access to objects at certain addresses may be controlled depending on such criteria as the current processor state and attributes of the process attempting to reference the object in question.

A passive protection mechanism is one that prevents or detects unauthorized use of the information associated with an object, even if access to the object itself is not prevented. In most cases, these techniques use cryptographic techniques to prevent unauthorized disclosure of information or checksum techniques to detect an unauthorized alteration of an object.

Protection mechanisms are often implemented in operating systems, hardware, or firmware. They control access to primitive objects such as memory, machine code instructions, and registers, which are used to control input/output operations.

Platform Protection

In the environment section, the topics discussed were the basics of how the platform components operate and some of the vulnerabilities and threats associated with the platform environment. In this topic, we look at several options that can be implemented to secure the operating system, memory, files, and objects.

Operating System Protection

Three of the security technologies used by operating systems to protect security features of the software are the trusted computing base (TCB), the reference monitor, and the security kernel.

Trusted Computing Base (TCB). The *trusted computing base (TCB)* is the totality of protection mechanisms within a computer system — including hardware, firmware, software, processes, and some inter-process communications — that, combined, are responsible for enforcing a security policy. The TCB consists of one or more components that together enforce a unified security policy over a product or system. The ability of the TCB to correctly enforce a security policy depends solely on the mechanisms within the TCB and on the correct input by system administrative personnel of parameters (e.g., a user's clearance) related to the security policy (e.g., TCSEC). While some operating systems implement a trusted computer base, the system could also be operated in such a manner as to negate much of the value derived from the TCB. Similarly, many operating systems do not implement a trusted computing base at all. If implemented, it usually follows the *reference monitor* concept, which is explained below.

The system architecture of trusted computing includes the ability of the TCB to protect itself from untrusted processes. For example, the TCSEC C2 system architecture criterion, described in the Assurance, Trust, and Confidence Mechanisms section of this chapter, includes three TCB requirements:

- The TCB must maintain for its own execution a domain protecting it from external interference and tampering.
- Resources controlled by the TCB may be a defined subset of subjects and objects.
- The TCB must isolate the resources to be protected so they are subject to access control and auditing.

The TCB maintains the confidentiality and integrity of each domain and monitors four basic functions:

- *Process activation.* In a multiprogramming environment, activation and deactivation of processes create the need for a complete change of registers, file access lists, process status information, and other pointers, much of which is security-sensitive information.
- *Execution domain switching.* Processes running in one domain often invoke processes in other domains to obtain more sensitive data or services. The TCB ensures that the processes provide security.

- *Memory protection.* Because each domain includes code and data stored in memory, the TCB must monitor memory references to ensure confidentiality and integrity for each domain.
- *I/O operations.* In some systems, software is involved in the transfer of characters to the I/O operation. This process connects a user program in the outermost domain with the I/O operation in the innermost domain. This cross-domain connection must be monitored.

A trusted system is one having undergone sufficient benchmark testing and validation to achieve the user's requirements and those established in the evaluation criteria. These requirements include those for reliability, security, and operational effectiveness with specified performance characteristics.

Trust can be measured by ensuring that the (1) System Security Policy states the rules enforced by a system's security features, and (2) System Assurance Policy states the trust placed in a system and the methodology used to develop, test, document, and deliver the system to the user in a trusted manner.

Reference Monitor. The *reference monitor* is an access control concept referring to an abstract machine that mediates all accesses to objects by subjects based on information in an access control database. The reference monitor must mediate all access, be protected from modification, be verifiable as correct, and must always be invoked. The reference monitor, in accordance with the security policy, controls the checks that are made in the access control database.

Historical Perspective. In early days of computing, the term "monitor" was used to identify the program in the system that controlled the actions of other programs. As monitors became bigger, they began to be called "operating systems." The term "monitor" began to mean only the most primitive types of operating systems. The term "reference monitor" was coined to refer to a special-purpose monitor dealing only with access control to resources.

Security Kernel. The *security kernel* is the hardware, firmware, and software elements of a *trusted computing base* (TCB) implementing the *reference monitor concept.* The security kernel must satisfy three principles:

- It must mediate all accesses (completeness).
- It must be protected from modification (isolation).
- It must be verifiable as correct (verifiable).

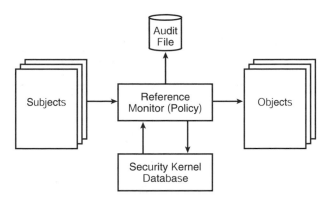

Exhibit 11. Security Kernel

The security kernel must be implemented to prevent users from modifying the operating system. If a user were able to disable or circumvent the protection mechanisms by modifying the operating system, the integrity of the system could be compromised.

As shown in Exhibit 11, the reference monitor is an abstract concept, the security kernel is the implementation of the reference monitor, and the TCB contains the security kernel along with other protection mechanisms.

Security Perimeter. The term "security perimeter" is sometimes used to refer to the security kernel, as well as other security related system functions, being within the (imaginary) boundary of the Trusted Computing Base (i.e., the security perimeter). This is a different definition than traditionally associated with the term. In this case, the security perimeter refers to the boundaries surrounding the security kernel and TCB. System elements outside the security perimeter are not to be trusted.

Layering. A primary concept of operating system design is to place the security mechanisms in one of the lower system layers. An example of this is shown in Exhibit 12. A layered operating system looks like a stack of systems, each having an interface for use by the layers above. Layers in the system are hierarchical, wherein the lower layers provide primitive functions and the upper layers provide more complex functions. Remember that a vulnerability may exist if an unauthorized user could get access to a layer below and thus compromise the layer above. Additional protection for the data can be achieved through layering above the operating system in the applications the system is executing for the user community.

One technique in the layering approach is called *data hiding* — when the software in each layer maintains its own global data and does not directly reference data outside its layers. Having a single security layer is not possible because each layer has its own set of objects requiring secure

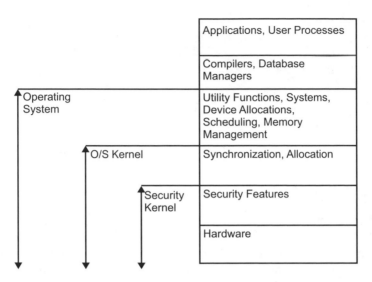

Exhibit 12. Layering

management. Thus, each layer must be able to make security decisions. For example, if one layer is able to control all security decisions, that particular layer would need to know too many details about the other layers, thus violating the data-hiding principles of layering. If an entire operating system existed in each layer, with no pass-through features, such knowledge would not be required because each layer would be capable of protecting all of its objects. The use of a layered architecture can help increase the reliability of a secure operating system.

TOC/TOU Protection. The safest solution for TOC/TOU is for the operating system to copy the parameters to a location safe from asynchronous modification prior to validation. It is also necessary for the operating system to prevent an asynchronous change to all information on which the validation depends, not just to the parameters themselves. For example, if at a higher level a system call is invoked to read a file, the operating system must first read a directory to find out the caller's mode of access and to obtain the location of the file on the storage disk. During the time that the file on the disk is read, the file may have been deleted and a new file put in its place, which may be a file to which the caller did not originally have access. To control this, operating systems can put appropriate locks on files.

While locking can help avoid the TOC/TOU problem in situations where tables and operating systems databases are involved in checking access, a user's application database randomly located somewhere in a process's address space may not be subject to the same controls.

However, applications themselves typically provide similar mechanisms to protect the data and enforce access privileges.

Guard Protection. A logical *security guard* is (usually) an add-on security feature addressing a particular class of multi-level security problems. In some environments, users may need to communicate with a system although some of those users cannot be allowed direct access to the system because of weaknesses in the system's security controls.

For example, users may need access to a restricted set of data, and the system may not be strong enough to protect other highly sensitive data residing on that system. A guard can permit users logged onto a system running at a low access class to submit queries to a database running on a system at a high access class. The two systems are not allowed to communicate directly because neither system can be trusted. The guard is a trusted system authorized to communicate with both systems at the same time. Essentially, the guard is trusted to prevent a nonsecure flow of information from high to low.

Automated guards have been used for one-way traffic, such as sending mail from a low to a high system. The only information the low system needs to receive in response to a message is an acknowledgment that the guard has accepted the message. The guard has enough store-and-forward capability to ensure that little or no information about the status of the high system can be deduced by the low system. This eliminates the possibility of information loss or inference through a covert channel. Although the guard is an add-on security feature, it eliminates the need for a person to read a message on one terminal in the low system and then retype the message into another terminal on the high system.

Process Isolation. A basic role implemented in the architecture is the capability of the security system to protect itself. Process isolation involves the use of distinct address spaces and ensures that multiple processes running concurrently will not interfere with each other, either by accident or by design. It ensures that the system can keep track of everything (e.g., registers or status information) it needs to when switching from one process to another. On modern operating systems, this is typically a basic function. Built into the operating system are memory and process management facilities to prevent corruption of the applications, data, and operating system parameters. The operating system must abort or handle the request to prevent one process from executing instructions accessing another process's address space.

Enforcement of Least Privilege. Just as with least privilege assignments for a person, processes must have no more privilege than needed to perform functions. Only those modules needing complete system privileges are located in the security kernel, and other modules call on more privileged routines only as needed and as long as needed.

Hardening. Traditionally, the term "hardening" of any operating system referred to the protection of kernel (layers in the operating system), hardware, and memory from programs already executing on the host. Recently, it has been expanded to include the notion of strengthening network interfaces and limiting the activities and services permitted upon them. Hardening must include all aspects of the system, including physical and logical access, the operating systems, applications, and data interfaces.

Some hardware vendors are now providing hardened versions of their systems that may include a sandbox layer of access controls that separate resources from access requests. For example, one vendor requires each resource access from an application to use a security interface to reference an operating system component. If an access decision is needed before permitting the request to proceed, a logical security manager is invoked for resolution of the request.

General Operating System Protection. The following items are typical characteristics included in the design of a trusted operating system and associated processes that provide both the features (functions) and assurance necessary to ensure implementation of a trusted system:

- *User identification and authentication:* must authenticate or verify users to the system.
- *Mandatory access control:* access control policy decisions beyond the control of the object owner.
- *Discretionary access control:* all object access control left to the owner.
- *Complete mediation:* control all accesses; it is difficult as more paths are created.
- *Object reuse protection:* ensure sensitive information is purged from memory and magnetic media before assignment to a new subject.
- *Audit:* be able to generate security-relevant events.
- *Protection of audit logs:* ensure they cannot be modified after creation.
- *Audit log reduction:* since audit logs can become large, it is helpful to have some type of volume and analysis tools that can be used to simplify and/or correlate the security events (i.e., implement a clipping level).
- *Trusted path:* provide protection of critical operations (i.e., the path between a workstation and authentication server).
- *Intrusion detection:* provide capabilities for recognizing an intrusion event and invoking an analysis capability.

Memory Protection

One of the most basic hardware requirements for a secure system is memory protection. If a system runs a single process in memory at one time, on behalf of a single user, memory protection is needed to prevent the user's programs from affecting the operating system. If it is a multitasking system, memory protection will need to isolate the process's memory areas from each other.

Hardware techniques were developed to provide the necessary protection mechanisms in the computer hardware, and the concept of a "privileged" state of operation was introduced. This privileged state ensured that only the operating system could perform the operations that were critical to controlling and maintaining the protection mechanisms.

From a historical perspective, the security for RAM began to evolve with the move from mainframes to personal computers that ran MS-DOS operating systems. The MS-DOS operating system was developed to run on a microprocessor and did not provide any protection features. Protection was not deemed necessary because microprocessors and memory available were very limited, so it was not common to allow any sharing. Additionally, the design of the operating system allowed the execution of only a small number of programs with no multitasking capability. For example, while MS-DOS has the concept of Terminate and Stay Resident (TSR) programs, those programs were only resident in memory — they did not execute until an instruction from the user activated them. Because MS-DOS did not control the coexistence of programs in its memory, and because it did not provide protection mechanisms to protect files stored on disk, the computers running MS-DOS were vulnerable to programs that tried to interfere with other programs or files.

Even in the evolution of memory management, the underlying requirement for security in operating systems is still concerned with the ability of the operating system to enforce control over the storage and movement of information in and between the resources that the operating system supports. Because most systems today are multi-user systems requiring the ability to share resources, the operating system must ensure that the only way programs (acting on behalf of users) can interact with shared resources is through controls enforced by the operating system. To achieve this, various controls must be built into the operating system.

Typical memory protections are:

- Every reference is checked for protection.
- Many different data classes can be assigned different levels of protection.
- Two or more users can share access to the same segment with potentially different access rights.

- Users cannot access a memory or address segment outside what has been allocated for them.

Hardware segmentation is a hardware protection feature dividing virtual memory into segments. It ensures that a process occupies only those segments needed during execution. The operating system manages what memory is allocated for a process. If the process attempts to access memory or alter memory contents outside its allocated resource, the operating system issues a message to the application. This frequently results in abnormal termination of the application.

Isolation. A system's isolation capabilities determine its overall security robustness. There are two types: hardware isolation and software isolation. Hardware isolation involves the isolation of the TCB from untrusted parts of the system. Software isolation is the containment of subjects and objects, where they remain separate from each other. This is usually in addition to the protection controls provided by the operating system. Analysts tend to prefer hardware isolation because it is less vulnerable to subversion.

Binding. Binding is the process of limiting the independent activity of subjects by attaching them to each other or to objects, such as from user to program, program to data, subject to program, subject to object, or program to object. It is an active entity to a course of action that helps form a type of authorization. Binding denotes the principle of obligation.

CPU and Input/Output Device Protection

The protections for the I/O devices are based on the type of processor. For explanation purposes, we will look at an earlier version of the Intel processor, the 80486. The Intel 80486 (pr 486) is a 32-bit microprocessor containing a 2-bit field in the status register defining the four privilege levels or protection rings. The privilege level can only be changed by a single instruction that has to be executed at level O. Software could be assigned to the levels as (note that not all operating systems make use of all four levels and some use more):

- 0 = operating system kernel
- 1 = I/O drivers
- 2 = rest of the operating system
- 3 = application software

To explain how the security controls are implemented, a bit of background technical information is necessary. The 486 processor stores information about system objects in *descriptors*. The field of the descriptor stores the privilege level of the object. Descriptors are stored in the descriptor table and accessed via *selectors*. A selector is a 16-bit field containing an index pointing to the object's entry in the descriptor table and also a Requested Privilege Level (RPL). The operating system is only allowed access to selectors. When a subject requests access to an object, the relevant selectors are loaded into dedicated segment registers.

The security challenge occurs when an access is requested from a higher privilege. For example, an application operating in ring 3 needs a service from the operating system in ring 1. To solve this, the 486 processor uses *gates*. A gate is a system object pointing to a procedure where the gate has a privilege level different from that of the code to which it points.

When a procedure wants to use a gate, the gate must be in the same ring as the procedure. When invoking a subroutine through a gate, the current privilege level changes to the privilege level of the code to which the gate is pointing. When returning from the subroutine, the privilege level is restored to that of the calling procedure. In addition, a subroutine call saves the information indicating the state of the calling procedure or the return address on the stack. This process could also pose a security risk, because the return address of the subroutine could be left unprotected in the outer ring. To avoid the security risk, part of the stack is copied to a more privileged stack segment.

From an access control perspective, several other terms can be used to describe how hardware supports I/O. They are:

- *Programmed I/O.* It is synchronous because the processor is in direct control of every word of data transferred to or from the I/O device. This was the only type available before I/O became intelligent enough to operate without the help of the processor.
- *Unmapped I/O.* It is a direct memory access scheme where software sends the device an I/O command specifying the physical location of a buffer in memory. The device acts as a trusted subject and is allowed to read or write physical memory. It is trusted to execute the command correctly.
- *Premapped I/O.* This is also called virtual I/O. It allows software to specify virtual buffer addresses. When the I/O instruction is issued, the processor translates these virtual addresses into physical addresses; using the descriptor tables and mapping registers of the current process, the processor then passes the resulting physical address to the device. During the translation, the processor checks whether the process has the appropriate access permissions to the requested locations. From the viewpoint of the device, the I/O is physical; from the process's viewpoint, the I/O is virtual and the access control is enforced by hardware. Because it uses an unmapped I/O, the device must be trusted to access only the desired locations in memory.

- *Fully-mapped I/O.* This is a much safer form of virtual I/O and consists of hardware carrying out a virtual-to-physical translation on each memory reference made by the device. The device acts as an untrusted subject, presenting only virtual addresses as it reads or stores information in memory. The translation hardware within the security perimeter does the mapping and access checks. In addition, the translation and the access check are made on each word transferred. This prevents a security problem if the operating system were to reallocate memory during the I/O operation.

Application Layer Protection

All input received from a source external to the application must be validated prior to processing. This is true regardless of the source. Possible sources of data include:

- User input through data entry screens
- Output generated by an external program
- Access requests from an external program
- Operating system environment
- Command parameters

Input checking includes verifying that the input is of the proper type and within specified ranges. For example, if the data entry field is to contain only numbers, the input must be verified such that it contains only numbers. Invalid input must be rejected and an appropriate error and audit record written for later investigation and analysis. The data is not lost in this case and it is not processed, as doing so would inject errors and create data integrity problems.

Access requests from an external program occur through a data interface or link between the two applications. Requests must be properly validated for consistency and accuracy prior to allowing the application to validate the authorization level and access to the data.

Additionally, many commands reference configuration files and environment variables from the operating system. This input must also be properly validated prior to using it. As many operating systems allow the user to change environment variables, the application operation may be changed and allow for confidentiality and integrity issues. Similarly, command parameters provided when the command is executed must be properly evaluated to prevent undesirable operation and ensure that the user has the correct privilege levels for the desired operations.

Storage Device Protection

Access to server, workstations, and mobile computer storage devices needs security protection, such as:

- Removable storage media
- Encryption software for protection of sensitive files
- Physical locking devices
- Locking portable devices in a desk, file cabinet, or safe
- Fixed disk systems may need additional protection that can be provided by physical security mechanisms such as lockable enclosures, clamping devices, cable fastening devices, and movement alarms

Mobile computing brings a large number of risks such as the theft or accidental disclosure of information. These can be caused by the nature of the device or the connectivity used, such as wireless modems or network cards. Additionally, network services provided with public forums and hotels should also be considered risks to the security architecture. This can occur when users connect devices to external networks and then reconnect the device to the local network.

Users should be provided with the necessary tools and resources consistent with the organization's security policies. For example, users with laptop computers should be provided with locking cables. While these are not perfect, they will deter many would be thieves. Additionally, the adage "out of sight — out of mind" applies to portable devices. If the device is not visible, a thief is not aware of its existence.

Network Protection

This section provides examples of controls available at the system or application level providing security services that may not be available from the underlying security services. More specific technologies and approaches are covered in the telecommunications, cryptography, and access control chapters.

The decision to develop and use any of the controls presented should be made after a careful evaluation of the risks in your environment and an evaluation of the missing elements from your security infrastructure.

Data Transmission Controls. These are controls that could be used over and above any controls provided in the network (i.e., telecommunications) system. These are controls that would typically be implemented on the end system (host) as part of an overall application security strategy to secure the integrity of the transmissions. In older, more error-prone telecommunications environments, these types of controls would more likely be employed. In modern and relatively error-free networks and telecommunications systems, these controls may only be necessary for highly critical systems and data where the protection of data integrity is paramount. (More information on data transmission controls is located in the Telecommunications, Network, and Internet Security chapter [Chapter 8].)

The data transmission controls do not apply to just the hardware implementation, but equally apply to the application layer. The data transmission controls available to ensure transmission integrity include:

- Hash totals:
  - They are stored in the record before transmission
  - They identify errors and omissions
  - The workstation and server use the same hashing algorithm
  - The transmission is tested for accuracy at the destination
  - They can use a different hashing algorithm for each data type to strengthen security
- Recording of sequence checking:
  - Tests the accuracy and completeness of a transmission
  - The source assigns and stores a record sequence number for data or for files to ensure they are received and processed in the proper order
  - The sequence is tested at the destination to ensure all packets are received
  - Both host and client may have the feature
- Transmission logging:
  - Built into the front-end communication program
  - Records the transmission, date, time, origin, type
  - Provides an audit trail of the transmission
- Transmission error correction:
  - Provides extensive edit controls in the front-end communication program
  - Identifies hardware and software errors
- Invalid login, modem error, lost connections, CPU failure, disk error, line error, etc.
  - Provides detailed edit controls
  - Enables quick identification/correction of errors
  - Records errors in the error log
  - Uses the error log for trend analysis and to identify chronic error problems
- Retransmission control:
  - Used to detect/prevent duplicate transmission of data
  - The front-end communication program detects duplicate data transmission
  - Examines successive records
  - Duplicate transmissions of a file are difficult to identify
  - May need a downstream application to handle file retransmission control

> *Encryption.* More information on encryption controls for networks is provided in the Cryptography chapter (Chapter 6).
>
> *Telecommunications.* More information on telecommunication and Internet controls is provided in the Telecommunications, Network, and Internet Security chapter (Chapter 8).
>
> *Physical.* More information on physical controls for networks is provided in the Physical Security chapter (Chapter 7).

2.4 Assurance, Trust, and Confidence Mechanisms

As important as it is to design a secure architecture, it is also important to verify whether the architecture is secure. Because it is important for users to be assured that the products they use provide the necessary security requirements, evaluation methods have been developed to provide this assurance.

When looking at evaluation methods, it is necessary to first identify what is to be evaluated — a product or a system. An example of a product is a specific operating system that will be used in any number of applications or a specific application that will be operated in a set of defined conditions. Typically, a system is a collection of products that together meet the specific requirements of a given application. The differences between the two are helpful in understanding the various security evaluation criteria.

Some questions or factors involved in selecting products include:

- Security:
  - How secure is the system?
  - What access control and privilege management is available?
  - How secure is the encryption algorithm and process, if used?
  - Has any rigorous formal testing been conducted?
  - Can it connect to my existing security infrastructure?
  - Does privilege management to maintain a segregation of duties exist?
- Cost:
  - Are volume discounts/pricing alternatives/site licensing available?
  - What other costs impact the product selection? Hardware, maintenance, upgrades, etc., all contribute considerably to the cost.
- Flexibility considerations:
  - Length of company commitment
  - Ease of change to alternative product
  - Interface with other security products

- Environmental considerations:
  - Ability to accommodate hardware and operating system evolution
  - Ability to accommodate changes in user procedures
- User interface considerations:
  - User ease of operation
  - Number of rules to understand and follow
- System administration:
  - Initial effort and ongoing administration
  - Ability to centrally recover from user error
  - Specialized skills and training for the administrators
  - Integration with other applications
- Future developments of a product:
  - What and when planned?
  - Will it be easier for the user? Will it reduce administrative workload?
- Process:
  - What processes exist to provide ongoing operation as defined in the previous controls? Failing to provide processes to maintain the system operation provides a significant security risk.

The available methods used for evaluating products or systems include:

- Trusting the advertisements from the manufacturer/vendor
- Performing system tests internally within the organization
- Trusting an impartial, independent assessment authority

Because it is difficult for the general users to perform security tests, the preferred method is to trust an independent assessment authority. Throughout the world there are various assessment authorities that perform evaluations based on a previously designed set of criteria. The assessment authorities then rate the product or system according to the defined criteria. The manufacturers and vendors then use the established rating in the marketing and advertisement of their products.

The Trusted Computer Security Evaluation Criteria (TCSEC 1985) define evaluation as assessing whether a product has the security properties claimed for it. Typically, an evaluation tries to give assurance that a product or system is secure based on three principles:

- *Functionality:* the security features of the system, such as authentication and auditing.
- *Effectiveness:* the mechanisms used are appropriate to the stated security requirements.
- *Assurance:* the completeness of the evaluation identifying to what level the functionality can be trusted to perform.

This section begins by discussing historical evaluation criteria, such as the Trusted Computer Security Evaluation Criteria; and continues with one of the most recent evaluation schemes, the Common Criteria.

Trusted Computer Security Evaluation Criteria (TCSEC)

The first evaluation standard to gain widespread acceptance was the *Trusted Computer Security Evaluation Criteria (TCSEC)*. As a historical reference, in the late 1960s, the U.S. Department of Defense began to address the risks associated with implementing systems that were not secure. A result of this endeavor (and through various drafts), the National Computer Security Center (NCSC) produced the U.S. Department of Defense (DoD) Trusted Computer Security Evaluation Criteria (TCSEC) 5200.28-STD document (1985). It is also known as the "Orange Book" because it is part of the *Rainbow Series*, which contains several color-bounded reference documents about computer and information system security. The criteria were broken down into four divisions: A, B, C, and D. Those in the A division provided the most comprehensive security functionality and those in the D division provided none. The NCSC evaluated products against the criteria under the Trusted Product Evaluation Criteria. Even though the Orange Book only addressed confidentiality, it did provide guidelines for the evaluation of security products, such as hardware and operating systems.

The Orange Book's four evaluation classes are based on several elements from the following:

- *Security policy:* mandatory or discretionary access control policies.
- *Marking of objects:* labels indicate the sensitivity of objects.
- *Identification of subjects:* subjects must be identified and authenticated.
- *Accountability:* security-related events must be contained in audit logs.
- *Assurance:* refers to operational assurance, such as system architecture, protected execution domain, system integrity; and lifecycle assurance, such as design methodology, security testing, and configuration management.
- *Documentation:* users and system administrators need to know how to install and use the security features of a secure system, and evaluators need documentation for testing.
- *Continuous protection:* guarantees that security mechanisms cannot be tampered with or modified.

Based on these criteria, four security divisions and seven security classes are used as ratings. They are shown in Exhibit 13.

Exhibit 13. *Orange Book*'s Evaluation

Security Division	Explanation
A: Verified Protection	A1 is equivalent to B3; however, it achieves the highest assurance level through the use of formal methods. A system security administrator is supported. Very few products have been evaluated to class A1.
B: Mandatory Protection, includes B1, B2, and B3	The B class is intended for products that handle classified data and enforce the mandatory Bell-LaPadula access control policies. To achieve the B1 (Labeled Security Protection) rating, an informal or formal model of the security policy, data labeling, and mandatory access control over named subjects and objects is required. The capability must exist for accurately labeling exported information. Testing and documentation must be more thorough, and any flaws identified by testing must be removed. The design document, source code, and object code have to be analyzed. It is intended for system high environments with compartments. B2 (Structured Protection) increases assurance by adding requirements to the design of the system. A formal model of the security policy and a descriptive top-level specification of the system are required. A covert channel analysis needs to be conducted. Authentication mechanisms are strengthened, trusted facility management is provided in the form of support for system administrator and operator functions, and stringent configuration management controls are imposed. B3 (Security Domains) is graded as highly resistant to penetration. The new elements in B3 are related to security management, involving security administrator support and audit capabilities supporting automatic notification of suspicious activities. Trusted recovery after a system failure MUST be included.
C: Discretionary Protection, includes C1 and C2	C1 (Discretionary Security Protection) systems are intended for an environment where cooperating users process data at the same level of sensitivity. Users are able to protect information and keep other users from accidentally reading or destroying their data. C2 (Controlled Access Protection) systems make users individually accountable for their actions through login procedures, auditing of security-relevant events, and resource isolation. DACs are enforced at the granularity of single users. *Although C2 systems are considered weak, they are regarded as the most reasonable class for commercial applications.*
D: Minimal Protection	In this class, products were submitted for evaluation but did not meet the requirements of any higher TCSEC class.

The Trusted Network Interpretation (TNI)

The *Trusted Network Interpretation (TNI)*, also called the *Red Book,* was published in 1987. With the *Orange Book* as its basis, the *Red Book* addresses network and telecommunications. The purpose is to evaluate vendor products for use in trusted (secure) networks and let users know the level of trust they can expect from these products. The A, B, C, and D levels of trust described in the *Orange Book* are used.

Some key features of the *Red Book* are:

- *Integrity.* The Biba model for integrity is suggested as a formal integrity model. Information transfer integrity refers to the correctness of message transmission, including the authentication of source and destination of a message. Cryptography is introduced as protection against the modification of data.
- *Labels.* To guarantee mandatory access controls, which include mandatory integrity policies, *integrity labels* are introduced. An example of an integrity label is one that would indicate whether an object has ever been transmitted.
- *Other security services.* These include several types of security services grouped into three main categories:
  - *Communication integrity,* including authentication, communication field integrity, and non-repudiation
  - *Denial-of-service,* including continuity of operation, protocol-based protection, and network management
  - *Compromise protection,* including data confidentiality and traffic confidentiality

For each of these factors, the functionality, strength, and assurance must be specified.

Information Technology Security Evaluation Criteria (ITSEC)

Following the release of the *Orange Book*, several European countries issued their own criteria. The European *Information Technology Security Evaluation Criteria (ITSEC)* was first drafted in 1990 and became endorsed by the Council of the European Union in 1995. It was the result of Dutch, English, French, and German activities designed to define and harmonize European national security evaluation criteria. Although ITSEC includes concepts from the TCSEC, the *Orange Book* was thought to be too rigid. Thus, ITSEC attempted to provide a framework for security evaluation that would be more flexible. One major difference between the two is ITSEC's inclusion of integrity and availability as security goals, along with confidentiality.

The ITSEC recognizes that the security of an IT system can often be achieved through nontechnical measures, such as organizational and administrative controls. Technical security measures are used to counter remaining threats. The ITSEC ratings are based on *effectiveness* and *correctness*. Effectiveness describes how well a system is suited for countering the predicted threats. Correctness involves assurance aspects related to the development and operation of a system. The ITSEC makes a distinction between products and systems. A product can be a hardware and/or software package bought off the shelf and used in a variety of operational environments. A system is deployed in a specific real-world environment and designed and built for the needs of a specific user. Both products and systems are comprised of components.

To cover both options, ITSEC uses the term "Target of Evaluation" (TOE). The sponsor of the evaluation determines the operational requirements and threats. The *security objectives* for the TOE depend on legal or other regulations. The security objectives establish the required security functionality and evaluation level. The *security target* specifies all aspects of the TOE that are relevant for evaluation.

The security target may contain the following:

- Security objectives:
  - Statements about the system environment
  - Assumptions about the TOE environment
- Security functions:
  - Rationale for security functions
  - Required security mechanisms
  - Required evaluation level
- Security assurance:
  - The level of assurance required in the TOE

The *security functionality* is described as being able to answer the following:

- Security objectives: why is the functionality wanted?
- Security functions: what is actually done?
- Security assurance: how is it done?

The types of security functions include identification and authentication, access control, accountability, audit, object reuse, accuracy, reliability, and data exchange.

ITSEC ratings come in pairs: *Function (F)* (Exhibit 14) and *Assurance (E)* (Exhibit 15). The ratings are hierarchical; each class adds to the one above. The testing is done at the Assurance (E) level. The functionality of a TOE can be specified individually or by reference to one of the predefined functionality classes.

Exhibit 14. ITSEC Ratings: Functionality (F)

Functionality (F)	Class Characteristics
F1–F5	Mirror the functionality aspects of the *Orange Book* classes
F6	For systems with high integrity requirements for data and programs (e.g., databases)
F7	Sets requirements for the high availability of a complete system or special functions of a system
F8	Sets high requirements for data integrity during communications
F9	Addresses systems with high demands on data confidentiality during communications
F10	Intended for networks with high demands on the data confidentiality and integrity during communications

Exhibit 15. ITSEC Ratings: Assurance (E)

Assurance (E)	Class Characteristics
E0	Inadequate assurance; assigned to those that fail to meet E1
E1	There shall be a security target and an informal description of the TOE; functional testing must satisfy its security target
E2	Adds an informal description of detailed design; testing evidence is evaluated; requires configuration control; controlled distribution process
E3	Source code/drawings are evaluated; testing evidence of security mechanisms evaluated
E4	Formal model of security policy; semiformal specification of security enforcing functions, architectural design, and detailed design
E5	Close correspondence between detailed design and source code/drawings must be established; vulnerability analysis uses the source code
E6	Formal specifications of the security architecture of the TOE (enforcing functions and architectural design) that are consistent with the formal model of the security policy; it must be possible to relate portions of the executable form of the TOE to the source code

Assurance of correctness is expressed using seven evaluation fields, E0 through E6, each representing ascending levels of confidence. They refer to the construction and to the operation of the TOE, specify the list of documents that need to be provided by the sponsor, and the actions to be performed by the evaluator.

Currently, E3 is the most popular evaluation level for commercial security products. Secure operating systems or database management systems typically try for the combination of F2+E3.

During the early 1990s, the United States began to update the TCSEC. However, the update was stopped in favor of combining efforts with the Europeans and Canadians to develop a Common Criteria (CC). The CC evaluates software systems based on both functionality and assurance in terms of integrity, confidentiality, and availability.

The Common Criteria (CC)

The Common Criteria (CC) is an international standard to evaluate trust. It is based on the *U.S. Federal Criteria* that expanded on the ITSEC by giving more guidance in the definition of evaluation classes but retaining some degree of flexibility. The Federal Criteria kept the linkage between function and assurance in the evaluation classes and tried to overcome the rigid structure of the *Orange Book* by adding protection profiles. The Common Criteria merges ideas from its various predecessors. It leaves the total flexibility of ITSEC and follows the Federal Criteria by using protection profiles and predefined security classes.

The protection profiles include:

- *Descriptive elements*: includes the name of the protection profile and identifies the information protection problem that needs to be solved.
- *Rationale*: fundamental justification (threat/environment/usage) of the protection profile and some guidance on and the security policies that can be supported by the product conforming to the profile.
- *Functional requirements*: establishes the protection boundary that must be provided by the product, so that expected threats can be countered.
- *Development assurance requirements*: identifies the requirements for all phases of development, from the initial design through implementation.
- *Evaluation assurance requirements*: specifies the type and intensity of evaluation.

The protection profile developments include:

- Environment security analysis: threats/vulnerabilities, intended method of product use, environment assumptions, and policies/standards/regulations/directives
- Component requirement synthesis: functional and assurance components
- Technical soundness
- Usefulness
- Evaluation capability
- Distinctness from other profiles
- Consistency with other profiles

The functional requirements include:

- Enabling definition of different protection profiles
- Enabling harmonization with existing standards
- Grouping by trusted computing base (TCB) components

The security policy requirements include:

- *Accountability policy:* identification and authentication, system entry, trusted path, and audit
- *Access control policy:* confidentiality/integrity, and discretionary/non-discretionary
- *Availability policy:* resource allocation, fault tolerance
- *Security management policy:* security system maintenance, user administration, security policy parameter maintenance, control/maintenance of system resources, and audit trails

Only three profiles for commercial security ratings currently exist (see Exhibit 16).

Security evaluation criteria have been criticized as an expensive process required by governments. The European Computer Manufacturers Association (ECMA) has published a report that insists that a balance between cost, productivity, and security has too many competing factors. The ECMA warns that the high requirements for security are creating negligence for operational effectiveness. It states the cost of evaluation (which is between 10 and 40% of the development cost) and the time delays in getting the evaluation completed are areas of concern.

In addition to government-sponsored documents, private industry has developed criteria and processes for achieving information security. The ECMA, which is now a worldwide association with members from Europe, the United States, and Japan, has produced the Commercial Oriented Functionality Class (COFC). The COFC specifies a baseline security standard that is intended to reflect the minimum set of security functionality needed

Exhibit 16. Profiles for Commercial Security Ratings

Profile	
CS1	Equivalent to TCSEC C2
CS2	Separation of administrative functions
	Group and access control list access control
	Rigorous password control (optional)
	System entry and availability requirements
	Enhanced security administration and audit mechanisms
CS3	Role-based central control of access
	Non-discretionary integrity and confidentiality enforced (MACs)
	Stronger authentication, administration, and assurance

for the commercial market. The objective is to reduce the complexity of the government documents to allow cost- and time-effective applications and also to keep standards open for extension and adaptability to any future requirements.

The International Computer Security Association (ICSA) initiated a program for certifying information technology products and operating environments against a set of *de facto* industry standards. Because most organizations purchase commercial off-the-shelf (COTS) products, their approach is based on the principle of "secure enough." Their goal is to develop criteria for at least 80% of the products and at least 80% of customers and individuals that would rely on the certification. The criteria are based on threats that occur most frequently versus threats that might happen based on some abstract theory. ICSA has established several certification programs for Web sites, cryptography products, firewalls, anti-virus software, and biometric products.

Certification and Accreditation

Certification and Accreditation is a set of procedures and judgments assessing the suitability of a system to operate in a target operational environment.

Certification and Accreditation is used often for non-certified products, but not exclusively. It is sometimes used to evaluate a series of certified products to see, if together, they enforce the security policy of the organization. Every new system and application that goes into production should go through a process of certification and accreditation prior to implementation. Certification is the endorsement that the system/application meets their functional and security requirements, and accreditation is the formal approval by management.

Certification is the technical evaluation of compliance with security requirements for the purpose of accreditation. It is the comprehensive analysis of the security features and safeguards of a system to establish the extent to which the security requirements are satisfied. It uses a combination of security evaluation techniques: risk analysis; validation, verification, and testing; security countermeasure evaluation; and audit. It culminates in a technical judgment that describes the extent to which countermeasures meet security requirements.

Certification considers the system in its operational environment, such as the:

- Security mode of operations
- Specific users (and their training)
- Applications and data sensitivity
- System and facility configuration and location
- Interconnections with other systems

There are vulnerabilities associated with certification. The first is that organizations and users cannot count on the certified product being free of security flaws. Because new vulnerabilities are always being discovered, no product is ever completely secure. Second, most software products must be securely configured to meet certain protection mechanisms. For example, although the Windows NT 4.0 operating system offers auditing capabilities, by default, the auditing is not enabled. Thus, the system administrator needs to enable and configure the auditing capabilities. Another issue is that certifications are not the definitive answer to security. Information system security depends on more than just technical software protection mechanisms, such as personnel and physical security measures.

Accreditation is the official management decision to operate a system. It is management's formal acceptance of the adequacy of a system's security. Accreditation looks at the following:

- Particular security mode
- Prescribed set of countermeasures
- Defined threat; stated vulnerabilities
- Given operational concept and environment
- Stated interconnections to other systems
- Risk formally accepted
- Stated period of time

Ideally, certification and accreditation should be an ongoing process. A formal recertification and reaccreditation is required whenever a major change occurs, a major application is added, the security environment changes, or significant technology is upgraded.

In the United States, federal agencies are mandated to conduct security certification and accreditation of systems that process sensitive information or perform critical support functions. Various U.S. guidelines are provided. For example, the Department of Defense (DoD) has published #5200.40 "Defense Information Technology Security Certification and Accreditation Process (DITSCAP)" (December 1997); the National Security Agency (NSA) has published #NSTISSI No. 100 "National Information Assurance Certification and Accreditation Process (NIACAP)" (April 2000); and the National Institute of Standards and Technology (NIST) has published SP 800-37 "Guide for the Security Certification and Accreditation of Federal Information Systems (October 2002).

2.5 Information Protection and Management Services

Management activities for computer, system, and security architecture include:

- Hardware and software procurement and use policy
- Procurement procedures
- Program change control
- Staff training responsibilities
- Hardware, software data access provisions
- Server/other computer system access
- Data processing and nondisclosure controls
- Reporting unauthorized, irregular, fraudulent use
- Awareness and training
- Train systems personnel so they know how to use systems properly
- All employees should be aware of system security responsibilities
- Separation of duties: the process of separating processes into specific tasks and having different employees responsible for each of the tasks; this can prevent one individual from having total control of the process and circumventing security practices.
- Developing security policies, procedures, and guidelines: appropriate access control policies, procedures, and guidelines are an essential element in designing and developing a secure architecture. The policies and procedures must reflect the organizational culture regarding protection of the system resources, including all data processed and stored. This should include how to purchase, process, store, and dispose of media and equipment.

Summary

The security professional needs to have a basic understanding of how the system processes and secures information in order to understand the vulnerabilities of different environments, operating systems, and applications. This chapter identified some of the key components of the computer and network system as an introduction to computer, system, and security architecture. Memory protection, file protection, object/subject access controls, and user authentication play an important part when designing and developing a secure architecture.

One of the most important aspects of having a secure system is to design the architecture with security as part of the process. It is much more efficient to implement security from the beginning than to add security as an afterthought. A plan should be developed that provides guidelines on how the architecture should be built, including how the security goals will be implemented.

Key to including security during the design of the architecture is to develop a security policy for the organization. The security policy specifies the organization's goals on security and also who is responsible for implementing the security program. The security policy must then be communicated and enforced by those who have overall authority for the organization.

2.6 Common Body of Knowledge (CBK)

The current CBK for the Computer, System, and Security Architecture Domain is listed below to assist in determining topics for further review. Although this Study Guide is very detailed in many areas, it is not possible to thoroughly discuss every CBK topic in a single book; therefore, additional study of items may be advisable.

Expectation

The professional should fully understand:

- Security models in terms of confidentiality, integrity, and information flow
- Differences between commercial and government security requirements
- The role of system security evaluation criteria such as TCSEC, ITSEC, and CC
- Security practices for the Internet (IETF IPSec)
- Technical platforms in terms of hardware, firmware, and software
- System security techniques in terms of preventative, detective, and corrective controls

Components

- Principles of common computer and network organizations, architectures, and designs
- Addressing: physical and symbolic
- Address space, as contrasted with memory space
- Hardware, firmware, and software differences
- Machine types (real, virtual, multistate, multitasking, multi-user)
- Network protocol functions (OSI seven-layer model)
- Operating states
- Resource manager functions
- Storage types (primary, secondary, real, virtual)
- Principles of common security models, architectures, and evaluation criteria
- Accreditation and certification
- Closed and open systems
- Confinement, bounds, and isolation
- Controls: mandatory and discretionary
- IETF Security Architecture (IPSec)

- ITSEC classes and required assurance and functionality
- Objects and subjects (purpose and relationship)
- Reference monitors and kernels (purpose and function)
- Security models (Bell-LaPadula, Clark-Wilson, Biba)
- TCSEC classes and required functionality
- Tokens, capabilities, and labels (purpose and functions)
- Common flaws and security issues associated with system architectures and designs
- Covert channels (memory, storage, and communications)
- Initialization and failure states
- Input and parameter checking
- Maintenance hooks and privileged programs (superzap/su)
- Programming (techniques, compilers, APIs, and library issues)
- Timing (TOC/TOU), state changes, and communication disconnects
- Electromagnetic radiation

Examples

- Define process isolation.
- Describe enforcement of least privilege as it pertains to security architecture.
- Define hardware segmentation as it pertains to security architecture.
- Compare and contrast proper protection mechanisms.
- Define layering protection mechanism.
- Define abstraction as a protection mechanism.
- Define data hiding as a protection mechanism.
- Compare and contrast methods of protecting data/information storage.
- Define types of data/information storage (primary, secondary, real, virtual, random, sequential, volatile, real space, virtual space).
- Compare and contrast open systems and closed systems.
- Compare and contrast multitasking, multiprogramming, multiprocessing, multiprocessors.
- Compare and contrast single-state versus multistate machines.
- Define and describe the IT/IS "protection ring" architecture.
- Describe the C-I-A triad as it relates to security architecture.
- Define data objects as they pertain to confidentiality.
- Compare and contrast time of check versus time of use (TOC/TOU).
- Compare and contrast binding and handshaking as they pertain to integrity.
- Define system availability and fault tolerance.
- Compare and contrast system high mode and multi-level secure (mls) mode.
- Define what is meant by a "security perimeter."
- Define what makes up a security kernel.

- Describe what is meant by the term "reference monitor."
- Define the term "trusted computing base" (TCB).
- Identify and define the design objectives of security architecture.
- Identify and define vulnerabilities to data/information systems.
- Describe the Bell-LaPadula confidentiality model.
- Compare and contrast the Biba and Clark-Wilson integrity models.
- Define noninterference, state machine, access matrix, and information flow integrity models.
- Define and describe lattice-based access controls.
- Define the term "trusted system" as related to IT/IS.
- Compare and contrast various information system evaluation standards such as TCSEC, ITSEC, CTCPEC, and Common Criteria.
- Define and describe the TCSEC classes of trust.
- Describe the minimum requirements for a TCSEC C1 level of trust.
- Describe the minimum requirements for a TCSEC C2 level of trust.
- Describe the minimum requirements for a TCSEC B1 level of trust.
- Describe the minimum requirements for a TCSEC B2 level of trust.
- Describe the minimum requirements for a TCSEC B3 level of trust.
- Describe the minimum requirements for a TCSEC A1 level of trust.
- Compare and contrast the C, B, and A levels of trust as defined by the TCSEC.
- Define and describe the European Criteria (ITSEC).
- Define and describe the European Criteria (ITSEC) functionality classes.
- Compare and contrast the ITSEC levels of trust with the TCSEC levels of trust.
- Define and describe the ITSEC assurance classes.
- Define certification as it pertains to IT/IS.
- Define accreditation as it pertains to IT/IS.
- Compare and contrast access control as it pertains to host and PC.
- Define and describe micro-host security.
- Define data transmission control methodologies.
- Define and describe physical and environmental control methodologies.
- Define and describe software and data integrity control methodologies.
- Define file backup.
- Describe the primary causes of programming environment security problems.
- Define possible management actions as potential solutions to programming environment security problems.
- Define possible programmer actions as potential solutions to programming environment security problems.
- Describe possible PC security problems caused by decentralization.
- Define PC security issues.

- Define PC security problem countermeasures.
- Identify security product selection criteria.
- Define security association (SA) bundling.
- Compare and contrast internal, external, and independent configuration auditing.

2.7 Sample Questions for the CISSP Exam

1. Why should security elements be located in a lower layer of the system architecture?
   a. They are easier to adjust according to user requirements.
   b. This may increase system performance.
   c. This allows for multitasking.
   d. It is simpler to install system security bypasses.
2. In pre-emptive multitasking mode, who controls the use of system resources?
   a. The user
   b. The application program
   c. Input/output devices
   d. The operating system
3. In cooperative mode, who controls the use of system resources?
   a. The user
   b. The application program
   c. Input/output devices
   d. The operating system
4. What is a vulnerability of a multiprocessing system?
   a. Different levels of users operating simultaneously
   b. Synchronous data attacks
   c. Object reuse
   d. Insufficient random memory
5. Which of the following cannot usually be referred to as a maintenance hook?
   a. Privileged program
   b. Backdoor program
   c. Wormhole
   d. Trojan horse
6. Which of the following is considered a general protection feature of a trusted operating system?
   a. Mandatory access controls and discretionary access controls
   b. Anti-virus controls
   c. Authentication of users to the system
   d. Audit logs cannot be modified after creation
7. What is the security risk with virtual storage?
   a. The data is volatile and may be lost when powering down.

b. The data may be read by other processes running simultaneously.

c. The temporary files may not delete after use.

d. System performance may be impacted.

8. What security risk can be associated with interrupt processing?

   a. An interrupted process may assume the priority of the higher-level process.

   b. An interrupted process may lose data integrity.

   c. A higher-level process may not receive sufficient CPU cycles.

   d. A low-level process may time-out before completion.

9. In dedicated security mode, the system must have all of the following EXCEPT:

   a. One classification of data running for a set time

   b. Access approval clearance for all users or nondisclosure agreements

   c. Need-to-know for all information within the system

   d. Direct access only to the system

10. A subject most commonly has:

   a. Authentication

   b. Clearance

   c. Classification

   d. Collusion

11. Biba's invocation property is intended to prevent:

   a. A subject requesting a service of an object at a lower classification

   b. An administrator granting an increased level of clearance to an authorized user

   c. A process from gaining elevated access through a higher-level process

   d. The deferring of processing until resources are available

12. Which of the following is NOT a rule of integrity?

   a. All users must be subject to need-to-know.

   b. Unauthorized users should make no changes.

   c. The system should maintain internal and external consistency.

   d. Authorized users should make no unauthorized changes.

13. Which is commonly associated with the Clark-Wilson security model?

   a. The access tuple

   b. Read down/write up

   c. Subject/program binding

   d. Lattice-based model

14. A capability listing is based on which primary item?

   a. A subject

   b. A program

   c. A system

   d. An object

15. State machine models are concerned with each of the following EXCEPT:
    a. Initial state
    b. State transition functions
    c. State variables
    d. State classification

16. The Chinese Wall model was associated with the work of:
    a. Harrison and Ullman
    b. Brewer and Nash
    c. Glasser
    d. El Gamal

17. Certification refers to:
    a. The technical review of a product or system
    b. Management's approval for an implementation
    c. A stringent evaluation of a system in a test environment
    d. Formal acceptance of risk

18. What is the Common Criteria (CC) suppose to do?
    a. Provide a forum for Europeans, Canadians, and Americans to discuss privacy laws.
    b. Document the international information warfare threats and create international cooperation to counter those threats.
    c. Provide an international center to track the outbreak of viruses across the globe in order to reduce infections.
    d. Document the international standards for evaluating trust in information systems and products.

19. A class of a system containing various levels of sensitive information that also permits users with different security clearances best describes:
    a. a multi-level security system
    b. a trusted computer based with security kernels
    c. a system using a state machine model to control subjects and objects
    d. a system using an information flow model to control subjects and objects

20. A trusted computing base is defined as:
    a. The totality of protection mechanisms within a computer system
    b. The ability to prevent and detect unauthorized use of an object
    c. Containing a security kernel and reference monitor with the ability to encrypt its processes
    d. A logical access control concept where the security kernel mediates all accesses to objects by subjects

References

Bell, D.E. and L.J. LaPadula (1973). "Secure Computer Systems: Mathematical Foundations and Model," M74-274. Mitre Corporation, Bedford, MA.

Biba, K.J. (1977). "Integrity Considerations for Secure Computing Systems," ESD-TR-76-372. Hanscom AFB, MA.

Brewer, D.F.C. and M.J. Nash (1989). "The Chinese Wall Security Policy." *Proceedings of the 1989 IEEE Symposium on Security and Privacy.*

Canadian System Security Center (1993). "The Canadian Trusted Computer Product Evaluation Criteria, Version 3.0e."

Commission of the European Communities (1991). "Information Technology Security Evaluation Criteria, Version 1.2."

Cooper, James (1989). *Computer and Communications Security.* McGraw-Hill, New York.

CSC-STD-004-85. "Technical Rational Behind SCS-STD-003-85: Computer Security Requirements. Guidance for Applying the Department of Defense Trusted Computer System Evaluation Criteria in Specific Environments." The Rainbow Series: National Institute of Standards and Technology, Gaithersburg, MD.

De Blasi, M. (1990). *Computer Architectures.* Addison-Wesley, Reading, MA.

European Computer Manufacturers Association (ECMA) (1995). "Commercially-Oriented Functionality Class for Security Evaluation (COFC)." Technical Report ECMA 205.

Gasser, Morrie (1988). *Building a Secure Computer System.* Van Nostrand Reinhold, New York.

Gollmann, Dieter (1999). *Computer Security.* John Wiley & Sons, Sussex, England.

Information Technology Security Evaluation Criteria (ITSEC) (1998). ITSEC Joint Interpretation Library (ITSEC JAL). Available at http://www.cesg.gov/uk/site/iacs/itsec/media/joint-int-lib/jil.pdf

King, Christopher, Curtis E. Dalton, and T. Ertem Osmanoglu (2001). *Security Architecture: Design Deployment & Operations.* RSA Press, McGraw-Hill, Berkeley, CA.

Kingston Technology (2002). "Ultimate Memory Guide." Kingston Technology Company, Fountain Valley. CA. http://www.kingston.com/tools/umg/default.asp

McDonald, Tim (2002). "Group Announces New Flash Memory Security Spec." *Newsfactor Network*, July 26, 2002. www.newsfactor.com.

National Computer Security Center (NCSC) (1985). *DoD Trusted Computer System Evaluation Criteria (Orange Book).* 5200.28-STD.

National Computer Security Center (NCSC) (1987). *The Trusted Network Interpretation (Red Book).* NCSC-TG-005, Version 1.0.

Pfleeger, Charles P. (1997). *Security in Computing, 2nd edition.* Prentice Hall, Saddle River, NJ.

Ramachandran, Jay (2002). *Designing Security Architecture Solutions.* John Wiley & Sons, New York.

Sandisk (2002). "Background Information on the M-Commerce Extension Specification." July 2002. www.sandisk.com.

U.S. GAO Executive Guide (April 2003). Information Technology: A Framework for Assessing and Improving Enterprise Architecture Management, Version 1.1. Document #GAO-03-584G.

Web Sites

www.radium.ncsc.mil — for evaluation criteria documents.

www.itsec.gov.uk — for ITSEC evaluation criteria documents.

www.csrc.ncsl.nist.gov.cc — for Common Criteria documents.

www.commoncriteria.org — for Common Criteria documents.

www.microsoft.com/technet/ — for technical vulnerabilities and threats.

Chapter 3
Access Control Systems and Methodology

Laissez faire, laissez passer. No interference and complete freedom of movement.

—Francois Quesnay, 1694–1774

Introduction

The Access Control Domain outlines various information system security options that control access to an organization's information and data processing resources. It builds on the basic issues addressed in the Information Security Management Domain, with an emphasis on various administrative, physical, and technical/logical controls.

Controls for gaining physical access to an area or to information have been used for centuries. One of the earliest examples is the use of shared secret words in a simplified challenge–response system. The sender would speak the first secret word and wait for the correct secret word in response. If the response was not part of the shared secret words, access would not be granted. These early access controls techniques have evolved to include our modern-day access controls; in many instances, the fundamental concepts remain the same, the only difference being the technological implementation.

Prohibition and Access Controls?

In the U.S. during the 1930s, many Prohibition speakeasies were "clubs." Some charged a 50-cent entrance or membership fee; some issued much-sought-after identification cards to their regulars, which would be flashed at the peephole or to the doorman; others were "key clubs," giving door keys to regular patrons. It was the first time many Americans talked about clubs, key clubs, identification cards, or even peepholes (Flexner, 1976).

Although some access control techniques are also used for physical security access, the primary focus of this chapter looks at controlling access to the information system. As such, there is some crossover between the technologies presented here and those in the Physical Security chapter (Chapter 7). When studying for the CISSP exam, it is important for the candidate to understand the various access domains and the corresponding entry points that might be used for unauthorized entry. When taking the exam, it is recommended to carefully read the question to determine whether it is referring to an access control system for the information system or to the physical environment.

The CISSP candidate should be able to:

- Describe the access control concepts and methodologies and their enterprisewide implementation in a centralized or decentralized environment.
- Identify the access control security tools and technologies used to minimize or avoid risks, exposures, and vulnerabilities.
- Describe the auditing mechanisms for analyzing behavior, use, and content of the IT system.

This chapter is divided into five topic areas. The first section (Information Protection Requirements) begins by defining the concept of access control and its requirements. The Information Protection Environment section identifies the access control environment and outlines some of the threats associated with unauthorized users gaining access to the information system and its resources. The third section (Security Technology and Tools) provides an explanation of the types of controls available to mitigate the threats. In this section, access controls are separated into two areas: access to the network and access to the data. The final topics outline what organizations can do to ensure that the access controls are effective, such as using audit tools and intrusion detection tools. Finally, a few specific management controls are mentioned.

3.1 Information Protection Requirements

Defining Access Controls

Access controls are the collection of mechanisms that specify what users can do on the system, such as what resources they can access and what operations they can perform. They are the countermeasures for ensuring that only users with the proper need and authority can access the system, are allowed to execute programs, and can read, edit, add, and delete the appropriate information on that system.

The A-I-C Triad

Access controls are implemented to ensure the availability, integrity, and confidentiality needs of the organization. One of the primary goals of an access control system is to identify and authenticate (I&A) users to a system. I&A is the process of differentiating users based on some type of unique characteristic and its corresponding tool/mechanism. There must also be an access control policy that documents who is allowed access and a standard that specifies what type of mechanism and distinguishing characteristic are used to control that access. The access control mechanism should also trigger an event in an audit log that describes the access as successful or failed. In addition to providing access controls to the system, there must also be a mechanism that provides access controls to data. Data access controls should provide appropriate protection for the information that is stored and processed on a system.

An important element of access control is the organizational policy. For example, a written policy should define who can access and what type of access will be given to information contained on the system. This written policy, also called the access control policy, can be based on two standards of practice: separation of duties and least privilege.

Separation of Duties

Separation of duties means that a process is designed so that separate steps must be performed by different people. The first step in implementing the practice of separation of duties is to define the elements of a process or work function. Once completed, the defined elements are then divided among different employees. This prevents one individual from having control of an entire process and having the capability to manipulate the process for personal gain. Separation of duties forces individuals to create collusion in order to manipulate the system for personal gain. Collusion is an agreement among two or more people to commit fraud.

Separation of Duties

In some organizations, system staff is grouped into specific functional categories, such as those in Firewall Administration, Network Administration, User Account Management, and Help Desk Support. For example, if separation of duties were implemented, those maintaining the user account software would not be able to make changes to the firewall configuration. Thus, they could not open a port in the firewall that would allow an unauthorized user to gain access to the network.

An example of separation of duties can be found in accounting departments. If the staff is large enough, there will one individual who records the accounts payable invoices, a second individual who writes the checks, and third individual who reconciles the bank statements. This helps eliminate the possibility that individuals authorized to write checks could write a fraudulent check to themselves without detection unless in collusion with another individual. In situations where there are not enough people to provide this level of separation, other controls must be established to reduce the chance of unauthorized activity. In the information system, the company may have a software application that also enforces this type of separation, such as instituting different access levels based on the individual performing the function.

Least Privilege

Least privilege is a policy that limits both the system's users and processes to access only those resources necessary to perform assigned functions. Ensuring least privilege requires identifying what each user's job is, outlining the minimum set of privileges required to perform that job, and restricting the user to only those privileges on a system/network. Users only get access to those resources necessary to do their job — no more and no less. By restricting access to only those privileges necessary for performing job duties, access is denied to privileges that might be used to circumvent security. In some organizations, this is also referred to as "need-to-know."

In addition to separation of duties and least privilege, policies are based on the sensitivity of the data that is being processed and stored. For example, recognizable U.S. Government sensitivity classifications include top secret > secret > confidential > and unclassified. These sensitivity descriptors are used for both data and other resources, such as workstations and printers. In addition, individuals are granted access based on their security clearance. Thus, if the information were considered "secret," then access would be granted to only those individuals who have received a prior clearance to access "secret" information or higher.

Regardless of the method an organization uses to define how it will grant and limit access to the information system and its resources, this method should be documented in an approved access control policy.

3.2 Information Protection Environment

The environment for access controls is the technological infrastructure underlying the information processing system, the types of existing controls, and the sensitivity/criticality of the data and processes. This includes the system (hardware, operating system, and applications); networking platform; and additional network connections, such as intranets, extranets, and the Internet. It also includes the physical environment, such as entry points to buildings, computer centers, and even the specific user's workstation. When thinking of the Access Control environment, it is important to understand the threats to system resources.

Availability

An attack on availability is when an asset on the system is destroyed, rendered unavailable, or caused to be unusable.

Integrity

An attack on integrity occurs when an unauthorized entity gains access and tampers with a system resource. Another type of integrity attack occurs when an unauthorized entity inserts objects into the system or performs an unauthorized modification.

Confidentiality

An attack on confidentiality is when an entity, such as a person, program, or computer, gains unauthorized access to sensitive information.

Threats

There are several types of threats and several categories of threats. The following includes examples. Because threats can change on a daily basis, this list is not intended to be a totally comprehensive list, but rather a framework to begin to think about the type of threats to a system. (Note that these are presented in alphabetical order and not in order of most importance or most common.)

- *Buffer overflows.* The buffer overflow problem is one of the oldest and most common problems in software. It can result when a program fills up its buffer of memory with more data than its buffer can hold. When the program begins to write beyond the end of the buffer, the program's execution path can be changed. This can lead to the insertion of malicious code that can be used to destroy data or to gain administrative privileges on the program or machine. (More information on buffer overflows is provided in the Application Program Security chapter [Chapter 4].)
- *Covert channel.* A covert channel is one that violates the organization's security policy through an unintended communications path. Covert channels have the potential for occurring when two or more subjects or objects share a common resource. It includes the

unauthorized use of timing channels and/or storage channels to signal an accomplice. (More information on covert channels is provided in the Application Program Security chapter [Chapter 4].)

- *Timing channel.* A timing channel utilizes the timing of occurrences of an activity to transfer information in an unintended manner. Saturating or not saturating a communications path in a timed fashion can transfer information to a receiver observing the communication path in synchronism with the sender.
- *Storage channel.* A storage channel utilizes changes in stored data to transfer information in an unintended manner. The filling or clearing of a memory area by a sender can indicate a 1 or 0 to a receiver reading the same memory area.

- *Data remanence.* Data remanence occurs when some data, after the magnetic media is written over or degaussed, still remains on the magnetic media. Just because magnetic media was written over or degaussed, this does not mean that information cannot still be retrieved by accident or determined technical capabilities.
- *Dumpster diving.* This is when individuals access discarded trash to obtain user identifications, passwords, and other data.
- *Eavesdropping.* This is the use of software (sniffers) to monitor packets or wiretapping telecommunication links to read transmitted data.
- *Emanations.* Emanations are electronic signals that radiate from hardware devices (i.e., monitors, CPUs, transmission media, and power cords). If the electronic signals were intercepted and analyzed, they would disclose the information transmitted, received, handled, or otherwise processed by the telecommunications or computer equipment. Radio-frequency (RF) computer devices (i.e., cell phones, wireless PDAs, wireless LANs) are all susceptible to emanation interception. In the United States, TEMPEST equipment is designed to eliminate this problem.
- *Hackers.* Hackers are those people who have gained unauthorized access to a computer or its data. There are several forms of hackers: the "white-hat hacker;" the "malicious hacker," often called a "cracker;" and the "prankster." The white-hat hacker explores other people's computer systems for education, curiosity, competition, or just because they can. In some cases, these hackers point out the vulnerabilities of the networks to the owners or they notify software vendors of holes in operation systems or application software. The pranksters conduct tricks on others, but are not intending to inflict any long-lasting harm. Malicious hackers are those individuals with unauthorized access who intend to cause harm or loss.
- *Impersonation.* Impersonation is masquerading as an authorized user to gain unauthorized access.
- *Internal intruders.* Internal intruders are likely to use the same techniques as external intruders to gain access to systems and

information to which they are not normally entitled. Internal intruders include:

- Authorized users trying to gain access to data or resources beyond their need-to-know or access limitations.
- Authorized users trying to gain unauthorized physical access to network connections, server equipment, etc.

- *Loss of processing capability.* This includes losses due to natural disasters, user errors, malicious code, or technical failure of hardware or software.

- *Malicious code.* This is code that can gain access to a system and, in executing, violates security policy. More information is provided later in this section.

- *Masquerading/man-in-the-middle attacks.* This involves someone who intercepts and manipulates packets being sent to a networked computer. A masquerade takes place when one entity pretends to be a different entity. For example, authentication sequences can be captured and replayed after a valid authentication sequence has taken place, thus enabling an authorized entity with few privileges to obtain extra privileges by impersonating an entity that has those privileges. A man-in-the-middle attack occurs when an unauthorized third party intercepts a transmission and changes it before retransmitting it to the intended recipient.

- *Mobile code.* Executable content, or mobile code, is software that is transmitted across a network from a remote source to a local system and is then executed on that local system. The code is transferred by user actions and, in some cases, without the explicit action of the user. The code can arrive to the local system as attachments to email messages or through Web pages. Web developers create applications so that Web browsers can automatically download executable programming code. An example is Java applets written in the Java programming language that are transferred from a server to a client for execution. Java code executed inside a Web browser could reveal information that is on the local hard drive. Also, an HTTP header will report information that Web browsers will provide, such as the last addressed IP address, the machine IP address, username, password, or browser type. Mobile code can also be used as a computer attack. Once the code has downloaded onto the computer, a hacker could transmit data from the computer back to the hacker's computers without your knowledge. This could include stealing passwords or credit card information, erasing or transferring sensitive business files, and, in some cases, could cause the system to become inoperable. (More information on mobile code is provided in the Application Program Security chapter [Chapter 4].)

- *Object reuse.* This refers to the possibility that sensitive data is available to a new subject. It may occur when magnetic media or memory is reassigned to a new subject and the media or memory still contains one or more objects that have not been purged before the reassignment. Thus, the sensitive objects remain and may be available to another user who is not authorized access.

- *Password crackers.* These are software programs that can be used to reveal passwords stored in password files. Usually, passwords for user accounts are one-way encrypted (hashed) and stored in a system file. If unauthorized users can gain access to the file, they can break the passwords using a software password-cracking tool that includes dictionary attacks and brute-force attacks. Dictionary attacks are accomplished when the program hashes each word in a dictionary and successfully matches the result with an entry in the password file.

- *Physical access.* This refers to gaining physical access to network connections, equipment, and/or support systems, such as HVAC, power, etc. (More information on physical access is in the Physical Security chapter [Chapter 7].)

- *Replay.* This is the passive capture of a packet and its subsequent retransmission to produce an unauthorized effect.

- *Shoulder surfing.* This is the process of direct visual observation of monitor displays to obtain access to sensitive information.

- *Sniffers.* These are software mechanisms attached to network lines that read or capture packets that travel on the networks. Protocol analyzers used by network maintenance personnel are examples of authorized uses of sniffers. Sometimes, this is referred to as "sniffing the wire," which refers to the act of watching packets as they travel on the network.

- *Social engineering.* This occurs when an unauthorized user tries to con authorized users into providing the information needed to access systems. Passwords, network infrastructure, and employee identity are all targets of social engineering attacks.

- *Spoofing.* This is the act of masquerading as a different IP address. Packets can be formatted with false (or fake) addresses to hide the originator's true location. It involves an intruder connected to the network and pretending to be a trusted host. The intruder pretends to have the identity of another computer so as to obtain access to the other computers on the network.

- *Spying.* This refers to high-tech methods of eavesdropping that utilize cameras or microphones or light beams (can reflect sounds).

- *Targeted data mining.* This is the process of searching through databases for specific information. Targeted data-mining techniques can be used to search for sensitive information on a system.

- *Trapdoor.* A trapdoor is an opening that system developers use to bypass the user authentication process in software. It may be inadvertently left available after software delivery.

- *Tunneling.* This is a digital attack that attempts to get under a security system by accessing low-level system functions.

Transmission Threats

Since the opening of systems to outside connections, specific types of threats have developed and have become part of the information system security vernacular. Threats to transmissions on the system can be categorized as either passive or active attacks. Passive attacks involve monitoring or eavesdropping on transmissions. The objective is to obtain information that is being transmitted on the networks. Active attacks involve some modification of the data transmission or the creation of a false transmission. The following is not meant to be an all-inclusive list; however, we wanted to provide a list of some of the more well-known and legacy types of attacks. Although we usually provide the security controls for threats and vulnerabilities in the Security Technology and Tools section, for ease in reading this list, we have included some options that can be used to reduce the possibility of these types of attacks following the definition. (More information on transmission threats is provided in the Telecommunications, Network, and Internet Security chapter [Chapter 8].)

Denial-of-Service (DoS). This is the common name for attacks on resource availability. It occurs when invalid data is sent in such a way that it confuses the server software and causes it to crash. Another person or process tries to control the resources of the system and thus denies the resources to others. Denial-of-service attacks do not try to steal or damage information; instead, they attempt to disable a computer or network or deny access to authorized users. An example of a denial-of-service is email spamming. Spamming is the process of sending lots of junk email to clog the receiver's email box with unwanted mail and thus interfering with the delivery of business email. Other types of DoS attacks are Distributed Denial-of-Service, Ping of Death, Smurf, and SYN Flooding. Also, DoS attacks can happen in a variety of ways not related to invalid data, such as "backhoe transmission loss." A backhoe transmission loss can occur when a backhoe (earth moving equipment) or other construction equipment cuts into the cabling system carrying transmission links. In fact, recent initiatives and discussions have focused on the need for "smart pipes" that would provide damage detection information. Thus, if a cable were damaged, the smart pipe would be able to determine the type of damage to the cable, the physical position of the damage, and transmit a damage detection notification.

Distributed Denial-of-Service (DDoS). A DDoS attack requires the attacker to have many compromised hosts (this could be hundreds or thousands, depending on the type of attack), which overload a targeted server with

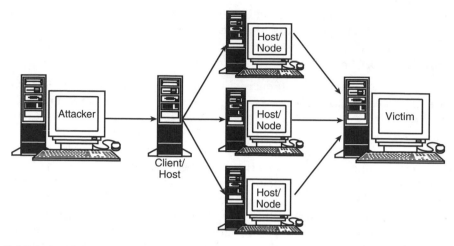

Exhibit 1. Distributed DoS

packets until the server crashes. An infected host computer is sometimes referred to as a zombie. (A zombie is a computer infected with a daemon/system agent without the owner's knowledge and subsequently controlled by an attacker.) The hosts are compromised using automated tools that then allow a master host to control them. The master host coordinates a simultaneous attack from all zombie hosts against the target server. The following steps, as shown in Exhibit 1, outline the basic steps of how a DDoS attack might occur:

- The attacker uses client software to send commands to the hosts or nodes. The hosts, in turn, send floods of packets, or malformed packets to the victim.
- In most cases, the attacker installs the client software on another system; usually a compromised host that is several router hops from the attacker's system (this can help prevent the attacker from being tracked). The client software is also installed on the nodes. Because this process can take less than five seconds, several hundred hosts can be compromised in an hour. The attacker very often releases a Trojan program, either through spam, posting to Usenet, or over a system such as IRC. The Trojan, when run by careless users, installs the DDoS agent software on systems and announces the availability of a new compromised system on a relatively anonymous channel, such as IRC, usually through a coded message.
- The attacker can send commands using the Internet Control Message Protocol (ICMP) [ICMP packets are used to handle errors and exchange control messages] packets or through some form of Telnet on an unusual port. One type of client software, called TFN2K, also

uses encryption on the ICMP packets. Some DDoS systems provide for password validation of commands.

- The infected nodes receive the commands from the client software and begin to send packets of useless information to the targeted victim. One node alone can send thousands of packets per minute. With a hundred nodes, millions of packets can be sent per minute, which can instantly use all of the victim's available bandwidth. If a thousand nodes are used, billions of packets could be sent instantaneously. So many packets could overwhelm even victims who have protection in place.
- The goal is to clog the site's routers and keep legitimate users from gaining access to the site. Although the packets contain useless information, the computer receiving the data spends time and resources trying to understand the influx of data that has been transmitted by the zombies. Thus, the overload of requests to the victim consumes the available network resources and can cause the victim computer to lock up or crash. Even if the target is capable of resisting the direct attack, legitimate users will not be able to connect due to lack of an available connection. (In 2000, several prominent Web sites — Yahoo!, Amazon, and CNN.com — were brought down by zombie DDoS attacks.)

Fixes to a Distributed Denial-of-Service (DDoS) Attack. The following measures can be taken to counter a DDoS attack:

- An attacker will attempt to find hosts or nodes on which to install the client attack software. This can be done by performing a DNS lookup of the address of the target or using the ping command. It may be possible to see this access in audit log files at the target location.
- Scan your machines to see if the attack software is installed. There are commercially available scanners that will perform this function. Also, ensure that your machines do not have known vulnerabilities still open.
- Install and set up a firewall with specific rules that limit outbound packets to only the traffic that should be sent. If a distributed attack is launched from your machines, the firewall will prevent the bad packets from leaving the network.
- Set up a firewall or intrusion detection system to identify and block a DDoS attack. To do this, you must be able to identify the source address of the incoming malicious packets. Once the source address has been identified, block all packets from that source address.

Ping of Death. Under normal circumstances, the ping program is used to determine whether a remote machine on the network is operating. The ping works like sonar. The originator sends an ICMP Echo Request, commonly called a "ping" packet (it is named after the application program used to send the packets). ICMP is used to convey status and error information, including notification of network congestion and other network transport problems. ICMP can also be a valuable tool in diagnosing host or network problems. The packet (a tiny piece of data) is sent to the machine and the program then waits to see if a reply is sent back. If the target machine receives that packet, that machine will return an ICMP echo reply packet. Typically, the attack does not damage the system it is attacking; rather, it prevents authorized users from accessing the system by flooding the target with pings.

The "Ping of Death" takes advantage of the ability of the Internet Protocol to fragment packets. The attack works as follows:

- The specification for the Internet Protocol (IP) says that a packet may be up to 65,535 bytes in length, including the packet header. However, the specifications for most current network technologies do not allow packets that large. For example, the maximum Ethernet packet size is 1500 bytes.
- The Ping of Death attack is initiated by sending a packet that is 65,536 bytes. Although the long packet is invalid, it is possible to create because packets are broken into fragments for transmission.
- The problem occurs in the way packet fragmentation is implemented by most systems. Typically, the systems do not attempt to process a packet until all the fragments have been received — after an attempt has been made to reassemble them into one large packet. The large packet can cause the internal system buffers to overflow, which in turn can result in system crashes or protocol hangs.

Fixes to the Ping of Death Attack. Note that the Ping of Death is an older vulnerability first discovered in 1996–1997. Because the problem is based on the implementation of fragmented packet reassembly, it has been easy to fix. Operating system vendors have released patches for the problem. In addition, firewalls can be configured to block IMCP echo request packets.

Smurfing. Another attack that exploits the ping program is called "smurfing." It is also called an "ICMP storm" or "ping flooding." The attacks have been referred to as "smurf" attacks because the name of one of the exploit programs that attackers use to execute this attack is called "smurf." There are three parties in these attacks: the attacker, the intermediary (the broadcast host), and the victim (note that the intermediary can also be a victim). The process is as follows:

- In a smurf attack, the attacker sends a large stream of spoofed ping packets to a broadcast address (an IP address that services a network of computers and will send messages to multiple recipients). The intermediary receives an ICMP echo request packet directed to the IP broadcast address of its network. If the intermediary does not filter ICMP traffic directed to IP broadcast addresses, many of the machines on the network would receive this ICMP echo request packet and send back an ICMP echo reply packet. Under certain conditions, the broadcast host will relay the packets to all the hosts on its network. Each broadcast address can support up to 255 hosts, so a single ping request can be multiplied 255 times.

- The return address of the ping request itself is spoofed; that is, it is not the originator's address, but the address of the victim.
- The hosts receiving the ping request will reply to the victim, each with an equivalent amount of data. The victim is then subjected to network congestion (all the ICMP echo requests) that could make the network unusable.
- The effect is to multiply the amount of data by a factor equal to the number of hosts that clog the victim's network and also that of the broadcast host. When all the machines on a network respond to this ICMP echo request, the result can be severe network congestion or outages.

Fixes to the Smurf Attack. The following provides options for limiting and responding to a smurf attack:

- One solution is to disable IP-directed broadcasts on all routers being used by the site (including internal routers). This will prevent the site from being used as an intermediary in this attack. By disabling these broadcasts, the router is configured to deny IP broadcast traffic onto your network from other networks. In almost all cases, IP-directed broadcast functionality is not needed.
- Some operating systems can be configured to prevent the machine from responding to ICMP packets sent to IP broadcast addresses. Configuring machines so that they do not respond to these packets can prevent your machines from being used as intermediaries in this type of attack.
- There are no good fixes for the victim. Good security practice involves reducing the capability for attacks to occur. Attacks like the smurf attack rely on the use of spoofed packets (those in which the attacker deliberately falsifies the origin address). With the current IP technology, it is impossible to eliminate IP-spoofed packets. However, administrators can use filtering tools to reduce the likelihood of their site's networks being used to initiate spoofed packets. One method to reduce the number of IP-spoofed packets exiting your network is to install filtering on the routers, which requires packets leaving the network to have a source address from the internal network. This type of filter prevents a source IP-spoofing attack from the site by filtering all outgoing packets that contain a source address from a different network.

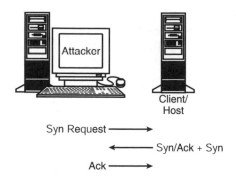

Syn Request ———→

←——— Syn/Ack + Syn

Ack ———→

Exhibit 2. Synchronous Flooding

SYN Flooding. This is a method of disabling a system by exploiting the synchronization protocol used to initiate an Internet connection. A brief explanation of Syn Flooding is when the "client" system attempts to establish a TCP connection to a system "server" providing a service, the client and server exchange a set sequence of messages. This connection technique applies to all TCP connections, such as Web requests, email, Telnet, etc. The connection technique is often referred to as a handshake. The process begins by the client system sending a SYN (synchronization) message to the server. The SYN message tells the server it would like to open a TCP connection. The server then acknowledges the SYN message by sending a SYN/ACK (synchronization-acknowledgment) message to the client and continues the handshake by sending a SYN message of its own. The client then finishes the establishment of the connection by responding with an ACK (acknowledgment) message in response to the server's SYN. The connection between the client and the server is then open, and the service-specific data can be exchanged between the client and the server. This handshake exchange is shown in Exhibit 2.

The potential for a SYN Flood attack occurs at the point where the server system has sent an acknowledgment (SYN/ACK) back to the client, but has not yet received the ACK message. During the connection process, this is referred to as a half-open connection. The server has built into its system memory a small database structure that keeps track of pending connections. Because this database structure is of finite size, it can be made to overflow by intentionally creating too many half-open connections.

Creating half-open connections is easily accomplished with IP spoofing. The attacking system sends SYN messages to the victim server system; these appear to be legitimate but in fact reference a client system with a phony return address. Because the SYN/ACK packet from the server goes nowhere, it is left in a half-open state waiting for the client to respond with the final ACK message.

Normally, there is a timeout associated with a pending connection, so the half-open connections will eventually expire and the server system will recover. However, if it receives false packets faster than the entries are removed, space will fill up, leaving no room to establish legitimate connections. In some cases, the server system may exhaust memory, crash, or be rendered otherwise inoperative.

Fixes to SYN Flooding. As of this writing, there were no generally accepted solutions to SYN Flooding based on the current IP technology. Although difficult, it is possible to reduce the time that connections remain half open: modern networks are generally faster than older ones. Also, stateful firewalls can be set to limit the number of connection requests per hour (or even minute) from the same address. A proper router configuration can reduce the likelihood that a site will be the source of one of these attacks.

For example, it may be necessary to install a filtering router that restricts the input to the external interface (known as an input filter) by not allowing a packet through if it has a source address from the internal network. In addition, filtering of outgoing packets should be done so that if a packet has a source address different from the internal network address, the packet should not be allowed to exit the network. This can prevent a source IP spoofing attack from originating from the site.

Some transmission attacks are mischievous in nature, such as defacing Web sites. Web sites usually have a low level of security, but are high visibility, which makes them a popular target. The Web sites are altered by either changing the information or inserting obscenities, pornographic images, and anti-government messages. Another damage to Web sites is tampering with Domain Name Servers (DNSs). The DNS is altered so that the site's domain name displays the IP address of another site. Users pointing their browsers to one site would be redirected to another site. The users would not be able to correct the problem unless they knew the correct IP address for the site they wanted.

Malicious Code Threats

Malicious code is code that can gain access to a system and, in executing, violates security policy. It includes various types of rogue code, such as viruses, worms, Trojan horses, and logic or time bombs. Symantec Corporation (2002) states that "at last count there were more than 53,000 virus threats on the loose."

A *virus* attaches itself to executable code and is executed when the software program begins to run or an infected file is opened. The virus can harm the computer system by displaying a certain message on the machine's monitor, perform a deletion or modification to a certain file or files, delete entire files, or even reformat the hard drive. Viruses do not necessarily carry a damaging payload: the most "successful" ones, in terms of spread, do not. However, viruses can create problems simply by their very existence within a system.

The virus can replicate itself within one computer and infect other programs as it reproduces. Viruses spread through the sharing of infected programs, documents, email attachments, infected diskettes, or other removable media.

Worms are programs that reproduce by copying themselves through computers on a network. A worm is different from a virus because it does not copy itself to a program; it remains an independent program and installs itself on the system. A worm can quickly spread itself to hundreds of thousands of machines via both the local networks and the Internet. Worms usually do not cause damage to data; instead, the worm absorbs the network's resources causing the damage. While replicating itself, a worm can take much of the network's memory capability and may eventually shut down the system. Worms are distinguished from viruses in that they do not require intervention from the user, whereas a virus does.

A *Trojan horse* is a code fragment that hides inside a program and performs a disguised function. Although the function is usually hidden, a Trojan can be, and frequently is, a stand-alone program with a single function. The Trojan horse is usually hidden in an independent executable program that performs a useful or appealing function, such as a screen saver or game. However, while the program is active, the Trojan horse is performing some other unauthorized operation. It does not replicate itself like a virus, nor does it make copies of itself like a worm. Trojan horses are usually spread by email attachments or Web downloads.

A *logic bomb* is a type of Trojan horse that releases some type of malicious code when a particular event occurs. Usually, it is triggered by an unsuspecting event, such as a date, time, or processing event. A time bomb is set to explode on a particular date or after a certain period of time has elapsed.

There are new viruses being discovered all the time, but at the same time, there are many *hoaxes* (i.e., rumors of viruses and other types of malicious code) that do not actually exist. However, the hoax itself can become a threat to network resources. For example, users will send everyone on their email list a warning about a hoax, and then the warning is then sent again by those recipients. The resources needed to announce the warning could clog the network bandwidth and also use excessive storage on the email server.

An independent research firm located in Carlsbad, California, has published some financial statistics about malicious code shown in Exhibit 3.

Exhibit 3. Financial Analysis by Incident

Year	Code Name	Worldwide Economic Impact, in $U.S.
2001	Nimda	$635 Million
2001	Code Red(s)	$2.62 Billion
2001	SirCam	$1.15 Billion
2000	Love Bug	$8.75 Billion
1999	Melissa	$1.10 Billion
1999	Explorer	$1.02 Billion

© 2002 Computer Economics, Inc., Computer Economics.

Fixes for Malicious Code. The following provides options for controlling malicious code attacks:

- Use anti-virus software to stop malicious code from entering the system.
- Update the anti-virus software definition files frequently.
- Provide awareness material to users that includes:
  - Never open email from people who you do not recognize — or emails from people you know but have odd or weird subject lines.
  - Only download executable files from sources with which you are familiar.
  - With anti-virus software tools, have users scan all email attachments and downloads before opening them. Generally, save to disk and scan, rather than relying on email system scanners. Attachment scanning is highly unreliable.

Password Threats

Ali Baba and the 40 Thieves

Ali Baba "eavesdropped" on the 40 thieves and overheard the "Open Sesame" password and thus was able to gain access to the den containing gold and jewels. Did Ali Baba, "an unauthorized user," do the right thing?

Because passwords are the most widely used type of authentication mechanism, we have included some of the most common types of threats:

- An unauthorized user attempts to steal the file that contains a list of the passwords. Although most current networking operating systems provide encryption algorithms (hashing) to protect the contents of the password file if it is stolen, there are password-cracking tools that can defeat this protection.

- Users may create weak passwords that are easily guessed. In this type of attack, the attacker will try to guess the passwords of users. For example, in the Washington, D.C., metropolitan area, the most widely used password was "Redskins," named for the local National Football League team, the Washington Redskins.
- Social engineering can be used to obtain passwords.
- Sniffers can be used to intercept a copy of the password as it travels from the client to the authentication mechanism.
- Hardware or software keyboard intercepts can be used to record all data typed into the keyboard.
- Trojan horse code can be installed on a workstation that will present an unauthorized login window to the user. Although the window may look valid to the user, it is simply a method of gaining the password information. The attacker, through the Trojan horse, can then intercept the data (user ID and password) that has been entered into the Trojan code.

The next section identifies the types of controls available to mitigate the various threats and vulnerabilities when accessing a system and its information.

3.3 Security Technology and Tools

In this section we look at the technology and tools available to control access to the information system resources. The first section defines the types of controls available, followed by the specific technologies available to restrict both access to the network and access to data.

Definition of Controls

Controls that limit access are traditionally grouped into three types: Administrative (including personnel), Physical, and Technical (Logical). All are involved in controlling access to the system and resources. Administrative controls consist of management activities such as organizational policies and procedures. Personnel controls involve items such as background investigations and security clearances. Physical controls include locks and badge systems. System technical or logical controls are those installed or implemented as part of the information system, such as antivirus software, password filters, or encryption technologies. A few examples of each type of control are shown in Exhibit 4.

For most organizations, it is cost-prohibitive or not necessary to employ all possible controls. Thus, organizations must strive to reach a balance between what is available and what is needed to ensure that access controls are reasonable and realistic, and yet still fulfill the security policy objectives.

Exhibit 4. Examples of Access Control Methods

Technical (Logical) Controls
- Access control software, such as firewalls, proxy servers
- Anti-virus software
- Passwords
- Smart cards/biometrics/badge systems
- Encryption
- Dial-up callback systems
- Audit trails
- Intrusion detection systems (IDSs)

Administrative Controls
- Policies and procedures
- Security awareness training
- Separation of duties
- Security reviews and audits
- Rotation of duties
- Procedures for recruiting and terminating employees
- Security clearances
- Background checks
- Alert supervision
- Performance evaluations
- Mandatory vacation time

Physical Controls
- Badges
- Mantraps
- Turnstiles
- Limiting access to physical resources through the use of bollards, locks, alarms, or guards

---

For ease in understanding what type of access is being discussed, the next section is separated into (1) Access to the System and (2) Access to Data. The first section discusses access controls for the system, while the second section focuses on controlling access to information once the user has gained access to the system.

Access to the System

In this section, the concept of *identification and authentication* is discussed, as well as *remote, centralized,* and *decentralized* access control methods.

Identification and Authentication. Access to the system is the process of limiting and controlling access to system resources. An initial aspect of this control is to identify and authenticate each user and system process. Most users will recognize the identification and authentication process as entering a user ID and password to log on to the system.

In the context of users, the first step is to identify the user to the system. The second step authenticates the first step; that is, it is some type of credential that proves the user (i.e., John) is who he says he is. Be careful not to confuse authentication with authorization. Authentication is the process of verifying the identity of the sender and/or receiver of information. Authorization establishes what the user is allowed to do once the user has been identified and authenticated by the system. Another "A" term sometimes misinterpreted is accountability, which is the ability to track actions to users.

Types of Identification. Identification is the cornerstone for all aspects of information system security. All system entities must have a unique identifier that differentiates it from other entities. It is the key component to the access control process.

User identification provides the following:

- Asserts user identity
- Provides accountability (when combined with an audit trail)
  - Enables activities to be traced to individuals
  - Individuals can be held responsible for actions

The user identification can be called the logon ID, user ID, or account number. However, the most common type of user identification is a *username*. It is what users present to the system to say who they are. In addition to users, there are entities within the system that also need to be identified, such as software services and hardware components. Any function or requirement that will be granted access to the system requires a unique identifier.

Because today's networked systems have a large volume of users and entities that must be accounted for, some type of formal management process of identification should be established. A simple management procedure is establishing the format of a user's name. Some organizations use the last name and first initial of the first name. Others use both the first name and last name separated by an underscore. Regardless of which method is employed, it is important to establish a procedure that is consistent throughout the organization, regardless of the system.

Another type of user identification is a badge or card system. *Badge systems* are usually identified with physical access controls that are implemented to control access to restricted locations such as buildings or server rooms. However, some badge systems are also integrated into access for the network system. For example, smart card systems have been installed that allow access into the physical room as well as entry to the network.

Biometric devices, such as fingerprint, hand geometry, and voice recognition systems, can also be used as a form of identification for physical access control systems, as well as authentication for logical access control to a network or host.

An important component of identification is accountability. As such, a unique identifier allows actions initiated and created by an entity (i.e., system user) to be traced via audit trails to specific individuals or system services. Thus, an individual attempting to gain access to system resources will be identified to the system by the unique identifier and can be held responsible for the activity.

The following are guidelines for user identification:

- *Issuance.* The process of issuing identifiers must be secure and documented. The quality of the identifier is, in part, based on the quality of how it is issued.
- *Naming standards.* In simple user identifiers, such as the user's name, a standardized format should be followed. For example, all user identifiers would be Last Name, First Initial, Middle Initial, so that the user ID for John R. Smith would be "SMITHJR."
- *Non-descriptive of job function.* The identifier should not easily identify the user's job functions. For example, the system administrator should not use a user ID called "administrator."
- *No sharing.* Identifiers should belong to one user throughout the entire system and, if possible, throughout the entire network or organization. Also, sharing of identifiers reduces accountability.
- *Verifiable.* The identifier must be simple and easily validated. The verification process needs to be available at all times and standardized so that reviewing of user identification is automated, regardless of the entry point.
- *Unique.* Identifiers must be unique so that each user can be positively identified.

Types of Authentication. *Authentication* verifies the identification. In almost all enterprise information systems, the user must present identification, and the system must authenticate the identification before the user is allowed access to the system. The three factors or methods of authentication are presenting something *you know*, something *you have*, or something *you are*. An important concept and term you may hear is one-factor or two-factor (also referred to as multi-factor) authentication. One-factor authentication requires the use of one authentication method, such as something you know, like a password, while two-factor requires two authentication methods, such as something you know, followed by something you have, such as an access card. Another example of two-factor authentication is the use of a password (or PIN [personal identification number]) (something you know) and a fingerprint reader (something you are). When an authentication system uses two or three factors, it is

Exhibit 5. Authentication Factors

Authentication Type	Example	Pros	Cons
Something you know	Password, passphrase, or personal identification number (PIN)	Easy and inexpensive to implement	Easy to guess; subject to password sniffers and dictionary attacks; users do not keep their passwords secret
Something you have	Token, memory card, or smart card	Difficult to attack	Can be lost or stolen; can be expensive to implement
Something you are	Biometric devices, such as fingerprint, voice recognition, eye scanners, etc.	Portable and provides an easy method of authenticating	Can be expensive to implement; user acceptance can be difficult; false rejection and false acceptance rates must meet security objectives

sometimes referred to as providing "strong authentication." Exhibit 5 provides a brief overview of the authentication factors.

What a User Knows. The most common type of user-known authentication is a *password*. The password is a protected word (or string of characters) that authenticates the user to the system. The theory is that a user has a secret password, something only the user knows; and when the password is entered into the system, it must be the user, because the user is the only one who knows the secret password.

The problem with this theory is the secrecy of passwords. Users might write it down, tape it to the monitor (or underneath the keyboard), share it with others, or make it so simple that it is easily guessed. Because of the ease in compromising reusable passwords, they are not considered to be an adequate control by themselves.

A *passphrase* is a sequence of characters or words used as an alternative to a password. There is no real difference between the two, except in the meaning of the terms themselves: "password" encourages users to think short and easy, whereas "passphrase" is meant to encourage the user to type in a complete phrase. Except when there are arbitrary length restrictions, there is nothing restricting a password from being a phrase. For example, a passphrase can be an acronym generated from the sentence, Roses Are Red Violets Are Blue, as RARVAB. Keep in mind that although

---

History of Passwords

In the early days of computers, access was controlled through physical access to the room housing the computer. People either worked with the computer directly or gave computer programs to the "operators" for processing. As the concept of "timesharing" developed (i.e., the ability to share a computer so that several people could simultaneously use the computer), the need for some type of technically controlling access also began. Fernando Corbato, at the Massachusetts Institute of Technology (MIT), first introduced the Compatible Time Sharing System (CTSS) in 1961. He envisioned a system that handled a large number of users, but also provided some privacy between the users' work. Through advancements, the CTSS began to incorporate a "memorized lock" for timesharing users. Users had to type in a username and a memorized private code. Corbato's memorized private code is now commonly called a password.

Of special note is that some early computer users, particularly the sophisticated ones called hackers, did not like the idea of usernames and passwords. They were outraged at the loss of individual control that was suddenly given to the computer. Hackers began to attack the CTSS and soon realized that one of the weak points was the password file itself. Legend has it that a hacker would occasionally manage to get a copy of the password file, print it out, and post the password file on an MIT bulletin board for all to see.

RARVAB may be more difficult to guess, it could still be defeated using an automated password cracker.

Passphrases are also used as keys in encryption systems. In these instances, the difference between passphrases and passwords is length. For example, passwords are usually six to ten characters, while passphrases can be up to 100 characters (or even more).

Recommendations for implementation and management of passwords and passphrases are:

- Password lifetime should be restricted. It is dependent on several variables, such as cost of replacement, risk if compromised, distribution risk, probability of guessing, number of times used, and level of work required to discover it by exhaustive trial and error. High security requirements may require passwords to change daily, while lower-security systems may require passwords to change monthly, quarterly, biannually, or annually.
- Users should create passwords that are not dictionary words or names.

- Users should create passwords using a mix of alphabetic, numeric, and special characters. In the United States, the National Security Agency (NSA) recommends that passwords contain a mixture of uppercase and lowercase alphabet letters, numbers, and special characters, such as ?RaRV19aB.
- Users should create longer passwords, which tend to be more secure. If the password is only a few characters, it is easier to try all possible combinations.
- Creating a good passphrase is one of the most important things that can be done to preserve the privacy of computer data and email messages. A passphrase should be:
  - Known only to the creator
  - Long enough to be secure
  - Hard to guess, even by someone who knows the user well
  - Easy to remember and easy to type accurately

Because passwords are a vital element of access control, it is important to protect access to the password file. Typically, passwords are stored in a password database file that uses a one-way encryption algorithm (hashing). For security measures, the operating system should offer both encryption and other access controls to protect the password file.

For example, in Windows NT systems, when the system manager or user enters the original password, it is first hashed before it is sent to the server for authentication. The hashed password is stored in the password file, not the entered cleartext. During the login process, the user enters the password, the system hashes the password, and this hash is compared to the encrypted hash stored in the password file. Although passwords are not stored in cleartext, password-cracking software can crack the hashed passwords by brute-force or dictionary attacks.

LC4 is the 2003 version of the L0phtCrack password auditing and recovery application (formerly called a password-cracking tool). LC4 can be used to discover passwords stored in the Windows NT or 2000 operating system. If an encrypted password file can be accessed and imported to the LC4 application, the program can compare the hashed password stored in the password file with an internal LC4 file that has hashed dictionary words (over 250,000 English words are in the internal LC4 dictionary). When the hashes match, the password is displayed in cleartext. It will also perform a brute-force crack that, given enough time, will crack passwords on a character-by-character basis. To counter this threat, stronger hashing schemes can be used. Stronger hashing algorithms make it more difficult for password-cracking software to crack passwords in a short timeframe. Microsoft released a patch for Windows NT, called SysKey, that offered a 128-bit hashing algorithm to counter the LC4 software. By default, Windows 2000 contains the 128-bit hashing algorithm. However, LC4 advertises that it can crack back Windows passwords, regardless of whether the 128-bit algorithm has been installed. A similar tool, Crack, is the classic password cracker for the Unix system.

The Unix system originated at the Bell Laboratories (United States) in the late 1960s. Its logon process was developed in the 1970s and provided user authentication and eventually password hashing. In early versions, the Unix program ran a utility called /bin/login when a user began the logon process. The utility would read the username and extract the password for that user. The utility would then read the user's entered password; hash it along with a salt (random generated value) from the stored password entry. If the results matched the hash stored in the password file, the user would be logged on. Current versions of Unix offer more or different logon security features, such as keeping records of logon attempts and delays after bad guesses. Early attacks focused on the attacker gaining a copy of the password file and then using password-cracking tools to obtain the passwords. To prevent this attack, Unix has added the ability to shadow password files, which hide the hash values contained in the password file from unauthorized users.

In addition, it is important to protect the password file by limiting physical access to the servers that contain the original or a backup copy of the file, such as those found on emergency repair disks. Also, the access permissions for the password file should be set so that only authorized system administrators have the right to access the file.

Another aspect of protecting the password is to limit the number of attempts that a user may have to enter the password. If the user exceeds the number of attempts, the user account is locked until a specified amount of time has expired or the system administrator unlocks the account. Note that this could make the system vulnerable to a denial-of-service attack, wherein the perpetrator is able to lock out many users by discovering their user identifications and entering a specified number of invalid passwords. This type of denial-of-service attack can be easily launched if the attacker has knowledge of the organization's standard account-naming convention and a copy of the organization's employee directory.

Account Lockout Example

Lock account after three bad logon attempts.

Lock account for 60 minutes or "forever." The forever option requires the system administrator to unlock the account, regardless of the time the account has been locked.

Although password authentication is virtually useless, it is the most widely used mechanism for logon authentication. Users often share their passwords with colleagues, friends, and family. Users may write down their password on a piece of paper or a post-it note and leave it where it can be found by others. If the user does not safeguard the password, the system is subject to unauthorized access via an authorized account. In addition, passwords are easy to crack using password-cracking software. An option to counter the inherent vulnerabilities of passwords is to use another authentication method or require two authentication methods (two-factor authentication), such as something the user knows and something the user has.

What a User Has. Technical solutions include one-time passwords and some type of memory card or smart card solution. These options eliminate the vulnerabilities associated with traditional user password creation and use. Smart cards can help because they perform security tasks, like remembering difficult passwords that users find a burdensome task. For example, most smart card systems provide a two-factor authentication. The user uses both the card and a personal identification number (PIN) for access. Thus, even if the card is stolen or lost, other users could not use the card for access unless they also had the PIN.

One-Time Passwords (OTPs). An OTP is not like a traditional password that is used multiple times; the OTP is only used once — it is changed after every use. One of the security features is that if someone were eavesdropping on the transmission link, they would not be able to make use of a stolen password. Because the OTP is only valid for one access, if a captured OTP was tried on a second attempt, the second access would be denied.

One type of OTP does not require a computer to operate; it can be a list of passwords printed out on paper and used only once. However, most uses are through a handheld token device.

Of course, security is only as good as the person protecting the password list or token device. Thus, to provide protection, the password list or device that generates the OTP must be protected and stored securely.

One type of OTP token uses a secret key to encrypt an internal value that yields a password that works only once; this is often referred to as synchronous OTP. Another type uses a challenge–response technique, where the tokens encrypt the challenge to yield a single-use password, sometimes referred to as asynchronous OTP.

Synchronous Tokens

There are two general methods for generating synchronous OTP tokens. The first is a *counter-based* token that combines the base secret with a synchronized counter to generate the OTP. The second is a *clock-based* token

---

History: An Attack That Forced the Use of OTP

In 1994, an international team of thieves gained unauthorized access to the Citibank Cash Management System. The Citibank system allowed major Citibank customers to transfer money from their Citibank accounts to other financial institutions around the world. The scheme was organized by Vladimir Levin, the head systems operator at a computer company in St. Petersburg, Russia. Levin and his accomplices acquired and shared passwords that authorized over 40 transactions, totaling over $10 million. By using authentic passwords, they were perceived by the system as legitimate account managers and moved money between bank accounts in several countries. Citibank noticed the discrepancies and began to work directly with the FBI. Levin was arrested by the Scotland Yard Computer Crime Unit (based on a U.S. federal warrant) at Heathrow Airport in 1995. He was later extradited to the United States to stand trial for bank fraud and wire fraud, and was sentenced in 1998 to jail for three years and ordered to pay back $240,015. Citibank managed to cancel or reverse all except $400,000 of the unauthorized transactions.

To prevent this from occurring again, Citibank installed a counter-based OTP system for authenticating cash management accounts. Each account manager was issued a token that had to be used for all transactions. This eliminated the problem of having an account manager share a password or having a trusted insider (like a systems administrator) gain access to messages that may contain an account's password.

---

that uses a synchronized clock to generate the OTP. One vendor has developed a product that combines both a counter-based and clock-based solution. Both of these token techniques rely on a random base secret stored in the OTP token. New passwords combine the base secret with some arbitrary value, either a counter, a clock, or both. What makes them synchronous is that the server and token must remain synchronized with respect to the passwords they generate. Once the token and the server lose synchronization, the user cannot authenticate. Clock-based tokens usually will search a few minutes on either side of the time to find a match and resynchronize with every use. An example of a synchronous token is provided in Exhibit 6.

Counter-Based Token. To use a counter-based token, the administrator must first insert a specific base secret and internal counter into the token device and copy this information to the server device. The owner of the token pushes a button on the token to activate the OTP service. The token increments the internal counter, combines it with the owner's unique base secret, and computes a one-way hash result. The token formats the result and displays the new OTP. Refer to Exhibit 7 for an

1. Every minute, clock reading is enciphered with secret key and displayed. This is one-time password.

2. User reads secret key, and along with the PIN, enters the data into workstation.

3. Authentication Server knows secret keys of all cards by clock synchronizing with the cards. It verifies the entered data.

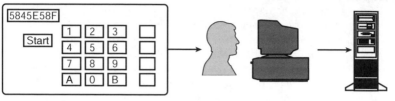

Exhibit 6. Synchronous Token

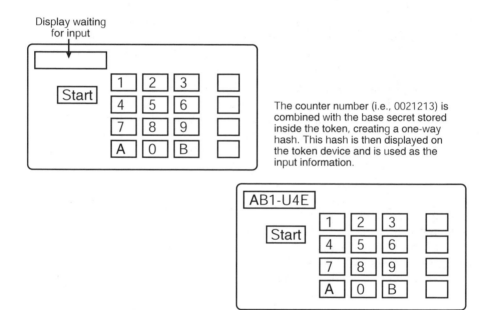

Display waiting for input

The counter number (i.e., 0021213) is combined with the base secret stored inside the token, creating a one-way hash. This hash is then displayed on the token device and is used as the input information.

Exhibit 7. Counter-Based Token

example of a counter-based token. If an attacker intercepts the password and tries to reuse it, the server device will not recognize the password as valid.

Clock-Based Token. The clock-based token uses internal clocks instead of counters. An internal clock value is combined with a base secret key to generate a time-based password each time the user needs one. The token device displays the generated result for the user to use when logging into the system.

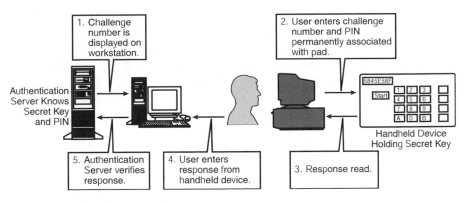

Exhibit 8. Asynchronous Tokens

The server performs a similar process by combining its own clock value with a copy of the token's base secret key. In case there is a time delay between the token and the server, the server can be programmed to accept any password derived from a clock value within an established time window.

Asynchronous Tokens: Challenge–Response Devices. This type of token generates a password based on a challenge or nonce from the server that is then combined with a base secret key within the token. The user, in response to the server's challenge, uses the result of this combination as its reply. To begin, the authentication server sends a challenge number to a workstation. This challenge number is entered into the token device. The challenge number is combined with the base secret key to generate the result that is displayed in the token device. The user enters the generated token result. The server, which also knows the token device's secret key, performs a similar function. The server's result is then compared with the result that the user entered. A visual diagram of an asynchronous token is shown in Exhibit 8.

One of the advantages of asynchronous or challenge–response authentication is that the servers do not need to maintain synchronization with the token devices. By generating a random challenge each time, the server ensures that previously valid passwords will not be valid for the next logon. A security feature of challenge–response passwords ensures each password is for a specific logon attempt. If the logon attempt fails, another challenge is issued. This can help eliminate the risk of an attacker intercepting and reusing the OTP.

More recently, many people are using software on their workstations (instead of physical token devices) to automatically handle challenge–response authentication. This software is sometimes referred to as "soft tokens." It is even available for personal digital assistants like the Palm organizer. Using the soft tokens, the server site generates the initial base secrets (similar to the physical token devices) and sends them to the users as data files. Once the user has properly installed the data files, the software token will work the same as the physical token during the logon process. Another type of soft token is a paper-based "codebook" that provides a list of OTPs to use. In most cases, the authentication system will generate a separate codebook that indicates the valid dates for the codebook.

Smart Cards. A *smart card* is a credit card-sized plastic card (some are metal) that, unlike a credit card, has an embedded semiconductor chip that accepts, stores, and sends information. It can hold significantly more data than magnetic stripe cards. The semiconductor chip can be either a memory chip with nonprogrammable logic or a microprocessor with internal memory.

Smart cards typically fall into two general categories: *contact* or *contactless* (see Exhibit 9). The embedded chip communicates either directly via a physical contact or remotely via a contactless electromagnetic interface. Contact smart cards need to be inserted into smart card readers that touch a conductive module on the surface of the card. Data, encryption algorithms, and other types of information are transmitted via the physical contacts. Another security feature of smart cards is that data stored on cards is encrypted using a variety of encryption algorithms.

A contactless card makes use of an electromagnetic signal and an antenna on each smart card to create the conversation between the card and the card reader. The microwave frequencies employed provide the card with its power source. These non-battery-powered cards need to come within a certain distance of the card reader to be powered. One example is the transportation fare cards at tollbooths that allow the card to be near the device, instead of inserting and removing the card.

A third category is commonly referred to as hybrid or combi, although the two are fundamentally different. The hybrid cards are dual-chip cards; each chip has both a contact and contactless interface that are not connected to one another inside the card. Combi cards carry only a single chip, which has both a contact and a contactless interface, and either can communicate between the chip and card reader.

In addition to differences in card interfaces, there are two types of chips used inside smart cards: memory chips and microprocessor chips. Smart cards with only memory cards are simply storage devices that cannot process information. These cards are very similar to magnetic stripe cards, although they hold more data.

Memory cards provide nonvolatile storage in a variety of card and storage sizes. For example, storage size can range between 4 and 320 MB. The

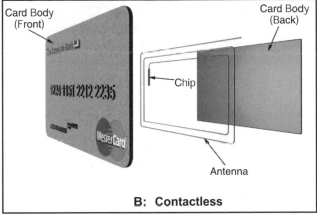

Exhibit 9. Contact and Contactless Smart Cards

chip in a memory card consists only of storage and a little extra hardware that prevents access to the stored data. Memory cards store files and keep them available without power and while detached from the information systems network. The authentication aspect of memory cards is to manage passwords on the memory cards. For example, one system provides for every entry on the card to consist of a password and a description that gives information about the password. All data on the memory card is stored encrypted so that if the card is stolen or lost, the data would not be usable. Memory cards are less expensive than microprocessor cards and have correspondingly less security. Memory cards can support basic applications, such as telephone cards.

Smart cards with microprocessor chips can do far more than memory chip cards. Essentially, they are miniature computers on a plastic card. The microprocessor provides storage for information and also the ability to add, delete, and manipulate the data in its memory. Because of these capabilities, chip cards offer higher levels of security. The microprocessor chip has three elements: the central processing unit, memory, and input/output.

These components are integrated into the same circuit chip with electrical connections tying them together. Because it is difficult for outside signals to tamper with the interconnections of the elements inside the chips, the security of the smart card is improved.

The value of a smart card is its capability to store personal information with a high degree of security and portability. It can provide hacker-resistant storage for protecting private keys, account numbers, passwords, and other forms of personal data. Smart cards also isolate security-critical computations involving authentication, digital signatures, and key exchange from other parts of the system. The cards can store the digital signatures, and thus enhance authentication between parties, control access to intranets and extranets from outside a firewall, and protect the privacy of data, files, and email. In addition, smart cards can provide portability for securely moving private information among systems at work, home, or on the road.

Smart cards also offer an enterprisewide authentication system. For example, the user enters the card into a smart card reader, enters a personal identification number, and is then provided access to all available applications. The benefit is using a single card versus several authentication passwords to access multiple applications across the enterprise network. Smart card users do not need to memorize their passwords or employ a different password for every application; instead, they simply carry the smart card with them.

Smart cards are also used for encryption systems. The smart card can securely store the keys and in sophisticated systems, encryption algorithms can be performed on the card. This eliminates the need for the encryption process to appear on the desktop system where a malicious program can view it.

Finally, smart cards provide security for the logon path because user authentication is done between the reader at the workstation and the smart card. Therefore, the user's ID and password are not exposed during the transmission from the workstation to the authentication computer. The reader has a "handshake" with the computer to provide authentication.

There are several weaknesses and types of attacks against smart cards. Because a smart card is essentially a computer, similar types of attacks can be used against the smart card. The attacks can be either invasive or non-invasive. In an invasive attack, the method used to analyze the card might render the card inoperative, so it is usually used to gain information about the card and chip. The information can then be used in a later noninvasive attack. Kaommerling and Kuhn (1999, p. 2) distinguish four major attack categories:

- *Microprobing* techniques can be used to access the chip surface directly; thus, we can observe, manipulate, and interfere with the integrated circuit (invasive attack).
- *Software attacks* use the normal communication interface of the processor and exploit security vulnerabilities found in the protocols, cryptographic algorithms, or their implementation (noninvasive attack).
- *Eavesdropping techniques* monitor, with high time resolution, the analog characteristics of all supply and interface connections and any other electromagnetic radiation produced by the processor during normal operation (noninvasive attack).
- *Fault generation* techniques use abnormal environmental conditions to generate malfunctions in the processor that provide additional access (noninvasive attack).

One of the weaknesses is the lack of global standards for e-commerce smart cards. Although there are several international standards for card design, there is a lack of global standards for how data is embedded (stored) on the card. As a contrast, credit card standards, such as name, unique number, signature, and expiration date, have become recognized throughout the world.

Another vulnerable aspect is the card interface to the reader. The smart card needs to resist unauthorized instructions and unspecified bit combinations via the software interface. E-commerce attacks of this sort concentrate on destroying or extracting the uploaded credit on the card with the most probable goal being stealing valid e-cash from the cardholder (Karppinen, 2000). Although cryptographic algorithms will reduce this type of attack, adding cryptography also adds complexity.

More recently (May 2002), University of Cambridge researchers revealed in a paper presented at an Institute of Electrical and Electronics Engineers (IEEE) symposium in California that a camera's electronic flashgun duct-taped to a microscope could be used to reveal private data directly from a smart card's microprocessor.

Sergei Skorobogatov and Ross Anderson, in their paper entitled "Optical Fault Induction Attacks," wrote that by scraping away the protective layer to reveal the microprocessor, they were able to direct a camera's flash through the microscope and alter the contents of a smart card's brain. Although current-generation devices have countermeasures in place to make these types of attacks not feasible, these devices are generally used for higher-end applications, such as in the banking or the health field. Lower-end applications, such as telephone debit cards or parking fee cards, may not employ the protections.

An interesting side about the May 2002 University of Cambridge release was the response from Gemplus (a smart card manufacturer), stating that the company has been aware of such attacks for some time, and has implemented effective countermeasures notably against side channel and fault attacks. "The light attack publicized by Cambridge University researchers is a type of fault attack, which has been widely studied for years, but about which Gemplus is also well aware. The attack presented shows how a fault can be generated, but not how sensitive information can actually be recovered. This is not straightforward. The attacker must adapt his or her attack to any one of more than 60 chip designs used in smart cards. Recent products benefit from the most advanced countermeasures, but earlier products in the field may prove vulnerable. Smart cards remain the most efficient and cost-effective device to protect privacy and security of access to digital information and electronic transactions. It has proven, over many years and with broad use, to offer the strongest security at the most competitive price" (Gemplus Press Release, 2002).

What a User Is. The most common method of authentication based on physical attributes is through *biometric devices*. Because each individual has physical characteristics that are distinct from another, they can be used to authenticate a user. Biometric verification is an automated method whereby an individual's identity is confirmed by examining a unique physiological trait (e.g., palm print or iris pattern) or behavioral characteristic (e.g., voice or signature). Although the initial cost of a biometric security authentication system is expensive, biometric devices are the most secure access control method. Exhibit 10 provides a list of some biometric devices and their related attributes.

Physiological traits are stable physical characteristics and this type of measurement is essentially unalterable. A behavioral characteristic is influenced by both controllable actions and less controllable psychological factors. Also, because behavioral characteristics can change over time, the enrolled biometric reference template must be updated periodically.

Although behavior-based biometrics can be less expensive and less threatening to users, physiological traits tend to offer greater accuracy and security. Regardless, both systems provide a significantly higher level of identification accuracy than passwords or ID cards alone.

Important elements of biometric devices are accuracy, processing speed, and user acceptability.

Accuracy. Accuracy is the most critical characteristic of a biometric identification/authentication system. The system must be able to accurately separate authentic users from imposters. The terms associated with accuracy are "false reject rate," "false accept rate," and "crossover error rate." All are stated in terms of percentages. The false accept rate is usually considered the most important error for a biometric system, while the crossover rate is considered the most important measure of biometric system accuracy. Exhibit 11 provides a brief overview of accuracy terms in biometric systems.

The crossover error rate (CER) as shown in Exhibit 12 provides a single measurement that is fair and impartial in comparing the accuracy of various systems. A 1% CER indicates a 2% total error, 1% false acceptance plus 1% false rejection. Also, it is not difficult to find a situation where the CER is not the lowest error or best setting.

For example, if a biometric device is set to ensure that the false acceptance rate is low, it may guarantee that no unauthenticated users can gain access. On the opposite side, if a biometric device is set to ensure that the false reject rate is low, the system will only access input data that approximates a match with the enrollment data. If a device is tested in this configuration, the system can achieve a near-zero false rejection rate. The reality is, however, that a biometric system can only operate on one sensitivity setting at a time. Thus, published data about a system's accuracy does not always tell the entire story. This is why the crossover error rate measurement was created.

Processing Speed. Processing speed is related to the data processing capability of the system and is stated as how fast the accept or reject decision is annunciated or presented to the user. It involves the entire authentication process, from input of the physical characteristic, the process of matching the input to the stored data, and the annunciation of the accept or reject decision. A generally accepted standard for system speed is five to ten seconds from start-up through decision annunciation.

User Acceptability. Another important factor is the acceptance rate by users. Because users must be comfortable and willing to use the system, the biometric device needs to be accepted by the users. If users are not comfortable/willing, they may overtly or covertly damage or sabotage the system devices. The best method of ensuring user acceptance is to first have users agree that resources must be protected. The next step is to convince users that the system is not dangerous to their health. Finally, users should be assured that their health information is not collected and personnel movement will not be unreasonably restricted.

Types of Biometric Devices

There are three physical characteristics that are entirely unique for each individual: the fingerprint, the retina of the eye (i.e., blood vessel patterns inside the eyeball), and the iris of the eye (i.e., random patterns of granularity in the colored portion of the eye). There are several other types of biometric devices that provide authentication services. Exhibit 10 provides information

Exhibit 10. Biometric Attributes

Attribute	Enrollment Process and Time	Input File Size	User Input Action	System Response Time	Accuracy
Fingerprint	Users press their finger(s) against a glass or polycarbonate plate. The location of the ridges, whorls, lines, bifurcations, and intersections are stored in an enrolled user database file and later compared with user input data. The process is repeated several times for calibration. Total enrollment time is less than two minutes.	500–1500 bytes	User places finger(s) against the reader plate.	5–7 seconds	Varies — a good CER would be 5%
Hand geometry	A three-dimensional record of the length, width, and height of the hand and fingers is acquired by simultaneous vertical and horizontal camera images. The images are recorded several times and averaged into a single code. Total enrollment time is less than two minutes.	~9 bytes	User places the hand flat on the reader plate. Lights confirm correct hand placement and data is captured.	3–5 seconds	CER rates of 2.2%
Voice pattern	Nasal tones, larynx, throat vibrations, and air pressure from the voice are captured by audio and other sensors. The user picks up a handset and speaks a personal access phrase (four to six words). This process is repeated up to four times. Total enrollment time is less than two minutes.	1000–10,000 bytes	User speaks into a handset.	10–14 seconds	CER rates of 10%

Retina pattern	The blood vessel patterns of the retina on the inside rear portion of the eyeball are recorded using a camera. The user's eye is positioned approximately two inches from the camera. An ultra-low invisible light enables reading 320 points on a 45° circle on the retina. Total enrollment time is less than two minutes.	96 bytes	The user positions an eye in front of the camera and focuses on a pulsing green dot.	4–7 seconds	CER rate of 1.5%
Iris pattern	The colored portion of the eye surrounding the pupil (iris) has unique patterns of striations, pits, freckles, rifts, fibers, filaments, rings, coronas, furrows, and vasculature. These patterns are captured by a 1/2-inch video camera capturing 30 images per second. The camera creates zones of analysis on the iris image and locates the patterns within the zones to create an Iriscode. Total enrollment time is less than two minutes.	256 bytes	The user looks into the optical unit's LCD that produces a feedback image of the eye. The user centers and focuses the image.	2–4 seconds	CER less than 0.5%
Signature dynamics	Small sensors in the pen or writing surface record the pen-stroke speed, direction, and pressure. The user signs (at least five times) a normal signature using the pen (or stylus) and a specialized surface to create a template. Templates are then encrypted. Total enrollment time is less than two minutes.	1500 bytes	The user's signature is written by using the pen and special writing surface.	5–10 seconds	Testing is in progress

Source: Richards, Donald R., 2000. "Biometric Identification," in *The Handbook of Information Security Management.* Auerbach Publications and CRC Press, Boca Raton, FL.

Exhibit 11. Biometric Accuracy Terms

Accuracy Terms	Description	Error Type
False reject rate	Authentic users are rejected as unidentified or unverified	Type I error
False accept rate	Imposters are accepted as authentic	Type II error
Crossover error rate	The point at which the false rejection rates and the false acceptance rates are equal	

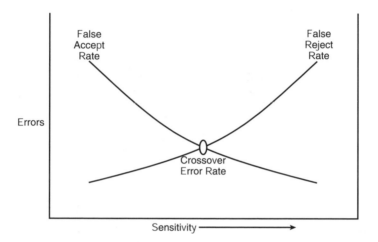

Exhibit 12. Crossover Error Rate

on a few characteristics for several popular biometric systems in use today. As an example, hand topography (side-view elevations of the hand) has proved insufficiently unique for accurate use, but in combination with the top view of the hand (hand geometry), it has become very successful.

Centralized Access Control Methodologies

Providing remote user access to network resources is a security challenge. Remote access includes dial-in users and access from the Internet through a firewall or Virtual Private Network (VPN) service. The challenge is to provide a secure form of *authentication, authorization,* and *accounting (AAA)* for the network system.

Authentication *verifies who the user is and whether the user is allowed access to the network.*

Authorization *determines what the user is allowed to do.*

Accounting *tracks what the user did and when it was done. It can be used for an audit trail or for billing for connection or resource time.*

The Internet Engineering Task Force (IETF) chartered an AAA Working Group to develop the AAA requirements for network access. The objective was to produce a base protocol that supported a number of different network access models, including traditional dial-in network access servers, mobile-IP, and roaming operations. Prior to this AAA Working Group were the RADIUS and TACACS standards for remote access. The task of the Working Group was to build on the current models to produce a standard that would provide the key features of a centralized AAA service.

The AAA service should include:

- *A distributed (i.e., client/server) security model.* Distributed security separates the authentication process from the communications process, thus making it possible to consolidate user authentication information into a single centralized database.
- *Authenticated transactions.* Transmissions between the client and server are authenticated to ensure both the integrity and the source of the transactions. Sensitive information is encrypted to ensure confidentiality and prevent passwords and other authentication information from being monitored or captured during transmission.
- *Flexible authentication mechanisms.* AAA servers are able to support a variety of authentication mechanisms, such as the Password Authentication Protocol (PAP), Challenge Handshake Authentication Protocol (CHAP), the standard Unix login process, or the Microsoft domain controller. Also, calling number identification (CLID) and callback features can be used to enhance secure connections.
- *An extensible protocol.* Due to changes in technology, AAA servers are designed with extensible protocols so that new protocols will be supported without disabling existing protocols.

RADIUS, TACACS, and DIAMETER (a draft Internet RFC) are centralized authentication protocols to improve remote access security and reduce the time and effort required to manage the process. The RADIUS and TACACS protocols are principally used by Internet service providers and in the remote access systems of large businesses. Typically, they are used as a protocol between a terminal server and the host to handle the AAA requirements for those devices. All three are characterized as AAA servers.

The basic steps of an AAA service are shown in Exhibit 13:

1. Remote user sends a user ID and password to the NAS (network access server).
2. The NAS collects the remote user's user ID and password.
3. The NAS sends an authentication request to the AAA server.
4. The AAA server returns connection parameters, authorization, and protocol information.
5. The NAS confirms connection and writes the audit record.

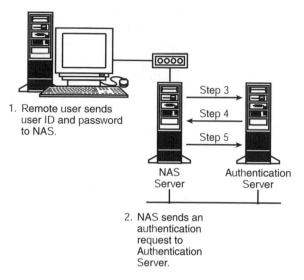

1. Remote user sends user ID and password to NAS.

Step 3
Step 4
Step 5

NAS
Server

Authentication
Server

2. NAS sends an authentication request to Authentication Server.

Exhibit 13. Network Access Server

RADIUS — Remote Authentication Dial-In User Service

RADIUS was developed by Livingston Enterprises for their Network Access Servers (NASs) to assist Internet Service Providers (ISPs) with billing information and connection configuration. Because it was one of the first products, it is considered the most popular AAA service in use today. Since its release in the early 1990s, much advancement has been made that has increased its capability and scalability. Note that the popularity and advancements could be attributed to the fact that Livingston openly distributed the RADIUS source code.

A RADIUS environment includes a RADIUS client, a RADIUS server, and a UDP/IP-based frame protocol. The RADIUS client is situated on the NAS, which accepts the login credentials from the user, and then submits them to the RADIUS server for authentication. Thus, a NAS operates as a client of RADIUS. The RADIUS client is responsible for passing user information to the designated RADIUS server and then acting on the response that is returned. RADIUS servers are responsible for receiving user connection requests, authenticating the user, and then returning all configuration information necessary for the client to deliver service to the user. The RADIUS servers can also act as a proxy client to other kinds of authentication servers.

RADIUS Authentication is done through eight standard transaction types: access-request, access-accept, access-reject, accounting-request, accounting-response, access-challenge, status-server, and status-client. Authentication occurs by decrypting a NAS access-request packet, authenticating the NAS source, and validating the access-request parameters against the user file. The server then returns one of three authentication responses — access-accept, access-reject, or access-challenge — which asks for more information.

The transactions between the RADIUS client and server are authenticated through the use of a shared secret that is never sent over the network. Also, any user password is encrypted between the client and RADIUS server to eliminate the possibility that someone eavesdropping on an unsecured network could determine the user's password. RADIUS also enables use of a dynamic (one-time) password.

RADIUS Authorization is part of the authentication reply. When a RADIUS server validates an access-request, it returns to the NAS client all the connection attributes specified in the user file, such as access to network specifications like TCP/IP.

RADIUS Accounting is an independent function and must be implemented separately. The NAS client configured to use RADIUS accounting will generate an accounting-start packet once the user has been authenticated and also an accounting-stop packet when the user disconnects.

TACACS — Terminal Access Controller Access Control Systems

TACACS and subsequent versions are authentication protocols that allow a remote access server to communicate with an authentication server to determine if the user has access to the network. There are at least three versions of the protocol. The first one, TACACS, has been in use for many years. The original TACACS daemon, using a UDP transport, was used in the early days of ARPANET and was adopted by Cisco Systems in the early 1990s to support AAA services on its products. The first extension to the protocol was to include additional functionality and change the transport service to TCP. This first protocol extension was called XTACACS, that is, extended TACACS. The third version, TACACS+ (TACACS Plus), is an expanded version that offers enhanced security and supports additional types of authentication requests and response codes. The TACACS+ protocol specification is a proposed IETF Standard. Because Cisco freely distributes the TACACS and TACACS+ source code, the implementations vary considerably.

TACACS+ uses an AAA architecture that separates authentication, authorization, and accounting. This allows an organization to implement another type of authentication solution, but still use TACACS+ for authorization and accounting. For example, Kerberos, a third-party authentication service based on a Ticket Granting Ticket (TGT) system, could be used for authentication and TACACS+ for authorization and accounting. After NAS authenticates on a Kerberos server, it then requests authorization information from a TACACS+ server without having to reauthenticate. The NAS informs the TACACS+ server that it has successfully authenticated on a Kerberos server, and the server then provides authorization information.

TACACS Authentication has three packet types: Start, Continue, and Reply. The client begins the authentication with a Start packet that describes the type of authentication to be performed. The server responds with a Reply packet. If additional information is required, the server responds with either Continue or Reply packets. Transactions include login and password change using various authentication protocols, such as the Challenge Handshake Authentication Protocol (CHAP) or the Password Authentication Protocol (PAP). A successful authentication returns attribute value pairs (AVPs) for connection configuration. TACACS uses a fixed password while TACACS+ enables use of a dynamic password.

TACACS Authorization consists of Request and Response Attribute Value Pairs (AVPs) to permit or deny certain commands, addresses, services, or protocols. Authorization also includes the ability to set user privilege levels, invoke input and output packet filters, set access control lists (ACLs), invoke callback actions, and assign a specific network address.

TACACS Accounting functions include Start, Stop, More, and Watchdog. The Watchdog function is used to validate TCP sessions when data is not sent for extended periods of time. This functionality is often referred to as TOC/TOU (Time of Check versus Time of Use) validation. TACACS has an audit event logging capability that can record system-level changes in access rights or privileges. The reason for the event as well as the traffic totals associated with it can also be logged.

DIAMETER

DIAMETER is a *draft* Internet RFC. As such, it is a "work in progress." DIAMETER is not an acronym, but a twist on the RADIUS name. Although it is still a draft Internet RFC, it is presented here so that the information system security professional is aware of the potentially new authentication protocol.

DIAMETER was designed to support roaming applications and to overcome the extension limitations of the RADIUS protocol. RADIUS was designed to function only with Serial Line Internet Protocol (SLIP) and Point-to-Point Protocol (PPP) for standard analog modems. It is not extensible and thus cannot be used for access authentication of handheld or other wireless computer devices, cellular phones, or VPNs. DIAMETER is built upon the RADIUS protocol and is designed to do more than RADIUS in terms of authenticating more types of users, but yet maintain compatibility with RADIUS-based systems.

It is a peer-based AAA protocol designed to offer a scalable foundation for introducing new policy and AAA services over existing and emerging network technologies. It is divided into two parts: the Base Protocol and the Extensions. The Base Protocol defines the message format, transport, error reporting, and security services used by all DIAMETER Extensions. DIAMETER Extensions are modules designed to conduct specific types of AAA transactions, such as NAS, Mobile-IP, and Secure Proxy.

DIAMETER uses a UDP transport but in a peer-to-peer rather than client/server configuration, encoded attribute value pairs (AVPs), and proxy server support. The peer-to-peer configuration allows servers to initiate requests and handle transmission errors locally, plus it uses reliable transport extensions to reduce transmissions, improve failed node detection, and reduce node congestion.

DIAMETER Authentication is ruled by the Extension used, but all follow a similar structure. The NAS issues an authentication request to the server containing the AAA Request Command, a session-ID, and the client's address and host name followed by the user's name and password and a state value. The server validates the user's credentials and returns an AAA Answer Packet containing either a Failed-Attribute Value Pair (AVP) or the accompanying Result-Code AVP or the authorized AVP for the service being provided. An example of an AVP is "user ID and smithj" or "password and #123$ABC." Essentially, the DIAMETER server issues the user ID attribute as a challenge; the NAS or other system responds with the user value — the ID. Then the server issues the password attribute. If the user values are correct, the user is considered authentic.

DIAMETER Authorization can be combined with authentication requests or conducted separately. The specifics of the transaction are ruled by the Extension used. Authorization requests must take place over an existing session; they cannot be used to initiate sessions but they can be forwarded using a DIAMETER proxy. By using other value pairs, the server can further qualify the user to determine the specific resources that the user is granted access. For example, if access to a high-security application were requested, the user would be required to supply an additional key code.

DIAMETER Accounting significantly improves upon the accounting capabilities of RADIUS and TACACS+ by adding event monitoring, periodic reporting, real-time record transfer, and support for the roaming operations (ROAMOPS) accounting data interchange format. While a RADIUS server cannot send unsolicited comments to a client, DIAMETER permits such interaction. This may be useful if the server needs to instruct the NAS to perform specific accounting functions or terminate a connection. The ability of the server to send messages may also be helpful with troubleshooting connections or for accounting data. For example, the DIAMETER server can force a client to send current accounting data.

A major difference between RADIUS and DIAMETER is the scope of AVP use. The RADIUS address space is limited to 256 value pairs. DIAMETER features a 32-bit AVP address space, enough for a million or more pairs. This AVP potential is what gives DIAMETER extensibility and this is what allows for mobile access. For example, a mobile user calling from a cell phone might use a home-agent address as the attribute and an IP address as the value. This information is passed through the DIAMETER server of the home ISP in order to authenticate the user ID and password value pairs. DIAMETER also supports both PAP and CHAP challenge–response protocols.

For more information, check the Internet Engineering Task Force (IETF) Authentication, Authorization, and Accounting (AAA) Working Group Charter at http://www.ietf.org/html.charters/aaa-charter.html.

Decentralized/Distributed Access Control Methodologies

Single Sign-On (SSO)

Some network enterprise systems provide users with access to many different computer systems or applications for their daily work. This wide range of access may require the user to have a user ID and password for each available resource. This need for multiple user IDs and passwords could cause the user to practice bad password protection, such as creating easy passwords or writing them down. As shown in Exhibit 14, the user does not need to log on to each individualized system or program; instead, a SSO solution is implemented that enables the user to log on once to the enterprise and then access all additional authorized network resources. SSO can minimize either the number of times users must log on within a site or the number of authentication characteristics they need, or both. Thus, Single Sign-On means the user is never prompted to enter additional authentication credentials for the session. The alternative is Single Login, which is where the user has a single user ID and password used on every system in the organization. Users must still log in/authenticate to each system; they just use the same credentials.

As an access control method, SSO addresses the identification and authentication need across multiple platforms. The need for SSO includes:

- The multiple number of entry points, including Internet access.
- The management of large numbers of workstations dictates that some control be placed over how they are used.
- The multiple number of applications used by enterprises.
- The administration of access control needs to be simplified to increase efficiency.

The advantages of SSO are:

- SSO provides a more efficient user logon process. Users only need to type their user ID and password once. When additional resources

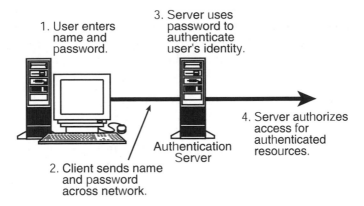

1. User enters name and password.

3. Server uses password to authenticate user's identity.

4. Server authorizes access for authenticated resources.

Authentication Server

2. Client sends name and password across network.

Exhibit 14. Single Sign-On (SSO)

are needed, the user does not need to enter another user ID and password.

- Because there are fewer passwords to remember, users can create stronger passwords.
- The need for multiple passwords and change synchronization is avoided.
- Inactivity timeout and attempt thresholds are applied closer to the user point of entry.
- The effectiveness and timelines of disabling all network/computer accounts for terminated users improve. SSO systems allow a single administrator to add and delete accounts across the entire network from a centralized database and one user interface.

The disadvantages of SSO include:

- Once a user's ID and password are compromised in the system, an intruder could have access to all of the resources authorized for the user without constraint.
- The system security policy must be followed to ensure access is granted and/or limited to appropriate users.
- Implementation with microcomputer systems is difficult and can prevent full implementation.

In most SSO systems, the user provides a user ID and password to a primary login program that authenticates the user against a master system. Once authenticated, the user can request access to additional resources. When the user requests access, the SSO system retrieves the user's password for the new system and starts a session with the new system using that password. In some systems, the authenticated user is presented with a constrained user interface containing only those applications they are authorized to use. Users then select an application or service from the desktop and are transparently logged into that application by the SSO system. If authentication fails, the SSO system prevents the user from gaining unauthorized access to the enterprise's applications and services. The defined security policy determines whether the user is given an explanation for the failure.

To allow mobile users to log on from a modem, an SSO can offer encryption techniques such as one-way encryption (hashing) algorithms for password protection. Authorized remote (i.e., dial-in or Internet) users should be recognized by their remote login address and telephone number to authenticate to the privileges associated with their own desktop, allowing these remote users access to their own applications or services.

The enterprisewide SSO auditing capability needs to track all the actions carried out by users to ensure user accountability. A logged event should specify the user, activity, workstation or terminal used, and the date and time of the session.

Kerberos

Kerberos may be one of the best-tested authentication protocols in use today. It was designed and implemented in the mid-1980s as part of Project Athena at the Massachusetts Institute of Technology (MIT). It is an authentication protocol that provides security services for large, heterogeneous networks.

> *In Greek mythology, Kerberos was a three-headed dog that served as the guardian to the entrance to Hades. Just as the Greek Kerberos had three heads, the modern Kerberos was intended to have three elements to guard a network's entrance: authentication, accounting, and auditing.*

The basic idea of Kerberos is that a trusted third party, the Kerberos Authentication Server (also called the Key Distribution Center [KDC]), performs secure verification of users and services. The constituents can be any hardware or software that communicates across the network. It uses the U.S. Data Encryption Standard (DES) cryptographic algorithm for encrypting authentication information. In addition to authentication, Kerberos offers confidentiality and integrity for network messages.

In small, closed environments where all systems are owned and operated by a single organization, Kerberos is probably not needed. In these situations, clients can authenticate themselves to servers and the servers can be relied upon to enforce a security policy based on the user ID. Kerberos is effective in open, distributed environments where network connections to other heterogeneous machines are supported and the user must prove identity for each application and service. Kerberos assumes a distributed architecture and employs one or more Kerberos servers to provide an authentication service. This redundancy can avoid a potential single point of failure issue. The primary use of Kerberos is to verify that users are who they claim to be and the network components they use are contained within their permission profile. To accomplish this, a trusted Kerberos server issues "tickets" to users. These tickets have a limited life span and are stored in the user's credential cache.

Kerberos has four basic requirements:

- *Security.* A network eavesdropper should not be able to obtain the necessary information to impersonate a user.
- *Reliability.* It must be available for users when needed and provide a distributed server architecture so that one system can back up another.
- *Transparency.* After initial authentication, the user should not be aware of the authentication process.
- *Scalability.* It must support a small or large number of computer systems.

The Kerberos protocol has many elements, and the actual exchanges and subsequent security features are complicated. Refer to additional resources such as RFC 1510 for specific details. However, the following steps provide a simplified explanation of how Kerberos works; in this instance, a user would like to use a sensitive printer for output of a document. Note that the following description is client/server, but the process is true for any network. A very simplified view of Kerberos is shown in Exhibit 15.

1. The Kerberos client has knowledge of an encryption key known only to the user and the trusted key distribution center (KDC). Also, the application server shares an encryption key with the KDC. When the client wants to create an association with a particular application server, the client uses the authentication request and response to first obtain a ticket and session key from the KDC. The KDC holds the secret keys of all users and resources on the network. The KDC performs Authentication Service (AS) and Ticket Granting Service (TGS) functions.
2. The user enters user ID and password into the local workstation that contains the Kerberos client software. The workstation uses the password to generate the user's secret key that will reside *temporarily* on the client workstation. On behalf of a user, a Kerberos client on the workstation transmits the user's ID to the Ticket Granting Service (TGS), in order to obtain a Ticket Granting Ticket (TGT). The request contains the user's identity, a requested expiration time

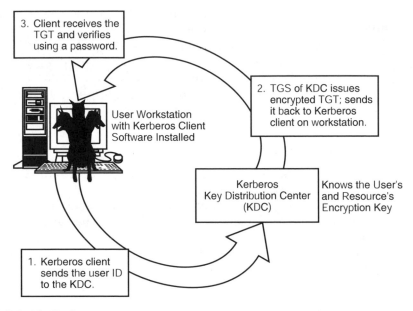

3. Client receives the TGT and verifies using a password.

User Workstation with Kerberos Client Software Installed

2. TGS of KDC issues encrypted TGT; sends it back to Kerberos client on workstation.

Kerberos Key Distribution Center (KDC)

Knows the User's and Resource's Encryption Key

1. Kerberos client sends the user ID to the KDC.

Exhibit 15. Kerberos

for the ticket, and a random number that will be used to match the authentication response with the request.

3. TGS sends the client a TGS-Client Session Key (KTGSc) encrypted with the user's secret key and a Ticket Granting Ticket (TGT) encrypted with a key known only to the TGS. The TGT contains the client ID, the TGS-client session key (KTGSc), and start and expiration times. The TGT is so named because it is used to obtain tickets for the services that the user wants to access. This information is all encrypted with the user's password, which was registered with the Authentication Server. When the client receives the authentication reply, it prompts the user for the password. The password is used to decrypt the session key. The client is now ready to communicate with the resource.

4. When the user selects the resource, the Kerberos client software on the workstation asks the Kerberos security server for the credentials necessary to use that resource. The client sends the Kerberos ticket and an authenticator that includes information such as the current time, a checksum, and an optional encryption key. This information is all encrypted with the session key.

5. After receiving the request, the resource decrypts the ticket, extracts the session key, and uses the session key to decrypt the authenticator. If the checksum and timestamp match, the verifier accepts the request as authentic. Because the Authenticator and

Ticket are timestamped, these transactions are subject to time expiration.

The degree to which Kerberos can be trusted depends on how carefully it is implemented. Kerberos requires trusted, synchronized clocks in the network. Enforcing limited lifetimes for authentication credentials based on timestamps can minimize the threats of replaced credentials. In addition, Kerberos and its authentication are based on trust. The KDC and clients must trust one another to be who they represent themselves to be. Because the KDC contains all of the shared secrets and provides security services, it must be physically secured and must not allow any non-Kerberos network activity.

A major issue affecting the level of use of Kerberos involves the awareness of the client. The client software must be compiled with the Kerberos software.

SESAME

The Secure European System for Applications in a Multi-Vendor Environment (SESAME) is a European research and development project funded by the European Commission. It is also the name of the technology that came from the project. It offers SSO with added distributed access controls using symmetric and asymmetric cryptographic techniques for protection of interchanged data. It builds on work done in international standards and is an Open System solution to distributed access control.

As shown in Exhibit 16, to access the network system, the user first authenticates to an Authentication Server to get a cryptographic protected token. The token is used to prove the user's identity. The user then presents the token to a Privileged Attribute Server to obtain a guaranteed set of access rights contained in a Privileged Attribute Certificate (PAC). The PAC is digitally signed to prevent tampering. The PAC is cryptographically protected from the point it leaves the Privileged Attribute Server to the final requested resource. The PAC conforms to standards set by the European Computer Manufacturer's Association (ECMA) and the International Standards Organization (ISO/ITU-T).

The promulgation, protection, and use of the PACs are the central features of the SESAME design. The user presents the PAC to a requested application/resource whenever access is needed. The requested application makes an access control decision according to the user's security attributes contained in the PAC and any other access control information that is located on the resource, such as an Access Control List (ACL).

It is similar to Kerberos in that SESAME components can be accessible through the Kerberos V5 protocol. This allows for the use of Kerberos data structures, as well as new SESAME structures.

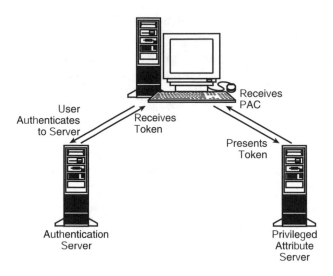

Exhibit 16. SESAME

SESAME is accessed through the Generic Security Services Application Programming Interface (GSS-API). The GSS-API is an Internet and X/Open Standard and provides several security features: the interface hides from its users the details of the specific underlying security mechanism that leads to better application portability, and GSS-API completely separates the choice of security mechanism from choice of communications protocols.

Additional Distributed Security Controls

Security Domains. A domain is typically referred to as a group of computers that share a similar mission and single point of management responsibility. An Enterprise Resource Program (ERP), such as SAP or Peoplesoft, among others, would be structured into a single domain. Domains are often composed of subdomains for functional groups. The ERP system would discriminate between payroll and HR benefits databases. A *security domain* is based on trust between resources or services on a domain that share a single security policy and single management. The trust is the unique context in which a program is operating. The security policy must define the set of objects that each user has the ability to access. Think of a security domain as a concept in which the principle of separation protects each resource and each domain is encapsulated into distinct address spaces.

Security domains (refer to Exhibit 17) examine the establishment of a trust relationship where access control management and administration can be compartmentalized to make distributed management more feasible. Each security domain would have an access control permissions matrix for the resources within that security domain.

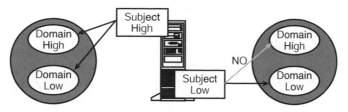

Exhibit 17. Security Domains 1

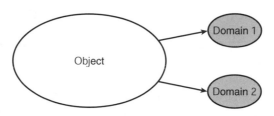

Exhibit 18. Security Domains 2

In a hierarchical domain relationship, subjects can access objects in equal or lower domains, while domains of higher privilege are protected from domains of lower privilege. As shown in Exhibit 18, in an equivalence class of subjects, each domain is encapsulated in a single subject. The domain contains a separate address map to achieve isolation and allows shared objects to map to two or more domains. It is possible to have more than one domain on a server and the subject's domain is the set of objects to which it has access.

Thin Clients. Thin-client systems is one of the new security (and cost-saving) alternatives available for distributed networks. It appears that as thin clients gain in popularity and usage, they may be the next wave. Vendors that specialize in providing thin-client systems have been promoting the use of thin clients for several years and continue to develop the hardware and software capabilities to meet the needs of large network systems.

The idea behind thin-client systems is to centralize the computing power, storage, applications, and data on powerful servers (remember mainframes). Users are provided with an inexpensive client device that is an alternative to desktop personal computers. The client connects to the server through the network to process applications, access files, print, and perform any other network service. Many thin-client systems send and receive only keystroke information rather than actual data; thus, data is not processed on the thin client, but on the servers.

The advantages are many, including providing more security to the system. They include:

- *Lower technology costs.* As technology advances occur, only the servers would need to be replaced.
- *Centralized administration provides a cost-saving benefit.* An example of this type of capability is the Citrix thin-client model. Citrix Independent Computing Architecture (ICA®) and Citrix MetaFrame are two of a number of implementations of this model. (See http://www.citrix.com for more information.)
- *Access controls can be centrally located on the server.* Because the applications reside on the server, the server is then responsible for ensuring only authorized access.
- *Reduced virus infections.* Because the thin client does not have access entry points (i.e., floppy, CD-ROM, or DVD drives), the risk of a virus entering the system is reduced.
- For corporate computing, the advantage of thin-client computing is that an employee can tap into the workplace from any computer — one in a different office, one at home, a kiosk in an airport — without having to worry about synchronizing files between different systems or having a laptop with corporate secrets stolen. Also, administrators have a much easier time managing computers because they have to control a relatively small number of servers while the thin clients require almost no care and feeding (CNET New Com, April 2002).

Scott McNealy (2002) of Sun Microsystems describes thin capabilities as "This is out-of-the-box thinking at its best. Literally out of the box." Although McNealy's focus is on marketing the Sun Ray architecture, he does make a valid point about what thin-client systems provide — "this is computing the way it was meant to be: simple."

The security advantages are similar to those of mainframe environments — because the access points are centrally managed, the client-side vulnerabilities are decreased. Also, because data/information is stored on a central server and not at the client workstation, the potential for more security and reliability (i.e., centralized backup plans) exists.

The downside to thin clients is that users have become accustomed to having powerful workstations at their desktop. They like the control that personal computers provide, such as being able to install software and play music or games.

This technology is also referred to as a class of products known as Network Computers (NCs). An NC is any type of computer with minimal processor power, memory, and disk storage that is designed to connect to a network. The NC relies on the power of a network server, rather than on its own hardware power. In the same line are new hardware technologies that provide a modified thin-client environment. These client machines can be locked to prevent users from physically altering their configuration; however, they are different from true thin clients because they process data locally instead of on the servers.

The next section looks at the access controls available to protect information or data.

Access to Data

Discretionary Access Controls (DACs)

DACs are an access control policy that restricts access to files and other system resources based on the identity and assignment of the user and/or the groups to which the user belongs. DACs are considered a policy-based control. In contrast to Mandatory Access Controls (MACs), where the system controls access, DACs permit resource owners to specify who has access and what privileges other users will have. DACs can be implemented through Access Control Lists (ACLs).

File Structure and DACs

DACs can also be used for the file structure on the storage system. In a tree-structured file system, there are directories and files. DACs can be applied to both. This control allows users to not only specify who has access, but also what type of access others will have. For example, in most systems there are generic types of access to files — none, read, write, execute, delete, change, and full control. Exhibit 19 provides a sample list of available file access permissions.

The important aspect of DACs is resource ownership. For example, in some systems, the user who creates the file is considered the owner of the file. This user is then granted full control over the file, including the ability

Exhibit 19. File Permissions

Access Type	Permissions
No Access or Null	No access permissions are granted
Read (r)	Ability to read a file but not make changes
Write (w)	Ability to write to a file, such as making editing changes
Execute (x)	Ability to execute a program
Delete (d)	Ability to delete a file
Change (c)	Ability to read, write, execute, and delete a file, but not allowed to change the access control permissions
Full Control	All abilities are allowed — read, write, execute, delete, and change the access control permissions

Exhibit 20. Sample Access Control Matrix

	UserMary Directory	UserBob Directory	UserBruce Directory	Printer001
Mary	Full Control	Write	Write	Execute
Bob	Read	Full Control	Write	Execute
Bruce	No Access	Write	Full Control	Execute
Sally	No Access	No Access	No Access	No Access

to set access permissions on the file. If the user is not the owner of the file, the user does not have the ability to set access controls. Some organizations control policies by setting the system administrator as the owner of all files and directories or by limiting full control permissions to only the system administrator. The disadvantage of this option is that the system administrator may have too much control. Thus, a shared level of control may offer more security.

Access Control Matrix

DAC mechanisms are based entirely on the identities of users and objects. This information can be outlined in an access control matrix consisting of rows (users) and columns (objects). Each entry in the matrix represents the access type held by that user to that object. A sample access control matrix is shown in Exhibit 20.

Access Control Lists (ACLs)

ACLs allow any particular user to be allowed or disallowed access to a particular protected object. They work like DACs and access control matrices. The ACL implements the access control matrix by representing the columns as lists of users attached to the protected objects.

Access to ACLs should be protected just as other objects are protected. In addition, the creation of groups must be controlled, since becoming a member of a group can allow access to objects. Also, the possibility of conflicts between groups and individual users must be resolved in the design of the mechanism. The security element can be designed to limit the ability of creating groups to only system security administrators who can monitor the group access level.

ACLs provide an easy method of specifying a list of users who are allowed access to each object. Providing access to defined groups can be done with ACL-based mechanisms for controlling groups and individual users.

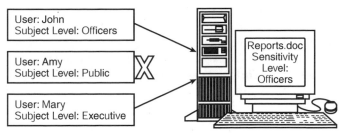

Security Policy:
- Public: has access only to public level
- Officers: has access only to officers and public level
- Executive: has access only to public, officers, and executive

Exhibit 21. MACs

Mandatory Access Controls (MACs)

Mandatory Access Controls (MACs) are an access control policy supported for information systems that process highly sensitive data. MACs are considered a policy-based control. The information system providing MACs must assign sensitivity labels to all system subjects (i.e., users or programs) and all system objects (i.e., files or devices), as shown in Exhibit 21. The definition of the level and degree of security policy is specified in a control document.

For example, the subject (i.e., the user) has a sensitivity level based on a clearance level. A file called "report.doc," which is the object, also has a sensitivity level based on confidentiality requirements. The file's sensitivity level specifies the level of privilege and need-to-know that a user must have to be able to access that file. MACs use sensitivity labels to determine who can access what information. Because MACs are based on an organization's security policies, the system administrator and the owner of the information manage the policies. The system administrator should install the clearance levels and the owner should establish the file sensitivity levels. MACs require that users be authorized to access objects by the object owner, just like in DACs, but additionally must be allowed access by the system in accordance with the labeling.

Access decisions are based on the owner's authorization, the subject's label, the object's label, and the security policy. Based on the security policy in this scenario, if authorized User John with a subject level of officers (or classified — secret) and User Mary with a subject label of executive (or classified — top secret) will have access to the "reports.doc" file with an object label of officers (or classified — secret). User Amy, however, with a subject label of public (or unclassified) will not have access. The important element of MACs is to limit user access so that a user at a lower level cannot access information labeled at a higher level.

The term *system high policy* was once used to indicate that everyone who had access to the system would have authorization and a specific clearance level required by the highest classification of information stored on the system. For example, some government organizations might label information as secret. Thus, all users who had authorized access to a system processing or storing secret information would need a secret clearance level. A multi-level security policy is a policy for processing multiple information classifications at a number of different security levels on the same computer system. This is accomplished by dividing the data and then labeling the data according to its sensitivity level. These types of systems allow users with the highest and lowest clearances to only access the data (objects) with the same or lower sensitivity label. (More information on multi-level security can be found in Chapter 2, "Computer, Systems, and Security Architecture.")

One of the important aspects of a MAC security policy is controlling the import of information from other systems and the export of information to other systems. Because this could create unauthorized access, information systems using MACs have many rules about how information can be imported and exported. This may also include how information is printed, such as specifying the use of printers located in a private or controlled area.

Rule-Based Access Control

In a rule-based system, access is based on a list of rules that determine if authorization should be granted. The rules, created or authorized by system owners, specify the privileges granted to users (i.e., read, write, execute, etc.). The rules have a mediation mechanism that evaluates attributes of both the user and the resource. The mediation mechanism is sometimes called the reference monitor (it is implemented by the security kernel). In a rule-based access control system, the mediation mechanism intercepts every user request to access the resources and refers to the established rules in order to make an access decision.

Role-Based Access Control

In many organizations, access control decisions are based on the user's role as part of the organization. A role-based access control policy bases the access control decisions on the functions that a user is allowed to perform within an organization. The tasks capable of being performed by a given role can be associated with a specific authorization and granted to any user trusted in that role. It requires that common attributes be defined that apply to each task so that a comparison can be made. The attribute can include the time of day, time of week, or any data value that can be detected by the system.

Exhibit 22. Simple Version of a Role-Based Capability Table

Role	Access
Patient	All information for the patient
Doctor	All information for the patient
Medical laboratory	Name, address, clinical data
Administrative staff	Name, address

The determination of membership to a role is not in accordance with discretionary decisions on the part of the system administrator, but rather in compliance with the organization's security access control policy and guidelines implemented by the owner. Also, within the role-based access control policy, the concern is protecting the integrity of the information, essentially who can perform what acts on what information.

An advantage of role-based access controls is the ease of administration. Once the access rules, called transactions, of a role have been established, the system administrator grants and revokes membership to the specified roles. When a new user is added, membership is granted to an existing role and the privileges of that role are inherited. When a user is deleted, membership to all roles is deleted.

Capability Tables

Capability tables are sometimes seen in conjunction with role-based access controls. Within the role-based system is a back-end array of tables that contain protected identifiers that identify the subject and specify the access rights allowed to a subject possessing the capability. It uses an authorization table — a type of access matrix that relates subjects, objects, and rights. The row is a capability list that defines the capabilities that a subject has with respect to all objects in the table. The column is a control list and defines the subjects and their corresponding capabilities relative to a specific object. It supports security by limiting the capabilities to write and/or read objects. An example of a simplified capability table for medical information is shown in Exhibit 22.

Access Controls Typically Associated with Databases

There are several options available for controlling access to databases. First we want to control the connection capabilities that users have through authentication mechanisms. The second involves controlling the transfer or availability of data to the user — that is, what data the user is allowed to access. For example, we can limit the data that is available to the user by controlling the view. A brief description of several access controls for databases is provided in this chapter. However, please refer to the

Application Program Security chapter (Chapter 4) for more information on database security.

Content-Based Access Control

Content-based access controls use knowledge of the context in which the decision is to be made. Key attributes include:

- Utilizes information in object being accessed.
- Provides more access control granularity; in addition to having a label on an object, the contents of the object can be reviewed for access.
- Content of record, such as comparing data within an object against a preset policy.
- Arbiter program controls access, such as a software product that looks for specific types of content (i.e., dictionary word checking).

An example of content-based access controls is a software program that limits certain Web sites on the Internet. For example, organizations can restrict employees from accessing certain Web sites while using company computers. For example, the company would block access to all gambling sites. To assist in this type of access control, the World Wide Web Consortium has published the Platform for Internet Content Selection (PICS). PICS established Internet conventions for label formats and distribution methods. However, it provides neither a labeling vocabulary nor who should pay attention to which labels. It is similar to specifying where on a package a label should appear and in what font, but not what the label should say. Prior to the PICS format, there was no standard format for Web labeling. Thus, organizations that wanted to provide Internet content access controls needed to develop the software and provide the labels. Now, PICS provides a common format for labels, so that any PICS-compliant selection software can process any PICS-compliant label.

Another example of content-based access controls is to check text in emails and/or Web pages against dictionaries of restricted material. The dictionaries are supplied with words and phrases and can be preset or custom designed. The policies may include restricting access to sensitive content, logging access to restricted content, or copying restricted emails to an administrator or information system security officer.

Constrained User Interfaces

The term "user interface" describes the methods and devices used to accommodate interaction between machines and the human beings who use them (i.e., users). Essentially, the user interface communicates information from the machine to the user and from the user to the machine.

Constrained user interfaces restrict the user's access to specific system resources by not allowing them to request the function, information, or access to specific system resources. For example, graphical icons in an application may be grayed to indicate that they are not available for use. Other examples include limiting access to database views available to users, to menus and shells, and the number of options to select.

The next section focuses on how to provide assurances that the defined access control technologies and tools are doing what is needed — essentially, what mechanisms are in place to ensure that access control policies are providing the appropriate access control levels.

3.4 Assurance, Trust, and Confidence Mechanisms

Not only is it important to put access control measures in place, but it is also important to verify whether or not an intruder has breached the access controls. To fully protect an organization, it is necessary to audit the network on a regular basis for intrusion attempts. An intrusion is any set of actions that attempts to compromise the availability, integrity, or confidentiality of the system. To make auditing easier, a new category of software has emerged — Intrusion Detection Systems (IDSs). IDSs are similar to a home burglar alarm — the alarm alerts neighbors, homeowners, or law enforcement officers that someone or something has broken through the security measures. An IDS attempts to detect either an intruder breaking into the system or an authorized user misusing system resources. The IDS operates in the background of the system and sends alert messages when it notices something suspicious.

Misuse intrusions are well-defined attacks on known weak points of a system. They are detected by watching for specific actions being performed on certain objects.

Anomaly intrusions are based on looking for deviations from normal system usage patterns. They are detected by creating a profile, or baseline, of the user being monitored, and detecting significant deviations from this profile.

Intrusion Detection

Intrusion detection techniques attempt to identify and isolate computer and network attacks by observing traffic logs or other audit data. An IDS is based on the idea that an intruder can be detected through the examination of various elements, such as network traffic, packet elements, CPU utilization, I/O utilization, and file activities. These elements or system activities are chronologically organized into audit data. Thus, the audit data refers to the audit records of all activities on a system.

The most common data for an IDS is the audit data. Although it may be possible to manually analyze each record of activity, the vastness of the audit data provided makes a manual analysis impractical. To resolve this, automated intrusion detection systems provide this type of analysis. Automated IDSs examine current audit records of user activity and compare these with profiles of expected activity to infer in real-time if an intrusion is occurring.

There are three basic components of an IDS: a sensor (also called an agent), an analyzer, and a user (security administrator) interface. The sensor collects data and forwards it to an analyzer. The analyzer receives the input from the sensor and determines if an intrusion has been attempted or has occurred. The user interface displays the output from the analyzer to the security administrator.

There are two main types of IDS: network based and host based. The best approach for an IDS is to use both network-based and host-based IDSs. The network-based system can monitor network traffic and the host-based system can review internal audit logs for suspicious activity.

Network-Based IDS (NIDS)

A network-based IDS (NIDS) monitors network traffic on the transmission links in real-time. It is considered a passive device and does not consume the resources of the host network. Passive devices take advantage of "promiscuous mode" access. A promiscuous mode device obtains copies of packets directly from the network transmission media. The system examines the details of the packet payloads before they reach their destination. The system is looking for denial-of-service attacks or malicious code located in the data payloads. The NIDS analyzes the protocols used on the network and other relevant information about the packets. When suspicious activity is noticed, the NIDS is capable of sending alerts and terminating the offending connection. Some IDSs can integrate with a firewall and automatically define new rules to shut out similar types of attacks in the future.

The NIDS requires a dedicated host to operate. A dedicated host is viewed as an advantage to a network-based IDS because no software is installed on production machines. A disadvantage of the NIDS is scalability. As transmission speeds increase, there is more data traffic for the NIDS box to monitor. Thus, to be effective, the NIDS must be capable of supporting increased data transfer rates.

A problem with the NIDS is the increasing use of encryption techniques to protect confidentiality of data packets. When encryption is used, the

NIDS may not be capable of interpreting the data packets and thus might allow unauthorized or suspicious packets to enter the network. Additionally, the data collected by the NIDS should be transmitted through a management network to keep the alerts and other information out of the production environment.

Host-Based IDS (HIDS)

A host-based IDS (HIDS) uses an agent that resides on a single host to detect intrusions. The agent scrutinizes event logs, critical system files, and other auditable resources, looking for unauthorized changes or suspicious patterns of behavior or activity. The HIDS will detect an attack on the host and provide the ability to respond more effectively to an attack. If configured correctly, when something unusual is noticed, some type of alert is immediately given. There are also multi-host IDSs that audit data from multiple hosts. Host-based IDSs consume some of the host's resources.

Several types of analysis engines exist for both the NIDS and the HIDS, such as Statistical-Based, Rule-Based, Signature-Based, and Anomaly-Based. In some systems, the analysis methods are combined to provide higher levels of security.

Analysis Engine Methods

Rule-Based Intrusion Detection

Rule-based intrusion detection systems are based on the premise that intrusion attempts can be characterized by sequences of user activities that lead to compromised system states. Rule-based IDSs are characterized by their expert system properties that create rules to detect system status information or when audit records begin to indicate intrusion attempts.

Two approaches to rule-based IDSs are state based and model based. In a state-based system, the rule base is codified using the terminology found in the audit trails. Intrusion attempts are defined as sequences of system states — as defined by audit trail information — leading from an initial, limited access state to a final compromised state. As data is analyzed, the system makes transitions from one state to another. For example, a user opening a file would change the state of the system. According to Sundaram (1996), there are also a few problems with state transition systems. "First, attack patterns can specify only a sequence of events, rather than more complex forms. Second, there are no general-purpose methods to prune the search except through the assertion primitives. And finally, they cannot detect denial-of-service attacks, failed logins, variations from normal usage, and passive listening — this is because these items are either not recorded by the audit trail mechanism, or they cannot be represented by state transition diagrams."

In a model-based system, known intrusion attempts are modeled as sequences of user behavior. These events can then be modeled as events in an audit trail. Scenarios are inferred by observable activities, and when these activities are monitored, it is possible to discover intrusion attempts by reviewing activities that infer a certain intrusion scenario. For example, if a known DoS attack involves three unique phases and during each phase the attacker sends a packet specific to that DoS attack, the IDS analyzes the first packet and recognizes it is the first phase of the known DoS attack method.

Snort is an example of a rule-based network IDS for Unix systems. Snort is free software available by download and, as such, is considered open source software. It uses a flexible rules language to describe traffic that it should collect or pass, as well as a detection engine that utilizes modular plug-in architecture. Snort claims to perform protocol analysis and content searching/matching, and can be used to detect a variety of attacks and probes, such as buffer overflows, stealth port scans, CGI attacks, SMB probes, OS fingerprinting attempts, and much more. It also has a real-time alerting capability that works with several types of software.

Rule-based IDSs are affected by system hardware and software changes. Thus, if a system is changed, the rule-based IDS must also be changed to reflect such differences. It also requires that security personnel know how various activities can be represented in audit trails.

Statistical-Based/Anomaly-Based Intrusion Detection Systems

A rule-based IDS seeks to identify intrusion attempts by matching audit data with known patterns of intrusive behavior. Because these systems rely on a set of rules of known intrusions, attempts not represented in the set of rules will not be noticed. To overcome this limitation, statistical methods, also called anomaly-based, have been developed to identify audit data that may indicate potential intrusive or abusive behavior. This is known as a statistical-based intrusion detection system. Such IDSs analyze audit trail data by comparing it to typical or predicted profiles in an effort to find potential security breaches. Thus, they attempt to identify suspicious behavior by analyzing audit data for deviations from a predicted norm.

The IDS starts with a generalized set of rules for the system, then learns or adapts to local conditions that would otherwise be viewed as unusual. Expected behavior must be defined in advance by either a manually developed profile or an automatically developed profile. These profiles typically represent sequences of events that can be found in the audit logs. To generate a normal profile, statistical samples of the system are taken over a period of normal operation and use. This data is then used to create metrics of certain system operations such as memory usage, CPU utilization, and network packet traffic. The profiles are subsequently used to define expected behavior. Any sequence of events deviating from the expected profile by a statistically significant amount is flagged as an intrusion attempt. The automatic development of a profile occurs when the software collects characteristics of user behavior over time and forms a statistically valid sample of such behavior. After the initial learning process, the system understands how people interact with the system, and then deviations from this behavior are flagged.

A deviation might include:

- Multiple, failed logon attempts
- Users logging in at strange hours
- Unexplained changes to system clocks
- Unusual error messages
- Unexplained system shutdowns or restarts

An advantage of statistical-based IDSs is that they are able to detect new attacks that might be bypassed by a signature-based system. IDSs can adaptively learn the behavior of the users they monitor and thus are potentially more sensitive to intrusion attempts.

A disadvantage is they tend to produce more data. Anything outside the expected behavior is reported, which means they also tend to report more false-positives as expected behavior patterns change. In addition, an attacker may try to outsmart the IDS by modifying behavior over time and create a new behavior pattern. Once the pattern has been established, the attacker would launch an attack.

An important consideration is to determine an appropriate threshold for significant deviations. If the threshold is set too low, anomalous activities that are intrusions are not flagged. If the threshold is set too high, anomalous activities that are not intrusive are flagged. A second consideration is that this technology requires personnel who are experienced in statistical and IDS techniques to both properly configure the system and monitor the alerts.

Using the combination of signature and anomaly detection systems can provide the capability to detect more diverse intrusion attempts. Also, if configured correctly, the anomaly system could program the new attempt into the signature system's database of attacks.

Signature-Based Intrusion Detection

Signature-based intrusion detection systems, sometimes called "misuse detections," are the most common type of IDS. The signature-based IDS compares data in packet headers with known attack signatures stored in a signature database. It is similar to anti-virus software in that the vendor produces a list of patterns that it believes could be suspicious or indicative of an attack. Note that all forms of IDS have a corresponding form of anti-virus — signature-based IDSs are similar to signature scanners, rule-based IDSs are similar to activity monitors, and anomaly-based IDSs are similar to change detection.

The system scans the network, looking for a match to the known patterns. The system must be programmed to interpret a certain series of packets, or data contained within the packets, as an intrusion attempt. The programming consists of models of attacks that are based on past intrusions and the system tries to recognize the "signature" of these attacks.

A disadvantage is that signature-based IDSs assume that the attack signature is known and is programmed into the database. This leaves the system vulnerable to new types of attacks. However, it is much easier to configure a signature-based IDS than an anomaly-based IDS. The anomaly detection system requires more data collection, analysis, and updating to create the system profiles.

Intrusion Response

Intrusion detection and intrusion response systems have traditionally been thought of as separate entities. However, as technologies continue to evolve, the differences between the two have started to merge into a single system that provides both capabilities.

Responses to intrusion attempts include:

- Dropping suspicious data packets at the firewall
- Denying user access to resources if they display suspicious behavior
- Reporting the activity to other hosts of sites involved in the intrusion attempt
- Updating configurations within the IDS

Intrusion Alarms and Signals

Through some type of user interface, an IDS will alert the system manager or information system security officer of intrusion attempts. The alert mechanism might be an instant message appearing on a workstation or server screen, an email message, a pager message, or some type of audible message. The type of alert depends on the capabilities of the IDS software vendor product. Events that require immediate administrator or security officer intervention need to be given the highest priority and should be designated as alerts. Most IDS mechanisms provide some form of alerting capability for specified events.

For the IDS to be effective, a technically knowledgeable person must be employed to select, install, configure, operate, and maintain the IDS. A trained analyst is needed to keep the system updated with new signature attacks and also to evaluate expected behavior profiles. This is considered to be a candidate for outsourcing because of the manpower requirements.

A new concern of IDSs is that the systems are also vulnerable to attacks. Intruders who realize that an IDS has been implemented will first try to disable the IDS by providing false information or trying to overload the system. These types of events may distract the IDS observer while the real attack occurs.

Audit Trail Monitoring

An audit trail is a record of system activities. To create an audit trail, the system must be configured to capture and record various kinds of system activity. Collecting data generated by system, network, application, and user activities is essential for reviewing and analyzing the security of the information system. System events are activities generated on behalf of the operating system or applications operating on the system. User events are generated by user interactions, such as logging on to the network.

The audit trail data can be used to examine the sequence of events that occurred on the network, such as reviewing the audit trails to detect computer intrusions and misuse.

There is no standard format for audit data; thus, each system has its own methodology for format and content. However, the system administrator or information system security officer should identify the logging mechanism available, such as system access, file access, process access, or application access. In some organizations it is necessary to supplement an operating system's or application's auditing capabilities with specialized auditing software that watches for signs of intrusions or misuse, such as previously noted intrusion detection systems (IDSs). If properly configured and monitored, audit trails can:

- Alert management and administrative staff to suspicious activity that may require further investigation
- Provide details on the extent of an intruder's activity
- Provide information required for legal proceedings

One example of the use of audit trails is the creation of violation reports. Violation reports identify activities that may portend a breach or attempted breach of the system access controls. An example is numerous attempts at logging into a secured system trying different passwords. The violation reports present significant, security-oriented events that may indicate either actual or attempted policy deviations reflected in an audit trail. Information system security officers should review the violation reports on a frequent basis to identify unauthorized access attempts.

Auditing events include:

- Monitoring and identifying system resource use
- Monitoring and analyzing network traffic and connections
- Monitoring and identifying user account and file access
- Scanning for malicious code, such as viruses
- Verifying file and data integrity
- Probing for system and network vulnerabilities

Type of Events Recorded

- Internet connection event data
  - Username
  - Host name
  - Source and destination IP address
  - Source and destination port numbers
  - Timestamp
- System-level event data
  - Logon attempts (successful and unsuccessful)
  - Logon ID
  - Date and time of each logon and logoff
  - Devices used
  - Functions performed
- Application-level event data
  - Data files opened/closed
  - Specific actions (read, edit, delete, print)
  - Record modification
  - Denied access
- User-level event data
  - User-initiated commands
  - Identification/authentication attempts
  - Files and resources accessed

Another element of audit trails is the ability to hold individuals accountable for their actions on the network. Operating systems offering auditing capabilities will allow all objects on the system to be configured for auditing purposes, such as successful or failed access attempts. This type of auditing trail can be helpful in resolving incidents that occur from insiders. For example, if the president of an organization awoke to see newspaper headlines announcing the results of the year-end tax reports, which was two days ahead of their official release, the security officer could use the audit data to help identify who had access to the file. The audit data will reveal that a specific user accessed the file, the time of access, and the type of access.

Just as important as it is to configure the auditing capabilities correctly, it is equally important to let users know that the system is being monitored. Regardless of the work environment (not to mention legal reasons), users must be notified that the activities they perform on the system are subject to auditing and monitoring. A common method of notifying users is to display a banner message immediately before the user completes the login process. In the scenario of an insider leaking sensitive information, the audit data might reveal who could be responsible; and if there is a monitoring warning, the data could be presented in a criminal case (refer to the chapter on Law, Investigations and Ethics [Chapter 10] for more details).

Another type of monitoring is recording all keystroke activity by users. Keystroke monitoring can be performed on a specific sequence of keystrokes, such as inputting a password, or can be conducted on all keystroke activity. Because many people are sensitive to this type of monitoring, an organization wishing to implement keystroke monitoring should follow a few guidelines: it must (1) be based on an organizational information security policy, (2) be well communicated, and (3) must apply to all employees in the organization. These actions legitimize its use.

An issue with audit trails is the volume of data that is collected. Depending on how the audit system is configured and the number of users on the system, thousands (and even tens of thousands) of system events will be captured and recorded in the audit log. The audit logs may well exceed the administrative time and skills available to review and investigate events that seem suspicious. Therefore, it may be necessary to use some type of event filtering or "clipping level" to properly determine the amount of log detail captured. Clipping levels are established by first producing a baseline of normal user mistake activity or expected "fat finger" behavior on the system. Anything that occurs beyond the baseline would be considered worth reviewing in more detail.

It is important that procedures are established in advance and that personnel are trained in what log events are pertinent. There are automated tools that can help reduce the audit logs to a manageable size for finding suspicious activity. This process is sometimes referred to as selective auditing.

Because auditing data could expose intrusion attempts or misuse, it is common for an unauthorized user to either disable the auditing or clear/delete the audit logs. To counter this, control mechanisms should be in place that allow only authorized system administrators or security officers to read, print, or delete the audit log files. In addition, the storage location of audit logs should also be protected. If the storage location is on the system via an electronic file, some type of encryption would be prudent. Although encryption would not keep the audit log from being deleted, it would provide confidentiality for the data. If the logs are stored on tapes or disks, the media should be in a secure container, such as a locking file cabinet. Storing audit data on CD-ROMs is an effective way of preventing them from being changed. Also, the audit trail data should be protected at the most sensitive system level.

The next section looks at the managerial responsibilities to access controls.

3.5 Information Protection and Management Services

Security function activity for access control includes:

- *Developing security policies, procedures, and guidelines.* Appropriate access control policies, procedures, baselines, standards, and guidelines are essential to an effective information system security program. The policies must reflect the organizational culture regarding the protecting of the system resources, including all data processed and stored. Procedures should include how to purchase, process, store, and dispose of media and equipment and should apply to all internal and external personnel whether they are employees, partners, contractors, or suppliers.
- *Personnel controls.* Such controls should indicate how employees are expected to interact and follow the security controls, such as:
  - *Separation of duties.* This is the process of separating processes into specific tasks and having different employees responsible for different tasks. This can prevent one individual from having total control of the process and circumventing security practices without being in collusion with others.
  - *Rotation of duties.* This is useful in breaking up collusion and reaffirming authorizations.
  - *Collusion.* More than one person in collaboration with another commit a fraudulent act.
  - *Procedures for recruiting and terminating employees.* During recruiting, depending on the sensitivity level of the information being processed and stored on the system, a thorough background check should be conducted. During termination, all authorizations that have been granted to an employee must be disabled or deleted upon departure or when the assigned job function changes. All keys, badges, and other devices used to gain access to premises, information, or any other resource must be retrieved from the employee and disabled. User accounts on the system should immediately be disabled or deleted to prevent any further access to the system resources; shared administrative passwords should be changed. This includes all voice and data services, such as voice mail and PBX access codes.
- *Security awareness and training.* This is a measure that helps end users understand their role in protecting the information system

resources. For example, users should be aware of how to create good passwords and properly protect their passwords. Security awareness programs are intended to change employee attitudes toward the need for information security.

- *Testing of access controls.* An essential role of management is to ensure that all access controls and mechanisms are tested on a periodic basis to ensure they are working properly and meet the security policy, goals, and objectives. A type of testing is penetration testing to assess the weaknesses within the system.

Penetration Testing

Penetration testing is the process of simulating an attack on an information system at the request of the owner, or at least with the owner's permission. A penetration team is an organized group of people who attempt to penetrate the security of an information system. The goal is to assess the security of the system and find the vulnerabilities or security gaps in the security measures of the organization.

Penetration tests are typically aimed at environments prevalent in most organizations, including Internet, intranet, extranet, or remote dial-in connections. The penetration team will use several methods, based on the environment, to attack the system.

A zero-knowledge attack is one that is performed by a team that has no relevant information about the target environment. It is designed to provide the most realistic external penetration test. It usually includes gathering a significant amount of information about the target system before launching an attack. Typically, an independent third party performs this type of test because internal system and security personnel are too knowledgeable about their own system. A full-knowledge attack is one that is performed by a team that has intimate knowledge of the target environment. In this type of attack (an internal penetration test), all the security information related to an environment is considered when formulating the attack methods.

The penetration test must have clearly defined methodologies and goals. For the most useful results, the team should use the same methodology or techniques that an adversary would use as well as the same level of known information.

A generic method of penetration testing is discovery, enumeration, vulnerability mapping, and exploitation. During the first step (i.e., discovery), information about the target system is identified and documented. The second step, enumeration, attempts to gain more information about the target, but this time the penetration team will use more intrusive methods. Additional information is recorded by trying to connect to network resources. Vulnerability mapping is one of the most important steps in the process. The team maps the profile of the environment to known vulnerabilities. For example, if the system is operating the Microsoft Internet Information Server (IIS), the team will map a known vulnerability to the relevant hardware or software component. The final step, exploitation, involves actually attempting to gain access through vulnerabilities identified in the vulnerability-mapping phase. Usually, the goal is to gain user-level and privileged (administrator) access to the system.

In addition to finding holes in the security measures, a penetration test can be initiated to test an intrusion detection system and intrusion response capability. It can provide information on whether anyone is monitoring the system or the audit logs. It can also provide a good indication of how suspicious activity is reported.

Following the simulated attack, the penetration team prepares a report for the owner of the system, outlining the vulnerabilities and suggesting countermeasures. It is then the system owner's responsibility to implement the appropriate additional security controls based on a cost/benefit analysis.

Summary

When deciding on an access control strategy, it is important to balance the goals of the organization's access control policy with the technical mechanisms. This includes reviewing the legal requirements necessary to protect access, conducting a risk analysis that identifies the typical threats to the system, reviewing accepted industry practices, identifying users who need access and what type of access they need, and identifying the sensitivity of the information stored and processed on the system. After answering these questions, it is possible to plan for a combination of access controls necessary to meet the security goals.

3.6 Common Body of Knowledge (CBK)

The current CBK for the Access Control Domain is listed below to assist in determining topics for further review. Although this Study Guide is very detailed in many areas, it is not possible to thoroughly discuss every CBK topic in a single book; therefore, additional study of items may be advisable.

The professional should fully understand the following:

- *Accountability.* Understand the importance of accountability in order to hold individuals responsible for their actions.

- *Identification and authentication.* Understand the methods for identification and authentication (knowledge based, token based, and characteristic based).
- *Passwords.* Understand effective password management.
- *Access control techniques.* Understand the following access control techniques:
  - Discretionary Access Control (DAC)
  - Mandatory Access Control (MAC)
- *Access control administration.* Understand the following access control administration concepts:
  - The process that grants users, programs, and processes the right to access information, to include files and directories
  - The process used to identify a user, program, or process and validate the claimed identity
  - Account administration (opening, closing, transfers, suspensions, temporary accounts, etc.)
  - Account, log, journal monitoring, and audit in a timely manner
  - Access control concepts and methodologies and their enterprise-wide implementation in a centralized and decentralized environment
  - Access control preventive, detective, and corrective technologies used to minimize or avoid risks, exposures, and vulnerabilities
  - Mechanisms for directing or restraining influence over the behavior, use, and content of the system for availability, integrity, and confidentiality
- *Rule of least privilege.* Understand the importance of this rule in the technical and procedural design of systems.
- *Intrusion detection.* Understand the types of intrusions and tools available on the various computing platforms, operating systems, and specific security software used for anomaly and attack signature identification.
- *Attack methods.* Understand the following attack methods: brute force, denial-of-service, password dictionary attacks, and spoofing.

Components

- Access Controls
- Access Control techniques
- Discretionary Access Control and Mandatory Access Control
- Lattice-Based Access Control, Rule-Based Access Control, Role-Based Access Control, Access Control Lists
- Rule of Least Privilege
- Segregation of Duties and Responsibilities

- Single Sign-On (SSO)
- Access Control administration
- Access Control Models: Bell-LaPadula, Biba, Clark-Wilson, Non-interference Model, State Machine Model, Access Matrix Model, Information Flow Model
- Access Rights and Permissions: Establishment, Maintenance, Revocation, Accountability
- Identification and Authentication techniques
- Knowledge-based (passwords, personal identification numbers [PINs], phrases)
- Characteristic-based access controls (biometrics, behavior)
- Tickets
- One-time passwords
- Token-based (smart card, key card)
- Administrative
- Passwords: Selection, Management, Control
- Centralized/Remote Authentication Access Controls: RADIUS, TACACS
- Decentralized Access Control
- Domains
- Trust
- File and Data Ownership and Custodianship
- Methods of Attack: brute force, denial-of-service, password dictionary attacks, spoofing
- Monitoring and Intrusion Detection
- Types of intrusions
- Intrusion prevention (identification, authentication)
- Intrusion detection (data extraction, sampling, recognition, traffic)
- Attack Signature Identification
- Intrusion reactive response, alarms, signals
- Anomaly identification
- Audit trails
- Violation reports
- Corrections
- Penetration testing

Examples

- Compare and contrast principles of access control.
- Compare and contrast responsibilities of users, data owners, and custodians.
- Identify the role of biometrics in access control.
- Identify and define the confidentiality/integrity/availability triad as relating to access control.
- Identify preventive physical access controls.

- Identify preventive administrative access controls.
- Define privacy issues in regard to access control.
- Identify electronic radiation vulnerabilities and countermeasures.
- Compare and contrast the types of biometric identification methods.
- Distinguish between passwords and passphrases.
- Define password management techniques.
- Define Single Sign-On.
- Compare and contrast centralized access control methodologies with decentralized/distributed access control methodologies.
- Identify the two application-independent integrity rules.
- Compare and contrast mandatory and discretionary access control.
- Compare and contrast access control technologies.
- Define methodologies of access control monitoring.
- Compare and contrast the various intrusion detection methodologies.
- Define the concept of penetration testing.
- Describe methods of penetration testing.
- Identify the steps of penetration testing.
- Describe various attack methods.

3.7 Sample Questions for the CISSP Exam

1. Two types of covert channels are storage based or:
   a. Accidental
   b. Timing
   c. Cooperative
   d. Malicious
2. Data remanence is:
   a. When residual data remains on a storage medium following degaussing
   b. The permanence of the data resisting accidental deletion
   c. Data that exceeds the boundaries of its memory buffers
   d. The process of overwriting data
3. Internal intruders are NOT usually defined as:
   a. Authorized users exceeding their authority
   b. Persons who have defeated the physical access controls of a facility
   c. Employees gaining access to controlled areas
   d. Users who access unintended areas of the network
4. How might an attacker with little systems experience gain privileged systems access?
   a. Dictionary attack
   b. Brute force attack
   c. Birthday attack
   d. Shoulder-surfing attack

5. Which of the following is not a characteristic of a virus?
   a. Its primary effect is to consume system resources.
   b. It may or may not carry a malicious payload.
   c. It spreads through user action.
   d. It attaches itself to executable code.

6. Requiring approval before granting system access would be:
   a. A physical control
   b. A logical control
   c. A compensating control
   d. An administrative control

7. Granting of access privileges to certain files is:
   a. Authentication
   b. Identification
   c. Authorization
   d. Accountability

8. What is the best method of reducing a brute-force denial-of-service (DoS) attack against a password file?
   a. Setting a higher clipping level
   b. Locking out a user for a set time period
   c. Establishing a lockout that requires administrator intervention
   d. Using a stronger cryptographic algorithm

9. Which of the following is a characteristic of a synchronous token?
   a. Challenge–response based
   b. Counter based
   c. Random number based
   d. Nonce based

10. Which of the following is NOT a common attack performed against smart cards?
    a. Etching
    b. Microprobing
    c. Fault generation
    d. Eavesdropping

11. Important elements in choosing a biometric system include all of the following EXCEPT:
    a. User acceptance
    b. Accuracy
    c. Productivity
    d. Processing speed

12. TACACS+ has a "watchdog" function to prevent what kind of attacks?
    a. Synchronous
    b. Side channel
    c. Fault
    d. TOC/TOU

13. What is a security benefit related to thin-client architecture?
    a. Reduced total cost of ownership of desktops

    b. Standardized access control

    c. Easier training for users

    d. Wider availability of applications

14. Discretionary access control (DAC) involves:

    a. Review of the classification of the object

    b. The data owner granting permission to access a file

    c. The system authorizing access based on labels

    d. Sensitive programs only running during specific time periods

15. Mandatory access control (MAC) requires all of the following EXCEPT:

    a. Data owner's permission

    b. Enforcement of security policy

    c. Sensitivity labels on all critical files

    d. Need-to-know authorization

16. What is the most secure method for controlling privileged access to a system available for use in a public area?

    a. Mandatory Access Control (MAC)

    b. Role-Based Access Control (RBAC)

    c. Database Views

    d. Constrained User Interfaces

17. What is NOT a basic component of an IDS?

    a. Analyzer

    b. Notifier

    c. Sensor

    d. User interface

18. What does a host-based IDS use for analysis?

    a. Audit logs

    b. Traffic patterns

    c. Packet structure

    d. Promiscuous mode

19. An IDS does NOT use which of the following techniques for detecting intrusions?

    a. Model based

    b. Statistical based

    c. Authorization based

    d. State based

20. Audit logs should record all of the following EXCEPT:

    a. Successful access attempts

    b. System performance measurements

    c. Failed access attempts

    d. Changes to user permissions

21. Clipping levels help prevent:

    a. Unnecessary investigation by administrators

    b. Denial-of-service attacks

    c. Unauthorized users from logging on

    d. "Fat finger" attacks
22. Audit logs should be protected for all of the reasons below EXCEPT:
    a. Modification may impede an investigation.
    b. An attacker may try to alter them.
    c. Audit logs may contain confidential information.
    d. Standard format is critical for automated processing.
23. A penetration test is not designed to:
    a. Find vulnerabilities in a network
    b. Test incident response capabilities
    c. Alter system access permissions
    d. Exploit social engineering opportunities

References

Allen, Julia, Alan Christie, William Fithen, John McHugh, Jed Pickel, and Ed Stoner, 2000. "State of the Practice of Intrusion Detection Technologies." Technical Report, CMU/SEI-00, TR-028, ESC-99-028.

Carrington, Robert, Karen A. Moore, and John Richardson, September 2002. "Smart Pipe Integral Communication, Damage, Detection, and Multiple Sensor Application in Pipelines." Idaho National Engineering and Environmental Laboratory. http://www.netl.doe.gov/publications/proceedings/02/naturalgas/.

Denning, Dorothy, 1999. *Information Warfare and Security.* ACM Press, New York.

Ferraiolo, David and Richard Kuhn, 1995. "Role-Based Access Control." National Institute of Standards and Technology (NIST). Web site: http://hissa.nist.gov/rbac/paper/rbac1.html.

Flexner, Stuart Bert, 1988. *I Hear America Talking: An Illustrated History of American Words and Phrases.* Simon & Schuster: New York.

Ilgun, Koral, 1993. "USTAT: A Real-Time Intrusion Detection System for UNIX," pp. 16–28. *Proceedings of the 1993 Computer Society Symposium on Research in Security and Privacy.* Oakland, California, May 24–26, 1993. IEEE Computer Society Press, Los Alamitos, CA.

Kaeo, Merike, 1999. *Designing Network Security.* Cisco Press, Indianapolis.

Kaommerling, O. and M.G. Kuhn, 1999. "Design Principles for Tamper-Resistant Smartcard Processors." *Proceedings of the USENIX Workshop on Smartcard Technology Smartcard '99,* pp. 9–20, Chicago, Illinois, 1999. Available online at: http://www.usenix.org/publications/library/proceedings/smartcard99/full_papers/kommerling/kommerling.pdf.

Karppinen, Lauri, 2000. "Attacks Related to the Smart Card Used in Electronic Payment and Cash Cards." *Proceedings of the Helsinki University of Technology "Seminar on Network Security Fall 2000."* Article is available online at: http://www.tcm.hut.fi/Opinnot/Tik110.501/2000/papers/karppinen.pdf.

Leo, Ross, 2001. "Single Sign-On," in the *Information Security Management Handbook,* Harold Tipton and Micki Krause, Editors. Auerbach Publications and CRC Press, Boca Raton, FL.

McGraw, Gary and John Viega, September 2000. "Protecting Passwords: Part 2," on the Web site: http://www-106.ibm.com/developerworks/library/pass2/index.html.

McNealy, Scott (2002). Think Outside the Box. Available at http://www.sun.com/executives/perspectives/think-outside.html.

National Computer Security Center, 1987. "A Guide to Understanding Discretionary Access Controls in Trusted Systems." Rainbow Series #NCSC-TG-003. Web site: www.radium.ncsc.mil/tpep/library/rainbow/NCSC-TG-003.html.

Pipkin, Donald, 2000. *Information Security, Protecting the Global Enterprise.* Prentice Hall, Englewood Cliffs, NJ.

Ptacek, Thomas H. and Timothy N. Newsham, 1998. "Insertion, Evasion, and Denial of Service: Eluding Network Intrusion Detection. " Web site: http://secinf.net/info/ids/idspaper/idspaper.html.

Richards, Donald R. 2000. "Biometric Identification," in the *Information Security Management Handbook*, Harold Tipton and Micki Krause, Editors. Auerbach Publications and CRC Press, Boca Raton, FL.

Sandhu, Ravi S. "Lattice-Based Access Control Models." *IEEE Computer,* 26(11), 9–19, November 1998.

Shankland, Stephen (2002). Sun keeps plugging at thin clients. CNET News Com: Available at http://news.com.com/2100-1001_3-881467.html?tag=mainstry.

Skorobogatov, Sergei and Ross Anderson (2002). Optical Fault Induction Attacks. University of Cambridge, Computer Laboratories. Available by download from: http://www.ftp.cl.cam.ac.uk/ftp/users/rja14/faultpap3.pdf.

Smith, Richard E., 2002. *Authentication: From Passwords to Public Keys*. Addison-Wesley, Upper Saddle Creek, NJ.

Stackpole, Bill, 2001. "Centralized Authentication Services (RADIUS, TACACS, DIAMETER)," in the *Information Security Management Handbook*, Harold Tipton and Micki Krause, Editors. Auerbach Publications and CRC Press, Boca Raton, FL.

Sundaram, Aurobindo, 1996. "An Introduction to Intrusion Detection. ACM Crossroads." http://www.acm.org/crossroads/xrds2-4/intrus.html.

Tipton, Harold. "Access Control Principles and Objectives: Types of Information Security Controls," in the *Information Security Management Handbook,* Harold Tipton and Micki Krause, Editors. Auerbach Publications and CRC Press, Boca Raton, FL.

Vacca, John, 2000. "Single Sign-On for the Enterprise," in the *Information Security Management Handbook,* Harold Tipton and Micki Krause, Editors. Auerbach Publications and CRC Press, Boca Raton, FL.

Web Sites

The Diceware Passphrase home page: http://www.diceware.com.

The official SESAME home page: www.cosic.esat.luleuven.ac.be/sesame/.

http://www.eskimo.com/~joelm/tempest.html for information on emanations.

http://razor.bindview for information on system vulnerabilities and threats.

http://www.cert.org/advisories/CA-1998-01.html for information on system vulnerabilities and threats.

http://www.computereconomics.com/cei/press/pr92101.html. Michael Erbschloe, vice president of research at Computer Economics and author of *Information Warfare: How to Survive Cyber Attacks*. For information on "2001 Economic Impact of Malicious Code Attacks."

http://www.symantec.com/securitycheck/maliciouscode.html for information on malicious code.

http://www.dell.com/us/en/gen/topics/power_ps1q02-lowery.htm for information on attacks.

http://larch-www.lcs.mit.edu:8001/corbato for information on Professor Fernando Corbato.

http://www.proximalconsulting.com/WhitePapers/WhitePaper5.htm for information on Vladimir Levin and the Citibank attack (also discovery.com — most well known hackers).

http://news.com.com/2100-1001-881467.html for article, "Sun Keeps Plugging at Thin Clients" by Stephen Shankland, April 11, 2002.

http://www.gemplus.com/companyinfo/press/2002/security/smart_card_security.html — response to smart card attacks.

http://www.snort.org for information on Snort IDS.

http://www.atstake.com for further information on LC4 and LOphtCrack.

Chapter 4

Applications and Systems Development

Introduction

This chapter addresses the important security concepts that apply during the software development, operation, and maintenance processes. Software is defined to include both operating system software (the software that manages the operations of a computer system) and application software (the software that provides functionality for the user, such as word processing programs and games). In the Computer, Systems, and Security Architecture chapter (Chapter 2), the focus was on how the operating system interacts with and controls the hardware and software components.

In Chapter 2, it was recommended that the platform environment be based on a layered approach, beginning with the end user at the top. The user interacts with data and the network resources through applications (see Exhibit 1). The applications sit on top of the utilities and operating system. The operating system provides management of the computer hardware resources. In this chapter, the focus is on the software, primarily for applications that users use to do their jobs and interact with the operating system. While some of the fundamental concepts of application development also apply to operating system software development, most users purchase an existing (commercial off-the-shelf) operating system. Thus, general users do not usually develop operating system code; however, they do design, develop, operate, and maintain proprietary applications relevant to their business needs.

It is a well-known fact in computer security that security problems are very often a direct result of software bugs. That leads security researchers to pay lots of attention to software engineering. The hope is to avoid the ever-present penetrate-and-patch approach to security by developing more secure code in the first place.

—McGraw and Felton, 1999

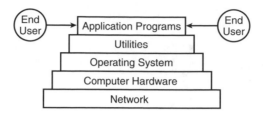

Exhibit 1. Applications

Operating system and application software consists of relatively complex computer programs. Without this software it would be impossible to operate the computer. In the early days of computers, users (programmers) had to write code for each instruction (action to be undertaken by the computer) using a machine language (i.e., languages understandable by the computer). This was a difficult and cumbersome task, so programmers began to write sets of code that would implement many of the more common instructions. Soon, new languages were developed that permitted programmers to write computer programs in a format that more closely resembled English.

The CISSP should know:

- The knowledge, practices, and principles for securing systems and applications during the processes known as lifecycle management
- The security controls to be included in the systems development process, application controls, change and configuration control, data warehousing, data mining, knowledge-based systems, program interfaces, and the concepts used to ensure software and overall system availability, integrity, and confidentiality
- The principles related to designing secure information system software
- That security is a system level attribute
- The various types of malicious code and how malicious code can be introduced into the computing environment, and the tools and techniques that can be used to prevent, detect, and correct malicious code attacks

It should be noted that the CISSP is not required to be an expert programmer or know the inner workings of the developing application software code, like C++ or how to develop Web code using Java. Because the CISSP may be the person responsible for ensuring that security is included in such developments, the CISSP should know the basic procedures and concepts involved during the design and development of software programming. That is, for the CISSP to "manage" the software development process and verify that security is included, he or she must understand the fundamental concepts of programming developments and the security strengths and weaknesses of various application development processes.

Throughout this chapter, insight is provided into the security-related problems that can (and do) occur during the design and development of computer software. The environment where software is designed and developed is outlined, and the critical role that software plays in providing security for the system is explained. This chapter begins by outlining software protection requirements. The second section focuses on the software environment, such as the role software plays in the functioning of the computer. The security technology and tools section looks at various protection mechanisms that can be used to overcome the threats and vulnerabilities to software, such as using a Systems Development Life Cycle (SDLC) methodology. It also outlines some of the core programming languages used to develop software. The section entitled Assurance, Trust, and Confidence Mechanisms provides information on how to make sure appropriate software protection mechanisms are implemented and operating properly. The final section briefly discusses the role that security management plays in software design, development, implementation, operation, and maintenance. Also, throughout this chapter, the many issues of designing and implementing secure databases are also discussed.

4.1 Information Protection Requirements

The A-I-C Triad

The security of data and information is one of the most important elements of information system security. Through hardware and software mechanisms, we process and access the data on the system. Thus, it is important for organizations to make an effort to prevent unauthorized access and to protect the system from harm. The objective is to make sure that the system and its resources are available when needed, that the integrity of the processing of the data and the data itself is ensured, and that the confidentiality of the data is protected.

Application development procedures are absolutely vital to the integrity of systems. If applications are not developed properly, data may be processed in such a way that the integrity of the data is corrupted. In addition, the integrity of the application software itself must be maintained, both in terms of change control and in terms of attack from malicious software such as viruses. Also, if confidentiality is required for data, encryption mechanisms should be built into the programming code from the beginning, and not added on as an afterthought.

Information systems are becoming more distributed and open, with a substantial increase in the sharing of resources. Increased sharing requires that all resources be protected against unauthorized access. Many of these safeguards are provided through software controls, especially operating system mechanisms. Therefore, the operating system must offer controls that protect the computer's resources. In addition, the relationship between applications and the operating system is important. Controls must be included in operating systems so that applications cannot damage or circumvent the operating system controls. If there is a lack of application software protection mechanisms, the operating system and critical computer resources can be open to corruption and attack.

Some of the main security requirements for applications and databases are to ensure that only valid, authorized, and authenticated users can access the data; permissions related to use of the data are controlled; the software provides some type of granularity for controlling the permissions; encryption is available for protecting sensitive information such as password storage; and audit trails can be implemented and reviewed.

Essentially, security requirements in operating systems, applications, and databases focus on the ability of the software to enforce controls over the storage and transfer of information in and between objects. Remember that the underlying foundation of the software security controls is the organization's security policy. The security policy reflects the security requirements of the organization. Therefore, if the security policy requires that only one set of users can access information, then the software must have the capability to limit access to that specific group of users. Keep in mind that the ability to refer to a system as secure is based upon the reliable enforcement of the organization's security policy.

4.2 Information Protection Environment

The environment in which software operates is fundamental to computer operations. This environment begins with the hardware resources, such as the central processing unit (CPU), memory, input/output (I/O) requests, and storage devices. The operating system is responsible for controlling these resources and providing security mechanisms to protect them. The applications employed by the end users make requests or calls to the operating system to provide the required computer services. In some applications, there are security features built into the software that allow the users more control over their information, such as access controls or auditing capabilities. There are also vulnerabilities that can be introduced in the application, such as when a buffer overflow attack takes advantage of improper parameter checking within the application.

Open Source Code and Closed Source Code

Before we begin the discussion on the software environment, a distinction should be made between open source and closed source software. *Open source* is when the vendor releases the software source code so that others can comment or assist in debugging the code. *Closed source* is when the vendor conceals the source code and releases an executable version in machine code. Keep in mind that although there is a trend toward "open source," most software companies still keep their source code secret.

The term "security by obscurity" was originally coined to refer to the idea that if the code is released in compiled form, it will stay secret. Essentially, the threat of hackers or unintentional accidents could be avoided because the source code is not available for review. Although this may sound good, the concept is a fallacy — hackers, through observation, trial-and-error, and simply luck may be able to find security vulnerabilities.

Many advocates of open source software believe that security can be improved when source code is available to the public. The "many eyeballs" phenomenon lets other developers/programmers review the code and help find the security vulnerabilities. The idea is that this openness leads to quick identification and repair of the problem. The risk in this theory is whether others will be able to find all of the security vulnerabilities. Just releasing the source code does not ensure that all security bugs will be found, which can then lead to a false sense of security. Another security issue concerns the honesty of those reviewing the open source code. What would happen if a black-hat hacker/developer found a security vulnerability but did not disclose the problem? In recent years, there have been notable instances of black-hat hackers discovering security vulnerabilities and then attempting to blackmail software vendors. On the opposite side are the software developers and white-hat hackers who believe in "full disclosure." Full disclosure means that individuals who find security vulnerabilities will publicly disseminate the information in an effort to help organizations patch the risk. In most cases, they first try to contact the vendor of the software and ask that the vulnerability and a subsequent fix be released to the public.

Instead of trying to decide whether to purchase (or design) open source or closed source software, for security purposes it is better to look at how the software was designed. The essential question is whether security was part of the design process. Was security thought of when the developers chose the programming language, designed the features, programmed the features, and tested and evaluated the features?

Software Environment

Threats to the Software Environment

The threats to software during design, development, and operation include the following:

Buffer Overflow. The buffer overflow problem is one of the oldest and most common problems to software. It results when a program fills up its buffer of memory with more data than the buffer can hold. When the program begins to write beyond the end of the buffer, the program's execution path can be changed. This can lead to the insertion of malicious code that can be used to destroy data or to gain administrative privileges on the program or machine.

The following is a generic example of how a buffer overflow works:

- A program that is the target of an attack is provided with more data than the application was intended or expected to handle.
- The attacked program (target) overruns the memory allocated for input data, and writes the excess data into the system memory.
- The excess data can contain machine language instructions so that when the next step is executed, the attack code, like a Trojan horse or other type of malicious code, is run.

An actual attack method is far more detailed and is highly dependent on the target operating system and hardware architecture. In most buffer overflows, the desired result is to put attack instructions into memory. These instructions usually do something malicious such as patch the kernel in such a way as to execute another program at an elevated privilege level or disable the program.

Citizen Programmers. This is a common practice that can have extremely harmful consequences and may violate the principle of separation of duties. If this type of unsupervised programming is allowed, then a single user may have complete control over an application or process. It can occur when general users are allowed access to programming languages in order to modify the software program. Visual Basic, included in the Microsoft Office suite, is often used by citizen programmers to develop their applications or extend existing ones. Citizen programmers are unlikely to be trained in, or bound by, system development practices that involve proper application design, change control, and support for the application. Therefore, application development in such a manner is likely to be chaotic and lack any form of assurance in regard to security. It is discussed in more detail in the Information Security Management chapter (Chapter 1).

Covert Channel. A covert channel or confinement problem is an information flow issue. It is a communication channel allowing two cooperating processes to transfer information in such a way that it violates the system's security policy. Although there are protection mechanisms in place, if unauthorized information can be transferred using a signaling mechanism or other objects, then a covert channel may exist. In simplified terms, it is any flow of information — intentional or inadvertent — that enables an observer not authorized to have the information to infer what it is or that it exists. This is primarily a concern in systems containing highly sensitive information.

There are two commonly defined types of covert channels: storage and timing. A *covert storage channel* involves the direct or indirect reading of a storage location by one process and a direct or indirect reading of the same storage location by another process. Typically, a covert storage channel involves a finite resource, such as a sector on a disk that is shared by two subjects at different security levels.

A *covert timing channel* depends upon being able to influence the rate that some other process is able to acquire resources such as the CPU, memory, or I/O devices. The variation in rate may be used to pass signals. Essentially, the process signals information to another by modulating its own use of system resources in such a way that this manipulation affects the real response time observed by the second process. Timing channels are normally considerably less efficient than storage channels because they have reduced bandwidth and are usually more difficult to control.

Malicious Code/Malware. This is software (sometimes referred to as "hostile" software) designed specifically to include functions for penetrating a system, breaking security policies, or to carry malicious or damaging payloads.

"Malware" is a relatively new term abbreviated from MALicious software. Various researchers have debated over the linguistics; but in the literature, the terms "malicious code" and "malware" are used interchangeably. Heiser (2002) defines malware as "… a huge category of unwanted code…. Electronic burglar tools like password crackers, traffic sniffers, keystroke loggers, data scroungers and remote access Trojans (RATs) are being used by attackers both inside and outside organizations to capture passwords, spy on network traffic, record private communications, and stealthily receive and transmit unauthorized commands to and from remote hosts."

In November 2002, SearchSecurity.com conducted a survey about the use of the term "virus" as a catchall term for unwanted code. Results indicated that 20% felt that "malicious code" was the better term, while 5% thought "malware" was better. The article pointed out that a recent Google search found 38,000 hits for "malware" and 153,000 for "malicious code." However, the term "computer virus" dwarfed both with 343,000 results.

It has long been known that the number of variants of viruses or other forms of malware is directly connected to the number of instances of a given platform. The success of a given piece of malware is also related to the relative proportion of a given platform in the overall computing environment.

Although it may not seem so, the modern computing environment is one of extreme consistency. Consider the use of the Intel platform in hardware and Microsoft software on the desktop. In addition, compatible application software (and the addition of functional programming capabilities in those applications) can mean that malware from one hardware and operating system environment can work perfectly well in another.

The functionality added to application macro and script languages has given them the capability either to directly address computer hardware and resources, or to easily call upon utilities or processes that have such access. This means that objects previously considered data, and therefore immune to malicious programming, must now be checked for malicious functions or payloads.

There are a variety of types of malware. Although functions can be combined, these types do have specific characteristics, and it can be important to keep the distinctions in mind. However, it should be noted that there is an increasing convergence in malware. Viruses and Trojans are being used to spread and plant RATs and RATs are being used to install zombies. In some cases, hoax virus warnings are being used to spread viruses. Also, virus and Trojan payloads may contain logic bombs and "data diddlers." The types of malicious code include:

- *Virus.* A virus is a fragment of code that attaches itself to other executable computer instructions, including software application code, the code used to boot the computer, and macro instructions placed in documents. A key component of a virus is the ability to replicate and reproduce itself on the system. Generally, a virus requires some type of action by the user or a process to activate. For example, when a user (or process) activates something on the system, such as starting an application, the virus code would also be initiated. A virus can search for uninfected executable objects and append itself to the object; it checks to see if a trigger condition is met and then executes the rest of the program. A virus may or may not carry payloads and, if it is carrying a payload, the payload may or may not be damaging.
- *File infector or file-infecting virus.* A file infector (or file-infecting virus) contaminates files that contain computer code, especially .exe and .com files, but also files such as .sys and .dll. Whenever the user starts the application and runs an infected file, the virus is activated.

- *Boot sector infector or virus.* The boot sector infector or virus infects the boot sector and related areas on a hard or floppy storage disk. Because every disk has a boot sector, any disk is vulnerable to infection. The boot virus moves or overwrites the original boot sector with the virus code. And because it is part of the boot process, every time the machine is powered on, the virus will be activated. Some boot sector infectors create bad sectors on the disk in order to hide more virus code.
- *System infector.* This is a somewhat vague term. Some use the term to indicate viruses that infect operating system files, or boot sectors, such that the virus is called at boot time, and has or may have preemptive control over some functions of the operating system. (The Lehigh virus infected only COMMAND.COM on MS-DOS machines.) In other usage, a system infector modifies other system structures, such as the linking pointers in directory tables or the MS Windows system Registry, in order to be called first when programs are invoked on the host computer. An example of directory table linking is the DIR virus family.
- *Multipartite virus.* Originally, this term was used to indicate a virus that was able to infect both boot sectors and program files. Current usage tends to mean a virus that can infect more than one type of object, or to infect or reproduce in more than one way. Examples are Telefonica, One Half, and Junkie. Traditional multipartites are not very successful.
- *Email virus.* A virus that specifically, rather than accidentally, uses the email system to spread. While virus-infected files may be accidentally sent as email attachments, email viruses are aware of email system functions. They generally target a specific type of email system (Microsoft's Outlook is the most commonly used), harvest email addresses from various sources, and may append copies of themselves to all email sent, or may generate email messages containing copies of themselves as attachments. Some email viruses monitor all network traffic, and follow up legitimate messages with messages that they generate. Most email viruses are technically considered worms because they often do not infect other program files on the target computer, but this is not a hard and fast distinction. There are known examples of email viruses that are file infectors, macro viruses, script viruses, and worms. Melissa, Loveletter, Hybris, and SirCam are all widespread examples, and the CHRISTMA exec is an example of an older one. Email viruses have made something of a change to the epidemiology of viruses. Traditionally, viruses took many months to spread, but stayed around for many years in the computing environment. Many email viruses have become "fast burners" that can spread around the world, infecting hundreds of thousands or even millions of machines within hours.

However, once characteristic indicators of these viruses become known, they die off almost immediately.

- *Macro virus.* This is a virus that uses macro programming of an application such as a word processor. (Most known macro viruses use Visual Basic for Applications in Microsoft Word: some are able to cross between applications and function in, for example, a PowerPoint presentation and a Word document, but this ability is rare.) Macro viruses infect data files, and tend to remain resident in the application itself by infecting a configuration template such as MS Word's NORMAL.DOT. Although macro viruses infect data files, they are not generally considered to be file infectors: a distinction is generally made between program and data files. Macro viruses can operate across hardware or operating system platforms as long as the required application platform is present. (For example, many MS Word macro viruses can operate on both the Windows and MAC versions of Word.) Examples are Concept and CAP. Melissa is also a macro virus, in addition to being an email virus; it mailed itself around as an infected document. One of the most destructive was FormatC that deleted files on the hard disk.

- *Script virus.* Script viruses are generally differentiated from macro viruses in that script viruses are usually stand-alone files that can be executed by an interpreter, such as Microsoft's Windows Script Host (.vbs files). A script virus file can be seen as a data file in that it is generally a simple text file, but it usually does not contain other data, and generally has some indicator (such as the .vbs extension) that it is executable. Loveletter is a script virus.

- *Worms.* A worm is a program that self-propagates from one computer to another over a network, using the resources on one machine to attack other machines. The term has evolved to distinguish between programs that involve the user in some way (viruses) and programs that do not involve the user, but directly probe network-attached computers trying to exploit a specific weakness or loophole (worms). Worms differ from viruses in that they do not need input from users — worms are independently capable of transferring between computers. Once in a computer, the code replicates itself to the host for execution. In general, worms look for a specific piece of server or utility software that will respond to network queries or activity. Examples of worms are the Internet/Morris Worm of 1998, and more recently Code Red and a number of Linux worms such as Lion. (Nimda is an example of a worm, but it also spreads in a number of other ways, so it could be considered to be an email virus and multipartite as well.)

> *The earliest worm infection was the "Internet Worm" in 1988. The worm was released onto the Internet network and, within hours, the program replicated copies of itself on 3000 to 4000 of 60,000 hosts (the affected machines were VAX and Sun computers). Although the worm did not destroy files, intercept private mail, reveal passwords, or corrupt databases, it did compete for CPU time with, and eventually overwhelm, ordinary user processes. In an effort to isolate the worm, several administrators needed to shut down nationwide network gateways that resulted in a shutdown of some portions of the Internet.*

- *Trojan horses.* A Trojan horse is a program that appears useful but contains hidden code that is designed to perform unauthorized functions. Trojan programs have been distributed by mass email campaigns, by posting on Usenet newsgroup discussion groups, or through automated distribution agents (bots) on Internet Relay Chat (IRC) channels. Because source identification in these communications channels can be easily hidden, Trojan programs can be redistributed in a number of disguises and specific identification of a malicious program has become much more difficult.

The Trojan Horse Story

When the invading Greeks wanted to sack Troy, they built a large wooden horse as a gift for the Trojans and pretended to abandon their siege of the city. The Trojans brought the horse inside their city walls as a trophy, and unbeknown to the Trojans, a number of Greek soldiers hid inside the horse. At night, the soldiers emerged from their hiding place and opened the city gates, allowing the Greek armies into the city. In the context of computer security, a Trojan horse is any code that has apparently or actually useful features, but also contains hidden malicious functionality that exploits any privileges the program may have when executing.

- *Remote Access Trojan (RAT).* The authors of RATs would generally like RATs to be referred to as Remote Administration Tools (conveys a sense of legitimacy). All networking software can, in a sense, be considered remote access tools: we have file transfer sites and clients, World Wide Web servers and browsers, and terminal emulation software that allow a microcomputer user to log on to a distant computer and use it as if he or she were on-site. The RATs considered to be in the malware camp tend to fall somewhere in the middle of the spectrum. Once a client, such as Back Orifice, Netbus, Bionet, or SubSeven, is installed on the target computer, the controlling computer is able to obtain information about the target computer. The master computer will be able to download files from, and upload files to, the target. The control computer will also be able to submit commands to the victim, which basically allows the distant operator to do pretty much anything to the prey. One other function is quite important: all of this activity goes on without any alert being given to the owner or operator of the targeted computer.

When a RAT program has been run on a computer, it will install itself in such a way as to be active every time the computer is turned on after that. Information is sent back to the controlling computer (sometimes via an anonymous channel such as IRC) noting that the system is active. The user of the command computer is now able to explore the target, escalate access to other resources, and install other software, such as distributed denial-of-service zombies.

- *Bomb.* A bomb is malicious code hidden within a program that is set to activate under particular conditions. There are two main categories: logic bomb and time bomb. A logic bomb is triggered when a specific event (or series of events) occurs within the system. A time bomb is activated after a period of time has elapsed or when a specific date or time is reached.
- *Data diddler.* This is a term that refers to the payload in a Trojan or virus that deliberately corrupts data, generally by small increments over time.
- *Hoax.* Hoaxes are usually warnings about new viruses that do not exist. In addition, hoaxes generally carry a directive to the user to forward the warning to all addresses available to them. Hoaxes have characteristics that can be used to determine warnings that may or may not be valid. The following are general characteristics of hoaxes:
  - Ask the reader to forward the message.
  - Make reference to false authorities such as Microsoft, AOL, IBM, and the FCC (none of which issue virus alerts), or completely false entities.
  - Do not provide specific information about the individual or office responsible for analyzing the virus or issuing the alert.
  - State that the new virus is unknown to authorities or researchers.
  - Often state that there is no means of detecting or removing the virus, and do not give any means of removing an infection — many of the original hoax warnings stated only that you should not open a message with a certain phrase in the subject line. (The warning, of course, usually contained that phrase in the subject line.)

- Often state that the virus does tremendous damage, and is incredibly virulent — hoax warnings very often contain A LOT OF CAPITAL LETTER SHOUTING AND EXCLAMATION MARKS!!!!!!!!!!
- Often contain technical sounding nonsense (technobabble, such as "nth complexity binary loops").

- *Pranks.* Pranks are intended as humor and usually do not cause harm to the system. A fairly common thread running through most pranks is that the computer is, in some way, nonfunctional. Many pretend to have detected some kind of fault in the computer (and some pretend to rectify such faults, of course making things worse). One entry in the virus field is PARASCAN, the paranoid scanner. It pretends to find large numbers of infected files, although it does not actually check for any infections. One specific type of joke is the "Easter egg," a function hidden in a program and generally accessible only by a specific sequence of commands. Although they may seem harmless, they do consume resources, even if only disk space, and also make the task of ensuring program integrity more difficult.

Memory Reuse (Object Reuse). Memory management involves sections of memory allocated to one process for awhile, then deallocated, then reallocated to another process. Because residual information may remain when a section of memory is reassigned to a new process after a previous process is finished with it, a security violation may occur. When memory is reallocated, the operating system should ensure that memory is zeroed out or completely overwritten before it can be accessed by a new process. Thus, there is no residual information in memory carrying over from one process to another.

Executable Content/Mobile Code. Executable content, or mobile code, is software that is transmitted across a network from a remote source to a local system and is then executed on that local system. The code is transferred by user actions and in some cases without the explicit action of the user. The code can arrive at the local system as attachments to email messages or through Web pages.

The concepts of mobile code have been called by many names: mobile agents, mobile code, downloadable code, executable content, active capsules, remote code, etc. Although the terms seem the same, there are slight differences. For example, mobile agents are defined as "programs that can migrate from host to host in a network, at times and to places of their own choosing. The state of the running program is saved, transported to the new host, and restored, allowing the program to continue where it left off. Mobile agents differ from 'applets,' which are programs downloaded as the result of a user action, then executed from beginning to end on one host" (Kotz and Gray, 1999). Examples include ActiveX controls, Java applets, and scripts run within the browser. All of these deal with the local execution of remotely sourced code.

One way of looking at mobile code is in terms of current security architectures. Typically, security in the operating system could answer the question, "Can subject X use object Y?" The challenge with mobile code is how to resolve when one subject may be acting on behalf of another, or may be acting on its own behalf. Thus, security mechanisms must be implemented to resolve whether these requests should be allowed or denied.

Social Engineering. One method of compromising a system is to befriend users in order to gain information; especially vulnerable are individuals with system administrator access. Social engineering is the art of getting people to divulge sensitive information to others, either in a friendly manner, as an attempt to be helpful, or through intimidation. It is sometimes referred to as "people hacking" because it relies on vulnerabilities in people rather than those found in software or hardware.

Social engineering comes in many forms, but all based on the principle of disguising oneself as a non-hacker who needs or deserves the information to gain access to the system. For example, one method is for attackers to pretend they are new to the system and need assistance with gaining access. Another method is when attackers pretend to be a system staff member and try to gain information by helping to fix a computer problem, although there is no problem.

Time of Check/Time of Use (TOC/TOU). This is a type of asynchronous attack that occurs when some control information is changed between the time the system security functions check the contents of variables and the time the variables actually are used during operations. For example, a user logs on to a system in the morning and is fired later in the day. As a result of the termination, the security administrator removes the user from the user database. Because the user did not log off, he or she still has access to the system and might try to disrupt operations or cause damage.

Trapdoor/Backdoor. A trapdoor or backdoor (can also be called a maintenance hook) is a hidden mechanism that bypasses access control measures. It is an entry point into a program that is inserted in software by designers/programmers during the program's development to provide a method of gaining access into the program for modification if the access control mechanism malfunctions and locks them out. They can be useful for error correction, but they are dangerous opportunities for unauthorized access if left in a production system. A programmer or someone who knows about the backdoor can exploit the trapdoor as a covert means of access after the program has been implemented in the system. An unauthorized user may also discover the entry point while trying to penetrate the system.

This list of software threats is to be used as a reminder of the types of threats that developers and managers of software development should be aware. It is not intended to be an inclusive list, as there are new threats developed every day. As a reminder, countermeasures for software threats are provided in the Security Technology and Tools section.

The Database and Data Warehousing Environment

In the early history of information systems, data processing occurred on stand-alone systems that used separate applications that contained their own set of master files. As systems expanded and more applications were run on the same machine, redundant files were gathered. Several complexities and conflicts also arose, mainly the possibility of having duplicate information within each application contained on the same system. For example, an employee's address might be duplicated in several application systems within the organization, once in the payroll system and again in the personnel system. This duplication of information not only wasted storage space, but also led to the possibility of inconsistency in the data. If an employee moved and notified payroll (to make sure the payroll check still arrived), only the database in payroll would be updated. If the personnel department needed to send something to the employee, the address contained within its application would not show the change. Another danger might occur if the personnel department sees the change in the payroll system, thinks it is an error, and overwrites the newer payroll data with data from the personnel files.

To resolve the potential inconsistencies of having information replicated in several files on a system, databases were developed to incorporate the information from multiple sources. They are an attempt to integrate and manage the data required for several applications into a common storage area that will support an organization's business needs.

DBMS Architecture

Organizations tend to collect data from many separate databases into one large database system, where it is available for viewing, updating, and processing by either programs or users. A *Database Management System (DBMS)* is a suite of application programs that typically manage large, structured sets of persistent data. It stores, maintains, and provides access to data using ad hoc query capabilities. The DBMS provides the structure for the data and some type of language for accessing and manipulating the data. The primary objective is to store data and allow users to view the data. DBMSs have transformed greatly since their introduction in the late 1960s. The earliest file access systems evolved into network databases in

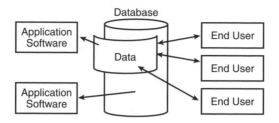

Exhibit 2. DBMS

the 1970s. In the 1980s, relational databases became dominant. Most recently, in the 1990s, object-oriented databases emerged. Since companies have become increasingly dependent upon the successful operation of the DBMS, it is anticipated that future demands will drive more innovations and product improvements.

Typically, a DBMS has four major elements: database, hardware, software, and users (see Exhibit 2). The database element consists of one (or more) large structured sets or tables of persistent data. Databases are usually associated with another element, the software that updates and queries the data. In a simple database, a single file may contain several records that contain the same set of fields and each field is a certain fixed width. The DBMS uses software programs that allow it to manage the large, structured sets of data, and provide access to the data for multiple, concurrent users while at the same time maintaining the integrity of the data. The applications and data reside on hardware and are displayed to the user via some sort of display unit, such as a monitor.

The data consists of individual entities and entities with relationships linking them together. The mapping or organization of the data entities is based on a database model. The database model describes the relationship between the data elements and provides a framework for organizing the data. The data model is fundamental to the design because it provides a mechanism for representing the data and any correlations between the data.

The database model should provide for:

- *Transaction persistence.* The state of the database is the same after a transaction (process) has occurred as it was prior to the transaction.
- *Fault tolerance and recovery.* In the event of a hardware or software failure, the data should remain in its original state. Two types of recovery systems available are rollback and shadowing. Rollback recovery is when incomplete or invalid transactions are backed out. Shadow recovery occurs when transactions are reapplied to a

previous version of the database. Shadow recovery requires the use of transaction logging to identify the last good transaction.

- *Sharing by multiple users.* The data should be available to multiple users at the same time without endangering the integrity of the data (i.e., locking of data).
- *Security controls.* These include controls such as access controls, integrity checking, and view definitions.

DBMSs typically operate on hardware that has been implemented to run only databases and often only specific database systems. This allows hardware designers to increase the number and speed of network connections, incorporate multiple processors and storage disks to increase the speed time of searching for information, and also increase the amount of memory and cache.

When an organization is designing a database, the first step is to understand the requirements for the database and then design a system that meets those requirements. This includes what information will be stored, who is allowed access, and estimating how many people will need to access the data at the same time.

In most database developments, the database design is usually done by either a database design specialist or a combination of database administrators and software analysts. The database designers produce a schema that defines what and how the data is stored, how it relates to other data, and who can access, add, and modify the data.

The data in a database can be structured in several different ways, depending upon the types of information being stored. Different data storage techniques can exist on practically any machine level, from a PC to mainframe, and in various architectures, such as stand-alone, distributed, or client/server.

The various architecture models that exist for databases are:

- Hierarchical Database Management Systems
- Network Database Management Systems
- Relational Database Management Systems (i.e., Oracle, DB2)
- Object-Oriented Database Management Systems
- End-User Database Management Systems (i.e., dBase, Paradox, Access)
- Spreadsheets (i.e., Excel, Quattro Pro)

Hierarchical Database Management Model

The *hierarchical model* is the oldest of the database models and is derived from the Information Management Systems of the 1950s and 1960s. Even today, there are hierarchical legacy systems that are still being operated by banks, insurance companies, government agencies, and hospitals. Such a system stores data in a series of records that have field values attached. It collects all the instances of a specific record together as a record type. These record types are the equivalent of tables in the relational model, with the individual records being the equivalent of rows. To create links between the record types, the hierarchical model uses parent/child relationships through the use of trees. A weakness is that the hierarchical model is only able to cope with a single tree, and is not able to link between branches or over multiple layers. For example, an organization could have several divisions and several sub-trees that represent employees, facilities, and products. If an employee worked for several divisions, the hierarchical model would not be able to provide a link between the two divisions for one employee. The hierarchical model is no longer used in current, commercially available DBMS products; however, it still exists in legacy systems.

Network Database Management Model

The *network database management model*, introduced in 1971, is an extended form of the hierarchical data structure. It does not refer to the fact that the database is stored on the network, but rather to the method of how data is linked to other data. The network model represents its data in the form of a network of records and sets that are related to each other, forming a network of links. Records are sets of related data values and are the equivalent of rows in the relational model. They store the name of the record type, the attributes associated with it, and the format for these attributes. For example, an employee record type could contain the last name, first name, address, etc., of the employee. Record types are sets of records of the same type. These are the equivalent of tables in the relational model. Set types are the relationships between two record types, such as an organization's division and the employees in that division. The set types allow the network model to run some queries faster; however, it does not offer the flexibility of a relational model. The network model is not commonly used today to design database systems; however, there are some legacy systems remaining.

Relational Database Management Model

The majority of organizations use software based on the relational database management model. The *relational model* is based on set theory and predicate logic, and provides a high level of abstraction. The use of set theory allows data to be structured in a series of tables that have columns representing the variables and rows that contain specific instances of data. These tables are organized using "normal forms." The relational model outlines how programmers should design the DBMS so that different database systems used by the organization can communicate with each other.

The basic relational model consists of three elements:

- *Data structures* that are called either tables or relations
- *Integrity rules* on allowable values and combinations of values in tables
- *Data manipulation agents* that provide the relational mathematical basis and an assignment operator

Each table or relation in the relational model consists of a set of attributes and a set of tuples or entries in the table. *Attributes* correspond to a column in a table. Attributes are unordered left to right and thus are referenced by name and not position. All data values in the relational model are *atomic*. Atomic values mean that at every row/column position in every table there is always exactly one data value and never a set of values. There are no links or pointers connecting tables; thus, the representation of relationships is contained as data in another table.

A *tuple* of a table corresponds to a row in the table. Tuples are unordered top to bottom because a relation is a mathematical set and not a list. Also, because tuples are based on tables that are mathematical sets, there are no duplicate tuples in a table (sets in mathematics, by definition, do not include duplicate elements).

In Exhibit 3, using the Author Table as an example, the entity is the author and the attributes would be author identifier, author last name, author first name, and the state in which the author lives. The unique attribute in the table is author identifier; thus; the primary key is author identifier.

The *primary key* is an attribute or set of attributes that uniquely identifies a specific instance of an entity. Each table in a database must have a primary key that is unique to that table. It is a subset of the candidate key. Any key that could be a primary key is called a candidate key. The candidate key is an attribute that is a unique identifier within a given table. One of the candidate keys is chosen to be the primary key and the others are called alternate keys. Primary keys provide the sole tuple-level addressing mechanism within the relational model. They are the only guaranteed method of pinpointing an individual tuple; therefore, they are fundamental to the operation of the overall relational model. Because they are critical to the relational model, the primary keys cannot contain a null value and cannot change or become null during the life of each entity. When the primary key of one relation is used as an attribute in another relation, then it is the foreign key in that relation.

The *foreign key* in a relational model is different from the primary key. The foreign key value represents a reference to an entry in some other table. If an attribute (value) in one table matches those of the primary key of some other relation, it is considered the foreign key. The link (or

243

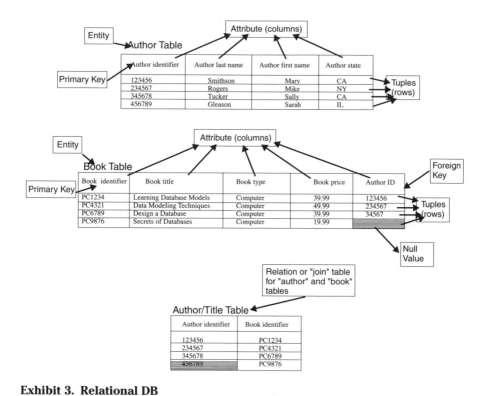

Exhibit 3. Relational DB

matches) between the foreign and primary keys represents the relationships between tuples. Thus, the matches represent references and allow
one table to be referenced to another table. The primary key and foreign
key links are the binding factor that holds the database together. Foreign
keys also provide a method for maintaining referential integrity in the data
and for navigating between different instances of an entity.

Integrity

To solve the problems of concurrency and security within a database,
the database must provide some integrity. The user's program may carry
out many operations on the data retrieved from the database, but the
DBMS is only concerned about what data is read/written from or to the
database — the transaction. *Concurrency* occurs when the DBMS inter-
leaves actions (read/write of database objects) of various transactions.
For concurrency to be secure each transaction must leave the database in
a consistent state if the database is consistent when the transaction
begins.

The DBMS does not really understand the semantics of the data; that is, it does not understand how an operation on data occurs, such as when interest on a bank account is computed. A transaction might "commit" after completing all its actions, or it could "abort" (or be aborted by the DBMS) after executing some actions. A very important property guaranteed by the DBMS for all transactions is that they are atomic. Atomic transactions imply that a user can think of "X" as always executing all its actions in one step, or not executing any actions at all. To help with concurrency, the DBMS logs all actions so that it can undo the actions of aborted transactions.

The security issues of concurrency can occur if several users who are attempting to query data from the database interfere with each other's requests. The two integrity rules of the relational model are entity integrity and referential integrity. The two rules apply to every relational model and focus on the primary and foreign keys. In the *entity integrity rule*, the tuple cannot have a *null value* in the primary key. This guarantees that the tuple is uniquely identified by the primary key value. *Entity integrity rule: no component of the primary key is allowed to accept null values.* This is shown in Exhibit 3 in the Book Table — the author ID for the book number PC9876 has a null value that would violate the entity integrity rule and possibly corrupt the data.

The *referential integrity rule* states that for any foreign key value, the referenced relation must have a tuple with the same value for its primary key. *Referential integrity rule: the database must not contain unmatched foreign key values.*

Essentially, every table relation or join must be accomplished by coincidence of the primary keys or of a primary key and a foreign key that is the primary key of the other table. As shown in Exhibit 3 as the Author/Title Table, each table participating in the join must demonstrate entity integrity and in the referenced relation must have a similar primary key/foreign key relationship. Another example of the loss of referential integrity is to assign a tuple to a nonexistent attribute. If this occurs, the tuple could not be referenced — with no attribute, it would be impossible to know what it represented.

Structured Query Language (SQL)

The relational model also has several standardized languages; one is called the Structured Query Language (SQL) that users use to issue commands. An advantage of having a standard language is that organizations can switch between different vendor systems without having to rewrite all their software or retrain their staff.

SQL was developed by IBM and is an International Standards Organization (ISO) and American National Standards Institute (ANSI) standard. (ANSI is a private, nonprofit organization that administers and coordinates the U.S. voluntary standardization and conformity assessment system.) Because SQL is a standard, the commands for most systems are similar. There are several different types of queries, such as those for normal users that are predesigned and included in applications, and often direct ad hoc queries that are usually done by database experts.

The main components of a database using SQL include:

- *Schemas:* describe the structure of the database, including any access controls limiting how the users will view the information contained in the tables
- *Tables:* the columns and rows of the data are contained in tables
- *Views:* define what information a user can view in the tables — the view can be customized so that an entire table may be visible or a user may be limited to only being able to see just a row or a column; views are created dynamically by the system for each user and provide access control granularity

The simplicity of SQL is achieved by giving the users a high-level view of the data. A view is a feature that allows for virtual tables in a database; these virtual tables are created from one or more real tables in the database. For example, a view can be set up for each user (or group of users) on the system; the user can then only view those virtual tables (or views). In addition, access can be restricted so that only rows or columns are visible in the view. The value of views is to have control over what users can see. For example, we can allow users to see their own salary information in an employee database, but not other employee salaries unless they have sufficient authorization.

This view feature removes many of the technical aspects of the system from the users, and instead places the technical burden on the DBMS software applications. As an example, assume that all employees in the personnel department have the same boss, the director of personnel. To avoid repeating the data for each employee, this type of data would be stored in a separate table. This saves storage space and reduces the time it would take for queries to execute. This process is known as *normalization*, because it comes from the study of normal forms.

Object-Oriented Database Model

The *object-oriented (OO) database model* is one of the most recent database models. Similar to OO programming languages, the OO database model stores data as objects. The OO objects are a collection of public and private data items and the set of operations that can be executed on the data — that is, objects contain both methods and data. It was designed to overcome some of the limitations of relational databases that contain large amounts of data. The object-oriented model does not have a high-level language such as SQL. An advantage of not having a standard language allows the OO DBMS to interact with applications without the unnecessary overhead of a standard language.

Relational models are starting to add object-oriented functions and interfaces, to create an object-relational model. An *object-relational database* system is a hybrid system. It is a relational DBMS that has an object-oriented interface built on top of the original software. This can be accomplished either by adding a separate interface or by adding additional commands to the current system. The hybrid model allows organizations to maintain their current relational database software, and at the same time provide an upgrade path for future technologies.

Database Interface Languages

The existence of legacy databases has proven a difficult challenge for managing new database access requirements. To provide an interface that combines newer systems and legacy systems, several standardized access methods have evolved, such as Open DataBase Connectivity (ODBC), Object Linking and Embedding Database (OLE DB), ActiveX Data Objects (ADO), Java Database Connectivity (JDBC), eXtensible Markup Language (XML), and Security Assertion Markup Language (SAML). These systems provide a gateway to the data contained in the legacy systems as well as the newer systems.

Open DataBase Connectivity (ODBC)

ODBC is the dominant means of standardized data access. It is a standard developed and maintained by Microsoft. Almost all database vendors use it as an interface method to allow an application to communicate with a database either locally or remotely over a network. It is an Application Programming Interface (API) that is used to provide a connection between applications and databases. It was designed so that databases could connect without having to use specific database commands and features.

ODBC commands are used in application programs, which translate them into the commands required by the specific database system. This allows programs to be linked between DBMSs with a minimum of code changes. It allows users to specify which database is being used, and can be easily updated as new database technologies enter the market.

ODBC is a powerful tool; however, because it operates as a system entity, it can be exploited. The following are issues with ODBC security:

- The username and password for the database are stored in plaintext. To prevent disclosure of this information, the files should be protected. For example, if an HTML document is calling an ODBC data source, the HTML source must be protected to ensure that the username and password in plaintext cannot be read. (The HTML should call a CGI that has the authentication details, because HTML can be viewed in a browser.)

- The actual call and the returned data are sent as cleartext over the network.
- Substandard verification of the access level of the user using the ODBC application.
- Calling applications must be checked to ensure they do not attempt to combine data from multiple data sources, thus allowing data aggregation.
- Calling applications must be checked to ensure they do not attempt to exploit the ODBC drivers and gain elevated system access.

Object Linking and Embedding Database (OLE DB)

OLE DB is, according to Microsoft, replacing ODBC as the standard database development API. Before OLE DB is defined, an explanation of OLE is provided. The Component Object Model (COM) is the protocol that allows OLE to work.

Microsoft Web site support (1999) defines OLE as: "Object *linking* allows users to share a single source of data for a particular object. The document contains the name of the file containing the data, along with a picture of the data. When the source is updated, all the documents using the data are updated as well. On the other hand, with object *embedding*, one application (the source) provides data or an image that will be contained in the document of another application (the destination). The destination application contains the data or graphic image, but does not understand it or have the ability to edit it. It simply displays, prints, and/or plays the embedded item. To edit or update the embedded object, it must be opened in the source application that created it. This occurs automatically when you double-click the item or choose the appropriate edit command while the object is highlighted."

OLE DB is a low-level interface designed by Microsoft to link data across various DBMSs. It is an open specification that is designed to build on the success of ODBC by providing an open standard for accessing all kinds of data. It enables organizations to easily take advantage of information contained not only in data within a DBMS, but also when accessing data from other types of data sources.

Essentially, the OLE DB interfaces are designed to provide access to all data, regardless of type, format, or location. For example, in some enterprise environments, the organization's critical information is located outside of traditional production databases, and instead is stored in containers such as Microsoft Access, spreadsheets, project management planners, or Web applications. The OLE DB interfaces are based on the Component Object Model (COM) and they provide applications with uniform access to data regardless of the information source. The OLE DB separates the data into interoperable components that can run as middleware on a client or server across a wide variety of applications. The OLE DB architecture provides for components such as direct data access interfaces, query engines, cursor engines, optimizers, business rules, and transaction managers.

When developing databases and determining how data might be linked through applications, whether through an ODBC interface or an OLE DB interface, security must be considered during the development stage. If OLE DB is considered, there are optional OLE DB interfaces that can be implemented to support the administration of security information. The security OLE DB interfaces allow for authenticated and authorized access to data among components and applications. The OLE DB can provide a unified view of the security mechanisms that are supported by the operating system and the database components.

Accessing Databases through the Internet

Many database developers are supporting the use of the Internet and corporate intranets to allow users to access the centralized back-end servers. Several types of application programming interfaces (APIs) can be used to connect the end-user applications to the back-end database. Although we will highlight a couple of available APIs — namely, ActiveX Data Objects (ADO) and Java Database Connectivity (JDBC) — there are several security issues about any of the API technologies that must be reviewed. These include authentication of users, authorizations of users, encryption, protection of the data from unauthorized entry, accountability, and auditing, and availability of current data.

One approach for Internet access is to create a "tiered" application approach that manages data in layers. There can be any number of layers; however, the most typical architecture is to use a three-tier approach: Presentation Layer, Business Logic Layer, and the Data Layer. This is sometimes referred to as the "Internet Computing Model" because the browser is used to connect to an application server that then connects to a database.

Three-Tier Approach.

- Presentation Layer: user/client level
- Business Logic Layer: accepts commands from the presentation layer and hands off the commands to the data layer
- Data Layer: typically the database

Depending on the implementation, it can be good or bad for security. The tier approach can add to security because the users do not connect directly to the data. Instead, the users are connecting to a middle layer, the business logic layer that connects directly to the database on behalf of the users. The bad side of security is that if the database provides security features, they may be lost in the translation through the middle layer. Thus, when looking at providing security, it is important to analyze not only how the security features are implemented, but also where they are implemented and how the configuration of the application with the back-end database affects the security features. Additional concerns for security are user authentication, user access control, auditing of user actions, protecting data as it travels between tiers, managing identities across tiers, scalability of the system, and setting privileges for the different tiers.

ActiveX Data Objects (ADO)

ADO is a Microsoft high-level interface for all kinds of data. It can be used to create a front-end database client or a middle-tier business object using an application, tool, or Internet browser. Developers can simplify the development of OLE DB by using ADO. Objects can be the building blocks of Java, JavaScript, Visual Basic, and other object-oriented languages. By using common and reusable data access components (Component Object Model [COM]), different applications can access all data regardless of data location or data format. ADO can support typical client/server applications, HTML tables, spreadsheets, and mail engine information.

Java Database Connectivity (JDBC)

JDBC is an API from Sun Microsystems used to connect Java programs to databases. It is used to connect a Java program to a database either directly or by connecting through ODBC, depending on whether the database vendor has created the necessary drivers for Java.

Regardless of the interface used to connect the user to the database, security items to consider include how and where the user will be authenticated, controlling user access, and auditing user actions.

eXtensible Markup Language (XML)

XML is a World Wide Web Consortium (W3C) standard for putting structured data in a text file so that both the format of the data and the data can be shared on intranets and the Web. A markup language, such as the Hypertext Markup Language (HTML), is simply a system of symbols and rules to identify structures (format) in a document. XML is called "extensible" because the symbols are unlimited and can be defined by the user or author. The format for XML can represent data in a neutral format that is independent of the database, application, and the underlying DBMS.

XML became a W3C standard in 1998 and many believe it will become the *de facto* standard for integrating data and content during the next few years. It offers the ability to exchange data and bridge different technologies, such as object models and programming languages. Because of this advantage, XML is expected to transform data and documents of current DBMSs and data access standards (i.e., ODBC, JDBC, etc.) by Web-enabling these standards and providing a common data format. Another, and probably more important, advantage is the ability to create one underlying XML document and display it in a variety of different ways and devices. Like the Wireless Markup Language (WML), which is a markup language based on XML, WML delivers content to devices such as cell phones, pagers, and personal digital assistants (PDAs).

As with any of the other programs used to make database interface calls, XML applications must also be reviewed for how authentication of users is established; access controls are implemented; auditing of user actions is implemented and stored; and how confidentiality of sensitive data can be achieved.

Security Assertion Markup Language (SAML)

SAML is a new technology standard being developed by the OASIS XML-Based Security Services Technical Committee (SSTC). It is based on XML and can be used to express security credentials, such as authentication and authorization, in a common format.

Data Warehousing

A data warehouse is a repository for information collected from a variety of data sources. Bill Inmon (1996) defines the data warehouse as a "subject-oriented, integrated, time-variant, and nonvolatile collection of data in support of management's decision-making process." Theriault and Newman (2001) define the use of data warehouses as many layers of management being able to see the same information at the same time and thus making more timely and educated decisions. Data warehouses essentially *unsecure* the organization's information in order to enable sharing of that information to more levels of employees.

Data warehouses (Exhibit 4) do not contain operational data, which is their distinguishing characteristic. That is, the data stored in a data warehouse is not used for operational tasks, but rather for analytical purposes. The data warehouse combines all of the data from various databases into one large data container. Because the data is collected into one central location for analysis, instead of several smaller databases, the combined data can be used by executives to make business decisions.

A current term associated with data warehouses is "data marts." Data marts are smaller versions of data warehouses. While a data warehouse is

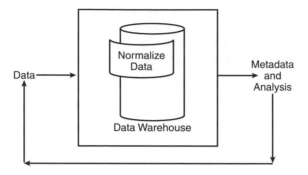

Exhibit 4. Data Warehouse

meant to contain all of an organization's information, a data mart may contain the information from just a division or only about a specific topic. In most instances, the creation of a data mart is less time consuming and, thus, the data can be available for analysis sooner than if a data warehouse was created.

The following tasks illustrate a simplified process of building a data warehouse:

- Feed all data into a large, high-availability, and high-integrity database that resides at the confidentiality level of the most sensitive data.
- Normalize the data. Regardless of how the data is characterized in each system, it must be structured the same when moved into the data warehouse. For example, one database could categorize birthdate as "month/date/year," another as "date/month/year," and still another as "year/month/date." The data warehouse must "normalize" the various data categories into only one category. Normalization will also remove redundancies in the data.
- Mine the data for correlations to produce metadata.
- Sanitize and export the metadata to its intended users.
- Feed all new incoming data and the metadata into the data warehouse.

In traditional database administration, rules and policies are implemented to ensure the confidentiality and integrity of the database, such as defining user views and setting access permissions. Security is even more critical for data warehouses. Rules and policies must be in place to control access to the data. This includes items such as defining the user groups, the type of data each group can access, and outlining the user's security responsibilities and procedures. Another danger of data warehouses is if the physical or logical security perimeter of the database servers were breached, the unauthorized user could gain access to all of the organization's data.

In addition to confidentiality controls, security for the data also includes the integrity and availability of the information. For example, if the data warehouse were accidentally or intentionally destroyed, a valuable repository of the organization's historical and compiled data would also be destroyed. To avoid such a total loss, appropriate plans for backups must be implemented and maintained, as well as recovery options for hardware and software applications.

Metadata

The information about the data, called "metadata" (literally data about data or knowledge about data), provides a systematic method for describing resources and improving the retrieval of information. The objective is to help users search through a wide range of sources with better precision. It includes the data associated with either an information system or an information object for the purposes of description, administration, legal requirements, technical functionality, usage, and preservation. It is considered the key component for exploiting and using a data warehouse. Metadata is useful because it provides valuable information about the unseen relationships between data and the ability to correlate data previously considered unrelated.

Note that the data warehouse is usually at the highest classification level possible; however, users of the metadata are usually not at that level and therefore any data that should not be publicly available must be removed from the metadata. Generally, this involves just handing over the correlations, but not the underlying data from which the correlations came.

The Dublin Core metadata element set was developed during the first metadata workshops in Dublin, Ohio, in 1995 and 1996. It was a response to the need to improve retrieval of information resources, especially on the Web. It continues to be developed by an international working group as a generic metadata standard for use by libraries, archives, governments, and publishers of online information. The Dublin Core Metadata Initiative (DCMI) standard has received widespread acceptance among the electronic information community and has become the *de facto* Internet metadata standard.

Data contained in a data warehouse is typically accessed through front-end analysis tools such as Online Analytical Processing (OLAP) or Knowledge-Discovery in Databases (KDD) methods.

Online Analytical Processing (OLAP)

OLAP technologies provide an analyst with the ability to formulate queries and, based on the outcome of the queries, to define further queries.

The analyst can collect information by roaming through the data. The collected information is then presented to management. Because the data analyst interprets aspects of the data, the data analyst should possess in-depth knowledge about the organization and also what type of knowledge the organization needs in order to adequately retrieve the information that can be useful for decision making.

For example, a retail chain may have several locations that locally capture product sales. If management decided to review data on a specific promotional item without a data warehouse, there would be no easy method of capturing sales for all stores on the one item. However, a data warehouse could effectively combine the data from each store into one central repository. The analyst could then query the data warehouse for specific information on the promotional item and present the results to those people in management who are responsible for promotional items.

Data Mining

In addition to OLAP, data mining is another process (or tool) of discovering information in data warehouses by running queries on the data. A large repository of data is required to perform data mining. Data mining is used to reveal hidden relationships, patterns, and trends in the data warehouse. Data mining is a decision-making technique that is based on a series of analytical techniques taken from the fields of mathematics, statistics, cybernetics, and genetics. The techniques are used independently and in cooperation with one another to uncover information from data warehouses.

There are several advantages to using data-mining techniques, including the ability to provide better information to managers that outlines the organization's trends, its customers, and the competitive marketplace for its industry. There are also disadvantages, especially for security. The detailed data about individuals obtained by data mining might risk a violation of privacy. The danger increases when private information is stored on the Web or an unprotected area of the network and thus becomes available to unauthorized users. In addition, the integrity of the data may be at risk. Because a large amount of data must be collected, the chance of errors through human data entry may result in inaccurate relationships or patterns. These errors are also referred to as data contamination.

One positive security function of data mining is the use of tools to review audit logs for intrusion attempts. Because audit logs usually contain thousands of entries, data-mining tools can help to discover abnormal events by drilling down into the data for specific trends or unusual behaviors. Information systems security officers can use a data-mining tool in a testing environment to try to view unauthorized data. For example, testers could log in with the rights assigned to a general user, then use a data-mining tool to access various levels of data. If during this test environment, they were able to successfully view sensitive or unauthorized data, appropriate security controls, such as limiting views, could be implemented.

Data mining is still an evolving technology; thus, standards and procedures need to be formalized so that organizations will be able to use their data for a variety of business decisions and uses. The challenge will be to provide the business need and yet still comply with security requirements that will protect the data from unauthorized users.

Database Vulnerabilities and Threats

One of the primary concerns for the DBMS is the confidentiality of sensitive data. A major concern for most people is that many databases contain health and financial information, both of which are protected by privacy laws in many countries. Another primary concern for the DBMS is enforcing the controls to assure the continued integrity of the data. A compromise of data integrity through an invalid input, or an incorrect definition, could jeopardize the entire viability of the database. In such an instance, the work required to restore the database or manually write queries to correct the data could have a serious impact on operations.

The threats to a DBMS include:

- *Aggregation.* This is the ability to combine nonsensitive data from separate sources to create sensitive information. For example, a user takes two or more unclassified pieces of data and combines them to form a classified piece of data that then becomes unauthorized for that user. Thus, the combined data sensitivity can be greater than the classification of individual parts. For years, mathematicians have been struggling unsuccessfully with the problem of determining when the aggregation of data results in data at a higher classification.
- *Bypass attacks.* Users attempt to bypass controls at the front end of the database application to access information. If the query engine does not have any security controls, the engine may have complete access to the information; thus, users may try to bypass the query engine and directly access and manipulate the data.
- *Compromising database views used for access control.* A view restricts the data a user can see or request from a database. One of the threats is that users may try to access restricted views or modify an existing view. Another problem with view-based access control is the difficulty in verifying how the software performs the view processing. Because all objects must have a security label identifying the sensitivity of the information in the database, the software used to classify the information must also have a mechanism to verify the sensitivity

of the information. Combining this with a query language adds even more complexity. Also, the view just limits the data the user sees; it does not limit the operations that can be performed on the views.

- *Concurrency.* When actions or processes run at the same time, they are said to be concurrent. Problems with concurrency include running processes that use old data, updates that are inconsistent, or having a deadlock occur.

- *Data contamination.* This is the corruption of data integrity by input data errors or erroneous processing. It can occur in a file, report, or a database.

- *Deadlocking.* This occurs when two users try to access the information at the same time and both are denied. According to sql-server-performance.com (2001), "In an SQL database, deadlocking occurs when two user processes have locks on separate objects and each process is trying to acquire a lock on the object that the other process has. When this happens, SQL Server ends the deadlock by automatically choosing one and aborting the process, allowing the other process to continue. The aborted transaction is rolled back and an error message is sent to the user of the aborted process. Generally, the transaction that requires the least amount of overhead to rollback is the transaction that is aborted."

- *Denial-of-service.* This refers to any type of attack or action that could prevent authorized users from gaining access to the information. Often, this can happen through a poorly designed application or query that locks up the table and requires intensive processing (such as a table scan where every row in the table must be examined to return the requested data to the calling application). This can be partially prevented by limiting the number of rows of data returned from any one query.

- *Improper modification of information.* Unauthorized or authorized users may intentionally or accidentally modify information improperly.

- *Inference.* Inference is the ability to deduce (infer) information from observing available information. Essentially, users may be able to determine unauthorized information from what information they can access and may never need to directly access unauthorized data. For example, if a user is reviewing authorized information about patients, such as the medications they have been prescribed, the user may be able to determine the illness. Inference is one of the most difficult threats to control. This is sometimes called a statistical attack.

- *Interception of data.* If dial-up or some other type of remote access is allowed, the threat of interception of the session and modification of the data in transit must be controlled.

- *Polyinstantiation.* In the database world polyinstantiation is referred to as an environment characterized by information stored in more than one location in the database. Within a security model, this permits multiple levels-of-view and authorization. The security challenge is to ensure the integrity of the information in the database. Thus, without an effective method for simultaneously updating all occurrences of the same data element, integrity cannot be guaranteed.

- *Query attacks.* Users try to use query tools to access data not normally allowed by the trusted front end (e.g., those views controlled by the query application).
- *Server access.* The server where the database resides must be protected not only from unauthorized logical access, but also from unauthorized physical access to prevent the disabling of logical controls.
- *Time of check/time of use (TOC/TOU).* TOC/TOU can also occur in databases. An example is when some type of malicious code or privileged access could change data between the time that a user's query was approved and the time the data is displayed to the user.
- *Web security.* Many DBMSs allow access to data through Web technologies. Static Web pages (HTML or XML files) are methods of displaying data stored on a server. One method is when an application queries information from the database and the HTML page displays the data. Another is through dynamic Web pages that are stored on the Web server with a template for the query and HTML display code, but no actual data is stored. When the Web page is accessed, the query is dynamically created and executed and the information is displayed within the HTML display. Providing security control includes measures for protecting against unauthorized access during a login process, protecting the information while it is transferred from the server to the Web server, and protecting the information from being stored on or downloaded to the user's machine.
- *Unauthorized access.* This type of access allows the release of information, either intentionally or accidentally, to unauthorized users.

The next section focuses on the tools and technologies available to provide security controls for application development and database management systems.

4.3 Security Technology and Tools

System Life Cycle and Systems Development

During the 1960s, the development and maintenance of software for the computer system made up the predominant cost of a systems project almost 75%. Because of the expenses associated with software development, industry research began to provide the best methods of reducing costs, which subsequently led to the discipline of software engineering. *Software engineering* simply stated that software products had to be planned, designed, constructed, and released according to engineering principles. It included software metrics, modeling, methods, and techniques associated with the designing of the system before it was developed, and tracking project progress through the entire development process. By the 1980s, the software-engineering field had developed structured methods and modeling that culminated in the development of object-oriented programming in the 1990s.

Since the beginning, software development has faced numerous problems that can result in higher costs and lower quality. In fact, budget and schedule overruns are two of the largest problems for software development. Remember that Windows 95 was released about 18 months late and it is estimated that the budget was exceeded by 25%. On the other side, if software development is rushed and software developers are expected to complete projects within a shortened timeframe, the quality of the software product could be reduced.

Brooks's Law

"Adding manpower to a late software project makes it later." Fred Brooks, a manager of IBM's OS/360 project, stated that the expected advantage from splitting development work among N programmers is O(N) (that is, proportional to N), but the complexity and communications cost associated with coordinating and then merging their work is O(N^2) (that is, proportional to the square of N).

Fred Brooks, 1975, "The Mythical Man-Month"

System (Software) Development Methods

Several System Development Methods (SDMs) have evolved to satisfy different requirements for software programming. The term "SDM" is used to describe the various models used by software developers to provide guidance during the analysis, design, development, and maintenance of information systems. Note that the term "Systems Development Model" (SDM) is not used universally; instead, you may see terms such as "process model" or "development guidelines."

Although there are several different ways to categorize the various software development methods, the approach presented here was to group the current software development methods under three primary approaches: Ad-Hoc Development, Waterfall Method, and the Iterative process.

Ad-Hoc Software Development

Ad-Hoc Development is when development takes place in a chaotic and haphazard manner. It relies entirely on the skills of the individuals performing the work. Generally, schedules, budgets, and functionality are inconsistent — performance can be predicted only by individual rather than organizational capability.

Waterfall and Related Models

The traditional waterfall life cycle model is probably the oldest known model for developing software systems. It was developed in the early 1970s and provided a sense of order to the process. Each phase contains a list of activities that must be performed and documented before the next phase begins. The disadvantage of the waterfall model is that it does not always scale well for large and complex projects. Also, because each phase must be completed before the next, it can inhibit a development team from pursuing concurrent phases or activities. Usually, this method is not good for projects that must be developed in quick turnaround time periods (i.e., less than six months). Although it has been viewed as too rigid or unrealistic, it is still widely used.

Other models developed around the same timeframe include:

- *Systems Development Life Cycle (SDLC).* Sometimes referred to as the waterfall model, it is a project management tool used to plan, execute, and control a software development project. The SDLC is a process that includes systems analysts, software engineers, programmers, and end users in the project design and development. Because there is no industrywide SDLC, an organization can use any one or a combination of SDLC methods. The SDLC simply provides a framework for the phases of a software development project, from defining the functional requirements to implementation. Regardless of the method used, the SDLC outlines the essential phases, which can be shown together or as separate elements. The model chosen should be based on the project. For example, some models work better with long-term, complex projects, while others are more suited for short-term projects.
- *Structured Programming Development (SDM).* SDM is a method that programmers use to write programs, allowing considerable influence on the quality of the finished products in terms of coherence, comprehensibility, freedom from faults, and security. It is one of the most widely known programming development models. The methodology promotes discipline, allows introspection, and provides controlled flexibility. It requires defined processes, modular development, and each phase is subject to reviews and approvals. It also allows for security to be added in a formalized, structured approach. Because

it is one of the more commonly used methods, the following provides a look at some of the security features of the model:

- Layering: when developing an operating system, the reference monitor is usually implemented as a layer, or a module. When developing an application, a reference monitor for that application can also be developed to provide more security for the application.
  - Processes are constructed in layers that can protect the security features.
  - Specific activity and access rights are developed for each layer.
- Modularity (agents, applets, objects):
  - Segmenting activities so that pieces can be tested and correctness can be proven for both functionality and security features.
- Identifying and documenting activities performed provides the ability to audit the procedures during the development phases.
- Identifying data flows supporting activities:
  - Data elements/data flows are defined in a data dictionary.
  - Automatic flow diagrams are linked with dictionaries. For example, CASE tools can be very valuable in an object-oriented world. The tools can make the controlling of who is using an object and how it is referenced an almost trivial task.

- *Computer Aided Software Engineering (CASE)*. CASE is the technique of using computers to help with the systematic analysis, design, development, implementation, and maintenance of software. It was designed in the 1970s but has evolved to include visual programming tools and object-oriented programming. It is most often used on large, complex projects involving multiple software components and many people. It provides a mechanism for planners, designers, code writers, testers, and managers to share a common view of where a software project is at each phase of the lifecycle process. By having an organized approach, code and design can be reused, which can reduce costs and improve quality. The CASE approach requires building and maintaining software tools and training for the developers who will use them.

Iterative Development. The problems with the waterfall model created a demand for new models of developing software that provided greater flexibility. In the iterative approach, the project is fragmented into smaller components and each component is a regular waterfall model. This model allows for successive refinements of requirements, design, and coding. One advantage is that system users can provide feedback earlier in the process. Thus, one of the challenges of this model is ensuring involvement from the user community. Allowing refinements during the process requires that a change control mechanism be implemented. Also, the scope of the project may be exceeded if clients change requirements after each release.

Several models have developed from the Iterative Development approach, such as:

- *Prototyping.* The prototyping method was formally introduced in the early 1980s to combat the weaknesses of the waterfall model. The objective is to build a simplified version (prototype) of the application, release it for review, and use the feedback from the user's (or client's) review to build a second, better version. This is repeated until the users are satisfied with the product. It is a four-step process: initial concept, design and implement initial prototype, refine prototype until acceptable, complete and release final version.
    - *Rapid Application Development (RAD).* RAD is a form of prototyping that requires strict time limits on each phase and relies on application tools that enable quick development. This may be a disadvantage if decisions are made so rapidly that it leads to poor design.
    - *Joint Analysis Development (JAD).* JAD was originally invented to enhance the development of large mainframe systems. Recently, JAD facilitation techniques have become an integral part of RAD, Web development, and other methods. It is a management process that helps developers work directly with users to develop a working application. The success of JAD is based on having key players communicating at critical phases of the project. The focus is on having the people who actually perform the job (they usually have the best knowledge of the job) work together with those who have the best understanding of the technologies available to design a solution. JAD facilitation techniques bring together a team of users, expert systems developers, and technical experts throughout the development life cycle.
    - *Modified Prototype Model (MPM):* MPM is a form of prototyping that is ideal for Web application development. It allows for the basic functionality of a desired system or component to be formally deployed in a quick timeframe. The maintenance phase is set to begin after deployment. The goal is to have the process be flexible enough so the application is not based on the state of the organization at any given time. As the organization grows and the environment changes, the application evolves with it rather than being frozen in time.
- *Exploratory Model.* A set of requirements is built with what is currently available. In some projects it may be difficult to identify any of the requirements at the beginning. Thus, assumptions are made as to how the system might work, and then rapid iterations are used to quickly incorporate suggested changes to create a usable system.

The distinguishing characteristic of the exploratory model is the lack of precise specifications.

- *Spiral Model.* The spiral model is a combination of both the waterfall and prototyping methods, and introduces a new component — risk assessment. Similar to prototyping, an initial version of the application is developed. However, the development of each iterated version is carefully designed using the waterfall model. Beginning at the center and working outward (the spiral), each iteration provides a more complete version of the product. A distinguishing feature of the spiral model is that in each phase, a risk assessment review is added. During the risk assessment, an evaluation is completed to determine whether or not development should continue. Estimated costs to complete and schedules are revised each time the risk assessment is performed. Based on the results of the risk assessment, a decision is made to continue or cancel the project, such as the customer or developer determining that increased cost or lengthened timeframe makes the project impractical.

- *Object-Oriented Programming (OOP).* OOP is considered by some to be a revolutionary concept that changed the rules in computer program development. It is organized around *objects* rather than *actions*. OOP is a programming method that makes a self-sufficient object. The object is a block of pre-assembled programming code in a self-contained module. The module encapsulates a chunk of data and the processing instructions that may be called to process the data. Once a block of programming code is written, it can be reused in any number of programs. Examples of object-oriented languages are Eiffel, Smalltalk (one of the first), Ruby, Java (one of the most popular today), C++ (also one of the most popular today), Python, Perl, and Visual Basic. More information on object-oriented programming is provided in the Programming Languages section.
  - *Reuse Model:* an application built from existing components. This model is best suited for projects using object-oriented development because objects can be exported, reused, or modified.
  - *Component-Based Development:* the process of using standardized building blocks to assemble, rather than develop, an application. The components are encapsulated sets of standardized data and standardized methods of processing data, together offering economic and scheduling benefits to the development process. This is similar to object-oriented programming (OOP).

- *Extreme Programming.* Extreme programming is a discipline of software development based on values of simplicity, communication, feedback, and courage. The goal is to bring the entire team (including developers, managers, and customers) together in the presence of simple practices and provide enough feedback to enable the team to see where they are to evaluate their unique software development situation. It uses a simple form of planning and tracking to decide what should be done next and to predict when the project will be finished. The team produces the software in a series of small, fully integrated releases that fulfill the customer-defined needs for the software.

- *Cleanroom.* Developed in the 1990s as an engineering process for the development of high-quality software, it is named after the process of cleaning electronic wafers in a wafer fabrication plant. (Instead of cleaning the crud from the wafer after it has been made, the objective is to prevent the crud from getting into the fabrication environment.) In software application development, it is a method of controlling defects (bugs) in the software. The goal is to write code correctly the first time, rather than trying to find the problems once they are there. Essentially, cleanroom software development focuses on "defect prevention" rather than "defect removal." To achieve this, more time is spent in the design phase; however, the time spent in other phases, such as testing, is reduced (i.e., quality is achieved through design and not testing). Because testing can often consume the majority of a project timeline, the savings of less time during the testing phase could result in substantial savings.

To improve and control software development, the Software Engineering Institute released the Capability Maturity Model^{SM} for Software (CMM or SW-CMM) in 1991. The SW-CMM focuses on quality management processes and has five maturity levels that contain several key practices within each maturity level. The five levels describe an evolutionary path from chaotic processes to mature, disciplined software processes (see Exhibit 5).

The result of using SW-CMM should be higher-quality software products produced by more competitive companies. The SW-CMM framework establishes a basis for which the following can occur:

- Practices can be repeated; if an activity is not repeated, there is no reason to improve it. Organizations must commit to having policies, procedures, and practices and to using them so that the organization can perform in a consistent manner.
- Best practices can be rapidly transferred across groups. Practices need to be defined in such a manner as to allow for transfer across project boundaries. This can provide for standardization for the entire organization.
- Quantitative objectives are established for tasks. Measures are established, done, and maintained to form a baseline from which an assessment is possible. This can ensure that best practices are followed and deviations are reduced.
- Practices are continuously improved to enhance capability (optimizing).

Exhibit 5. SW-CMM

Level	Focus and Key Process Area
Level 1: Initial	The software process is characterized as ad hoc, and occasionally even chaotic. Few processes are defined, and success depends on individual effort and heroics.
Level 2: Repeatable	Basic project management processes are established to track cost, schedule, and functionality. The necessary process discipline is in place to repeat earlier successes on projects with similar applications.
Level 3: Defined	Management and engineering activities are documented, standardized, and integrated into a family of standard software processes for the organization. Projects use a tailored version of the organization's standard software processes for developing and maintaining software.
Level 4: Quantitatively Managed	Detailed measures of the software process and product quality are collected. Software processes and products are quantitatively understood and controlled.
Level 5: Optimizing	Continuous process improvement is facilitated by quantitative feedback from the process and from piloting innovative ideas and technologies.

Mark C. Paulk, Software Engineering Institute, USA. Effective CMM-Based Process Improvement © 1996 by Carnegie Mellon University. CMM, Capability Maturity Model, and IDEAL are service marks of Carnegie Mellon University.

When followed, the SW-CMM provides key practices to improve the ability of organizations to meet goals for cost, schedule, functionality, and product quality. The model establishes a yardstick against which it is possible to judge, in a repeatable way, the maturity of an organization's software process and also compare it to the state of the practice of the industry. The CMM can also be used by an organization to plan improvements to its software process. According to Paulk (1996), "The SW-CMM represents a 'common sense engineering' approach to software process improvement."

The International Standards Organization (ISO) has included software development in its ISO 9000 standards. Both the ISO and SEI efforts are intended to reduce software development failures, improve cost estimates, meet schedules, and produce a higher-quality product. In the United States, more and more organizations are pushing software developers to be SEI-CMM and ISO 9000 compliant.

Depending on the application project and the organization, models can be combined to fit the specific design and development process. For example, an application may need a certain set of activities to take place to achieve success, or the organization may require certain standards or processes to meet industry or government requirements.

Including Security in a Systems Development Method

When deciding on the programming model, security must be a consideration. Many developers focus on functionality and not security: thus, it is important to educate those individuals responsible for the development and the managers who oversee the projects. If developers are brought into the project knowing there is a focus on security, they may better understand the importance of coding both functionality and security.

Regardless of which software development model is used, there are typical phases that need to be included. The basic phases are:

- Project initiation and planning
- Functional requirements definition
- System design specifications
- Build (develop) and document
- Acceptance
- Transition to production (installation)
- Operations and maintenance support (post-installation)
- Revisions and system replacement

Based on these typical phases, the next section provides a correlation of where security tasks should be included during the activities completed at each of these basic phases.

Project Initiation and Planning

In the beginning phase, the business needs (functional requirements) are identified along with the proposed technical solution. This information is contained in a document that outlines the project's objectives, scope, strategies, and other factors such as cost or schedule. Management approval for the project is based on this project plan document.

During this phase, security should also be considered. Exhibit 6 represents security activities that should be done in parallel with the project initiation activities.

A service level agreement, as identified in the security tasks under Identify Security Framework, is a contract that defines the technical support or business parameters that an application service provider will provide to its clients. Typically, the agreement defines the measures for performance and any consequences for failure.

The security officer checklist during the project initiation phase includes:

- Does information have special value or require protection?
- Has the system owner determined the information's value? What are the assigned classifications?

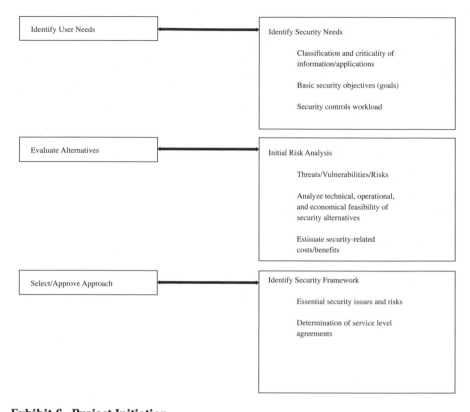

Exhibit 6. Project Initiation

- Will application operation risk exposure of sensitive information?
- Will control of output displays or reports require special measures?
- Will data be generated in public or semi-public places? Are controlled areas required for operation?

Functional Requirements Definition

During this phase, the project management and systems development teams conduct a comprehensive analysis of current and possible future functional requirements to ensure that the new system will meet end-user needs. The teams also review the documents from the project initiation phase and make any revisions or updates as needed. This phase is often included in the project initiation phase.

Exhibit 7 outlines the security activities that should occur in parallel with defining the functional requirements.

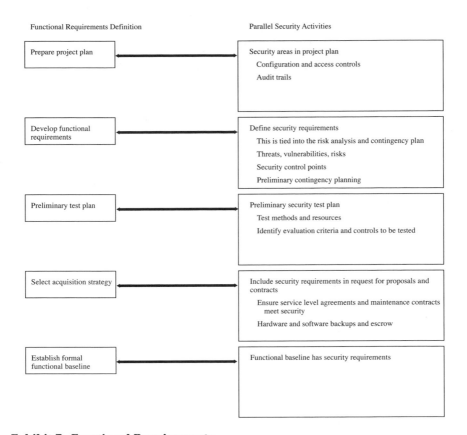

Functional Requirements Definition   Parallel Security Activities

| Prepare project plan | Security areas in project plan
Configuration and access controls
Audit trails |

| Develop functional requirements | Define security requirements
This is tied into the risk analysis and contingency plan
Threats, vulnerabilities, risks
Security control points
Preliminary contingency planning |

| Preliminary test plan | Preliminary security test plan
Test methods and resources
Identify evaluation criteria and controls to be tested |

| Select acquisition strategy | Include security requirements in request for proposals and contracts
Ensure service level agreements and maintenance contracts meet security
Hardware and software backups and escrow |

| Establish formal functional baseline | Functional baseline has security requirements |

Exhibit 7. Functional Requirements

System Design Specifications

This phase includes all activities related to designing the system and software. In this phase, the system architecture, system outputs, and system interfaces are designed. Data input, data flow, and output requirements are established and security features are designed.

The security activities outlined in Exhibit 8 should be done in parallel with the system design phase.

Build/Development and Documentation

During this phase, the source code is generated, test scenarios and test cases are developed, unit and integration testing is conducted, and the program and system are documented for maintenance and for turnover to acceptance testing and production. The parallel security activities are shown in Exhibit 9.

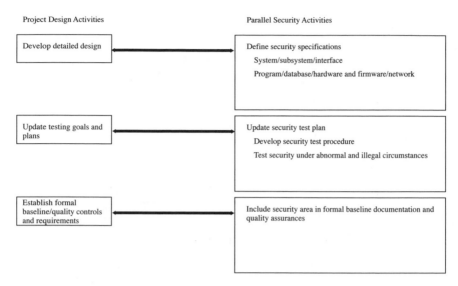

Project Design Activities

Parallel Security Activities

Develop detailed design

Define security specifications
System/subsystem/interface
Program/database/hardware and firmware/network

Update testing goals and plans

Update security test plan
Develop security test procedure
Test security under abnormal and illegal circumstances

Establish formal baseline/quality controls and requirements

Include security area in formal baseline documentation and quality assurances

Exhibit 8. System Design

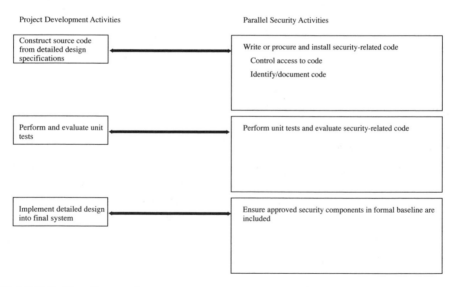

Project Development Activities

Parallel Security Activities

Construct source code from detailed design specifications

Write or procure and install security-related code
Control access to code
Identify/document code

Perform and evaluate unit tests

Perform unit tests and evaluate security-related code

Implement detailed design into final system

Ensure approved security components in formal baseline are included

Exhibit 9. Development

Documentation and Common Program Controls

These are controls used when editing the data within the program, the types of logging the program should be doing, and how the program versions should be stored.

- Program/application:
  - Operating instructions/procedures
  - Utilities
  - Privileged functions
- Job and system documentation:
  - Components: hardware, software, files, databases, reports, users
  - Restart and recovery procedures
- Common program controls:
  - Edits, such as syntax, reasonableness, range checks, and check digits
- Logs:
  - Who, what, when
  - Timestamps
  - Before and after images
- Counts: useful for process integrity checks, and includes total transactions, batch totals, hash totals, and balances
- Internal checks: checks for data integrity within the program from when it gets the data to when it is done with the data:
  - Parameter ranges and data types
  - Valid and legal address references
  - Completion codes
- Peer review: the process of having peers of the programmer review the code
- Program or data library when developing software applications:
  - Automated control system
  - Current versions: programs and documentation
  - Record of changes made:
    - By whom, when authorized, what changed
    - Test data verifying changes
    - User signoffs indicating correct testing
    - A librarian ensures program or data library is controlled in accordance with policy and procedures
    - Controls all copies of data dictionaries, programs, load modules, and documentation and can provide version controls
    - Ensures no programs are added unless properly tested and authorized
- Erroneous/invalid transactions detected are written to a report and reviewed by developers and management

Acceptance

In the acceptance phase, an independent group develops test data and tests the code to ensure that it will function within the organization's environment and that it meets all the functional and security requirements. It is essential that an independent group test the code during all applicable stages of development to prevent a separation of duties issue. A goal of security testing is to ensure that the application meets its security requirements and specifications.

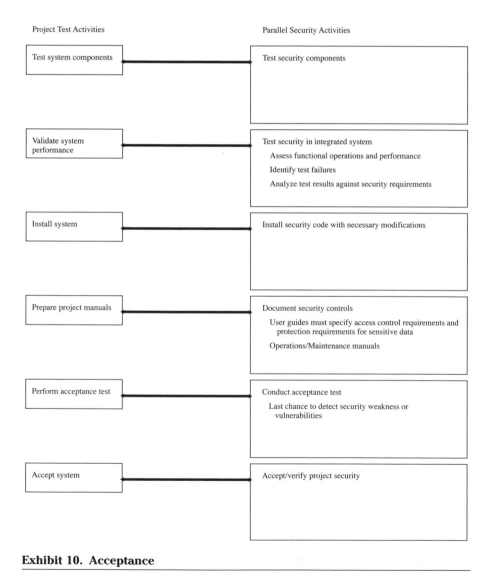

Exhibit 10. Acceptance

The security testing should uncover all design and implementation flaws that would allow a user to violate the software security policy and requirements. To ensure test validity, the application should be tested in an environment that simulates the production environment. This should include a security certification package and any user documentation. This is the first phase of what is commonly referred to as the Certification and Accreditation process (C & A). Exhibit 10 outlines the parallel security activities.

Testing and Evaluation Controls

During the test and evaluation phase, the following guidelines can be included as appropriate to the environment:

- Test data should include data at the ends of the acceptable data ranges, various points in between, and data beyond the expected and allowable data points.
- Test with known good data.
- Data validation: before and after each test, review the data to ensure that it has not been modified inadvertently.
- Bounds checking — field size, time, date, etc. Bounds checking prevents buffer overflows.
- Sanitize test data to ensure that sensitive production data is not exposed through the test process.
- Test data should not be production data until preparing for final user acceptance tests.

Testing controls include:

- Test all changes.
- Management acknowledges the results of the test.
- Program librarian retains implementation test data.
  - Use this data to test modifications.
- Parallel run requires a separate copy of production data.
  - Use copies of master files, not production versions.

Certification and Accreditation. Certification begins with the process of evaluating the security stance of the software or system against a predetermined set of security standards. Certification also involves how well the system performs its intended functional requirements. The evaluation results should be documented in some type of security certification document. The document should contain an analysis of the technical and nontechnical security features and countermeasures and the extent that the software/system meets the security requirements for its mission and operational environment. A certifying officer then verifies that the software has been tested and meets all applicable policies, regulations, and standards

271

for securing information systems. Any exceptions are noted for the accreditation officer (usually a senior management official). (Note: certification and accreditation are two separate steps.)

The accreditation officer, after reviewing the certification, authorizes the software/system to be implemented in a production status, in a specific environment, for a specific period of time. There are two types of accreditation: provisional and full. Provisional accreditation is for a specific time period and outlines required changes to the applications, system, or accreditation documentation. Full accreditation implies that no changes are required for making the accreditation decision.

Transition to Production (Implementation)

During this phase, the new system is transitioned from the acceptance phase into the live production environment. Activities during this phase include obtaining security accreditation (if not included in the system accreditation process); training the new users according to the implementation and training schedules; implementing the system, including installation, data conversions; and, if necessary, conducting any parallel operations.

Security activities verify that the data conversion and data entry are controlled and only those who need to have access during this process are allowed on the system. Also, an acceptable level of risk is determined and the security accreditation is obtained (note that this should have been done earlier). Additionally, appropriate controls must be in place to reconcile and validate the accuracy of information after it is entered into the system. It should also test the ability to substantiate processing. The acceptance of risk is based on the identified risks and operational needs of the application to meet the organization's mission.

Operations and Maintenance Support (Post-Installation)

During this phase, the system is in general use throughout the organization. The activities involve monitoring the performance of the system and ensuring continuity of operations. This includes detecting defects or weaknesses, managing and preventing system problems, recovering from system problems, and implementing system changes.

The operating security activities during this phase include testing backup and recovery procedures, ensuring proper controls for data and report handling, and the effectiveness of security processes.

During the maintenance phase, periodic risk analysis and recertification of sensitive applications are required when significant changes occur. Significant changes include a change in data sensitivity or criticality, relocation or major change to the physical environment, new equipment, new external interfaces, new operating system software, or new application software. Throughout the operation and maintenance phase, it is important to verify that any changes to procedures or functionality do not disable or circumvent the security features. Also, someone should be assigned the task of verifying compliance with applicable service level agreements according to the initial operational and security baselines.

Revisions and System Replacement

As systems are in production mode, the hardware and software baselines should be subject to periodic evaluations and audits. In some instances, problems with the application may not be defects or flaws, but rather additional functions not currently developed in the application. Any changes to the application must follow the same SDM and be recorded in a change management system.

Revision reviews should include security planning and procedures to avoid future problems. Periodic application audits should be conducted and include documenting security incidents when problems occur. Documenting system failures is a valuable resource for justifying future system enhancements.

Programming Languages

In the development phase, programmers have the option of writing code in several different programming languages. A programming language is a set of rules telling the computer what operations to perform. Programming languages have evolved in "generations," and each language is characterized into one of the generations.

The five generations of programming languages are:

- Machine language
- Assembly language
- High-level language
- Very high level language
- Natural language

Those in the lower level are closer in form to the binary language of the computer. Both machine and assembly languages are considered low-level languages. As the languages become easier and more similar to the language people use to communicate, they become higher level. High-level languages are easier to use than lower levels and can be used to produce programs more quickly. In addition, high-level languages are beneficial because they enforce coding standards and can provide more security. Exhibit 11 provides a brief overview of the characteristics associated with each generation language.

Exhibit 11. Characteristics of Each Generation Language

Generation	Language	Characteristics
First-generation	Machine language	Very simple instructions that can be executed directly by the CPU of a computer (i.e., they do not need to be translated). Each type of computer has its own machine language.
Second-generation	Assembly language	Uses symbols as abbreviations for major instructions instead of long combinations of binary digits. Procedural language.
Third-generation	High-level language — COBOL, FORTRAN, Basic, and C	Considered procedural languages because the program instructions tell the computer what to do and how to do it.
Fourth-generation	Very high level language — query languages, report generators, and application generators	Not considered procedural because it allows programmers to specify what the computer is suppose to do without specifying how it is to be done. Thus, they need much fewer programming statements to achieve the same result as an earlier-generation language.
Fifth-generation	Natural language — expert systems, artificial intelligence	Eliminates the need for programmers to learn a specific vocabulary, grammar, or syntax. The text of a natural language statement very closely resembles human speech. They take the user further away from dealing directly with the computer hardware and software.

Assembly languages and high-level languages must be translated into an appropriate machine language. Because it is easier to write code in a high-level language, most programs are first written in one of these languages and then translated into machine code.

A language translator converts the source code into machine language so that the program will work on the computer. The translation is performed by another type of program, such as an assembler, compiler, or interpreter.

Assemblers, Compilers, and Interpreters

An *assembler* is a program that translates an assembly language program into machine language. High-level languages are translated into machine language by a program called a compiler. A *compiler* takes a high-level program (referred to as the source code) and translates it into an executable machine-language program (known as object code). The translation occurs in a single process — the entire program is translated at one time. Once the translation is complete, the machine-language program can be run any number of times, but it can only be run on one type of computer. To run the program on another type of computer, the program must be retranslated (using a different compiler) into the appropriate machine language.

Another alternative to compiling a high-level language is to use an *interpreter* program. Instead of compiling a program all at once and storing it for future use, the interpreter translates it instruction-by-instruction at the time of execution. The interpreter program acts like a CPU with a fetch-and-execute cycle. To execute a program, the interpreter runs in a loop that repeatedly reads one instruction from the program, decides what is necessary to carry out that instruction, and then performs the appropriate machine-language command. Interpreters are commonly used when developing small and simple programs.

The major difference between using a compiler or an interpreter is speed. Compiled programs typically execute up to five times faster than interpreted programs. For the most part, vendors compile software before it is distributed. Thus, end users are typically never able to look at the source code. This protects the vendors from having to publish and release their application source, which often contains proprietary secrets.

There are also decompilers and disassemblers. *Decompilers* are the reverse of compilers, in that they attempt to translate machine language back into a high-level programming language, and *disassemblers* translate machine language into an assembly-language program. Essentially, it is the process of translating the machine language into code that can be read more easily. Sometimes, this can be a form of reverse-engineering. It is important for security professionals to remember that most vendors prohibit the use of reverse-engineering techniques to disassemble their software. On the other hand, security personnel may use decompilers and disassemblers for software forensics and forensic programming. A hybrid approach is done using Java, bytecode, and the Java Virtual Machine (JVM); more information is provided in the Java section.

The next section provides a brief overview of the most common programming languages used to develop applications, including:

- *C and C++.* The C programming language was devised in the early 1970s as a system implementation language for the Unix operating system. (It was named C because its predecessor was named B.) C is a high-level programming language forming the basis of other programming languages such as C++, Perl, and Java. Programs are first written in C and the code is later compiled into binary language for the computer to understand.

- *Hypertext Markup Language (HTML).* HTML is a simple data format used to create hypertext documents that are portable from one platform to another. In the true sense of programming languages, HTML would not itself be one. However, because of the advent of the Web, it is a common language used for programming information in a format that is viewable in browsers. HTML is an application of the Standard Generalized Markup Language (SGML). SGML documents with generic semantics are appropriate for representing information in a wide range of domains. HTML has been in use since 1990 by the WWW information initiative. It consists of text displayed to the reader of the HTML document and tags that tell the browser how to format the text.
- *Java.* Java is a relatively new language (1995) developed and released by Sun Microsystems as part of Sun's HotJava Web browser. It is a high-level programming language that compiles and interprets. In many ways it is similar to C++. Both provide support for object-oriented programming, share many keywords, and can be used to develop stand-alone applications. Java is different from C++ in that Java is type-safe, supports only single inheritance, and has support for concurrency.

Programs written in Java are compiled into machine language, but it is a machine for a computer that does not really exist. This so-called "virtual" computer is known as the *Java Virtual Machine (Java VM, JVM).* The machine language for the Java VM is an independent-machine bytecode that can be transmitted across a network and then interpreted or compiled to native code by the Java runtime system in Java VM. Note that Java can also be compiled into native object code.

One of the advantages of using Java is that it can be used on any type of computer. All the computer needs is an interpreter for the Java bytecode. A different Java bytecode is needed for each type of computer; but once the computer has a Java bytecode interpreter, it can run any Java bytecode program. The same Java bytecode program can be run on any computer that has such an interpreter. This is one of the essential features of Java — the same compiled program can be run on many different types of computers (see Exhibit 12).

In Exhibit 12, the program is first translated (compiled) into an intermediate language called *Java Bytecode.* The Java interpreter parses and runs each Java bytecode instruction on the computer. Compilation happens just once; however, interpretation occurs each time the program is executed. The Java bytecode is similar to the machine code instructions for the Java VM. Every Java interpreter, whether it is a development tool or a Web browser, is an implementation of the Java VM.

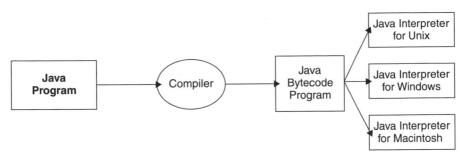

Exhibit 12. Java

The Java Application Programming Interface (Java API) is a large collection of ready-made software components that provide useful capabilities. The most common Java programs are applications and applets. *Applications* are stand-alone programs. Applets are similar to applications, except that they are not stand-alone; they run within a Java-compatible browser. An applet is a small program (executable content) written in the Java programming language that can be included in an HTML page. When a browser is enabled with Java technology, the applet's code is transferred to the system and executed by the browser's Java VM. Embedded in the Java API is the applet security manager that enforces several applet restrictions.

Java Security

The original Java security model implemented a *sandbox* that imposed strict controls on what Java programs could and could not do. An alternative to the sandbox approach of handling mobile code is to run only code that is trusted. For example, ActiveX controls should be run only when you completely trust the entity (person or corporation) that signed the control. Currently, the trend for mobile code systems is to have both a sandbox model and a code-signing trust model — Java is already including both code-signing and sandbox approaches for securely running applets on a local machine.

The Java programming language runs its components (applets) in a restricted environment, called the sandbox. All activities in the sandbox are carefully checked, and any dangerous activity, such as the code attempting to access the hard drive, is prevented.

The three parts (sometimes referred to as layers) of the Java secure sandbox approach include:

- *Verifier* (or *interpreter*), which helps to ensure type safety. It is primarily responsible for memory and bounds checking.
- *Class loader,* which loads and unloads classes dynamically from the Java runtime environment

- *Security manager,* which acts as a security gatekeeper protecting against rogue functionality

The Web browser defines and implements a security policy for running downloaded Java code, such as an applet. A Java-enabled Web browser includes a Java Verifier and runtime library, along with Classes (in Java, all objects belong to classes) to implement a Security Manager. The Security Manager controls the access to critical system resources and ensures that the Web browser's version of the Security Manager is implemented correctly. In the extreme, if a Java-enabled Web browser did not install a system Security Manager, an applet would have the same access as a local Java application.

The verifier is responsible for scrutinizing the bytecode (regardless of how it was created) before it can run on a local Java VM. Because many programs written in Java are intended to be downloaded from the network, the Java verifier acts as a buffer between the computer and the downloaded program. And because the computer is actually running the verifier, which is executing the downloaded program, the verifier can protect the computer from dangerous actions that can be caused by the downloaded program. The verifier is built into the Java VM and, by design, cannot be accessed by programmers or users.

The verifier can check bytecode at a number of different levels. The simplest check ensures that the format of a code fragment is correct. The verifier also applies a built-in theorem prover to each code fragment. The theorem prover can ensure that the bytecode does not have rogue code, such as the ability to forge pointers, violate access restrictions, or access objects using incorrect type information. If the verifier discovers rogue code within a class file, it executes an exception and the class file is not executed.

A criticism of the Java verifier is the length of time it takes to verify bytecodes. Although the delay time is minimal, Web business owners thought that any delay, such as 10 to 20 seconds, would prevent customers from using their sites. This could be viewed as an example of a technology that is not quite ready for the argument (trade-off) between functionality and security.

In most Java implementations, when the bytecode arrives at the Java VM, the Class Loader forms it into a Class, which the verifier automatically examines. The class loader is responsible for loading the mobile code. The class loaders are responsible for determining when and how classes can be added to a running Java environment. For security purposes, the class loaders ensure that important parts of the Java runtime environment are not replaced by imposter code (known as class spoofing). For security purposes, class loaders typically divide classes into distinct namespaces according to origin. This is an important security element — to keep local classes distinct from external classes. However, a weakness was discovered in the class loader — in some instances, it was possible for the namespaces to overlap. This has subsequently been protected with an additional security class loader.

The third part of the model is the Security Manager, which is responsible for restricting the ways an applet uses visible interfaces (Java API calls). It is a single Java object that performs runtime checks on dangerous operations. Essentially, code in the Java library consults the Security Manager whenever a potentially dangerous operation is attempted. The Security Manager has veto authority and can generate a "security exception." A standard browser Security Manager will disallow most operations when they are requested by untrusted code, and will allow trusted code to perform all of its operations. It is the responsibility of the Security Manager to make all final decisions as to whether a particular operation is permitted or rejected.

A weakness of the three-part model is that if any of the three parts fail to operate, the security model is completely compromised. Since Java's introduction, several additional security features have been released, including the "java.security package." This package is an API that includes both a cryptographic provider interface and APIs for common cryptographic algorithms. It provides the ability to implement cryptography and manage/modify default security protection for a specific application.

Other new Java releases focusing on security include:

- *Java Certification Path API* for building and validating certification paths and managing certificate revocation lists.
- *Java GSS-API* for securely exchanging messages between communication applications using Kerberos. Support for single sign-on using Kerberos is also included.
- *Java Authentication and Authorization Service (JAAS)* that enables services to authenticate and enforce access controls upon users.
- *Java Cryptography Extension (JCE)* provides a framework and implementation for encryption, key generation and key agreement, and Message Authentication Code (MAC) algorithms.
- *Java Secure Socket Extension (JSSE)* enables secure Internet connections. It implements a Java version of the Secure Socket Layer (SSL) and Transport Layer Security (TLS) protocols and includes functionality for data encryption, server authentication, message integrity, and optional client authentication.

As a side note, *JavaScript* is a source-level scripting language embedded in HTML documents. It is *not* Java and has no relation to Java. It was originally named LiveScript and was renamed as a marketing strategy. It is interpreted by the user's Web browser and allows control over most of the features of the Web browser. It has access to most of the contents of the HTML document and has full interaction with the displayed content. Its security management is minimal — it is either enabled or disabled.

Visual Programming: Visual Basic, Delphi, and Visual C. These are examples of visual programming languages allowing programmers to make connections between objects by drawing, pointing, and clicking on diagrams and icons. The goal is to make programming easier by borrowing from the object-orientation language. However, it is done in a graphical or visual manner. It enables the programmer to focus on solving a problem versus handling the programming language. For example, Visual Basic, built by Microsoft, offers a visual environment allowing the programmer to build various components using buttons, scroll bars, and menus.

Object-Oriented Technology

When defining an object-oriented language, the following are some of the key characteristics:

- *Encapsulation* (also known as data hiding). A class defines only the data it needs to be concerned with; thus, when an instance of that class (i.e., an object) is run, the code will not be able to accidentally access other data.
- *Polymorphism.* This is a programming language's ability to process objects differently, depending on their data type. Essentially, a resource can accept arguments of different types at different times and still remain type-safe. This allows for programming generality and software reuse (Nuemann, 1995).
- *Inheritance.* This is the concept of related classes of objects behaving similarly and those subclasses should inherit the proper behavior of their ancestors. This allows for reusability of code across related classes (Nuemann, 1995).
- *All predefined types are objects.* A data type in a programming language is a set of data with values having predefined characteristics, such as integer, character, string, and pointer. In most programming languages, a limited number of such data types are built into the language. The programming language usually specifies (1) the range of values for a given data type, (2) how the values are processed by the computer, and (3) how they are stored.
- All user-defined types are objects.
- All operations are performed by sending messages to objects.

The first step in using an object-oriented language is to identify all the objects you want to manipulate and how they relate to each other; this is often known as *data modeling*. Once the object is identified, it is (1) generalized as a class of objects, (2) defined as the kind of data it contains, and (3) defined as any logic sequences that can manipulate it. Each distinct logic sequence is known as a method. A real instance of a class is called an "object" or an "instance of a class," and this is what is run in the computer. The object's "methods" provide computer instructions and the "class object characteristics" provide relevant data. Communication with objects, and objects' communication with each other, are established through interfaces called messages.

In an object-oriented system, there are three main items: classes, objects, and messages. Classes tell the system how to make objects. The act of creating an object using the directions in a class is called instantiation — the created object is called an instance of the class. An object contains both procedures, which are called methods, and data, which are called attributes. Procedures let the object do things, while data lets the object remember things. Objects perform work by sending messages to other objects. For example, the message may ask the other object to execute one of its methods and return the result to the sender of the message, or the message may ask the object to return the value of one of its attributes to the sender of the message.

When building traditional programs, the programmers must write every line of code from scratch. With object-oriented languages, programmers can use the predetermined blocks of code (objects) instead of starting from scratch. Consequently, an object can be used repeatedly in different applications and by different programmers. This reuse reduces development time and thus reduces programming costs. C++ is an example of an OOP language — it combines the traditional C programming language with object-oriented capabilities.

The advantages of object-oriented languages include:

- Compressed time and maximization of resources
- Speeds development: cuts programming time by 75%
- Increases developer productivity, which can save money
- Facilitates changes
- Assembled applications closely resemble things that people see in the business world
- Self-contained objects: encapsulation provides some security
- Ability to communicate with other objects: strict enforcement of standards is necessary for communication between objects to occur
- Reuse of key portions of application programs: must maintain a library of critical objects

Object-Oriented Security

Object-oriented systems provide security by applying controls that are based on policy. For example, in a CORBA system, a policy applies to a domain. System administrators apply policy to an object by putting the object into a domain and setting up policies for the domain.

In object-oriented systems, objects are encapsulated. *Encapsulation* protects the object by denying access to view what is located inside the object

— it is not possible to see what is contained in the object because it is encapsulated. Encapsulation of the object does provide protection of private data from outside access. For security purposes, no object should be able to access another object's internal data. On the other hand, it could be difficult for system administrators to apply the proper policies to an object if they cannot identify what the object contains.

Some of the security issues can be found in the use of polymorphism and inheritance. In object-oriented programming, *Polymorphism* refers to a programming language's ability to process objects differently, depending on their data type. The term is sometimes used to describe a variable that may refer to objects whose class is not known at compile time, but will respond at runtime according to the actual class of the object to which they refer. Although polymorphism seems straightforward, if used incorrectly, it can lead to security problems. Refer to the insert, which was taken from an article by Todd Sundsted (2002) in the *Java Security Newsletter.*

Secure Code and Polymorphism

In Java, inheritance dictates interface but does not constrain behavior. Without language support for techniques such as Design by Contract, it is easy to use inheritance in ways that introduce security flaws.

Subclassing allows a programmer to redefine core functionality of a superclass in a subclass. Polymorphism permits the substitution of that subclass anywhere the superclass could be used — with altered functionality in place. Together, these two characteristics of object-oriented programming allow developers to change the behavior of a set of classes in ways that cannot be anticipated by the original authors.

Consider a design in which a randomness source is passed to a cryptographic algorithm during key generation. To make the design flexible, the randomness source is modeled as an interface. Concrete randomness sources implement this interface.

Now imagine that a novice programmer uses the framework and implements a randomness source that returns less than random numbers (an infinitely long sequence of 1s, for example). This change in behavior introduces a flaw that compromises the security of the entire framework, if not the entire application. These kinds of programming errors are easy to make, and difficult to spot.

For this reason, consider making critical classes and methods final. In this way, you reduce the likelihood of malicious or accidentally flawed attempts at subclassing.

— Todd Sundsted (July 2002)
Java Security Newsletter © 2002 Accela Communications, Inc.

One of the basic activities of an object-oriented design is establishing relationships between classes. One fundamental way to relate classes is through *inheritance*. Inheritance is when a class of objects is first defined as the superclass, and any subclass that is defined can inherit the definitions of the general or super class. Inheritance allows a programmer to build a new class similar to an existing class without duplicating all the code. The new class inherits the old classes' definitions and adds to them. Essentially, for the programmer, an object in a subclass need not have its own definition of data and methods that are generic to the class it is a part of. This can help decrease program development time — what works for the superclass will also work for the subclass.

Exhibit 13A shows an example of a *single* inheritance, where one single inheritance and entity directly inherits state and behaviors from only one category. A typical OOP example uses the bank account. The superclass account has the operations that all bank accounts would need — add money and subtract money. Accounts are often split into types, such as checking and savings accounts; these would be the subclasses. Both of these accounts would inherit their parent's (superclass) operations: Add Money and Subtract Money. This example assumes checking accounts and their variations (such as plan B) have checks, and savings accounts and their variations (plans C and D) have interest. One of the problems with inheritance is what to do if one subclass has the same properties of another subclass. Using the banking example, this would be a checking account also having interest, or a savings account also having checks.

Multiple inheritance allows an entity to directly inherit state and behavior from two or more categories. In Exhibit 13B, Mary Smith is both a manager and a security officer; thus, she would inherit the capabilities of being both a manager and security officer.

Multiple inheritances can introduce complexity and may result in security breaches for object accesses. Issues such as name clashes and ambiguities must be resolved by the programming language to avoid a subclass inheriting inappropriate privileges from a superclass.

Distributed Object-Oriented Systems

Applications today are being constructed with software systems that are based on distributed objects, such as the Common Object Request Broker Architecture (CORBA), Java Remote Method Invocation (JRMI), Enterprise JavaBeans (EJB), and Distributed Component Object Model (DCOM). A distributed object-oriented system allows parts of the system to be located on separate computers within an enterprise network. The object system itself is a compilation of reusable self-contained objects of code designed to perform specific business functions.

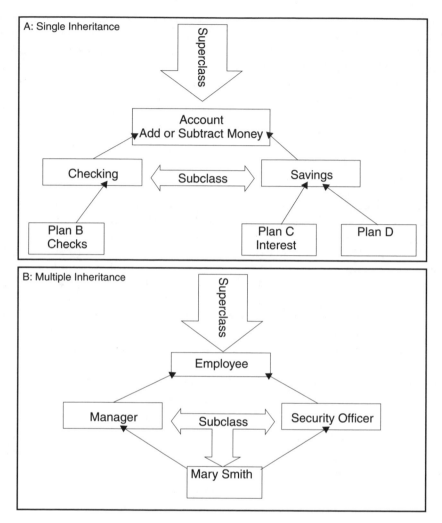

Exhibit 13. Single Inheritance and Multiple Inheritance

Using Object Linking and Embedding (OLE), applications can share functionality through live data exchange and embedded data. OLE architecture is based on software pieces called components. The capability to call one program from another is linking. The capability to put a piece of data in a foreign program is embedding. Note that embedding can embed programs as well, including malware.

As the age of mainframe-based applications began to wane, the new era of distributed computing emerged. Distributed development architectures allow applications to be divided into pieces called components, and each component can exist in different locations. This development paradigm allows programs to "download" code from remote machines onto a user's local host in a seamless manner to the user.

Some distributed computing characteristics are:

- *Enhanced transaction processing.* In a distributed environment, single transactions can span multiple hosts and multiple processes. However, applications must still guarantee the atomic integrity of transactions.
- *Portable clients and servers.* In a distributed environment, the user and the application can move. Users can access applications from just about anywhere using an Internet connection. In addition, system managers can move applications/components among various machines, depending on factors such as workload or hardware failures.
- *Enhanced datasets.* Applications no longer deal with only simple data types. Current technologies allow system designers to incorporate enhanced objects such as video, audio, and multimedia into the most basic applications.

How objects communicate with one another is complex, especially because objects may not reside on the same machine, but may be located across machines on the network. To standardize this process, the Object Management Group (OMG) created a standard for finding objects, initiating objects, and sending requests to the objects. The standard is the Object Request Broker (ORB), which is part of the Common Object Request Broker Architecture (CORBA).

For security purposes, each of the models/technologies has different characteristics that should be considered when making a distributed object choice. The following is a brief overview of the major technologies in this area.

Distributed Component Object Model (DCOM)

DCOM is a Microsoft networking standard (it is only used for Microsoft platforms) that allows different software components to interact with each other as an integrated application. DCOM provides for authentication, data integrity, and confidentiality through a single property called the *authentication* level. Authentication levels only apply to server objects, and each object can have its own level set. The higher levels of DCOM provide additional security, but at a greater cost. Exhibit 14 defines the DCOM authentication levels.

ActiveX

ActiveX is a set of technologies enabling software components to interact with one another in a networked environment, regardless of the language in

Exhibit 14. DCOM Authentication Levels

Level	Authentication Features
1	No authentication. Allows the application in question to interact with any machine without any requirements regarding the identity associated with the remote object.
2	Connect authentication. The client will only be authenticated on connection. Subsequent packets are not authenticated, which can lead to a hijacking attack.
3	Default authentication. Currently default authentication is exactly the same as connect authentication.
4	Call-level authentication. Individually authenticates every method call in an object. The remote user's machine will cache the password; thus, the authentication of each call does not necessarily require the user to input a password each time a remote method is called. The extra authentication is primarily used to prevent hijacking attacks. However, calls are generally broken into multiple packets and only one packet carries the authentication information; the other packets can be completely replaced.
5	Packet-level authentication. Authenticates each packet separately. This is used to fix the authentication weakness in level 4. However, the authenticated packets can be modified as long as the authentication information is not changed.
6	Packet integrity-level authentication. Improves on packet-level authentication by adding a checksum to each packet to avoid tampering. However, the contents of the packets could still be viewed.
7	Packet privacy-level authentication. Fully encrypts all data, preventing attacks as long as the underlying encryption is sufficiently strong.

From Viega and McGraw, 2002, pp. 57–58.

which the components were created. It was developed by Microsoft as an alternative to Sun Microsystems' Java technology. ActiveX controls are based on the Component Object Model (COM) technology. It is the underlying architecture forming the foundation for higher-level software services, such as transferring and sharing information among applications. For example, Microsoft uses it to develop programs for the Windows CE operating system used in palm-sized PCs.

An interesting note about security and ActiveX is the use of Authenticode to help mitigate some of the risks associated with software developed using ActiveX. Microsoft client applications, such as Internet Explorer, Exchange, Outlook, and Outlook Express, come with security features that incorporate Authenticode. These applications are often used to obtain other pieces of software. In a component model, such as ActiveX, applications are often used to obtain other pieces of software — in many instances without the end user being aware of it. For example, when a user visits a Web page that uses executable files to provide animation or sound, code is often downloaded to the end user's machine to achieve the effects. While this may be useful and valuable for getting information, the user risks downloading malicious code from a disreputable publisher.

To avoid this risk to users, Microsoft Authenticode working with Digital IDs from VeriSign™ (provider of digital certificate services) uses digital signatures to enable software developers to include information about themselves and their code with their programs. This is sometimes referred to as "code-signing." Both Microsoft and Netscape use some form of code-signing, which allows users to verify whether downloaded software is from a reputable source.

If the Authenticode is in use and the developer does not have an Authenticode signature, the user would see a security warning verifying whether the user wanted to download the software. If the developer did have an Authenticode signature, a message box would appear telling the user (1) the identity of the publisher, (2) a place to find out more about the control, and (3) the authenticity of the information provided by VeriSign.

As a code-signing technique, Authenticode works well and does what it is intended to do. However, one of the security risks is that there are only two categories: those who you trust and those who you do not trust. For example, if users see the developer as Microsoft, they assume that Microsoft is trusted and will accept the software. If the users see an unknown developer, they may assume that the code cannot be trusted and thus deny access to smaller software companies. Another risk is that Authenticode does not currently support signed scripts in Internet Explorer and is limited to ActiveX objects. In addition, code-signing can only detect whether a file has been tampered with since the time it was signed; it does not prevent damage from malicious (or error-prone) programmers before the code is signed.

Another security risk is how the Certificate Revocation List (CRL) is distributed and updated to users. (The CRL is a document maintained and published by a certification authority [CA] that lists certificates issued by the CA that are no longer valid.) In March 2001, VeriSign Inc. discovered through its routine fraud screening procedures that on January 29 and 30, 2001, it issued two digital certificates to an individual who fraudulently claimed to be a representative of Microsoft Corporation. VeriSign immediately revoked the certificates. The certificates were VeriSign Class 3 Software Publisher certificates and could be used to sign executable content under the name "Microsoft Corporation." The risk associated with these certificates is that the fraudulent party could produce digitally signed code and appear to be Microsoft Corporation. In this scenario, it is possible that the fraudulent party could create a destructive program or ActiveX control, then sign it using either certificate and host it on a Web site or distribute it to other Web sites (VeriSign Security Alert, March 2001). VeriSign worked closely with Microsoft to develop an update to protect customer

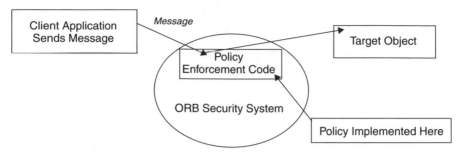

Exhibit 15. ORB Security System

desktops. Refer to Microsoft Security Bulletin MS01-017 for more information on the update.

To counter some of these risks, Microsoft has developed "security
zones" and Netscape has developed "Java Capabilities API" to improve the
granularity of access control beyond the all-or-nothing decision. Although
it is an improvement, neither provides for the granularity needed for highly
sensitive systems.

Common Object Request Broker Architecture (CORBA)

CORBA is a set of standards that address the need for interoperability
between hardware and software products. CORBA allows applications to
communicate with one another, regardless of where they are stored. The
Object Request Broker (ORB) is the middleware that establishes a cli-
ent/server relationship between objects. Using an ORB, a client can transparently locate and activate a method on a server object, either on the
same machine or across a network. The ORB operates regardless of processor type or programming language.

Not only does the ORB handle all the requests on the system, but also
enforces the system's security policy (see Exhibit 15). The policy describes
what the users (and the system) are allowed to do and also what user (or
system) actions will be restricted. The security provided by the ORB
should be transparent to the user's applications. The CORBA security service supports four types of policies: access control, data protection, non-
repudiation, and auditing.

The client application (through an object) sends a request (message) to
the target object.

- The message is sent through the ORB Security System. Inside the
  ORB Security System is the Policy Enforcement Code, which contains
  the organization's policy regarding objects.

- If the policy allows the requester to access the targeted object, the request is then forwarded to the target object for processing.

CORBA is different from DCOM and Enterprise JavaBeans because CORBA is a non-vendor-specific standard. CORBA relies on software vendors to provide implementations. More recently, the CORBA and Enterprise JavaBeans approaches are merging to provide for greater interoperability on enterprise networks.

When reviewing CORBA implementations, consider the following:

- The specific CORBA security features that are supported
- The implementation of CORBA security building blocks, such as cryptography blocks or support for Kerberos systems
- The ease with which system administrators can use the CORBA interfaces to set up the organization's security policies
- Types of access control mechanisms that are supported
- Types, granularity, and tools for capturing and reviewing audit logs
- Any technical evaluations (i.e., Common Criteria)

Java's Remote Method Invocation (RMI) and Enterprise JavaBeans (EJB)

EJB is a Sun Microsystems model providing an API specification for building scalable, distributed, multi-tier, component-based applications. EJB uses Java's RMI implementations for communications. The EBJ server provides a standard set of services for transactions, security, and resource sharing. One of the security advantages is that EJB allows the person assembling the components to control access. Instead of a component developer hard-coding the security policies, the end user (i.e., system administrator or security officer) can specify the policy. Other security features are also available to the end user. A vulnerability of EJB is the noted weakness of the RMI. For example, the RMI is typically configured to allow clients to download code automatically from the server when it is not present. Thus, before the client can make a secure connection, it can still download code or a malicious attacker could masquerade as the client to the server and download code. Although improvements have been made to increase the security of RMI, all implementations must be reviewed for security features.

Programming Language and Security

The choice of which programming language to use is fundamental to the security needs of the project. CISSPs who are managing software development need to be aware of the risks of using various programming languages. For example, if a project requires processing data containing sensitive information, then a programming language that offers more security features would need to be used. On the opposite site, if the project were to distribute an organization's forms on an internal intranet where access from unauthorized users is protected, less security would be needed from the programming language.

When deciding on which programming language and the level of security needed, Nuemann (1995) suggests that the following issues be taken into consideration: modernization, encapsulation, strong type checking, program definable extensions, initialization and finalization, synchronization, aliasing, control of argument passing, handling of exceptions, and runtime libraries.

Software Protection Mechanisms

This section provides a brief overview of many of the software protection controls that can be designed and developed in applications.

Security Kernels

A *security kernel* is responsible for enforcing a security policy. It is a strict implementation of a reference monitor mechanism. The architecture of a kernel operating system is typically layered (see Exhibit 16). The kernel is the lowest and most primitive level. It is a small portion of the operating system. All references to information and all changes to authorizations must pass through the security kernel. In theory, the kernel implements access control and information flow control between implemented objects according to the security policy it is required to enforce.

To be secure, the kernel must meet three basic conditions:

- *Completeness.* All accesses to information must go through the kernel.
- *Isolation.* The kernel itself must be protected from any type of unauthorized access.
- *Verifiability.* The kernel must be proven to meet design specifications.

The reference monitor, also called the reference validator, usually runs inside the security kernel and is responsible for performing security access checks on objects, manipulating privileges, and generating any resulting security audit messages. The reference monitor guards the operating system resources that are performing runtime object protection and auditing.

A term associated with security kernels and the reference monitor is the Trusted Computing Base (TCB). The TCB is the portion of a computer system that contains all elements of the system responsible for supporting the security policy and the isolation of objects. The security capabilities of products for use in the TCB can be verified through various evaluation cri-

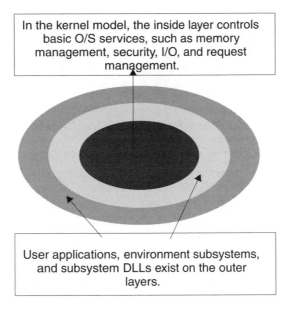

In the kernel model, the inside layer controls basic O/S services, such as memory management, security, I/O, and request management.

User applications, environment subsystems, and subsystem DLLs exist on the outer layers.

Exhibit 16. Security Kernels

teria, such as the earlier Trusted Computer System Evaluation Criteria and the current Common Criteria standard.

Many of these security terms — reference monitor, security kernel, and TCB — are used by vendors for marketing, instead of rigorous standards that must be adhered to. Thus, it is necessary for security professionals to read between the lines and read the small print to fully understand what the vendor is offering with regard to security features.

Processor Privilege States

The *processor privilege states* protect the processor and the activities that it performs. The earliest method of doing this was to record the processor state in a register that could only be altered when the processor was operating in a privileged state. Instructions such as I/O requests were designed to include a reference to this register. If the register was not in a privileged state, the instructions were aborted. The hardware and firmware typically control entry into the privilege mode. For example, the Intel 486 processor defines four privilege rings to protect system code and data from being overwritten.

The privilege level mechanism prevents memory access (programs or data) from less privileged to more privileged levels. The privileged levels are called *rings*.

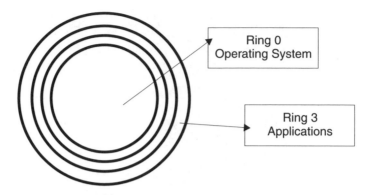

Exhibit 17. Privilege Ring Level

To illustrate this point, many operating systems, including Unix and Windows 2000, use two processor access modes: user mode and kernel mode. User application code runs in user mode and operating system code runs in kernel mode. The privileged processor mode is called kernel mode. Kernel mode allows the processor access to all system memory and all CPU instructions. Application code runs in a non-privileged mode (the user mode) and has a limited set of interfaces available, limited access to system data, and no direct access to hardware resources. An advantage of the operating system having a higher privilege level than the application software is that problematic application software cannot disrupt the system's functioning. As a side note, if the processor has four privilege rings, as in the Intel X486, the kernel mode uses the "0" privilege level ring, while the user mode (applications) uses the "3" privilege level ring, with the rings numbered from the inside out (see Exhibit 17).

When a user-mode program calls a system service (such as reading a document from storage), the processor catches the call and switches the calling request to kernel mode. When the call is complete, the operating system switches the call back to user mode and allows the user-mode program to continue.

Again, in the Microsoft model, the operating system and device drivers operate at ring level 0, also known as kernel-level or system-level privilege. At this privilege level, there are no restrictions on what a program can do. Because programs at this level have unlimited access, users should be concerned about the source of device drivers for machines that contain sensitive information. One of the problems for the ring level 0 is that if the operating system (or a device driver) makes a memory or access mistake, the operating system halts with a trap screen (known as the blue screen of death).

Applications and services operate at ring level 3, also known as user-level or application-level privilege. Note that if an application or service fails at this level, a trap screen will appear (also known as a general protection fault) that can be dismissed and the operating system does not care. The decision to have services run at the same privilege level as regular applications is based on the idea that if the service traps, the operating system should continue to operate.

As a side note, Windows 2000 is considered a monolithic operating system. A monolithic operating system exists as a large program consisting of a set of procedures; there are no restrictions on what procedures may be called by any other procedures.

> *A relatively recent attack against Microsoft operating systems using the Win32 API was the Shatter Attack. Refer to the article "Exploiting design flaws in the Win32 API for privilege escalation OR Shatter Attacks — How to Break Windows."*
>
> — http://security.tombom.co.uk/shatter.html

In the Windows 2000 model, this means that the majority of the operating system and device driver codes share the kernel-mode protected memory space. Soloman and Russinovich (2000) outline how Windows 2000 does not provide any protection mechanisms to components running in kernel mode. Thus, once in kernel mode, operating system and device driver code have complete access to system space memory and can bypass Windows 2000 security to access objects. Because most of the Windows 2000 operating system code runs in kernel mode, it is critical that kernel-mode components be carefully designed to ensure they do not violate security features. If a system administrator installs a third-party device driver, it operates in kernel mode and then has access to all operating system data. If the device driver installation software also contains malicious code, that code will also be installed and could open the system to unauthorized accesses.

A privileged state failure can occur if an application program fails. The safest place for an application to fail is to a system halt. For example, if an application has an error, it will fail to the operating system program, and the user can then use the operating system to recover the application and data. This vulnerability could also be exploited by allowing an attacker to crash an application to get to the operating system with the identity and privileges of the person who started the application.

Security Controls for Buffer Overflows

Another issue with privilege states is called *ineffective binding,* which causes buffer overflows. Buffer overflows are perhaps the oldest software problem in existence, and still the most prevalent. If correctly executed by the attacker, the attacker can control the machine. A *buffer overflow* is caused by improper or lack of bounds checking in a program. Essentially, the program fails to see if too much data is provided for an allocated space of memory. Because programs are loaded into memory when run, when there is an overflow, the data has to go somewhere. If that data happens to be executable malicious code that is loaded, it will run as if it were the program.

Buffer overflows must be corrected by the programmer or by directly patching system memory. They can be detected and fixed by reverse-engineering (disassembling programs) and looking at their operations. Hardware states and other hardware controls can make buffer overflows impossible. Bounds enforcement and proper error checking will also stop buffer overflows.

Controls for Incomplete Parameter Check and Enforcement

A security risk exists when all parameters have not been fully checked for accuracy and consistency by the operating systems. The lack of parameter checking can lead to buffer overflow attacks. A recent parameter check attack involved an email attachment with a name longer than 64K. Because the application required attachment names to be less than 64K, attachments that had longer names would overwrite program instructions.

To counter the vulnerability, operating systems must offer some type of buffer management. Parameter checking is implemented by the programmer and involves checking the input data for disallowed characters, length, data type, and format.

Memory Protection

Memory protection is concerned with controlling access to main memory. When several processes are running at the same time, it is necessary to protect the memory used by one process from unauthorized access by another. Thus, it is necessary to partition memory to ensure processes cannot interfere with each other's local memory and to ensure common memory areas are protected against unauthorized access. For example, an operating system can use secondary memory (storage devices) to give the illusion of a larger main memory, or it can partition the main memory among users so that each user sees a virtual machine that has memory smaller than that on the real machine.

The memory used by the operating system needs to be protected to maintain the integrity of privileged code and data. Because memory protection deals with addressing, many protection mechanisms protect memory by placing it outside the address space available to a process. Using Windows 2000 as an example, Solomon (2000) outlines the four methods Windows 2000 uses to provide memory protection so no user process can inadvertently or deliberately corrupt the address space of another process, or the operating system itself.

The first method ensures that all systemwide data structures and memory pools used by kernel-mode system components can be accessed only while in kernel mode; thus, user-mode requests cannot access these pages. If they attempt to do so, the hardware will generate a fault and then the memory manager will create an access violation. In early Windows operating systems, such as Windows 95 and Windows 98, some pages in the system address space were writable from user mode, thus allowing an errant application to corrupt key system data structures and crash the system.

Second, each process has a separate, private address space protected from being accessed by any request belonging to another process, with a few exceptions. Each time a request references an address, the virtual memory hardware, in conjunction with the memory manager, intervenes and translates the virtual address into a physical one. Because Windows 2000 is controlling how virtual addresses are translated, requests running in one process do not inappropriately access a page belonging to another process.

Third, most modern processors provide some form of hardware-controlled memory protection, such as read or write access. The type of protection offered depends on the processor. For example, a memory protection option is page_noaccess. If an attempt is made to read from, write to, or execute code in this region, an access violation will occur.

The fourth protection mechanism uses Access Control Lists to protect shared memory objects and are checked when processes attempt to open them. Another security feature involves access to mapped files. To map to a file, the object (or user) performing the request must have at least read access to the underlying file object or the operation will fail.

Covert Channel Controls

A covert channel or confinement problem is an information flow that is not controlled by a security control. It is a communication channel that allows two cooperating processes to transfer information in such a way that violates the system's security policy. Although there are protection mechanisms in place, if unauthorized information can be transferred using a signaling mechanism or other objects, then a covert channel may exist.

In TCP/IP, there are a number of methods available whereby covert channels can be established and data can be surreptitiously passed between hosts. These methods could be used in many areas, such as network sniffers or bypassing packet filters. For example, one method would be to store information inside the TCP/IP header in a covert manner (Rowland, 1996).

Examples of Covert Channel Attacks

The attacker can use a covert channel to secretly operate remote hacking tools to search for vulnerabilities to be exploited in other networks. Should the activities be discovered by the protection mechanisms in the other network, it would appear that the probe originated from the compromised network, not from the IP address of the attacker.

Most content filtering applications restrict an internal user's access to Web sites whose URL is contained in a database of Web sites that are not permitted. The malicious user can establish a covert channel over HTTP to a PC outside the protected network. To the content filter it appears that the user is connected to a Web site that is not in the database of Web sites that have been restricted. The user is able to freely surf the dark side if the Internet is unimpeded by the organization's content filtering application.

— Excerpted from a white paper by Paul A. Henry MCP+I, MCSE, CISSP

© CyberGuard Corporation, 2000

The only channels of interest are those breaching the security policy; those channels that parallel legitimate communications paths are not of concern. Although there are differences for each type of covert channel, there is a common condition — the transmitting and receiving objects over the channel must have access to a shared resource.

To counter covert channels, the first step is to identify any potential covert channels; the second is to analyze any potential covert channels to determine whether a channel actually exists. The next steps are based on manual inspection and appropriate testing techniques to verify if the channel creates security concerns. The final step is to close the covert channel by installing patches or adding additional security software, such as packet-filtering.

Cryptography

Cryptographic techniques protect information by transforming the data through encryption schemes. They are used to protect the confidentiality and integrity of information. Most cryptographic techniques are used in telecommunications systems; however, because of the increase in distributed systems, they are becoming increasingly used in operating systems.

One method is to encrypt objects using a checksum. The encrypted object includes a checksum calculated from the value of the decrypted object. This allows the decryption element to verify that decryption has taken place; that is, the correct key has been used in the decryption operation.

Encryption algorithms are also used to encrypt specific files located within the operating system. For example, database files that contain user information, such as group rights, are encrypted using one-way hashing algorithms to ensure higher protection of the data. Another cryptographic technique of operating systems is to offer users, through simple application interfaces, the capability to encrypt and decrypt specific files. Cryptography and related issues are discussed in the Cryptography chapter (Chapter 6).

Password Protection Techniques

Operating systems and application software use passwords as a convenient mechanism to authenticate users. Typically, operating systems use passwords to authenticate the user and establish access controls for resources, including the system, files, and applications.

Password protections offered by the operating system include:

- How the password is selected: can users generate their own password?
- Password lifetime limits
- Password complexity: a mix of uppercase/lowercase letters, numbers, special characters
- Password length

Password files stored within a computer system must be secured by the protection mechanisms of the operating system. Because password files are prone to unauthorized access, the most common solution is to encrypt password files using one-way encryption algorithms (hashing). These, however, are very susceptible to a dictionary attack if the passwords chosen appear in any dictionary.

Another feature offered by an operating system for password security involves an overstrike or password-masking feature. This prevents others from reading the typed password.

Inadequate Granularity of Controls

If there is not enough granularity of security, users will get more access permission than needed. One of the primary goals of unauthorized users is to gain system administrator or root access. With this level of access, an unauthorized user has full control over the system and can bypass security protection measures. However, depending on the desired resource, system administrator privilege may not be needed. For example, accessing a file owned by another user or application account only involves obtaining that user's privileges.

Another example occurs when a system feature permits a program to run with privileges and capabilities other than those assigned to the user. If the user is unable to access object A, but the user has access to a program that can access object A, then the security mechanisms could be bypassed.

Inadequate granularity of controls can be addressed in the following ways:

- *Implement the concept of least privilege.* Set reasonable limits.
- *Separation of duties/functions.* During development, this includes programming, quality assurance/approval, and production. Programmers should never be system administrators. Grant users only those permissions necessary to do their jobs.
- *Roles should be performed by different people;* examples include:
  - *Users.* Users should have no access to computer rooms or legacy programs.
  - *Information systems development.* Programmers and system analysts should not have write access to production programs, allowing them to change the installed program code. Programmers should have no ongoing direct access to production programs. Access to fix crashed applications should be limited to the time required to repair the problem causing the failure.
  - *Information systems processing.* Mainframe operators should not be allowed to do programming.
  - *Information system support.* Maintenance programmers should not have access to programs under development.
- *Assignment of system privileges.* This must be tightly controlled and a shared responsibility.

Control and Separation of Environments

The following environmental types can exist in software development:

- Development environment
- Quality assurance environment
- Application (production) environment
- Blended environment

The security issue is to control how each environment can access the application and the data, and then provide mechanisms to keep them separate. For example, systems analysts and programmers write, compile, and perform initial testing of the application's implementation and functionality in the *development environment*. As the application reaches maturity and is moving toward production readiness, users and quality assurance people perform functional testing within the *quality assurance environment*. The quality assurance configuration should simulate the production environment as closely as possible. Once the user community has accepted the application, it is moved into the *production environment*. *Blended environments* combine one or more of these individual environments and are generally the most difficult to control.

Control measures protecting the various environments include:

- Physical environment controls:
  - Physical isolation of environment
  - Physical separation of data for each environment
- Logical environment controls:
  - Access control lists
  - Content-dependent access control
  - Rule-based access control
  - Role-based access control: primary benefit is speed and ease of use, change the role, change the access
    - Role-based advantages
      - Change management is easier
        - As people change jobs, administrator changes their roles
        - As people come and go, administrator changes the user database
        - As applications/transactions change, owner assigns roles allowed access
    - Role-based constraints
      - Role definition stability
      - Accountability and separation of duty
        - User ID in audit trail for accountability
        - Assign different duties to mutually exclusive roles for separation of duties
        - Be careful of users with multiple roles
        - The part of the organization where role-based constraints are determined should also dictate which data objects those users can access
      - Organizational affiliation
        - The part of the organization where role-based constraints are determined should also dictate which data objects users may access
  - Capabilities and tokens
  - Passwords/authentication

     –   Read/write/execute control

Time of Check/Time of Use (TOC/TOU)

If there are multiple threads of execution at the same time, a TOC/TOU is possible. The most common TOC/TOU hazards are file-based race conditions that occur when there is a check on some property of the file that precedes the use of that file.

Viega and McGraw (2002) point out that to avoid TOC/TOU problems, especially file-based issues, the programmer should avoid any file system call that takes a filename for an input, instead of a file handle or a file descriptor. When using file descriptors, it is possible to ensure that the file being used does not change after it is first called. In addition, files that are to be used should be kept in their own directory, where the directory is only accessible by the Universal ID (UID) of the program performing the file operation. In this manner, even when using symbolic names, attackers are not able to exploit a race condition, unless they already have the proper UID. (If they have a proper UID, there is no reason to exploit the race condition.)

Social Engineering

The best method of preventing social engineering is to make users aware of the threat and give them the proper procedures for handling unusual (or what may seem usual) requests for information. For example, if a user were to receive a phone call from a "system administrator" asking for his password, users should be aware of social-engineering threats and ask that the system administrator come to their office to discuss the problems in a face-to-face format. Unless the user is 100% sure that the person on the phone is the system administrator and the phone line cannot be tampered with, it is better to never give out a password using the phone lines.

Backup Controls

Backing up operating system and application software is a method of ensuring productivity in the event of a system crash. Some controls include:

- Operation copies of software should be available in the event of a system crash. Also, storing copies of software at an off-site location can be useful if the building is no longer available.
- Data, programs, documentation, computing, and communications equipment redundancy can ensure that information is available in the event of an emergency.
- Require that the source code for custom-designed software is kept in escrow. If the software vendor was to go out of business, the

source code would be available to use or can be given to another vendor in the event upgrades or assistance is needed.

- Contingency planning documents help provide a plan for returning operations to normal in the event of an emergency.
- Disk mirroring, Redundant Arrays of Independent Disks (RAID), etc., provide protection for information in the event of a production server crashing.

Malicious Code/Malware Controls

Although most organizations rely on anti-virus software to detect malicious code, some forms of malware may not be detected by the anti-virus software. Some anti-virus or signature scanning software vendors do provide the capability to detect malware code and this can be used in conjunction with anti-virus software to provide greater screening capabilities. There are also controls called *behavior blockers* that prevent hostile code from executing on a host. For example, if executable code attempted to access a file or network resource, the behavior blocker would prevent the access. Another option is to review the system for integrity changes; vendors offer software with the ability to create a baseline of the system, which is subsequently, over a predetermined timeframe, reviewed for changes.

Virus Protection Controls

The methods for detecting a virus include:

- Checking unexpected file size increases
- Noting changes in timestamps
- Experiencing sudden decreases of free space
- Calculation of checksums
- Saving images of internal control tables and noting unexplained changes

Methods for preventing a virus include the following:

- Install and use anti-virus software.
- Conduct frequent backups. (In the event that a backup tape is infected, backups should be periodically stored for an extended period of time so that information can be restored from a clean backup.)
- Only use software from trusted sources and perform virus scans on all software that is installed on the system.
- Back up or make a copy of new software immediately after installation. The original should be stored and the backup copy kept active. If the software becomes infected, the original copy should be used for restoration.

- Know your system so that you can recognize abnormal operation.
- Prohibit the introduction of unauthorized computer products of software by users — only system administrators should be allowed to add new equipment or software.
- Set policies and procedures for users and system administrators so that unauthorized software or equipment cannot be added without proper authorization.
- When appropriate, issue periodic warnings to users so that they are aware of what to do if they suspect unusual emails.
- Establish procedures for reporting suspected incidents.
- Implement programs to reward employees for reporting or assisting in discovery of viruses.

Mobile Code Controls

The concept of attaching programs to Web pages has very real security implications. However, through the use of appropriate technical controls, the user does not have to consider the security consequences of viewing the page. Rather, the controls determine if the user can view the page. Secured systems should limit mobile code (applets) access to system resources such as the file system, the CPU, the network, the graphics display, and the browser's internal state. Additionally, the system should garbage-collect memory to prevent both malicious and accidental memory leakage. The system must manage system calls and other methods that allow applets to affect each other as well as the environment beyond the browser.

Fundamentally, the issue of safe execution of code comes down to a concern with access to system resources. Any running program has to access system resources in order to perform its task. Traditionally, that access has been given to all normal user resources. Mobile code must have restricted access to resources for safety. However, it must be allowed some access in order to perform its required functions.

When creating a secure environment for an executable program, such as mobile code, it is important to identify the resources the program needs and then provide certain types of limited access to these resources to protect against threats. Examples of threats to resources include:

- Disclosure of information about a user or the host machine
- Denial-of-service attacks that make a resource unavailable for legitimate purposes
- Damaging or modifying data
- Annoyance attacks such as displaying obscene pictures on a user's screen

Some resources are clearly more dangerous to give full access to than others. For example, it is difficult to imagine any security policy where an unknown program should be given full access to the file system. On the other hand, most security policies would not limit a program from almost full access to the monitor display. Thus, one of the key issues in providing for safe execution of mobile code is determining which resources a particular piece of code is allowed access. That is, there is a need for a security policy that specifies what type of access any mobile code can have.

Two basic mechanisms can be used to limit the risk to the user:

- Attempt to run code in a restricted environment where it cannot do harm, such as in a sandbox.
- Cryptographic authentication can be used to attempt to show the user who is responsible for the code.

Sandbox

One of the control mechanisms for mobile code is the *sandbox*. The sandbox provides a protective area for program execution. Limits are placed on the amount of memory and processor resources the program can consume. If the program exceeds these limits, the Web browser terminates the process and logs an error code. This can ensure the safety of the browser's performance. A sandbox can be created on the client side to protect the resource usage from Java applets.

There are commercial products available, such as Janus for Linux and Solaris and Subdomain for Linux, that provide these types of isolation protection. For example, one product has access control list permissions, such as read, write, execute, and delete. The program allows or denies access to directories, local drives, network drives, and executable program files.

In the Java Sandbox Security model, which is included in Java API releases, there is an option to provide an area for the Java code to do what it needs to do, including restricting the bounds of this area. A sandbox cannot confine code and its behavior without some type of enforcement mechanism. In the Java arena, the Java Security Manager makes sure all restricted code stays in the sandbox. Trusted code resides outside the sandbox; untrusted code is confined within it. By default, Java applications live outside the sandbox and Java applets are confined within. The sandbox ensures that an untrusted application cannot gain access to system resources.

This confined area is needed for applet security. As an example, if a user is viewing an applet showing an environmental picture show of endangered dolphins, the applet could also, unbeknownst to the user, search the hard drive for private information. A sandbox can prevent this type of intrusion by controlling the boundaries/limits of the program.

Programming Language Support

A method of providing safe execution of programs is to use a type-safe programming language (also known as "strong typing") such as Java. A type-safe language or *safe language* is a program that will never go wrong in certain ways. These ensure that arrays stay in bounds, that pointers are always valid, and that code cannot violate variable typing (such as placing code in a string and then executing it). From a security perspective, the absence of pointers is important. Memory access through pointers is one of the main causes for weaknesses (bugs) and security problems in C or C++. Java does an internal check, called static type checking, which examines whether the arguments an operand may get during execution are always of the correct type (Gollman, 1999).

DBMS Controls

The future of the database environment is becoming more technically complex. Organizations must find solutions to easily and quickly support their end users' requirements. This includes user-friendly interfaces to access data stored in different DBMSs, from many different locations and on a variety of platforms. Additionally, users want to manipulate the data from their own workstation using their own software tools and then transmit updates to other locations in the network environment.

The challenge for both security and database managers is to retain control over the organization's data and ensure that business rules are consistently applied when core data is accessed or manipulated. The DBMS provides security controls in a variety of forms, both to prevent unauthorized access and to prevent authorized users from accessing data simultaneously or accidentally or intentionally overwriting information.

As a first line of security to prevent unauthorized users from accessing the system, the DBMS should use usernames and passwords to identify users, programs, and individual machines. Most databases have some type of logon and password authentication control that limits access to tables in the database based on a user account. Another initial step is to assign permissions to the authorized users, such as the ability to read, write, update, query, and delete data in the database.

Typically, there are fewer users with add or update privileges than users with read and query privileges. For example, in an organization's personnel database, general users would be allowed to change their own mailing address, office number, etc., but only personnel officers would be allowed to change an employee's job title or salary.

Lock Controls

The DBMS can control who is able to read and write data through the use of *locks*. Locks are used for read and write access to specific rows of data in relational systems, or objects in object-oriented systems.

In a multi-user system, if two or more people wish to modify a piece of data at the same time, a deadlock occurs. A *deadlock* is when two transactions try to access the same resource; however, the resource cannot handle two requests simultaneously without an integrity problem. The system will not release the resource to either transaction, thereby refusing to process both of the transactions. To prevent a deadlock so that no one can access the data, the access controls lock part of the data so that only one user can access the data. The access control locking methods include:

- *Page locking*: an entire memory page is locked.
- *Table locking:* an entire table is locked.
- *Row locking:* a row of data is locked.
- *Field locking:* the single field that is being changed is locked.

Using locks, only one user at a time can perform an action on the data. For example, in an airline reservation system, there may be two requests to book the last remaining seat on the airplane. If the DBMS allowed more than one user (or process) to write information to a row at the same time, then both transactions could occur simultaneously. To prevent this, the DBMS takes both transactions and gives one transaction a write lock on the account. Once the first transaction has finished, it releases its lock and then the other transaction, that has been held in a queue, can acquire the lock and make its action or, as in this example, be denied the action.

The technical term for these requirements is the "ACID test," which stands for Atomicity, Consistency, Isolation, and Durability.

- *Atomicity* is when all the parts of a transaction's execution are either all committed or all rolled back — do it all or not at all. Essentially, all changes take effect, or none do. Atomicity ensures that there is no erroneous data in the system or data that does not correspond to other data as it should.
- *Consistency* occurs when the database is transformed from one valid state to another valid state. A transaction is allowed only if it follows user-defined integrity constraints. Illegal transactions are not allowed and, if an integrity constraint cannot be satisfied, the transaction is rolled back to its previously valid state and the user is informed that the transaction has failed.
- *Isolation* is the process that guarantees that the results of a transaction are invisible to other transactions until the transaction is complete.

- *Durability* ensures that the results of a completed transaction are permanent and can survive future system and media failures; that is, once they are done, they cannot be undone.

For access control, the relational and object-oriented database models use both discretionary access control (DAC) and mandatory access control (MAC). MACs assign sensitivity labels to data subjects and objects and provide a higher level of security. A brief description follows, but refer to the Access Control chapter (Chapter 3) for more information.

Access Controls

Security for databases can be implemented either at the user level by restricting the operations (views) available to a user or placing permissions on each individual data item or in an object-oriented database, the object. Objects can be tables, views of tables, and the columns in those tables or views. For example, in the SQL-92 standard, rights to objects can be individually assigned. However, not all databases provide this capability as outlined in the SQL-92 standard. The types of actions available in SQL include Select (allows the reading of data), Insert (allows adding new data to a table), Delete (allows removing data from a table), and Update (allows changing data in a table). Thus, it is possible to grant a set of actions to a particular table for a specific object.

Discretionary Access Controls (DACs). In relational DBMSs, all users must be authorized explicit or implicit access to perform any function. Explicit access is granted or revoked by the system administrator, allowing an individual to access or not access the resource. The system administrator can provide grant authority to others who can, in turn, authorize grant authority to still others. The data owner authorizes the system administrator to grant the authority to access data to specific users, and relies on the system administrator to configure the access levels appropriately. Implicit access in a relational DBMS is assigned by the system to specific system roles.

Mandatory Access Controls (MACs). MACs are based on security labels applied to fields, rows, columns, views, etc. However, because labels affect performance, they are rarely used for elements more granular than views. The system, rather than the owner or system administrators, does enforcement. This is the main difference between DACs and MACs — DACs allow owners discretion or control over access, while MACs are controlled and enforced by the system; the owner does not completely control access.

Access Matrix. An access matrix is a model of a protection system originally intended for modeling and analyzing access control mechanisms. An access matrix is represented as a two-dimensional matrix where the horizontal row is labeled with a subject and the vertical column is labeled with the name of an object. An access matrix is often used to implement Access Control Lists.

View-Based Access Controls. In some DBMSs, security can be achieved through the appropriate use and manipulation of views. A trusted front end is built to control assignment of views to users. View-based access control allows the database to be logically divided into pieces that allow sensitive data to be hidden from unauthorized users. It is important that controls are in place so that a user cannot bypass the front end and directly access and manipulate the data.

Because the system controls what the user can access, views are considered a type of MAC. The database manager can set up a view for each type of user, and then each user can only access the view that is assigned to that user. Some database views allow the restriction of both rows and columns, while others allow for views that read-write (not just read-only).

Grant and Revoke Access Controls. Grant and revoke statements allow users who have the "grant authority" permission to grant permission and revoke permission to other users. In a grant and revoke system, if a user is granted permission without the grant option, the user should not be able to pass grant authority to other users. However, the security risk is that a user granted access, but not grant authority, could make a complete copy of the relation and subvert the system. Because the user, who is not the owner, created a copy, the user (now the owner of the copy) could provide grant authority over the copy to other users, leading to unauthorized users being able to access the same information contained in the original relation. Although the copy is not updated with the original relation, the user making the copy could continue making similar copies of the relation, and continue to provide the same data to other users.

The revoke statement functions like the grant statement. One of the characteristics of the revoke statement is its cascading effect. When the rights previously granted to a user are subsequently revoked, all similar rights are revoked for all users who may have been granted access by the newly revoked user.

Security for Object-Oriented (OO) Databases

Most of the models for securing databases have been designed for relational databases. Because of the complexity of object-oriented databases, the security models for object-oriented databases are also more complex. Adding to this complexity, the views of the object-oriented model differ; therefore, each security model has to make some assumptions about the object-oriented model used for its particular database.

Because several models for secure object-oriented databases have been proposed, we briefly mention a few. If you will be working with database security in your profession, it is recommended that you review books specifically related to database security. Keep in mind that the security models differ in their capabilities and protections. The differences are based on how the security problem is defined, how a secure database is defined, and what is the basis of the object-oriented model.

ORION: Explicit Authorizations

One method of security for an object-oriented (OO) DBMS is the ORION authorization model that provides DACs. The ORION system allows access to data on the basis of explicit authorizations provided to each group of users. These authorizations are classified as positive authorizations because they specifically allow a user access to an object. On the same line, a negative authorization is used to deny a user access to an object. Also, there are several implicit authorizations, such as group membership, that can be used to allow access.

SORION MACs

The SORION security policy was developed for OO DMBSs to extend the ORION model by adding Mandatory Access Controls. The SORION model specifies subjects, objects, and access modes within the system and assigns sensitivity labels to each entity. Specific properties regulate the assignment of the sensitivity labels to each subject, object, and access mode.

SODA

Dr. Thomas Keefe of Penn State University developed the Secure Object-Oriented Database (SODA) model. It was one of the first models to address the specific concepts in the object-oriented paradigm. SODA is often used as a standard example of secure OO models. It complies with MAC properties and can be executed in systems operating at a multi-level.

SODA assigns classification levels to the data through the use of inheritance. However, multiple inheritance is not supported in the SODA model. SODA assigns security levels to subjects and sensitivity levels to objects. The security classifications of subjects are checked against the sensitivity levels of the information before access is allowed.

SODA allows the use of polyinstantiation as a solution to the multi-party update conflict. This problem occurs when users with different security levels attempt to use the same information. The variety of clearances and sensitivities in a secure database system result in conflicts between the objects that can be accessed and modified by the users. Through the use of polyinstantiation, information resides in more than one location, usually with different security levels. The more sensitive information is omitted from the instances with lower security levels. Although polyinstantiation solves the multi-party update conflict problem, it raises a potentially greater problem in the form of ensuring the integrity of the data within the database. Without some method of simultaneously updating all occurrences of the data in the database, the integrity of the information quickly disappears. In essence, the system becomes a collection of several distinct database systems, each with its own data.

Metadata Controls

In addition to facilitating the effective retrieving of information, metadata can also manage restricted access to information. Metadata can serve as a gatekeeper function to filter access and thus provide security controls.

Some security controls for metadata are:

- Apply change control processes to the procedures of developing and maintaining metadata.
- Ensure that metadata information is as well protected as the underlying databases.
- When used, the metadata must be appropriately secured. All measures for control and destruction of data must meet the classification level of the data. Often, this is accomplished through sanitizing the data by making it more general. This is done to remove the individually identifiable sensitive components of the data.

Data Contamination Controls

To ensure the integrity of data, there are two types of controls: input and output controls. Input controls consist of transaction counts, dollar counts, hash totals, error detection, error correction, resubmission, self-checking digits, control totals, and label processing. Output controls include the validity of transactions through reconciliation, physical handling procedures, authorization controls, verification with expected results, and audit trails.

Online Transaction Processing (OLTP)

OLTP is designed to record all of the business transactions of an organization as they occur. It is a data processing system facilitating and managing transaction-oriented applications. These are characterized as a system used by many concurrent users who are actively adding and modifying data to effectively change real-time data. OLTP environments are frequently found in the finance, telecommunications, insurance, retail, transportation, and travel industries. For example, airline ticket agents enter data in the database in real-time by creating and modifying travel reservations.

The security concerns for OLTP systems are concurrency and atomicity. Concurrency controls ensure that two users cannot simultaneously change the same data, or that one user cannot make changes before another user is finished with it. In an airline ticket system, it is critical for an agent processing a reservation to complete the transaction, especially if it is the last seat available on the plane. Atomicity ensures all of the steps involved in the transaction complete successfully. If one step should fail, then the other steps should not be able to complete. Again, in an airline ticketing system, if the agent does not enter a name into the name data field correctly, the transaction should not be able to complete.

OLTP systems should act as a monitoring system and provide the following:

- Detect when individual processes abort
- Automatically restart an aborted process
- Back out of a transaction if necessary
- Allow distribution of multiple copies of application servers across machines
- Perform dynamic load balancing

A security feature uses transaction logs to record information on a transaction before it is processed, and then mark it as processed after it is done. If the system fails during the transaction, the transaction can be recovered by reviewing the transaction logs. Checkpoint restart is the process of using the transaction logs to restart the machine by running through the log to the last checkpoint or good transaction. All transactions following the last checkpoint are applied before allowing users to access the data again.

Knowledge Management

Knowledge management (KM) involves several existing research areas tied together by their common application environment, that is, the enterprise. Some topics listed under the Knowledge Management category are workflow management, business process modeling, document management, databases and information systems, knowledge-based systems, and several methodologies to model diverse aspects relevant to the knowledge in an enterprise environment.

A key term for knowledge management is "corporate memory" or "organizational memory." The memory serves for storing the enterprise knowledge that has to be managed. Corporate memory contains several kinds of information stored in databases, including employee knowledge, and lists of customers, suppliers, products, or specific documents relating to the organization. Essentially, it is all of the information, data, and knowledge about an organization that can be obtained from several different sources.

For data to be helpful, it must have meaning. The interpretation of the data into meaning requires knowledge. This knowledge is an integral aspect of interpreting the data. When an organization attempts to understand the raw data from various sources, it can have a knowledgeable employee attempt to interpret the data into some meaning for the organization. To automate this process, knowledge-based systems (KBSs) are used by problem-solving methods for inference. In the first case, the user knows or learns something; whereas in the KBS, the system contains the knowledge.

Knowledge Discovery in Databases (KDD) are mathematical, statistical, and visualization methods of identifying valid and useful patterns in data. It is an evolving field of study to provide automated analysis solutions. The knowledge discovery process takes the data from data mining and accurately transforms it into useful and understandable information. This information is usually not retrievable through standard retrieval techniques, but is uncovered through the use of artificial intelligence (AI) techniques.

The main approaches of KDD include:

- *Probabilistic approach:* uses graphical representation models to compare different knowledge representations. The models are based on probabilities and data independencies. The probabilistic models are useful for applications involving uncertainty, such as those used in planning and control systems.
- *Statistical approach:* uses rule discovery and is based on data relationships. A learning algorithm can automatically select useful data relationship paths and attributes. These paths and attributes are then used to construct rules for discovering meaningful information. This approach is used to generalize patterns in the data and to construct rules from the noted patterns. An example of the statistical approach is OLAP.
- *Classification approach:* groups data according to similarities. One example is a pattern discovery and data-cleaning model that reduces a large database to only a few specific records. By eliminating redundant and non-important data, the discovery of patterns in the data is simplified.
- *Deviation and trend analysis:* uses filtering techniques to detect patterns. An example is an intrusion detection system that filters a large volume of data so that only the pertinent data is analyzed.
- *Neural networks:* methods used to develop classification, regression, association, and segmentation models. A neural net method organizes data into nodes that are arranged in layers, and links between the nodes have specific weighting classifications. The neural net is helpful in detecting the associations among the input patterns or relationships.

It is also considered a learning system because new information is automatically incorporated into the system. However, the value and relevance of the decisions made by the neural network are only as good as the experience it is given. The greater the experience, the better the decision. Note that neural nets have a specific problem in terms of an individual's ability to substantiate processing in that they are subject to superstitious knowledge, which is a tendency to identify relations when no relations actually exist. More sophisticated neural nets are less subject to this problem.

- *Expert system approach:* uses a knowledge base (a collection of all the data, or knowledge, on a particular matter) and a set of algorithms and/or rules that infer new facts from knowledge and incoming data. The knowledge base could be the human experience that is available in an organization. Because the system reacts to a set of rules, if the rules are faulty, the response will also be faulty. Also, because human decision is removed from the point of action, if an error were to occur, the reaction time from a human would be longer.
- *Hybrid approach:* a combination of more than one approach that provides a more powerful and useful system.

Security controls include:

- Protecting the knowledge base as you would any database
- Routinely verifying the decisions based on what outcomes are expected from specific inputs
- If using a rule-based approach, changes to the rules must go through a change control process
- If the data output seems suspicious or out of the ordinary, performing additional and different queries to verify the information
- Making risk management decisions because decisions that are based on data warehouse analysis techniques may be incorrect
- Developing a baseline of expected performance from the analytical tool

4.4 Assurance, Trust, and Confidence Mechanisms

Software is frequently delivered with vulnerabilities that are not discovered until after the software has been installed and operational. Both Unix and Microsoft products have numerous security weaknesses that have been discovered after their release. However, this is not a new problem. Early operating systems also had security vulnerabilities. Because this is an ongoing problem, organizations must implement policies and procedures to limit the vulnerabilities that are inherent in the software by expeditious implementation of applicable vendor patches.

Information Integrity

Procedures should be applied to compare or reconcile what was processed against what was supposed to be processed. For example, controls can compare totals or check sequence numbers. This would check that the right operation was performed on the right data.

Information Accuracy

To check input accuracy, data validation and verification checks should be able to perform the following tasks:

- Character checks compare input characters against the expected type of characters, such as numbers or letters.
- Range checks verify input data against predetermined upper and lower limits.
- Relationship checks compare input data to data on a master record file.
- Reasonableness checks compare input data to an expected standard.
- Transaction limits check input data against administratively set ceilings on specified transactions.

Information Auditing

Because vulnerabilities exist in the software life cycle, there is the likelihood that attacks will occur. Auditing procedures assist in detecting any abnormal activities. A secure information system must provide authorized personnel with the ability to audit any action that can potentially cause access to, damage to, or in some way affect the release of sensitive information. The level and type of auditing depend on the auditing requirements for the installed software and the sensitivity of data that is processed and stored on the system. The key element is that the audit data provides information on what types of unauthorized activities have taken place and who or what processes took the action.

Some criteria that should exist in secure software include:

- The system resources should be protected when they are available for use.
- If security software or security features of software are disabled in any way, notification should be given to appropriate individuals.
- The ability to bypass security features must be limited to only those individuals who need that level of access, such as system administrators or information system security officers.
- Hardware and software should be evaluated for compatibility.

Evaluation/Certification and Accreditation

Refer to the Computer, Systems, and Security Architecture chapter (section entitled Assurance, Trust, and Confidence Mechanisms in Chapter 2) for detailed information on Evaluation Criteria and Certification and Accreditation. It provides information on TCSEC, ITSEC, Common Criteria, and Certification and Accreditation.

4.5 Information Protection and Management Services

If software is shared, it should be protected from unauthorized modification by ensuring that policies, developmental controls, and lifecycle controls are in place. In addition, users should be trained in security policies and procedures.

Software controls and policies should require procedures for changing, accepting, and testing software prior to implementation. These controls and policies require management approval for any software changes and compliance with change control procedures.

Configuration Management

For software, configuration management refers to monitoring and managing changes to a program or documentation. The goal is to guarantee integrity, availability, and usage of the correct version of all system components, such as the software code, design documents, documentation, and control files.

Configuration management consists of reviewing every change made to a system. This includes identifying, controlling, accounting for, and auditing all changes. The first step is to identify any changes that are made. The control task occurs when every change is subject to some type of documentation that must be reviewed and approved by an authorized individual. Accounting refers to recording and reporting on the configuration of the software throughout any change procedures. Finally, the auditing task allows the completed change to be verified; especially ensuring that any changes have not affected the security policy or protection mechanisms implemented.

The best method of controlling changes is to have a configuration management plan that ensures that changes are performed in an agreed-upon manner. Any deviations from the plan could change the configuration of the entire system and could essentially void any certification that it is a secure trusted system.

In a project, configuration management often refers to the controlling of changes to the scope or requirements of the project. Often called "scope creep," a lack of configuration management can lead to a project never being completed or structured because its requirements are continuously changing.

Summary

Choosing a programming language is one of most important technology choices made for a software project. Some developers choose familiarity or comfort with a language as their deciding factors. Although efficiency is usually one of the primary factors that may impact the choice, the impact of not considering security could be a primary mistake. Security must be considered an equal factor when making decisions of which programming language to design and develop the application. For example, C and C++ are known for being efficient; however, they are also known for being vulnerable to buffer overflow attacks. Java is new and requires developers to learn a new language, but it offers increased security. Perl offers significant security features but is one of the slowest languages to run. Thus, when deciding on a language, it is often a balance (trade-off) between the benefits and weaknesses.

When implementing security in an application program environment, it is important to consider security throughout the entire lifecycle process, especially in the requirements and design phases. As a final note, I have included Viega and McGraw's (2002, p. 92) ten principles for building secure software. The goal of these principles is to identify and to highlight the most important objectives when designing and building a secure system.

> ### "90/10" Strategy
>
> *Avoid 90% of the potential problems by following these ten guidelines:*
>
> 1. *Secure the weakest link.*
> 2. *Practice defense-in-depth.*
> 3. *Fail securely.*
> 4. *Follow the principle of least privilege.*
> 5. *Compartmentalize.*
> 6. *Keep it simple.*
> 7. *Promote privacy.*
> 8. *Remember that hiding secrets is difficult.*
> 9. *Be reluctant to trust.*
> 10. *Use your community resources.*

4.6 Common Body of Knowledge (CBK)

The current CBK for the Application Program Domain is listed below to assist in determining topics for further review. Although this Study Guide is very detailed in many areas, it is not possible to thoroughly discuss every CBK topic in a single book; therefore, additional study of items may be advisable.

The professional should fully understand:

- Security and controls of the systems development process, application controls, change controls, data warehousing, data mining, knowledge-based systems, program interfaces, and concepts used to ensure data and application integrity, confidentiality, and availability
- The security and controls that should be included within systems and application software
- The steps and security controls in the software life cycle and change control process
- Concepts used to ensure data and software integrity, confidentiality, and availability
- Computer viruses and other forms of malicious code, including ActiveX and Java
- How malicious code can be introduced into the computing environment
- Mechanisms that can be used to prevent, detect, and correct malicious code and their attacks

Components

- Application Issues
- Distributed Environment: Agents, Applets, ActiveX, Java, Objects
- Local/Non-distributed Environment Attacks: Viruses, Trojan Horses, Logic Bombs, Worms
- Databases and Data Warehousing: Aggregation, Data Mining, Inference, Polyinstantiation, Multi-Level Security
- DBMS Architecture
- Knowledge-based Systems: Expert Systems, Neural Networks
- Systems Development Controls
- System Development Life Cycle: Requirements Determination, Protection Specifications Development, Design Review, System Test Review, Certification and Accreditation, Maintenance, Service Level Agreement
- Malicious code: Definitions, Jargon, Myths/Hoaxes
- The concept of hackers, crackers, phreaks, and virus writers
- Anti-viral protection, Anti-viral software
- Various types of computer viruses
- Methods of attack: Trapdoors, Brute-Force, Denial-of-Service, Dictionary attacks, Spoofing, Pseudo Flaw, Alteration of authorized code, Flooding, Cramming

Examples

- Define the A-I-C triad as it relates to application security.
- Define programming-related aggregation.
- Define security-related aggregation.

- Define and describe applet as it refers to IT/IS.
- Define architectural neural distribution format (ANDF).
- Describe artificial neural network (ANN).
- Define "backdoor" as related to IT/IS.
- Define Common Object Request Broker Architecture (CORBA).
- Compare and contrast input controls, output controls, and transaction controls.
- Define covert channel, covert storage channel, and covert timing channel.
- Define data contamination.
- Define data integrity.
- Define data mining.
- Define distributed systems environment.
- Define encapsulation as related to IT/IS.
- Define file protection.
- Define garbage collection.
- Define granularity as related to IT/IS.
- Describe potential types of malicious code threats.
- Define logic bomb.
- Define neural network.
- Define Object Linkage and Embedding (OLE).
- Define object-oriented design (OOD).
- Define object-oriented programming (OOP).
- Define polyinstantiation.
- Define polymorphism.
- Define scalability as it refers to IT/IS.
- Compare and contrast trapdoors, Trojan horses, and worms as related to IT/IS.
- Distinguish between various IT/IS-related threats and attacks.
- Identify system lifecycle phases.
- Describe functional design analysis and planning.
- Compare and contrast project design activities and parallel security activities.
- Describe system design specifications.
- Compare and contrast project test activities and parallel security activities.
- Identify maintenance support/operations in relation to IT/IS.
- Define development methodology controls.
- Define object-oriented technology.
- Describe object request brokers (ORBs).
- Define object-oriented techniques.
- Describe the benefits of object-oriented programming (OOP).
- Describe methods of object-oriented programming (OOP).
- Define the distinguishing features of object-oriented programming (OOP).

- Define Online Transaction Processing (OLTP).
- Define baseline and supplementary security design controls.
- Describe a multi-partite virus.
- Describe master record or boot virus.
- Describe a macro virus.
- Describe a file infector virus.
- Describe a Macintosh virus.
- Understand the difference between a worm, virus, and Trojan horse.
- Define the term "worm."
- Define the term "virus."
- Define the term "Trojan horse."
- Define the terms "backdoor" and "trapdoor."
- Describe the symptoms of a computer virus.
- Describe anti-virus software.
- Describe flooding, spamming, and cramming.
- Describe ICMP redirects.
- Define "sleath."
- Define "polymorphic."
- Define heuristic scanning.
- Understand virus behaviors.
- Describe event- or date-activated viruses.
- Describe how worms work.
- Describe how logic bombs work.
- Describe how Trojan horses work.
- Define a Java applet.
- Define an ActiveX applet.
- Describe a hostile Java applet.
- Describe a hostile ActiveX applet.
- Define the term "malware."
- Define the concept of Prank.
- Define the salami technique.
- Describe an integrity checker.
- Define a false-positive.
- Define denial-of-service.
- Define a false-negative.
- Define change detection software.
- Understand which viruses can cross platforms.
- Compare and contrast strengths and weaknesses of various anti-virus programs.
- Describe active content.

4.7 Sample Questions for the CISSP Exam

1. What is the correct definition of "transaction persistence"?

    a. A transaction that repeats until all affected records are changed

    b. A timing-based transaction that executes on a regular basis

    c. A transaction that requires user intervention to complete

    d. A transaction that preserves the state of the database

2. Shadow recovery of a database is accomplished through:

    a. Applying journalized transactions to an earlier copy of a database

    b. Having a mirror copy of the database in case of interruption

    c. Doing hourly backups of the database to prevent failure

    d. Having all transactions recorded in a transaction file and updated in batch mode at a later time

3. When designing a database, what is LEAST important?

    a. Knowing the quantity of data

    b. Knowing the sensitivity of the data

    c. Knowing the hardware platform

    d. Knowing user access requirements

4. In database terminology, "atomic" refers to:

    a. Each field can be changed dynamically by any user.

    b. All relational items are linked through keys and indexes.

    c. The database is a single independent unit.

    d. All fields can contain only one value.

5. A database "view" is:

    a. A logical subset of a database

    b. The layout of the database

    c. The relationship between the records and the key

    d. A method of disguising data by creating duplicate records

6. One of the greatest risks with many driver programs is:

    a. The drivers are not standard across vendors.

    b. Use of a driver may grant high-level access to the calling program.

    c. A driver may execute unwanted actions.

    d. The drivers may contain backdoors or maintenance hooks.

7. One method of protecting confidential corporate data accessed through an Internet-based application is:

    a. Refusing remote access to all users

    b. Placing stringent security policies on the data storage system

    c. Having tiers of applications and storage

    d. Storing the data on an isolated Web server

8. Which of the following is NOT true of a data warehouse?

    a. It contains data from many sources and databases.

    b. It is used for operational data storage.

    c. It provides analysis and management support.

    d. It can increase the risk of privacy violations.

9. What is one of the differences between a virus and a worm?

    a. Only the virus is distributed through email attachments.

    b. Only the worm is capable of executing without user interaction.

    c. Only the worm is capable of attaching to an application and creating it's own macro programming infections.

    d. Only the virus is a stand-alone file that can be executed by an interpreter.

10. Which of the following best describes a remote access Trojan considered to be malware?

    a. Software is installed on a remote target computer that allows the target computer and its information to be accessed via remote connection, without the target's knowledge.

    b. Software is executed on a remote target computer and is activated when a specific event occurs, such as Friday the 13th.

    c. The user at the target machine downloads software from the Internet and in addition to the legitimate software; malware is also wrapped into the software and installed on the machine.

    d. Software is executed on a remote target machine and immediately installs itself into the boot sector of the machine and allows the attacker to take control over the machine.

11. What is a security risk of allowing mobile code to execute on a target machine?

    a. The time delay from when it is downloaded and executed could initiate an asynchronous attack.

    b. Malware may be included in the downloaded code and infect the target machine.

    c. It will move or overwrite the original boot process so that every time the machine is powered on, the code will be activated.

    d. It will contaminate files that contain computer code, especially .exe and .com files.

12. The ability to combine nonsensitive data from separate sources to create sensitive information is referred to as _____.

    a. Concurrency

    b. Inference

    c. Polyinstantiation

    d. Aggregation

13. Which of the following best describes data contamination in a database?

    a. Occurs when two users try to access the information at the same time and the original information becomes corrupted.

    b. Occurs when two users try to access the information at the same time and the original information is deleted.

    c. Occurs when data entry personnel corrupt the data integrity by input data errors or erroneous processing.

    d. Occurs when users bypass the front end controls and manipulate the backend database information.

14. Company XYZ has decided to develop its own travel manager software that will allow employees to expense travel reports electronically. It is

important for several of the employees who travel a lot to have input into the design and development. Based on this scenario, which software development model may be best suited for this project?

    a. Ad-hoc model

    b. Prototype model

    c. Exploratory model

    d. Cleanroom

15. During which phase of the software project will the team conduct a comprehensive analysis of current and possible future security requirements?

    a. Project initiation and planning

    b. Functional requirements definition

    c. System design specifications

    d. System development specifications

16. What is the process of conducting an independent evaluation of the software to determine whether the planned security standards or features have been implemented?

    a. Certification

    b. Accreditation

    c. Authorization

    d. Acceptance

17. Which of the following would be the best method for a software developer to limit the vulnerability of buffer overflows in software?

    a. Reduce the number of backdoor entry points.

    b. Ensure that the software runs only in Level 0 of the processor ring.

    c. Budget more time into production to allow for more bounds checking in the software.

    d. Ensure that the software is certified and accredited before allowing full-scale entry of production data.

18. What is defined as an information flow that is not controlled by a security control?

    a. TOC/TOU

    b. Incomplete parameter check

    c. Buffer overflow

    d. Covert channel

19. Which type of the following password controls, if added, would NOT provide adequate security to the software?

    a. Password complexity requirements

    b. Encryption of the password file

    c. Overstrike or password masking feature

    d. Reference monitor authorization

20. If following the concept of separation of duties during software production, which of the following would NOT occur?

    a. Separation between programmers.

b. Separation between programmers and system administrators.
c. Separation between programmers and quality assurance personnel.
d. Separation between programmers and production personnel.

References

CSC-STD-001-83; NCSC-WA-001-85 (covert channel definitions).

AlBanna Sami J. and Joe Ohsterhaus, 1998. "Meeting the Software Challenge: A Model for IS Transformation," in the *Information Systems Management Journal*, Winter 1998.

Anderson, Ross, 2001. *Security Engineering*. John Wiley & Sons, New York.

Atluri, Vijay and Pierangela Samarati, 2000. *Security of Data and Transaction Processing*. Kluwer Academic Publishers, New York.

Barman, Scott, 2001. *Writing Information Security Policies*. New Riders Publishing, Indianapolis.

Blakeley, Jose A., 1996. "OLE DB: A Component DBMS Architecture." *Proceedings of the 12th International Conference on Data Engineering (ICDE '96)*. Published on the Web site: http://www.computer.org/proceedings/icde/7240/72400203.pdf.

Blakley, Bob, 2000. *CORBA Security: An Introduction to Safe Computing with Objects*. Addison-Wesley, Reading, MA.

Brooks, Frederick P., 1995 (first edition 1974). *The Mythical Man-Month: Essays on Software Engineering, Anniversary Edition (2nd edition)*. Addison-Wesley, Reading, MA.

Castano, Silvano, Maria Grazia Fugini, and Giancarlo Martella, 1994. *Database Security*. Addison/Wesley/ACM Press Books, New York.

Dean, Drew, Edward W. Felten, and Dan S. Wallach, 1996. "Java Security: From HotJava to Netscape and Beyond." *1996 IEEE Symposium on Security and Privacy* (Oakland, CA).

Erdmann, Micheal, 1997. "The Data Warehouse as a Means to Support Knowledge Management," an accepted paper for the 21st Annual German Conference on Artificial Intelligence 1997. http://dfki.uni-kl.de.

Foon, AKA Chris Paget, 2002. "Exploiting design flaws in the Win32 API for privilege escalation OR Shatter Attacks — How to Break Windows." http://security.tombom.co.uk/shatter.html.

Forcht, Karen Anne, 1994. *Computer Security Management*. Boyd & Fraser Publishing Company, Danvers, MA.

Gollman, Dieter, 1999. *Computer Security*. John Wiley & Sons, West Sussex, England.

Grimes, Roger A., 2001. *Malicious Mobile Code: Virus Protection for Windows*. O'Reilly Computer Security, Cambridge, MA.

Harley, C. David, Robert Slade, David Harley, Urs E. Gattiker, and Eugene H. Spafford, 2002. *Viruses Revealed*. McGraw-Hill Osborne Media, Berkeley, CA.

Heiser, Jay, 2002. "Combating Nonviral Malware: Trojans, Sniffers and Spyware, Oh My!" *Information System Security*, May 2002.

Henry, Paul, 2000. "Covert Channels Provided Hackers the Opportunity and the Means for the Current Distributed Denial of Service Attacks." A White Paper for CyberGuard Corporation, Ft. Lauderdale, FL, © CyberGuard Corporation, 2000.

Hurley, Edward, 2002. "The lexicon of viruses, worms and malicious code." SearchSecurity.com, November 19, 2002. http://searchsecurity.techtarget.com/originalContent/0,289142,sid14_gci864280,00.html.

Inmon, W.H., 1996. *Building the Data Warehouse, 2nd edition*. John Wiley & Sons, New York.

Kelley, Al, Ira Phol, and Carter Shanklin, 1992. *C by Dissection: The Essentials of C Programming*. Addison-Wesley Publishing, Reading, MA.

Kotz, David and Robert S. Gray, 1999. "Mobile Agents and the Future of the Internet," articles from the Thayer School of Engineering, Dartmouth College: http://www.cs.dartmouth.edu/~dfk/papers/kotz:future2/.

Krehnke, M.E. and D.K. Bradley, 2001. "Data Marts and Data Warehouses: Keys to the Future or Keys to the Kingdom," in *Information Security Handbook*, Tipton, Hal and Micki Krause (editors), Auerbach Publications, Boca Raton, FL.

McGraw, Gary and Ed Felton, 1999. *Securing Java: Getting Down to Business with Mobile Code.* John Wiley & Sons, New York.

McInnis, Kirby, 2000. "Component-Based Development: The Concepts, Technology and Methodology." Copyright © 2000 Castek Software Factory Inc. http://www.cbd-hq.com/PDFs/cbdhq_000901km_cbd_con_tech_method.pdf.

Microsoft Knowledge Base Article #122263, 1999. "Common Questions: Object Linking and Embedding, Data Exchange." http://support.microsoft.com/default.aspx?scid = KB;EN-US;q122263&.

Microsoft Security Bulletin MS01-017, March 28, 2001. "Erroneous VeriSign-Issued Digital Certificates Pose Spoofing Hazard." http://www.microsoft.com/technet/treeview/default.asp?url = /technet/security/bulletin/MS01-017.asp.

Neumann, Peter G., 1995. *Computer-Related Risks.* Addison-Wesley, Reading, MA.

Olivier, Martin S. and Sebastian H. von Solms. "A Taxonomy for Secure Object-Oriented Databases." *TODS,* 19(1), 3–46, 1994; http://dblp.uni-trier.de.

Olson, T.G., N.R. Reizer, and J.W. Over, 1994. "A Software Process Framework for the SEI Capability Maturity Model." Documents and Checklists for a Software Process Framework for CMM. Copyright 1994 by Carnegie Mellon University. http://www2.umassd.edu/swpi/sei/spf.html.

Paulk, Mark C., 1996. "Effective CMM-Based Process Improvement." © 1996 by Carnegie Mellon University. ftp://ftp.sei.cmu.edu/pub/cmm/Misc/effective-spi.pdf.

Pfleeger, Charles P., 1997. *Security in Computing.* Prentice Hall, Upper Saddle River, NJ.

Ramachandran, Jay, 2002. *Designing Security Architecture Solutions.* John Wiley & Sons, New York.

Rowland, Craig H., 1996. "Covert Channels in the TCP/IP Suite." *First Monday,* Peer Reviewed Journal on the Internet. http://www.firstmonday.dk/issues/issue2_5/rowland/.

Samarati, Pierangela and Ravi Sandhu, Editors, 1999. *Database Security: Status and Prospects.* Kluwer Academic Publishers, New York.

Slade, Robert, 1996. *Robert Slade's Guide to Computer Viruses: How to Avoid Them, How to Get Rid of Them, and How to Get Help.* Springer Verlag, New York.

Soloman, David and Mark Russinovich, 2000. See *Inside Microsoft Windows 2000* for more information on Windows security.

Sommerville, Ian, 2000. *Software Engineering, 6th edition.* Addison-Wesley, Reading, MA.

Sundsted, Todd, 2002. "Secure Code and Polymorphism," *Java Security Newsletter.* © 2002 Accela Communications, Inc. http://www.itworld.com/nl/java_sec/07052002/.

Theriault, Marlene, William Heney, and Debby Russell, 1998. *Oracle Security.* O'Reilly & Associates, Cambridge, MA.

Theriault, Marlene and Aaron Newman, 2001. *Oracle Security Handbook: Implement a Sound Security Plan in Your Oracle Environment.* Osborne McGraw-Hill, New York.

VeriSign Security Alert, March 22, 2001. "Security Alert Fraud Detected in Authenticode Code Signing Certificates." http://www.verisign.com/developer/notice/authenticode/.

Viega, John and Gary McGraw, 2002. *Building Secure Software: How to Avoid Security Problems the Right Way.* Addison-Wesley, Pearson Education Corporate Sales Division: Indianapolis.

Voegele, Jason, 2002. "Programming Language Comparison." Programmer's Corner Web site. http://www.jvoegele.com/software/langcomp.html.

Wiener, Lauren Ruth, 1993. *Digital Woes: Why We Should Not Depend on Software.* Perseus Publishing, Cambridge, MA.

Web Sites

http://www.rpbourret.com
http://www.info.cern.ch/
http://www.comp.glam.ac.uk
http://msdn.microsoft.com
http://www.utexas.edu
http://java.sun.com
http://www.cultdeadcow.com
http://www.beauvh.org
http://www.phase-one.com.au
http://www.phrack.com
http://www.ansi.org for information about the ANSI SQL92 standard
http://www.microsoft.com for information on ActiveX Data Object (ADO)
http://www.software.com.pl on the Internet worm in 1988
http://dublincore.org for Dublin Core metadata information on security and access controls
http://xml.coverpages.org/saml.html for information on SAML
http://www.sql-server-performance.com for deadlocking definition of SQL servers
http://www.xprogramming.com for extreme programming, written by Ronald E. Jeffries, © 2000–2002
http://crit.org for authenticode security risks
http://www.oasis-open.org for information on WAP Wireless Markup Language Specification (WML)

VeriSign is a registered trademark of VeriSign in the United States and/or other countries.

Chapter 5
Operations Security

Introduction

Operations security identifies the controls over hardware, media, and the operators and administrators with access privileges to these resources. It is the process of safeguarding information assets while the data is resident in the computer, storage media in transit through communication links, or otherwise associated with the data processing environment. Fisher considers operations security to be the heart of information security: it controls the way data is accessed and processed.[1] In essence, the operational controls should provide consistency across all operating systems, applications, and processes.

To obtain a complete understanding of "operations security," it is necessary to look at it from a historical perspective. In the 1960s and 1970s, the processing of information took place in one central location and was controlled by only a handful of people. The term "data center" referred to this central location, while "operations" referred to the day-to-day data processing that occurred within the data center. The "operators" included the experienced, knowledgeable staff who performed the day-to-day operation of the computers.

Although data center operations are still in existence today, the term "operations security" now refers to the central location of all IT processing areas, whether it is called a data center, server room, or computing center.

This chapter focuses on the security needs for this type of information system operations — that is, the needs of the data centers, server rooms, computer rooms — the back-end locations where information system processing is accomplished, and the personnel who have privileged access to the resources in these areas.

In the operations domain, the CISSP should be able to:

- Identify historical and real-time security events
- Capture subsequent actions
- Identify the key elements involved
- Alert appropriate authorities
- Take appropriate corrective or recovery actions

This chapter is divided into five topic areas. The first section begins by defining the goals and security requirements for operations security. The Information Protection Environment section identifies the operations environment and outlines some of the threats associated with hardware, software, data/media, telecommunications equipment, support systems, physical areas, and personnel. The third section, Security Technology and Tools, provides an explanation of the types of controls available to address the goals identified in the Requirements section and mitigate the vulnerabilities and threats identified in the Environment section. The Assurance, Trust, and Mechanisms Confidence section focuses on what is needed to ensure that the implemented countermeasures will provide the appropriate levels of security. This includes configuration management, contingency planning, change management, and audit reporting. The final section explains the role of management in protecting the operations environment, including security reviews and incident reporting.

> *If you have heard the term "OPSEC" before, note that it is NOT the same as what the CISSP CBK is referring to as "Operations Security." OPSEC, used primarily by U.S. military organizations, is a means of controlling information and observable actions about your own capabilities in order to keep them from being used by your adversary. Essentially, OPSEC is the ability to examine your organization's day-to-day activities from an adversary's point of view, assess the amount of risk to your organization, and then develop countermeasures to protect against the adversaries.[2] For example, if you leave your home every day at the same time and return home every day at the same time, would an adversary (i.e., house thief) be able to identify an advantageous time to enter your home? What is the likelihood that a thief will break into your house while you are work? Should you implement countermeasures to reduce this risk? There is an entire field devoted to OPSEC and if you would like further information about OPSEC, a good starting point is the Web site www.opsec.org.*

5.1 Information Protection Requirements

Data processing operations have traditionally been associated primarily with maintaining the availability of systems for the user groups. The highest level of availability has been the goal. However, operations security involves not only availability but also integrity and confidentiality. Processes and files are not useful unless an acceptable level of integrity is maintained, and operators/system administrators are ethically bound to ensure that the confidentiality of sensitive information is provided in accordance with the requirements established by the system owner.

The security requirements of an operations center will vary, depending on the type of information and the organizational needs. However, there are some consistent security goals that need to be met. These include:

- *Operations management* includes requirements for scheduling, processing, and monitoring data production for potential problems and incidents.
- *Problem management* determines the root cause of recurring, critical, and escalated incidents.
- *Service level management* translates the service plan into operational services, and establishes and manages service level agreements.
- *Application support* provides for software programming support to maintain and update software.
- *Performance and capacity management* defines, tracks, and controls service capacities to ensure that infrastructure improvements are ready to meet demands of customers.
- *Change management* logs all significant changes to the infrastructure, coordinates change-related work orders, prioritizes change requests, schedules resources, and assesses the risk of non-routine changes to the infrastructure.
- *Configuration management* centrally registers and controls configuration item attributes, status, and relationships; Configuration items are infrastructure components or assets, including system hardware, software, network components, software versions, and documentation.
- *Software control and distribution* documents centralized software licensing and distribution across the entire enterprise.
- *Availability and continuity management* defines, tracks, and controls IT resource availability to customers; determines plans and procedures for service continuity (disaster recovery) and physical and data security.
- *Security management* monitors the system to detect and respond to security-related incidents.

According to Fisher,[3] there are three critical requirements for operations controls: resource protection, privileged-entry control, and hardware control. It is helpful to understand these concepts in order to appreciate the security requirements for the "operations."

The first — *resource protection* — is the goal of protecting the organization's computing resources from loss or compromise. This includes the ability to:

- Reduce the vulnerabilities of compromise of availability, integrity, and confidentiality
- Balance ease of system use with the need for controls
- Ensure compliance with legislative requirements or industry guidelines
- Protect data processing resources

The controls used for reducing vulnerabilities frequently inhibit freedom of use of computer systems by authorized users as well as limit access by intruders. This often results in a need to achieve a compromise between the best security available and the need to provide the highest level of productivity for the user. This balance can depend on the value of the data and the ongoing business need for the data. The value of the data is stated in two ways. It has intrinsic or monetary value. Intrinsic value is the value of a company or an asset based on an underlying perception of the value — for example, the value of a brand name, which is difficult to calculate. The monetary value is the potential financial loss should the data fall into the hands of unauthorized persons. Another aspect of monetary value is the ongoing business need for the data and the impact to business operations should the data not be available.

Compliance with legislative requirements and industry guidelines reflects the need to protect certain sensitive information to avoid injury to personnel. Today, considerable attention is devoted to privacy regulations to protect personal information maintained in computer systems. The U.S. HIPAA (Health Insurance Portability and Accountability Act) regulations, for example, require that medical information related to individuals be protected from unauthorized access. More information on privacy is in Chapter 10, "Law, Investigations, and Ethics."

Protecting data processing resources involves safeguarding all the assets needed to process information for the organization. This includes, at a general level, people, facilities, processing equipment and peripherals, utilities, communications equipment, software, files/databases, storage media, documentation, archives, and sensitive forms/printouts.

The next requirement involves *privileged-entity controls.* Users on a network have certain access levels that allow them to complete their work. When we refer to a user having "privileged" access, it implies the user has the ability to modify control functions, such as access control, audit logging, or incident detection. Thus, these individuals (usually only systems staff and systems security staff) have administrative or super-user control capabilities.

The third requirement of operations security is *hardware controls.* Although security objectives are sometimes viewed as software and physical security, it is also important to remember that the hardware itself can be vulnerable to attack. For example, an unauthorized connection of a device to a processor or telecommunications link could expose the data to unauthorized disclosure. Thus, although access to the hardware is defined by the operating system, the hardware itself can be used to gain unauthorized access to system resources.

Another important operations requirement is to ensure *trusted recovery.* The objective of trusted recovery is to ensure the maintenance of the security and accountability properties of a system in the face of failures and discontinuities of service. To accomplish this, a system should incorporate mechanisms enabling it to remain in a secure state whenever a set of anticipated failures or discontinuities occurs. It should also include a set of procedures enabling administrators to bring the system to a secure state whenever unanticipated failures or discontinuities occur.

The Information Security Forum (ISF) (formerly the European Security Forum) is an international association composed of more than 250 organizations dedicated to meeting the increasing demand for solutions to information security problems. Every two years, the ISF publishes "The Standard for Good Practice for Information Security," which is a business-oriented process of assessing an organization's information security arrangements. The goal of the document is to provide organizations with a challenging, but achievable bench mark against which they can measure their performance. Although most of its reports are only available to members, The Forum's Standard of Good Practice: The Standard for Information Security (2000) report is available as a free download from their Web site, www.securityforum.org.

The ISF does not use the term "operations security;" instead, the ISF has a similar requirement (standard) called "information processing." Information processing is defined as how the requirements for computer services are identified and how the computers are set up and implemented to meet those requirements. They define a computer installation as:[4]

- Any type of system that supports one or more business applications
- Any size, from the largest mainframe to midrange systems and groups of personal computers
- Running in a specialized environment (i.e., data center) or in ordinary work environments (i.e., offices, factories, and warehouses)
- Using any kind of operating system, such as IBM MVS, Digital VMS, Windows NT/2000, or Unix

According to the ISF, the security requirements for information processing include system operation, change management, access control, incident management, physical security, and procedures for ensuring continuity of services. As you can see, regardless of the terminology used, there are similar requirements to ensure the security of the operational aspects of processing and storing data.

5.2 Information Protection Environment

The environment for operations security includes all computing resources of an organization — hardware, software, media, telecommunications equipment, support systems, personnel, and computer/server rooms. Of course, the building housing the rooms and its location with respect to external hazards play a role in the overall environment (those issues are covered in Chapter 7, "Physical Security"). This chapter focuses on the information processing elements within the operational facility.

Production systems are those run on a regular basis to conduct the business of the organization. They can contain critical or sensitive information, or both. Critical information is that which must be available to authorized users for the organization to remain in business. Sensitive information is that which must be protected by classification procedures to prevent it being seen by unauthorized persons. Examples of production systems include financial systems, manufacturing systems, management information systems, e-commerce systems, email systems, etc.

Various types of threats are specifically related to the operations environment for both data centers and distributed processing/network environments. Briefly stated, they are:

- *Disclosure* of sensitive information to unauthorized persons
- *Destruction of resources* (i.e., hardware/equipment or files of information)
- *Interruption* of processing due to the non-availability of information, software, hardware, or telecommunications
- *Corruption/modification* of processes due to the unauthorized alteration of information, system software, or applications
- *Theft/removal* of resources that result in the loss of information or equipment

It should be noted that these threats map directly to the information security triad. Disclosure is related to confidentiality; corruption/modification is related to integrity; and destruction, interruption, and theft relate directly to availability.

The next section in this chapter is divided into seven topic areas: hardware, software, operations, data/media, telecommunications equipment, support systems, and personnel — all elements upon which the organization relies for data processing support. These topic areas are repeated in format in the Security Technology and Tools section, which defines the controls necessary to ensure operations security.

Hardware Equipment

Hardware refers to the processing equipment that may be a combination of computers from mainframes to minis to micros, as well as peripherals such as printers, scanners, digital copiers, and facsimile machines. Mainframes are the large computers used for large-scale computing purposes by both government and private-sector organizations. They can be either centralized or decentralized, but are not usually considered to be distributed processing elements. Mainframes and minicomputers are normally controlled from an operator console that provides the interface between the operator and the system. The operators use the console to issue commands to the computer and to respond to instructions from the computer while it is processing activities on the system.

Mainframes, minicomputers, and microcomputers (workstations and servers) all face similar security issues, such as unauthorized access to the data/systems, unauthorized use of computing resources, denial-of-service attacks, and potential equipment failure.

A type of threat to hardware is that operators/system administrators have full access to the computers and thus have the ability to load a version of the operating system that bypasses any access control mechanism. This could also occur intentionally if the operator/system administrator was trying to quickly recover a crashed system.

Another threat to hardware is when the equipment provides hardware maintenance functions that allow main storage display and modification, as well as tracing all program instructions, while the system is running. These capabilities could enable someone to update system control block information, obtain system privileges, and thus compromise data/information. Still another hardware threat involves the unauthorized connection of a device or communications line to a processor that would allow the unauthorized exposure of information.

Software

Software refers to the operating system components and the applications that tell the computers what to do. The operating system components include the operating system utilities and libraries, directories, address tables, system logs, audit trails, and security services. These all are subject to abuse and must be protected not only from external attacks, but also from internal misuse. Examples of application programs and data include application program libraries, source and object code, vendor software, database management system, and proprietary packages.

Software and files/databases include system software; utilities; application programs; vendor software; communications software; sensitive/critical files and programs; logs, audit trails, and violation reports; backup files, etc.

Documentation and sensitive forms/printouts include system and application documentation, business continuity plans, contingency plans, phone books, blank check stock, classified listings, etc.

Archives contain historical information that may be sensitive and critical under certain circumstances, such as in litigation cases. Controls must be established to prevent this material from unauthorized access, corruption, or destruction. To minimize unnecessary exposure, archive management procedures must be implemented not only to remove obsolete material no longer required by the organization or government regulations, but also to ensure that it can be read by existing equipment, if needed.

Some of the operations issues related to the use of software include those that have plagued us for many years. Heading the list is the buffer overflow problem. This is usually the result of inadequate system testing during the development process. It is a good argument against only using operational data to conduct testing.

The problem of pirated software is more pervasive than many businesses think. According to Business Software Alliances (BSAs) Software Piracy Study, released in May 2001, 37% of software used by businesses has been copied illegally. The study highlights the serious impact of copyright infringement to the economy with piracy losses nearing $11.8 billion worldwide in 2000. Organizations caught having such software are subject to heavy fines and humiliation. Therefore, organizations should strictly enforce the conditions of software licenses, respect software copyright requirements, and ensure that copies of software not paid for by the organization are not finding their way into the facility.

February 2003: The United States Attorney's Office for the Northern District of California announced that Joseph Edwin Mitchell was sentenced yesterday to 46 months in prison for trafficking in counterfeit labels for copies of computer programs. The sentence was handed down by U.S. District Court Judge James Ware following a guilty plea to ten counts in violation of Title 18, United States Code, Section 2318. On July 8, 2002, Mr. Mitchell pleaded guilty to the ten counts of trafficking in counterfeit labels for copies of computer programs. Mr. Mitchell admitted that he trafficked in counterfeit labels for copies of computer programs and committed criminal copyright infringement. Specifically, Mr. Mitchell sold infringing copies of Autodesk Incorporated and other companies' computer aided design (CAD) software on Internet auction Web sites, including eBay, Yahoo, Up4sale, Ubid, and Lycos. In so doing, he used counterfeit labels for copies of many of the computer programs, which he sold. He sold copies of software from a number of companies, including Autodesk, Alias Wavefront, and Side Effects Software. Autodesk was his best-selling software. The defendant "burned" copies of software he received from other persons on his home computer. He had been warned via e-mail on numerous *occasions by auction Web sites that he was not allowed to sell the software he was selling, and several of his auction accounts were shut down by the Web site operators at eBay and Yahoo. Mr. Mitchell also received warnings from Autodesk. Nonetheless, he continued to sell infringing software with counterfeit labels. Judge Ware sentenced the Defendant to 46 months in federal prison, restitution totaling $1,943,404 ($1,520,404 to Autodesk, $304,000 to Alias Wavefront, and $119,000 to Side Effects Software), $1000 in special penalty assessments, as well as a three-year period of supervised release. The defendant will begin serving the sentence on April 23, 2003.*

— http://www.usdoj.gov

Backdoors or trapdoors are hidden software mechanisms that enable system access without going through the access control section of the program. This capability can be essential if the access control code fails and it becomes necessary to bypass it to obtain access to the program to fix the problem. Therefore, software developers often introduce trapdoors in their code that enable them to enter the system to make changes without going through the access control section. Sometimes, they include a password or random sequence of characters to activate the trapdoor as a simple security measure.

Unfortunately, they sometimes fail to remove this bypass when the program goes into production mode. Then, anyone able to discover the trapdoor and activation code can easily obtain unauthorized access. A special type of trapdoor is called a *maintenance hook*. This consists of special instructions in software to allow easy maintenance and additional future development. Maintenance hooks are not usually clearly defined in the design specifications and frequently allow system entry at unusual points or without the usual checks. Therefore, they can become a security risk if not removed before the system is placed into production.

Still another issue involves the manipulation of security software to change system privileges or controls, reallocate resources, halt the system, etc. Obviously, access control software should be implemented to control and monitor access to the system and data resources, but it must be protected from manipulation. Passwords, or similar authenticators, should be obscured by one-way encryption (hashing).

For more information on operating system vulnerabilities and threats, refer to Chapter 2, "Security Architecture and Models"; further information on application elements is provided in Chapter 4, "Applications and Systems Development."

Operations

This topic is tied to the personnel topic in that the personnel who run the data centers/server rooms have the potential to cause harm to the day-to-day processing of the data. For example, a user with privileged access modifies a device address that could result in rerouting input or output causing a compromise of confidentiality.

Another example is hijacking a server's network address to capture traffic to or from the server — a potential confidentiality compromise. A privileged user could force the server to boot from tape, CD, or floppy disk to bypass operating system security and thereby enable unauthorized access to the system and files. Sensitive data output could be rerouted to print at an insecure location where unauthorized persons could access it.

Forcing a system shutdown from the console or operations area, either accidentally or intentionally but inappropriately, is a potential exposure related to system availability.

Initially loading a program without required security features is a violation of organization policy and results in leaving the program open to unauthorized access.

Manipulating the generation of input/output can compromise the system and is a misuse of privileges. Also, stealing the password file or table from the server leads to dictionary attacks whereby compromise of passwords is possible and violation of accountability requirements is possible.

In the data processing environment, systems sometimes fail or experience other operating problems. There are several system problems that can cause a system to halt or require reboot. These include, as examples, crash, power failure, missing resource, inconsistent database, and system compromise. These conditions need to be prepared for so that system security is not breached while the system is in a vulnerable state during a system crash or failure. Essentially, prudent activities include preparing for system failure and planning for recovering the system while protecting the required secure state.

Data and Media

There are several types of data and media that need protection in the operations environment. These would include, for example, sensitive or critical files and programs. We have previously defined sensitive files as the confidentiality issue, whereby the files and programs that should not be accessible by unauthorized persons are protected, and critical files as the availability issue, whereby those files and programs needed for the organization to remain in business are protected.

The system logs, audit trails, and violation reports needed to hold users accountable for their activities and necessary for the investigation of security incidents are another class of data that must be protected. Obviously, if an abuser can manipulate these records, it may be impossible to identify and prosecute the culprit.

Backup files of all types should be protected to the same level as the files they are backing up to prevent them from being easy targets for someone intent upon unauthorized access. It should be noted that backup files play a role in all three aspects of the security triad. They must be protected to ensure the confidentiality of sensitive information; they enhance availability by being there when needed to replace a damaged or destroyed file; and they can be used as a replacement for a file that has been corrupted and thereby lost its integrity. Finally, sensitive forms, like blank check stock, and printouts containing sensitive information require protection against abuse or unauthorized access.

The media is the vehicle for storing data. Although we are familiar with paper documents, we usually think of protecting data on magnetic media. Therefore, paper documents (and microfilm) are often overlooked when it comes to proper access control. Magnetic media, known as storage devices, include computer hard drives and removable storage, including high-density devices such as CDs, tapes, cartridges, etc. It is necessary in this storage environment to ensure that media (including paper form) containing sensitive data are protected in accordance with the policies of the organization.

Disposal. Special effort or attention comes into play when considering the disposal, destruction, or loss of data. Some of the factors related to this aspect that must be considered include the sensitivity of the information; the quantity of information; the timing considerations (because the level of sensitivity can diminish over time and it may be discarded when its sensitivity value is gone); the medium on which it is stored (paper, magnetic, electronic, etc.); and the legal and regulatory requirements for its protection.

Also of concern is whether the data is susceptible to unauthorized access by dumpster diving. A dumpster is a large trash receptacle but the term as we use it relates to intruders looking through our trash wherever it is located to discover information about the organization that may help support an attack. Phone directories, floor plans, organization charts, listings containing user IDs, etc., can all provide the information needed to mount or support an attack. This type of information can be useful to attackers who use social-engineering techniques to obtain unauthorized access or are involved in identity theft — a rapidly growing problem. The specific disposal issues revolve around whether the information to be disposed of is government classified or sensitive data in the private or public sector.

Object Reuse. Another specific issue related to storage media deals with its reassignment, either within the computer or outside on removable media. Reassignment occurs when a user or group of users has finished using the storage media and it becomes available for another user or group. In this case, it is necessary to remove any sensitive data from the media before it is made available to the next set of users. This removal ensures that any sensitive data remaining on the media is not made available to unauthorized users. The term for this phenomenon is *object reuse* — the object being previously defined as the files or databases where the data is located.

Telecommunications Equipment

Although most of the discussion about telecommunications equipment is found in Chapter 8, "Telecommunications, Network, and Internet Security," it is a part of the operations environment and for completeness purposes should be briefly mentioned here. The types of equipment in this category include items such as network interface cards, routers, switches, firewalls, cables, telephone/cellular phones, etc. The hardware and other telecommunications equipment must be protected at the level used for other computing equipment. Generally, this involves housing this equipment in restricted areas using physical security controls.

Support Systems

Support systems are part of the computing infrastructure discussed in detail in Chapter 7, "Physical Security." As part of the operations environment, we mention them here. Included are items such as facility location and construction to house the operation, heating/ventilation/air conditioning (HVAC) and refrigeration to ensure a hospitable operational climate, electrical power to run the equipment, fire protection, and water. All need physical protection to ensure ongoing operations.

Personnel

Although many data center operations are being automated in ongoing efforts to reduce data processing operations costs, people are still a key ingredient in operations security. They are usually considered to be the weakest link from a security of operations viewpoint. Personnel security encompasses not only ensuring personnel needed to operate the data processing facilities have a safe and habitable working environment, but also that they can be trusted to conduct secure operations in accordance with organization policies and procedures.

Basically, personnel security is the process of ensuring that employees's backgrounds and workplace evaluations are consistent with the trust needed for them to be relied upon to perform sensitive or critical assignments. Personnel granted access must be trusted to not take advantage of their privileges to obtain access to information where they have no need to know. In addition, a sensitive and critical environment requires competent supervisors to ensure compliance with policies, standards, baselines, procedures, and guidelines. Depending on the type of organization, personnel may be required to submit to government security clearances or public trust clearances supported by independent investigations.

Key employees in the operations environment have job functions that provide them with the ability to control data processing activities. These are the operators in a data center, the network or system administrator in a network or distributed system, and the security administrator in both.

In a data center operation, operators control mainframe or minicomputer operations from the operator's console. Their responsibilities include, but are not necessarily limited to, the following:

- *Implementing the initial program load (IPL).* The program executed from the operator's console that starts the operating system of a computer.
- *Monitoring execution of the system.* Responding to console messages requesting operator action to handle errors, certain interrupts, etc.
- *Controlling the flow of jobs.* Initiating new jobs, etc.
- *Mounting input/output volumes* as required by the application being executed.
- *Bypassing label processing.* Using a utility program to enable the processing of foreign (not from that computing facility) tapes or cartridges with unreadable labels by allowing the system to bypass the label section. It is important that use of this utility be restricted to only authorized personnel, so other users are not able to use it to get access to media that they are not allowed access according to the label.
- *Renaming/relabeling resources, as necessary, to enable jobs to run.* If this capability is abused, sensitive data could be made available to unauthorized persons in violation of the organization's confidentiality policy.
- *Reassigning ports/lines to enable processing requirements.* If this capability is abused, sensitive printouts could be routed to insecure locations where they would be available to unauthorized persons.

In a data center operation, it is typical to have a built-in separation of responsibilities: the operators run the computers, the programmers and analysts create the software, the librarians control the media, the setup personnel prepare the jobs for the operators to run, and the security administrators assign privileges to the users. It is a different case in the network or distributed system environment because the network or system administrator can do it all and usually does, so there is no separation of responsibilities.

Fisher[6] states that the whole subject of operator and administrator privileges deserves much more attention than it normally receives. Because privileges provide users with the ability to invoke the commands needed to accomplish their work, every user has some degree of privilege. In the operations security context, the term has come to be applied to those individuals performing specialized tasks requiring broader capabilities than those assigned to a general user. In this environment, a privilege provides the authority necessary to modify control functions, such as access control, logging, and violation detection. It may also provide access to specific system vulnerabilities that can be used to gain unauthorized access to system components or data. Thus, individuals such as systems programmers, operators/system administrators, and systems monitoring personnel have privileges greater than general users.

The following privileges, common to operators and system administrators, create security issues if abused:

- Changing computer system privileges or controls
- Changing protective features or parameters affecting another
- Allocating resources
- Halting the computing system
- Controlling the allocation and sharing of system and data resources (e.g., memory, file space, CPU cycles, etc.)

A classic example of personnel threats involves commission of fraud by operators who have the privilege of fixing transactions identified by the system as erroneous. They can enter into the system a transaction that they know will be rejected as erroneous. Because they have the privilege of handling rejected transactions, they simply replace the erroneous transaction with one that appears to be valid but with the "pay to" account changed to benefit them or a friend.

Personnel who do not have an operations function, in either a data center or distributed processing environment, should not have physical access to system resources that are processing production systems.

Also, because operators are charged with running the system for the owners, they can easily interfere with its operation, either intentionally or accidentally, and cause production delays or denial-of-service incidents. Thus, operations personnel/systems administrators should be responsible to the system owners for running the systems in accordance with established security procedures intended to protect the availability, integrity, and confidentiality requirements of the systems.

Operators, and users as well, can use the system's computer time or vendor software for personal business or entertainment. I once heard a story of a system administrator running a computer repair shop using the organization's resources. It became suspicious when the administrator's boss received a phone call from one of the customers complaining about the level of service he had received from this repair shop. Just think: if the system administrator had provided a quality service, this could have gone unnoticed for a very long time.

Certainly, operators have the opportunity and the ability to be involved in unauthorized access to restricted files and obtain information later disclosed to unauthorized persons.

Investigating or reading another user's files is considered the same as reading papers on someone's desk — a violation of their privacy. In some organizations, policies are enacted that state that reading protected files, by whatever mechanism, is considered the same as "breaking and entering."

A general vulnerability of personnel is the discontinuity of operation caused by failures induced by users, operators, and administrators. They are caused by erroneous actions, such as unexpected system shutdown; for example, by turning off the power or by lack of action, such as ignoring the exhaustion of critical system resources warnings (e.g., audit trail is 95% full, insufficient swap space left, inadequate configuration installed, etc.).

Probably one of the most dangerous capabilities of operators is that of corrupting audit trails or system logs to hide their unauthorized activities. Because access and use of the system should be specific to an individual user, it must be possible to track access and use to that individual. An operational threat is when privileged users configure the system in such a manner as to allow their activity to bypass system logs and thus avoid a record being made. Another factor is the bypassing of security and access controls to enable unrestricted access in violation of organization policy.

Another important personnel control is the review of users who have privileged-entity access. As with all groups of users, privileged users should be subject to periodic recertification to maintain the broad level of privileges that have been assigned. The rationale for the recertification should be based on a business need that requires that privilege access. The business need, in this case, should be equal to the regular, assigned duties of the person and should never be allocated on the basis of organizational politics or backup. The recertification process should be conducted on a regular basis, either annually or semi-annually. The security officer or supervisors should verify each individual's need to retain assigned privileges. By structuring the recertification process to include authorization by managers, a natural separation of duties can occur. This separation is very important to ensure proper control and minimize the over-allocation of system privileges.

In some organizations, there is a rationale to give privilege access to more personnel than necessary to ensure theoretical emergency situations are covered. In most cases, this should be avoided. One option to consider is to have a privileged ID and password in a sealed envelope with the site security staff — which should only be used in emergency situations. When the privilege access is needed, the security officer should sign for the envelope — this will establish ownership of the administrative privileges and also alerts management that someone has the ability to access privileged functions. If necessary, audit records can be examined for details of what that account has accessed. Although misuse of administrative privileges cannot be prevented with this technique, it does provide a reasonable control to continue performing business functions efficiently.

In this section we introduced the operations environment and outlined some of the security issues involved. Certainly, this environment presents many opportunities for wrongdoing and calls for the implementation of security controls as well as close monitoring by supervisors. The next section presents the types of controls for ensuring secure operations.

5.3 Security Technology and Tools

This section discusses the controls needed for the operational environment. Before we begin outlining the specific type of operations security countermeasures, five distinct types of controls for use by security and audit personnel have been identified to manage the information security environment. Although these fit into any of the domains, we decided to include them here as general controls for the operational environment. As such, the CISSP should be aware of these types of controls when reviewing the CBK.

Type 1: Directive Controls. Often called administrative controls, these are intended to advise employees of the behavior expected of them during their interfaces with or use of the organization's information systems. Usually, these are presented as policies or related documents and specify what employees can and cannot do. Directive controls are considered mandatory requirements placed on employees. Frequently included in directive controls are deterrent controls that are intended to encourage personnel to obey the directive controls to avoid some form of punishment. Examples of directive controls include legislation, authorized use policies, anti-viral software standards, platform installation baselines, media classification procedures, etc. Further discussion of policies, standards, baselines, and procedures is available in Chapter 1, "Information Security Management."

It is important that the information security professional be able to implement appropriate directive controls and monitor personnel activity to ensure compliance. Directive controls should not be implemented unless the organization is willing and able to enforce them.

Type 2: Preventive Controls. Included in preventive controls are physical, administrative, and technical measures intended to preclude actions violating policy or increasing risk to system resources. In essence, these are mechanisms to prevent the occurrence of undesirable activity. Most information security professionals would be inclined to use as much preventive control as their user groups would tolerate and follow that level with appropriate detective controls. Once the tolerance level of user groups is reached, further preventive controls are considered to be overkill and usually result in the users discovering methods of working around or avoiding controls. The tolerance of user groups for preventive controls can usually be increased through effective security awareness programs designed to prove the need for additional control. Examples of preventive controls include guards, mantraps, backups, UPS systems, separation of duties, user registration, supervision, dial-up access control, encryption, access control software, and anti-viral software.

Type 3: Detective Controls. Detective controls involve the use of practices, processes, and tools that identify and possibly react to security violations. These include both historic and ongoing events. Examples of detective controls include audit trails, intrusion detection software, logs, integrity checks, violation reports, and security reviews and audits. Detective controls must be monitored frequently if they provide only historical information, and continuously if they are intended to be used as real-time controls.

Type 4: Corrective Controls. Corrective controls also involve physical, administrative, and technical measures designed to react to detection of an incident in order to reduce or eliminate the opportunity for the unwanted event to recur. Examples of corrective controls include procedures requiring more frequent updates of anti-viral software, more training for members of the guard force, additional security awareness training for employees, replacement of key locks with badge access systems, use of two-factor user authentication, implementation of more sophisticated firewalls, etc. In the event that adequate corrective or preventive controls are not available, it may be necessary to revert to compensating mechanisms to reduce risk to an acceptable level.

Type 5: Recovery Controls. Once an incident occurs that results in the compromise of integrity or availability, the implementation of recovery controls is necessary to restore the system or operation to a normal operating state. Recovery controls are often associated with business continuity and disaster recovery planning, but they could involve simply recovering a corrupted or destroyed file from a backup. Other examples of recovery controls include fault tolerance mechanisms, RAID, virus removal by anti-viral software, and resending lost or corrupted messages.

In discussing the tools available to get a handle on the issues identified in the operations environment, we will follow a similar list of topics as was used to address them there. These are hardware, software, operations, data and media, telecommunications equipment, support systems, physical areas, and personnel.

Hardware Controls

Hardware controls include the physical protection of the equipment. To protect the equipment, surge suppressors should be installed; and to ensure a reliable flow of power, UPS equipment should be utilized.

For configuration control (integrity), logs of hardware modifications, configuration changes, and maintenance performed must be maintained, reviewed, and retained for future reference.

To control the unauthorized connection of a device or communications link to a processor, there are several countermeasures available. The first is to physically secure individual machines and servers; for example, installing the equipment in a restricted area that has physical security controls, such as locks and alarms. Network cabling should be protected in conduits and not easily accessible to unauthorized individuals. Second, there are "anti-sniffer" tools available that can detect unauthorized connections on networks. Although this may seem extreme, a third option may be to encrypt all data on the equipment as well as data traveling on the telecommunication cables. This would ensure that if an unauthorized connection were made, the activity would not gain any useful data. A fourth control would be to install "switches" into the network to break up the passing of data packets to all broadcast nodes. Remember that in the non-switched environment, packets are visible to every node on the network. In a switched environment, packets are only delivered to the target address — this would reduce the level of packets available to every node.

Processing problems can often be hardware problems. To handle hardware problems, the first step is to categorize the problem and rank it in terms of its severity. This enables responsible personnel to concentrate their energies on solving those problems considered most severe, leaving those of lesser importance to a more convenient time. When a problem can be solved, a test can be conducted to confirm problem resolution. Often, however, problems cannot be easily solved or tested. In these instances, a more subjective approach may be more appropriate. For example, management may decide that if the problem does not recur within a predetermined number of days, the problem can be considered closed. Another way to close such problems is to reach a major milestone (e.g., completing the organization's year-end processing) without a recurrence of the problem.

Software Controls

In the following paragraphs we address several of the security controls related to software. Remember that the operating system software tells the internal hardware devices how to operate. An operating system control program can restrict the execution of certain computing functions, permitting them only when the processor is in a particular functional state (known as privileged or supervisor state) or when authorized by architecturally defined tables in control storage. These programs operate in various states, during which different commands are permitted. To be authorized to execute privileged hardware instructions, a program should be running in a restrictive state that allows these commands — this is sometimes referred to as a "security kernel" mode. Instructions permitting changes in the program state are classified as privileged and are available only to the operating systems and its extensions. Therefore, to ensure adequate protection of the system, only carefully selected individuals should be able to change the program state and execute these commands.

All levels of system privileges must be defined to the operating system when hardware is installed, brought online, and made available to the user community. As the operating system is implemented, each user ID, along with an associated level of system privileges, is assigned to a predefined class within the operating system. Each class is associated with a maximum level of activity. For example, operators are assigned to the class that has been assigned those functions that must be performed by operations personnel. Likewise, auditors are assigned to a class reserved for audit functions. Auditors should be permitted to perform only those tasks that both general users and auditors are authorized to perform, not those permitted for operators. By following this technique, the operating system can be partitioned to provide no more access than is absolutely necessary for each class of user. This is a classic way of implementing the fundamental security concept of least privilege.

If desired, input/output (I/O) instructions can be defined as privileged and issued only by the system control program after access authority has been verified. In this protection method, before the initiation of any I/O operations, a user's program must notify the system control program of both the specific data and type of process requested. The system control program then obtains information about the dataset location, boundaries, and characteristics it uses to confirm authorization to execute the I/O instruction.

The system control program controls the operation of user programs and isolates storage control blocks to protect them from access or alteration by an unauthorized program. Authorization mechanisms for programs using restricted system functions should not be confused with the mechanisms invoked when a general user requests a computing function. In fact, almost every system function (e.g., the user of any I/O device, including a display station or printer) implies the execution of some privileged system functions that do not require an authorized user.

The following privileges should be restricted and monitored:

- Changing computer system privileges or controls
- Changing protective features or parameters affecting another user
- Allocating resources
- Halting the computing system
- Controlling the allocation and sharing of system and data resources (e.g., memory, file space, CPU cycles, etc.)

A System Development Life Cycle (SDLC) procedure should be chosen from those described in Chapter 4, "Application Program Security." and implemented for all production program development efforts. This will ensure that all development processes are conducted in a consistent manner; address integrity, confidentiality, and availability issues; and include all of the requirements established by organization policy. This process includes, of course, determining the security requirements during the initial stages of development and revising them as necessary to accommodate any changes in classification, environment, processing equipment, etc.

To control buffer overflows, the programmer of the software must test and directly patch system memory limitations that could be exploited. These can be detected and fixed by reverse-engineering (disassembling programs) and looking at their operations. Hardware states and other hardware controls can make buffer overflows impossible. Bounds enforcement and proper error checking will also stop buffer overflows.

The company should strictly enforce the conditions of software licenses and respect software copyright requirements. This has been a serious issue worldwide for several years. As a result, law enforcement entities are actively tracking down organizations using unlicensed software and courts are awarding millions of dollars in damages to plaintiffs. Often, disgruntled or terminated employees lead investigators to the violations in progress. Not only is it costly to get caught using pirated software, but it can be very embarrassing to the organization. One method of ensuring that your organization uses only licensed software is to install a software program that will identify the use of unlicensed software. Another control is to establish an "authorized software" list and only software contained on that list can be installed on the network. The organization should then buy an enterprise license (with the appropriate number of end users) for the software.

All acquired software from any source — vendors, partners, freeware, etc. — must be examined for malicious code. Usually, it is desirable to use current anti-virus software products from several vendors for this process because, if one fails to identify a virus, another may discover it. There are also controls called "behavior blockers" that prevent hostile code from executing on a host.

Check software for backdoors and trapdoors. This can be easier said than done, particularly with respect to vendor-provided software that is delivered without the source code. If you are programming an application, it is important that your internal staff do not install backdoors that could be exploited by outsiders. Although they may be convenient for internal use, the risk of an outsider also using the entry point could allow for unauthorized release of data.

An integrity control that helps keep intruders and unauthorized changes out of production programs is the use of a program library. This is usually computer maintained and controlled by a program librarian. The program librarian is charged with ensuring that the program library is maintained and controlled in accordance with the organization's policy and procedures.

All copies of data dictionaries, programs, load modules, and documentation, including test data and results, should be under the control of the librarian. The librarian is responsible for ensuring that programs are not added to the production library until they have been properly tested and authorized. Only the librarian should be allowed to alter any production program.

The program library contains the current versions of programs and documentation with a record of any changes made, by whom, when, authorized by whom, and what the changes were. Also in the library should be the test data used to verify that changes were correctly applied and approved by user signoffs.

The responsibilities for software library maintenance need to be established by policy and include such items as maintaining a list of who has custody of the programs and who is allowed access, the number of backup versions of software for both on-site and off-site storage, and records of who had access to make changes.

Operation Controls

To maintain control of operations, either in a data center or a network environment, it is necessary to establish, document, and enforce operating procedures for all equipment and software. At a minimum, operating procedures should address system start-up, error conditions and how to handle them, system shutdown, and how to restore the system from backup media.

When a system crashes or experiences a system failure, the primary consideration from a security viewpoint is to ensure that security is not breached during the recovery process. Recovery and restart procedures enable the operations staff to minimize the outage duration in case of a system halt or failure. This is addressed in the Common Criteria using the term "fail secure." Fail secure means that the failure occurs with the preservation of a secure state. This requires that the security functions being utilized preserve a secure state in the face of the identified failures. To accomplish this preservation of a secure state, preparations must be made for handling the failure and the system must be recovered. A key element of system recovery is having current backups of all system-critical files. To ensure this availability, it is necessary to backup critical files on a regular basis. Depending on their volatility, the files should be backed up hourly, daily, or weekly — often enough to minimize the amount of recreation needed to obtain a current version. The goal is to ensure that the integrity of the system is restored.

Recovery actions can be classified into three general categories:

- *System reboot.* A reboot is performed after shutting down the system in a controlled manner.
- *Emergency system restart.* This is performed after a system fails in an uncontrolled manner in response to a security kernel or media failure. In such cases, security kernel and user objects on nonvolatile storage belonging to processes active at the time of failure may be left in an inconsistent state.
- *System cold start.* This is performed when unexpected security kernel or media failure occurs and the automated recovery procedures cannot bring the system back to a consistent state. This happens because the security kernel and user objects may remain in an inconsistent state following attempts to recover automatically. In this case, the intervention of administrative personnel is required to bring the system to a consistent state from the maintenance mode.

The available types of recovery include:

- *Manual recovery* allows an evaluated product to only provide mechanisms that involve human intervention to return to a secure state.

- *Automated recovery* provides for at least one type of service discontinuity recovery to a secure state without human intervention. Recovery for other discontinuities may require human intervention.
- *Automated recovery without undue loss* provides for automated recovery but strengthens the requirements by disallowing undue loss of protected objects.
- *Function recovery* provides for recovery at the level of particular security functions. It should ensure either successful completion of the security function or rollback to a secure state.

Controls after a system crash or failure ensure that the system is in a secure state before allowing user access. The steps to accomplish this involve rebooting the system and getting it running in single-user mode, recovering all file systems that were active at the time of failure, restoring any missing or damaged files and databases from the current backup, and checking security-critical files for integrity.

Because state-transaction failures occur often, recovery mechanisms are usually included in the system code to undo temporary modifications of system states, thus returning the system to a consistent state. If the recovery mechanism fails to undo the temporary modifications, the system may remain in an inconsistent state and crash. A crash is a failure that causes the processor's registers to be reset to some standard values. Because consistent system states cannot be recovered from processor and primary memory registers after a crash, these registers are referred to as volatile storage. Consistent system states can normally be recovered from magnetic media such as disks and tapes, which are called nonvolatile storage.

The crashes resulting from trusted computing base (security kernel) failures cause volatile storage to be lost, but nonvolatile storage usually survives crashes. Therefore, recovery mechanisms can reconstruct consistent states in a maintenance mode of operation. After reconstructing a consistent state, the recovery mechanisms restart the system with no processes executing; for example, processes that were active, blocked, or swapped out before the crash are aborted. New processes that run the code of aborted processes executing at the time of the crash can be started by users after the consistent state is reconstructed. Recovery mechanisms can reconstruct consistent states by either removing or completing incomplete updates of various objects represented on nonvolatile media.

Restart procedures in a mainframe facility involve backing the system to the last point where everything was operating normally and restarting it from that point. In systems that run for hours to complete processing a job, it is far more efficient to return to a recent point to restart. This point is identified in the system as a "checkpoint restart" location. Several can be programmed into long-running programs.

347

Media failures usually cause the system to crash unless the lost data can be retrieved from archival storage and rebuilt on a redundant storage device. If redundant media are not available, or if users and administrators fail to keep archival data current, media failures may result in unrecoverable failures. In such a case, administrative recovery procedures may need to be used to bring the system to a consistent state.

Data and Media

An operations concern with respect to data is to maintain the highest level of availability to users. The common operations environment tools to maintain availability of data include techniques such as backups, electronic vaulting, remote journaling, database shadowing, use of Direct Access Storage Devices (DASDs), fault tolerance, network data mirroring, redundant network connections and equipment, and Redundant Arrays of Independent Disks (RAID). A brief description of each of these follows; however, more specific information on how to conduct backups and recovery is in the Business Continuity Planning Domain and in the Telecommunications, Internet, and Network Security Domain.

Backups. The terminology used to describe the several types of backups varies by organization, the function being discussed, and often, the author. Because all types of backup are performed by operations, we will mention the types and their alternate terminology. Operators often speak of image backups, sometimes termed "ghost image backups," which mean the whole operating system, utilities, and standard applications used by the organization. They also speak of file backups as meaning the files or databases related to production systems. In their terms, a hybrid image and file backup would be a complete backup of everything on the system.

From a disaster recovery or business continuity perspective, backups use different terminology. Full volume is when the entire critical system disk volume is copied or full backup where everything on the mass storage of a specific system is copied. Differential backups copy all data that has changed since a specific date or event (usually everything since the last full backup). Incremental backups are a subset of the differential backup in that they copy everything changed since either the last full or incremental backup. Database backups are a special type of full-volume backup because they copy the database files, which may be on several different disk drives. A dataset backup is used to back up applications and inactive files that are headed for archives. Finally, a journal backup refers to the process of copying transactions that have been processed against a database. Backup tapes tend to deteriorate with time, so they should be read periodically if they are used for long-term storage and restored if they are critical and show signs of deterioration. Also, technological changes may inhibit the reading of archived tapes, so they should be restored as the technology changes.

Electronic Vaulting. Electronic vaulting actually consists of three types: online tape vaulting, remote transaction journaling, and database shadowing. In online tape vaulting, backup data is sent electronically to the selected recovery or backup storage location.

Remote Journaling. In remote transaction journaling, the same logging procedure used for a database management system to create the on-site journal is used to create a second journal at the off-site storage location. This enables the off-site storage location to recover the most recent files and minimize the amount of recreation necessary in the event of a disaster that destroys the active files.

Database Shadowing. In database shadowing, the system creates updates to the production system, journals them, and sends them to the alternate computer. There, the journal is used to update a copy of the production files.

Direct Access Storage Devices (DASDs). DASDs available at remote locations can also be used as an effective backup facility by causing the system to transmit critical files via a duplex (two-way) transmission link. This provides almost instant recovery of files if the originals are lost or corrupted.

Fault Tolerance. Fault tolerance is defined as ensuring the continuity of operations in the event of equipment failure. Some definitions also include software failure. It involves the use of such mechanisms as data mirroring, hot spares, and redundant servers. A fault-tolerance system must identify that a failure has occurred and then take corrective action to ensure that the continuity of operations is maintained with the least possible delay. The mechanisms available to support fault-tolerance systems include network data mirroring, hot spares, redundant servers, and clustering.

Network Data Mirroring. Network data mirroring, usually referred to as disk mirroring, has been available since at least the late 1980s with RAID systems. It provides duplicate copies of production disks so that disk failures result in limited or no damage to critical data. In addition to RAID, software systems exist that provide automatic copying of data onto separate disks in support of workstations and personal computers. Earlier software-based disk mirroring experienced slower responses when updating primary files because the system needed to complete outputting to the mirroring disk before releasing the application for continued processing. Now, however, software uses part of the system's memory as a buffer to minimize performance degradation. Mirrored files are normally not more than a few milliseconds behind the primary file.

349

Redundant Network Connections and Equipment. Redundant network connections and equipment are used to avoid availability problems resulting from the single point of failure issue. It is easy to overlook potential single point of failure problems, such as those related to authentication servers. If multiple hosts depend on a single authentication server and it fails, the entire organization could suffer a loss of system availability. This was originally a problem with third-party authentication servers (e.g., Kerberos before it became standard to employ a backup).

Hot spares or redundant servers are simply interconnected duplicate disks that are updated simultaneously with the primary disk and are immediately available to take over if the primary fails. This process results in no performance degradation when a failure occurs. Clustering consists of creating groups of disks or servers that are interconnected and can provide mutual support — in case one fails, another is readily available to take its place. This may result in some limited degradation of less important processes if the spare is used for processing while waiting to be used to support fault-tolerance procedures.

Redundant Arrays of Independent Disks (RAID). RAID is an assembly of disk drives, known as a disk array, that operates as one storage unit. The drives could be any storage system with random data access, such as magnetic hard drives, optical storage, or magnetic tapes. It is probably the most widely used method of providing fault tolerance in cases of hard disk crashes. RAID improves system performance when multiple disks are worked together to save large files simultaneously. RAID techniques include both mirroring and striping. Striping is the process of writing data across multiple disks rather than just one, as is done in mirroring, to maximize efficiency. RAID can be implemented as either hardware or software. A term associated with RAID is Extended Data Availability and Protection (EDAP). EDAP is the ability of a disk system to provide timely and continuous, online access to reliable data under certain conditions.

In 1993, a RAID Advisory Board (RAB) consisting of manufacturers and consumers was established to standardize RAID specifications, terminology, and concepts. In 1996, the RAB introduced an improved classification to the RAID system: (1) Failure Resistant Disk Systems (FRDSs) that protect against data loss due to disk failure and its enhancement, FRDS+, (2) Failure Tolerant Disk Systems (FTDSs) that protect against loss of data access due to failure of any single component, and (3) Disaster Tolerant Disk Systems (DTDSs) that consist of two or more independent zones, either of which provides access to stored data. For more information on RAID and RAB, refer to http://www.usbyte.com.

Additional data/media security guidelines include the following.

Store all media securely. This is a concept that applies to all three elements of the security triad: confidentiality because unauthorized access to sensitive information can be a threat where the data is stored; integrity because unauthorized changes or data corruption can occur if the storage media is not well secured; and availability because the loss or destruction of data is possible if data is not adequately secured.

With respect to controlling main storage, the use of address translation mechanisms can provide effective isolation between the storage locations of different users. In addition, main storage protection mechanisms protect main storage control blocks against unauthorized access.

One type of mechanism involves assignment of storage protection keys to portions of main storage to keep out unauthorized users. For example, the system control program can provide each user section of the system with a specific key to protect against read-only or update access. In this methodology, the system control program assigns a key to each task and manages all requests to change that key. To obtain access to a particular location in storage, the requesting routine must have an identical key or the master key.

Encrypt sensitive data. This is particularly true if the data will be transmitted through a network at any time and especially if a wireless network is involved.

Track and control all media. This is necessary to ensure that appropriate security is being applied at all media locations.

Label media. Label both internally, so the computers will know its level of sensitivity and accessibility, and externally, so operators and system administrators will be aware of its sensitivity and special handling requirements.

Secure all data. Secure data if the system or the secure area will be unattended. This is done to minimize the opportunity for personnel to gain unauthorized access.

Train users. Provide training in the procedures for proper media handling and storage. This training should be included in a security awareness program to ensure that users are fully cognizant of their responsibilities related to the protection of sensitive data.

Establish and train staff in media transport and transmittal procedures. Many times, media are particularly vulnerable to compromise while in transit and not under the protection of storage location.

Use a media library/librarian. This is the ideal way to protect media from unauthorized changes (the integrity issue) and to implement a separation of responsibilities condition that inhibits fraud and other undesirable activities.

Require human- and machine-readable volume labels. These contain, as a minimum, information such as the date created, the date to be destroyed (or retention period), who created it, the volume/file name and version, and the classification. This is a must for mandatory access control but is also important in the operations environment for proper media management and control.

Disposal controls. Government classified is disposed of in accordance with rigorous government regulations, depending on the level of classification involved. Private- or public-sector sensitive data that could cause personal or organizational damage if subject to unauthorized disclosure, alteration, loss, or destruction is disposed of in accordance with organizational procedures and government laws or regulations. The destruction procedures may include the physical alteration (destruction) of the media to prevent its use if it cannot be overwritten or degaussed to avoid exposing sensitive data to unauthorized disclosure. There may also be a need for emergency destruction procedures if the organization is in a hostile environment (terrorist threat) and the facility is about to be overtaken.

Object reuse controls. To ensure that media contain no residual data that could prevent a secure reassignment and depending on the computing environment, a procedure might require that disks be formatted before reassignment or, in the case of tapes or cartridges, be written over a number of times or degaussed with a magnetic field-generating device. The point is that simply erasing or deleting files is not sufficient because all that happens is that the pointers to the data are removed. These can be easily reestablished and the data compromised.

"Purging" is the term often used to describe the overwriting or degaussing operation to remove data. Hiding the data could also be accomplished by encryption, but this involves additional steps to protect encryption keys. The final term associated with object reuse is "remanance," which simply means that after purging is complete, there may still be some residual sensitive data that escaped during the purging process.

Access controls. Implement an access control policy that defines user and operations staff privileges in terms of who can access data and what capabilities they have (read, write, etc.). This is an opportunity to ensure that the concept of least privilege is implemented.

Data classification controls. Establish a data policy that requires the evaluation and classification of all data, even if most of the data can be classified for general employee access. Require that the data be protected in accordance with its classification.

Input/output controls. The following input/output controls were established years ago in data center operations to monitor and reconcile the movements of data into and out of the computer systems. The rush to distributed and client/server operations left these controls more or less in the dust. However, their value in keeping track of operations is being realized again and their use is making a comeback. They can be monitored and reconciled either manually or by computer.

Data input controls consist of data counts with online transactions recorded and timestamped, a record of data entered into the system, and a record of the data edited. For problem-solving efforts in cases of invalid operations or data corruption, this information can be very useful.

Data output controls enable a comparison of output control totals with input counts to ensure that all, and only all, transactions or data were included in the processing cycle. Output controls also ensure that the output reaches the people who it is intended to reach. This can be accomplished by restricting access to printed output reception areas so that only authorized persons can obtain the output. To enable this, it is necessary to print heading and trailing banners on the output that include the intended recipient's name and location. A signed receipt should be required before releasing any output containing sensitive material. When a report is processed but contains no information, there should be printed a "no output" message so that the recipient will not be concerned about lost or stolen data.

Telecommunications Equipment

In this section, we discuss the security controls associated with telecommunications equipment because it has been part of the operations environment for many years. However, most of the discussion and more information related to telecommunications can be found in Chapter 8, "Telecommunications, Network, and Internet Security."

Basic security guidelines for telecommunications equipment include:

- Communications equipment must be monitored for errors, inconsistencies, etc., just like any other data processing equipment.
- Penetration tests should be conducted to ensure that communications controls cannot be easily compromised or misused. Perfection with respect to these controls is an impossible goal but should be pursued, keeping an eye on what new controls do to productivity. This is an

area where the use of a cost/benefit analysis is very appropriate. Remember, as mentioned previously, you go as far with preventive controls as possible in your organization's environment; but when they become too restrictive, you fall back on detective controls.

- The organization's sensitive data — passwords and other sensitive information — being communicated electronically should be encrypted.
- Non-employee (vendor) personnel performing maintenance should be supervised by a knowledgeable employee or other trusted person who can understand the implications of the actions being taken. Remote maintenance should also be monitored and not be available except when actually performing work.
- The use of communications test equipment, communications software utilities, network monitoring tools, and diagnostics for monitoring the network that enable viewing traffic in cleartext must be controlled. This equipment is called "sniffers" and is commonly used to obtain unauthorized access to data passing through the network. Organizational policy must forbid the use of sniffers by anyone not required to use such equipment in the performance of their assigned jobs. Violation of the policy should be grounds for dismissal.
- All communications equipment (e.g., bridges, routers, switches, etc.) should be located in secured facilities. These restricted areas should be monitored continuously to ensure that unauthorized persons do not enter. Cabling for communications equipment must also be installed in protected spaces to make it difficult for intruders to tap in or accidents to cause damage.

Support Systems

Support systems are basically the infrastructure that makes it possible for data processing operations to exist. Because these are an integral part of operations, we mention them here but most of the discussion is found in Chapter 7, "Physical Security."

Maintaining an environmentally sound data center is key to ensuring the continued availability of an information system. Environmental objectives include maintaining appropriate temperature and humidity levels, maintaining air quality by installing a closed-loop recirculating air conditioning system, and maintaining positive pressurization and ventilation to minimize contamination.

In addition, procedures for the installation, monitoring, and maintenance of environmental support equipment, communications and electrical wiring and equipment, plumbing, and other utilities and services should be in accordance with the manufacturer's specifications.

Physical Areas

The data processing facilities and equipment should be located within a structure so as to minimize exposure to threats, such as fire, water, corrosive agents, smoke, and other potential hazards, from adjacent areas, explosion or shock, and unobserved unauthorized access.

Operational components should be located in a secure room with restricted access. Access to the room should include the use of an access request form (to ensure only specifically authorized persons can be granted entrance) and a guest or visitor log (to ensure that there is a record of who was allowed to enter the restricted area). Also, knowledgeable operations personnel should escort visitors in the operations center to ensure they do not obtain physical access to equipment.

When disks or tapes are brought into or taken out of the restricted room, they should be logged to ensure appropriate accountability. Also, for proper accountability, an inventory system that shows which user is assigned to specific pieces of equipment should be maintained. A hardware configuration chart needs to be maintained to indicate the location of hardware items.

Personnel

The security controls for personnel are the final piece of discussion related to the Security Technology and Tools section. Basic personnel controls begin with the hiring process, where it is necessary to conduct background checks to ensure, to the extent possible, the hiring of trustworthy people. These can be more detailed as the sensitivity or privilege level of the job increases. The implication is that the initial background check for an entry position can be less intensive than a future check for a person being promoted to a more responsible position. Security clearances, if required for government-classified work, should be provided and reviewed, as appropriate.

Following the hiring process, supervision of initial job training, ongoing training, and security awareness training is called for. Finally, employee transfers or terminations must be addressed in organization policy.

In network or distributed operations, the network or system administrators usually control all network operations, and in some environments, all security administrator tasks as well. This, of course, is a combination of functions that creates greater security risks. The separation of responsibilities concept is a control measure that was in use before computers ever existed. It is intended to prevent an individual from having control over all steps of an operation and, therefore, being able to manipulate it for personal benefit. With an effective separation of responsibilities, fraudulent use of a system can only be accomplished by collusion between all of those participating in its operation. Eventually, the collusion breaks down or is broken down by a rotation of duties and the fraudulent activities are discovered or at least discontinued until a new collusion can be assembled. So, what can be done to correct the lack of separation of responsibilities in the case of networks and distributed systems? From a security viewpoint, a security administrator position can be established to handle all the operational security-related tasks.

For example, the operator or network administrator should perform the operations-oriented functions such as server start-up and shutdown, and resetting of items such as time/date, network and operating system logs, and passwords. The security administrator should perform security tasks such as user-oriented activities (i.e., setting both user clearances [privileges] and initial passwords, setting other security parameters for new users, and changing security profiles for existing users); setting new or changing existing file sensitivity labels; setting the security characteristics of devices and communications channels; and reviewing audit data, violation reports, intrusion detection data, etc.

It is recognized that assigning a person to perform security administrator duties does not prevent the network/system administrator from actually doing these tasks. However, it should be obvious to an alert security administrator that unauthorized actions were performed by the network/system administrator and appropriate management action can be used to correct the situation.

Particular attention must be given to password management privileges. Some administrators must have the ability and, therefore, the authorization to change another user's password, and this activity should always be properly logged. The display password feature, which permits all passwords to be seen by the password administrator, should be disabled or blocked. If not disabled, this feature can adversely affect accountability, because it allows some users to see other user's passwords.

There are, of course, other personnel who are part of the operations environment and who need to be considered when establishing controls. These include programmers, local and remote end users, cleaning staff, maintenance staff, vendor support personnel, contract/temporary staff, and external partners.

Programmers should not be allowed to have ongoing direct access to computers running production systems (systems used by the organization to operate its business). To maintain system integrity, any changes they make to production systems should be tracked by the organization's change management control system. End users should not have change access to production programs, but should be limited to executing programs and to change access to data as required to perform their duties.

The cleaning staff should be supervised to prevent them from operating any computing resources. The maintenance staff should be closely supervised to avoid unauthorized changes.

Vendor service personnel should be escorted by knowledgeable staff personnel to ensure they do not engage in any unauthorized activities. Procedures and access controls for remote maintenance must be established. Remote maintenance by vendor personnel should never be unrestricted, but should be granted as needed to accomplish specific work for a specific time period upon a specific request by an authorized vendor representative.

If contract and temporary staff personnel seem to be particularly interested in exploring systems, they must have limited access privileges and be supervised to ensure they do not obtain access to areas they do not require to perform their assigned work. Controls over external partners must ensure that they are limited to system accesses consistent with the partnering agreement.

5.4 Assurance, Trust, and Confidence Mechanisms

There are several options that provide the information security professional with assurance that the security tools are effective.

Configuration Management

Configuration Management (CM), simply stated, deals with how organizations define and document their products and processes and how they manage changes as those products and processes evolve. An official definition of CM comes from the ANSI/EIA 649 Configuration Management Document: "CM is a process applied over the life cycle of any product that provides visibility and control of a product's functional, performance and physical attributes. The primary objective of CM is to assure that a product performs as intended and its physical configuration is adequately identified and documented to a level of detail sufficient to repeatably produce the product and meet anticipated needs for operation, maintenance, repair and replacement."[7]

A simpler definition might be: CM is the process of managing products, facilities, and processes by managing their requirements, including changes, and assuring conformance in each case. A good CM process is one that can (1) accommodate change; (2) accommodate the reuse of proven standards and best practices; (3) ensure that all requirements remain clear, concise, and valid; (4) ensure changes, standards, and requirements are communicated promptly and precisely; and (5) ensure that the results conform to each instance of the product (can be duplicated).

In the IT environment, CM involves the integrity issue of controlling modifications to system hardware, firmware, software, and documentation so that they are protected from unauthorized or improper changes. Organizations should have a CM document that provides for the processes followed regarding any events on the information systems.

Contingency Management

Contingency management, as discussed in Chapter 9, "Business Continuity Planning," involves establishing actions to be taken before, during, and after a threatening incident. This includes documented and tested procedures to ensure the availability of critical services and maintain the continuity of operations.

Contingency Plan

A contingency plan is defined as documented actions for items such as emergency response or backup operations. The IT contingency plan is a document providing the procedures for recovering a major application or local information system network in the event of an outage or disaster.

Continuity of Operations Plan (COOP)

A COOP is a document describing the procedures and capabilities to sustain an organization's essential strategic functions at an alternate site for up to 30 days.

Backup Planning

Backup planning is the process of documenting how the organization will conduct backups. The first step in creating a backup plan is to determine what data needs backup, where it is located, and how much your data changes from day to day. The next step is to determine what backup software, hardware, and media will be needed and then plan for growth (e.g., adding more servers). The type of backup used (i.e., full, incremental) should be documented, as well as how often. For example, some organizations conduct incremental or differential backups every hour and full backups every evening. The plan should also include where the backup tapes will be stored and for how long. Another important aspect of any plan, including a backup plan, is to provide training on the plan to those employees responsible for its implementation. The final step is to test the backup plan — can you recover documents in a timely fashion in a consistent manner? As they say, backups are only as good as how well they perform when you need a file restored.

Change Control Management

Change control management is the key ingredient that authorizes changes to production systems, including system and application software. Changes to production systems include the implementation of new applications, modifications of existing applications, removing old applications, and upgrading or patching system software. From a security viewpoint, we are concerned with the potential security impact of these changes, especially if they are not documented or approved by management.

Historically, the most easily sidestepped control is change control. Therefore, every computing facility should have a policy regarding changes to operating systems, computing equipment, networks, environmental facilities (e.g., HVAC, water, plumbing, electricity, and alarms), and applications. A policy is necessary for change to be effective and orderly. The process also allows for notifying affected people of the pending change. Remember: The purpose of the change control process is to manage changes within the computing environment.

Organizations normally customize the change management process to suit their unique requirements. Change management procedures should be designed to ensure that the costs and benefits of change are properly analyzed and that changes to systems are made in a controlled way. An outline of a generic Change Control Management Process is:

- A change is requested by completion of a change request form.
- A change request form is analyzed for validity.
- The ways the change could be implemented are analyzed.
- The costs associated with the changes are analyzed.
- The analysis and change recommendations are recorded.
- The change request is given to the change control board for final decision.
- Accepted changes are made and recorded.
- The change implementation is submitted to quality control for approval.

During this process, the security department and audit function should have an opportunity to review the changes to ensure that changes do not result in a bypass or erosion of required security controls. Thus, it is important for information system security or audit personnel to be involved in change review at the earliest point in the process.

According to Fisher,[8] the goals of the change management process are to eliminate problems and errors and to ensure that the entire environment is stable. To meet these goals, it is important to:

Ensure orderly change. In a facility requiring a high level of systems availability, all changes must be managed in a process to control any variables possibly affecting the environment. Because change can be a serious disruption, however, it must be carefully and consistently controlled.

Inform the computing community of the change. Changes assumed to affect only a small subsection of a site or group may actually affect a much broader cross-section of the computing community. Therefore, the entire computing community should receive adequate notification of impending changes. It is helpful to create a committee representing a broad cross-section of the user group to review proposed changes and their potential effect on users.

Analyze changes. The presentation of an intended change to an oversight committee, with the corresponding documentation of the change, often effectively exposes the change to careful scrutiny. This analysis clarifies the originator's intent before the change is implemented and is helpful in preventing erroneous or inadequately considered changes from entering the system.

Reduce the impact of changes on service. Computing resources must be available when the organization needs them. Poor judgment, erroneous changes, and inadequate preparation must not be allowed in the change process. A well-structured change management process prevents problems and keeps computing services running smoothly.

General procedures should be in place to support the change control policy. These procedures must, at the very least, include steps for instituting a major change to the site's physical facility or to major elements of the system's software or hardware. The following steps should be included.

Applying to introduce a change. A method must be established for applying to introduce a change affecting the computing environment in areas covered by the change control policy. Change requests must be presented to the individual who will manage the change through all of its subsequent steps. Once the change request is entered, it must be subsequently approved prior to scheduling. The approver must not be the same person who submitted the request, as doing so would introduce segregation of duties problems.

Cataloging the change. The change request should be entered into a change log, which provides documentation for the change itself (e.g., the timing and testing of the change). This log should be updated as the change moves through the process, providing a thorough audit trail of all changes.

Scheduling the change. After thorough preparation and testing by the sponsor, the change should be scheduled for review by a change control committee and for implementation. The implementation date should be set far enough in advance to provide the committee with sufficient review time. At the meeting with the change control committee, all known ramifications of the change should be discussed. If the committee members agree that the change has been thoroughly tested, it should be entered on the implementation schedule and noted as approved. All approvals and denials should be in writing, with appropriate reasons given for the denials.

Implementing the change. The final step in the change process is application of the change to the hardware and software environment. If the change works correctly, this should be noted on the change control form. When the change does not perform as expected, the corresponding information should be gathered, analyzed, and entered on the change control form, as a reference to help avoid a recurrence of the same problem in the future. Ideally, the change request should have appropriate information to demonstrate how a failed change would affect system operation or how the system is restored until the change can be implemented again.

Reporting changes to management. Periodically, a full report summarizing change activity should be submitted to management. This helps ensure that management is aware of any quality problems that may have developed and enables management to address any service problems.

These steps should be documented and made known to all involved in the change process. Once a change process has been established, someone must be assigned the responsibility for managing all changes throughout the process.

Intrusion Detection Systems (IDSs)

An IDS attempts to detect either an intruder breaking into the system or an authorized user misusing system resources. The IDS operates in the background of the system and sends alert messages when it notices something suspicious. Intrusion detection techniques attempt to identify and isolate computer and network attacks by observing traffic logs or other audit data. An IDS is based on the idea that an intruder can be detected through the examination of various elements, such as network traffic, packet elements, CPU utilization, I/O utilization, and file activities. These elements or system activities are chronologically organized into audit data. Thus, the audit data refers to the audit records of all activities on a system. More information on intrusion detection systems can be found in Chapter 3, "Access Control Systems and Methodology."

System Events/Audit Reports

The most common data for an IDS is the audit data. Although it may be possible to manually analyze each record of activity, the vastness of the audit data provided makes a manual analysis impractical. To resolve this, automated IDSs provide this type of analysis. Automated IDSs examine current audit records of user activity and compare these with profiles of expected activity to infer in real-time if an intrusion is occurring.

Audit and monitoring mechanisms, tools, and facilities permit the identification of security-oriented events and subsequent actions to identify the key elements and report pertinent information to the appropriate individual, group, or process.

Another method of determining excessive or unauthorized use by employees with privileged access is to use some type of system event tracking system (sometimes referred to as violation tracking). For a security administrator to get an understanding of what occurs during system operations, it may be helpful to have a mechanism that captures various system details, such as logon attempts, file access attempts, or processes/application access attempts. For system event tracking to be effective, rules need to be established as to what is acceptable. Any actions outside of those settings would be considered a violation.

Capturing system activity permits determination of whether a violation has occurred or whether elements of software and hardware implementation were merely omitted, therefore requiring modification. In this regard, tracking and analyzing violations are equally important. In some industries, it is mandatory to have some type of system event capturing software to satisfy the requirements for the due care of information. Without violation tracking, the ability to determine excesses or unauthorized use becomes extremely difficult, if not impossible. For example, a general user might discover that, because of an administrative error, he or she can access system control functions. Adequate, regular tracking and periodic review highlight such inappropriate privileges before errors occur.

A frequently overlooked component of violation processing is analysis. Violation analysis enables an organization to locate and understand specific trouble spots, both in security and in usability. Violation analysis can be used to find:

- Various types of violations, such as:
  - Are repetitive mistakes being made? This might be a sign of poor implementation or user training.
  - Are individuals exceeding their system access needs? This might be an indication of weak control implementation.
  - Do too many people have too many update abilities? This might be a result of inadequate system design or privilege assignment.
- Where the violations are occurring, which may help identify program or design problems
- Patterns that can provide early warning of serious intrusions (e.g., hackers or disgruntled employees) (Fisher, 1998)

An important element of system event analysis is to determine what is normal activity versus what is unusual or unauthorized activity. A term associated with this is to establish "clipping levels." For example, organizations may set a baseline that allows a particular type, number, or patterns of violations to occur before conducting an in-depth analysis. When the baseline is exceeded, a violation record is produced.

Clipping levels can also make the analysis of system events manageable. If an organization does not use some type of filtering software, the number of system events may become unmanageable to analyze. Imagine having to review over 10,000 lines of data each day. Thus, for violation tracking to be effective, a clipping level should be established. Note that this solution is particularly effective for small to medium-sized installations. Organizations with large-scale computing facilities often track all violations and use statistical routines to filter minor infractions.

Other activity reporting deals with the need to report all activity connected with privileged IDs (i.e., those with administrative-level privileges). This activity should be reported using logging and audit records and should be reviewed periodically to ensure privileged IDs are not being misused. Either a sample of the audit records should be reviewed using a predetermined methodology incorporating approved EDP auditing and review techniques, or all accesses should be reviewed using expert system applications. Transactions deviating from those normally conducted should be examined and, if necessary, fully investigated. Under no circumstances should management skip the regular review of these activities. Many organizations have found that a regular review process deters curiosity and even mischief within the site and often produces the first evidence of attempted hacking by outsiders.

Penetration Testing

Penetration testing is the process of simulating an attack on an information system at the request of the owner, or at least with the owner's permission. A penetration team is an organized group of people who attempt to penetrate the security of an information system. The goal is to assess the security of the system and find the vulnerabilities or security gaps in the security measures of the organization. More information on Penetration Testing can be found in Chapter 3, "Access Control Systems and Methodology."

5.5 Information Protection and Management Services

In this final section, Information Protection and Management Services, we outline some of the tasks that security and operations management needs to perform to ensure a secure operating environment.

Security Reviews

Security reviews by the information security staff enable an independent evaluation of how the security policies, procedures, standards, and baselines are being implemented and how well they are working to achieve the level of information security that has been intended. Areas to be reviewed include, but are not limited to, system access and authorization, procedures and controls (including operating procedures, input/output controls, detection and surveillance, etc.), security incident or problem reporting, and change control.

Operations management duties involve providing support and oversight for overall operations security, such as reviewing:

- *Implementation of vendor patches:* probably the greatest concern these days.
- *Operating logs:* to ensure that operators are not abusing the system.
- *Inventory:* documenting the status of resources.
- *Change control practices:* ensuring system integrity.
- *Incident reporting:* how well the controls are operating.
- *System/audit logs:* can their integrity be assured?
- *Audits/security reviews:* are findings properly addressed/corrected?

An insight as to how well access control and authorization are being handled can be obtained from a regular review of the violation reports and a follow-up on how resulting breaches are controlled and how well both violations and breaches are reported. Violations must be detected and verified to eliminate false alarms. A large number of false alarms might indicate that the parameters of the violation reporting bases are either faulty or not implemented correctly. If breaches are not properly controlled, the potential losses to the organization will increase. Also, if these incidents are not properly reported, it is difficult to understand how well the security controls are performing. Organizational, regulatory, and discretionary reporting is addressed in Chapter 10, "Law, Investigations, and Ethics."

Incident Reporting

What type of activity you should report, and the level of detail included in your report, depend on who will receive your report and what type of industry regulations exist or the sensitivity of your data. The organization's local policies and procedures should have detailed information about what types of activity should be reported, as well as the appropriate person to whom you should report. Additionally, there are several outside organizations located within each country that also want to receive incident reports. For example, in the United States, the CERT® Coordination Center (CERT/CC) would like to hear of incidents occurring. When asked why organizations (or individuals) should send incident reports to CERT/CC, their response was: "There are several reasons to report an incident to the CERT Coordination Center. We may be able to provide technical assistance in responding to the incident, or put you in touch with other sites involved in the same activity. Your reports allow us to collect and distribute better information about intruder activity through our statistics and documents. Reporting incidents to the CERT/CC and others helps to promote greater security awareness and improve the security of the Internet. Your organizational policies or local laws may require you to report the activity to us or some other CSIRT. Finally, notifying other sites of possible security intrusions is an important part of being a good Internet citizen."[9]

Problem Management

Although problem management can affect different areas within computing services, from an operations perspective, it is most often encountered in dealing with hardware. This control process reports, tracks, and resolves problems affecting computer services. Management should be structured to measure the number and types of problems against predetermined service levels for the area in which the problem occurs. This area of management has three objectives:

- Reducing failures to an acceptable level
- Preventing recurrences of problems
- Reducing the problem impact on service

Problems should be organized according to their types. Examples of problem types include:

- Performance and availability for the hardware, software, network/telecommunications equipment, and environment equipment (e.g., air conditioning, plumbing, power, heating)
- Safety
- Security
- Operating procedures

All functional areas in the organization affected by these problems should be included in the control process. Problem management, as part of computing operations, should investigate deviations from operations standards, unusual or unexplained occurrences, unscheduled initial program loads (in a data center), or other abnormal conditions.

Regarding the deviation from standards issue, organizations should have standards against which computing services are measured. Actual performance should be measured against the standard and the deviation determined. Significant deviations should be investigated and resolved.

When unusual or unexplained occurrences happen, they must be investigated to determine their source. Because these problems can appear to be random or sporadic, tracking over a period of time can identify patterns that, in turn, can lead to solutions.

For example, unscheduled initial program loads in a data center usually occur when a problem has happened. The reason may be that some portion of the hardware is malfunctioning and slowing down, or software may be experiencing an error condition from which recovery is not possible. In any case, manual recovery procedures must be initiated and the event must be reported in the problem tracking system.

Other abnormal conditions include problems not specifically addressed above. These could involve performance degradation, intermittent or unusual software failures, and corrupted system software. All should be tracked in the problem management system.

Finally, as with most of the other chapters, the operations staff may be involved in security awareness training. In the operations arena, this involves training of operators, system administrators, and network administrators so that they are prepared to deal appropriately with intruders and social engineers.

Summary

This chapter addressed issues related to data center operations as well as distributed and network operations. Both types of operations are well represented throughout the world. A key issue is ensuring that operations personnel — operators in a data center and system/network administrators in the distributed environment — do not abuse the special privileges they must have to perform their duties. The distributed environment presents special concerns because the built-in separation of responsibilities available in the data center operation has been eliminated. This requires that extra precautions and supervision are necessary.

5.6 Common Body of Knowledge (CBK)

The current CBK for the Operations Security Domain is listed below to assist in determining topics for further review. Although this Study Guide is very detailed in many areas, it is not possible to thoroughly discuss every CBK topic in a single book; therefore, additional study of items from the bibliography may be advisable.

Expectation

Professionals should fully understand the following:

- *Information security controls.* Understand information security controls, including the mechanisms, tools, and facilities (both passive and active) that permit:
  - The identification of security events (historical and real-time)
  - The capture of subsequent actions
  - The identification of the events' key elements
  - The alerting of appropriate authorities
  - The taking of corrective or recovery actions
- *Security audits.* Understand how to perform a security audit, including:
  - The difference between internal and external security audits
  - How to perform an evaluation of the controls employed to ensure (1) the appropriate protection of the organization's information assets (including hardware, software, firmware, and data) from all significant anticipated threats or hazards, and (2) the accuracy and reliability of the data maintained by a system
  - Standard of due care
  - Frequency of review
- *Violation analysis.* Understand the elements of violation analysis, including:
  - Types of violations, including repetitive mistakes, individuals exceeding their authority, too many people with unrestricted access, hackers, disgruntled employees, potential abuses to operations security, and fraud. A rejected transaction example might include erroneous transaction entered and rejected, perpetrator handles rejects, replaces with apparently valid transaction but "pay to" account is changed. Violations could also include interference with operations, denial-of-service, production delays, conversion to personal use of computing time, vendor software with trapdoors, unauthorized access/disclosure, off-hours access, and audit trail/system log corruption.
  - Potential hardware and software exposures, including:
    - Device address modification, such as rerouting output, obtaining supervisory terminal functions, or bypassing system logs
    - System shutdown/downtime, such as shutdown handled from console/operations area
    - IPL from tape, such as initial program load without security
    - I/O system generation, including terminals/printers/disks and tape drives
    - Network
    - Server bootup sequence from tape, CD, or floppy disk that can bypass O/S security
    - "Highjack" server's network address in order to capture traffic to and from server or modify user/application data

- Steal password file/table from the server
- Gain access to OS or application user accounts
- Where it is occurring, including patterns indicating serious intrusion attempts
  - The need to determine clipping levels, which establish a baseline violation count to ignore normal user errors
- *Audit trails*. Understand how to implement an effective audit trail to ensure:
  - Individual accountability
  - Reconstruction of events
  - Intrusion detection
  - Problem identification
- *Audit reporting*. Understand how to generate audit reports that are accurate, supported by evidence, meaningful, constructive, and lead to action.
- *Monitoring*. Understand:
  - Warning banners
  - Keystroke monitoring
  - Pattern recognition
  - Trend analysis
  - Tools available on the various computing platforms, operating systems, and specific security software used by the practitioner for audit reduction and variance techniques
- *Resource protection*. Understand what resources must be protected and privileges that must be restricted to attain operations security. Resources that must be protected to achieve operations security include:
  - Password files
  - Application program libraries
  - Source code
  - Vendor software
  - Operating systems, such as libraries, utilities, directories, and address tables
  - Proprietary packages
  - Communication software and hardware
  - Main storage
  - Disk and tape storage media
  - Processing equipment
  - Stand-alone computers
  - Printers
  - People
  - Sensitive/critical data
  - Files
  - Programs
  - System utilities

- System logs/audit trails
- Violation report
- Backup files (all)
- Sensitive forms/printouts
- Appropriate system administrator privileges include:
  - Server start-up and shutdown
  - File system(s)
  - Database(s)
  - Application(s)
  - Reset
  - Time/date
  - Operating system log(s)
- Appropriate operator privileges include:
  - Initial program load
  - Program starts OS controlled from console
  - Operator could load wrong program
  - Bypass label processing
  - Rename/relabel resources
  - Reset
  - Time/date
  - Passwords
  - Reassign ports/lines
- Possible recovery procedures include:
  - Reboot system and get running in single-user mode
  - Recover all files systems active at time of failure
  - Restore missing/damaged files and database from most recent backup
  - Check security-critical files
  - Operating systems' responses to failures can be classified into three general categories: (1) system reboot, (2) emergency system restart, and (3) system cold start
- *Operations controls.* Understand the following operations controls: (1) Resource Protection, (2) Privileged-Entity Control, (3) Change Control Management, (4) Hardware Controls, (5) Input/Output Controls, (6) Media Controls, (7) Separation of Duties and Responsibilities, (8) Rotation of Duties, (9) Least Privilege, and (10) Trusted Recovery Process
  - Change Control Management that can be employed to attain operations security includes:
    - Authorize changes to production systems:
      - New applications
      - Modify existing applications
      - Remove old applications
    - Use input from problem management to initiate changes

- Block changes that adversely affect security of applications/data
- Hardware Controls that can be employed to attain operations security include:
  - Hardware area locks and alarms
  - Operator terminals
  - Server/router rooms
  - Modem/circuit rooms
  - Magnetic media rooms/cabinets
  - Sensitive
  - Critical
- Input/Output Controls that can be employed to attain operations security include:
  - Input data counted
  - Online transactions recorded and timestamped
  - Data entered and data edited
  - Output control totals compared with input counts
  - Ensure output reaches proper people
  - Restrict access to printed output storage areas
  - Print heading and trailing banners with recipients' names and locations
  - Require signed receipt before releasing sensitive output
  - Print "No Output" with banners when report is empty
- Media Controls that can be employed to attain operations security include:
  - Media labels: human- and machine-readable form:
    - Magnetic tape, disk, diskette, optical disk external label required
    - Volume label required
    - Date created
    - Date to be destroyed (or retention period)
    - Who created
    - Volume/file name
    - Volume/file version
    - Classification
  - Audit trail of who checked out and when
  - Separation of responsibilities
  - Controlled by media librarian
  - No programmer access
  - Backup procedures:
    - Original copy
    - Copy on-site (away from computers)
    - Copy off-site
- *Separation of duties and responsibilities.* The operator and administrator functions must be separated because combination of func-

tions creates greater security risks. The primary purpose behind the separation of the Operator and Administrator functions is to limit the potential damage that untrusted, or errant, code can inflict on the information the TCB uses to enforce the security policy. Any code executed with Operator or Administrator privileges has the ability to change the TCB data structures, thus affecting the enforcement of policy. Through the application of the principle of least privilege and the separation of Operator and Administrator functions so that they are prevented from executing untrusted code, the TCB data structures can be protected.

- *Rotation of duties.* The rotation of duties is used to interrupt opportunity to create collusion to subvert an operation for fraudulent purposes.
- *Least privilege.* The principle of least privilege requires that each subject be granted the most restrictive set of privileges needed for the specific task. In the case of the operator and administrator functions, the privileges need to be established at a low level of granularity so that the processes that implement those functions do not have unnecessary privileges.
- *Trusted recovery process.* Before allowing user access:
  - Reboot system
  - Get running in single user-mode
    - Recover all files and systems active at time of failure
    - Restore missing/damaged files and databases from most recent backup
    - Check security critical files
- *Attack methods.* Understand the potential for abuse or access to IT/IS systems:
  - Threats and countermeasures to media library:
    - *Errors and omissions.* A sound training and awareness program can be used to reduce this threat.
    - *Fraud and theft (from inside or outside).* Proper access control can be used to reduce this threat.
    - *Employee sabotage.* Separation of duties and responsibilities, multiple backups, and proper access control can be used to reduce this threat.
    - *Loss of physical and infrastructure support.* Multiple backups can be used to reduce this threat.
    - *Malicious hackers/crackers.* Proper access control can be used to reduce this threat.
    - *Industrial espionage.* Proper access control can be used to reduce this threat.
    - *Malicious code.* Malicious code checkers with periodic updates and multiple backups can be used to reduce this threat.

   • *Foreign government espionage.* Proper access control can be used to reduce this threat.

5.7 Sample Questions for the CISSP Exam

1. Critical data is:
   a. Subject to classification by regulatory bodies or legislation
   b. Data of high integrity
   c. Always protected at the highest level
   d. Instrumental for business operations
2. When an organization is determining which data is sensitive, it must consider all of the following EXCEPT:
   a. Expectations of customers
   b Legislation or regulations
   c. Quantity of data
   d. Age of the data
3. All of the following are examples of a preventative control EXCEPT:
   a. Intrusion detection systems
   b. Human resources policies
   c. Anti-virus software
   d. Fences
4. Recovery controls attempt to:
   a. Establish countermeasures to prevent further incidents
   b. Return to normal operations
   c. Compensate for vulnerabilities in other controls
   d. Ensure that audit logs are reviewed regularly
5. Privileged access permissions should:
   a. Never be granted
   b. Be subject to recertification
   c. Only be granted on an emergency basis
   d. Be provided to all trusted personnel
6. Transparency of controls does all of the following EXCEPT:
   a. Allow authorized access without hindering business operations.
   b. Deny unauthorized access without revealing system knowledge to attackers.
   c. Log all important activity without identifying monitoring techniques.
   d. Ensure that security activity does not impact system performance.
7. Change management must include all of the following EXCEPT:
   a. Be reviewed by security
   b. Be a formal process
   c. Be ready to handle unexpected events
   d. Be subject to acceptance

8. Which of the following is NOT a class of failures identified in the "Trusted Recovery Guide" by the National Computer Security Center:
   a. State transition
   b. Trusted computing base (TCB)
   c. Buffer overflow
   d. Discontinuity of operation
9. Separation of duties controls can be defeated through:
   a. Mutual exclusivity
   b. Collusion
   c. Dual control
   d. Accreditation
10. The best technique for preventing and detecting abuse by a user with privileged access is:
    a. Good policy
    b. Review by management
    c. Strong authentication
    d. Audit logs
11. Fault tolerance can be defined as:
    a. The ability to detect and attempt recovery from failure
    b. A robust system that resists failure
    c. A system that is backed up to prevent data loss
    d. Preparing alternate processing in case of loss of primary system
12. To speed up RAID disk access, an organization can:
    a. Use larger hard drives.
    b. Stripe the data across several drives.
    c. Mirror critical drives.
    d. Disallow ad hoc queries.
13. The Common Criteria define the term "fail secure" as:
    a. A system that is tolerant of component failure
    b. The ability of a system to fail in a controlled manner
    c. A system failure does not affect normal business operations
    d. The preservation of a secure state in the event of a failure
14. If a report contains no data, should it be printed anyway?
    a. No, save paper and be environmentally conscious.
    b. No, there is no need to print an empty report.
    c. Yes, so that the owner knows the report is empty — and not just lost.
    d. Yes, to preserve the regular job flow and prevent errors.
15. When contracting a vendor for software or hardware provisioning, care must be taken to:
    a. Ensure all changes are kept up-to-date.
    b. Ensure all changes go through a change management process.
    c. Ensure that in-house technical staff learn the system.
    d. Ensure that all activity on the system is monitored.

16. System documentation must contain all of the following EXCEPT:
    a. A description of the system functionality
    b. A record of all changes to a system
    c. The identity of the person or position responsible for the system
    d. The volume of transactions processed by the system
17. When an employee transfers within an organization:
    a. The employee must undergo a new security review.
    b. All old system IDs must be disabled.
    c. All access permissions should be reviewed.
    d. The employee must turn in all remote access devices.
18. Emergency fixes to a system must:
    a. Be implemented as rapidly as possible
    b. Be scrutinized subsequently to ensure they were performed correctly
    c. Be performed only by following normal change control procedures
    d. Be made permanent within 72 hours

Notes

1. Patricia A.P. Fisher, "Operations Security and Controls," in *Information Security Management Handbook*, Harold F. Tipton and Micki Krause (eds.), Boca Raton, FL: Auerbach Publications, 1999, p. 699.
2. Zhi Hamby, "What Is OPSEC?" www.opsec.org/who, p.3.
3. Fisher, p. 699.
4. Information Security Forum, *The Standard for Good Practice for Information Security*, London: Internet Security Forum, 2003, p. 17.
5. "Florida Man Sentenced for Selling Counterfeit Software Labels on Auction Web Site," www.usdoj.gov/criminal/cybercrime/mitchellSent.htm, February 4, 2003.
6. Fisher, p. 705.
7. National Consensus Standard for Configuration Management (ANSI/EIA 649), p. 7.
8. Fisher, p. 710.
9. CERT Coordination Center Incident Reporting Guidelines, www.cert.org/tech_tips/_incident_reporting.html#Introduction.

References

American National Standards Institute, National Consensus Standard for Configuration Management (ANSI/EIA).

Bosworth, S. and M.E. Kabay (eds), *Computer Security Handbook, 4th edition*, New York: John Wiley & Sons, 2002.

Drury, Jason, "Sniffers: What They Are and How to Protect from Them," www.securityfocus.com, 2000.

Fisher, Patricia A.P., "Operations Security and Controls," in *Handbook of Information Security Management*, Harold F. Tipton and Micki Krause (eds.), Boca Raton, FL: Auerbach Publications, 1999.

Fites, P. and M.P.J. Kratz, *Information Systems Security: A Practitioner's Reference*, New York: Van Nostrand Reinhold, 1993.

Hunter, Laura, "Top Ten Backup Planning Considerations," Searchwindowsmanageability.techtarget.com, August 2, 2002.

Peltier, Thomas, *Information Security Policies and Procedures: A Practitioner's Reference*, Boca Raton, FL: Auerbach Publications, 1999.

Web sites

OPSEC Professionals Society: www.opsec.org.

Information Security Forum, *The Forum's Standard of Good Practice,* The Information Security Forum, 2001. At www.isfsecuritystandard.com.

Websense Press Releases, 2001. Increased Popularity of Pirated Software Creates Legal Liability and Bandwidth Headaches for Corporations, Warns Websense Inc. http://www.Websense.com.

U.S. Department of Justice Press Release, 2003. Florida Man Sentenced for Selling Counterfeit Software Labels on Auction Web Sites. http://www.usdoj.gov.

RAID Systems, 2002. http://www.usbyte.com. Copyright © 1999–2002, USByte.com.

Institute of Configuration Management: http://www.icmhq.com.

CERT Coordination Center Incident Reporting Guidelines: http://www.cert.org.

Chapter 6
Cryptography

Introduction

Cryptography addresses the principles, means, and methods of disguising information to ensure its integrity, confidentiality, and authenticity.

The CISSP candidate should be able to understand:

- The business and security requirements for cryptography and how to apply the appropriate use of cryptography to achieve the desired business effect.
  - *Confidentiality.* Understand the strength of various cryptographic applications, impacts on system performance, and when to apply; the concepts of synchronization of parameters between end systems; and how to recognize the use of confidentiality functions.
  - *Integrity.* Understand how the integrity function works and how it differs from the authentication and confidentiality functions, when to apply, and how to recognize its use.
  - *Authentication.* Understand how the authentication function works, how it differs from integrity and non-repudiation, what a digital signature is, and how to apply this function to messaging, web, and commerce applications.
  - *Non-repudiation.* Understand how non-repudiation works, how it differs from authentication, what to apply, and how to recognize its use.
- Cryptographic concepts, methodologies, and practices:
  - Understand the difference between symmetric and asymmetric cryptography, public and private keys.
  - Understand public and private key algorithms in terms of their applications and uses.
  - Understand construction and use of digital signatures.
  - Understand the basic functionality of hash/crypto algorithms (DES, RSA, SHA, MD5, HMAC, DSA), and effects of key length.
  - Understand the basic functions involved in key management, including creation, distribution, verification, revocation, destruction, storage, recovery and life span, and how these functions affect cryptographic integrity.
  - Understand major key distribution methods and algorithms (e.g., manual, Kerberos, ISAKMP).

377

- Vulnerabilities to cryptographic functions:
  - Understand the strengths and weaknesses of algorithms and key strengths.
  - Understand cryptographic key administration and storage in terms of vulnerability increases (compromise).
  - Understand attack methods (COA, KPA, CTA [including CPA, AC-PA, and CCA], brute force, CRACK, replay, MIM, and birthday) and how to recognize attacks against cryptographic functions.
  - Understand which attacks work against which types of algorithms.
- Use and function of CAs and PKI:
  - Understand how certificates are issued, verified, distributed, and revoked (hierarchy chain).
  - Understand types and classes of certificates (standards).
  - Understand and recognize the components of a CA and the hierarchical structure of PKI.
- System architecture requirements for implementing cryptographic functions:
  - Understand cryptography algorithm construction.
  - Understand the use of application and network-based protocols, such as PEM, S/MIME, SSL, HTTPS (also SHTTP), SET, IPSec.
  - Understand the application of hardware components, such as smart cards, tokens, etc.
  - Understand the application of cryptographic components, such as IPSec nodes and ISAKMP.

6.1 Information Protection Requirements

The A-I-C Triad

In this chapter we will learn how cryptography and encryption techniques will help us address the issues associated with Confidentiality and Integrity as they relate to our A-I-C triad (Exhibit 1). The goal is to protect

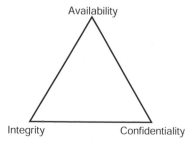

Exhibit 1. A-I-C Triad

the information that is stored and transmitted using cryptographic techniques, which is related to the Confidentiality goal. Cryptography also allows us to address the issue of Integrity, by providing techniques that will allow us to identify the unauthorized modification of information.

6.2 Information Protection Environment

Introduction

Oddly enough, some of the earliest cryptographers were not really trying to hide anything. Rather, they were trying to draw attention to their subject and show off their language skills by playing with words.

When knowledge of the written language was not widespread, for example, during Julius Caesar's time (see Exhibit 2), ciphers did not need to be very complex. Because few people knew how to read, Caesar's cipher, simple as it was, was very effective.

As history unfolded and more people were able to read and write, something had to be done to better deal with the growing number of potential adversaries. Throughout history, cryptography has been used mainly to secure communications belonging to the powerful and the influential, usually governments, the military, and royalty. The powerful people of this world have always used ciphers. They have exchanged coded messages among one another and decoded the messages of others for their own advantage. But with the advent of the computer, the widespread use of computer technology has expanded the need for secure communications around the world and the need for secure storage of sensitive information. The advent of computers has changed many things, but not the fundamentals of cryptography. The fundamentals of cryptography are the same today as they were hundreds and even thousands of years ago. They have just been applied to today's technology, in order to provide some very good methods of ensuring the confidentiality, integrity, and availability of information.

Computers have made adding complexity to cryptography very easy. They have also made solving complexity easier. Because of rapidly advancing technology, secure systems must constantly be assessed for the possibility of new attacks if security is to be maintained. Secret sharing, a necessity in today's world, is still a tug-of-war between clever cryptographers and ingenious cryptanalysts with new tools in their belts.

Definitions

Cryptography is about writing secrets. The first secret messages were exchanged thousands of years ago. Cryptography involves scrambling some kind of useful information, in its original form called plaintext, into a

Exhibit 2. History of Cryptography

~1900 BC	An Egyptian scribe used non-standard hieroglyphics in an inscription. Kahn lists this as the first documented example of written cryptography.[1]
1500 BC	A Mesopotamian tablet contains an enciphered formula for the making of glazes for pottery.[1]
500–600 BC	Hebrew scribes writing down the book of Jeremiah used a reversed-alphabet simple substitution cipher known as ATBASH. (Jeremiah started dictating to Baruch in 605 BC but the chapters containing these bits of cipher are attributed to a source labeled "C" [believed not to be Baruch], which could be an editor writing after the Babylonian exile in 587 BC, someone contemporaneous with Baruch or even Jeremiah himself.) ATBASH was one of a few Hebrew ciphers of the time.[1]
487 BC	The Greeks used a device called the "skytale" — a staff around which a long, thin strip of leather was wrapped and written on. The leather was taken off and worn as a belt. Presumably, the recipient would have a matching staff and the encrypting staff would be left home. [*Note:* an article in *Cryptologia* late in 1998 makes the case that the cryptographic use of the skytale may be a myth.][1]
50–60 BC	**Julius Caesar** (100–44 BC) used a simple substitution with the normal alphabet (just shifting the letters a fixed amount) in government communications. This cipher was weaker than ATBASH, by a small amount; but in a day when few people read in the first place, it was good enough. He also used transliteration of Latin into Greek letters and a number of other simple ciphers.[1]
0–400?	The *Kama Sutra of Vatsayana* lists cryptography as the 44th and 45th of 64 arts (yogas) men and women should know and practice. The date of this work is unclear but is believed to be between the 1st and 4th centuries, AD. [Another expert, John W. Spellman, will commit only to the range between the 4th century BC and the 5th century AD.] Vatsayana says that his *Kama Sutra* is a compilation of much earlier works, making the dating of the cryptography references even more uncertain.
	Part I, Chapter III lists the 64 arts and opens with: "Man should study the *Kama Sutra* and the arts and sciences subordinate thereto [....] Even young maids should study this *Kama Sutra*, along with its arts and sciences, before marriage, and after it they should continue to do so with the consent of their husbands." These arts are clearly not the province of a government or even of academics, but rather are practices of laymen.

(continued)

Exhibit 2. History of Cryptography (Continued)

	In this list of arts, the 44th and 45th read:
	The art of understanding writing in cipher, and the writing of words in a peculiar way.
	The art of speaking by changing the forms of words. It is of various kinds. Some speak by changing the beginning and end of words, others by adding unnecessary letters between every syllable of a word, and so on.[2]
200s	"The so-called Leiden papyrus [...] employs ciphers to conceal the crucial portions of important [magic] recipes."[1]
725–790?	**Abu `Abd al-Rahman al-Khalil ibn Ahmad ibn `Amr ibn Tammam al Farahidi al-Zadi al Yahmadi** wrote a (now lost) book on cryptography, inspired by his solution of a cryptogram in Greek for the Byzantine emperor. His solution was based on known (correctly guessed) plaintext at the message start — a standard cryptanalytic method, used even in World War II against Enigma messages.[1]
855	**Abu Bakr Ahmad ben `Ali ben Wahshiyya an-Nabati** published several cipher alphabets that were traditionally used for magic.[1]
—	"A few documents with ciphertext survive from the Ghaznavid government of conquered Persia, and one chronicler reports that high officials were supplied with a personal cipher before setting out for new posts. But the general lack of continuity of Islamic states and the consequent failure to develop a permanent civil service and to set up permanent embassies in other countries militated against cryptography's more widespread use."[1]
1226	"As early as 1226, a faint political cryptography appeared in the archives of Venice, where dots or crosses replaced the vowels in a few scattered words."[1]
~1250	**Roger Bacon** not only described several ciphers but wrote: "A man is crazy who writes a secret in any other way than one which will conceal it from the vulgar."[1]
1379	**Gabrieli di Lavinde,** at the request of Clement VII, compiled a combination substitution alphabet and small code — the first example of the *nomenclator* Kahn has found. This class of code/cipher was to remain in general use among diplomats and some civilians for the next 450 years, despite the fact that there were stronger ciphers being invented in the meantime, possibly because of its relative convenience.[1]
1300s	**`Abd al-Rahman Ibn Khaldun** wrote "The Muqaddimah," a substantial survey of history that cites the use of "names of perfumes, fruits, birds, or flowers to indicate the letters, or [...] of forms different from the accepted forms of the letters" as a cipher among tax and army bureaus. He also includes a reference to cryptanalysis, noting that "Well-known writings on the subject are in the possession of the people" [p. 97].[1]

(continued)

Exhibit 2. History of Cryptography (Continued)

1392	"The Equatorie of the Planetis," possibly written by **Geoffrey Chaucer**, contains passages in cipher. The cipher is a simple substitution with a cipher alphabet consisting of letters, digits, and symbols.[3]
1412	**Shihab al-Din abu `l-`Abbas Ahmad ben `Ali ben Ahmad `Abd Allah al-Qalqashandi** wrote *Subh al-a `sha,* a 14-volume Arabic encyclopedia that included a section on cryptology. This information was attributed to **Taj ad-Din `Ali ibn al-Duraihim ben Muhammad ath-Tha`alibi al-Mausili,** who lived from 1312 to 1361 but whose writings on cryptology have been lost. The list of ciphers in this work included both substitution and transposition and, for the first time, a cipher with multiple substitutions for each plaintext letter. Also traced to Ibn al-Duraihim is an exposition on and worked example of cryptanalysis, including the use of tables of letter frequencies, and sets of letters that cannot occur together in one word.[1]
1466–1467	**Leon Battista Alberti** (a friend of **Leonardo Dato**, a political secretary who might have instructed Alberti in the state-of-the-art of cryptology) invented and published the first polyalphabetic cipher, designing a cipher disk (known to us as the Captain Midnight Decoder Badge) to simplify the process. This class of cipher was apparently not broken until the 1800s. Alberti also wrote extensively on the state-of-the-art in ciphers, in addition to his own invention. Alberti also used his disk for enciphered code. These systems were much stronger than the nomenclator in use by the diplomats of the day and for centuries to come.[1]
1473–1490	"A manuscript [...] by **Arnaldus de Bruxella** uses five lines of cipher to conceal the crucial part of the operation of making a philosopher's stone."[1]
1518	**Johannes Trithemius** wrote the first printed book on cryptology. He invented a steganographic cipher in which each letter was represented as a word taken from a succession of columns. The resulting series of words would be a legitimate prayer. He also described polyalphabetic ciphers in the now-standard form of rectangular substitution tables. He introduced the notion of changing alphabets with each letter.[1]
1553	**Giovan Batista Belaso** introduced the notion of using a passphrase as the key for a repeated polyalphabetic cipher. (This is the standard polyalphabetic cipher operation mis-named "Vigenère" by most writers to this day.)[1]
1563	**Giovanni Battista Porta** wrote a text on ciphers, introducing the digraphic cipher. He classified ciphers as transposition, substitution, and symbol substitution (use of a strange alphabet). He suggested use of synonyms and misspellings to confuse the cryptanalyst. He apparently introduced the notion of a mixed alphabet in a polyalphabetic tableau.[1]

(continued)

Exhibit 2. History of Cryptography (Continued)

1564	Bellaso published an autokey cipher improving on the work of **Cardano,** who appears to have invented the idea.[1]
1623	**Sir Francis Bacon** described a cipher that now bears his name — a biliteral cipher, known today as a 5-bit binary encoding. He advanced it as a steganographic device — by using variation in type face to carry each bit of the encoding.[4]
1585	**Blaise de Vigenère** wrote a book on ciphers, including the first authentic plaintext and ciphertext autokey systems (in which previous plaintext or ciphertext letters are used for the current letter's key). Both of these were forgotten and reinvented in the late 19th century.[1] The autokey idea survives today in the DES, CBC, and CFB modes.[1]
1790s	**Thomas Jefferson**, possibly aided by **Dr. Robert Patterson** (a mathematician at U. Penn), invented his wheel cipher. This was reinvented in several forms later and used in World War II by the U.S. Navy as the Strip Cipher, M-138-A.[1,5]
1817	**Colonel Decius Wadsworth** produced a geared cipher disk with a different number of letters in the plain and cipher alphabets — resulting in a progressive cipher in which alphabets are used irregularly, depending on the plaintext used.[1]
1854	**Charles Wheatstone** invented what has become known as the Playfair cipher, having been publicized by his friend **Lyon Playfair**. This cipher uses a keyed array of letters to make a digraphic cipher that is easy to use in the field. He also reinvented the Wadsworth device and is known for that one.[1]
1857	**Admiral Sir Francis Beaufort's** cipher (a variant of what is called "Vigenère") was published by his brother, after the admiral's death, in the form of a 4×5-inch card.[1]
1859	**Pliny Earle Chase** published the first description of a fractionating (tomographic) cipher.[1]
1854	**Charles Babbage** seems to have re-invented the wheel cipher.[5]
1861–1980	"A study of United States patents from the issuance of the first cryptographic patent in 1861 through 1980 identified 1,769 patents which are primarily related to cryptography" [p. 1].[6]
1861	**Friedrich W. Kasiski** published a book giving the first general solution of a polyalphabetic cipher with repeating passphrase, thus marking the end of several hundred years of strength for the polyalphabetic cipher.[1]
1861–1865	During the Civil War, possibly among other ciphers, the Union used substitution of select words followed by word columnar-transposition while the Confederacy used Vigenère (the solution of which had just been published by Kasiski).[1]

(continued)

Exhibit 2. History of Cryptography (Continued)

1891	**Major Etienne Bazeries** did his version of the wheel cipher and published the design in 1901 after the French Army rejected it. [Although he was a military cryptologist, the fact that he published it leads me to rate this as (Civ) as well as Gov.][5]
1913	**Captain Parket Hitt** reinvented the wheel cipher, in strip form, leading to the M-138-A of World War II.[5]
1916	**Major Joseph O. Mauborgne** put Hitt's strip cipher back in wheel form, strengthened the alphabet construction, and produced what led to the M-94 cipher device.[5]
1917	**William Frederick Friedman**, later to be honored as the father of U.S. cryptanalysis (and the man who coined that term), was employed as a civilian cryptanalyst (along with his wife Elizabeth) at **Riverbank Laboratories** and performed cryptanalysis for the U.S. Government, which had no cryptanalytic expertise of its own. Friedman went on to start a school for military cryptanalysts at Riverbank — later taking that work to Washington and leaving Riverbank.[1]
1917	**Gilbert S. Vernam**, working for AT&T, invented a practical polyalphabetic cipher machine capable of using a key that is totally random and never repeats — a one-time tape. This is the only provably secure cipher, as far as we know. This machine was offered to the government for use in World War I, but it was rejected. It was put on the commercial market in 1920.[1]
1918	The ADFGVX system was put into service by the Germans near the end of World War I. This was a cipher that performed a substitution (through a keyed array), fractionation, and then transposition of the letter fractions. It was broken by the French cryptanalyst, **Lieutenant Georges Painvin**.[1]
1919	**Hugo Alexander Koch** filed a patent in the Netherlands on a rotor-based cipher machine. He assigned these patent rights in 1927 to Arthur Scherbius, who invented and had been marketing the Enigma machine since about 1923.[1]
1919	**Arvid Gerhard Damm** applied for a patent in Sweden for a mechanical rotor cipher machine. This machine grew into a family of cipher machines under the direction of **Boris Caesar Wilhelm Hagelin,** who took over the business and was the only one of the commercial cryptographers of this period to make a thriving business. After the war, a Swedish law that enabled the government to appropriate inventions it felt important to defense caused Hagelin to move the company to Zug, Switzerland, where it was incorporated as Crypto AG. The company is still in operation, although facing controversy for having allegedly weakened a cipher product for sale to Iran.[1]

(continued)

Exhibit 2. History of Cryptography (Continued)

1921	**Edward Hugh Hebern** incorporated "Hebern Electric Code," a company making electromechanical cipher machines based on rotors that turn, odometer style, with each character enciphered.[1]
1923	**Arthur Scherbius** incorporated "Chiffriermaschinen Aktiengesellschaft" to make and sell his Enigma machine.[1]
1924	**Alexander von Kryha** produced his "coding machine," which was used, even by the German Diplomatic Corps, into the 1950s. However, it was cryptographically weak — having a small period. A test cryptogram of 1135 characters was solved by the U.S. cryptanalysts **Friedman, Kullback, Rowlett,** and **Sinkov** in 2 hours and 41 minutes. Nevertheless, the machine continued to be sold and used — a triumph of salesmanship and a lesson to consumers of cryptographic devices.[6]
1927–1933	Users of cryptography were not limited to legitimate bankers, lovers, experimenters, etc. There were also a handful of criminals. "The greatest era of international smuggling — Prohibition — created the greatest era of criminal cryptology" [p. 817]. To this day, the FBI runs a cryptanalytic office to deal with criminal cryptography. [As of Kahn's writing in 1967, that office was located at 215 Pennsylvania Avenue SE, Washington, D.C.] "A retired lieutenant commander of the Royal Navy devised the systems for Consolidated Exporters' Pacific operation, though its Gulf and Atlantic groups made up their own as needed." His name was unknown but his cryptologic expertise was apparent. The smugglers' systems grew increasingly more complicated. Some of these are of a complexity never even attempted by any government for its most secret communications, wrote **Mrs. [Elizebeth Smith] Friedman** in a report in mid-1930. "At no time during the World War, when secret methods of communication reached their highest development, were there used such involved ramifications as are to be found in some of the correspondence of West Coast rum running vessels" [p. 804].[1]
1929	**Lester S. Hill** published "Cryptography in an Algebraic Alphabet" in which a block of plaintext is enciphered by a matrix operation.[1]
1933–1945	The Enigma machine was not a commercial success, but it was taken over and improved upon to become the cryptographic workhorse of Nazi Germany. [It was broken by the Polish mathematician, **Marian Rejewski**, based only on captured ciphertext and one list of three months' worth of daily keys obtained through a spy. Continued breaks were based on developments during the war by **Alan Turing, Gordon Welchman,** and others at Bletchley Park in England.][1]

Exhibit 2. History of Cryptography (Continued)

(continued)

1937	The Japanese Purple machine was invented in response to revelations by **Herbert O. Yardley** and broken by a team headed by **William Frederick Friedman**. The Purple machine used telephone stepping relays instead of rotors and thus had a totally different permutation at each step rather than the related permutations of one rotor in different positions.[1]
1930s	Kahn attributes the American SIGABA (M-134-C) to **William F. Friedman** while Deavours attributes it to an idea of **Frank Rowlett**, one of Friedman's first hires. It improved on the rotor inventions of Hebern and Scherbius by using pseudo-random stepping of multiple rotors on each enciphering step rather than having uniform, odometer-like stepping of rotors as in Enigma. It also used 15 rotors (10 for character transformation, 5 probably for controlling stepping) rather than the Enigma's 3 or 4.[1]
1930s	The British TYPEX machine was an offshoot of the commercial Enigma purchased by the British for study in the 1920s. It was a five-rotor machine with the two initial rotors being stators, serving the purpose of the German Enigma's plugboard.[6]
1970	**Dr. Horst Feistel** led a research project at the IBM Watson Research Lab in the 1960s that developed the Lucifer cipher. This later inspired the U.S. DES (below) and other product ciphers, creating a family labeled "Feistel ciphers."[7]
1976	A design by IBM, based on the Lucifer cipher and with changes (including both S-box improvements and reduction of key size) by the U.S. NSA, was chosen to be the U.S. Data Encryption Standard. It has since found worldwide acceptance, largely because it has shown itself strong against 20 years of attacks. Even some who believe it is past its useful life use it as a component — e.g., of three-key Triple-DES.[8]
1976	**Whitfield Diffie** and **Martin Hellman** published "New Directions in Cryptography," introducing the idea of public key cryptography. They also put forth the idea of authentication by powers of a one-way function, now used in the S/Key challenge–response utility. They closed their paper with an observation for which this timeline Web page gives detailed evidence: "Skill in production cryptanalysis has always been heavily on the side of the professionals, but innovation, particularly in the design of new types of cryptographic systems, has come primarily from amateurs."[9]

(continued)

Exhibit 2. History of Cryptography (Continued)

April 1977	Inspired by the Diffie-Hellman paper and acting as complete novices in cryptography, **Ronald L. Rivest, Adi Shamir,** and **Leonard M. Adleman** had been discussing how to make a practical public key system. One night in April, Ron Rivest was laid up with a massive headache and the RSA algorithm came to him. He wrote it up for Shamir and Adleman and sent it to them the next morning. It was a practical public key cipher for both confidentiality and digital signatures, based on the difficulty of factoring large, prime numbers. They submitted this to Martin Gardner on April 4 for publication in *Scientific American.* It appeared in the September 1977 issue. The *Scientific American* article included an offer to send the full technical report to anyone submitting a self-addressed, stamped envelope. There were thousands of such requests from all over the world.

Someone at NSA objected to the distribution of this report to foreign nationals and for awhile, RS&A suspended mailings — but when NSA failed to respond to inquiries asking for the legal basis of their request, RS&A resumed mailings. Adi Shamir believes this is the origin of the current policy [as of August 1995] that technical reports or papers can be freely distributed. [*Note.* Two international journals, *Cryptologia* and *The Journal of Cryptology,* were founded shortly after this attempt by NSA to restrain publication.]

Contrary to rumor, RS&A apparently had no knowledge of ITAR or patent secrecy orders. They did not publish before applying for international patents because they wanted to avoid such restraints on free expression, but rather because they were not thinking about patents for the algorithm. They just wanted to get the idea out.[10]

1978	The **RSA** algorithm was published in the *Communications of the ACM.*[11]
1984–1985?	The rot13 cipher was introduced into USENET News software to permit the encryption of postings in order to prevent innocent eyes from being assaulted by objectionable text. This is the first example I know of in which a cipher with a key everyone knows actually was effective.[12]
1990	**Xuejia Lai** and **James Massey** in Switzerland published "A Proposal for a New Block Encryption Standard," a proposed International Data Encryption Algorithm (IDEA) — to replace DES. IDEA uses a 128-bit key and employs operations that are convenient for general-purpose computers, therefore making software implementations more efficient.[13]

(continued)

Exhibit 2. History of Cryptography (Continued)

1990	**Charles H. Bennett, Gilles Brassard,** et al. published their experimental results on Quantum Cryptography (QC), which uses single photons to communicate a stream of key bits for some later Vernam encipherment of a message (or other uses). Assuming the laws of quantum mechanics hold, Quantum Cryptography provides not only secrecy, but also a positive indication of eavesdropping and a measurement of the maximum number of bits an eavesdropper might have captured. On the downside, QC currently requires a fiber-optic cable between the two parties.[13]
1991	**Phil Zimmermann** released his first version of PGP (Pretty Good Privacy) in response to the threat by the FBI to demand access to the cleartext of the communications of citizens. PGP offered high security to the general citizen and as such could have been seen as a competitor to commercial products like Mailsafe from RSADSI. However, PGP is especially notable because it was released as freeware and has become a worldwide standard as a result, while its competitors of the time remain effectively unknown.[14]
1994	**Professor Ron Rivest**, author of the earlier RC2 and RC4 algorithms included in RSADSI's BSAFE cryptographic library, published a proposed algorithm, RC5, on the Internet. This algorithm uses data-dependent rotation as its nonlinear operation and is parameterized so that the user can vary the block size, number of rounds, and key length. It is still too new to have been analyzed enough to enable one to know what parameters to use for a desired strength — although an analysis by RSA Labs, reported at CRYPTO'95, suggests that $w = 32$, $r = 12$ gives strength superior to DES. It should be remembered, however, that this is just a first analysis.[15]
2000	**Rijndael** was announced as the winner of the three-year AES (Advanced Encryption Standard) competition involving some of the world's leading cryptographers. Computer scientists at the National Institute of Standards and Technology organized the international competition in a drive to develop a strong encryption formula to protect sensitive information in federal computer systems. Many businesses are expected to use the AES as well. The Rijndael developers are Belgian cryptographers Joan Daemen and Vincent Rijmen. It is expected that the AES will eventually replace DES and since hundreds of encryption products currently employ DES or Triple-DES, the selection of the AES may affect millions of consumers and businesses.[15]

(continued)

Exhibit 2. History of Cryptography (Continued)

1. David Kahn, *The Codebreakers,* Macmillan, 1967.
2. Sir Richard F. Burton, trans., *The Kama Sutra of Vatsayana,* Arkana/Penguin, 1991.
3. Derek J. Price, *The Equatorie of the Planetis,* edited from Peterhouse MS 75.I, Cambridge University Press, 1955.
4. Sir Francis Bacon, "De Augmentis Scientarum," Book 6, Chapter i [as quoted in C. Stopes, "Bacon-Shakspere Question," 1889].
5. *Cryptologia,* Vol. 5, No. 4, pp. 193–208.
6. Cipher A. Deavours and Louis Kruh, *Machine Cryptography and Modern Cryptanalysis,* Artech House, 1985.
7. Horst Feistel, "Cryptographic Coding for Data-Bank Privacy," IBM Research Report RC2827.
8. Federal Information Processing Standards Publications (FIPS PUBS), "Data Encryption Standard (DES)," Pub. 46.
9. Whitfield Diffie and Martin Hellman, "New Directions in Cryptography," *IEEE Transactions on Information Theory,* November 1976.
10. Adi Shamir, "Myths and Realities."
11. Rivest, Shamir, and Adleman, "A Method for Obtaining Digital Signatures and Public Key Cryptosystems," *Communications of the ACM,* February 1978, pp. 120–126.
12. Steve Bellovin and Marcus Ranum, individual personal communications, July 1995.
13. *Proceedings,* EUROCRYPT '90, Springer-Verlag.
14. Simson Garfinkel, *PGP: Pretty Good Privacy,* O'Reilly & Associates, Inc., 1995.
15. Ronald L. Rivest, "The RC5 Encryption Algorithm," document made available by FTP and World Wide Web, 1994.

garbled form, called ciphertext. The intent is to allow two or more parties to communicate the information while preventing other parties from being privy to it.

Cryptanalysis and Attacks

Cryptanalysis is the science of cracking codes, decoding secrets, violating authentication schemes and breaking cryptographic protocols. It is also the science devoted to finding and correcting weaknesses in cryptographic algorithms. It is understood within the field of Cryptology that an algorithm should not rely on its secrecy. An algorithm should always be made available for public scrutiny. It is this scrutiny that will make it a well-trusted algorithm. Inevitably, an algorithm will be discovered and its weaknesses will be exploited.

There are various techniques involved in cryptanalysis, but generally they are referred to as "attacks." Cryptanalytic attacks are usually classified into six categories that distinguish them from each other. In each case, the name comes from the type of information that is available to the attacker. The six categories are:

- *Ciphertext-only attack.* The attacker has a sample of ciphertext, without having the associated plaintext. In this case, the attacker is trying to recover the plaintext.
- *Known-plaintext attack.* The attacker obtains a sample of ciphertext and the corresponding plaintext as well. In this case, the attacker is trying to recover the key.
- *Chosen-plaintext attack.* The cryptanalyst is able to choose a quantity of plaintext and then obtain the corresponding encrypted text in order to try and recover the key.
- *Adaptive-chosen-plaintext attack.* This is a special case of the chosen-plaintext attack in which the attacker is able to choose plaintext samples dynamically, and alter his or her choices based on the results of the previous operation.
- *Chosen-ciphertext attack.* In a chosen-ciphertext attack, the attacker selects the ciphertext and can obtain the corresponding plaintext in order to try and recover the key.
- *Adaptive-chosen-ciphertext attack.* This is the adaptive version of the chosen-ciphertext attack, where the attacker is able to choose ciphertext samples dynamically, depending on previous outcomes of the attack.

Brute-Force Attacks

Brute-force attacks are also referred to as exhaustive search attacks. This technique involves trying every possible combination (key) until the correct one is identified. Brute-force attacks can be mounted on any type of cipher. Advances in technology and computing performance have made brute-force attacks increasingly practical against keys of a fixed length. For example, when DES was designed, it was considered secure against brute-force attacks. Over the years, this type of attack has become increasingly attractive to attackers because the cost and time involved in finding a DES key has been reduced dramatically. With today's technology, DES only offers a few hours of protection from brute-force attacks, mainly because of the growth of the Internet. An exhaustive search of DES's 56-bit key space would still take tens or hundreds of years on the fastest general-purpose computer available today, but the growth of the Internet has made it possible to utilize thousands of machines in a distributed search by splitting the key space and allocating those key spaces to each computer.

The current rate of increase in computing power is such that an 80-bit key should offer an acceptable level of security for another 10 or 15 years. At that point, however, an 80-bit key will be as vulnerable to brute force as a 64-bit key is today. Given this rate of advancement, it is unlikely that 128-bit keys, such as those used by the new Advanced Encryption Standard (AES), Rijndael, will be broken by brute force in the foreseeable future.

Symmetric Block Cipher Attacks

A block cipher takes a certain number of letters and encrypts them all at once. The encryption algorithm takes a fixed-length block of plaintext data and creates a fixed length block of ciphertext of the same length.

There are several attacks that are specific to block ciphers. Because there are too many attacks to discuss here, we will concentrate on the four that are considered most relevant:

- *Differential cryptanalysis.* A type of attack that can be mounted against block ciphers. It is basically a chosen-plaintext attack that relies on the analysis of the evolution of the differences between two related plaintext samples as they are encrypted using the same key. By carefully analyzing the available data, probabilities can be assigned to each possible key, and eventually the most probable key is identified as the correct one.
- *Linear cryptanalysis.* A known-plaintext attack using linear approximations to describe the behavior of the block cipher. Given enough pairs of plaintext and corresponding ciphertext, information about the key can be obtained, which eventually will yield a higher probability of success in cracking the key.
- *Weak keys.* Secret keys with a certain value for which the block cipher in question will exhibit certain regularities in encryption, or in other cases, a poor level of encryption. For example, with DES, there are four keys for which encryption is exactly the same as decryption. This means that if someone were to encrypt twice with one of these weak keys, then the original plaintext would be recovered. There is a similar problem with the IDEA algorithm, where there is a class of keys for which cryptanalysis is greatly facilitated. In both cases, the number of weak keys is so small that the chance of picking one at random is exceptionally slight.
- *Algebraic attacks.* A class of techniques that rely on the block ciphers exhibiting a high degree of mathematical structure. For example, it is conceivable that a block cipher might exhibit a group structure where encrypting a plaintext under one key and then encrypting the result under another key would always be equivalent to single encryption under some other key. If this is the case, the block cipher would be considered weaker because the use of multiple encryption would offer no additional security over single encryption.

Stream Cipher Attacks

Stream ciphers usually take a "keystream," which is somehow randomly generated and encrypted using (combined with) a secret key, and combine that keystream with the message being encrypted, normally using the XOR

(Exclusive OR) operation. The sender and receiver must use the same algorithm and key to generate the keystream. For stream ciphers to be effective, they must use a keystream that is totally random. This means that an attacker should have no additional advantage in being able to predict any of the subsequent bits of the sequence. It is imperative that a keystream generated by the stream cipher have no structural weaknesses that would allow an attacker to deduce some of the keystream and, eventually, the key itself.

Hash Function Attacks

There are two essential functions of a hash algorithm that are most important. The hash function has to be one-way and collision-free. A good hash function should not produce the same hash value from two different inputs. If it does, this is known as a collision. Most attacks against hash functions involve choosing inputs to the hash function at random until an input that gives us the target output is found, or finding two inputs that produce the same output is found.

Message Authentication Code (MAC) Attacks

There are a variety of threats to the security of a MAC. These include the following. The use of a MAC should not reveal information about the secret key being used. Also, it should not be possible for an attacker to forge the correct MAC to some message without knowing the secret key, even after being able to see many messages and their associated MACs. It should also not be possible to replace the message in a message/MAC pair with another message for which the MAC remains legitimate. The most pertinent attacks against MAC involve the sophisticated application of the birthday paradox, which is described below. The birthday paradox can also be used in attacking hash functions.

The Birthday Paradox

The birthday paradox says that the probability that two or more people in a group of 23 share the same birthday is greater than 50%. This paradox can be applied mathematically to attack types of hashing functions. The birthday paradox shows that the probability that two messages will end up with the same hash is high even if the number of messages is considerably less than the number of hashes possible. The good hashing algorithms will resist, as much as possible, the possibilities that duplicate hashes will be produced. The birthday paradox attack is considered a type of brute-force attack because the attacker keeps trying to hash messages until ones that yield the same hash are obtained.

Man-in-the-Middle Attacks

This type of attack is relevant for cryptographic communication and key exchange protocols. The idea is that when two parties are exchanging keys for secure communications (e.g., using Diffie-Hellman), an adversary puts himself between the parties on the communication line. The adversary then performs a separate key exchange with each party. The parties will end up using a different key, each of which is known to the adversary. The adversary will then decrypt any communications with the proper key, and encrypt them with the other key for sending to the other party. The parties will think they are communicating directly with each other securely but, in fact, the adversary is seeing everything. One way to prevent man-in-the-middle attacks is for both sides to compute a cryptographic hash function of the key exchange (or at least the encryption keys), sign it using a digital signature algorithm, and send the signature to the other side. The recipient then verifies that the signature came from the desired other party, and that the hash in the signature received matches that computed locally.

Import/Export Issues

COCOM (Coordinating Committee for Multilateral Export Controls) was an international organization for the mutual control of the export of strategic products and technical data from country members to proscribed destinations. It maintained, among others, the International Industrial List and the International Munitions List. In 1991, COCOM decided to allow export of mass-market cryptographic software (including public-domain software). Most member countries of COCOM followed its regulations, but the United States maintained separate regulations.

Its 17 members were Australia, Belgium, Canada, Denmark, France, Germany, Greece, Italy, Japan, Luxembourg, the Netherlands, Norway, Portugal, Spain, Turkey, the United Kingdom, and the United States. Cooperating members included Austria, Finland, Hungary, Ireland, New Zealand, Poland, Singapore, Slovakia, South Korea, Sweden, Switzerland, and Taiwan.

The main goal of the COCOM regulations was to prevent cryptography from being exported to "dangerous" countries — usually the countries thought to maintain friendly ties with terrorist organizations, such as Libya, Iraq, Iran, and North Korea. Exporting to other countries is usually allowed, although states often require a license to be granted.

COCOM was dissolved in March 1994. Pending the signing of a new treaty, most members of COCOM agreed in principle to maintain the status quo, and cryptography remained on export control lists.

Wassenaar Arrangement

In 1995, 28 countries decided to establish a follow-up to COCOM, the *Wassenaar Arrangement on Export Controls for Conventional Arms and Dual-Use Goods and Technologies*. The negotiations on the Arrangement were finished in July 1996, and the agreement was signed by 31 countries (Argentina, Australia, Austria, Belgium, Canada, the Czech Republic, Denmark, Finland, France, Germany, Greece, Hungary, Ireland, Italy, Japan, Luxembourg, the Netherlands, New Zealand, Norway, Poland, Portugal, the Republic of Korea, Romania, the Russian Federation, the Slovak Republic, Spain, Sweden, Switzerland, Turkey, the United Kingdom, and the United States). Later, Bulgaria and Ukraine also became participants in the Arrangement.

The Wassenaar Arrangement controls the export of weapons and of dual-use goods, that is, goods that can be used both for military and for civil purposes; cryptography is such a dual-use good. The initial provisions were largely the same as the old COCOM regulations. The General Software Note (GSN) (applicable until the December 1998 revision) excepted mass-market and public-domain crypto software from the controls. Australia, France, New Zealand, Russia, and the United States deviated from the GSN and controlled the export of mass-market and public-domain crypto software. Export via the Internet did not seem to be covered by the regulations. There is a personal-use exemption, allowing export of products "accompanying their user for the user's personal use" (e.g., on a laptop).

In September 1998, Wassenaar negotiations in Vienna did not lead to changes in the crypto controls, although it was apparently considered to restrict the GSN and possibly also to ease controls for key-recovery crypto.

The Wassenaar Arrangement was revised in December 1998. Negotiations were held on December 2 and 3, 1998, in Vienna, which resulted in restrictions on the General Software Note and in some relaxations:

- Free for export includes all symmetric crypto products of up to 56-bit keys, all asymmetric crypto products of up to 512-bit keys, and all subgroup-based crypto products (including elliptic curve) of up to 112-bit keys
- Mass-market symmetric crypto software and hardware of up to 64-bit keys are free for export (the 64-bit key limit was deleted on December 1, 2000; see below)
- The export of products that use encryption to protect intellectual property (such as DVDs) is relaxed
- Export of all other crypto still requires a license

There were no changes in the provisions on public-domain crypto, such that all public-domain crypto software is still free for export. Nothing was said about electronic exports (e.g., via the Internet), which consequently remain unclear.

In its meeting of November 30–December 1, 2000, the Wassenaar states lifted the 64-bit key limit for export controls on mass-market crypto software and hardware.

The Wassenaar provisions are not directly applicable in each country; each member state has to implement them in national legislation for them to have effect.

European Union Controls

Export of dual-use goods, including cryptography, is regulated by the Council Regulation (EC) No. 1334/2000 setting up a Community regime for the control of exports of dual-use items and technology (Official Journal L159, 30.1.2000), in force since September 29, 2000. This replaces the earlier 1994 Council Regulation that covered crypto controls. In general, export within the EU is liberalized, and remaining export licensing procedures have been simplified.

Export to other EU countries is entirely liberalized, with the exception of some highly specialized products, such as cryptanalysis items. For these items, member states can issue General Intra-Community Licenses valid for export to one or more designated EU countries provided basic requirements are met, such as a statement of the end use to be made of exported items. For re-exports after intra-EU export, an information-exchange mechanism is established.

For export to Australia, Canada, the Czech Republic, Hungary, Japan, New Zealand, Norway, Poland, Switzerland, and the United States, a Community General Export Authorization (CGEA) can be applied for, which is valid for export from all EU countries.

For export to other countries, a General National License can be applied for (except for cryptanalysis items), which are valid for export to one particular country. Otherwise, exporters have to apply for an individual license.

United States Controls

There are no import restrictions on cryptography in the United States. It is a different story when it comes to export controls. The United States has signed the Wassenaar Arrangement, but generally maintains stricter controls. This statement is generally true, although the United States has relaxed export controls a number of times over the years. Since October 2000, a further liberalization of export controls is effective, triggered by changes in the European Union export regulations. The liberalization was announced on July 17, 2000. The major components of the updated policy include the following:

- Any crypto of any key length can be exported under a license exception, after a technical review, to any country except the seven "terrorist countries."
- Retail crypto, which is defined as crypto that does not require substantial support and is sold in tangible form through retail outlets, or that has been specifically designed for individual consumer use, of any key length can, after a technical review, be exported to any recipient in non-terrorist countries.
- Unrestricted crypto source code, such as most "open source" software, and publicly available commercial source code, can be exported to any end user under a license exception without a technical review. One may not, however, knowingly export source code to a terrorist country, although source code may be posted on the World Wide Web for downloading with the poster having to check whether it is downloaded from a terrorist country.
- Any crypto can be exported to foreign subsidiaries of U.S. firms without a technical review. Foreign nationals working in the United States no longer require an export license to work for U.S. firms on encryption.

The "terrorist countries" include Cuba, Iran, Iraq, Libya, North Korea, Sudan, and Syria. It is important to note that within the restrictions, U.S. exporters can ship products immediately after filing a commodity classification request, without waiting for the technical review results.

6.3 Security Technology and Tools

Basic Concepts of Cryptography

Fundamentals: Method and Key

Let's take a practical example that will help understand the basic concepts of cryptography. When people buy locks from the hardware store, they do so to protect some type of asset. Hardware stores will sell a number of identical locks to different people, but these people realize and rely on the fact that all of them, although they have bought the same lock, will not have the opportunity and means to get into everyone else's locks. The lock design may be identical in each lock, but it is the *combination* that sets them apart from each other, and makes each lock individually secure. Cryptography is both the lock and the combination. Think of the combination as the "key" and think of the lock itself as the "method" or the "algorithm." Together, the method and the key determine the overall security strength of a cryptographic technique.

When a person buys a lock, that person wants the assurance that it would take an attacker a very long time to try all the possible combinations to open the lock, which is the work factor. How long we want someone to try different combinations determines what kind of lock we buy. For example, if our concern is to protect our asset for only a few minutes, we will use a lock with fewer combinations. However, if our concern is to protect our asset for a very long time, we will need a lock with more combinations, realizing that it will take an attacker a very long time to try all the possible combinations. A lock with 1000 possible combinations is much more secure than a lock with 100 possible combinations. This is true for cryptography as well; the algorithm that supports many more keys is usually the one that provides much more security.

The important concept to remember about cryptography is that anyone can have the method, but it is the key that provides the security. The secrets that we have protected using cryptography are only as secure as the "secret" key. We have to assume that an attacker will know our encryption method; it is the joining of the encryption method with your unique secret key that provides the security.

Block Ciphers versus Stream Ciphers

There are two ways that encryption algorithms will apply their methods on information. These are *block* and *stream*. A block cipher takes a certain number of letters (actually bits) and encrypts them all at once. The encryption algorithm is taking a fixed-length block of plaintext data and creating a block of ciphertext data of the same length. This transformation takes place under the action of the user's secret key. Decryption is performed by applying the reverse transformation to the ciphertext using the same secret key. The fixed length is called the block size, and for many block ciphers the size is 64 bits.

While block ciphers operate on a fixed block size, stream ciphers typically operate on smaller units of plaintext, usually bits. A stream cipher generates a keystream, which is a sequence of bits used as a key. Encryption is accomplished by combining the keystream with the plaintext, usually with an XOR operation. Stream ciphers can be designed to be exceptionally fast, much faster than any block cipher.

The XOR operation is very simple. It takes a simple bit of plaintext and combines it with a simple bit of the keystream. The operation is simple binary arithmetic, which states that when you combine two bits that are identical, the result will be a 0; and when bits are different, they will yield a 1. The following example shows the results of a simple XOR operation:

```
Keystream:   10010000000
Plaintext:   01110011011
XOR result:  11100011011
```

It is important to realize that for the stream cipher to be effective, the keystream needs to be the exact same length as the plaintext that is being encrypted. The generation of the keystream is usually done by the algorithm, based on input from the user (the key). Also, the generation of the keystream should be independent of the plaintext and the ciphertext.

One-Time Pad

Current interests in stream ciphers are most commonly equated to what is referred to as a One-Time Pad. A One-Time Pad uses a keystream string of bits that is generated completely at random. The keystream will be the same length as the plaintext message, and again, both are combined using the XOR operation described above. Because the entire keystream is totally random and is used only once, a One-Time Pad is said to have perfect secrecy (unable to be defeated by a brute-force attack). Stream ciphers were developed to try and apply the action of a One-Time Pad. While current stream ciphers are unable to provide the "true" theoretical security of a One-Time Pad, they are at least very practical.

Information Security and Encryption

There are two purposes for using encryption. The first is to protect stored information, and the other is to protect transmitted information while in transit. To understand how cryptography and encryption allow us to address certain aspects of information security, an understanding of certain aspects of information security in general is necessary. Over time, various protocols and mechanisms have been developed to address the security requirements of information. The following outlines some of the most common information security objectives that are needed in today's technology:

- *Confidentiality:* keeping information secret from those who are unauthorized to see it
- *Data integrity:* ensuring information has not been altered in unexpected ways
- *Availability:* ensuring information is available to those authorized at all times
- *Entity authentication:* being able to prove the identity of an entity (person, process, etc.)
- *Data origin authentication:* being able to prove the source of information
- *Signature:* binding information to a specific entity
- *Access control:* restricting access to resources
- *Receipt:* acknowledging that information has been received
- *Confirmation:* acknowledging that services have been provided

- *Authorization:* giving an entity the authorization to perform or be something
- *Ownership:* providing an entity with the legal right to use or transfer information to others
- *Timestamping:* recording the time of creation of information
- *Non-repudiation:* preventing the denial of previous actions
- *Certification:* endorsing information by a trusted entity
- *Revocation:* retracting a certification or authorization
- *Anonymity:* concealing the identity of an entity involved in some process
- *Validation:* providing timeliness of authorization to use or change information

Achieving information security in an electronic society where information is mostly stored and transmitted in electronic form requires a vast array of technical solutions. The means for these technical solutions is provided through cryptography.

Of all the objectives listed above, four of them provide a framework upon which the others can be derived. The four are:

- *Confidentiality* is a service that ensures keeping information secret from those who are not authorized to have it. Secrecy is a term often used to mean confidentiality.
- *Data integrity* is a service that prevents data from being altered in unexpected ways. To ensure this, one must have the ability to detect manipulation by unauthorized parties or prevent unauthorized parties from gaining access to make unauthorized changes.
- *Authentication* is a service that allows entities wanting to communicate with each other to positively identify each other. Information delivered over a channel should be authenticated as to origin, date of origin, data content, time sent, etc.
- *Non-repudiation* is a service that prevents an entity from denying having participated in a previous action.

A fundamental goal of cryptography is to adequately address these four areas in both theory and practice. Confidentiality is normally achieved by encrypting the message content, data integrity is achieved through cryptographic hashing functions, authentication is achieved through the use of asymmetric cryptography, and non-repudiation is normally achieved through the use of cryptographic digital signatures.

Symmetric Key Cryptography

Secret key cryptography is technically referred to as symmetric cryptography. It is the more traditional form of cryptography, in which a single key — a secret key — is used to encrypt and decrypt a message. Users

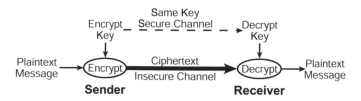

Exhibit 3. Symmetric Key Cryptography

share a secret key, keeping the key to themselves. Data encrypted with a secret key can be decrypted only with the same secret key. Exhibit 3 shows how symmetric key cryptography works.

Symmetric key algorithms are relatively fast, and are therefore suitable for encrypting large amounts of data. Some algorithms, such as RC6, Twofish, and Rijndael, are essentially uncrackable by any currently known or imaginable technology, given adequate key management and implementation.

The primary problem is with key management, which is really related to how two parties can agree upon and exchange a certain key, without the possibility of an attacker getting access to it. This means that two parties wanting to communicate securely with each other need to exchange sensitive information beforehand. They will need to agree on the key being used and how to exchange that key. This communication should be done through means other than what will be used for transmission of the secret information. This is referred to as "out-of-band" messaging. Out-of-band messaging means using transmission methods other than what is usual, or expected. Another problem deals with scalability, which relates to how there is an explosion in the number of keys required as the number of communicating pairs increases, if each pair requires a separate key.

For example, if two people want to communicate securely using symmetric key cryptography, the number of keys required is one. With three people, the number of keys required is three. With four people, the number increases to six; and with five people, the number of keys required is ten. This "explosion" continues dramatically. To allow any pair of 1000 users to communicate securely with each other, it would require the creation and management of 499,500 distinct keys, which could be considered an unmanageable number. The formula for calculating the number of keys required is represented by $n(n-1)/2$.

Yet another problem with symmetric key cryptography is the limited information security services that it can provide. Cryptography offers some core information security services, namely, confidentiality, data integrity, authentication, and non-repudiation. Symmetric key cryptography certainly offers us confidentiality, data integrity, and authentication.

However, it does not offer the non-repudiation or secure key exchange services that asymmetric key cryptography provides.

The following represents a summarization of the advantages and disadvantages of symmetric key cryptography:

- Advantages:
  - Speed
  - Strength of algorithms
  - Availability of algorithms
- Disadvantages:
  - Key management and implementation
  - Key distribution
  - Scalability
  - Limited security (provides only limited information security services)

Asymmetric Cryptography

With private key, or symmetric key cryptography, the sender and receiver of a secret message know and use the same key to encrypt and decrypt the data. As we have learned, this method is referred to as secret key, single key, or symmetric key cryptography. As we have also learned, the main challenge is to get the sender and receiver to agree on a secret key and how to exchange that key without having anyone else find out. If the sender and receiver find themselves in different physical locations, this could be very challenging. They will have to trust a phone system, a courier, a network connection, or some other type of transmission medium to prevent the disclosure of the private key. That is, the problem with symmetric key cryptography is "key management."

To solve the key management problem, Whitfield Diffie and Martin Hellman introduced the concept of "public key'" cryptography in 1976. In public key cryptography, also referred to as asymmetric key cryptography, each user has a *public key* and a *private key*. The public key is made public, while the private key always remains secret. The need for the sender and receiver to share secret key information is eliminated. All communications involve only the public keys, and no private key is ever transmitted or shared. The idea behind asymmetric key cryptography is simple: if you encrypt with either the private or public key (either will work), then you can only decrypt with the other key of the matched pair. How can this work? The two keys are linked to each other mathematically. Therefore, it is theoretically possible to attack an asymmetric key system by deriving the private key from knowledge of the public key. Typically, the defense against this is to make the problem of deriving the private key from the public key as difficult as possible. Asymmetric key cryptography uses the concept of "hard math" problems or "trapdoor one-way functions" to

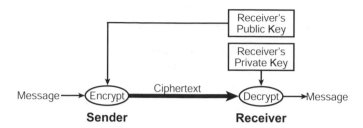

Exhibit 4. Asymmetric Key Cryptography

provide this defense. Most asymmetric algorithms involve fairly sophisticated mathematics such as numbers theory, finite fields, abelian groups, and elliptic curves. More about this later.

To encrypt a message using asymmetric key cryptography, the sender would use the receiver's public key to encrypt the message and would send it off. The receiver would then use his private key to decrypt the message and read it. No one listening in on the communications line can decrypt the message, because the receiver is the only party that has the corresponding private key that can decrypt that message. Exhibit 4 shows how asymmetric key cryptography works.

The advantage of asymmetric cryptography over symmetric cryptography is obviously key distribution. The problem of having to have a secure distribution channel is gone. Another advantage deals with key scalability. When using asymmetric key cryptography, one distinct key for each communicating pair of users is not needed. Each person has exactly two keys, or more precisely one matched key pair. One of the keys is considered the public key, which is made available to anyone, typically even published in a directory. The other key is the corresponding private key and is never revealed to anyone other than the key owner. By comparison to symmetric key cryptography, if 1000 people need to communicate securely with each other, a total of 2000 keys (1000 matched pairs) are needed. This is obviously easier than trying to manage 499,500 symmetric keys.

Another advantage of asymmetric key cryptography is that it provides a full range of information security services. In addition to being able to provide privacy through encryption, asymmetric key cryptography also provides forms of access control, authentication, data integrity, and non-repudiation.

All of this sounds great, but there are some disadvantages to asymmetric key cryptography. Algorithms using this technology are computationally intensive because of the mathematics involved, and this makes the algorithms very slow compared to symmetric key cryptography. They are often up to1000 times slower in terms of bytes per second processed than symmetric key algorithms.

The following represents a summarization of the advantages and disadvantages of asymmetric key cryptography:

- Advantages:
  - Key management and distribution
  - Scalability
  - Provides five elements of security:
    - Confidentiality/privacy
    - Access control
    - Authentication
    - Data integrity
    - Non-repudiation
- Disadvantages:
  - Computationally intensive
  - Slow

Hybrid Systems

So, we have symmetric key algorithms that are very fast and strong, but are really bad at key management. We have asymmetric key algorithms that are really good at key management, but are terribly slow. Real-world systems are usually hybrids, using each technology, symmetric or asymmetric, where it is strong. Normally, these hybrid systems will use asymmetric key cryptography to do the key management, and use symmetric key cryptography to do the bulk encryption/decryption. As an example, we could use symmetric key cryptography to encrypt a long message, and then use asymmetric key cryptography to exchange the symmetric key used in the encryption process.

Encryption Systems

For as long as people have been communicating, they have looked for secure ways to share and hide messages. To stay a step ahead of cryptanalysts, cryptographers have invented very ingenious ways to hide messages. To understand how complexity affects a cryptographic system, we need to understand the simple methods that lead up to the more complex ones that are used in today's computer methods.

Substitution Ciphers

If your mission is to win a war, maintaining secrecy is very important. Throughout the ages, those engaged in wars, such as Julius Caesar, have been eager to disguise written messages. Caesar came up with a cipher that is very simple but is not particularly secure once the method is known. Substitution ciphers involve replacing each letter of the plaintext with another that is farther down the alphabet. If we remember, most encryption systems will combine a method, usually called the algorithm, and a key. With substitution ciphers, the method is "add," the key "how many times to do it." In Caesar's case, the key was 3, making his cipher look like the following:

Plaintext:	A	B	C	D	E	F	G	H	I	J
Ciphertext:	D	E	F	G	H	I	J	K	L	M

If Caesar's message to his generals was to "attack at eleven pm," his encrypted message would look like: dwwdfn dw hohyhq sp.

An attacker trying to decrypt Caesar's cipher would repeatedly increase each letter one alphabetic position until the plaintext jumps out upon inspection and makes sense. It is important to realize that Caesar's cipher has only 25 possible keys. The objective to Caesar's cipher, and indeed with cryptography in general, is to make your adversary work a long time trying many keys. Hopefully, by the time the attacker finds the correct key, the encrypted message has little value. In our example above, at 11:01 p.m., the value of "attack at eleven pm" has been greatly reduced.

Transposition Ciphers

Transposition (also called permutation) ciphers involve changing the positions of plaintext letters. Most of us have seen these types of ciphers, because many newspapers will carry a page that has "jumble" puzzles. Here is an example. A simple transposition of "eleven pm" could move each letter one position to the left. The ciphertext would then become "leven pme." Although the letters have been moved around, all the ciphertext letters are the same as the plaintext letters. There is no replacement or substitution of letters. Obviously, we can get more complex on how we do the transposition to offer more security. For example, we could offer the following example. The message "attack at eleven pm" could be enciphered in the following manner:

A	T	T	A
C	K	A	T
E	L	E	V
E	N	P	M

We could read down the columns, so that our message "attack at eleven pm" would become "aceetklntaepatvm." In this case, the intended receiver would have to know two things: the length and width of the grid and the way letters are read from the grid.

Problems with Substitution and Transposition Ciphers

The encrypted example above, "dwwdfn dw hohyhq sp," certainly looks like garbage, but not to a distinguished cryptanalyst, who would instantly see that there are three Hs and three Ws (and three Ds). Because E is the most used letter in the English alphabet, the cryptanalyst would substitute E for all the Hs and then substitute T, the second most used letter, for all the Ws, and so on. It will not take the cryptanalyst very long to figure out the correct message. In these cases, although we may have the possibility for millions of different keys, it would not necessarily slow cryptanalysts very much. The problem is that substitution and transposition ciphers do not disguise the linguistic patterns of letters and word frequency in the encrypted message, so they are easily cracked using frequency analysis.

Some of the facts that can be used for frequency analysis from the English language include the following:

- E is the letter most often used, followed by T, O, A, and N.
- T is the most common letter at the beginning of a word. E is the most common letter at the end of a word.
- A and I are the only single-letter words in English. The words OF, TO, and IN are the most frequent two-letter words; THE and AND are the most frequent three-letter words; THAT is the most common four-letter word.
- The most common double letters are II, EE, OO, TT, FF, RR, NN, PP, and CC. TH, HE, AN, RE, and IN are the most frequent two-letter combinations. THE, ING, AND, ION, and ENT are the most frequent three-letter combinations.
- N is the consonant that most often follows a vowel.
- U always follows Q.

You might be wondering why these types of ciphers are used if they are so easy to crack. It is because they can be more difficult to crack if they are combined and repeated numerous times. As cryptographers looked for innovative ways to hide secret messages, they found that using both substitution and transposition ciphers together created much better concealment than either method alone. In fact, using substitution and transposition cipher methods repeatedly on ciphertext does such a good job of disguising patterns that the encoded message is very difficult to decipher, unless the cryptanalyst has other kinds of clues. Modern computer cryptography has made the most of combining transposition and substitution methods to provide very efficient encryption methods. This is because computers are very good at performing simple operations numerous times, without making mistakes.

Today's leading symmetric key cryptography methods such as DES and Rijndael use multiple combinations of transposition and substitution.

These types of ciphers, coupled with frequently changed keys, can be very difficult to crack.

Polyalphabetic Ciphers

Adding complexity to a substitution cipher can make the disguise more effective. We can use several alphabets to provide more security. The idea is simple: instead of having one alphabet, you have many. Using several alphabets with letters randomly rearranged and then substituting letters from each alphabet for letters in plaintext provides a system that can defeat frequency analysis because, for example, the E would be represented by a different character in each alphabet. These types of ciphers are very effective because they disguise simple linguistic patterns.

The Vigenere Cipher: An Example of a Polyalphabetic Cipher

One of the main problems with simple substitution ciphers is that they are vulnerable to frequency analysis. Given a sufficiently large ciphertext, it can easily be broken by mapping the frequency of its letters to the known frequencies of, say, the English language. Therefore, to make ciphers more secure, cryptographers have long been interested in developing enciphering techniques that are immune to frequency analysis. One of the most common approaches is to suppress the normal frequency data by using more than one alphabet to encrypt the message. A polyalphabetic cipher involves the use of two or more cipher alphabets. Instead of there being a one-to-one relationship between each letter and its substitute, there is a one-to-many relationship between each letter and its substitutes.

The Vigenere cipher, proposed by Blaise de Vigenere from the court of Henry III of France in the 16th century, is a polyalphabetic substitution cipher based on the table shown in Exhibit 5.

Note that each row of the table corresponds to a Caesar cipher. The first row is a shift of 0; the second is a shift of 1; and the last is a shift of 25.

The Vigenere cipher uses this table together with a *keyword* to encipher a message. For example, suppose we wanted to encipher the plaintext message:

```
PASSING THE CISSP EXAM IS CHALLENGING
```

Use the keyword CAESAR. We begin by writing the keyword, repeated as many times as necessary, above the plaintext message. To derive the ciphertext using the table, for each letter in the plaintext, one finds the intersection of the row given by the corresponding keyword letter and the column given by the plaintext letter itself to pick out the ciphertext letter.

Cryptography

Exhibit 5. The Vigenere Cipher

	A	B	C	D	E	F	G	H	I	J	K	L	M	N	O	P	Q	R	S	T	U	V	W	X	Y	Z
A	A	B	C	D	E	F	G	H	I	J	K	L	M	N	O	P	Q	R	S	T	U	V	W	X	Y	Z
B	B	C	D	E	F	G	H	I	J	K	L	M	N	O	P	Q	R	S	T	U	V	W	X	Y	Z	A
C	C	D	E	F	G	H	I	J	K	L	M	N	O	P	Q	R	S	T	U	V	W	X	Y	Z	A	B
D	D	E	F	G	H	I	J	K	L	M	N	O	P	Q	R	S	T	U	V	W	X	Y	Z	A	B	C
E	E	F	G	H	I	J	K	L	M	N	O	P	Q	R	S	T	U	V	W	X	Y	Z	A	B	C	D
F	F	G	H	I	J	K	L	M	N	O	P	Q	R	S	T	U	V	W	X	Y	Z	A	B	C	D	E
G	G	H	I	J	K	L	M	N	O	P	Q	R	S	T	U	V	W	X	Y	Z	A	B	C	D	E	F
H	H	I	J	K	L	M	N	O	P	Q	R	S	T	U	V	W	X	Y	Z	A	B	C	D	E	F	G
I	I	J	K	L	M	N	O	P	Q	R	S	T	U	V	W	X	Y	Z	A	B	C	D	E	F	G	H
J	J	K	L	M	N	O	P	Q	R	S	T	U	V	W	X	Y	Z	A	B	C	D	E	F	G	H	I
K	K	L	M	N	O	P	Q	R	S	T	U	V	W	X	Y	Z	A	B	C	D	E	F	G	H	I	J
L	L	M	N	O	P	Q	R	S	T	U	V	W	X	Y	Z	A	B	C	D	E	F	G	H	I	J	K
M	M	N	O	P	Q	R	S	T	U	V	W	X	Y	Z	A	B	C	D	E	F	G	H	I	J	K	L
N	N	O	P	Q	R	S	T	U	V	W	X	Y	Z	A	B	C	D	E	F	G	H	I	J	K	L	M
O	O	P	Q	R	S	T	U	V	W	X	Y	Z	A	B	C	D	E	F	G	H	I	J	K	L	M	N
P	P	Q	R	S	T	U	V	W	X	Y	Z	A	B	C	D	E	F	G	H	I	J	K	L	M	N	O
Q	Q	R	S	T	U	V	W	X	Y	Z	A	B	C	D	E	F	G	H	I	J	K	L	M	N	O	P
R	R	S	T	U	V	W	X	Y	Z	A	B	C	D	E	F	G	H	I	J	K	L	M	N	O	P	Q
S	S	T	U	V	W	X	Y	Z	A	B	C	D	E	F	G	H	I	J	K	L	M	N	O	P	Q	R
T	T	U	V	W	X	Y	Z	A	B	C	D	E	F	G	H	I	J	K	L	M	N	O	P	Q	R	S
U	U	V	W	X	Y	Z	A	B	C	D	E	F	G	H	I	J	K	L	M	N	O	P	Q	R	S	T
V	V	W	X	Y	Z	A	B	C	D	E	F	G	H	I	J	K	L	M	N	O	P	Q	R	S	T	U
W	W	X	Y	Z	A	B	C	D	E	F	G	H	I	J	K	L	M	N	O	P	Q	R	S	T	U	V
X	X	Y	Z	A	B	C	D	E	F	G	H	I	J	K	L	M	N	O	P	Q	R	S	T	U	V	W
Y	Y	Z	A	B	C	D	E	F	G	H	I	J	K	L	M	N	O	P	Q	R	S	T	U	V	W	X
Z	Z	A	B	C	D	E	F	G	H	I	J	K	L	M	N	O	P	Q	R	S	T	U	V	W	X	Y

```
Keyword:     CAESA RCAES ARCAE SARCA ESARC AESAR CA
Plaintext:   PASSI NGTHE CISSP EXAMI SCHAL LENGI NG
Ciphertext:  RAWKI EITLW CZUST WXROI WUARN LIFGZ PG
```

Decipherment of the message is equally straightforward; one simply writes the keyword repeatedly above the message:

```
Keyword:     CAESA RCAES ARCAE SARCA ESARC AESAR CA
Ciphertext:  RAWKI EITLW CZUST WXROI WUARN LIFGZ PG
Plaintext:   PASSI NGTHE CISSP EXAMI SCHAL LENGI NG
```

This time, one uses the keyword letter to pick a column of the table, and then traces down the column to the row containing the ciphertext letter. The index of that row is the plaintext letter.

The strength of the Vigenere cipher against frequency analysis can be seen by examining the above ciphertext. Note that there are five Ss in the plaintext message and that they have been encrypted by W, K, U, S, and W, respectively. This successfully masks the frequency characteristics of the English S. One way to look at this is to notice that each letter of our keyword CAESAR picks out one of the 26 possible substitution alphabets given in the Vigenere table. Thus, any message encrypted by a Vigenere cipher is a collection of as many simple substitution ciphers as there are letters in the keyword.

Symmetric Key Cryptography Algorithms

Data Encryption Standard (DES)

The 1960s was really the decade that computer cryptography began. It was during the 1960s that companies began needing secure ways to transmit information. Because there was no standard, financial institutions wanted a standard encryption method that they could have confidence in and could use for secure data exchange. Because of this need, in 1972, the National Institute of Standards and Technology (NIST) assisted in the development of a secure cryptographic algorithm for sensitive, not government classified, information. In 1974, it settled on DES, a method submitted by IBM. Despite some controversy, DES was finally adopted as the federal standard for unclassified documents in 1977 and is the most widely used cryptographic method in history.

NIST made the DES design public, and the proliferation of computer technology permitted faster processing, making software implementations of DES feasible. The 1977 DES mandated a review every five years. In 1983, DES was approved for an additional five years. In 1987, DES was approved for another five years, with the provision that it would expire before 1992. Then, in 1993, DES was again approved for yet another five years. In 1997,

NIST solicited candidates for a new symmetric key cryptography standard, which they called the Advanced Encryption Standard (AES).

DES is a symmetric key cryptography algorithm that uses a key of 56 bits and 16 rounds of transposition and substitution to encrypt each group of eight (64-bit) plaintext letters. The original IBM design proposed a key length of 128 bits, but the NSA (National Security Agency), assisting NIST on the DES development, shortened it to 56 bits. DES has probably been subjected to more cryptanalysis than any other encryption method in history, but, no practical holes have yet been found. The best attack on DES is brute force — to try each possible key. In 1977, a 56-bit key was considered an excellent defense. A cryptanalyst without the key would have to try all 56 combinations of 0s and 1s (72 quadrillion possibilities) to find the correct key. Working at one million keys per second, this would take an attacker 1000 years to try them all.

With the advent of faster computer chips, this requirement has been greatly reduced. A 1975 computer could try half of the possible DES keys in about 100,000 days (300 years). That provided very good security. But during the past quarter century or so, computers have become about 100,000 times more powerful.

This pattern of computers becoming stronger is dictated by Moore's law. The observation made in 1965 by Gordon Moore, co-founder of Intel, was that the number of transistors per square inch on integrated circuits had doubled every year since the integrated circuit was invented. Moore predicted that this trend would continue for the foreseeable future. In subsequent years, the pace slowed a bit, but data density has doubled approximately every 18 months, and this is the current definition of Moore's law, which Moore himself has blessed. Most experts, including Moore, expect Moore's law to hold for at least another two decades.

The pattern is clear. If you need a strong cryptographic method, DES does not provide it anymore. Probably no one is going to try and crack your current financial budget; but if your company's livelihood depends on e-business and multi-million dollar deals, DES may not be strong enough.

DES Modes

DES and some other ciphers as well can be used in different modes. Within DES, there are four modes. Two of these are considered stream ciphers: Cipher Feedback (CFB) and Output Feedback (OFB). The other two modes are considered block ciphers: Electronic Code Book (ECB) and Cipher Block Chaining (CBC). The two stream modes are usually implemented in hardware, whereas the two block modes are usually implemented in software.

Cipher Feedback (CFB)

Cipher feedback (CFB) is considered a stream cipher. In this mode, the ciphertext is fed back into the key-generating device to create the next key-stream. Each encryption depends on previous ciphertext. CFB is best for encrypting a stream of data one character at a time (e.g., between a terminal and a host). With 8-bit CFB, encryption is able to start and operate on each 8-bit character. Sometimes, it is desirable to use a block cipher in a mode that approximates a stream cipher — where the receiver or transmitter can begin to play with the block before its transmission is complete. This is exactly what CFB does. With CFB, we view a block-sized buffer as a shift register composed of *units*. After filling this register for the first time with a seed, we encode it using our encryption function. We then take the left-most byte of the output and consider it to be "live." That is to say, we use it as the key to encrypt the next unit of plaintext. We then take that unit of plaintext and push it into the right side of the register, shifting the register left. Now we can repeat the process and encode the next unit of plaintext.

CFB requires a unique initialization vector for each message to avoid being vulnerable to replay attacks. An initialization vector is defined as a non-secret binary vector used as the initializing input algorithm for the encryption of a plaintext block sequence to increase security by introducing additional cryptographic variance and to synchronize cryptographic equipment.

Errors in this mode of DES will propagate. For example, 8-bit CFB will produce 9 bytes of garbled plaintext from the point of error if a 1-bit error has occurred in the ciphertext.

Output Feedback (OFB)

Output feedback mode (OFB) is an additive stream cipher in which errors in the ciphertext are not extended to cause additional errors in the decrypted plaintext. Note that the keystream that is XOR'd with the message stream is constantly changing because of the feedback process used to generate the keystream. OFB is best for error-prone environments. It is used for handling asynchronous data streams (keyboard input) because most of the "cipher" is performed based on prior input and is ready when the last *n*-bit character is typed in. OFB requires an initialization vector. This prevents codebook collection problems, but OFB remains susceptible to block replay attacks. Errors do not propagate or extend. However, several analyses have shown that unless the *n*-bit feedback size is the same as the block size, the algorithm strength will be significantly reduced.

Electronic Code Book (ECB)

With a block cipher, to process more than 64 bits of data (for example, an email message of several thousand bytes), the simplest approach is to start at the beginning of the plaintext file and process 64-bit blocks one block at a time until you reach the end of the file. Decrypting would begin at the start of the ciphertext file and process 64-bit blocks one block at a time until you reach the end of the file. This approach is called Electronic Code Book (ECB), and is simple and fast to implement but has the following problems:

- Each 64-bit chunk of ciphertext is a separately attackable problem, using exactly the same key. In many files, the first few bytes may be known or guessable, possibly allowing a known plaintext attack, and the recovered key could then be used to decrypt the remaining blocks.
- A given 64-bit value in the plaintext will always produce the same ciphertext.
- A given message and key will always produce the same ciphertext.

ECB mode is not normally used for encrypting messages; rather, it is primarily used for sending keys and creating initialization vectors.

Cipher Block Chaining (CBC)

A simple modification to ECB mode that adds encryptive feedback across the blocks effectively solves the problems associated with Electronic Code Book. This also makes the file or message encryption much stronger. The basic idea is to generate a block of 64 randomly chosen bits, and the keyword is "randomly." This is called an initialization vector, or IV. The IV itself is encrypted with DES in ECB mode and sent as the first block of ciphertext. You then exclusive OR (XOR) this IV with the first 64-bit block of plaintext, and then encrypt the resulting value with DES to produce the second block of ciphertext. The next block of plaintext is XOR'd not with the IV, but with the ciphertext from the previous block, then encrypted with DES to make the next block of ciphertext. This is repeated until the end of the file.

To decrypt the file, you recover the original IV by decrypting the first 64-bit block of ciphertext with the key. You then decrypt the second block of ciphertext with DES and XOR the result with the IV to recover the first block of plaintext. You decrypt the third block of ciphertext and XOR the result with the previous block of ciphertext to recover the next block of plaintext. This is repeated until the end of the file, and then the recovered IV can be discarded.

The advantages of CBC over ECB include:

- Even if the plaintext is simple ASCII text, decrypting any block does not produce any recognizable pattern.
- The encryptive feedback (chaining) between blocks destroys any long-running pattern — even a file of all 0s would produce no repeating 64-bit groups in the ciphertext.
- If the IV is chosen differently each time, even the exact same file will produce different ciphertext each time it is sent.

Double-DES and Triple-DES

As previously mentioned, a successful attack against the DES algorithm involves finding the correct key. As technology has evolved, in today's world, this has become very feasible. Increasing the key length is an effective defense against a brute-force (trying every key) attack. Ways to improve the DES algorithm's resistance to a brute-force attack have been developed. These are Double-DES and Triple-DES.

Double-DES refers to the use of two DES encryptions with two separate keys, effectively doubling the size of the DES key from 56 to 112 bits. This dramatic increase in key size much more than doubles the strength of the cipher. Each increase of a single bit doubles the number of keys. This means that a 57-bit key is twice as big as a 56-bit key. A 58-bit key is four times as big, etc. This seems like a vast improvement; however, there is an attack on Double-DES that reduces its effective number of keys to about the same number in DES. This attack is known as the "meet-in-the-middle" attack and it reduces the strength of Double-DES to almost the same as DES.

Triple-DES is much more secure, so much so that although attacks on it have been proposed, the data requirements of these have made them impractical. With Triple-DES, you use three DES encryptions with either three or two different and separate keys. Managing three keys is difficult; thus, many implementations will use the two-key methods. The various ways of using Triple-DES include:

- DES-EEE3: three DES encryptions with three different keys.
- DES-EDE3: three DES operations in the sequence encrypt-decrypt-encrypt with three different keys.
- DES-EEE2 and DES-EDE2: same as the previous formats except that the first and third operations use the same key.

Rijndael

As previously discussed, the DES algorithm is becoming obsolete and is in need of replacement. To this end, the National Institute of Standards and Technology (NIST) held a competition to develop the Advanced Encryption

Standard (AES) as a replacement for DES. The winner of this competition was Rijndael, a block cipher designed by John Daemen and Vincent Rijmen.

The design of the Rijndael algorithm was strongly influenced by the design of the block cipher Square, which was also created by Daemen and Rijmen. The Rijndael algorithm can be implemented very efficiently on a wide variety of processors and in hardware or software. It is considered very secure and has no known weaknesses.

Rijndael's key length is variable, meaning that it can be set to be 128, 192, or 256 bits. It must be one of these three lengths, and not anything arbitrary. It also has a variable block size of 128, 192, or 256 bits. All nine combinations of key length and block size are possible, although the official AES block size is said to be 128. The number of rounds, or iterations of the main algorithm, can vary from 10 to 14 and depends on the block size and key length. The low number of rounds has been one of the main criticisms of Rijndael; but if this ever becomes a problem, the number of rounds can easily be increased at little extra cost by increasing the block size and key length.

IDEA

The International Data Encryption Algorithm (IDEA) is another example of a symmetric block cipher. It operates on a plaintext block size of 64 bits and, like DES, the same algorithm is used for encryption and decryption. Many consider IDEA to be superior to DES simply because it offers a 128-bit key size.

The IDEA algorithm takes a 64-bit input block and divides into four 16-bit blocks — X1, X2, X3, and X4 — which become the input blocks to the first round of the algorithm. In each of the eight total rounds, the four sub-blocks are XOR'd, added, and multiplied with one another and with six 16-bit sub-blocks of key material. Between each round, the second and third sub-blocks are swapped.

Because IDEA was developed as a possible replacement for DES, many will compare IDEA to the capabilities of DES. As far as speed is concerned, software implementations of IDEA are comparable to those of DES, and hardware implementations are just slightly faster.

RC5

RC5 is a fast block cipher designed by Ron Rivest. The algorithm itself is used in many existing security products and in a number of Internet protocols. It was explicitly designed to be simple to implement in software; therefore, the algorithm does not support any type of bit permutations. Even with this characteristic, speed tests only show a 50% speed increase over DES, using highly optimized versions of both algorithms.

The lackluster performance is likely due to key-setup times, which seem to be slow within RC5. Rivest designed a lengthy sub-key generation phase into the algorithm to make brute-force key searching substantially more difficult without slowing down conventional one-key uses of RC5.

Today's RC5 is a parameterized algorithm with a variable block size, a variable key size, and a variable number of rounds. Allowable choices for the block size are 32, 64, and 128 bits. The number of rounds can range from 0 to 255, while the key can range from 0 to 2040 bits in size.

There are three routines in RC5: key expansion, encryption, and decryption. In the key expansion routine, the user-provided secret key is expanded to fill a key table whose size depends on the number of rounds. The key table is then used in both encryption and decryption. The encryption routine consists of three primitive operations: integer addition, bitwise XOR, and variable rotation.

RC6

RC6 is a block cipher based on RC5 and, just like its predecessor, it is a parameterized algorithm where the block size, the key size, and the number of rounds are variable. The upper limit on the key size is 2040 bits, which should certainly make it strong for quite a few years. There are two new features in RC6 compared to RC5. The first is the inclusion of integer multiplication and the use of four 4-bit working registers instead of two 2-bit working registers. Integer multiplication is used to increase the diffusion achieved per round, so that fewer rounds are needed and the speed of the cipher can be increased.

Asymmetric Key Cryptography Algorithms

Asymmetric key (public key) cryptography has only been around for approximately 30 years. In fact, the idea of asymmetric key cryptography was invented in 1976. History shows that it was first invented by researchers in the British military, and classified by them until very recently. The British never came up with a practical implementation, and computers of the time were not fast enough to have made much use of it anyway. The first public invention of asymmetric key cryptography was by Whitfield Diffie and Martin Hellman, in the mid-1970s in the United States. This implementation is widely recognized as the most important advance in cryptography in the past 2000 years.

Simply stated, it differs from symmetric key cryptography in one important aspect. Instead of having to decrypt with the same key that you encrypted with, each user now has a *pair* of related keys (one called the *public key*, and the other called the *private key*). If you encrypt with one of these (either will work), you can only decrypt with the other key of the matched pair. In fact, the key that you encrypted with cannot decrypt the information.

Asymmetric Algorithm Bases and Trapdoor Functions

All asymmetric key algorithms are based on the concept of a trapdoor function. Most symmetric key (private key) algorithms do not really involve that much in the way of arithmetic operations (add, subtract, multiply, etc.); they primarily involve "bit fiddling" operations (shifts, ands, transpositions, etc.) Asymmetric key (public key) algorithms involve fairly sophisticated mathematics such as number theory, finite fields, abelian groups, elliptic curves, etc.

One-Way Functions and Trapdoor Functions

A One-Way Function is one in which there is an enormous difference in the time required to perform the function itself ("forward or fast direction") compared to how quickly you can perform its inverse ("reverse or slow direction"). For example, the RSA encryption algorithm is based on the fact that you can easily and fairly quickly multiply two large prime numbers together, but it takes a very long time to **factor** that number into its two prime factors. If the product is large enough (for example, 500 digits, or even larger), then there is a factor of millions or billions difference in the time required. Think of this concept as an "information diode." A diode is an electronic circuit device that allows current to flow easily in one direction, but poorly, if at all, in the other direction.

Asymmetric key cryptography is based on this concept of one-way functions described above. The two keys — the private and public keys — are mathematically related to each other through one-way functions. That is, they were created using this mathematical concept of one-way functions. In theory, it is possible to derive one from the other. To create the key pair requires performing the trapdoor in the fast direction (e.g., multiplying the two large prime numbers together). To crack the system, by deriving the private key from knowledge of the public key, requires performing the one-way function in the slow direction (e.g., factoring the product into its two prime factors). This means that you can create a key-pair in a reasonable amount of time (a few seconds); but to derive the private key from the public one would take an unreasonable amount of time (for 300 digits of 1024-bit products, many years or even decades).

In summary, a one-way function is a mathematical function that is significantly easier to compute in one direction (the forward direction) than in the opposite direction (the inverse direction). It might be possible, for example, to compute the function in the forward direction in seconds, but to compute its inverse could take months or years. A trapdoor one-way function is a one-way function for which the inverse direction is easy, given a certain piece of information (the trapdoor), but difficult otherwise. Public key cryptosystems are based on (presumed) trapdoor one-way functions. The public key gives information about the particular instance of the function; the private key gives information about the trapdoor. Whoever knows the trapdoor can compute the function easily in both directions, but anyone lacking the trapdoor can only perform the function easily in the forward direction. The forward direction is used for encryption and signature verification; the inverse direction is used for decryption and signature generation. In almost all public key systems, the size of the key corresponds to the size of the inputs to the one-way function; the larger the key, the greater the difference between the efforts necessary to compute the function in the forward and inverse directions (for someone lacking the trapdoor). For a digital signature to be secure for years, for example, it is necessary to use a trapdoor one-way function with inputs large enough that someone without the trapdoor would need many years to compute the inverse function (i.e., to generate a legitimate signature).

All practical public key cryptosystems are based on functions that are believed to be one-way, but no function has been proven to be so. This means that it is theoretically possible to discover algorithms that can easily compute the inverse direction without a trapdoor for some of the one-way functions; this development would render insecure and useless any cryptosystem based on these one-way functions. On the other hand, further research into theoretical computer science may result in concrete lower bounds on the difficulty of inverting certain functions; this would be a landmark event with significant positive ramifications for cryptography.

As mentioned, all asymmetric key cryptography algorithms are based on these trapdoor one-way functions, also known as "hard" problems. The RSA algorithm is the only one that uses the factoring problem. All of the others, including Diffie-Hellman, El Gamal, ECC, etc., use a discrete logarithm problem. The discrete logarithm problem is similar to the factoring problem in that it provides the mathematical concepts for the strength of the algorithm. Instead of factoring, the problem here is related to finding logarithms of large numbers that have been exponentiated.

Open, Secure, and Signed and Secure Messages Using Asymmetric Key Cryptography

There are different ways of using the concepts of asymmetric key cryptography to address information security services. The simplest one to understand is the secure message.

Let's review the concepts of public key cryptography through an analogy. Public key cryptography is like a postal mailbox. Anyone can drop a letter into a mailbox, but only the person with the key, hopefully the postal employee, can open the mailbox and retrieve the mail. Similarly, anyone

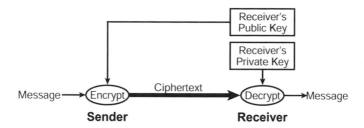

Exhibit 6. Asymmetric Key Cryptography (Secure Message)

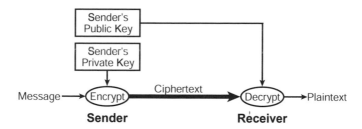

Exhibit 7. Asymmetric Key Cryptography (Open Message)

can use your public key to encrypt a message, but only you can decrypt the message. This is assuming, of course, that no one else has access to your private key.

If our goal is to send someone a confidential message using public key cryptography, it is achieved by encrypting the message using the recipient's *public* key. This ensures that the only key that will be able to decrypt the information will be the recipient's *private* key. Because this private key is only known to the recipient, a high degree of assurance that the message remains confidential is provided. Exhibit 6 depicts the process.

Public key cryptography can be used to achieve other results. Assume, for example, that message confidentiality is not our goal. Disclosure of the message is not important, but it is very important to verify the identity of the sender. This goal can also be achieved using asymmetric key cryptography. In this case, the sender of the message would encrypt the message using his own *private* key. This would ensure that the only key that would be able to decrypt the information is the sender's *public* key. Because the public key is not kept secret, this method does not ensure message confidentiality. However, because the message was encrypted using the sender's private key, it offers us a way to prove that it was actually encrypted by the sender. The sender, at this point, cannot deny having sent the message. Exhibit 7 depicts the process.

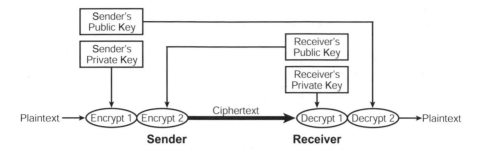

Exhibit 8. Using Public Key Cryptography to Verify the Sender Identity

What if the goal is to provide confidentiality of the message and to prove the source of it? Public key cryptography solves this for us as well. It requires, however, two encrypting steps. In this scenario, encryption is done first using the sender's private key. A second encrypting step is now necessary. The message is encrypted again using the receiver's public key. This will ensure that only the recipient will be able to decrypt the message because we have to assume that his private key is kept confidential. At the other end, the following is necessary. First, the receiver will need to decrypt using his own private key, and then decrypt again using the sender's public key. This series of steps does two things: proves the message came from the actual sender and provides confidentiality of the message. Exhibit 8 depicts the process.

Exhibit 9 shows a summary chart of some of the asymmetric (public key) algorithms that are available.

Exhibit 9. Asymmetric (Public Key) Algorithms

Public Key Algorithms	Usage	Features
RSA	Encryption and digital signature	Key length: 768, 1024 bits (Modulo length) Specified in ANSI X9.31-1 (Digital signature)
El Gamal	Encryption and digital signature	Key length: 768, 1024 bits (Modulo length) 180-bit exponent
DSA	Digital signature	512- to 1024-bit key Specified in ANSI X9.30-1 and FIPS 186
Diffie-Hellman	Key agreement procedure	Key length: 768, 1024 bits (Modulo length) 180-bit exponent Specified in ANSI X9.42

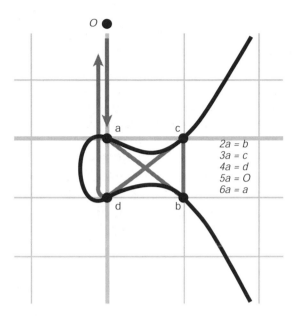

$2a = b$
$3a = c$
$4a = d$
$5a = O$
$6a = a$

Exhibit 10. Elliptic Curve

RSA Algorithm

RSA is a public key cryptosystem that offers both encryption and digital signatures (authentication). Ron Rivest, Adi Shamir, and Leonard Adleman developed RSA in 1977; RSA stands for the first letter in each of its inventors' surnames.

The RSA public (asymmetric) key algorithm is one of the most popular and secure encryption methods available in the asymmetric cryptography area. The algorithm capitalizes on the fact that there is no efficient way to factor very large (100 to 200 digit) numbers (prime integers).

Thus, the security of RSA is based on the assumption that factoring is difficult. The discovery of an easy method of factoring would "break" RSA. Here is how RSA can be used for encryption and digital signatures.

Elliptic Curve Cryptography (ECC)

The study of elliptic curves (see Exhibit 10) is a branch of mathematics. Elliptic curves are simple functions that can be drawn as gently looping lines in the (X,Y) plane. The study of elliptic curves has yielded some very significant results in the area of cryptography.

Traditional public key cryptography bases its strength on the computational difficulty of two problems: integer factoring, and discrete logarithms over finite fields. The two problems (factoring and discrete logarithms) appear to be computationally very difficult. There are, however, *subexponential* algorithms for both problems. These algorithms use both the additive and multiplicative structure of the fields (or rings) in which they operate.

There has been considerable recent activity in the implementation of *elliptic curve cryptosystems*. These systems use the Abelian group of the points of an elliptic curve on which a certain type of point addition can be defined. The elliptic curve discrete log problem is different and somewhat harder than discrete log in ordinary groups. Implementations of elliptic curve cryptography can exploit this difference to provide both increased speed and decreased key size for a given level of security.

Because elliptic curve cryptography is heavily dependent on mathematics, the exact explanation of how it works is beyond the scope of this chapter. However, a summary of how elliptic curve cryptography works follows.

First, imagine a huge piece of paper on which is printed a series of vertical and horizontal lines. Each line represents an integer with the vertical lines forming x class components and horizontal lines forming the y class components. The intersection of a horizontal and vertical line gives a set of coordinates (x,y). In the highly simplified example below, we have an elliptic curve that is defined by the equation:

$$y^2 + y = x^3 \cdot x^2$$

This is way too small for use in a real-life application, but it will illustrate the general idea.

For the above, given a definable operator, we can determine any third point on the curve given any two other points. This definable operator forms a "group" of finite length. To add two points on an elliptic curve, we first need to understand that any straight line that passes through this curve intersects it at precisely three points. Now we define two of these points as u and v: we can then draw a straight line through two of these points to find another intersecting point, at w. We can then draw a vertical line through w to find the final intersecting point at x. Now we can see that u + v = x. This rule works when we define another imaginary point, the origin, or O, which exists at (theoretically) extreme points on the curve. As strange as this problem may seem, it does permit for an effective encryption system, but it does have its detractors.

On the positive side, the problem appears to be quite intractable, requiring a shorter key length (thus allowing for quicker processing time) for equivalent security levels as compared to the Integer Factorization Problem and the Discrete Logarithm Problem. On the negative side, critics contend that this problem, because it has only recently begun to be implemented in cryptography, has not had the intense scrutiny of many years that is required to give it a sufficient level of trust as being secure.

The crucial property of an elliptic curve is that we can define a rule for "adding" two points that are on the curve, to obtain a third point that is also on the curve. This addition rule satisfies the normal properties of addition. In math jargon, the points and the addition law form a finite Abelian group. These concepts can be applied mathematically to provide effective security for elliptic curve cryptography.

The promise of elliptic curve cryptography is this. Traditional cryptography bases its strength on the computational difficulty of two problems: integer factoring and discrete logarithms over finite fields. Just about all commercial public key cryptography, except for the RSA algorithm, relies on the difficulty of a discrete log problem. As discrete log gets easier, longer bit-lengths are required to keep the method safe. Discrete logs in ordinary number groups are now much easier to solve than in elliptic curve groups. The discrete log problem for ordinary groups has been getting steadily easier, due to the discovery of what is called Number Field Sieve (NFS) techniques. In contrast, elliptic curve group discrete log techniques have not seen significant improvement in the past 20 years. This is obviously good news for elliptic methods because it allows us to use reduced key sizes to provide the same level of security as traditional public key cryptography methods. Future breakthroughs in mathematics and NFS techniques could impact the effectiveness of elliptic curve methods.

Diffie-Hellman

The Diffie-Hellman algorithm is used as a key agreement protocol, and not as an encryption algorithm. Sometimes, this algorithm is also called the exponential key agreement. It was developed by Whitfield Diffie and Martin Hellman in 1976, allowing two users to exchange a secret key over an insecure medium without having to exchange any prior secrets.

The Diffie-Hellman key agreement protocol, whereby two parties, without any prior arrangements, can agree upon a secret key that is known only to them (and, in particular, is not known to an eavesdropper listening to the dialogue by which the parties agree on the key). This secret key can then be used, for example, to encrypt further communications between the parties from that point on.

The Diffie-Hellman key agreement requires that both the sender and recipient of a message have key-pairs. By combining one's private key and the other party's public key, both parties can compute the same shared secret number. This number can then be converted into cryptographic keying material for encrypting subsequent communications.

In more mathematical terms, the Diffie-Hellman key exchange protocol can be described as follows. The protocol has two system parameters p and g. They are both public and may be used by all the users in a system.

Parameter p is a prime number and parameter g (usually called a generator) is an integer less than p, with the following property: for every number n between 1 and $p-1$ inclusive, there is a power k of g such that $n = g^k$ mod p.

Suppose Alice and Bob want to agree on a shared secret key using the Diffie-Hellman key agreement protocol. They proceed as follows. First, Alice generates a random private value a and Bob generates a random private value b. Both a and b are drawn from the set of integers $\{1, \, ^1/_4, \, p-2\}$. Then they derive their public values using parameters p and g and their private values. Alice's public value is g^a mod p and Bob's public value is g^b mod p. They then exchange their public values. Finally, Alice computes $g^{ab} = (g^b)^a$ mod p, and Bob computes $g^{ba} = (g^a)^b$ mod p. Because $g^{ab} = g^{ba} = k$, Alice and Bob now have a shared secret key k.

The protocol depends on the discrete logarithm problem for its security. The Diffie-Hellman key exchange is vulnerable to a man-in-the-middle (sometimes referred to as the "middle person") attack. In this attack, an opponent, Carol, intercepts Alice's public value and sends her own public value to Bob. When Bob transmits his public value, Carol substitutes it with her own and sends it to Alice. Carol and Alice thus agree on one shared key and Carol and Bob agree on another shared key. After this exchange, Carol simply decrypts any messages sent out by Alice or Bob, and then reads and possibly modifies them before re-encrypting with the appropriate key and transmitting them to the other party. This vulnerability is present because Diffie-Hellman key exchange does not authenticate the participants. Possible solutions include the use of digital signatures and authentication mechanisms.

El Gamal

The El Gamal system is a public key cryptosystem based on the discrete logarithm problem. Just like RSA, it allows both encryption and digital signature services. The encryption algorithm is very similar to the Diffie-Hellman key agreement protocol, but obviously better because it allows for message encryption as well. Analysis of these algorithms shows that the RSA system and the El Gamal system have a similar strength of security for equivalent key lengths. The main disadvantage of El Gamal is the need for randomness and its slower speed, especially for signing. El Gamal is really an extension of the Diffie-Hellman key exchange protocol with some added functionality such as message encryption capabilities. Its security, however, is very dependent on the randomness of some of the parameters used within the algorithm. If these parameters are not very random, El Gamal is susceptible to some of the same problems as Diffie-Hellman. A real disadvantage of El Gamal is its speed. The algorithm is very slow, especially when used for its signature capabilities.

Merkle-Hellman Knapsack

The Merkle-Hellman Knapsack cryptosystem is a public key cryptosystem first published in 1978. Again, because of the advanced mathematics involved, it would be beyond the scope of this chapter to fully describe its properties. However, in simple terms, it is based on the problem of selecting a number of objects with given weights from a large set such that the sum of the weights is equal to a prespecified weight. This is considered to be a difficult problem to solve in general, but certain special cases of the problem are relatively easy to solve, making this the weakness of the Merkle-Hellman algorithm.

Chor Rivest Knapsack

The Chor Rivest Knapsack problem was first published in 1984, followed by a revision in 1988. It is the only knapsack-like system that does not use modular multiplication. It is also considered to be the only knapsack cryptosystem that was secure for any extended period of time. An attack based on improved lattice reduction has been developed that reduces to hours the amount of time needed to crack the system for certain parameter values.

LUC

LUC is a public key cryptosystem developed by a group of researchers in Australia and New Zealand. The cipher implements the best features of the El Gamal system and those of the RSA and Diffie-Hellman systems, although recent publications have shown that many of the supposed security advantages of LUC over cryptosystems based on modular exponentiation are either not present or not as substantial as claimed.

Message Integrity Controls

When receiving messages over untrusted networks such as the Internet, it is very important to ensure the integrity of the message. Integrity means receiving exactly what was sent. The principle of integrity assures that no one can change the sender's messages without being detected. This principle is sometimes also referred to as message authentication. Message authentication can be achieved using Message Digest security features. Message digests come in two flavors: keyed and non-keyed (see Exhibit 11).

Non-keyed message digests are made without a secret key and are called Message Integrity Codes (MICs) or Modification Detection Codes (MDCs). Most public key digital signature schemes use non-keyed message digests.

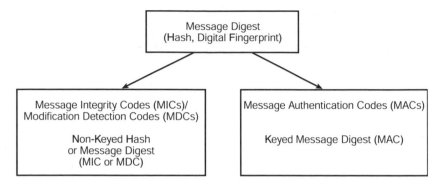

Exhibit 11. Message Digests

Keyed message digests, known as Message Authentication Codes (MACs), combine a message and a secret key. MACs require the sender and the receiver to share a secret key.

It is important to realize that the word "keyed" does not mean that the message digest is signed (private key encrypted); instead, it means that the digest is encrypted with a secret key.

Message Authentication Codes (MAC): Keyed Message Digests

In a typical situation, the sender and receiver of a message can obtain message integrity assurances by using their secret key and the message to create a "message fingerprint" known as a Message Authentication Code (MAC). The message and fingerprint (sometime referred to as a "hash") are a closely tied, matched pair. Any change in the message changes the fingerprint. Any small bit change in the message would also create a different MAC. Think of the MAC as a numeric representation of the message. A MACing algorithm compresses large files to a very few bytes and is considered one-way, meaning there is no way to decompress a MAC to reclaim the original underlying text.

The sender of a message would create a MAC from the secret key and the message, and would send both the message and the associated MAC to the receiver. Once the message has been received at the other end, the receiver would use the message and his/her copy of their shared secret key to independently calculate another message fingerprint (MAC). If the independently calculated message fingerprint is exactly equal to the message fingerprint received from the sender, the receiver is assured that the message has not been changed in transit.

The receiver can feel secure because no one else can duplicate the message fingerprint without knowing the secret key that he/she shares with the sender. It is important to realize here that the message sent along with the MAC is sent as plaintext; the message is not treated as being confidential. It must be noted that this does not prevent forgery by the receiver or anyone else who knows the secret key because all that would be necessary is to change the plaintext message and re-MAC it. Therefore, while the receiver can "feel secure," the sender cannot.

Message Integrity Codes (MICs)/Modification Detection Codes (MDCs): Non-Keyed Message Digests

Non-keyed message digests are made without the use of a secret key, and are simply algorithms that produce a numeric equivalent of the message being represented. This numeric equivalent is usually referred to as a *hash* or a *message digest*. The two most popular non-keyed message digest programs are Message Digest 5 (MD5) and Secure Hash Algorithm-1 (SHA-1). MD5 is simply the latest version of a series of hashing algorithms developed by Ron Rivest. SHA-1 is a NIST (National Institute of Standards and Technology) enhancement of MD4, an earlier version of MD5.

MD5 produces a 128-bit digest, meaning that a message of any length will produce a 128-bit message digest using MD5. SHA-1, often abbreviated as SHA, produces a 160-bit digest. Although not as widely known as MD5 and SHA-1, RIPEMD-160 is another secure 160-bit non-keyed digest. Like MD5 and SHA-1, it is also based, in large part, on MD4.

It is important to note that MD5 is more susceptible to Birthday Attacks (an attack that is very pertinent to hashing algorithms). Because MD5 produces 128-bit digests, it means that a birthday attack can be mounted against MD5 using 64 bits (128/2), and that is considered too vulnerable. SHA-1, on the other hand, produces a 160-bit digest, meaning that a birthday attack can be mounted using 80 bits (160/2). Mounting an 80-bit birthday attack requires nearly 65,000 times more effort than mounting a 64-bit attack. To put this in perspective, a successful one-hour attack against MD5 would need 65,000 hours to be successful against SHA-1. So far, SHA-1 has been immune to cryptanalytic attacks successfully mounted against MD5.

Hashed MAC

MACs execute much more slowly than non-keyed digest functions such as MD5 or SHA-1 because of the encryption involved. Cryptographers have proposed ways to combine MACs with non-keyed digest functions to speed up processing. One of these methods, HMAC, has become the *de facto* standard. HMACs (see Exhibit 12) use a secret key and a non-keyed hash function. Most HMACs use SHA-1 or MD5 and are as secure as MACs. Current real-world systems such as SSL and IPSec have standardized on HMAC. In summary, the need for processing speed prompted the invention of another message digest function. HMAC combines a MAC (secret key) and an MDC (hash function) to make a secure and more rapid message digest.

Exhibit 12. Hashed Algorithms

Hash Algorithms	Features
SHA-1	Message length: <2^64 bits 512-bit block 160-bit digest Specified in ANSI X9.30-2 and FIPS 180-1
HMAC-SHA-1	Keyed version of SHA-1 Specified in IETF RFC 2104
MD5	Message length: <2^64 bits 512-bit block 160-bit digest Specified in IETF RFC 1321
HMAC-MD5	Keyed version of MD5 Specified in IETF RFC 2104

6.4   Assurance, Trust, and Confidence Mechanisms

Digital Signatures and Certificate Authorities

Digital signatures are all about authenticating computer-based business information. Digital signatures are used to detect unauthorized modifications to data and to authenticate the identity of the signatory or the creator of the document. In addition, the recipient of signed data can use a digital signature in proving to a third party that the signature was in fact generated by the signatory. This is known as non-repudiation because the signatory cannot, at a later time, repudiate the signature.

Digital signatures are created and verified by cryptography, the branch of applied mathematics that concerns itself with transforming messages into seemingly unintelligible forms and back again. Digital signatures use what is known as "public key cryptography," which employs an algorithm using two different but mathematically related "keys," one for creating a digital signature by transforming message digest data into a seemingly unintelligible form, and another key for verifying a digital signature by returning the message digest to its original form. Computer equipment and software utilizing two such keys are often collectively termed an "asymmetric cryptosystem."

The complementary keys of an asymmetric cryptosystem for digital signatures are arbitrarily termed the private key, which is known only to the signer and used to create the digital signature, and the public key, which is ordinarily more widely known and is used by a relying party to verify the digital signature. If many people need to verify the signer's digital signatures, the public key must be available or distributed to all of them, perhaps by publication in an online repository or directory where it is easily accessible. Although the keys of the pair are mathematically related, if the asymmetric cryptosystem has been designed and implemented securely, it is computationally infeasible to derive the private key from knowledge of the public key. Thus, although many people may know the public key of a given signer and use it to verify that signer's signatures, they cannot discover that signer's private key and use it to forge digital signatures. This is sometimes referred to as the *principle of irreversibility.*

A fundamental process known as a hash function is used in both creating and verifying a digital signature. A hash function is an algorithm that creates a digital representation, or "fingerprint," in the form of a "hash value" or "hash result" of a standard length, which is usually much smaller than the message but nevertheless substantially unique to it. Any change to the message invariably produces a different hash result when the same hash function is used. In the case of a secure hash function, sometimes termed a "one-way hash function," it is also computationally infeasible to derive the original message from knowledge of its hash value. Hash functions, therefore, enable the software for creating digital signatures to operate on smaller and predictable amounts of data, while still providing robust evidentiary correlation to the original message content, thereby efficiently providing assurance that there has been no modification of the message since it was digitally signed.

Thus, use of digital signatures usually involves two processes, one performed by the signer and the other by the receiver of the digital signature:

- *Digital signature creation* uses a hash result derived from and unique to both the signed message and a given private key. For the hash result to be secure, there must be only a negligible possibility that the same digital signature could be created by the combination of any other message or private key.
- *Digital signature verification* is the process of checking the digital signature by reference to the original message and a given public key, thereby determining whether the digital signature was created for that same message using the private key that corresponds to the referenced public key.

To sign a document or any other item of information, the signer first delimits precisely the borders of what is to be signed. The delimited information to be signed is termed the "message." Then a hash function in the signer's software computes a hash result unique (for all practical purposes) to the message. The signer's software then transforms the hash result, called the message digest, into a digital signature using the signer's private key. The resulting digital signature is thus unique to both the message and the private key used to create it.

Typically, a digital signature (a digitally signed hash result of the message) is attached to its message and stored or transmitted with its message. However, it may also be sent or stored as a separate data element, so long as it maintains a reliable association with its message. Because a digital signature is unique to its message, it is useless if wholly disassociated from its message.

Verification of a digital signature is accomplished by computing a new hash result (message digest) of the original message by means of the same hash function used to create the digital signature. Then, using the public key and the new hash result, the verifier checks: (1) whether the digital signature was created using the corresponding private key and (2) whether the newly computed hash result matches the original hash result that was transformed into the digital signature during the signing process. The verification software will confirm the digital signature as "verified" if (1) the signer's private key was used to digitally sign the message, which is known to be the case if the signer's public key was used to verify the signature because the signer's public key will verify only a digital signature created with the signer's private key; and (2) the message was unaltered, which is known to be the case if the hash result computed by the verifier is identical to the hash result extracted from the digital signature during the verification process.

Various asymmetric cryptosystems create and verify digital signatures using different algorithms and procedures, but share this overall operational pattern.

The processes of creating a digital signature and verifying it accomplish the essential effects desired of a signature for many legal purposes:

- *Signer authentication.* If a public and private key-pair is associated with an identified signer, the digital signature attributes the message to the signer. The digital signature cannot be forged unless the signer loses control of the private key (a "compromise" of the private key), such as by divulging it or losing the media or device in which it is contained.
- *Message authentication.* The digital signature also identifies the signed message, typically with far greater certainty and precision than paper signatures. Verification reveals any tampering, because the comparison of the hash results (one made at signing and the other made at verifying) shows whether the message is the same as when signed.
- *Affirmative act.* Creating a digital signature requires the signer to use the signer's private key. This act can perform the "ceremonial" function of alerting the signer to the fact that the signer is consummating a transaction with legal consequences.

- *Efficiency.* The processes of creating and verifying a digital signature provide a high level of assurance that the digital signature is genuinely that of the signer. As with the case of modern electronic data interchange (EDI), the creation and verification processes are capable of complete automation (sometimes referred to as "machinable"), with human interaction required on an exception basis only. Compared to paper methods such as checking specimen signature cards — methods so tedious and labor-intensive that they are rarely actually used in practice — digital signatures yield a high degree of assurance without significantly adding to the resources required for processing.

The processes used for digital signatures have undergone thorough technological peer review for over a decade. Digital signatures have been accepted in several national and international standards developed in cooperation with and accepted by many corporations, banks, and government agencies. The likelihood of malfunction or a security problem in a digital signature cryptosystem designed and implemented as prescribed in the industry standards is extremely remote, and is far less than the risk of undetected forgery or alteration on paper or of using other less secure electronic signature techniques.

Public Key Certificates and Certificate Authorities

To verify a digital signature, the verifier must have access to the signer's public key and have assurance that it corresponds to the signer's private key. However, a public and private key-pair has no intrinsic association with any person; it is simply a pair of numbers. Some convincing strategy is necessary to reliably associate a particular person or entity to the key-pair.

In a transaction involving only two parties, each party can simply communicate (by a relatively secure out-of-band channel such as a courier or a secure voice telephone) with the public key of the key-pair each party will use. Such an identification strategy is no small task, especially when the parties are geographically distant from each other, normally conduct communication over a convenient but insecure channel such as the Internet, are not natural persons but rather corporations or similar artificial entities, and act through agents whose authority must be ascertained. As electronic commerce increasingly moves from a bilateral setting to the many-on-many architecture of the World Wide Web on the Internet, where significant transactions will occur among strangers who have no prior contractual relationship and will never deal with each other again, the problem of authentication/non-repudiation becomes not merely one of efficiency, but also of reliability. An open system of communication such as the Internet needs a system of identity authentication to handle this scenario.

To that end, a prospective signer might issue a public statement such as: "Signatures verifiable by the following public key are mine." However, others doing business with the signer may, for good reason, be unwilling to accept the statement, especially where there is no prior contract establishing the legal effect of that published statement with certainty. A party relying on such an unsupported published statement in an open system would run a great risk of trusting a phantom or an imposter, or of attempting to disprove a false denial of a digital signature (non-repudiation) if a transaction should turn out to prove disadvantageous for the purported signer.

The solution to these problems is the use of one or more trusted third parties to associate an identified signer with a specific public key. That trusted third party is referred to as a *certificate authority*.

To associate a key-pair with a prospective signer, a certification authority issues a certificate, an electronic record, which lists a public key as the *subject* of the certificate, and confirms that the prospective signer identified in the certificate holds the corresponding private key. The prospective signer is termed the *subscriber*. A certificate's principal function is to bind a key-pair to a particular subscriber. A *recipient* of the certificate desiring to rely on a digital signature created by the subscriber named in the certificate (whereupon the recipient becomes a *relying party*) can use the public key listed in the certificate to verify that the digital signature was created with the corresponding private key. If such verification is successful, this chain of reasoning provides assurance that the corresponding private key is held by the subscriber named in the certificate, and that the digital signature was created by that particular subscriber.

To ensure both message and identity authenticity of the certificate, the certification authority digitally signs it. The issuing certification authority's digital signature on the certificate can be verified using the public key of the certification authority listed in another certificate by another certificate authority (which may but need not be on a higher level in a hierarchy), and that other certificate can in turn be authenticated by the public key listed in yet another certificate, and so on until the person relying on the digital signature is adequately assured of its genuineness. In each case, the issuing certification authority must digitally sign its own certificate during the operational period of the other certificate used to verify the certification authority's digital signature.

A digital signature, whether created by a subscriber to authenticate a message or by a certification authority to authenticate its certificate (in effect, a specialized message), should be reliably timestamped to allow the verifier to determine reliably whether the digital signature was created during the "operational period" stated in the certificate, which is a condition of verifiability of a digital signature. To make a public key and its identification with a specific subscriber readily available for use in verification, the certificate may be published in a repository or made available by other means. Repositories are online databases of certificates and other information available for retrieval and use in verifying digital signatures. Retrieval can be accomplished automatically by having the verification program directly inquire of the repository to obtain certificates as needed.

Once issued, a certificate may prove to be unreliable, such as in situations where the subscriber misrepresents his identity to the certification authority. In other situations, a certificate may be reliable enough when issued but come to be unreliable sometime thereafter. If the subscriber loses control of the private key (*compromise* of the private key), the certificate has become unreliable, and the certification authority (either with or without the subscriber's request, depending on the circumstances) may suspend (temporarily invalidate) or revoke (permanently invalidate) the certificate. Immediately upon suspending or revoking a certificate, the certification authority must publish notice of the revocation or suspension or notify persons who inquire or who are known to have received a digital signature verifiable by reference to the unreliable certificate.

Public Key Infrastructure (PKI)

A PKI (Public Key Infrastructure) enables users of an insecure public network, such as the Internet, to securely and privately exchange data through the use of public key-pairs that are obtained and shared through a trusted authority, usually referred to as a Certificate Authority. The PKI provides for digital certificates that can vouch for the identity of individuals or organizations, and for directory services that can store, and when necessary, revoke those digital certificates. A PKI is the underlying technology that addresses the issue of trust in a normally untrusted environment.

A PKI is a pervasive security infrastructure whose services are implemented and delivered using public key concepts and techniques. A PKI consists of:

- A Certificate Authority that issues and verifies digital certificates
- A Registration Authority that acts as the verifier for the certificate authority before a digital certificate is issued to a requester
- One or more directories where the certificates (with their public keys) are held
- A certificate management system

A PKI consists of many components. They are discussed briefly here.

- *Certificate authority.* One of the fundamental ideas of public key cryptography is that two strangers should be able to communicate securely. For this to happen, there must be a function of binding a public key-pair to a given identity. Authorities that provide this function are referred to as Certification Authorities (CAs). In PKI

431

terms, they certify the key-pair/identity binding by digitally signing a data structure that contains some representation of the identity and a corresponding public key. This data structure is referred to as a *public key certificate*, or more simply a *certificate.*

- *Certificate repository.* Certificates issued by the CAs associate public keys with their owners, but there is still a fundamental problem that requires a PKI to allow someone to locate the certificate easily and readily. A good PKI solution will involve a robust, scalable, online repository system that will allow users to easily locate certificates as they are needed. There are numerous repository technologies available, including X.500, LDAP, Web servers, FTP servers, DNS, corporate databases, etc.

- *Certificate revocation.* The CA signs a certificate binding a public key-pair to a specific individual. There are times, however, when a breaking of that binding is necessary. These could include when identities change, such as changing from a maiden name to a married name, or when a compromise, such as a discovery by a hacker of a private key, has occurred. A PKI must have an efficient way of alerting the rest of the user population that it is no longer acceptable to use a specific public key for an individual.

- *Key backup and recovery.* In a PKI environment, users will undoubtedly lose their private keys due to any number of reasons such as a forgotten password or destruction of a medium, such as a hard drive. In these cases, it will become critical to be able to recover the lost key. A system that provides the ability to recover a lost private key would be part of an efficient PKI solution.

- *Automatic key update.* All certificates should have a lifetime, meaning that at some point they will expire and be replaced with a new certificate. Manual procedures to do this will be cumbersome and annoying; therefore, most PKI implementations will have an automated way of updating certificates without user intervention. When an expiration date is approaching, a renewal operation occurs and a new certificate is generated.

- *Key history.* The concept of automatic key update implies that, over time, a given user will have multiple old certificates and at least one current certificate. This collection of certificates and corresponding private keys is known as the user's key history. The PKI needs to keep track of this history so that encryption and decryption of data are done using the correct keys. Again, this part of the PKI solution should be totally automatic.

- *Cross-certification.* In today's world, we have multiple PKIs, independently implemented and operated, serving different environments and user communities. However, there is a need for some of these independent PKIs to be interconnected, so that secure communications between them and between their clients can occur. The concept of cross-certification allows unrelated PKI installations to form trust relationships so that users of one PKI community will be able to validate the certificates of users in another PKI community because the certificate authorities agree to accept each others certificates. However, in real life, cross-certification is very difficult to achieve until both certificate authorities involved have suitably demonstrated their policies, procedures, and measures to generate, revoke, and protect all keys involved.

- *Non-repudiation.* A PKI must be able to address the issue of non-repudiation, which means that a specific user must not be able to deny having participated in a transaction at an earlier time. Such denial is called repudiation of an action, so a PKI must be able to support the avoidance or prevention of repudiation by certifying the sending user's public key used to verify the digital signature.
- *Timestamping.* One of the critical elements in support of non-repudiation services is the use of secure timestamping, which means that all users must trust the time source for the PKI.
- *Client software.* Client software is an essential component of a full-featured, fully operational PKI solution. Client software is code that will be able to implement the required PKI services and make them available to the individual users.

PKI Core Services: Authentication, Integrity, and Confidentiality

A PKI is usually associated with three primary services:

- *Authentication:* the assurance to a user that another user is who he/she claims to be
- *Integrity:* the assurance to a user that data has not been altered, either intentionally or unintentionally
- *Confidentiality:* the assurance to a user that no one can read a particular piece of data except the intended receiver

PKI-Enabled Services

Authentication, integrity, and confidentiality are the three core services provided by a PKI. There are also other security services that in some way can be enabled by a PKI; however, these are not services inherent or fundamental to any PKI, but rather services that can include and build on the core PKI services mentioned above. The comprehensive list of security services and components that may be part of any PKI include the following:

- Certification authority
- Certification repository
- Certificate revocation
- Key backup
- Key recovery

- Automatic key update
- Key history management
- Cross-certification
- Client software
- Authentication
- Integrity
- Confidentiality
- Secure timestamping
- Notarization
- Non-repudiation
- Secure data archive
- Privilege/policy creation
- Privilege/policy verification

The above list describes an architecture that can be called the "comprehensive PKI." These would satisfy the requirements of virtually every environment. However, the reality is that in today's world, PKIs are often implemented to solve only a particular problem or set of problems; and in these cases, many of the above features may not be implemented. What has been described above are the components, core services, and PKI-enabled services that together make up the "comprehensive PKI." Many current and single-use PKIs may include subsets of this comprehensive architecture.

6.5 Information Protection and Management Services

Key Management[1]

Key management can be defined as the generation, recording, transcription, distribution, installation, storage, change, disposition, and control of cryptographic keys. History suggests that key management is very important. It suggests that each of these steps is an opportunity to compromise the cryptographic system. Further, it suggests that attacks against keys and key management are far more likely and efficient than attacks against algorithms.

Key management is not obvious or intuitive. It is very easy to get it wrong. For example, years ago, students found that a release of Netscape's SSL implementation chose the key from a recognizable sub-space of the total keyspace. While the total space would have been prohibitively expensive to exhaust, the sub-space was quite easy. Key management provides all kinds of opportunities for these kinds of errors.

As a consequence, key management must be rigorous and disciplined. History tells us that this is extremely difficult to accomplish. The most productive cryptanalytic attacks in history have exploited poor key management. Modern, automated key management attempts to use the computer to provide the necessary rigor and discipline. Moreover, it can be used to compensate for the inherent limitations in the algorithms we use.

Key Management Functions

This section addresses the functions that define key management in more detail. It identifies the issues surrounding each of these functions that the security manager needs to consider.

Key Generation

Key generation is the selection of the characters that are going to be used to tailor an encryption mechanism to a particular use. The use may be a sender and receiver pair, a domain, an application, a device, or a data object. The key must be chosen in such a way that it is not predictable and that knowledge of it is not leaked by the process.

It is necessary, but not sufficient, that the key be randomly chosen. In an early implementation of the Secure Socket Layer (SSL) protocol, Netscape chose the key in such a manner that it would, per force, be chosen from a small subset of the total set of possible keys. Thus, an otherwise secure algorithm and secure protocol was weakened to the strength of a toy. Students, having examined how the keys were chosen, found that they could find the keys chosen by examining a very small set of possible keys.

In addition to choosing keys randomly, it is also important that the chosen key not be disclosed at the time of the selection. While a key may be stored securely after its generation, it may be vulnerable to disclosure at the time of its generation when it may appear in the clear. Alternatively, information used in the generation of the key may be recorded at the time it is collected, thus making the key more predictable than might otherwise be expected by the size of the keyspace. For example, some key generation routines, requiring random numbers, ask the user for noisy data. They may ask the user to run his hands over the keyboard. While knowledge of the result of this action might not enable an attacker to immediately predict the key, it might dramatically reduce the set of keys that the attacker must search.

Distribution

Key distribution is the process of getting a key from the point of its generation to the point of its intended use. This problem is more difficult in symmetric key algorithms, where it is necessary to protect the key from disclosure in the process. This step must be performed using a channel separate from the one in which the traffic moves.

During World War II, the Germans used a different key each day but distributed the keys in advance. In at least one instance, the table of (future keys), recorded on water-soluble paper, was captured from a sinking submarine.

Installation

Key installation is the process of getting the key into the storage of the device or process that is going to use it. Traditionally, this step has involved some manual operations. Such operations might result in leakage of information about the key, error in its transcription, or might be so cumbersome as to discourage its use.

The German Enigma machine had two mechanisms for installing keys. One was a set of three (later four) rotors. The other was a set of plug wires. In one instance, the British succeeded in inserting a listening device in a code room in Vichy, France. The clicking of the rotors leaked information about the delta between key n and key n+1.

The plugging of the wires was so cumbersome and error-prone as to discourage its routine use. The British found that the assumption that today's plug setting was the same as yesterday's was usually valid.

Storage

Keys may be protected by the integrity of the storage mechanism itself. For example, the mechanism can be designed so that once the key is installed, it cannot be observed from outside the encryption machine itself. Indeed, some key storage devices are designed to self-destruct when subjected to forces that might disclose the key.

Alternatively, the key can be stored in an encrypted form, so that knowledge of the stored form does not disclose information about the behavior of the device under the key.

Visual observation of the Enigma machine was sufficient to disclose the rotor setting and might disclose some information about the plug-board setting.

Change

Key change is ending the use of one key and beginning that of another. This is determined by convention or protocol. Traditionally, the time at which information about the key was most likely to leak was at key change time. Thus, there was value to key stability. On the other hand, the longer the key is in use, the more traffic that is encrypted under it, the higher the probability that it will be discovered, and the more traffic that will be compromised. Thus, there is value to changing the key.

The Germans changed the key every day but used it for all the traffic in an entire theater of operations for that day. Thus, the compromise of the key resulted in the compromise of a large quantity of traffic and a large amount of information or intelligence.

Control

Control of the key is the ability to exercise a directing or restraining influence over its content or use. For example, selecting which key, from a set of keys, is to be used for a particular application or party is part of key control. Ensuring that a key that is intended for encrypting keys cannot be used for data is part of key control. This is such a subtle concept that its existence is often overlooked. On the other hand, it is usually essential to the proper functioning of a system.

The inventors of modern key management believe that this concept of *key control* and the mechanism that they invented for it, that they call the "control vector," is one of their biggest contributions to the cryptography field.

Disposal

Keys must be disposed of in such a way as to resist disclosure. This was more of a problem in the past when keys were used for a long time and when they were distributed in persistent storage media than it is now. For example, Enigma keys for submarines were distributed in books with the keys for the future. In at least one instance, such a book was captured.

Modern Key Management

Modern key management was invented by an IBM team in the 1970s. It was described in the *IBM Systems Journal* at the same time as the publication of the Data Encryption Standard (DES). However, while the DES has inspired great notice, comment, and research, key management has not received the recognition that it deserves. While commentators were complaining about the length of the DES key, IBM was treating it as a solved problem; they always knew how they would compensate for fixed key length and believed that they had told the world.

Modern key management is fully automated; manual steps are neither required nor permitted. Users do not select, communicate, or transcribe keys. Not only would such steps require the user to know the key and permit him to disclose it, accidentally or deliberately, but they would also be very error-prone.

Modern key management permits and facilitates frequent key changes. For example, most modern systems provide that a different key will be used for each object (e.g., file, session, message, or transaction) to be encrypted. These keys are generated at the time of the application of encryption to the object and specifically for that object. Its life is no greater than the life of the object itself. The most obvious example is a session key. It is created at the time of the session, exchanged under a key-encrypting key, and automatically discarded at the end of the session. (Because of the persistence of TCP sessions, even this may result in too much traffic under a single key. The IBM proposal for secure-IP is to run two channels [TCP sessions], one for data and one for keys. The data key might change many times per session.)

One can compare the idea of changing the key for each object or method with the practices used during World War II. The Germans used the same key across all traffic for a service or theater for an entire day. Because the British were recording all traffic, the discovery of one key resulted in the recovery of a large amount of traffic.

Manual systems of key management were always in a difficult bind; the more often one changed the key, the greater the opportunity for error and compromise. On the other hand, the more data encrypted under a single key, the easier an attack against that key and the more data that might be compromised with that key. To change or not to change — how to decide?

Automating the system changes the balance. It permits frequent secure key changes that raise the cost of attack to the cryptanalyst. The more keys used for a given amount of data, the higher the cost of attack, the more keys to be found; and the lower the value of success, the less data for each key. All other things being equal, as the number of keys increases, the cost of attack approaches infinity and the value of success approaches zero. The cost of changing keys increases the cost of encryption linearly, but it increases the cost of attack exponentially. All other things being equal, changing keys increases the effective key length of an algorithm.

Because many algorithms employ a fixed-length key, because one can almost always find the key in use by exhausting the finite set of keys, and because the falling cost and increasing speed of computers is always lowering the cost and elapsed time for such an attack, the finite length of the key might be a serious limitation to the effectiveness of the algorithm. In the world of the Internet, in which thousands of computers have been used simultaneously to find one key, it is at least conceivable that one might find the key within its useful life. Automatic key change compensates for this limitation.

By definition, the life of a key is equal to the duration of attack. Automated key management enables us to keep the life of most keys to minutes to days, rather than days to months. However, modern key management has other advantages in addition to greater effective key length and shorter life. It can be used to ensure the involvement of multiple people having sensitive duties. This is normally referred to as *separation of duties*. The concept is simple: multiple people have to be involved in completing a task. This ensures that if anyone is contemplating doing something unethical or illegal, it will require collusion among multiple people.

Key management can also be used to reduce the risk associated with a lost or damaged key. While in a communication application there is no need to worry about lost keys, in a file encryption application, a lost key might be the equivalent of loss of the data. Key management can protect against that. For example, one of my colleagues has information about one of my keys that would enable him to recover it if anything should happen to me. In this case, he can recover the key all by himself. Because a copy of a key halves its security, the implementation that we are using permits me to compensate by specifying how many people must participate in recovering the key.

Key management may be a stand-alone computer application or it can be integrated into another application. Key management must provide for the protection of keys in storage and during exchange. Smart cards can be used to accomplish this. For example, if one wishes to exchange one key with another, one can put it in a smart card and mail it. It would be useless to anyone who took it from the mail.

Principles of Key Management

A number of principles guide the use and implementation of key management. These principles are necessary, but may not be sufficient, for safe implementation. That is, even implementations that adhere to these principles may be weak, but all implementations that do not adhere to these principles are weak.

First, *key management must be fully automated.* There cannot be any manual operations. This principle is necessary both for discipline and for the secrecy of the keys.

Second, *no key may ever appear in the clear* outside a cryptographic device. This principle is necessary for the secrecy of the keys. It also resists known-plaintext attacks against keys.

Keys must be randomly chosen from the entire keyspace. If there is any pattern to the manner in which keys are chosen, this pattern can be exploited by an attacker to reduce his work. If the keys are drawn in such a way that all possible keys do not have an equal opportunity to be drawn, then the work of the attacker is reduced. For example, if keys are chosen so as to correspond to natural language words, then only keys that have such a correspondence, rather than the whole space, must be searched.

Key-encrypting keys must be separate from data keys. Keys that are used to encrypt other keys must not be used to encrypt data, and vice versa. Nothing that has ever appeared in the clear can be encrypted under a key-encrypting key. If keys are truly randomly chosen and are never used to encrypt anything that has appeared in the clear, then they are not vulnerable to an exhaustive or brute-force attack. To understand this, it is necessary to understand how a brute-force attack works.

In a brute-force attack, one tries keys one after another until one finds the key in use. The problem that the attacker has is that he must be able to recognize the correct key when he tries it. There are two ways to do this: corresponding cleartext and ciphertext attacks, and ciphertext-only attacks. In the former, the attacker keeps trying keys on the ciphertext until he finds the one that produces the expected cleartext.

At a minimum, the attacker must have a copy of the algorithm and a copy of the cryptogram. In modern cryptography, the algorithm is assumed to be public. Encrypted keys will sometimes appear in the environment and encrypted data, ciphertext, is expected to appear there.

For the first attack, the attacker must have corresponding cleartext and ciphertext. In historical cryptography, when keys were used widely or for an extended period of time, the attacker could get corresponding cleartext and ciphertext by duping the cryptographer into encrypting a message that he already knew. In modern cryptography, where a key is used only once and then discarded, this is much more difficult to do.

In the ciphertext-only attack, the attacker tries a key on the ciphertext until it produces recognizable cleartext. Cleartext can be recognized because it is not random. In the recent RSA DES Key Challenge, the correct cleartext message could be recognized because the message was known to begin with the words "The correct message is…." However, even if this had not been the case, the message would have been recognizable because it was encoded in ASCII.

To resist ciphertext-only attacks, good practice requires that all such *patterns* as format — for example, file or email message, language (e.g., English), alphabet (e.g., Roman), and public code (e.g., ASCII or EBCDIC) — *in the cleartext object must be disguised* before the object is encrypted.

Note that neither of these attacks will work on a key-encrypting key if the principles of key management are adhered to. The first one cannot be made to work because the crypto engine cannot be duped into encrypting a known value under a key-encrypting key. The only thing that it will encrypt under a key-encrypting key is a random value that it produced inside itself. The ciphertext-only attack cannot be made to work because there is no information in the cleartext key that will allow the attacker to recognize it. That is, the cleartext key is, by definition, totally random, without recognizable pattern, information, or entropy.

Keys with a long life must be sparsely used. There are keys, such as the Visa master key whose application is such that a very long life is desirable. As we have already noted, the more a key is used, the more likely a successful attack and the greater the consequences of its compromise. Therefore, we compensate by using this key very sparsely and only for a few other keys. There is so little data encrypted under this key and the data is so narrowly held that a successful attack is unlikely. Because only this limited number of keys is encrypted under this key, changing it is not prohibitively expensive.

Summary

Cryptography has been around for thousands of years but, other than military applications, did not see much use until the past 25 years or so. Even then, except for financial organizations, there was not much interest in crypto until the past few years — with the growth of networks and the need to protect information in transit. Now, crypto techniques are used in many different ways to protect the confidentiality and integrity of information. The key management problems of symmetric encryption and the e-business need for non-repudiation have been solved by the development of asymmetric encryption. Digital signatures have come of age because of asymmetric cryptography and the need to verify the owner of a public key has spawned the PKI line of business. The use of cryptography in business has come of age and is one of the most important tools available to information security personnel today.

6.6 Common Body of Knowledge (CBK)

The current CBK for the Cryptography Domain is listed below to assist in determining topics for further review. Although this Study Guide is very detailed in many areas, it is not possible to thoroughly discuss every CBK topic in a single book. Therefore, additional study of items from the bibliography may be advisable.

Components

The professional can meet the expectations defined at the beginning of this chapter by understanding such cryptography-related topics and methodologies as:

- Symmetric Algorithms
- Asymmetric Algorithms
- Message Authentication
- Certificate Authority
- Digital Signatures/Non-repudiation

- Encryption
- Error Detecting/Correcting Features
- Hash Functions
- Key Escrow
- Message Digests:
  - MD5
  - SHA
  - HMAC
- One-Time Cipher Keys (Pads)
- Private Key Algorithms:
  - Applications and Uses
  - Algorithm Methodology
  - Key Distribution and Management:
    - Key Generation/Distribution
    - Key Recovery
    - Key Storage and Destruction
    - Key Strength:
      - Complexity
      - Secrecy
      - Weak Keys
    - Methods of Attack
- Public Key Infrastructure
- Public Key Algorithms:
  - Applications and Uses
  - Algorithm Methodology
  - Key Distribution and Management:
    - Key Generation
    - Key Recovery
    - Key Storage and Destruction
    - Key Strength:
      - Complexity
      - Secrecy
      - Weak Keys
    - Methods of Attack
  - Stream Ciphers and Block Ciphers

Examples

- Describe the ancient history of cryptography.
- Describe the history of cryptography in the United States.
- Define plaintext and ciphertext.
- Compare and contrast the terms "encipher" and "decipher."
- Define cryptanalysis.
- Define key as it refers to cryptography.
- Define cryptovariable.

- Define the strength of key as it pertains to key length.
- Define ciphertext-only attack (COA).
- Define known-plaintext attack (KPA).
- Define chosen-text attack (CTA).
- Describe stream ciphers.
- Define block ciphers.
- Describe features of stream cipher algorithm.
- Identify the applications of cryptography.
- Identify the uses of cryptography.
- Compare and contrast symmetric and asymmetric key cryptography.
- Identify types of encryption systems.
- Compare and contrast substitution ciphers and transposition ciphers.
- Describe the concept of polyalphabetic ciphers.
- Describe the concept of concealment ciphers.
- Define and describe steganography.
- Describe digital system encryption.
- Define the word "codes" as it pertains to cryptography.
- Compare and contrast Hagelin and rotor cryptography machines.
- Describe the use and characteristics of "one-time pad" encryption.
- Describe the history of the DES algorithm.
- Describe the DES algorithm.
- Compare and contrast the modes of the DES algorithm.
- Describe the characteristics and usage of Double/Triple-DES.
- Compare and contrast the relative benefits of escrowed encryption.
- Describe the basis of public key algorithms.
- Define elliptic curve cryptosystem (ECC).
- Describe the advantages of the elliptic curve cryptosystem (ECC).
- Identify the standard activities involving elliptic curve cryptosystems (ECCs).
- Describe Pretty Good Privacy (PGP), S/MIME, SHTTP, SSL, and PEM.
- Compare and contrast El Gamal and Diffie-Hellman algorithms.
- Compare and contrast cryptographic module configurations.
- Identify the activities related to key management.
- Compare and contrast the types of key management.
- Describe the principles of key management.
- Describe the concept of key recovery and key recovery systems.
- Define digital signature as it pertains to cryptography.
- Describe the Digital Signature Standard (DSS).
- Define the operation of the Digital Signature Standard.
- Identify the benefits of digital signatures.
- Define non-repudiation as it pertains to cryptography.
- Define hash functions as they pertain to cryptography.
- Describe public key infrastructure (PKI).
- Describe the use of certification authorities (CAs).

- Define electronic document authorization (EDA).
- Define and distinguish between message authentication codes (MACs) and code generation.
- Describe bitstream authentication.
- Describe brute-force attacks as they pertain to cryptography.
- Compare and contrast the cost and time taken in brute-force attacks.
- Compare and contrast brute-force, analytic, statistical, and implementation attacks.
- Describe the Commercial COMSEC Endorsement Program (CCEP).
- Define the levels of encryption as defined in STUs.
- Describe the export issues regarding encryption.

6.7 Sample Questions for the CISSP Exam

1. The act of scrambling data to make it difficult for an unauthorized person from seeing it is called all of the following EXCEPT:
   a. Encode
   b. Emboss
   c. Encrypt
   d. Encipher
2. The key used in a cryptographic operation is also called:
   a. Cryptovariable
   b. Cryptosequence
   c. Cryptoform
   d. Cryptolock
3. What determines the correct choice of cryptographic algorithm?
   a. Cost
   b. Availability
   c. Business Risk
   d. Government Regulations
4. Most cryptographic algorithms operate in either block mode or:
   a. Cipher mode
   b. Logical mode
   c. Stream mode
   d. Decryption mode
5. Work factor is defined as:
   a. The time taken by a system to perform a ciphering operation
   b. The computer resources required to compute a cryptographic algorithm
   c. The problem of finding the two prime numbers used in RSA
   d. The time and effort required to break a security function
6. A one-time pad operates as a(an):
   a. Stream
   b. Linear

    c. S-box

    d. Differential

7. Which of the following is NOT one of the four primary objectives of cryptography?

    a. Non-repudiation

    b. Authentication

    c. Data integrity

    d. Authorization

8. Another name for symmetric key cryptography is:

    a. Shared

    b. Public

    c. Elliptic curve

    d. Key clustering

9. One of the greatest disadvantages of symmetric key cryptography is:

    a. Scalability

    b. Availability

    c. Computing resource requirements

    d. Confidentiality

10. Encrypting a message with a private key in an asymmetric system provides:

    a. Proof of receipt

    b. Confidentiality

    c. Proof of origin

    d. Message availability

11. How many keys would need to be managed for a public key system with 500 users (n)?

    a. $N(n-1)/2$

    b. $N \times 2$

    c. N

    d. N/2

12. A hybrid system uses:

    a. Symmetric algorithms for key distribution

    b. Asymmetric algorithms for message confidentiality

    c. Symmetric algorithms for proof of origin

    d. Symmetric algorithms for fast encryption

13. Which of the following techniques is not commonly used by encryption systems?

    a. Transposition

    b. Diffusion

    c. Substitution

    d. Transformation

14. Which mode of DES is best suited for communication between a terminal and a server?

    a. Output feedback

    b. Electronic Code Book (ECB)

    c. Cipher block chaining

    d. Cipher feedback

15. How many keys are required to operate Triple-DES?

    a. 1, 2, or 3

    b. 2 or 3

    c. 2

    d. 3

16. Which of the following does not support variable block sizes?

    a. Rijndael

    b. RC5

    c. Triple-DES

    d. Rivest Cipher 6

17. Message integrity codes are especially useful for:

    a. Detecting changes to a message

    b. Authenticating the source of a message

    c. Verifying the confidentiality of a message

    d. Ensuring that the message was sent from a reputable source

18. Birthday attacks are used against:

    a. Digital signatures

    b. Message integrity codes

    c. Asymmetric algorithms

    d. Brute-force attacks

19. Hashed MACing using SHA-1 is:

    a. RFC 1087

    b. X.509

    c. RFC 2104

    d. ANSI 9.9

20. Digital signatures do not allow for:

    a. Unauthorized modifications to a message

    b. Authentication of the signatory

    c. Third-party verification of a sender

    d. Confidentiality of a document

21. What does a certificate issued by a trusted third party indicate?

    a. It binds a public key to a person or organization.

    b. It proves the authenticity of a message.

    c. It allows for secure e-commerce transactions.

    d. It prevents ciphertext attacks.

22. Who "signs" the certificate?

    a. The registration authority

    b. The subscriber to the certificate

    c. The certificate authority

    d. The recipient of the message

23. When a certificate is invalidated, what is the proper process to follow?

    a. The certificate authority must issue a new key-pair.

b. The user must re-issue all documents produced under the old certificate.

c. The recipient must re-authenticate all documents received from that individual.

d. The certificate authority must place the certificate on a CRL.

24. What is a common error in key management?

a. Keys are too long for the algorithm to compute effectively.

b. Keys are stored in secure areas and are not recoverable.

c. Keys are chosen from a small or predictable portion of the key-space.

d. Key lifetimes are not long enough to be cost-effective.

References

Carlisle Adams and Steve Lloyd, *Understanding Public Key Infrastructure, Concepts, Standards & Deployment Considerations*, Indianapolis: New Riders Publishing, 1999.

(ISC)², Cryptography, in CISSP CBK Review Seminar, Framingham, MA: (ISC)², 2002.

Lars Klander, *Hacker Proof: The Ultimate Guide to Network Security*, Las Vegas, NV: Jamsa Press, 1997.

H.X. Mel and Doris Baker, *Cryptography Decrypted*, Reading, MA: Addison-Wesley, 2001.

William Hugh Murray, "Principles and Applications of Key Management," *Handbook of Information Security Management, 1999 ed.*, Harold F. Tipton and Micki Krause, Eds., Boca Raton, FL: CRC Press LLC, 2002.

RSA Laboratories, "RSA Laboratories' Frequently Asked Questions about Today's Cryptography, Version 4.1," Bedford, MA: RSA Security, Inc., 2000.

Chapter 7
Physical Security

The Physical Security Domain discusses the importance of physical security in the protection of valuable information assets of the business enterprise. It provides protection techniques for the entire facility, from the outside perimeter to the inside office space, including the data center or server room.

In the early days of computers, much of the security focus was built on providing physical security protections. Think of the data center that contained the mainframe servers and all the information processed and stored on the system. In this environment, the majority of the protections were for physical protection of that one area, such as restricting personnel from the area, enforcing physical access controls with locks and alarms, and implementing environmental controls to ensure the equipment was protected from heat and moisture. The advent of distributed systems changed this focus; resources and information were now in various places within the organization, and in many cases, not even contained within the building. For example, mobile devices, such as laptops and personal digital assistants, provided the ability to carry information outside a limiting physical environment.

According to many information system security surveys, such as the CSI/FBI "Computer Crime and Security Survey" annual report (2003), the majority of threats occur from insiders — that is, those individuals who have physical access to their own resources. Because of this, physical security is just as relevant today as it was 30 years ago. It is still necessary to protect server rooms by limiting access and installing appropriate locks. Let's look at an example. An authorized user (a.k.a. the insider) attempts to gain access to sensitive information that is stored on the file server. A logical control could be implemented by limiting the authorized user's account to only those files necessary to perform his or her job duties. However, if the authorized user can simply walk into the server room and "borrow" the daily backup tapes containing the file server's data, the logical controls are simply circumvented by a lack of physical controls.

Another factor impacting physical security is the new government and private sector initiatives to protect critical infrastructures, such as power and water supplies. Because information system assets require some type of power source to operate, the need for clean, constant power is a primary physical security concern. Threats to infrastructures are evolving and pose different types of threats. Although this may appear to be dramatic, chemical and biological threats have become increasingly more viable methods of attack.

In the United States in 2001, the biological agent Anthrax became a major scare when the agent was sent through the U.S. mail system to news organizations and politicians. This attack caused the death of five people who came into contact with the airborne spores through handling contaminated mail. Since that time, all U.S. Government mail is irradiated to kill Anthrax; however, both chemical and biological agents can easily be transported through a building via mechanical means, such as HVAC systems. Since the Anthrax attacks in 2001, many U.S. building owners and developers are demanding that design criteria for their projects include security master plans. In addition, those individuals responsible for protecting infrastructures have begun to develop protocols to protect power, water, wastewater, and other systems. According to Powers et al. (2002), the simplest protection from any threat is distance, which brings it back to the physical security controls. Although this chapter does not delve into these types of threats, it is important to note that threats to infrastructures have multiple effects, including the risks to the information system (Anthrax spores can be anywhere, including a computer keyboard).

One of the challenges for information system security professionals is to understand the security challenges associated with the physical environment. Although physical security is documented according to some specific technologies, such as closed-circuit television (CCTV) and alarm systems, there has not been much literature that combines the physical security field with the information system security field. There is also a dichotomy between the "traditional" security professionals who focus primarily on personnel and access controls and the information system security professionals who focus on logical controls. Many organizations still struggle for control over who will provide security — the traditional security divisions or the information management divisions. This lack of coordination and, in many cases, political maneuvering, has created difficulties for organizations to accomplish goals. However, as most security professionals will note, if both sides (security and information management) begin to work together, they will realize that indeed their goals are the same — and what is needed is better communication and coordination about how to achieve those goals. That is, by capitalizing on the strength and knowledge of both functions, they will achieve the goals of information system security — protecting the organization's valuable resources.

Although the challenges have changed along with the technologies, physical security still plays a critical role in protecting the resources of an organization. It requires solidly constructed buildings, emergency preparedness, adequate environmental protection, reliable power supplies, appropriate climate control, and external and internal protection from intruders.

The CISSP candidate should be able to:

- Describe the vulnerabilities, threats, and countermeasures related to physically protecting the enterprise's sensitive information assets.
- Identify the risks to facilities, data, media, equipment, support systems, and supplies as they relate to physical security.

Following the introduction, this chapter is divided into five main topic areas:

- *Information Protection Requirements:* outlines the requirements for physical security protection.
- *Information Protection Environment:* outlines the elements of the physical environment of concern to information system security professionals.
- *Security Technology and Tools:* provides the countermeasure techniques and tools that can be used to protect the physical environment. This includes external and internal boundary controls such as construction concerns, fencing, gates, lighting, access control devices, and reliable power.
- *Assurance, Trust, and Confidence Mechanisms:* discusses several methods to ensure that installed controls are effective.
- *Information Protection and Management Services:* discusses the managerial issues involved in securing the physical environment for information systems.

Introduction

The goal of physical security is to provide a safe environment for all assets and interests of the organization, including information system activities. Historically, protecting the computer system was simple because all equipment was located in a single area with appropriate locks. Only authorized personnel had access to the area containing the equipment. Even in the mainframe environments, the critical elements that might contain sensitive information or assets were located within a single area, a computer room. During this time, organizations began to realize the importance of mainframe processing and began to introduce measures to ensure that the mainframe equipment was protected. These measures included mechanical combination locks, card access systems, fire suppression systems, and disaster recovery plans. In today's distributed environments where desktop computers are considered critical and sensitive resources, physical security measures need to go beyond the computer room and must also address desktop resources. Recently, the growth of telecommuting and portable computers has expanded the need for physical security beyond the desktop to the user. Thus, protecting the physical environment has become even more challenging.

Physical security provides protection for the building, other building structures, or a vehicle housing the system, and/or other network components. Systems are characterized as static, mobile, or portable:

- *Static systems* are installed in structures at fixed locations.
- *Mobile systems* are installed in vehicles or vessels performing the function of a structure (i.e., not at a fixed location).
- *Portable systems* can be operated in buildings, vehicles, or in the open.

In many ways, physical security is the most obvious type of security. This is because, in most instances, it is visible; that is, people can see locks, alarm panels, and security guards. Because both employees and outsiders can see the controls, those controls can be a visual cue as to the security posture of the organization. If a possible intruder, during the first impression, sees several physical security measures, the intruder will suspect there is a need to work harder on circumventing the protection to gain access to the building.

Among some security professionals, information system countermeasures and protections seem to focus on logical controls. Although logical controls help protect resources, they cannot stop those who may have physical access. With physical access, an intruder can easily bypass or disable logical controls. Due to the inherent dangers associated with physical access to system resources by authorized and unauthorized personnel, physical security is still a very basic component of an organization's total security plan.

7.1 Information Protection Requirements

The A-I-C Triad

As with other security goals, the objective of physical security controls is to ensure the system and its resources are available when needed, the integrity of the data and system resources is ensured, and the confidentiality of the data is protected. It is the combination of all countermeasures, including physical controls, that provides a level of assurance that these three goals will be met.

Physical attacks can be directed against any element of an information system, including computers, printers, storage devices, communication systems, support systems, printed material, and personnel. Information system resources have been sabotaged using both physical and technical

Exhibit 1. Threats

Natural/environmental	Earthquakes, floods, storms (i.e., thunder, hail, lightning, electrical, snow, ice), tornadoes, hurricanes, volcanic eruptions, natural fires, extreme temperatures, high humidity, building collapse
Supply systems	Communication outages, power distribution (i.e., blackouts, brownouts, surges, spikes), burst pipes
Man-made	Explosions, disgruntled employees, unauthorized access (i.e., hackers, crackers), employee errors, arson/fires, sabotage, hazardous/toxic spills, chemical contamination, malicious code, vandalism and theft, fraud and embezzlement, intruders, unintentional acts (i.e., spilled drinks, overloaded electrical outlets)
Political events	Bombings, terrorist attacks, espionage, riots or civil disturbances, strikes

weapons. These attacks compromise the integrity and confidentiality of resources, and could also make them unavailable to authorized users. If an attack is successful, some resources may be destroyed and require a complete replacement, often requiring considerable time and effort. Even when resources can be recovered, the attack could harm the public image of the organization. This loss of confidence could subsequently result in lost customers or revenue.

An external threat may also interrupt the normal operations of the system. The extent of the losses depends on the duration and timing of the service interruptions and the characteristics of the operations performed by end users. Even simple damage to equipment — whether intentional or unintentional — can interrupt normal business operations. Damaged equipment can cause corruption of data, and can also increase the costs of doing business by requiring the purchase of new equipment.

The threats to the physical environment can be grouped into the following types of events: natural/environmental, supply systems, man-made, and political (see Exhibit 1).

While planning for physical security, it is helpful to perform a risk analysis that focuses on existing threats to the computing resources and determines where countermeasures can be most cost-effective. It is important to consider all potential threats that represent an exposure, even the unlikely ones.

When considering physical security, it is important not to cause conflict with *life safety* goals. Life safety focuses on providing a safe exit from a facility under dangerous conditions. Life safety concerns will always override other security issues; however, it is possible to achieve an effective balance between the two goals. The most newsworthy cases have been those where organizations barred exits to prevent employees from opening the doors. In several tragic instances, a fire occurred inside a building and locked doors prevented employees from exiting the building, thus causing unnecessary deaths. Because of these incidents, several countries have implemented fire-safety regulations that ensure adequate exit points from buildings. A common example is installing emergency exit doors with a time delay. When the panic bar is depressed, a loud alarm sounds and the door is released after a brief delay. This allows time for a security guard to assess the situation. Although people are refrained from using these exits improperly, they can be used effectively during an emergency evacuation.

7.2 Information Protection Environment

Physical security requires that the building site be protected in such a manner that it minimizes the risk of theft, destruction, and unauthorized access. An easy method of viewing the physical security environment is to think of it as a layered defense model.

As shown in Exhibit 2, beginning from the outside and progressing inward, the perimeter is the area surrounding the building. This could include sidewalks, roads, and any area that is immediately outside the building grounds. The building grounds include the area inside the perimeter that surrounds the building (i.e., grassy areas) as well as the physical barriers. The next layer includes all entry points into the building, such as obvious entries like doors and windows, and also rooftop entries, fire escape stairs, or other non-common entry areas. Once inside the building,

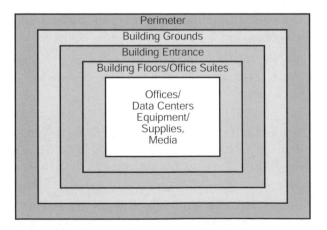

Exhibit 2. Layered Approach

physical security involves protecting floors or office spaces containing sensitive information and the data center or server room. Once inside an office, resources such as equipment, media, and documents must also be satisfactorily protected.

The subtopic areas for the Information Protection Environment include:

- Crime Prevention through Environmental Design
- Site Location
- Construction Impacts
- Facility Impacts

Crime Prevention through Environmental Design (CPTED)

Crime Prevention through Environmental Design (CPTED) is a concept that, as its basic premise, states that the physical environment of a building can be changed or managed to produce behavioral effects that will reduce the incidence and fear of crime.

> *CPTED as a concept began during the 1960s. Many of the programs and practices established in the CPTED movement were carried forward into the 1970s by police officers and security professionals. Throughout the 1980s, a handful of architects, planners, and academics advanced the field. In the 1990s, an International CPTED Association (ICA) was formed and initiatives are under way to establish standard criteria for CPTED accreditation.*

CPTED is a branch of situational crime prevention that aims to reduce the opportunity for specific crimes or incidents to occur. By combining security hardware, psychology, and site design, a physical environment can be created that would, by its very nature, discourage crime. The focus on the relationships between the social behavior of people and their environment is the essence of the CPTED concept. It contains elements that make legitimate users of a space feel safe and make illegal users feel unsafe in pursuing undesirable behavior. For example, outside lighting may make employees feel safe, but may also provide deterrence to intruders.

CPTED builds on several key strategies: territoriality, natural surveillance, and access control. Remember that CPTED is a psychological and sociological method of looking at security — it helps answer the question of how the physical environment might impact the security of an area or building. A brief description is provided to help explain some of the issues involved with designing an external physical security environment.

- *Territoriality:* People protect territory that they feel is their own and people have a certain respect for the territory of others. CPTED encourages the use of physical attributes that express ownership, such as fences, pavement treatments, art, signs, good maintenance, and landscaping. Identifying intruders is much easier in a well-defined space. Maintenance allows for the continued use of the space for its intended purpose. Deterioration and disrepair indicate a lack of concern and a tolerance for disorder.

- *Surveillance:* Intruders do not want to be seen. Surveillance is a principal tool in the protection of a space. Environments where occupants can exercise a high degree of visual control increase the likelihood of criminal acts being observed and reported. Implementing physical features, conducting activities, and locating people in ways that maximize the ability to see what is going on discourages crime. For example, landscaping and lighting can be planned to promote natural surveillance from inside a building and from the outside by people passing by. Formal surveillance, such as closed-circuit television (CCTV) or organized security patrols, is often used as an additional deterrent.

- *Access control:* Properly located entrances, exits, fencing, and landscaping can control the flow or limit access to both foot and automobile traffic in ways that discourage crime. Most intruders will try to find an unrestricted way into an area. Limiting access keeps them out altogether or marks them as an intruder.

CPTED works best when combined with a comprehensive physical security program. It is important for security practitioners to be brought into the discussions early and to share their knowledge of how security can be designed from the beginning. Because many traditionalists view physical security programs as installing tools, such as locks, lighting, and alarms, they miss the important CPTED design elements. It is how the tools are used that makes the difference, and this is what the security professional will offer to the development. Essentially, the security program must be integrated into the environment, not just tools added on after the construction.

Site Location

Physical security should begin with a detailed site selection process. If you are involved in the selection of where and how a building should be built, there are several questions to consider from a security perspective; they should include:

- Does our business have specific physical security concerns regarding the facility location?
- Is it vulnerable to crime, riots, demonstrations, or terrorism attacks?
- Is it vulnerable to natural disasters? In a high flood plain? Earthquake zone?

- Where is it located in relationship to adjacent buildings and/or other businesses? Is it located next to a chemical factory?
- How far away is it to other types of threats? Nearest airport? Interstate highway? Fertilizer plant? Landfill? Military base?
- What are neighborhood crime rates and types?
- What type of emergency support response is provided to the area? Can the fire department or other emergency vehicles respond within an acceptable timeframe?

Construction Impacts

Construction controls involve designing walls, windows, doors, and infrastructure support elements, such as water or gas lines, in a secure fashion. This includes constructing walls that are fire-rated to meet area zone requirements, penetration resistant, windowless or have non-opening windows. Questions to consider include: Could the structure withstand relevant natural threats, such as hurricane-force winds? Is it earthquake resistant? Does the business require specific building enhancements (i.e., a bank may have different building concerns than a warehouse)?

Facility Impacts

The actual facility design can affect the level of physical security available. The following elements are briefly reviewed:

- Entry points
- Infrastructure support systems
- Electrical power
- Heating, ventilation, air conditioning (and refrigeration)
- Internal sensitive or compartmentalized areas
- Portable computing

Entry Points

External entry points include doors, windows, roof access, service or delivery doors, fire-escape entries, and other secondary entrances. Internal entry points can include elevators, stairs, and doors to internal offices. Questions include:

- Does the building meet current building codes for construction and safety requirements?
- Is the building secured at ground or grade level by solid, locked doors, using heavy-duty commercial hardware (locks, hinges)?
- How many doors does it have? Where are they located?
- Do doors need to be fire resistant?
- Are trade entrances locked or controlled? Are they wide open to strangers?

- What type of roof access is needed? Is there a helicopter pad? Are rooftop openings locked with heavy-duty commercial hardware if accessible from outside the building?
- Does the building have an outside ladder? Fire-escape stairs?
- Are there windows at ground level? If so, are they fixed or locked with heavy-duty commercial hardware, bars, or grills?
- Do windows need wire-mesh controls?
- Do windows need to be opened?
- Is there sufficient lighting surrounding the entry points and an ability to observe them?

Infrastructure Support Systems

Infrastructure support systems include power; water/plumbing; and heating, ventilation, and air conditioning (HVAC). Support services are described as the underpinning of the operation of the system — the failure or substandard performance of the support systems may interrupt operation of the system and may cause physical damage to system hardware or stored data.

Physical security for the infrastructure support systems involves not only the area containing the operational hardware, but also locations of wiring used to connect elements of the system. For example, cabling, plugs, sockets, loose wires, and exposed cabling could be exploited if left open and physically accessible.

Electrical Power

Because information system processing depends on electrical power, a disruption in the electrical power supply can have a serious business impact. Even if a long-lasting (more than 30 minutes) battery UPS is installed, the loss of electrical power will halt the organization's ability to conduct business. A continuous power supply ensures the availability of resources. Note that companies involved in the manufacture of integrated circuit chips cannot tolerate a power outage at all — the failure of a laser while burning into a wafer can result in a loss of hundreds of thousands of dollars (i.e., the price of one wafer). Also, there is a need for continuous availability of power for telecommunications and other information system equipment; thus, security professionals must understand how power can be protected.

By working with utility providers, an approach can be planned for identifying and configuring a protection strategy toward information system needs that suit the organization's processing demands and system availability requirements. The way a power system is configured, even within a controlled environment, is the critical difference in availability.

One of the first steps is to understand the cost of downtime. In 2001, the Electric Power Research Institute (EPRI) released a study that said power outages and voltage fluctuations cost the U.S. economy up to $188 billion a year. The EPRI report estimated that the loss of power for one hour could cause an online network connection company to lose fees ranging from U.S.$24,000 to 28,000, an airline reservation center might lose U.S.$67,000 to 112,000, and a credit card sales operations loss could range in the millions of dollars. The good news is that the EPRI study showed that digital businesses (those that are most susceptible to outages) showed the least losses. The report stated that digital firms understand the implications of power to their equipment, so they invest in equipment and generators to protect their systems from unstable power.

Vulnerabilities include total power loss of short or long duration or degradation in power quality, such as brownouts, spikes, or sags. From the utility perspective, an outage occurs when a component of the distribution system is not available to provide its normal function. Short power unavailability (seconds) is not considered an outage, but an interruption.

Complete power loss includes:

- *Blackout:* complete loss of commercial power
- *Fault:* momentary power outage

Power degradation includes:

- *Brownout:* an intentional reduction of voltage by a utility company. It is usually in response to a power demand in excess of its generation capability.
- *Sag/dip:* a short period of low voltage. The duration is usually from one cycle to a few seconds. The American "sag" and the British "dip" have the same meaning. Most voltage sags originate from within the facility; they can be caused by starting an electrical motor that requires a large amount of power, loose or defective wiring, or faults or short circuits. They can also originate from the power company by faults on distant circuits or voltage regulator failures.
- *Surge:* a sudden rise in voltage in the power supply. A strong power surge can easily harm unprotected computers and other microprocessor circuits. It also puts a stress on anything else powered by the electric supply, from air conditioning motors to light bulbs. Electrical surges can be caused by a strong lightning strike, when a large plant or generating station goes on- or offline, or when something like a car hits a power pole and the power grid has to shift. In addition, electrical equipment inside the business can create power surges and fluctuations.
- *Transient:* line noise or disturbance is superimposed on the supply circuit and can cause fluctuations in electrical power.

- *In-rush current:* the initial surge of current required by a load before it reaches normal operation. Some electrical equipment (i.e., a refrigerator) when first turned on demands a higher level of power. (A motor may require two to five times more power to start than that required during normal operation.) This extra demand causes an in-rush of electrical current to the equipment. Due to the internal resistance inherent in any power source, this increased current will cause a diminution in the voltage level and a sag may occur in other areas of the power circuit.
- *Electrostatic discharge:* another type of electrical surge can occur when two nonconducting materials rub together, causing electrons to transfer from one material to another. (Think of your childhood, shuffling your shoes on carpet, and then "shocking" your sibling by touching them — on a grander scale, think of the large electrostatic discharge known as lightning.) Other causes include air that is very dry or handling certain types of materials. Although static is often overlooked, it can damage electronic equipment. This electrical static charge is the reason why manufacturers of computer equipment use anti-static bags to ship equipment and also why technicians must wear grounding straps and pads when working on susceptible computer equipment, such as CPUs.

Interference

To generate electricity, three things are needed: a conductor, a magnetic field, and relative motion. When an electrical current flows through a conductor, there is a corresponding proportional electromagnetic field that develops around the conductor. As the current increases, the electromagnetic field also increases in strength. Because the power we receive from the power company is alternating current, there is a constantly rising and falling electromagnetic field around most power conductors that is proportional in size to the amount of current flowing through the conductor. We now have the magnetic field and the relative motion needed to induce (or generate) an electric current in a nearby conductor. It is this changing electromagnetic field that can cause interference. (Building this magnetic field is also the reason for the in-rush current.)

Interference (sometimes called noise) is a random disturbance interfering with device operation. It may cause erratic program operation or it might cause errors in data processing. For example, a computer monitor display may fluctuate or audio equipment may reproduce noise from other electrical equipment, such as fluorescent lights. Electromagnetic interference and radio frequency interference are the two types.

- *Electromagnetic interference (EMI)* is defined as the interference in a circuit, for example, disturbance on a computer monitor that is caused by the radiation of an electric or magnetic field (or the operation of a nearby electric motor).

- EMI is categorized as either common-mode noise or traverse-mode noise. Common-mode noise occurs between hot and ground wires. Traverse-mode noise occurs between hot and neutral wires.

- *Radio frequency interference (RFI)* is the reception of radio signals. It is similar to EMI, except it is at a higher frequency. Radio waves can interfere with each other when they bounce off buildings in cities and cause distortion to the radio signal. Small electrical discharges generate RFI and can be created by components of electrical systems, various transmitting devices, or lightning. In addition, radio stations, cellular phones, small office equipment, fluorescent lights, loose electrical connections, or defective power plugs, cords, or sockets can be sources of this type of interference. Fluorescent lighting is a particular concern — running network cabling, such as unshielded twisted pairs, too close to fluorescent lighting can be a source of interference.

Water/Plumbing

Water damage, caused by leaks or condensation, can cause damage to information system resources. Common sources of water problems are broken pipes, fire-suppression systems, and improper installation of air conditioners, evaporative coolers, or condensers. Water damage can also lead to problems with mold and mildew that may affect the proper functioning of the computer resources and create health hazards. Left untreated, mold and mildew can quickly grow and potentially make the workspace uninhabitable. Review the locations of washrooms, showers, etc., that could affect the safety of personnel or equipment. In addition, check other facilities in the building, for example, a pool that could leak and cause power problems.

Heating, Ventilation, and Air Conditioning (HVAC)

HVAC is defined as a system that provides, either collectively or individually, the processes of comfort heating, ventilation, and/or air conditioning within a space. Recently, refrigeration has been added to the common HVAC term, so you may sometimes see HVAC&R.

One HVAC issue involves where and how the support systems are installed, such as the location for the main controls and the cable runs. When looking at it from a security perspective, the question is whether the location of these areas could allow for unauthorized access or some type of sabotage. For example, if the HVAC equipment is located in the basement of the building, how many people could access the basement? Are there dead-bolt locks on the door? Many HVAC systems are now networked for remote control, monitoring, and maintenance. Hackers have been known to remotely control temperatures making offices too hot or too cold. Thus, controlling remote access should be a key concern.

Also of concern is the computerization of these systems. In most systems, the functions are controlled through some type of digital/smart device. For example, sensors are installed to ensure that temperatures are maintained at required levels. HVAC services maintain appropriate temperature and humidity levels within a facility. However, HVAC services also manage air quality. Ventilation is the process of supplying or removing air by natural or mechanical means to or from any space. Mechanical ventilation uses HVAC equipment to heat or cool air, deliver either outdoor air or recirculated air to a space, and remove stale air from a space. Natural ventilation is the movement of outdoor air into a space through intentional openings, such as windows and doors.

A term associated with air quality is "pressurization." Positive or negative pressurization refers to the air movement between areas within a building or the building as a whole to the outdoors. Negative pressurization occurs when a building pulls air in from the outdoors or other adjacent areas through doors or other openings. When the air tries to escape through doors or other openings, it is referred to as positive pressurization. Think of a door opening and the inside air goes out while the outside air does not come in. This can be important in controlling contamination of an area from dangerous air quality levels, such as a chemical leak. If the area is positively pressurized, the HVAC system will not pull it in — essentially the ventilation system will prevent the contamination. If a fire were to occur, positive pressurization would force the smoke to exit the building and external particles (or smoke) could not enter (or re-enter) from the same exit point.

Positive pressurization is particularly important in computer rooms and data centers where sensitive equipment could become affected by airborne particles. For example, if a facility was being remodeled, the dust from the construction could affect a computer's ability to function by infiltrating the fan or external drive devices.

A vulnerability of HVAC systems is the risk of chemical and biological agents entering a building through the system. Remember that in March 1995, terrorists released sarin, an organophosphate (OP) nerve gas, at several points in the Tokyo subway system, killing 11 and injuring more than 5500 people. Similarly, there is a possibility that attackers could carry a biological or chemical agent into a public building, scatter it through various places in the public area, especially near ventilation registers. The spores would quickly enter the HVAC systems and be distributed throughout the facility.

Internal Sensitive or Compartmentalized Areas

Inside of the building are several areas that need additional physical protection. These areas include the data center or server room, communication centers, switching centers, or end-user areas where highly sensitive information is processed and stored.

Portable Computing

The growth of portable computing has transformed how organizations perform business. It includes remote connectivity to the home office by a terminal and remote computing on a stand-alone microcomputer that has desktop capabilities and storage. Both of these portable computing methods have environment-specific threats that require protection measures. Because the organization's data is being accessed and processed outside the normal physical protections of the office, the risk of loss, theft, data exposure, and data destruction can be significantly greater.

Remote access to a network can be done two ways: direct dial-in (private connection) or from a virtual dial-in via an Internet service provider (public connection). Remote connectivity can be between an organization's various locations, such as a branch office to a headquarters location, telecommuters, or mobile users.

Remote access introduces vulnerabilities to the physical equipment. For example, a telecommuter working from a home office may not have equivalent physical security controls as in an office building. Vulnerabilities include non-employees accessing the system, paper files left unprotected, or inappropriate disposal of magnetic media and paper. Also, an employee who travels with a laptop introduces additional physical security vulnerabilities for both the equipment and information. Each year there are reports from both industry and government highlighting the large numbers of laptops lost or stolen. Those losses result from user error, such as forgetting the laptop in a taxi or checking the laptop as luggage, and simply theft from a hotel room.

Because a large amount of information can be stored on a laptop, its loss can be devastating for both the user and the organization. Although laptops and portable digital assistants (PDAs) create a large security risk, the increased popularity of portable computing means that they are here to stay.

The next section discusses the controls that can be used to counter the physical environment threats and vulnerabilities.

7.3 Security Technology and Tools

Physical security tools are comprised of controls such as fences, door locking systems, surveillance devices, intrusion detection equipment, alarms, power generators, fire suppression, and locking file cabinets or safes. Collectively, these controls, along with organizational practices and procedures, are intended to deter, delay, detect, assess, and appropriately respond to an unauthorized activity. Each organization has unique resources and assets that vary, depending on the type of business that is conducted. Thus, the level of physical controls that an organization will implement depends on factors such as the facility location, size of the facility, sensitivity of the data, and specific industry regulations.

With regard to providing physical security measures, the environment should be considered multi-layered. Typically, this starts with the perimeter of the facility and continues through the building grounds, the building entry points, and inside the building. Once again, the objective of physical controls is to prevent or deter unauthorized or illegal events from occurring and, if they do occur, to detect the event and delay the activity to allow for a timely response. It is often said that a determined intruder will eventually gain unauthorized access regardless of any constraints. Given enough time, money, and access, an intruder could defeat anything. One method of making it difficult for intruders to gain access is to create a layered defense.

Layered Defense

Every facility should have a reception area that is accessed directly from the public access zone. This ensures that visitors and maintenance personnel cannot proceed to an operational or secure zone without escorted access. If this process cannot be accommodated, then securing each floor should be considered. Whether each floor must be secured depends on the sensitivity of the information and costs versus the security alternatives.

Let's look at an example (see Exhibit 3):

- A fence protects the perimeter.
  - Vulnerability: unlocked gate
  - Attack: the intruder enters through an unlocked gate at closing time
- The building entry points are protected with a card access control system.
  - Vulnerability: cleaning crew has badge cards for access but is not trained in security practices

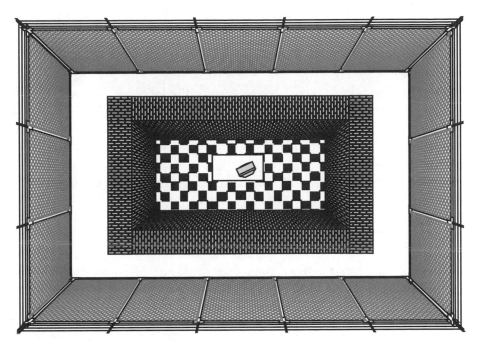

Exhibit 3. Layered Design

- Attack: intruder enters the building by "tailgating" with the cleaning crew; the cleaning crew does not stop or question the individual
- Inside the building, a card access control system protects the elevators and door locks secure the stairwells.
  - Vulnerability: to avoid waiting for the elevator or to sneak a cigarette in the stairwell, employees prop open the stairwell doors
  - Attack: intruder enters through unlocked stairwell
- The office doors are also secured with locks.
  - Vulnerability: door is pushed shut but employee does not ensure that it actually clicked shut all the way.
  - Attack: intruder easily pushes the door open (at this point, the intruder has managed to defeat the security control and gain access to an employee's office)
- Inside the office, the employee has locked all sensitive information in an office safe.
  - Vulnerability: employee did not put all information in the safe or did not close the safe properly
  - Attack: although information was left out of the safe, its content was not sensitive. (The employee did practice good security by

putting all sensitive information in the safe and properly closing the safe. Unfortunately for the intruder, the safe has a high-security combination lock that cannot be easily circumvented. Intruder was not successful!)

This is the concept of a layered defense: if the intruder can bypass one layer of controls, the next layer of controls should provide additional deterrence or detection capabilities.

Another key element is using multiple types of security controls within each of the layers. For example, if the same key is used to unlock the front door, the elevator, and the office suite, the layered defense is minimized or neutralized because an intruder only has to subvert one layer — gaining access to the front door key. However, using several types of controls, such as augmenting the locked front door with a surveillance system, can increase the ability to prevent, detect, or deter the event.

The next items in this topic focus on several specific security technologies and tools that provide physical protection control. It follows the layering model (i.e., perimeter to office suite) and outlines the controls that can be implemented at each layer. Note that some controls can be implemented at various levels. For example, locks are used for both building entry points and office suite entry points. The subtopics include:

- Perimeter and building grounds
- Building entry points
- Inside the building: building floors, office suites, and offices

Perimeter and Building Grounds Boundary Protection

The perimeter security controls are the first line of defense and are usually located as far away as possible from the main buildings. They should delay an intruder long enough for guards (discussed later) to react appropriately.

Protective Barriers: Landscaping, Fences, Gates, Bollards, Walls, and Doors

Physical security barriers are used to control, impede, or deny access, and also to effectively direct the flow of personnel through entry points. They are designed to reduce the number of entry and exit points, delay an intruder to enable interception, and protect personnel from hostile actions.

There are two types of protective barriers: natural and structural. Natural protective barriers include terrain features that are difficult to cross, such as thickets, heavy bush growth, bodies of water, or deserts and wide-open spaces that are easier to monitor. Structural barriers involve man-made devices such as fences, gates, bollards, and facility walls.

Landscaping. Landscaping can be designed to provide a measure of security. For example, shrubs or trees can provide a barrier or an entry point. Spiny shrubs may make it more difficult for an intruder to cross the barrier. On the other hand, a tall tree might provide a means for bypassing entry controls. Too much landscaping can also make it difficult to monitor. Consequently, there must be a good balance, such as thick growth followed by a wide gap.

Fences or Wall Structures. Fences or wall structures are used to secure an area and to designate a property boundary. For high-security facilities, fence structures are often supplemented by security patrols, continuous observation, or an intrusion detection system. Although fences or walls provide only minimal deterrence to a determined intruder, they are seen as a psychological deterrent. An additional advantage of a fence is that it is difficult to enter an area without the use of specific tools, such as wire cutters.

Chain-Link Fencing Guidelines. The design of chain-link fences should provide the following:

- Specific gauge and fabric specifications
- A top guard (i.e., be topped with barbed wire configurations)
- Fence construction must be taut and securely fastened to steel or concrete posts
- Posts should be secured in concrete or buried deep enough to compensate for the shifting or erosion of soil
- Adequate height specifications to meet security needs
- Be located in reasonable areas (i.e., some terrain may not be suited for chain-link fences)

The height of a fence provides various levels of protection. Exhibit 4 outlines some general guidelines for fence height.

For medium- to high-level security, the chain-link fabric mesh should be no greater than 2×2 inches with 9-gauge or heavier wire. A facility with critical security needs, such as a nuclear reactor plant, would need to meet

Exhibit 4. Guidelines for Fence Height

Height	Protection
1 meter/3–4 feet	Deters casual trespassers
2 meters/6–7 feet	Too high to climb easily
2.4 meters/8 feet with top guard	Deters determined intruder

higher security requirements. As an example, the U.S. Army has published guidelines for physical security in Field Manual (FM) 3-19.30 "Physical Security," January 2001. These guidelines specify the following for fences:

> *Chain-link fence (including gates) must be constructed of 6-foot material, excluding the top guard. Chain-link fences must be constructed with 9-gauge or heavier wire. They must be galvanized with mesh openings not larger than 2 inches per side and have twisted and barbed selvages at the top and the bottom. The wire must be taut and securely fastened to rigid metal or reinforced-concrete posts set in concrete. It must reach within 2 inches of hard ground or pavement. On soft ground, it must reach below the surface deep enough to compensate for shifting soil or sand.*

Fencing (see Exhibit 5) must be checked and repaired on a regular basis. It is important to ensure that fence fabric is properly attached to the support poles, especially if the fence fabric does not extend below the surface. Erosion of the ground under the fence may result in gaps or washouts that could permit someone to crawl under the fence. Another issue is controlling the vegetation that grows close to the fence. If the vegetation is too close or too high to the fence, it could provide cover for potential intruders or assistance for climbing the fence. An intruder could also use unprotected pipes or wires that pass over the fence to gain access. When constructing or checking fences, it is necessary to look at the proximity of other buildings or structures on either side of the fence that could provide a bridging capability from the outside to the inside. In addition, if using CCTV for perimeter security along the fence line, be sure to review how the fence looks through the camera lens. For example, if the camera lens angle is too narrow, the fence may look opaque or the entire fence line will not be seen.

Gates. A gate is defined as "a moving barrier, such as a swinging, sliding, raising, lowering, rolling, or like barrier that is a passage barrier. It is also that portion of a wall or fence system that controls entrance and/or egress by persons or vehicles and completes the perimeter of a defined area" (UL Standard 325 definition). The types of gates include barrier arm operator or system, vertical pivot gate, horizontal slide gates, horizontal swing gates, vertical lift gates, vertical pivot gates, and overhead pivot gates.

A term associated with gates is *entrapment*. As it relates to gates, it is defined as the condition when an object is caught or held in a position that may cause the risk of injury. Gates are evaluated based on their entrapment features and vary based on the type of gate. For example, a gate with "inherent entrapment" functionality has an automatic sensor system that senses the entrapment of a solid object and responds to that entrapment within a specified timeframe (i.e., two to five seconds).

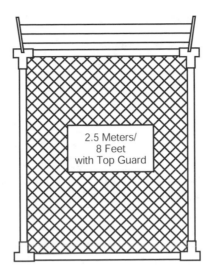

Exhibit 5. Fences

Exhibit 6. Vehicle Gate

Vehicular gates (Exhibit 6) are separated into classes:

- Class I: residential gate operation
- Class II: commercial, such as a parking lot or garage
- Class III: industrial/limited access, such as a warehouse, factory, or loading dock
- Class IV: restricted access operation that requires supervision by security personnel, such as those at a prison or airport security area

As a security measure, the gate must prevent a second party from entering while the gate is open: this is known as *tailgating*. Thus, the timeframe it takes to open and close a gate should be a consideration. For example, if a gate is opened for an authorized vehicle, a second unauthorized vehicle should be stopped by the gate system. The gate operation should sense a second attempt at entry; the gate operation (whether controlled automatically or by human presence) should stop the gate travel and go into a lockdown state that stops passage.

Another feature of gates is to have an audio alarm activate whenever the gate is operated. Just before the gate begins to operate and during the gate's travel, an audio alarm device will trigger. Depending on the gate class (i.e., I, II, III, or IV), it may be required to have this audio feature.

An important aspect for pedestrian gates is that the gate matches the type of fencing. The gate frames should consist of steel or aluminum tubes and conform to the specifications of the material used in the fence line. Also, the fence fabric should be of the same type of material used in the fence posts and frames.

Bollards/Vehicle Barriers. A bollard (Exhibit 7) is a heavy-duty rising post designed for use in traffic control and protecting property premises. It provides an effective visible and physical barrier to vehicles, providing security against ram raids or vehicle theft, and provides restriction to unauthorized access.

Depending on the organization, aesthetic considerations may play a part in the choice of bollards. There are a variety of shapes, sizes, and finishes that would fit in with the architecture. Another criterion would be to meet any city or county restrictions.

A secondary security feature of bollards is to use them for lighting controls. Bollards with lights can illuminate surfaces and provide lighting for parks, paths, or around shrubbery. Depending on security needs, bollards can divide, align, or structure outside space by their size and function.

Lighting. Lighting (Exhibit 8) provides a mechanism for continuing a degree of coverage during hours of darkness that, at a minimum, approaches the requirements maintained during daylight hours. It is an

Exhibit 7. Bollards

essential element in an integrated physical security system. For maximum effectiveness, it should be used with other controls, such as fences, patrols, and/or alarms.

Good protective lighting is achieved by having even light upon bordering areas, glaring lights in the eyes of an intruder, and little light on security patrol routes. Increasing the level of illumination allows greater visibility. For example, high brightness contrast between an intruder and the background should be the first consideration. If the same amount of light falls on an object and the background, the observer must depend on contrasts in the amount of light reflected. The ability to distinguish poor contrasts is improved by increasing the level of illumination. In addition, the perimeter area should be cleared of obstructions, trees, or other elements that could conceal a person.

There are several common types of protective lighting systems:

- *Continuous lighting* is the most common and consists of a series of fixed luminaries arranged to flood a given area continuously during hours of darkness. This includes glare projection lighting where the glare of lights is directed across the surrounding territory. Flood lighting uses luminaries that project their output in a forward direction (i.e., not up, down, sideways, or backward). Another type of continuous lighting is called controlled lighting. It is used where the width of the lighted area outside the perimeter must be controlled.

471

Exhibit 8. Lighting

- *Trip lighting* is activated by some trigger point, such as an intruder crossing a sensor. If the trigger point is activated, a light will shine. Note that these systems can be prone to nuisance tripping by pranksters or false alarms by animals and can also be used by intruders to create several false alarms that cause the security team to respond to various entry points. Because not every point can be monitored, an intruder may be able to gain access.
- *Standby lighting* is similar to continuous lighting. The difference is that the luminaries are not continuously lit, but are either automatically or manually turned on when suspicious activity is suspected. Because incandescent lamps tend to burn out more often than gaseous discharge lamps, standby lighting could prove to be a valuable resource — especially in a high-security area.
- *Emergency lighting* is used for limited times of power failures or other emergencies that render the normal system inoperative.
- *Gaseous discharge* lamps such as high-pressure sodium and mercury vapor lamps have an inherent security weakness in that they can take several minutes to re-ignite after even a brief power interruption. In some high-security areas, such as maximum-security prisons, you may additionally find incandescent lighting as a supplemental light source to provide lighting during this re-ignition period. Another security weakness associated with this type of lighting is that they are often equipped with photovoltaic sensors that allow

the lamps to automatically turn on at dusk and off at dawn. There is often a timing feature to prevent the lights from switching off due to transient bright lights such as lightning or passing car headlights that happen to strike the photocell. However, a determined intruder could point a high-powered light, even an invisible infrared beam, at the sensor for 30 to 60 seconds and cause the lamps to switch off. This would give the intruder approximately three to four minutes of darkness before the lamps could re-ignite and reach full brilliance again.

To be effective, security personnel must be trained in how to distinguish intruders using protective lighting and also where weaknesses in the system may allow an intruder to be undetected. They should be given the opportunity to observe dark-clothed intruders attempting to gain entry and should also experience the effects of facing glaring lights. By understanding what is normal, personnel should be able to determine what is abnormal.

Perimeter Intrusion Detection Systems (IDSs)

Sensors can be installed along the perimeter and on the building grounds to detect unauthorized access into an area. Perimeter sensors include those that can detect intrusion across or under a land boundary or through a physical barrier, such as a chain-link fence. It can also detect someone approaching or touching an object, such as a vehicle. A disadvantage in perimeter IDSs is they are susceptible to false alarms caused by non-intruders, such as animals, weather, etc. The section on Building Entry Points provides more details on sensor systems.

Surveillance Devices

An added security dimension for locked buildings is to use surveillance devices, such as video motion detectors or detectors utilizing microwave, infrared, ultrasonic, laser, or audio technologies. Video motion detectors and other detector types are considered both perimeter and building entry controls. For perimeter use they do not provide the same protection as a fence; however, if properly installed, they can provide an intrusion alert warning.

Closed-Circuit Television (CCTV)

CCTV (see Exhibit 9) is a television transmission system that uses video cameras to transmit pictures by a transmission medium (wired or wireless) to connected monitors. Because many surveillance systems are based on this type of transmission, we have provided more detailed information.

Exhibit 9. CCTV Camera

The CCTV system, if installed and configured correctly, can assist in providing information about an event, such as who, what, where, and how many. From this information, an assessment of the event can be determined. This assessment requires human intervention to determine whether an adversary or a nuisance alarm caused the event.

CCTV levels:

- *Detection* is the ability to detect the presence of an object.
- *Recognition* is the ability to determine the type of object.
- *Identification* is the ability to determine object details.

Originally, a domestic television system received transmission signals from various transmitters that did not have a physical connection. The television signals were commercially "broadcast" to the end users. This is referred to as an "open system." A CCTV system usually does not use broadcast technology to transmit; instead, it has some type of hard-wired capability. Thus, it is considered a "closed system." However, some recently configured CCTV systems are using broadcast to transmit signals between facilities.

The simplest CCTV system has one camera connected by cable to a monitor. A multi-camera system has more than one camera connected to the monitor. Viewing the picture from each of the cameras is done one at a time by a simple switcher that sequences through each camera. Viewing only one camera shot at a time has security limitations. For example, an intruder could find out the sequence pattern and enter at a time when the camera shot is not displayed on the monitor. One solution is to install a splitter (also called a multiplexer) that enables multiple simultaneous camera shots (i.e., four, nine, or sixteen shots) to be viewed at the same time.

A multiplexer is a device for sending several different transmission streams down a single communications link and for splitting a received multiple stream into component parts. This can be helpful if there are a large number of cameras in the facility. Another use of a multiplexer is to record several camera images simultaneously. It will synchronize the camera signals and mark each one with a code, allowing each camera to be replayed separately, irrespective of how many camera images were recorded.

The three main components of a CCTV system are the camera, transmission media, and monitor. The camera design and lens capabilities are the key components for successfully capturing movement. The transmission media, such as cabling, is used to transmit the camera images to the display monitor. First, let's look at the camera and lens capabilities.

Camera and Lens. The goal of the camera and lens is to capture an optical image and convert the image into a video signal that is then transmitted to a remote monitor display. The selection of the camera and the type of lens is based on various physical and environmental considerations, such as the size of the image that needs to be displayed, the natural and unnatural lighting, and the ability to focus on images when motion occurs.

Today, the most common camera type is a charge-coupled discharge (CCD) camera. Older cameras used a cathode ray tube (CRT) design and were referred to as tube cameras (brand names include Vidicon, Ultricon, and Newvicon). In a tube camera, a vacuum tube image was used to convert reflected light into electrical impulses. The CCD cameras provide an advantage over the tube camera by forming a better camera scene. CCD cameras have a light-sensitive integrated circuit that stores and displays the data for an image. Each picture element (pixel) is converted into an electrical charge related to a color in the color spectrum. Because CCDs generate less heat within them, the electronic components last longer and thus have a much longer life expectancy (5 to 25 years). Also used are infrared cameras, which provide night-vision capabilities that use the difference in temperature of scene objects to produce a video image.

In addition to the camera, various types of camera lenses are available. The camera lens can be either fixed (called fixed focal length) or zoom lens. Fixed lenses include manual, motorized, motorized with auto-iris, and others. Wide ranges of focal lengths and lens speeds are available. A zoom lens, such as 16 to 160 mm, allows the user to change the field of view without changing the lenses. The adjustment can be made either manually or with a motorized remote control. This allows one area to be viewed from a wide angle, then zoomed in for telephoto viewing of just one portion of the area.

An element of the lens is the iris. The iris opens or closes the aperture to control the light level passing through the lens to the camera. It can be controlled either manually or automatically. For example, a manual iris can be used in an area where the level of light is fixed, such as inside an office building. Because an automatic iris self-adjusts optically to light level changes, it can be useful in an area where there are variations in the expected light level. Many security cameras are installed with fixed exposure, so that changes in background lighting do not cause objects near the camera to be darkened and not distinguishable.

There are also pinhole lenses that are designed for covert use. The lens and camera are kept out of view so that anyone entering the area will not know they are being watched. These types of camera can be mounted in a wall, door, or ceiling.

The most important element about lenses is to understand depth-of-field (also called focal length) and field-of-view (see Exhibit 10). These concepts can be helpful when determining the proper lens for each location. The placement of exterior cameras requires more attention than that of interior cameras because of weather and illumination extremes. The field-of-view alignment, illumination range, and balanced lighting are major design factors.

Depth-of-field is the area between the nearest and farthest points that appear to be in focus. When a CCTV camera is focused on an object at a specific range, there are other objects both nearer and farther that are also in focus. As the focal length of the lens increases, the depth-of-field decreases. Depth-of-field becomes critical as light level decreases. As the aperture opens to compensate for the low light, the depth-of-field shortens.

Field-of-view is the entire area that can be captured by the camera lens. Once the field-of-view spreads to a certain distance, the low resolution at the outer areas can make the camera and lens unusable for assessing events.

Cameras and Lighting. One of the first steps in determining what camera to use is to identify the illumination available at the scene. To do this, a light meter (device that captures light in either foot candles or lux) can be used to identify the amount of light available at various times, such as full daylight, overcast day, dusk, twilight, full moon, moonless, etc. A second aspect is the amount of reflected light in the scene. For example, a black asphalt surface will reflect less light than the same surface covered with snow. To get a true picture of how much light is needed, multiply the

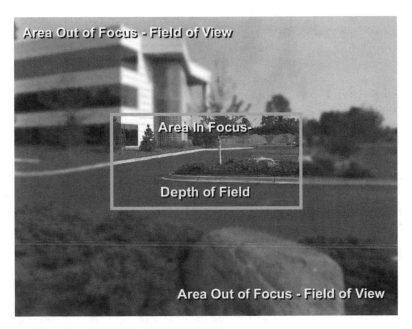

Exhibit 10. Depth-of-Field and Field-of-View

minimum amount of light available (an overcast day) and the percentage of reflection of the observed area (fresh snow).

> *Illumination and camera sensitivity are often listed in foot candles (fc) or lux (lx). To convert fc to lux, it is acceptable to approximate; thus,1 fc = 1 lx (0.0929 fc = 1 lx). For example, if a camera needs to see a scene with 1 fc of illumination against old concrete, which has a reflection of 25%, the light sensitivity rating would need to be 0.025 fc or 2.5 lx (Colombo, 2000).*

The lighting surrounding the CCTV camera must be sufficient for images to be viewed accurately. If a camera is placed in an interior location and the scene illumination is constant, then it is best to specify the manually adjustable iris. This allows a manual iris adjustment appropriate for each particular area's illumination level at the time of installation. If a camera is placed in an exterior (outside of a building) location that is subject to a wide dynamic range of illumination levels, it is best to specify the automatically adjusted iris feature. This allows the camera lens iris to adjust to the present lighting conditions.

Lights should never be pointed at CCTV cameras. Often, cameras are mounted on poles or on a building at an elevation that is above the elevation of lighting fixtures. The lighting fixtures themselves often have recessed lamps or point down and away from the cameras to avoid having the camera's auto-iris feature close the lens, thereby reducing available light and providing poor contrast.

Transmission Media. Several transmission media can be used to transmit the video signal from the camera to the monitor. A security concern is the possibility that the transmission media may be tampered with by intruders to hide their entry. The most common type of cable is coaxial cable because it is readily available and inexpensive. Fiber-optic cables can be used to extend the distances and provide clearer transmission resolution. Other types use wireless transmission systems such as microwave or laser beams. (Recently, the risks involved with wireless transmission [explained in Chapter 8] have led several organizations to restrict the use of wireless transmissions for perimeter security transmissions.)

Display Monitors. The CCTV monitor converts and displays the electronic signals transmitted over the transmission media. An important characteristic of CCTV monitors is to receive a crisp, highly detailed picture from the security cameras. When looking at types of monitors, vendors offer capabilities such as a number of lines per second. For background information, the following standards apply to video systems. In the United States and Japan, the National Television Systems Committee (NTSC) specifies 525 horizontal lines of interlace scanning at 30 frames per second. In Europe, Australia, and parts of Africa and the Middle East, the Phase Alternative Line (PAL) specifies 625 horizontal lines of interlace scanning at 25 frames per second (International Radio Consultative Committee standard). The French television standard, Sequential Couleur A'Memorie (Sequential Color and Memory; SECAM), has similar specifications as PAL (black and white is the same, while color encoding is different). One of the newest standards is High-Definition Television (HDTV). Although CCTV monitors and television monitors share similar characteristics, they are not the same. Televisions are designed to receive broadcasts signals, while CCTV monitors are designed to receive composite video signals directly from a coaxial or fiber cable (or wireless link). Another difference is the life expectancy of a CCTV monitor. Because a CCTV monitor is used 24 hours a day, 7 days a week, a commercial-grade CCTV monitor is needed to get maximum efficiency.

Depending on where the monitor is located, the size of the monitor may be an important consideration. How far away will the person be who is monitoring the images? If personnel are two to three feet away, a nine-inch monitor may be sufficient; however, if personnel are 12 feet away, a 15-inch monitor is needed. As a general rule, if personnel are farther away, the monitor should be larger. Deciding on whether to use a black-and-white or color monitor will depend on the security needs of the organization and what types of detail are needed from the images.

In addition to the camera, transmission media, and monitor, several other types of equipment are included in CCTV systems. These include:

- *Pan and tilt units.* These devices are designed for remote control positioning of cameras in both the horizontal (pan) and vertical (tilt) planes. The devices are available in either fixed- or variable-speed versions.
- *Panning device.* These devices rotate the camera back and forth in the horizontal plane only, although the camera tilt position could be manually adjustable. Auto panning devices provide an oscillating surveillance sweep back and forth across a preselected area or field-of-view.
- *Mountings.* The camera support mounting can be a horizontal or suspended ceiling mount, fixed or adjustable mount, or indoor/outdoor mount — there are mountings available for every possible application.
- *Multiplexers or switchers.* These combine several cameras onto a single line or allow selected viewing of multiple cameras. They allow personnel to switch between cameras — either manually or automatically.
- *Controls.* These include single, multiple, digital, and microprocessor-based controls that provide for remote operation of pan and tilt units, scanners, lenses, infrared illuminators, etc.
- *Infrared illuminators.* These are not visible to the human eye and are used in low-light conditions to provide greater viewing capability.
- *Time/date generators.* These generators automatically insert the time and date onto the video film. Most offer the capability to display and record the time in hours, minutes, seconds, and hundredths of a second.
- *Videotape recorders.* Capabilities are based on length of time and quality of image. Recording the images can significantly increase the cost, especially for time-lapse recorders and purchasing tapes and cameras that will produce images of a significant quality. Digital recording devices are replacing time-lapse video recorders.
- *Digital recorders.* These devices use compression techniques and hard drives (no tapes). They offer enhanced search features, including motion sensing, speedy time searching, selective pixel change, and light changes.

Another option for the CCTV system is to install video motion detectors. The sensors detect and report movement. Essentially, an alarm is activated when there are changes detected on the viewable image from the camera. However, this is not as effective as a dedicated motion detection system.

Computers are also used to preprogram and automate CCTV systems. The functions include items such as entering date/time notices, or directing automatic switching functions. These systems can provide expanded capabilities, ease of operation, and greater flexibility.

The key to a successful CCTV system lies in understanding the facility's total surveillance requirements. This requires a site survey to know where the cameras should be placed for maximum effectiveness. Also, for total facility control and effective use of the equipment, it is important that there is both an automatic and human intervention. The speed of the lens used, the system's resolution capabilities, and the field-of-view are all characteristics of the equipment that determine how well the system is able to meet the expectations of its performance.

The size of the area to be monitored must also be taken into consideration. Thus, the depth, height, and width of the area should be measured to determine the necessary field-of-view of the camera lens. These measurements impact the size of the lens that is needed. The field-of-view is a function of the size of the scene (the height × width) and the distance between the camera lens and the image sensor. This field-of-view calculation, pan/tilt speed, and the size of the image tube determine what the lens length should be.

Characteristics of the scene being viewed also affect the quality of the image and the choice of equipment to be used. Thus, lighting is important for successful CCTV systems. Different lamps and lighting will provide various levels of effectiveness of the system after dark. Lamp types include filament, tungsten-halogen, fluorescent, sodium discharge, and high-intensity discharge lamps that use mercury, metal halide, and high-pressure sodium. (Note that a disadvantage of high-density discharge lamps is if there is a slight power interruption, they do not provide illumination for several minutes.) Each kind of light source produces light of different wavelengths or colors. Natural light and tungsten lamps fall in the sensitivity range of most cameras. Also, knowing what type of light exists in an area to be covered by CCTV is important, as is knowing what type of illumination is needed to get a suitable image. For example, the camera should not be pointed at a light source. Also, if the camera is on a horizontal plane with the sun rising or setting, the intensity may burn into the camera image. A good point to remember is that cameras should be above what you want to see, pointed down, and the light fixtures should be outside the field-of-view.

The lighting of the scene as well as the contrast between the objects being watched and the background of the scene are influential factors. For example, in a dimly lit area, detecting a person dressed in clothing of approximately the same color or darkness as the background is different from detecting someone wearing dark clothes against a light-colored background. The relative "busy-ness" of the area also affects image quality. A cluttered scene makes detecting specifics with CCTV difficult. For example, spotting movement against a busy background is more difficult than spotting movement in front of a contrasting background.

Building Entry Points

Facility Wall Structures

In addition to mandatory building codes, there are security requirements for the outside building structure. The total area of the building includes all openings, walls, ceilings, roofs, floors, and basements.

Basic kinds of building construction include:

- *Light frame:* typical of most houses; fire survival ability is rated as 30 minutes.
- *Heavy timber:* structural elements with a minimum thickness of four inches with a fire survival ability of one hour.
- *Incombustible:* steel constructed, fire survival will weaken based on high temperatures that cause the steel to lose its strength and then cause the structure to collapse (the exact reason that led to the collapse of the World Trade Center).
- *Fire resistant:* structural elements are incombustible and concrete encases steel for added protection.

Building materials must be solid and offer penetration resistance to, and evidence of, unauthorized entry.

Doors

There are several methods of gaining entry through a locked door, such as through sheer brute force — that is, kicking in the door. Another is prying open the door using a tool such as a crowbar, jimmy bar, a large screwdriver, or, in some cases, a credit card or wire loop. Many lock cylinders can be easily pried out of the lockset with a minimal amount of effort. A high-security lock or an external guard plate installed over the cylinder facing will protect against this. The quality of the door, frame, and hinges, and how it is installed are critical factors for protecting against unauthorized entry.

Hollow-Core versus Solid-Core Doors. A typical door is a hollow-core wood door that contains a top and bottom rail as well as stiles. The top and bottom rails are the main horizontal structural members, and the stiles are the vertical structural members. They usually have a lock rail somewhere near the midpoint. The lock rail allows the lockset (lock and knob or handle) to be installed in a solid portion of the door. The doors are usually constructed of thin sheets or panels of wood veneer covering either side of an inner lightweight frame. Hollow-core doors are only slightly less resistant to attack than drywall. They can be easily kicked in, cut, or sawed.

A solid-core door is one in which the structural inner part of the door is solid. This inner core can be made of a variety of materials, such as a mineral-based material that is used in fire-rated doors, particleboard, wood blocks, or composition materials. Whether hollow or solid core, all doors have face panels on the exterior. In critically sensitive environments, such as data centers or server rooms, it is better to have solid-core doors. Doors should offer resistance to forced entry and, if necessary, reinforcement may be required for doorjambs (the top and two sides of a door or window frame that contact the door) or for the doorframe. It is not usually recommended to put a solid-core door in a wall made only of gypsum drywall. An intruder can literally kick through the drywall and bypass the solid-core door.

The door is installed in a doorframe. At the top of the frame is a header, also sometimes referred to as a head frame. The side on which the lock fits is called the strike frame, and it is where the strike plate for the lock is installed. The side in which the hinges are set is the hinge frame. At the bottom are the sill and threshold. For security purposes, hinges and strike plates on exterior doors should be firmly secured. Hinge pins should be welded or pinned in place.

The doorframe is often the weakest point in a typical door assembly. Because of this weakness, it is usually the first point of attack for intruders. Doors can be kicked in or pried from the frame. The frame can also be weakened over time by standard use. Frames may shrink or separate from the door; wood is subject to weather conditions and may dry, crack, or rot (doors swell with moisture and contract with dryness); and fasteners may corrode or otherwise deteriorate. Even a solid-core door with strong locks can be easily defeated if mounted in a weak frame.

Emergency Panic Bars. Panic bars, also referred to as emergency exit bars/devices or touch-bars, are door-locking devices designed to allow instant exit by pressing on a cross bar that releases the locking bolt. Several disasters have occurred in buildings when non-primary exit doors have been secured to keep intruders out, but have also prevented exit during emergency situations. For this reason, panic bars and emergency exit devices are designed (often by having lock hardware only on one side) to allow safe exit but controlled entrance.

Contact or Switch Devices. Often, some type of signaling device is required on a door or window to indicate whether it is open or closed. This is usually a switch (i.e., an electrical circuit) that can be activated by pressure or by a magnetic field. When the door or window is open, the switch is opened or closed and triggers the alarm signal. The devices can be installed in both surface and flush-type mountings.

Mantraps. A mantrap system interlocks two controlled doors and routes personnel through the double-doored facility. The key characteristic is that only one door should be opened at a time. The designs specify that the inner door will not unlock if the outer door is open, or vice versa. Usually, the person produces some type of identification to enter through the second door. This might include showing a badge, swiping an access control card, or some type of biometric device. If the identification cannot be made, the person is trapped between the two doors and cannot enter or leave until a security officer intercedes.

Windows

The most common type of window in residential homes is standard plate glass. It is easy to cut for any size window and can shatter into dangerous jagged shards if broken. The next level up is tempered glass, which is five to seven times more break resistant. Once cut or pierced at any point, it shatters into small fragments. Because of this shattering, tempered glass must be pre-formed to the exact size of the window (i.e., it cannot be cut to size like plate glass).

Windows can also be made from acrylic material. Standard acrylics are not as strong as polycarbonate acrylics, but they are more resistant to breakage than standard plate glass. The disadvantages to acrylic are that they support flames and produce toxic fumes if burned; scratch easily; and can be drilled, cut, or sawed. Polycarbonate windows are made from lightweight, see-through plastic that is 20 times stronger than standard acrylic of the same thickness. Glass-clad polycarbonate combines the best qualities of glass and acrylics. Windows made from glass-clad polycarbonate are resistant to abrasion, chemicals, fires, and are even anti-ballistic. Because they are expensive, they are usually limited to high-security areas.

For windows, shatter-resistant, laminated glass of a minimum thickness should be used. Also, the windows should be installed in fixed frames so that the windowpanes are not removable from the outside. It is essential that window frames are securely anchored in the wall, and windows can be locked from the inside. If the organization has high-security needs, windows could be alarmed, contain steel wire mesh, or be protected by steel bars.

Security controls for windows include:

* *Laminated glass.* Glass is made by bonding a plastic inner layer between two outer layers of glass under high pressure and heat. When the glass layer is broken, it does not separate significantly from the bonding layer. Increasing the number of layers can strengthen its resistance to impact. For example, if the layers are increased to a half-inch, it is considered burglar resistant and, if an

inch thick, it is considered resistant to bullets from a small-caliber gun. It is more expensive than plate or tempered glass and cannot be easily cut; thus, it is usually ordered to size. As an example, in the United States, most car windows, except the windshield, are tempered glass. The windshield is usually made from laminated glass to provide better protection.

- *Wired glass.* Glass is made by embedding a continuous sheet of wire mesh between two layers of ordinary glass. The glass tends to cling to the wire mesh, which prevents it from shattering if broken.
- *Solar window films.* Materials that are affixed to windows to, for the most part, offer window efficiency for heating and cooling purposes. They filter out the majority of the sun's damaging ultraviolet rays and also offer security features by preventing those on the outside from viewing activities on the inside. They also improve security by protecting the glass from shattering if broken. Solar films are used on both building and vehicle windows. Note that films can be damaged by cleaning chemicals, mechanical wash brushes, and harmful environmental conditions such as ultraviolet sunlight.
- *Window security film.* Similar to solar film, this commercially available film is a transparent overlay applied over a window to protect it from unwanted entries, storm damage, and in some cases, bomb blasts. It is similar to transparent contact paper and keeps the glass underneath it from fragmenting. It is the most effective way to improve the integrity of plate and tempered glass windows.
- *Glass breakage sensors.* Small specialty microphones are tuned to the resonant frequency of breaking glass.

Locks

The lock is the most accepted and used physical security device. Locks are considered delay devices and not foolproof bars to entry. They keep honest people out, but for unauthorized people who wish to gain access, most locks are easily bypassed and most keys can be readily duplicated. Although it may take time and expertise to break the lock, all lock types are subject to force and there are a variety of special tools that can be used to gain entry. Because of these vulnerabilities, locking systems should be just one aspect of many physical controls.

Before describing locks, it is important to note the vulnerability of locks. The basic lock-picking tools are the tension wrench and the pick; either can be bought from locksmith supply houses or made at home. The tension wrench imparts a rotary motion to the key plug of the lock and aids in finding the locking tumblers of the lock. The pick is used to move the binding tumblers, one at a time, to the shear line. When all tumblers are aligned properly with the shear line, the lock opens.

Another technique to defeat locks is called raking and is considered much easier than actually picking a lock. To "rake" a lock, a pick with a wider tip is inserted all the way to the back of the plug. The pick is quickly pulled out so that it bounces all of the pins up on its way out. As the rake exits, you turn the plug using a tension wrench. Some of the upper pins, while moving up and down, will happen to fall on the ledge created by the turning plug. Because it is easier to rake a lock, locksmiths will start by raking the pins, and then pick any remaining pins individually.

The typical lockset consists of the lock body, the strike, and the key. The lock body is the metal casing that encloses the cylinder and holds the protruding bolt that actually fastens the door. The cylinder consists of a key plug enclosed in its own barrel and is attached to the lock bolt by a cam at the outer edge of the lock body. The strike and strike plate form a separate rectangular metal piece that is inserted into the doorjamb. The strike plate contains the strike that is the slot to receive the matching bolt attached to the lock body. The key matches the tumblers in the lock's cylinder and releases them from the locked position. The cylinder accepts the key and causes the bolt to move in or out of its receptacle in the strike. The tumblers inside the cylinder come in various forms, but are usually tiny metal rods or pins that prevent the key plug from rotating, unless the key is inserted.

Lock cylinders are rated as low security, medium security, and high security. High-security cylinders use special keyways and tumbler arrangements to resist picking, drilling, or other mechanical attacks. A good security cylinder is the Medeco cylinder. It uses a double-locking system involving both cylinder pins and a sidebar with projections that move into matching slots in the bottom of the tumblers. The result is a system with a pin that has both depth and rotational angle. Also, Medeco keys are not easily duplicated, requiring special cutting machines with limited distribution.

The type of lock system used depends on what needs to be protected, the identified threat, existing barriers, and other protection measures. When reviewing locks, it is best to look closely at the lock specifications to ensure they will meet the organization's security needs.

How easy is it to pick a lock? Quite — picking a lock can be quite simple; thus, locks are said to be pick resistant, not pickproof.

The types of locking devices are:

- *Key locks.* A key lock requires a key to open the lock. An expert, in a few minutes, can pick most key locks.
  - One type of key-operated lock is the "warded lock." Wards are defined as obstructions in the keyhole (and/or inside the lock) that prevent all but the properly cut key from entering or working

the lock. The key must have the proper ward cuts to bypass the wards in the keyhole. There are keys, sometimes called skeleton keys, that are made to bypass the wards.

–   Wafer or disc tumbler locks are used on most automobiles, desks, and cabinets. Several wafers are located in the core or plug of the lock. The wafers are under spring tension and protrude outside the diameter of the plug into a shell formed by the body of the lock. This keeps the plug from turning and keeping the lock locked. Insertion of the proper key causes the wafers to be pulled out of the shell into the diameter of the plug, thereby allowing the plug to be turned. If a wafer lock is in a door or a desk and has a spring-operated bolt, it is usually easy to circumvent. If it is in an automobile, the lock can often be picked open.

–   Pin tumbler locks are used extensively in commercial, military, and residential security and are more secure than warded and wafer tumbler locks. The key moves pins so that a shear line can be obtained, thus allowing the key to turn the plug and operate the lock.

–   Interchangeable cores use a lock with a core that can be removed and replaced by another core using a special-change key. This is helpful in making multiple locks work with the same key.

- *Combination locks.* Using a sequence of numbers in a specific order opens a combination lock. The lock contains wheels and a dial-face. The more wheels, the better the protection; for example, those with four or more wheels offer higher penetration resistance.

- *Electronic combination locks.* There are several new electronic combination locks on the market that do not use wheels. They have a digital readout and obtain their operating power from the energy generated by turning the dial. While they do offer a higher level of security, they are currently much more expensive than the older-style, wheel-type combination locks.

- *Deadbolt locks.* A bolt is inserted into the frame of the door for added security. To be most effective, the bolt of the latch should be applied so that the bolt slides into the door-casing frame or into a keeper firmly attached to the doorframe. Combination locks can also be deadbolt locks.

- *Keyless locks.* Push-button locks have buttons that are pushed in sequence to open the lock. Digital push-button locks are sometimes called cipher locks (Simplex is a brand name and is often used to describe push-button locks). The advantage of push-button locks is that there are no key control issues. The disadvantages are that the combination must be remembered, someone may be able to watch the input of the combination, the buttons for the code always show more wear than the unused buttons, and the combination code must be changed periodically. In addition, the combination must be shared; this means any person with the code can enter — therefore, no accountability. This may be acceptable in some situations, but not others.

- *Smart locks.* Smart locks are designed to permit only authorized people into certain doors, at certain times. An example is the key system used in some hotels. The key is a plastic card that is programmed at a central computer to permit the guest access into a specific door. Another type of smart lock is the combination keypad–electronic deadbolt. It replaces the manual deadbolt in the door to provide keyless entry. To lock the door, simply touch the lock button on the keypad and the deadbolt slides into place. To unlock the door, enter the combination and the deadbolt slides into the unlocked position. An alarm can be added that will activate after consecutive incorrect codes are entered.

Lock Security Measures. Effective control must be maintained to ensure that locks, keys, and combinations are used appropriately. One of the important issues is having a lock-and-key control system. Key control procedures must be documented and followed. Accurate records must be maintained that identify who had access to the keys. Procedures for issue, sign-out, inventory, and destruction, as well as appropriate procedures for dealing with lost keys, must be established.

Combinations must be changed at specified times and under specified circumstances. For example, combinations to safe locks should be changed at least every 12 months, when possible compromise has occurred, or when someone who knew the combination has left the facility.

Relocking Devices. Relocking devices offer special protection against attempted intrusions. A relocking device responds to tampering by triggering additional locking mechanisms.

Master Keying. A master key system (Exhibit 11) can be used in a large organization or facility, and contains a "master key" and a series of "submaster keys." The master key opens all the locks in the system, although each lock also has its own unique key. To do this, locks are designed to work with two different keys. The submaster key will open only that specific lock, while the master key will open that lock and several others in a group. This type of scheme permits organizing master key systems along departmental or other functional lines to allow supervisory or emergency access.

When locks are master-keyed, a plan must be developed that establishes the scope of the keys. The plan begins with identifying the master and submaster keys, describing the existing doors, identifying the users and what

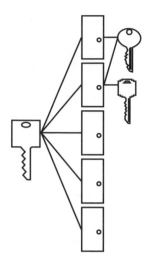

Exhibit 11. Master Keys

access is required, and the quantities of each key. Other guidelines for a master key system include:

- The security officer in charge of facility security should be aware of the master key plan for the lock system and know how keys are distributed to the users.
- Measures must be in place for controlling who has access to the master or submaster keys.
- The security requirements for the storage of such keys must be documented and users must be trained.
- All perimeter doors should be keyed alike and not placed on the master key system.
- Restricted access areas should be keyed differently and not placed on the master key system.
- All utility rooms should be keyed alike in groups.

Guard Stations

High-level guard stations are specially constructed enclosures that are often manned 24 hours per day, seven days a week. They are equipped to monitor the security of the facility through TV monitors, alarm systems, intercoms, automatic photographing of persons entering the facility, radio police scanners tuned to emergency channels, and radio devices such as walkie-talkies for emergency communications. In a high-threat environment, they are constructed with bulletproof walls, doors, or windows.

Guards, or some type of security force, can provide deterrence and a flexible security and safety response in the event of an unauthorized intrusion or other incident. Questions to consider when deciding on whether a security force is needed are:

- Is hiring or contracting more cost-effective?
- Should the guards be certified or licensed?
- Should the guards be armed or unarmed?
- Are there union considerations?
- What personnel screening procedures does the guard agency or the company use?
- Is bonding necessary?
- Is specific training required?
- Is insurance impacted?

Annunciation Panels

Annunciation panels are used to display signals of abnormal conditions in electrical power, fire detectors, water detectors, power generators, coolant pumps, and entry and intrusion detection systems.

Card Access Control or Biometric Systems

It is very popular today to use some type of card access control system. In a card access system, the user presents a unique card to a card reader at a controlled location. The reader extracts information from the card, which translates that information into a code number and sends it to the main processing center. The number is compared with the card or user's programmed access criteria and either grants or denies entry. (*Note:* Card-based access control does not imply that the user is the "owner" of the card — only that the card is valid to access the desired area.) A biometric device is similar; however, instead of a card used for access, a biometric characteristic, such as a fingerprint or retinal pattern, is used. For more information on card access and biometric controls, refer to the Access Control chapter (Chapter 3).

Inside the Building: Building Floors, Office Suites, Offices

Supply System Controls

Electric Power Controls. Because all electronic equipment needs electrical power to operate, the security controls for electrical power require specific technical training and expert consultants. However, the CISSP should be aware of some basic control concepts.

Surge Suppressors. Surge suppressors originally were designed to prevent (potentially) the most destructive power disturbances — sudden spikes or surges that damage microprocessor circuitry. A surge protector acts as a filter to stop the surge by sending the excess power to the ground.

Thus, the incoming power never exceeds optimal levels. Eliminating electric power surges can extend the service life of electrical equipment by over 50%. Because electronic equipment located inside the building can also create power surges and fluctuations, point-of-service protectors that plug into the wall socket between the building system and the equipment may also be needed.

Controlling Interference. To control interference, a single-socket stand-alone power line filter suppressor or a wire-in filter suppressor will solve the problem. Industrial equipment may require twist-type, extreme duty, or other high-current filter suppressors. It is important to install filter-suppressor equipment on problematic equipment.

Verify that all required grounding is in place and that grounding screws are securely tightened. Providing shielding to power lines can help to protect against EMI and RFI.

Uninterruptible Power Supply (UPS). An essential element for today's power system is a UPS. A UPS, from a battery or generator, provides clean power in the event of a shutdown or lengthy interruption from the primary source of electrical power. UPSs range from a small battery that will provide minutes of power to large diesel generators that will provide unlimited hours of power.

Manufacturers offer a wide range of UPSs and related protection equipment for just about every environment. Keep in mind that different requirements are needed for a workstation, such as small stand-alone UPS, while more power is needed for servers and clustered network nodes. Because stand-alone solutions are not the most efficient, most organizations connect networks to a large, full-featured UPS.

It is important to first think about what you are trying to protect and what is needed. For example, a network server needs enough power for a graceful shutdown; this is called a "fail soft." A telecommunication system that may need to stay operational for a longer time period may need a generator that provides power for hours.

Whether it is a generator or other form of backup power, it should meet the organization's requirements for lighting, physical security systems, fire detection/protection systems, HVAC systems, computers and communication equipment, proprietary telephone systems, etc. Remember that UPS systems need maintenance. In the event of a very extended outage, a generator will need fuel. This must be figured into the plan and operation of the system. As a monthly test, the facility should be operated on the backup generator for a predetermined timeframe to ensure it will be ready when needed.

Static Controls. Static is minimized by controlling the humidity. Anti-static mats under chairs and machines may be necessary for low-humidity climates, as well as anti-static carpet with special filaments to reduce static electricity in data centers or server rooms. Anti-static sprays can also help control static around computer equipment.

Good Practices. The goal of an installation's electrical power system design and installation is to provide "clean power" (no noise or voltage fluctuations) at appropriate levels and quality, without interruption. This goal is usually met by:

- Receiving power from the primary power source (the source that provides day-to-day power to information system operations; i.e., the power company)
- Having an alternate power source in the event of a failure of the primary power source
- Having dedicated feeder(s) and dedicated circuits from one or more utility substations or power grids
- Having access controls for the location of the equipment, especially for the distribution panels, master circuit breakers, and transformers/feeder cables
- Having an Emergency Power Off (EPO) switch that is readily accessible in case of an emergency that requires someone inside the building to shut down the power (in some cases, this may be a building code requirement)
- Installing a line filter on the computer's main power supply to regulate the flow of power
- Installing a power line monitor that detects and records frequency and voltage amplitude changes
- Installing a power regulator to condition the line to keep voltage steady and also provide filtering for noise
- Conducting tests on the power capacities by using voltage monitors and recorders
- Ensuring there is enough backup power to conduct an orderly shutdown to avoid data loss or device damage
- Avoiding inrush current problems by not switching all equipment on simultaneously, especially after a shutdown
- Keeping strong magnets away from computers; magnetic interference can create problems
- Avoiding fluorescent lights (noisy ballasts) near electrical circuitry
- Prohibiting radio/TV use near computer equipment to reduce RFI
- Shielding long cable runs and nearby electric motors

Keep in mind that electrical requirements are often regulated and must be adhered to for specific equipment. For example, life support equipment is typically regulated and must meet certain electrical conditions and requirements (i.e., filtered outlets, etc.). Also, there are special conditions for large UPS systems using lead acid batteries. Battery rooms must be secured, have limited access, and have Self-Contained Breathing Apparatus (SCBA) equipment available both inside and outside the room.

HVAC Controls. The air conditioning controls for a data center or server room should be separated from other controls for the building. This allows for greater control in areas that contain sensitive equipment. Thus, separate automatic humidity and temperature monitoring devices should be installed in these areas. Also, if possible, the computer facility should have an air conditioning system that is independent of the rest of the building.

The control centers or the rooms containing HVAC equipment should be monitored for ease of access. Penetration by intruders into the building's support systems area, such as electrical room, heating system, furnace areas, ductwork on the roof, and underground ventilation shafts, could enable them to shut down the entire facility.

Maintenance procedures for HVAC services should include documentation of all activity. Records should be kept for at least one year and reviewed quarterly. The reports should contain faults, actions, resolutions, expansions, upgrades, and any change in capability or function.

Water Control. Because water and computers do not mix, controls should be in place to limit damage. Simple things — such as making sure the computer room is not located next to or directly below areas where floods might occur — can reduce the possibility of damage. Also, check for pipes under raised floors that could damage equipment if they leaked. In situations where they cannot be checked, water detection sensors are a must.

If the location is prone to flooding, the data center or server room and physical security control center should be located well above ground level — never placed underground in basements. In hilly areas, the center should be located at the high end of the slope and well above ground level.

Consider emergency shut-off valves as requirements for chilled water. In the event of an emergency, the shut-off valve would automatically stop the flow of water in the pipeline; this could ensure the safety of the water supply in the system and prevent any outside contaminants from infiltrating the water supply.

In the event of water damage, to prevent problems with mold and mildew, it may be necessary to hire/contract high-powered air movers and commercial dehumidifiers combined with authorized water damage disinfectants and sanitizers to reduce the potential health hazards.

Gas Lines. If the facility has natural gas, the following safety precautions should be implemented:

- Identify the location of the natural gas main incoming shut-off valve.
- Verify that the shut-off valves are operational. In some locations, shut-off valves have not been moved in years and may even be inoperable. Special sealants and equipment may be needed to keep the valves operational.
- Identify the main shut-off valve in some manner. This could be especially important if several shut-off valves are located in the same area, such as for gas or water.
- If required, attach a shut-off wrench or tool to a location near the shut-off valve.
- The incoming natural gas main line should be secured in a fenced and locked area and have appropriate access controls.
- Know your natural gas distribution system to identify how the piping is networked and where system shut-off valves are located throughout the building. Make sure that the shut-off valves are accessible.
- Communicate the location of the shut-off valves to the local fire department.
- Paint shut-off valves with white or fluorescent paint to increase visibility.

Fire Protection

Fire Prevention, Detection, and Suppression Controls. Fire prevention refers to avoiding any problems with fire before they occur. If prevention does not work, fire detection becomes the primary concern. The goal of fire detection is to realize there is a fire while it is small and controllable. Fire containment and suppression are the last layers of control and involve how to deal with a fire in the event of an emergency. Containment uses fire barriers (floor to ceiling walls), vents, dampers, and the HVAC system to keep the fire and smoke from spreading. Suppression uses either fixed or portable extinguishing systems. All of these combined make up "fire protection," which refers to detecting fires and minimizing the damage to people and equipment if a fire should occur. Life safety issues include communications, alarms, routes of exit, and refuge areas. Keep in mind that building occupants must be successfully removed from the danger area and the firefighters must be able to gain access to the fire area.

Fire Prevention. Most cities/counties have fire codes that outline specific requirements for minimum fire prevention measures. The materials used in construction should be as fireproof as possible. For example, doors can be fireproof up to a specified amount of time. Combustible materials (e.g., stacks of paper) should not be stored in computer rooms or around electrical equipment. A false ceiling should not be flammable. An option is to install fireproof walls and doors to help prevent a fire from spreading into a data center, server room, or other critical processing areas. Floor-to-ceiling walls should be installed to prevent the rapid spread of fire.

Magnetic tapes, if ignited, produce poisonous gases when they burn. Thus, backup tapes and software should be stored in fireproof containers, preferably in an off-site location. Critical documents should also be stored in fireproof containers to minimize the extent of damage in the event of a fire.

Another prevention measure is to provide fire-prevention training to employees. The training should include information on how to prevent fires, as well as what to do in case of a fire, such as how to exit the building, where extinguishing equipment is located, and the location of emergency power shut-offs. Remember, however, that life safety is the most important issue. The primary concern is to ensure that all persons leave the building safely in the event of a fire emergency.

Fire prevention training also includes fire drills. As part of the security plan, periodic fire drills should be practiced to ensure that people know how to safely exit the building. In addition, if individuals are required to shut off emergency power or other switches, they should know how to per-form the task while safely exiting the building. These drills should be con-ducted during all shifts — not only during normal daytime working hours. Also, it is typically a requirement to notify people of any drill or system testing.

Fire Detection. Fire detection systems are readily available and effective. Ionization-type smoke detectors react to the charged particles in smoke. Photoelectric detectors react to light blockage caused by smoke. Heat detectors react to the heat of a fire. Combinations of these detectors can detect a fire very quickly, often before it is a critical problem. Again, if the fire is detected, the first rule is to get the people out.

Fire Suppression. There are several types of fire-extinguishing systems that can be used for fire suppression (see Exhibit 12). Portable fire extin-guishers should be available near any electrical equipment. For computer equipment, type ABC extinguishers are appropriate because combustible solids (class A), combustible liquids (class B), and electricity (class C) are all common in computer room fires. The primary purpose of portable fire extinguishers is to provide an escape route so that people can get out. If a fire is small enough, the portable extinguishers can be used to extinguish the fire; however, attempts should only be made by trained personnel, after the evacuation of all other people.

Exhibit 12. Fire Classes

Class	Type	Suppression
A	Common combustibles (i.e., wood products, laminates)	Water, soda acid
B	Liquid (i.e., petroleum products, coolants)	Gas (Halon/Halon substitutes), CO_2, soda acid
C	Electrical (i.e., electrical equipment, wires)	Gas (Halon/Halon substitutes), CO_2
D	Combustible metals	Dry powder

Fixed extinguishing systems include carbon dioxide (CO_2) extinguishers, with or without directing hoses. These types of systems are usually expensive and chemically unsafe for people. CO_2 is a colorless, odorless chemical that displaces oxygen, which puts out the fire, but can also harm personnel. CO_2 is best used for unattended facilities; if used in attended facilities, the system should have a built-in delay so that personnel can completely evacuate before the gas is released.

Until 1987, when Canada, the United States, the European Community, and several other nations signed the *Montreal Protocol on Substances That Deplete the Ozone Layer* (subsequently amended in 1990 and 1992), Halon gas was used in fire-suppression systems. The Halon chemical is loaded into some type of dumping system, and when a fire is detected, the Halon is dumped onto the fire. It is a safe system for electronic equipment because it avoids water damage. However, Halon extinguishers contained chlorofluorocarbons (CFCs), which are believed to deplete the ozone layer. The signing of the *Montreal Protocol* put controls on the production and consumption of certain CFCs, including the Halon group, such as Halon 1211, 1301, and 2402.

The United Nations Environment Programme (UNEP) has prepared a *Montreal Protocol Handbook* that provides additional detail and explanation of the provisions. However, for purposes of studying the CISSP CBK, some of the basic principles of the *Montreal Protocol* agreement include:

- Full-scale implementation began in 1992.
- Any new installations of fire-suppression system must use alternative options.
- If testing existing Halon systems, full-discharge testing should be avoided in favor of alternate test procedures, such as a puff test.
- By the year 2000, production of Halon was to be stopped.
- If Halon in an existing system is discharged, it can be replaced from a recycling bank.

Some buildings have automatic sprinkler systems that spray water. One of the problems associated with the use of water for fire suppression in a computer room is that a computer fire usually involves electricity, and unpure water could be a conductor for electricity. Thus, it may compound the problem instead of helping. Although distilled water is not a conductor under normal circumstances, tap water and water that has been in a holding reservoir could contain contaminants. Therefore, if possible, equipment should be shut off before discharging the sprinkler system to avoid shorting out electrical components. Once a computer is wet, it should not be turned on until it is thoroughly dry. If the water is clean, it may be possible to let the computer completely dry and then try to recover any data. Although there is a danger in using water for electrical fires, many countries require the use of water for fire protection. For example, the U.S. Fire Protection and Insurance Industries support the use of water as the primary fire-extinguishing agent for all business environments because it suppresses the fire, regardless of the risk of ruining the electrical equipment.

In some sprinkler systems the water is held back remotely by a valve that is actuated by a sensing system. This is called a "pre-action" or "dry-pipe" system. In conventional (wet-pipe) systems, the water is held back by the sprinkler heads and immediately released when the sensor activates. A conventional system may allow a premature release of water if the sensor malfunctions or the sprinkler head is damaged. Thus, the location of the sprinkler heads should be placed so equipment cabinets and moving equipment cannot accidentally knock off or damage the sprinkler heads. Also, hard water may corrode the sprinkler heads and cause them to fail to discharge the water when the sensor activates.

An important consideration in the design and installation of fire-detection and -suppression systems is the need to control the disbursement of the suppression agent so that specific areas can be targeted. This includes installing detectors in "zones of coverage" that permit quick identification of the specific area where the alarm originated.

Often, to minimize the occurrence of false alarms due to sensor malfunction, disbursement of the suppression agent or sounding of an alarm is activated only when two or more sensors from different zones detect a fire. The second aspect is to have a delay, built into the automatic fire-suppression system, tied into the detectors for a designated period of time. By having a delayed activation, an investigation of the area may be possible to determine what sounded the alarm before releasing the suppressant. This includes having an override feature in the event of a false alarm.

Penetration (Intrusion) Detection Systems

Penetration sensors can be used for additional security protection. They can be installed on windows, doors, ceilings, walls, or any other entry point. The exterior door can be equipped with one or more balanced magnetic switches. The surface of an interior door or wall can be covered with a grid wire sensor or any type of system using the principle of breaking an electric circuit or modifying the electronic characteristics.

Basic types of physical intrusion detection systems include:

- *Breaking or making an electrical circuit*
- *Interrupting a light beam*
- *Detecting sound or changes in sound levels*
- *Detecting vibration*
- *Detecting changes in heat level through passive infrared (PIR) detectors*
- *Detecting a disturbance in an electrostatic, microwave, ultrasonic, or other type field*

The obvious places for penetration detection systems are entry points, such as doors and windows. However, it is wise to consider ventilation openings, construction openings, or air conditioning openings. If an opening must remain open, it is best to place a metal grill over the inside of the opening and install a sensor to deter and detect intruders.

Breaking an Electrical Circuit. Points of entry into the building or floors/offices inside the building can be wired by using electrically sensitized strips of metallic foil or wire. An action that breaks the foil or wire breaks the electrical circuit and activates an alarm. Doors and windows may be equipped with magnetic contact switches that sound an alarm when the door or window is opened. In addition, metallic wire can be installed through panels, walls, or ceilings.

The advantages are that it causes few nuisance alarms and is mostly trouble-free. The disadvantage is that it can be costly to install when there are many entry points.

Interrupting a Light Beam. A photoelectric device uses a light-sensitive cell and a projected light source. The visible or invisible light beam is transmitted at a frequency of several thousand vibrations per second. An infrared filter over the light source makes the beam invisible to intruders. The beam is projected onto the light-sensitive cell (often from a hidden source) and may be criss-crossed by means of hidden mirrors until it reaches the light cell. The cell is connected by wires to a control station. If an intruder crosses the beam, the contact with the photoelectric cell is broken, which activates the alarm.

The advantages are that it is a reliable source of detection and may be useful in open entry points where obstructions cannot be used. The disadvantages are that intruders may be able to climb under or over the beam (by wearing infrared or night-vision goggles enabling them to see the reflective spot) and, if used outside, fog, dust, rain, bright sunlight, or smoke may cause an interruption of the light beam.

Passive Infrared Detectors (PIRs). Infrared detectors emit a certain level of infrared energy in the form of light energy. The light energy in the infrared range is below the visible light spectrum. Infrared technology measures the emission of infrared energy from the area it views through its optical device. Lenses or mirrors are used to focus the received energy on the measuring element. The unit will go into an alarm condition when it measures a change in received energy caused by an intruder. Passive infrared movement detectors will react to the radiation of heat in conjunction with movement. PIR is becoming the preferred technology in motion detection due to the ability and flexibility to control the area viewed through a variety of precision lenses and mirrored optics.

Detecting Sound. Sensitive microphones can be installed on walls, ceilings, and floors to detect any changes in sound volume. The sensor detects any sound caused by attempted forced entry. The advantage is that it is economical and easily installed. The disadvantage is that it must be used in an area that has low extraneous sound (it should not be used outdoors) to avoid an unacceptable frequency of false alarms.

Detecting Vibration. Vibration sensors are attached to walls, ceilings, and floors of the area. The sensors detect any vibration caused by an attempted forced entry. The advantage is that they are economical and flexible. The disadvantage is that they must be used only in areas where a minimum of vibration exists — not next to a railroad station or interstate highway.

Detecting Motion. Motion detection systems that use ultrasonic or microwave motion sensors can be very effective for the protection of interior areas. These systems flood the protected area with acoustic or microwave energy and detect the Doppler shift in transmitted and received frequencies when motion occurs within the area.

Ultrasonic Systems

An ultrasonic system consists of transceivers (contains both a transmitter and receiver), electronic unit, and a control unit. The transmitter generates a pattern of acoustic energy that fills the enclosed room. Motion within the enclosed area disturbs the field and triggers an alarm.

The advantages of ultrasonic systems are that they provide effective security detection against intruders and, because the field is not visible, intruders do not see the system. The disadvantages are that loud external sounds may cause false alarms and it may require a lower sensitivity setting to reduce false alarms in the area.

Microwave Systems

A microwave system is similar to an ultrasonic system. A pattern of radio waves is transmitted and partially reflected back to an antenna. If all objects within the range of the radio waves are stationary, the reflected waves return at the same frequency. If they strike a moving object, they return at a different frequency. If a difference is detected, an alarm signal is initiated.

The advantage of a microwave system is that good coverage can be provided if antennas are properly placed and are not affected by air currents, noise, or sound. A disadvantage is that coverage is not easily confined to an area. The waves may penetrate thin wooden partitions and windows causing an accidental activation by persons outside the protected area. While both ultrasonic and microwave use the same principle to detect motion, a microwave uses a much higher frequency and, as a result, it can detect some motion through walls.

Electrostatic Field. An electrostatic detection system can be installed on a safe, wall, or other item to establish an electrostatic field around the object to be protected. This field is tuned by creating a balance between the electric capacitance and the electric inductance. The body capacitance of any intruder who enters the field unbalances the electrostatic energy of the field and activates the alarm.

The advantages are that it is a flexible system that can be used to protect safes, file cabinets, windows, doors, etc.; it is easy to install and operate; and the field is invisible to the intruder. The disadvantage is that it can only be applied to ungrounded equipment.

Sensor Control Unit Locations. A control unit is required in each secure area to receive signals from the sensors and to transmit signals to the monitor unit and alarm devices. The control unit should be periodically checked to make sure tampering has not occurred.

The alarm device may be either a locally audible alarm or a telephone dial system. A local audible alarm system will produce an alarm sound if activated. This is only effective if someone is in the area to hear the alarm. A telephone dial device sends an alarm to a preselected phone number. Note that telephone dial devices are subject to tampering and interruption.

Compartmentalized Areas

Compartmentalized areas are a little different from space or area protection in that the area must be protected at all times. This defines an actual location where sensitive equipment and information is operated and stored. It includes establishing restricted zones that are the only places where sensitive or classified information can be processed or stored.

They can be either active 24 hours a day or closed most of the time and only open to a select few at specific times. Usually, these areas are found in government facilities or chemical, aerospace, or electronic organizations. The space can be established wherever it has been determined, by the organization, that by compartmentalizing proprietary information and/or materials, the chance of a major loss can be minimized.

To be effective, compartmentalized areas must automatically control who is permitted entry and when. A key element of these areas is that those who have entry are subjected to frequent background investigations and "need-to-know" determinations. This can help security officers verify who can have access, when they can have access, and why they should have access.

Data Center or Server Room Security

Exhibit 13 lists a quick summary of good security practices for data center security. Use this list as a basis that can be added to, as appropriate for the building, organization, and type of information processing that will occur.

Computer Equipment Protection

Equipment Locks. There are several mechanisms for securing equipment; most are used to prevent theft. The simplest way is to bolt down the computer. Servers, workstations, and cables can be equipped with locks that require special keys, electronic tokens, or smart cards to unlock. Some equipment can be locked with cryptographic locks. These require a smart key that contains cryptographic algorithms and keys to access the equipment.

Portable Device Security. Portable devices include laptops, notebooks, and handheld devices such as personal digital assistants (PDAs). Portable security involves protecting the device, protecting the data on the device, *and* keeping the security controls easy for the user. Protecting portables may require multiple solutions, depending on how they are used.

For laptops that are in docking stations or another type of fixed location, several types of locks exist. Steel cords can be used to wrap around the laptop, thus securing it to a desk, or a crossbar can be cabled to the desk to prevent the laptop from being lifted out of the docking station.

Another option is to install software that provides a tracing feature. The software acts as a transmitter that sends homing signals to a monitoring

Exhibit 13. Good Security Practices for Data Center Security

Access Control

Depending on the sensitivity of the information being processed, some type of electronic access control may need to be installed. This includes badge/smart cards or biometric devices.

Alarm doors/area during non-working hours.

Post an access control list on the outside of the door indicating who is allowed unescorted access.

Have visitors sign in to document who was in the room and why they were there (i.e., maintenance, meetings, etc.).

Have access control policies for daytime use, after-hour use, or during an emergency.

Enforce strict key control for locks.

Door locks should provide both daytime locks, such as push-button locks (while the room is occupied), and 24-hour locks, such as deadbolt locks for after business hours.

Secondary access doors should be securely locked from the inside to prevent unauthorized access.

Lock combinations should be changed as appropriate (i.e., every six months, whenever someone leaves the data center, etc.)

CCTV to view visitors.

Site Location

Location within the building should not be easily accessible to visitors or to the general public.

Away from external windows or walls — best if it is centrally located inside the building.

Away from water pipes or other support system facilities.

Walls

Construct the room as a single unit.

Walls should not form part of an external wall of the building.

Roof, floors, and walls should not form part of a common barrier to an adjoining area where the security administrator does not have security control.

Walls should extend from the floor to the underside of the above floor slab (slab-to-slab). This ensures that intruders cannot enter locked offices simply by climbing over the walls and that fires cannot sweep unrestrained through the area.

If using glass as an external wall barrier, use shatter-resistant glass to limit damage from breakage. For some organizations, glass walls provide a sense of security because they can view who is in the server room at all times. For other organizations, the same reason may increase the security risk.

Doors

Doors should be solid core.

Doors should not open out.

Door hinges should be fixed to the frames with a minimum of three hinges per door.

Door frame should be permanently fixed to the adjoining wall studs.

Review emergency exit door locking mechanisms.

(continued)

Exhibit 13. Good Security Practices for Data Center Security (Continued)

HVAC

Should be on a separate system from the rest of building.

The size of the ducts and vents should ensure that they cannot be breached by an intruder.

There should be separate temperature and humidity controls in the computer/server room.

Positive pressure should be maintained.

Ducts may require some type of barrier bars.

Power Supply

A backup power supply (UPS or generator) should exist for a minimum amount of time as required by the organization's needs.

Backup power supply needs to be tested on a regular basis.

Electrical facilities that support the data center should be separate from the main building.

Electrical closets should be properly secured.

Cables and wiring should be properly secured and tested to ensure adequate power supply.

Emergency lighting capabilities should be provided.

Locate emergency power-off switches near all exits.

Protect an emergency power-off switch from unauthorized use by encasing it in a clear plastic covering.

Fire

Deploy portable extinguishers at exits and near equipment.

Install fire sensors/detection equipment.

Have documented and tested emergency plans.

Install water sensors under the raised floor.

network. The signals are transmitted over any Internet connection or phone line. If the portable is missing (i.e., stolen or lost), the user notifies the monitoring network, the next time the device is connected to the Internet, a message will be sent to the monitoring network indicating its location.

An audible motion alarm can be connected to any laptop, laptop bag, or other device so that if the item is moved beyond a certain perimeter, an alarm will activate. This type of device should be used only as a deterrent. It does not prevent someone from accessing information if the device is stolen; it only provides a warning that the device is being stolen. Other types of motion alarms are available that disable the boot routines and encrypt key data on the hard drive if the laptop is moved outside a predefined perimeter.

Encryption software can be installed on the hard drive. All data on the hard drive is then encrypted and can only be accessed through some type of access control system. This could include entering a password, inserting a smart card, or using a biometric device. For example, MS Windows 2000 offers file and disk encryption. A word of caution: in some software, if the access control mechanism is not correctly entered, the hard drive may automatically begin to erase all the data on the hard drive.

The most obvious and possibly the best protection for portable devices is common sense. First, the organization should establish a written policy for portable use, including security controls. The policy should be explained to users when they are issued the device and include information on where portables can (and cannot) be used and stored. This should also include the user's responsibility in the event that carelessness results in the loss of or damage to the device. Security controls to consider include:

- Laptop users should always keep the laptop close by and in their possession. Never leave the laptop unattended.
- Use a nondescript case that does not look like a computer bag. The case should be sturdy, weatherproof, and have a locking device.
- When traveling, users should never check the laptop as luggage.
- Many scams have been reported at airport security centers where two or three people work together to steal laptops. When passing through airport security, do not put the laptop on the conveyor belt until the user is next in line. Although this would be harder to accomplish with today's airport security controls, when the laptop is placed on the conveyer belt, one suspect creates a commotion that prevents the user from walking through the security control gate. The second suspect picks up the laptop from the conveyor belt and walks away. In some cases, they immediately pass it off to a third person who exits the building.
- Use a locking cable to secure the laptop to a desk or table.
- If using the laptop in a public place, do not position the monitor where others can observe the screen.
- Have backups of the data that are stored separately from the laptop. This can prevent a catastrophe if the laptop is missing.
- Have an inventory system that accounts for all portable devices.
- Engrave the laptop with an identifying number.
- Monitor how anti-virus software will be updated on laptops. Many organizations "push" anti-virus updates to connected workstations, which is transparent to the end user. However, most laptops may never be connected to the network servers; therefore, an action plan must exist that provides for how laptop users will receive the anti-virus updates. It may be something as simple as requiring all laptop users to return their laptops to the system manager on a

monthly basis so that the system manager can update the anti-virus definitions.

Object Protection

The final layer of security is at the object level. These items are usually placed inside security containers such as safes, vaults, or locking file cabinets. Typically, the word "safe" refers to any steel container with a lock. However, to be effective, safes should be theft resistant. Safes also exist for fire protection, but those are not usually associated with the same theft-resistant features. A fire-resistant safe protects paper records from being destroyed by fire. They are installed with insulating material that limits the transfer of heat to the inside of the safe. A theft-resistant safe is designed to protect valuable objects from theft. The body and doors of the safe are designed with steel or other metal alloys that are capable of resisting attack by tools, torches, or explosives. The degree of protection is determined by the type and amount of steel used.

Safes are designed to be resistant to attack, but not attack-proof. Given enough time, any safe can be stolen or destroyed. Underwriters Laboratory (UL) rates safes for both fire and theft resistance. For example, one test that UL performs is combination drilling. They attempt to knock off the combination dial and punch or drill the spindle so that the locking mechanism can be picked.

To decide what type of container is needed, it is important to understand what is to be protected. For sensitive paper objects, a high-security locking file cabinet may be appropriate. These types of containers should also be fireproof. Combination dials and key locks are the most common locking devices for safes; however, some have mechanical or electronic push-button locks.

Security measures for safes include:

- If the safe is lightweight, install the safe in reinforced concrete or anchor it to the building.
- Install the safe in a visible location and train users to watch for unauthorized personnel trying to gain access.
- Create good combinations, change them frequently, and monitor their distribution.
- Install a relocking device for greater security protection. A relocking device is a mechanism inside the lock that will activate if a forced entry is attempted. For example, if a drill is used, the heat may activate a device to provide additional protection.

In the next section, we look at the mechanisms available to ensure that physical security controls are doing what is intended.

7.4   Assurance, Trust, and Confidence Mechanisms

Drills/Exercises/Testing

When employees become familiar with the organization, they may begin to establish routine and repetitive behaviors that ignore the security controls. To keep personnel aware of their responsibilities, some type of testing is conducted. The tests are usually designed and conducted by the security manager.

For example, most countries require fire evacuation drills on a regular basis. The drills require employees to exit the building, the fire response team must arrive, and employees cannot re-enter the building until the building is deemed safe. These exercises help to prepare and train personnel on how to exit a building and respond appropriately in the event of an emergency.

Vulnerability/Penetration Tests

A vulnerability test provides an estimate of the vulnerabilities of the facility, tests the effectiveness of security controls, alerts personnel on the techniques that an intruder might use, and provides information for corrective measures. The test should identify weak entry points, such as through unguarded gates or the use of false or altered badges. It should also indicate whether personnel were able to detect any illegal entries.

Upon the completion of the vulnerability tests, a written report should be prepared. The security team should then analyze the report because it provides an evaluation of the security program and defines what measures can be implemented to resolve any weaknesses. In addition, the results of the tests should be controlled so that only those who have a need-to-know can review the evaluation.

Creating a Checklist

Establishing a checklist can be helpful in identifying those elements of physical security that need to be checked on a regular basis. Even if it is a semi-annual or annual checklist, it will provide a basis for where to begin in checking the effectiveness of the controls.

Maintenance and Service

Regardless of the quality designed into a system by the manufacturer or the level of installation used to implement any type of system, there will always be maintenance to keep the system operating at its full capability. For example, in a CCTV system, the exposed lenses must be cleaned on a regular basis to provide clear images. If the maintenance is critical to the operation of the system, it may be wise to consider maintenance contracts. However, if the system is highly sensitive or the organization is located in a high-threat environment, it may be necessary to screen maintenance personnel. It is a good practice to escort maintenance personnel at all times. Regardless of how it is done, the critical factor is that it is done — the physical security control systems must be maintained and upgraded throughout the life cycle of the equipment.

The final section reviews the role of management and its responsibilities to ensure the implementation and support for physical security controls necessary to protect the information system.

7.5   Information Protection and Management Services

The security manager has the task of overseeing and directing the work and behavior of other members of the security team or security force. The manager is often responsible for selection, installment, implementation, training, productivity, safety, and morale of the security team. Thus, to be effective, the manager should have an understanding of how to be a good manager and possess the skills necessary to obtain maximum performance from team members.

To maintain an alert and efficient security front, there should be constant supervision. For example, the supervisor/manager should inspect the physical security controls on a regular basis. This includes checking to see if sensors are working, verifying that security patrols are reviewing the monitors, briefing team members on their responsibilities, and inspecting posts, vehicles, and equipment.

The security manager is also responsible for reporting to management on the physical security posture of the facility. This includes helping to set policies and procedures, requesting budget money for countermeasures, and generally promoting a security consciousness throughout the organization.

Awareness and Training

To have a high-quality security team, proper training and supervision are necessary. If the organization has a security patrol team/force, it is a good idea to have employees cross-trained in various duties and then rotate assignments.

The objectives of a security training program are to acquaint all personnel with the reasons for security controls and to ensure their cooperation. In this respect, all members of the organization should be aware of the security policies and procedures. Many people are naive and trusting, which is counter to good security. Thus, a continuous program should be presented on timely and applicable topics to develop a high degree of security consciousness. A good program will provide constant awareness of how important each employee is to good security and will outline the specific responsibilities of each employee.

An important element of any security training program is to provide information on how employees should report any security deficiencies, violations, or hazards. They should be told what type of incidents to report and who should be notified of any issues. It is critical that the awareness and training program stress the absolute requirement for support of information security by every employee, regardless of their work assignment.

Summary

Controlling access to information system resources involves more than technical/logical controls; it also includes limiting the physical access to the resources. As organizations become more reliant on their information systems, the threats to the systems also become more sophisticated. Even with these advances in technical attacks, the basic requirements for securing the resources include front-line physical security procedures and protection.

To meet the technical advances, the physical security field has changed and expanded in the past 30 years. One aspect of the new arena is the protection of critical infrastructures, such as the support systems mentioned in this chapter (i.e., power, water, HVAC). Many nations have begun establishing requirements to protect these infrastructures from attack. As part of protecting the infrastructure and information system resources, CISSPs must also understand the physical security field so that they can work with those professionals dedicated to physical security.

7.6 Common Body of Knowledge (CBK)

The current CBK for the Physical Security chapter is listed below to assist in determining topics for further review. Although this Study Guide is very detailed in many areas, it is not possible to thoroughly discuss every CBK topic in a single book; therefore, additional study of items may be advisable.

The professional should fully understand:

- Threats, vulnerabilities, and countermeasures related to physically protecting the enterprise's sensitive information assets
- The risk to people, facilities, data, media, equipment, support systems, and supplies as it applies to physical security

Components

The professional can meet the expectations defined above by understanding such physical security topics and methodologies as:

- Facility Requirements
- Restricted Areas/Work Areas
- Escort Requirements/Visitor Control
- Fences, Gates, Turnstiles, Mantraps
- Security Guards/Dogs
- Badging
- Keys and Combination Locks
- Lighting
- Site Selection, Facility Design, and Configuration
- Motion Detectors, Sensors, and Alarms
- CCTV
- Technical Controls
- Smart/Dumb Cards
- Audit Trails/Access Logs
- Intrusion Detection
- Biometric Access Controls
- Environment/Life Safety
- Power and HVAC Considerations
- Water Leakage and Flooding
- Fire Detection and Suppression
- Natural Disasters

Examples

- Define physical security threats.
- Define and describe the elements of physical security.
- Define and describe elements of IS processing center security.
- Identify facility management and planning requirements for IT/IS.
- Identify and define pertinent personnel access controls.
- Identify and define physical controls pertinent to IT/IS.
- Distinguish between facility construction requirements pertinent to IT/IS.
- Define general facility issues pertinent to IT/IS.
- Define facility electrical requirements.
- Compare and contrast methods of electric power protection.
- Define electromagnetic interference (EMI).
- Define radio frequency interference (RFI).
- Identify and define possible protective measures for noise control.
- Define the effect of excessive humidity on computer equipment.
- Distinguish between fire classes.
- Define types of fire detection methods.

- Compare and contrast fire-suppression techniques.
- Identify replacements for halon in computer-related suppression devices.
- Identify characteristics of smoke and gas damage.
- Identify concerns of physical security as regards media storage.
- Define concerns of media storage.
- Define media storage protective measures.
- Identify magnetic media physical protection controls.
- Identify object reuse issues.
- Define data remanence.
- Define and describe restricted area access controls.
- Identify and define boundary protection considerations.
- Compare and contrast physical access controls.
- Compare and contrast personnel access controls.
- Compare and contrast various biometric devices.
- Identify and describe characteristics of biometric systems.
- Define distributed processing impact on physical security.

7.7 Sample Questions for the CISSP Exam

1. Physical security often follows which of the following models:
   a. High-security defense model
   b. Deterrent-based security model
   c. Layered defense model
   d. Trusted systems security model
2. Physical crime prevention is often a combination of all of the following EXCEPT:
   a. Disposition
   b. Psychology
   c. Hardware
   d. Site design
3. Crime prevention through environmental design builds on the strategies of access control, natural surveillance, and:
   a. Possession
   b. Territoriality
   c. Isolation
   d. Obscurity
4. Site location should consider all of the following EXCEPT:
   a. Lighting
   b. Crime
   c. Natural disaster
   d. Emergency response facilities

5. A fault is a(an):
   a. Electrostatic discharge
   b. Momentary loss of power
   c. Voltage spike
   d. Transient noise
6. Positive pressurization of a facility means:
   a. Positive ions in the air will prevent the adhesion of contaminants.
   b. Higher air pressure inside a building may reduce external contamination.
   c. Increased air pressure provides better working conditions.
   d. Opening a door may draw fresh air into a building.
7. The greatest risk to most organizations through portable computing is:
   a. Loss of expensive hardware
   b. Vulnerability of remote access
   c. Loss of confidential data
   d. Tracking and inventory of equipment
8. Standby lighting is:
   a. Operated only in hours of darkness
   b. Operated in the event of a power failure
   c. Operated to facilitate emergency evacuation
   d. Operated in response to suspicious activity
9. A microwave-based sensor provides which type of control?
   a. Deterrent
   b. Preventative
   c. Detective
   d. Compensating
10. A closed-circuit TV splitter is not effective for:
    a. Replaying individual camera scenes
    b. Switching between camera inputs sequentially
    c. Displaying many cameras at once
    d. Recording several camera inputs concurrently
11. Intensified camera lenses are effective for:
    a. Low light surveillance
    b. Using heat signatures to record activity
    c. Magnifying the detail of an incident
    d. Creating a stereoscopic image of the scene
12. Which is the most secure form of window?
    a. Wired glass
    b. Tempered glass
    c. Glass-clad polycarbonate
    d. Acrylic glass
13. What method is not effective for mitigating damage from static?
    a. Static mats and wrist straps
    b. Reducing humidity

    c. Anti-static sprays

    d. Anti-static flooring materials

14. What type of fire-suppression system does the insurance industry recommend for use in computer rooms?

    a. Carbon dioxide (CO_2)

    b. Water

    c. Halon 1211

    d. Dry powder

15. When determining the best physical security countermeasures to implement, which of the following should be the key factor?

    a. Initial financial costs

    b. Installation costs

    c. Maintenance costs

    d. Life safety concerns

16. Due to heightened security, your security officer has asked you for options that would control and monitor automobile traffic into the employee parking lot. Which of the following do you think would be a good option to recommend?

    a. Install trip lighting at the entrance area.

    b. Install vehicle barriers at the entrance area.

    c. Install a Class I vehicular gate.

    d. Install a Class II vehicular gate.

17. To improve security in the employee parking lot, the security officer has asked to recommend some lighting options. Which of the following do you think would be a good option to recommend?

    a. Continuous lighting

    b. Trip lighting

    c. Standby lighting

    d. Emergency lighting

18. What is an emergency panic bar on a door designed to do?

    a. Eliminate the shrinkage or cracking of the doorframe due to excessive use.

    b. Indicate whether the door is open or closed.

    c. Allow instant exit, but controlled entrance.

    d. Reinforce the hinge frame, so the door cannot be kicked in or pried open.

19. Where would you likely to find a mantrap installed?

    a. Prison entranceway

    b. Public library entranceway

    c. Amusement park entranceway

    d. Bridge toll-gate

20. The primary entrance door to the server room has a push-button lock for daytime control and a spin-dial lock for after hour access control. A secondary door to the server room should have what type of lock installed?

a. Same as the primary entrance door
b. Deadbolt on the inside, allowing no access from the outside
c. Electronic combination lock on the outside
d. Pushbutton lock on the outside for daytime control and spin-dial lock on the outside for after hour control.

References

Australian Communications-Electronic Security Instructions 33 (ACSI-33). Defense Signals Directorate © Commonwealth of Australia. www.dsd.gov.au/infosec/acsi33/.

Cherry, Don, 1986. *Total Facility Control.* Butterworth Publishing, Stoneham, MA.

Colombo, Al, 2000. "CCTV — Video Surveillance Cameras — Monitors — Security Monitoring Devices." Information System Security Portal. http://www.infosyssec.org/infosyssec/cctv_.htm.

CSI/FBI 8th Annual Computer Crime and Security Survey (2003). Available by download from www.gosci.com.

Department of Energy, September 2000. "Physical Security Systems Inspectors Guide." U.S. Department of Energy, Germantown, MD.

Electric Power Research Institute (EPRI), 2001. "The Cost of Power Disturbances to Industrial and Digital Economy Companies." Topical Report, #1006274, EPRI Order and Conference Center, Concord, CA.

Fennelly, Lawrence J., 1997. *Effective Physical Security.* Butterworth-Heinemann, Boston, MA.

Field Manual (FM) No. 19-30 (FM 19-30), 1979. *Physical Security.* U.S. Department of the Army, Washington, D.C.

Field Manual (FM) No. 3-19.30 (FM 3-19.30), 2001. *Physical Security.* U.S. Department of the Army, Washington, D.C.

Fites, Philip and Kratz, Martin, 1993. *Information Systems Security: A Practitioner's Reference.* Van Nostrand Reinhold Publishing, a division of International Thomson Publishing Company. *Note:* The book is out of print but can be ordered directly from Philip Fites.

Forcht, Karen, 1994. *Computer Security Management.* Fraser Publishing Company, a division of International Thomson Publishing, Danvers, MA.

Gallery, Shari Mendelson, Ed., 1986. *Physical Security: Readings from Security Management Magazine.* Butterworth Publishing, Stoneham, MA.

Garcia, Mary Lynn, 2001. *The Design and Evaluation of Physical Protection Systems.* Butterworth-Heinemann, Boston, MA.

Morita, H., Yanagisawa, N., Nakajima, T., et al., 1995. "Sarin Poisoning in Matsumoto, Japan." *Lancet,* 346, 290–293, 1995.

Power, Richard, 2002. "2002 CSI/FBI Computer Crime and Security Survey." *Computer Security Issues & Trends*, Volume VIII, No. 1, Spring 2002.

Powers, Mary B., Post, Nadine M., and Roe, Andrew G., 2002. "Chemical, Biological Threats Pose New Design Challenges." *Engineering News-Record,* May 25, 2002.

Roper, C.A., 1997. *Physical Security and the Inspection Process.* Butterworth-Heinemann, Boston, MA.

Schnabolk, Charles, 1983. *Physical Security.* Butterworth Publishing, Woburn, MA.

Underwriters Laboratory (UL) 325 Safety Standards for Automatic Gate Operators, September 1998. Available from www.info@sunbeltsystems.com. You can contact UL directly at (847) 272-8800 in the United States.

Walker, Philip, 1983. *Electronic Security Systems.* University Press, Cambridge, England.

Web Sites

www.industryclick.com — electric power issues
www.powerstandards.com
www.feelsafeagain.com
www.ciesin.org — 1987 Montreal Protocol on Substances That Deplete the Ozone Layer
http://www.adtdl.army.mil — physical security field manual
http://www.gai.org.uk — panic bars, emergency exit bars

Chapter 8
Telecommunications, Network, and Internet Security

The Telecommunications, Network, and Internet Security Domain encompasses the structures, transmission methods, transport formats, and security measures used to provide integrity, availability, authentication, and confidentiality for transmissions over private and public communications networks and media. Simply stated, a network consists of two or more devices connected together in such a way as to allow them to exchange information.

This chapter is divided into five topic areas. The first section deals with the requirements for telecommunications and network security. The Information Protection Environment section describes the telecommunications and network environment for security consideration. The third section, Security Technology and Tools, explains the types of controls available to mitigate the threats. The final two sections address the assurance aspects of the effectiveness of controls and the management actions used to implement appropriate security.

In this domain, the CISSP should be able to:

- Describe the telecommunications and network security elements as they relate to the transmission of information in local area, wide area, and remote access.
- Define the concepts associated with the Internet, intranet, and extranet communications, such as firewalls, gateways, and associated protocols.
- Identify the communications security management and techniques that prevent, detect, and correct errors so that the protection of information transmitted over networks is maintained.

8.1 Information Protection Requirements

Maintaining the security of a distributed environment is one of the greatest concerns for most organizations. The convergence of the Internet, the corporate network and technologies including microcomputer-based networks, wide area networking, intranets, extranets, e-commerce, wireless technologies, and electronic mail have increased the security exposure of most organizations. Information security managers and executives rely on the assistance of security and audit personnel to devise plans that effectively monitor the complex distributed environments of today and tomorrow.

An organization's information assets have differing levels of value. On one level, there are the costs of hardware, software, and technology used to develop and store data to generate information. On another level, there are the human resource costs of actually collecting and interpreting data in order to store meaningful information for ongoing decision making. Finally, there is the value of keeping the information confidential and secret from outside entities to maintain a competitive advantage.

The goal of network security is to preserve the varying levels of investment, maintaining trustworthy and accurate data, and ensuring a sustainable level of trust in the automated systems used to collect, store, and disseminate accurate, reliable information.

Elements making up network security objectives may include:

- Maintaining secure and accessible transmission channels and services.
- Interoperability of network security mechanisms are operational.
- Messages sent are the actual messages received.
- A given message link is between a valid source and destination node.
- Message non-repudiation is available.
- Unauthorized disclosure of messages is prevented.
- Unauthorized disclosure of traffic flows is prevented.
- Remote access mechanisms are secure.
- Security mechanisms are easy to implement and maintain.
- Security mechanisms are transparent to end users.

Today's security professionals have more tools, techniques, and methodologies to meet their objectives, with more becoming available daily.

8.2 Information Protection Environment

Data Networks

A network is an integrated, communicating aggregation of computers and peripherals linked through communications facilities; basically, two or more computers that share resources and data, linked by cabling, telephony, or wireless equipment. The term "data network" refers to the electronic transmission of data. Although the term is usually used to refer to data that is manipulated by computers, it also encompasses traffic derived from other types of systems that have been digitized for transmission, such as voice, video, and images.

Data Network Structures

Data network structures include local area networks (LANs), wide area networks (WANs), the Internet, intranets, extranets, value-added networks, and the World Wide Web. Networks typically contain systems acting as clients and servers. The client computer operates and requests resources from the server. The server provides dedicated and shared resources to the client, including applications, disk storage, printers, and databases. In small networks, the server may also be a client. However, larger networks make a distinction to allow for improved performance, capacity planning, and security.

Systems today include a network-aware or network operating system to coordinate resource allocation, sharing of network-based resources, device management, data protection, and error control. Current system implementations include a range of attached input/output devices, including printers, scanners, faxes, and CD-RW drives, all of which are shared resources for LAN users.

LAN/WAN Environment. The Local Area Network (LAN) is typically a small network, generally limited by geographic bounds such as a building or an office. When a connection of multiple LANs occurs within a larger area, such as a group of buildings, a campus, or a city, a Metropolitan Area Network (MAN) is formed. The final grouping covers many networks over a large geographic area such as a state, country, or the globe; these are called Wide Area Networks (WANs).

Regardless of the geographic area covered, all types of networks can carry information that is sensitive to the organization. Consequently, planning for the security and privacy of these networks is imperative. The network security plan covers all aspects of the network from architecture, access to the network to policies, user awareness, and appropriate practices for the management and operation of the network.

LAN (Local Area Network). A LAN is primarily limited to a small geographical area or one site, such as an office building. However, LANs may be limited for technical reasons as well, such as reaching the limits on network connections or cable length. Many of today's environments incorporate a vast array of computing equipment, including PCs, minicomputers and mainframes, network printers, and storage. Although a LAN itself has

517

certain limitations, LANs can be connected together to form larger networks. A LAN is either peer-to-peer or client/server (server based). Peer-to-peer networks share resources between computers and are directly connected. Client/server networks have a dedicated machine as a server that provides resources, data, and security.

LANs are interconnected using a backbone LAN. The backbone provides resources to each of the LANs and transmits data from one LAN to another, as required. Backbone networks are built like any other LAN; however, they tend to use high-capacity cabling, as the backbone must be capable of carrying a larger amount of traffic than each individual LAN. Additionally, the backbone has similar security risks, as it sees all the traffic flowing between devices on the backbone as well as traffic between the LAN segments.

WAN (Wide Area Network). A WAN is a data communications network that serves users across a broad geographic area and often uses transmission services provided by common carriers. These services include Frame Relay, SMDS, and X.25.

Internet. The Internet is a worldwide system of computer networks: a network of networks linking computers to computers sharing the TCP/IP protocols. If they have permission, users at any one computer can get information from any other computer. Each runs software to provide or serve information or to access and view information. The Internet is the transport vehicle for the information stored in files or documents on another computer.

Intranet. The term "intranet" commonly refers to the application of Internet technologies within an organization. Unlike the Internet, which must support all TCP/IP applications, a corporate intranet can be tailored to the specific requirements of an organization. For example, if users need to transfer files, a File Transfer Protocol (FTP) application must be obtained. Similarly, the ability to provide direct point-to-point communications between individuals or groups of employees can be satisfied through the Simple Mail Transfer Protocol (SMTP) application, and the ability to access computer systems remotely would be satisfied through the use of a terminal emulator such as Telnet or TN3270 for access to an IBM mainframe.

An intranet represents much more than installing a browser and letting users access a Web server connected to the corporate network. Although Web browsers and Web servers can play an important role in a corporate intranet, they represent just two of the many technologies that can be used on a TCP/IP network. An intranet can also support other non-Internet applications, such as transferring legacy SNA traffic from PCs using emulation boards or TCP/IP traffic from PCs connected to LANs.

Extranets. Extranets have been around as long as the first rudimentary LAN-to-LAN networks began connecting two different business entities together to form WANs. In its basic form, an extranet is the interconnection of two previously separate LANs or WANs with origins from different business entities. This term emerged to differentiate between the previous definitions of external "Internet" connection and just a company's internal intranet.

Value-Added Networks. Companies operating computers for others are known as service bureaus. Private companies, the common carrier, have operated communications systems on behalf of others for a century or more; the telephone companies are the best example. Certain vendors of communications services combine the message transmission of the common carriers with the specialized processing of the service bureaus. These are known as value-added networks (VANs).

Different VANs can respond differently to a company's needs. Some VANs have advantages in technology strength. Some offer low prices. Thus, the selection of communication type and VAN needs careful investigation to ensure that a company can gain maximum benefits from the service implementation, and the selected alternatives can serve a company's needs without introducing problems.

World Wide Web (WWW). The World Wide Web is a set of services on the Internet that provides archives of information accessible via browsers and search engines. The data is presented in hypertext format, with links to other Internet sites. Graphics, video, and audio can be included in the hypertext document, or as a linked document.

Data Network Components

There are four main components of a data communications system: a terminal or computer, network software or operating systems, a communications adapter, and the communications channel.

A terminal can be either dumb or intelligent. An example of the former is the 3270 terminal used in the mainframe environment; an example of the latter is a PC or workstation. The difference is that the terminal relies on a host for processing and storage, which provides economic advantages; a PC or workstation contains its own processing and storage resources. Through a technique called emulation, a PC or workstation can act like a traditional 3270 terminal to communicate with a host, to provide flexibility.

A network operating system is a special control program that sets up the connections and manages the flow of data over the communications channel. In addition to link setup and flow control, the communications software may perform other functions such as error correction, data compression, and encryption.

The communications adapter provides the interface between the terminal or PC and the communications facility. There are many kinds of communications adapters, the choice of which depends on the type of communications lines or services being used.

When analog lines are used for the communications channel, the device used is a modem. A modem, or modulator-demodulator, converts the digital signals generated by the terminal or PC into analog signals suitable for transmission over dial-up telephone lines or voice-grade leased lines. Another modem, located at the receiving end of the transmission, converts the analog signals back into digital form for manipulation by the data recipient. A modem can be used to transfer files, access remote electronic mail services, connect to mainframe or servers from remote sites, share printers and access file or applications servers, or connect to the Internet.

Another type of communications adapter is the channel service unit/digital service unit (CSU/DSU), which provides the interface between data communications equipment such as multiplexers and digital lines (i.e., T1). The CSU/DSU encodes serial data from terminals or computers and performs wave-shaping of the transmit signal before it is sent over the digital facility to ensure an acceptable level of network performance. This device is also used by the telephone company and the customer for routine testing and for isolating problems on the network.

Different types of communications adapters are also required for connection to other services, such as X.25 and Frame Relay, which are packet services. Among other things, these types of communications adapters assemble data into packets or frames for transmission over the network and perform disassembly at the receiving end. In addition, flow control and congestion management functions are performed.

The communications channel provides the means by which data is transmitted from one point on the network to another. In a wide area network, the channel is provided by a leased line or carrier-provided service. Perhaps the best-known example of a digital line or service is T1, which provides 1.544 Mbps of aggregate bandwidth. This amount of bandwidth can be used as a single channel for a high-speed data application or it can be divided into as many as 24 channels of 64Kbps each for use by many lower-speed applications. Channel derivation is usually accomplished through a T1 multiplexer. Computers and other equipment are plugged into the multiplexer on the terminal side and assigned a dedicated channel for transmission on the network side. At the receiving end, another multiplexer routes the channels to the appropriate computer or other equipment.

LAN/WAN Components. PCs are an integral part of the LAN, using a network interface adapter board, cabling or wireless, and software to access the data and devices on the network. Similarly, other computer systems can be connected to the LAN using similar components. PCs can also have dial-in access to a LAN via a modem and telephone line. The PC is the most vulnerable component of a LAN because it typically has weak security features.

Network adapter/network interface cards (NICs) are used to connect a PC to a network. The NIC provides a physical connection between the networking cable and the computer's internal bus. Most network adapters provide support for a category of unshielded, twisted pair, copper cabling popularly called Category 5 or CAT 5.

Hubs are used to connect together two or more Ethernet segments of any media type. One end of the link is attached to the hub and the other is attached to the computer. Hubs provide the signal amplification required to allow a segment to be extended a greater distance. A hub takes any incoming signal and repeats it out all ports.

Traditionally, three types of intelligent devices have been used for inter-networking: bridges, routers, and gateways. Each operates at different layers of the OSI Reference Model, which dictates the level of functionality they provide. These network devices typically also provide security features to assist in protecting the network.

A bridge is a device that connects two or more physical networks and forwards packets between them. Bridges can usually be made to filter packets; that is, to forward only certain traffic. As bridges evolved, more efficient bridges are now called switches.

The function of switches is to join segments together. They filter and forward packets between LAN segments. Switches actually read the destination address of each packet and then forward the packet to the correct port. The first series of LAN switches to reach the market operated at Layer 2 (data-link layer) of the OSI Reference Model. In doing so, they represented a multi-port bridge because they would forward, filter, or flood frames based on the destination MAC address in each frame. The first method of upper layer switching to be incorporated into LAN switches is what is referred to as Layer 3 (network layer) switching. A Layer 3 switch looks further into each Ethernet frame to determine the destination IP address being transported. The switch then uses the IP address as a mechanism for the delivery of frames. The key advantage associated with a Layer 3 switch is the fact that it can be configured to route frames based on network segment addressing.

If the organization needs to transport time-critical frames, one will probably want to use a Layer 2 switch. If the organization needs to move frames directly onto different networks, one will probably want to consider a

Layer 3 switch. If the organization requires the routing of traffic based on the application being transported, a Layer 4 (transport layer) switch should be considered. Layer 4 switches are now commonly referred to as application layer switches, of which load balancing represents one of several popular applications. Other applications included in certain Layer 4 LAN switches include authentication, authorization, and accounting (AAA), which were previously performed by a separate server connected to a LAN.

A router is a system responsible for making decisions about which of several paths network (or Internet) traffic will follow. To do this, it uses a routing protocol to gain information about the network, and algorithms to choose the best route based on several criteria known as "routing metrics." In OSI terminology, a router is a network layer intermediate system.

LANs are implemented using some form of transmission medium, such as cabling, and wireless technologies. Cabling can include thin and thick coaxial cable, twisted pair, and optical fiber. Optical fiber provides the highest bandwidth capacity and, when properly used, a very high degree of security. However, with the protections associated with optical fiber, it is also the most expensive to implement and maintain.

All cabling should be considered a method for an attacker to gain unauthorized access to your network through a network tap or electromagnetic interference. However, the varying cable types provide different levels of shielding and pose different challenges for tapping. For example, optical fiber is generally considered most resistant to tapping because there would be a degradation in the light source and consequently the network beyond the tap would experience problems, leading to an investigation. Additionally, the cost of the appropriate equipment to perform and use a network tap can still be beyond the budget of some hackers. Add to this the requirement to have physical access to the cable and it becomes clear this is not a first method of choice.

A wireless LAN (WLAN) is a flexible data communication system implementation as an extension to, or as an alternative for, a wired LAN within a building or campus. A WLAN is just like a wired LAN with the cable replaced by a radio-spread spectrum signal. Spread spectrum, as the name implies, uses multiple frequencies in the band to increase the immunity to noise at any specific frequency. Using electromagnetic waves, WLANs transmit and receive data over the air, thus minimizing the need for wired connections. Therefore, WLANs combine data connectivity with user mobility, and, through simplified configuration, enable movable LANs.

Wireless LANs using RF (radio frequency) or infrared signals pose an increased threat to the organization's data because the information can be retrieved without the need for physical access to a network. Due to current limitations in the wireless network technology, it is very easy to gain access to a wireless network and obtain the information being transferred over the network.

The IEEE 802.11 standard defines an 802-compatible MAC layer that can interoperate with the other 802 technologies. Three physical standards are defined: the FHSS, DSSS, and Infrared. At the moment, the focus standard is on the 2.4-GHz band, but this will likely shift to the 4 GHz bands as they are released for open use. Essentially, the 802.11 standard provides open, asynchronous networking that requires a distributed control function. The supported data rates are up to 54 Mbps.

Data Network Technologies

Most organizations find their networking solutions not in one technology, but in a mix of technologies. This section presents a brief overview of the relevant communications and transmission services that are part and parcel of the data communications manager's responsibilities.

Synchronous Communications. Synchronous communication is the transmission of data at very high speeds using parallel circuits in which the transfer of data is synchronized by electronic clock signals. Synchronous communication relies on the presence of a clocking system at both ends of the transmission, and these clocks must be synchronized at the beginning of the session. Effective communication between the devices relies on the clock and not start- and stop-bit encapsulation, the timing signals where data begins and ends. When binary data is transmitted, a unique 8-bit pattern is used to define the start of the data stream. To preserve the timing during the session, a special bit-transition pattern is embedded in the digital signal assisting in maintaining the timing between the sender and receiver. Synchronous communication can achieve much higher rates than asynchronous communication methods.

Asynchronous Communications. Asynchronous transmission is a data exchange format controlled by start and stop bits at the end of each character. It is also characterized by the lack of predetermined time intervals between the transmissions of characters.

Asynchronous communication is a continuous stream of data that uses a start bit to flag the beginning of a byte of information, and ends with a stop bit and sometimes a parity bit, used for error checking. This type of communication does not use a timing mechanism to control the flow of data or to interpret the start or end of discreet pieces of data; rather, it uses its own encapsulation overhead to ensure that data is received error-free, in the order transmitted.

With the reliance upon start and stop bits in the transmission, there is a higher overhead associated with asynchronous communication. Consequently, the data rates are much lower with asynchronous communication methods.

Analog Communications. An *analog signal* is the representation of information with a continuously variable physical quantity, such as voltage. Because of this constant changing of the wave shape with regard to its passing a given point in time or space, an analog signal might have a virtually infinite number of states or values. This contrasts with a digital signal that is expressed as a square wave and therefore has a very limited number of discrete states.

The transmission of analog signals is accomplished over wires or through the air where information is conveyed through the variation of some combination of signal amplitude, frequency, and phase. Analog transmissions include voice, facsimile, and data transmission using a modem.

Digital Communications. A *digital signal* is a discontinuous electrical signal that changes from one state to another in discrete steps, or on-off pulses, while analog signals are continuous waves capable of representing an unlimited number of values.

Traditional telephone systems use analog-switched lines to provide voice communications. Data communication over analog lines has limited transmission speeds because of the narrow bandwidth of voice lines. When transmitting data over phone lines, a modem is required to convert the digital data signals to analog signals, and vice versa. When analog signals are transmitted over long distances, they need to be amplified, which can distort the value of the data transmitted.

When analog data is converted to digital data, it can be transmitted over digital circuits faster and without distortion. Discrete samples of binary data make up the content of the payload. Digital data is precise but can never transmit the range of information available with analog.

Circuit-Switched Networks. *Circuit switching* was the first switching technology, installed worldwide for the public-switched telephone network (PSTN). Circuit switching requires that a dedicated circuit be established for the connection between the two endpoints. Signaling software sets up the call and arranges billing. Then the voice call is switched in hardware systems. Everything flows along the same path, with uniform quality and no loss or interruptions. Circuit-switched networks are networks in which a connection is established on demand and maintained between data stations allowing the exclusive use of the circuit until the connection is released.

A circuit connection is a physical, permanent connection lasting for the duration of a call. If a connection is made over a long distance, many circuits are dedicated to this one call, using substantial resources. Circuit calls are not shared by other traffic. Circuits isolate communicating parties from one another. Although you may hear noise on a line, a circuit-switched connection is meant to be a one-to-one connection, without interference. Voice communication requires a fixed-bit rate to transmit voice sound. Voice calls require fairly continuous transmission during the course of a connection, so a circuit-switched, rather than a packet-switched, connection is more effective.

Packet-Switched Networks. In *packet switching,* data is segmented, or broken up, into packets and sent across a circuit shared by multiple subscribers. As the packets travel over the network, switches read the packet addresses and route the packets to the proper destination. X.25 and Frame Relay are examples of packet-switching services. Packet switching is the process of routing and transferring data by means of addressed packets so a channel is occupied during the transmission of the packet only, and upon completion of the transmission the channel is made available for the transfer of other traffic.

When moving through the mesh of the network, the packet relies on a device, usually a switch or a router, which is actually a high-speed computer, to read its destination address and output its signal to the next link in the direction of its destination. At the destination, all the packets are reassembled using the "frame check sequence" number embedded in the frame surrounding the packet. Packets are small, so the time they take to go through any physical point is very short (timescales are in millionths of a second). As a result, many packets can travel over the same point without noticeable interference. The significant difference between packet- and circuit-switched networks is the lack of a dedicated circuit between the two users. Consequently, resources are better used in a packet-switched network.

Virtual Circuits. A virtual circuit is a logical circuit created over a packet-switched network. Two types of virtual circuits exist: switched virtual circuits (SVCs) and permanent virtual circuits (PVCs). SVCs are dynamically allocated virtual circuits established on demand and terminated when transmission is complete. Communication over an SVC consists of three phases: circuit establishment, data transfer, and circuit termination. The establishment phase involves creating the virtual circuit between the source and destination devices. Data transfer involves transmitting data between the devices over the virtual circuit, and the circuit termination phase involves tearing down the virtual circuit between the source and destination devices. SVCs are used in situations in which data transmission between devices is sporadic, largely because SVCs increase network setup

525

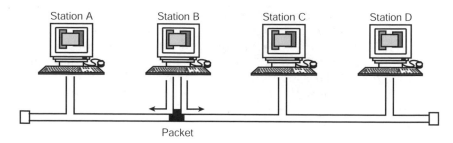

Exhibit 1. Bus Topology

time due to the circuit establishment and termination phases, but they decrease the cost associated with constant virtual circuit availability.

A PVC is a permanently established virtual circuit consisting of one mode: data transfer. PVCs are used in situations in which data transfer between devices is constant. PVCs eliminate the network delay associated with the establishment and termination of virtual circuits, but they increase costs due to constant virtual circuit availability. PVCs are generally configured by the service provider when an order is placed for service.

Network Topologies. Networks are connected using some access medium to provide an electrical connection to the various devices. The topology of the network defines how the signals move between the various systems. Network topologies include the bus, star, ring, or other combinations. The name associated with the topology describes the physical layout.

There are three principal topologies: bus, star, and ring. Other topologies include the mesh and tree, although they are variations of the basic three.

Bus Topology. A bus topology (Exhibit 1) connects each station on the network in an electrical configuration representing a bus. Each system on the network receives the data as the signal travels along the entire transmission medium, as illustrated here. This is the most commonly used topology covering the Ethernet IEEE 802.3 networks.

Ring Topology. In a ring topology (Exhibit 2), each station is connected through a unidirectional connection to another station, forming a closed loop. The Token Ring IEEE 802.5 and fiber-optic FDDI networks are implemented using ring topologies.

Star Topology. The star topology (Exhibit 3) uses a central hub or switch to connect each endpoint or device using dedicated links.

Tree Topology. A tree topology (Exhibit 4) is the same as a bus, but it uses branches to connect each device in the network. In Exhibit 4, the

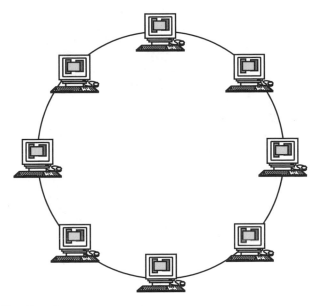

Exhibit 2. Ring Topology

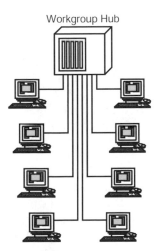

Exhibit 3. Star Topology

systems with connections to two networks require two network interface cards and must act as a router.

A tree network can also be constructed using hubs or switched by connecting one hub to another instead of computers.

527

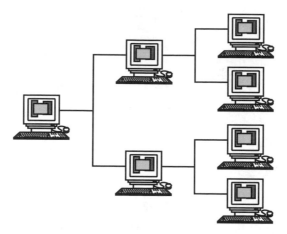

Exhibit 4. Tree Topology

Mesh Topology. Mesh topology (Exhibit 5) is implemented in larger, more complex networks due to its tolerance for node failures or congested network links. As each node in the network has more than one path to any other node, a failure on one link due to congestion or failure does not significantly impact network connectivity. Implementing a mesh network is very expensive when compared to other nework architectures, but the high levels of reliability and availability of the network often outweigh the implementation costs.

There are security issues with each of the topologies. Most visible, however, is the difference between the star and ring topologies. When sending data from one node to another through a star, the data is moved from the sender, through a central hub or switch, directly to the receiving station. However, with a ring or bus, the data is sent through each node on the network until it reaches its destination. Consequently, the other nodes on the network can intercept sensitive messages.

LAN Transmission Methods. LAN data is transmitted from the sender to one or more receiving stations using either a unicast, multicast, or broadcast transmission. Unicast transmissions send the data from the sender to a single receiver. The transmitting station obtains the network address of the receiver and addresses the packet only for the receiver. The packet is then transmitted on the network and all stations but the receiver ignore it because it is not addressed for it.

The same process occurs for multicast transmissions, except that the sending station sends the packet to a specific subset of the nodes on the network. This is accomplished using a multicast address. When a node receives the data, it processes the packet if it is in fact addressed to them.

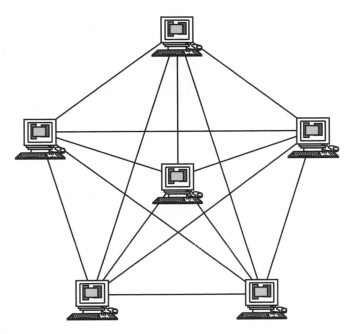

Exhibit 5. Mesh Topology

Finally, the broadcast address sends the data to all nodes in the network using a broadcast address. When the data is actually copied on the network, all the stations receive and process a copy of the data. Many networking protocols use broadcast packets to obtain information from nodes on the network. For example, the Address Resolution Protocol uses a broadcast packet to ask all the nodes on the network for the Ethernet address of the system with the specified IP address.

LAN Media Access Methods. Because LAN communications depend on transmitting an electrical signal on the access medium, no two systems can transmit at the same time. Consequently, some method must be used to detect when another station is transmitting and to mediate access to the network. This is accomplished using either Carrier Sense Multiple Access with Collision Detection (CSMA/CD) or token passing.

Networks using CSMA/CD, such as Ethernet, must share the available network resource. The network interface first listens to the network to see if another station is transmitting. If no station is transmitting, meaning there is no carrier present on the wire, the system transmits its data. Upon completion of the transmission, the station then listens to determine if a collision occurred, meaning two stations attempted to transmit simultaneously. If a collision occurred, each station waits a random period of time before attempting to retransmit the data. In the majority of situations, a collision will not occur again between those two devices. However, a collision may occur with other devices, which becomes more likely the more stations and the busier a network becomes. This is why the performance of an Ethernet network degrades as the volume of traffic increases.

The introduction of switch technology improved CSMA/CD network design. Using the network switch breaks the network into multiple collision domains by reducing the number of nodes per network segment. With smaller collision domains, network performance is increased significantly, without the need to reallocate network addresses.

Typically, CSMA/CD networks operate in a half-duplex mode, meaning that a device cannot simultaneously transmit and receive data. However, full-duplex capabilities are introduced when a switch is used. While network performance is increased, it is not as much as some claim. A 100-MB Ethernet segment can carry 200 MB of data, but only in one direction at a time; and because most network connections are asymmetric, meaning the same amount of data does not travel in both directions, the gain is less.

The alternative to CSMA/CD is token passing, commonly found in Token Ring and fiber-optic networks. In the token-passing network, a token is passed from station to station. When a device has data to transmit, it must wait until it has the token. When the data transmission is completed, the token is released for the next station. Should the token be lost, a part of the protocol regenerates the token to keep data moving on the network.

There are several advantages to the token-passing method. Clearly, collisions are not going to happen and it is possible to calculate the maximum time a device will have to wait before being able to send data. Because of the deterministic nature of the token-passing network, it is very popular in real-time networks where devices must be able to communicate at determined intervals.

Like Ethernet-based networks, token-based systems also benefit from switches, especially on larger networks. As the network grows, the contention can become significant. Using a network switch can reduce this delay by allowing simultaneous transmissions.

LAN Implementations. Network devices must be connected using some form of physical medium. Most commonly, this is done through cabling. However, today's networks also include wireless, which can be extended to desktop computers, or to laptop or palmtop devices connected to a cellular phone. There are several different connection methods; however, the most popular today are Ethernet and Token Ring.

Ethernet. Ethernet is, without a doubt, the most widely used local area network (LAN) technology. While the original and most popular version of Ethernet supported a data transmission speed of 10 Mbps, newer versions have evolved, called Fast Ethernet and Gigabit Ethernet, that support speeds of 100 and 1000 Mbps, respectively.

Ethernet LANs are constructed using coaxial cable, special grades of twisted pair wiring, or fiber-optic cable. Bus and star wiring configurations are the most popular by virtue of the connection methods to attach devices to the network. Ethernet devices compete for access to the network using a protocol called Carrier Sense Multiple Access with Collision Detection (CSMA/CD).

Token Ring. Token Ring is the second most widely used LAN technology after Ethernet. Stations on a Token Ring LAN are organized in a ring topology, with data being transmitted sequentially from one ring station to the next. Circulating a token initializes the ring. To transmit data on the ring, a station must capture the token. When a station transmits information, the token is replaced with a frame that carries the information to the stations. The frame circulates the ring and can be copied by one or more destination stations. When the frame returns to the transmitting station, it is removed from the ring and a new token is transmitted. The ring in a Token Ring network consists of the transmission medium or cabling and the ring station. While most people consider that Token Ring is a ring network-based topology, it is not. Token Ring uses a star-wired ring topology.

In a Token Ring network, each station in the ring receives its data from one neighbor, the nearest upstream neighbor, and then transmits the data to a downstream neighbor. This means that data in the Token Ring network moves sequentially from one station to another, while checking the data for errors. The station that is the intended recipient of the data copies the information as it passes. When the information reaches the originating station again, it is stripped, or removed from the ring. A station gains the right to transmit data, commonly referred to as frames, onto the network when it detects the empty token passing it. The token is itself a frame that contains a unique signaling sequence that circulates on the network following each frame transfer. After completing the transmission of its data, the station transmits a new token, thus allowing other stations on the ring to gain access to the ring and transmit data of their own.

With legacy Ethernet and Token Ring LANs getting bogged down from the added bandwidth requirements of engineering, document imaging, and electronic-mail applications, the need arose for higher-speed network solutions. One of the earliest solutions was FDDI (Fiber Distributed Data Interface), a token-based fiber backbone network operating at 100 Mbps. FDDI supports up to 1000 connections over a dual-fiber path. Each station regenerates and repeats frames sent to it, which also serves as the means for identifying new devices added to or deleted from the network.

Wireless Technology and Security Issues. Over the past ten years, the use of wireless communications devices such as mobile computers, cell phones, and pagers has exploded. These devices allow people to communicate over local and long-distance areas expanding their communications ability. The continued demand for wireless communications has expanded wireless communications networks and expanded into the data communications arena. Aside from the wireless technologies discussed previously, the use of wireless LANs in enterprises and personal networks has revolutionized information exchange.

Wireless LANs provide quick deployment and support for a highly mobile workforce and can be deployed in temporary and industrial situations where cabling may not be feasible. Additionally, the cost of deploying a wireless LAN is remarkably cost-effective. However, the wireless LAN typically lacks the security controls found in wired networks.

Technology Overview. Wireless LANs (WLANs) are intended as a flexible alternative or extension to wired LANs. The WLAN uses electromagnetic waves to transmit and receive data from other stations. WLANs enable mobile user connectivity, simplify installation, and enable a movable or relocatable network. WLANs have gained strong popularity in the healthcare, retail, manufacturing, warehousing, and academic areas. Both industry and the individual user have seen productivity benefits from using handheld and notebook computers to access information in real-time.

A WLAN uses a spread-spectrum radio signal instead of cabling as the transport medium. Installing a wireless network requires only a few components. First, a radio frequency must be allocated for the network. The allocation of radio frequencies for various purposes is managed by national regulatory agencies in the various countries.

The assigned WLAN radio frequencies do not require a license for use. Within North America, the assigned frequencies include the 2.42- to 2.483-GHz band. The Federal Communications Commission in the United States has restricted the power output of devices operating in the 2.4-GHz band to reduce interference with each other. Due to various noise sources within the same band, engineering a WLAN is more complicated than a traditional cable-based system. For example, consumer telephones operating in the 2.4-GHz band can cause interference for WLANs also operating in this frequency range.

The most obvious method of choosing a frequency is to simply select one and use it as the communications path. However, spurious noise emissions from other devices can interfere with the radio signal and may completely prevent a link from being established. The solution to this problem is to use spread-spectrum technology. Spread spectrum uses multiple frequencies in the band, decreasing the susceptibility to noise at any specific frequency. Today, two approaches are used to implement spread spectrum for WLAN transmissions:

- Frequency hopping spread spectrum (FHSS)
- Direct sequence spread spectrum (DSSS)

The Standards. There are several wireless LAN standards in use today, with continued evolution in the technology and protocol definitions. As with other network protocols, the WLAN standards are defined by the IEEE.

The IEEE 802.11 standard defines an 802-compatible MAC layer interoperable with the other 802 technologies. The FHSS, DSSS, and infrared communications technologies are available, with the focus on the 2.4-GHz band. As new bands are allocated for use, new technologies will be implemented to use them.

The original 802.11 standard provided an asynchronous networking model requiring a distributed control function. The data rates supported include 1 and 2 Mbps.

The typical 802.11 WLAN only had data transfer rates of 1 Mbps. While useful in some environments, it was not enough to support today's mainstream and mission-critical business applications. The IEEE approved the 802.11b (Wi-Fi) standard, increasing the data transfer rate to 11 Mbps. WLAN implementations using the 802.11b protocols still can communicate with devices from 50 to 300 feet away. This makes the 802.11b standard appropriate for both internal WLANs and building-to-building connectivity.

With the improvements in wireless data transfer rates, major communications vendors started to offer WLAN equipment in the form of access points. The access point had a 10baseT or 100baseT network port allowing the access point to be connected to the traditional cable network. Networking with WLANs can use an access point to connect to the wired LAN, which is called "infrastructure mode." The alternative is "ad hoc mode" that establishes a wireless link between individual systems.

The 802.11b standard has been evolving to the 802.11g standard, but is the current standard for wireless LAN communications. The 802.11g standard can provide network connection speeds up to 54 Mbps from the original 1 and 2 Mbps. Consequently, wireless LANs will likely become more prevalent. With the appropriate equipment, including directional antennas and access points, a wireless LAN can be extended a mile or more. With the range possible with WLANs, "war driving" has become a popular approach to locate wireless LAN access points and gain access to enterprise or personal networks.

Locating wireless LAN access points by driving or walking within a defined area is known as "war driving." Using a laptop or handheld computer with a wireless Ethernet card set to promiscuous mode and an antenna, a user can locate, determine the SSID, and possibly even connect to a wireless LAN. This is possible because wireless LANs can extend beyond the physical characteristics of the building where the access point is located. If the WLAN, and the wired LAN it is connected to, is not properly secured, an intruder may be able to access your network, steal network resources, or even steal your organization's data.

WLANs provide a limited, but still reasonably large wireless network. 802.15 Bluetooth is intended to provide smaller, short-range wireless networking, usually limited to approximately 10 meters or about 35 feet. Bluetooth allows various devices to form an "ad hoc" network to perform such functions as downloading voice mail from properly equipped IP telephones to a PDA. Bluetooth is intended primarily for use in PDAs, digital cameras, automobiles, and other consumer electronics.

Bluetooth uses spread-spectrum technology in the 2.4-GHz frequency range and is capable of allowing up to seven simultaneous connections in one location. The spread-spectrum technology used in Bluetooth performs up to 1600 frequency hops per second.

Despite the advantages to Bluetooth, some security problems do exist. If the transmission occurs in a public area between two Bluetooth-enabled devices, any other device in the vicinity is capable of intercepting those transmissions. Fortunately, Bluetooth includes an optional security specification that enables device authentication and line encryption.

Hardware. The acceptance of handheld computers and communication devices such as Palm Pilots, iPAQs, and BlackBerrys is changing the way mobile users access data. While many PDAs are capable of using a wireless LAN card, others require wireless LAN services delivered by a telecommunications tower operating in a cellular frequency range. Consequently, there must be sufficient transmitter (tower) coverage for the device to operate. If coverage is poor, the device cannot establish a connection, just like a cell phone.

PDA (personal digital assistant) and cellular technologies are merging, bringing both devices into a single package. Cell phones now include mini-browsers, allowing the user to view Internet services in a format suitable for the cell phone. Similarly, traditional PDAs now have cellular technology integrated, bringing the user both the cell phone and the extended user interface of the PDA.

Wireless LAN Architectures. In the majority of situations, a wireless LAN is connected to a traditional wired Ethernet LAN. When connected to the wired LAN, the wireless access point acts as a bridge to the wired LAN for the wireless devices. All wireless devices communicating at the same access point can access the same LAN resources.

The devices connected to a given access point are part of that network. The access point (AP) coordinates all communications inside and outside the cell. The AP is capable of communicating with other access points and the wired LAN. Additionally, the AP keeps the stations within the network synchronized so that collisions are minimized at the same time.

When there is only one access point and a group of associated wireless stations, the network is considered *stand-alone,* meaning there are no other access points with which to interact. The maximum number of stations supported by an access point varies, depending upon the amount of traffic carried by the WLAN. For high data throughput WLANS, 15 stations may be the maximum supportable.

PC Connectivity. When connecting a laptop or desktop PC to a WLAN, the traditional wired NIC is replaced with a wireless NIC appropriate for the computer type. All the necessary drivers and software must then be installed and configured to establish connectivity with the WLAN. Alternatively, the PC can be connected from the wired NIC card to an external wireless transceiver. The wireless transceiver bridges between the PC NIC and the WLAN, without the need for additional software installation on the PC.

Sources of Interference. Many different types of interference including multi-path propagation, microwave devices including cooking ovens, cordless telephones operating in the same frequency range, and other electromagnetic interference affect wireless LANs. Typically, the wireless NIC selects the strongest signal to connect to. With Frequency Hopping Spread Spectrum (FHSS) technology, the signal is spread over 79 hops of 1-MHz bands. The hops are changed frequently, from 30 to 80 times a second using a predefined order. The sending and receiving stations must be synchronized for data transfer to occur. When interference occurs, only one of the channels should experience the interference for a short period of time.

Benefits of Wireless LANs. The benefits of the wireless network should be obvious, but include:

- Mobility
- Ease of installation (which is also a detriment)
- Short-term usage
- Difficult wiring environments
- Installation flexibility

The wireless user no longer has to find a place to plug in and network managers can make changes without having to run additional cabling.

Consequently, wireless LANS can offer significant productivity, service, convenience, and cost benefits over traditional wired networks.

Mobility. The major benefit of a wireless LAN is user mobility. Users are no longer tied to their desk or a cable. They can use their laptops or other wireless-enabled devices to access information from anywhere in their organization. Increased mobility supports improved productivity and employee satisfaction over traditional wired networks. This has tremendous advantages in many organizations. Healthcare workers can now enter patient information at the bedside. Retail personnel can find inventory and product information while standing with a customer. Similarly, the reduction in information handling makes it less likely for errors to occur. If there is a business advantage to being with the customer and processing information, then a wireless network is the logical choice.

Short-Term Usage. Like mobility, short-term usage allows organizations to deploy wireless connectivity for the period of time it is required. WLAN access is deployed and modified as capabilities and requirements change. For example, auditors can be granted connectivity for the duration of the audit. Contractors can be given access to perform their contracted obligations. The operational flexibility gained supports ad hoc working groups. The ability to establish such short-term network connectivity can also provide a competitive advantage.

Simplicity and Flexibility. Unlike traditional networks, wireless LANs are quick and relatively simple to install, without the requirement to install network cabling. Similarly, wireless LANs can be installed in locations where traditional networks cannot, including difficult wiring locations such as historic buildings, factory floors, and open areas.

Open area examples include sports arenas and parks. Disaster recovery and relief efforts can also make use of wireless LANs as there is no need to locate, obtain, install, and test network cabling.

However, the ease of installation can also be a detriment. Because wireless LAN access points are relatively low cost, employees can purchase a rogue AP and plug it in at their desks. This AP is likely not configured to provide much, if any security, thereby allowing a gap in your overall network defense.

Scalability. The scalability of any network is particularly important. However, wired networks can be difficult to change due to cabling layouts and additional equipment requirements. Wireless LANs, however, are easily expanded by adding more access points to meet the mobile station requirements. Network topologies, access point locations, and configurations are easily changed.

Wired versus Wireless Security. Regardless of the transport medium, networks in general suffer from significant security risks, including:

- Physical network security threats
- Eavesdropping and data interception
- Attacks from the authorized user community

However, wireless LANS are especially vulnerable to these threats.

Aside from the physical cable, a wireless LAN has all the components and properties of a wired LAN. Consequently, some of the same countermeasures used to secure and protect the wired LAN can be used for the wireless LAN. Remember that the only difference between the wired and wireless LAN is the physical transport medium; many similar threats and vulnerabilities still apply.

Wireless Security

Security in all three 802.11 formats is handled in the same fashion. The network name, authentication, and encryption are the three mechanisms used to protect the wireless LAN.

Network Name. Each network device in a wireless LAN is called a station, which includes both clients and access points. The client stations can communicate directly with each other, known as ad hoc networking, or with an access point, known as infrastructure networking. Wireless clients wishing to communicate with a station on a wired LAN must use an access point to bridge the connection from the wireless LAN to the wired network.

In the infrastructure networking model, the wireless clients and access points form a group called the Basic Service Set (or BSS). The basic service set is assigned a name, which is called the Service Set Identifier (SSID). The SSID is also called the network name.

Those clients with the network name can join the BSS and communicate with the access point. However, the network name is effectively useless as a password. Most vendors use a well-known network name, which most people forget to change. Additionally, the access point periodically transmits frames, called beacon frames, including the SSID and other operational characteristics of the access point. Consequently, a wireless sniffer can retrieve the access point beacon frames and determine the SSID, allowing anyone to join the BSS. Even if users do not know the network name, they can generally configure the wireless station with a network name of ANY, and be granted access to the BSS.

Authentication. An authentication element is also included in the 802.11 standard to verify the identity of a given wireless station. The authentication model can be either open or a shared key. The open authentication mode means that a station's identity is not checked when it connects to the BSS. However, when using shared secret mode and encryption, the assumption is made that each station has the correct key and when operating in shared secret mode represents a valid user. However, the assumption has been proven incorrect due to successful eavesdropping attacks against the encryption mechanism.

Encryption. The third element in the wireless LAN security model is encryption. Encryption in a wireless LAN is called Wired Equivalent Privacy (WEP) and is intended to provide a level of privacy equivalent to a wired LAN. The goal of WEP is not to make the wireless LAN impregnable, but to provide the same level of protection as a wired LAN by making the "over-the-air" transmission difficult for the eavesdropper to understand.

However, WEP is disabled initially on the wireless LAN products available to the user today. Consequently, when users set up their wireless station and access point, no privacy of the air interface is initially configured. This makes acquiring the packets trivial for users with a directional antenna, a wireless station, and wireless sniffer software.

WEP encoding makes it more difficult for the attacker to decipher the traffic; however, the WEP design, despite using 64- and 128-bit keys, makes itself vulnerable to attack. WEP is used to create a pseudo-random binary string that is modulo-2 added to plaintext to create ciphertext using a stream cipher. The total key length consists of the initialization vector (IV) and the WEP key. The IV is 24 bits long and forms part of the key. This means that the 64-bit key is really only 40 bits supplied by the user, plus the initialization vector. The same is true for the 128-bit key, where 24 bits are used for the IV and 104 bits are supplied by the user. Consequently, a 128-bit WEP is not really a 128-bit key.

To avoid key reuse, a new IV is used with the WEP key for each frame. While this sounds good, the 24-bit IV used with the 40- or 104-bit WEP key can actually expose the key. Because the IV is only 24 bits in length, it will repeat periodically, meaning that capturing two or more identical IVs will allow the attacker to perform frequency analysis on the captured data. Consequently, the IV represents a weakness that compromises the WEP encryption process.

Researchers at Rice University and AT&T Laboratories discovered in mid-2001 that capturing five hours of wireless LAN traffic means that it is possible to determine the WEP key through mathematical computation, regardless of key length. Consequently, the shared secret key can be compromised through the weaknesses in the WEP key, thus rendering it almost useless as a means of validating the wireless station operator.

MAC Address Checking. One of the initial methods of compensating for the weaknesses associated with the network name, SSID and WEP, was MAC address checking. When used, the MAC addresses of allowed hosts are programmed into the access point. With this configuration, only stations with MAC addresses in the access point's configuration are permitted to associate with the access point. This fails because the MAC is sent unencrypted.

MAC address checking provides a significant improvement over the network name access control, but it does nothing to address the weaknesses in WEP. Consequently, several wireless vendors introduced dynamic WEP keys.

Dynamic WEP Keys. Using the same WEP key over a long duration of time means that an attacker can collect enough data to determine the key. Some wireless vendors introduced dynamic keys to configure the equipment to exchange keys on a frame-by-frame or periodic basis. This limits a third party's ability to collect sufficient traffic for either a frequency analysis of the encrypted data or to determine the WEP key.

While dynamic WEP keys would appear to be a good thing, the vendors offering this solution may do so in a proprietary manner. Consequently, it is unlikely that dynamic keys will work outside a homogeneous wireless LAN environment. Because it is unlikely that all devices will come from the same vendor, the LAN administrator and security manager cannot depend on dynamic WEP keys as a viable form of protection. There is still no integrity protection.

What Can Be Done to the Wired LANs? Any person who can gain access to the physical cable plant can damage the network or compromise the integrity and security of the information on it. While physical access to the cable plant must be protected, the vast amount of cabling found in most organizations makes protecting it a difficult task.

User authentication is a critical concern for managing authorized access to the network. The various remote access products allowing employees, contractors, vendors, and customers access to the network can leave the network open and vulnerable to attacks by hackers, viruses, and other intruders. The available countermeasures, including firewalls and intrusion detection systems, provide some measure of protection, but many remote access products bypass these countermeasures. Additionally, hackers are getting smarter at finding ways to circumvent the technology.

Capturing raw data and analyzing it for sensitive data is an ominous threat and very difficult to detect. Network data capture tools and software packet sniffers are readily available and range from low to no cost. Consequently, anyone with physical access to the network has the ability to capture data. Additionally, wired networks typically emanate more electromagnetic radiation, especially when using unshielded twisted pair cabling. Consequently, an intruder can sit outside the building and, if the radiation is sufficient, capture the packets without actually connecting to the network. The only effective countermeasure to this type of attack is network-level encryption, which is not in widespread use today.

Data security considerations apply equally to the wireless network as well and can impact the entire network architecture. However, the very different physical layer of the wireless network can provide additional benefits to protecting overall network security, but we do not use the same techniques.

The vast majority of wireless LAN systems available today use either Direct Sequence Spread Spectrum or Frequency Hopping Spread Spectrum radio technology. Spread-spectrum technology was developed by the military more than 60 years ago for message integrity and security, but we do not use the same techniques. Spread-spectrum systems are designed to be resistant to noise, interference, and jamming.

In contrast to traditional radio, where a large amount of power is transmitted on a single frequency, spread spectrum uses low power over a broad range of frequencies.

Data scrambling is also used by radio systems to assist in managing the timing and decoding of the radio signal. Consequently, the unauthorized receiver would also need to know the timing pattern. Many wireless products include encryption as a standard or optional component. However, the 802.11 standard, Wired Equivalent Privacy (WEP), is a less than adequate encryption method using 40-bit keys and the popular RC4 algorithm.

Wireless LAN products typically provide the ability to allow and exclude stations from connecting to the access point. The *station authentication* function requires that users know a variety of information, including the channel number being used, the radio domains, security IDs, and passwords. Consequently, by combining the security elements, the network administrator can make it difficult for hackers to gain network access even if they possess the right equipment.

Finally, wireless LANs eliminate the possibility of connecting to a physical access point through network cabling. Although linking the access points together still requires network cabling, the quantity is quite small compared to the traditional network. Consequently, it is much easier to safeguard the smaller amount of cable. Additionally, the access point acts as a bridge, keeping the majority of the LAN traffic away from the wireless user, making it more difficult for a wireless station to obtain access to the raw data packets.

WAN (Wide Area Network). A natural extension of the LAN is the wide area network (WAN). A WAN connects LANs, both locally and remotely, and thus connects remote computers together over long distances. The WAN provides the same functionality as the individual LAN, but on a larger scale where email, applications, and files now move throughout an organization-wide Internet. WANs are, by default, heterogeneous networks that consist of a variety of computers, operating systems, topologies, and protocols. The most popular internetworking devices for WANs are bridges and routers. Hybrid units are sometimes called brouters, or Layer 3 switches, capable of providing both bridging and routing functions. Today's technology is even offering Layer 4, and higher layer switches as well. The decision to bridge, route, or switch depends on protocols, network topology, and security requirements. Internetworking schemes often include a combination of bridges and routers.

Many organizations today support a variety of networking capabilities for different groups or divisions within their companies. These include LAN-to-LAN interconnection, gateways to outside company networks, and email backbone capabilities.

This section introduces the various protocols and technologies used in WAN environments. Topics summarized here include modems, ISDN, point-to-point links, xDSL and cable modems, SDLC and derivatives, X.25, Frame Relay, ATM, wireless, and multi-service access technologies.

Often, a network is located in multiple physical locations. Wide area networking combines multiple LANs that are geographically separate. This is accomplished by connecting the different LANs using services such as dedicated leased phone lines, satellite links, and data packet carrier services. Wide area networking can be as simple as a modem and remote access server for users to dial into, or it can be as complex as hundreds of branch offices globally linked using special routing protocols and filters to minimize the expense of sending data over vast distances, typically using facilities provided by the common carriers, such as the telephone companies. WAN technologies generally function at the lower three layers of the OSI Reference Model: the physical layer, the data-link layer, and the network layer.

Unlike LANs, which are designed to deliver data between many systems, WAN topologies are usually point-to-point. Point-to-point means that the technology was developed to support only two nodes sending and receiving data. If multiple nodes need access to the WAN, a LAN will be placed behind it to accommodate this functionality.

There are two ways to design WAN topologies. One is to use private circuits such as leased lines, dedicated lines, or by using T1 or T3. The other is to use Frame Relay or X.25, which are both packet-switched technologies.

WAN Modem Dial-up. Dial-up services sometimes offer cost-effective methods for connectivity across WANs. The two most popular dial-up implementations are dial-on-demand routing (DDR) and dial backup.

DDR is a technique whereby a router can dynamically initiate a call on a switched circuit when it needs to send data or when certain conditions have been met. In a DDR setup, the router is configured to initiate the call when certain criteria are met, such as a particular type of network traffic waiting to be transmitted, or when problems are experienced with certain other setups. When the connection is made, traffic passes over the line. The router configuration specifies an idle timer that tells the router to drop the connection when the circuit has remained idle for a certain period of time.

Dial backup is another way of configuring DDR. However, in dial backup, the switched circuit is used to provide backup service for another type of circuit, such as point-to-point or packet switching. The router is configured to fail-over to the backup when a failure is detected on the primary circuit. The dial backup line then supports the WAN connection until the primary circuit is restored. When the primary circuit is restored, the dial backup connection is terminated.

Integrated Services Digital Network (ISDN). Integrated services digital network (ISDN) is a worldwide public network service that can provide end-to-end digital communications and fully integrate technologies (including circuit switching, private line, and packet switching) and applications (voice, data, and image) over existing twisted pair cable. The objective of ISDN is to provide voice, video, and data on a single network. With such a communications network, increasingly diversified and complex data communications technology can be controlled and the installation and maintenance costs in communications facilities can be reduced.

There are two standard ISDN access interfaces (or two classes of services to customers): the basic rate interface and the primary rate interface. The basic rate interface (BRI) is the minimum ISDN service and is appropriate for residential and small business users. This service defines three channels and is referred to as 2B+D. The B channels are each of 64-Kbps bandwidth and are appropriate for either voice or data transmission. The D channel, which is a 16-Kbps signaling channel, is designed to control transmission of the B channels.

The primary rate interface (PRI) is referred to as 23B+D and is suitable for organizations that have heavier and stricter demand for data communications. It consists of 23 64-Kbps B channels and one 64-Kbps D channel. The PRI offers a high level of versatility for users. A transmission job that requires higher bandwidth can be performed by multiplexing two B channels to form one 128-Kbps channel, or by multiplexing four B channels to

Exhibit 6. Typical Point-to-Point Link through a WAN

form one 256-Kbps channel. In a similar manner, a 64-Kbps channel can be submultiplexed into two 32-Kbps or eight 8-Kbps channels.

Point-to-Point Links. A point-to-point link provides a single, preestablished WAN communications path from the customer premises through a carrier network, such as a telephone company, to a remote network. Point-to-point lines are usually leased from a carrier and thus are often called leased lines. For a point-to-point line, the carrier allocates pairs of wire and facility hardware to your line only. These circuits are generally priced based on bandwidth requirements and distance between the two connected points. Point-to-point links are generally more expensive than shared services such as Frame Relay. Exhibit 6 illustrates a typical point-to-point link through a WAN.

Leased lines are dedicated analog or digital circuits paid for on a flat-rate basis. This means that whether you use the circuit or not, you are paying a fixed monthly fee. Leased lines are point-to-point connections — they are used to connect one geographical location to another. Leased lines are generally capable of carrying a variety of services including voice, channelized data, or both.

T1, T2, T3, T4, Tx. A T1 is a general term for a digital carrier, typically leased from a local or long-distance provider, capable of transmitting 1.544 Mbps of electronic information. A T1 line is a point-to-point line, as opposed to a dial-able ISDN line. T1 lines may be used fractionally or at their full bandwidth. E1 is the approximate European equivalent, prevalent also in Mexico. T1 is a full-duplex signal (each end of the connection can transmit and receive simultaneously) over two-pair wire cabling.

T1s are used for dedicated point-to-point connections in the same way as leased lines. Bandwidth on a T1 is available in increments from 64 Kbps up to 1.544 Mbps. T1s use a technology known as "time division" to break the two wire pairs into 24 separate channels, each of 64K, which can carry either voice circuits or data. Time division is the allotment of available bandwidth based on time increments. This is extremely useful, as a T1 is capable of carrying both voice and data at the same time. This means an organization can use a single T1 to carry voice and data between two offices, reducing their overall network costs. However, when using a channelized approach, increasing capacity for either voice or data requires a similar change to decrease the other service.

- T2 connection: a T-carrier that can handle 6.312 Mbps or 96 voice channels.
- T3 connection: a T-carrier that can handle 44.736 Mbps or 672 voice channels.
- T4 connection: a T-carrier that can handle 274.176 Mbps or 4032 voice channels.

Cable Modem versus DSL. Internet access via cable modem has become available in many residential areas over the past few years. Cable has the capacity to transmit data at speeds as fast as Digital Subscriber Line (DSL) when configured properly and under optimal conditions. Due to the fact that cable lines are not available in the vast majority of commercial districts, cable does not compete with DSL in the enterprise market at all, in most cases. Cable was designed for residential use, and in some cases may be a cost-effective solution for residential high-bandwidth Internet access. Therefore, the challenge of cable versus DSL is primarily in the residential and telecommuter markets. The cable modem or DSL connection is normally always active and the bandwidth is very high compared to slower dial-up or ISDN methods. Consequently, these connections make easy targets for intrusion and disruption.

DSL, by using the existing telephone cabling infrastructure, is a technology backed by telephone enterprises that provides high-bandwidth services to the home and enterprise. Because DSL utilizes a greater range of frequencies than ordinary dial-up services (allowing for a super-fast connection), this high bandwidth is possible. Only a small fraction of one's telephone line capacity (bandwidth) is being used (that being only the low frequencies) when making an ordinary telephone call. By transporting data in the higher frequencies, DSL takes advantage of this idle bandwidth. This results in making it possible to talk on the phone and be on the Internet simultaneously.

There are several competing forms of DSL, each adapted to specific needs in the marketplace. Some forms of DSL are widely used standards, some are proprietary, and some are simply theoretical models. They can best be categorized within the modulation methods used to encode data. These technologies are sometimes collectively referred to as xDSL.

Asymmetric Digital Subscriber Line (ADSL) is the most popular form of DSL technology. The fact that the upstream and downstream bandwidths are asymmetric, or uneven, is the key to ADSL. In practice, the higher-speed path will be the bandwidth from the ISP to the user (downstream). This is mainly due to the desire to accommodate the typical Internet usage pattern, where the majority of data is being sent to the user (Web pages, graphics, programs, and video) with minimal upload capacity required (keystrokes and mouse-clicks). Speeds typically range from 144 Kbps to

1.5 Mbps downstream and from 144 Kbps to 1.5 Mbps upstream. Other forms of DSL include ADSL Lite, Consumer Digital Subscriber Line (CDSL), G.Lite, HDSL, IDSL, RADSL, SDSL, and VDSL.

A cable modem enables a personal computer (PC) to access the Internet via a common CATV coaxial cable at operating rates up to tens of millions of bits per second. Using traditional coaxial cable installed by CATV operators, these modems can deliver speeds of up to 1000 times that of today's analog modems. Cable modems are really not modems in the conventional sense. They modulate and demodulate signals like a conventional modem, but otherwise they are more like routers that are designed for installation on CATV networks, which themselves operate much like Ethernet LANs.

Cable modems (CMs) allow a form of high-speed shared access over media used for cable television (CATV) delivery. Standard CATV video channels are delivered over a frequency range from 54 MHz to several hundred megahertz. Cable modems simply use a relatively narrow band of those frequencies that are unused for TV signal delivery. CATV signals are normally delivered through a series of in-line amplifiers and signal splitters to a typical neighborhood cable segment. Along each of these final segments, additional signal splitters (or taps) distribute the CATV signals to users. Adding two-way data distribution to the segment is relatively easy because splitters are inherently two-way devices and no amplifiers are within the segment. However, the uplink signal from users in each segment must be retrieved at the head of the segment and either repeated into the next up-line segment or converted and transported separately.

A standard cable modem is essentially a two-way repeater connected between a user's PC (or local network) and the cable segment. As such, it repeats everything along your segment to your local PC network and everything on your network back out to the cable segment. Thus, all the "private" conversations one might have with one's network-connected printer or other local PCs are available to everyone on the segment. In addition, every TCP/IP packet that goes between a PC and the Internet is also available for eavesdropping along the cable segment. This is a very serious security risk, at least among those connected to a particular segment. It makes an entire group of cable modem users vulnerable to monitoring, or even intrusion.

Frame Relay and X.25. Frame Relay and X.25 are packet-switched technologies. Because data on a packet-switched network is capable of following any available circuit path, such networks are represented by clouds in graphical presentations. Both X.25 and Frame Relay must be configured as Permanent Virtual Circuits (PVCs), meaning that all data entering the cloud at point A is automatically forwarded to point B. These endpoints are defined at the time the service is leased. For large WAN environments,

Frame Relay can be far more cost-effective than dedicated circuits. This is because you can run multiple PVCs through a single WAN connection.

X.25 is an International Telecommunication Union-Telecommunication Standardization Sector (ITU-T) protocol standard for WAN communications defining how connections between user devices and network devices are established and maintained. X.25 is designed to operate effectively, regardless of the type of systems connected to the network. It is typically used in the packet-switched networks (PSNs) of common carriers, such as the telephone companies. Subscribers are charged based on their network usage. The development of the X.25 standard was initiated by the common carriers in the 1970s. At that time, there was a need for WAN protocols capable of providing connectivity across public data networks (PDNs). X.25 is now administered as an international standard by the ITU-T.

X.25 was designed to work in a world where network links are unreliable. X.25 suffers with overhead, and each packet is unpacked and repacked into frames at each hop (much like an IP router does). Flow control and error checking are performed on every frame at every hop, which can sometimes limit the speeds offered by X.25.

Frame Relay is a networking protocol, which means that unlike a point-to-point private line, there is a network switch between a location and a destination. Typically, the organization obtains a private, or leased, line to a node on the Frame Relay network, and the remote location gets a private line to a nearby Frame Relay node. When you send traffic over your line, the network gets it to the remote location by routing it through the Frame Relay network. The data is then passed to the remote location's line and, at this point, the data has reached its destination.

Exhibit 7 shows how DTE (Data Terminal Equipment) such as PCs, dumb terminals, and network hosts are connected to a WAN, and transmitted packets are switched through the WAN by Frame Relay switches. The Frame Relay switches are referred to as DCE (Data Circuit-terminating Equipment) and generally reside within telecommunications carrier-operated equipment.

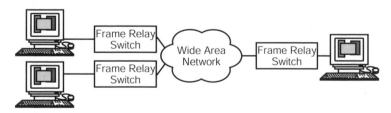

Exhibit 7. Frame Relay

Frame Relay started as a simplified version of X.25. Network advances had reduced the noise and error levels of modern networks to the point where the X.25 error checking was unnecessary. Frame Relay does not route packets like X.25 does: rather, Frame Relay forwards the frames. Unlike X.25, the frames are not unpacked at each node. Error checking is now also done at the endpoints, not in the network nodes. Speeds exceed 1 Mbps.

A critical concept in Frame Relay is the Committed Information Rate (CIR), which is the amount of bandwidth the service provider commits to carrying. The CIR is typically much lower than the full speed of the interface you purchase, and the carrier will allow your nodes to exceed the CIR under short bursts; but when the Frame Relay network is busy, the bursts may get dropped. That is, you get what you pay for.

Asynchronous Transfer Mode (ATM) is a network technology based on transferring data in cells or packets of a fixed size. The cell used with ATM is relatively small compared to units used with older technologies. The small, constant cell size allows ATM equipment to transmit video, audio, voice, and computer data over the same network, and minimizes delay of cells as they pass through switches.

ATM creates a fixed channel, or route, between two points whenever data transfer begins. This differs from TCP/IP, in which messages are divided into packets and each packet can take a different route from source to its destination. This difference makes it easier to track and bill data usage across an ATM network, but it makes it less adaptable to sudden surges in network traffic.

When purchasing ATM service, one generally has a choice of four different types of service:

- Constant Bit Rate (CBR) specifies a fixed bit rate so that data is sent in a steady stream. This is analogous to a leased line.
- Variable Bit Rate (VBR) provides a specified throughput capacity but data is not sent evenly. This is a popular choice for voice and videoconferencing data.
- Unspecified Bit Rate (UBR) does not guarantee any throughput levels. This is used for applications such as file transfers that can tolerate delays.
- Available Bit Rate (ABR) provides a guaranteed minimum capacity but allows data to be bursted at higher capacities when the network is free.

These classes of service affect availability and cost. The more you pay for, the more assurance your critical traffic will not get dropped. ATM switches provide high-speed switching and scalable bandwidths in the workgroup, the enterprise network backbone, and the wide area.

Wireless WANs use either infrared or radio waves. Infrared uses the same signal your remote control uses to control your TV. Infrared networks need clear lines-of-sight between communicating nodes but do not have severe bandwidth restrictions. Consequently, they can achieve normally acceptable data rates.

Radio waves use spread-spectrum technology, in which data is transmitted at low density over frequency ranges specified by national regulatory bodies. There are certain frequencies that are specified for data communications. Other ranges accommodate commercial radio, TV, and cellular phone communications. Spread-spectrum technology does not require line-of-sight but has limited bandwidth, which restricts data rates to less than ideal speeds for most networks. Higher frequencies have been authorized in the 18- to 19-GHz range, thus eliminating the bandwidth restrictions and interference problems of spread-spectrum technology.

Other technologies can include satellite links providing up to approximately 64 Kbps currently. Low Earth orbit (LEO) satellite can provide higher bandwidth. Satellite links usually experience high latency, which is normally caused by the long distances from Earth to the geosynchronous satellites hovering up to 23,000 miles above the Earth. LEO satellites travel at much lower altitudes, resulting in lower latency.

Terrestrial mobile phones can provide up to about 100 Kbps. This is an evolving technology and higher data rates are being evaluated by the ITU (International Telecommunication Union). New technology in the wireless area, specifically third-generation (3G) cellular technologies are providing significant improvements in data capacity. Further growth in the technology area and implementation by the telecommunications companies mean that we can expect speeds of 256 Kbps and higher to our mobile devices.

WAN Devices. WANs use numerous types of devices specific to WAN environments. WAN switches, access servers, modems, CSU/DSUs, and ISDN terminal adapters are discussed below. Other devices found in WAN environments include routers, ATM switches, and multiplexers.

A WAN switch is a multi-port internetworking device used in carrier networks. These devices typically switch such traffic as Frame Relay, X.25, and SMDS, and operate at the data-link layer of the OSI Reference Model.

An access server simply is a device, or series of devices, acting as a concentration point for dial-in and dial-out connections from the internal network.

A modem interprets digital and analog signals, enabling data to be transmitted over voice-grade telephone lines. At the source, digital signals are converted to sound, suitable for transmission over analog communication facilities. At the destination, these analog signals are returned to their digital form.

A channel service unit/digital service unit (CSU/DSU) is a digital-interface device (or sometimes two separate digital devices) that adapts the physical interface on a data terminal equipment (DTE) device (such as a terminal) to the interface of a data circuit-terminating (DCE) device (such as a switch) in a switched-carrier network. The CSU/DSU also provides signal timing for communication between these devices. A CSU/DSU is normally used to connect a router to a digital circuit like a T1.

An ISDN terminal adapter connects ISDN Basic Rate Interface (BRI) connections to other interfaces, such as an EIA/TIA-232 interface on a router. A terminal adapter is essentially an ISDN modem, although it is called a terminal adapter because it does not actually convert analog to digital signals.

Asynchronous Transfer Mode (ATM) switches provide high-speed switching and scalable bandwidths in the workgroup, the enterprise network backbone, and the wide area network. ATM switches support voice, video, and data applications and are designed to switch fixed-size information units.

The Wireless Application Protocol (WAP) is the *de facto* standard for providing Internet communications and advanced telephony-based services over digital mobile telephones, pagers, personal digital assistants, and other wireless terminals. The WAP is an open, global standard that empowers users of mobile telephones and wireless devices to securely access and instantly react with Internet information and services.

This single-industry, agreed-upon standard for wireless application interoperability uses an XML-compliant markup language called WML (Wireless Markup Language). The advantage of WML is that it provides a path for application developers as well as content providers to develop and deliver Web-based services. The WML user interface is a WAP microbrowser that maps into mobile phones and other wireless devices. Devices using WAP-based microbrowsers can access an array of innovative value-added services.

The basic concept of the WAP is to specify the network server, the mobile telephone software, and the communications between them. Communication is established between the mobile handset (client) and a gateway that serves as the gateway to the Internet. The gateway supports protocol and format conversion between a network application server, enabling communication with a WAP-enabled handset or client. The WAP is designed to function over any wireless network, including CDPD, CDMA, GSM, PDC, Mobitex, and others. An application server on the Internet provides the information or data desired by the client while the network serves as the bearer for the data.

Imode is an always-on, packet-switched service for mobile devices. This technology provides text messaging, Web browsing, e-commerce, and other Internet services. Imode is presently experiencing phenomenal usage in Japan and some European countries. The business community is taking notice of the high level of penetration within Japan, where 50% of the that country's cellular subscribers are using Imode. Similar penetration is expected elsewhere as the services become available in other countries.

Cellular. The evolution of cellular technology continues and standards are reviewed and revised. The AMPS analog system was primarily used in North and South America. As an analog-based system, AMPS had very little security and conversations were easily intercepted. Current technology standards include Time Division Multiple Access (TDMA), Code Division Multiple Access (CDMA), and Global System for Mobile Communications (GSM). GSM is predominately used outside North America, while TDMA and CDMA are still the predominant network technologies for North American cellular.

Both TDMA and CDMA protocols support data transmission, although at very slow speeds. Newer CDMA-based technology 1xRTT (single carrier radio transmission technology also known as CDMA 2000) will be capable of carrying data at speeds up to 144 Kbps. However, GSM currently supports high-rate digital data transmission using general packet radio services (GPRS).

Multi-Service Access. Multi-service networking combines all types of communications — data, voice, and video — over a single packet-cell-based infrastructure. The benefits of multi-service networking include reduced operational costs; increased performance; increased flexibility, integration, and control; and faster new application and service deployment. Multi-service networking supports Voice-over-IP (Internet Protocol), which will ultimately be a key component of the migration of telephony to the LAN infrastructure.

Significant advances in technology made during the past few years have also enabled the transmission of voice traffic over traditional public networks, to include Frame Relay (Voice-over-Frame Relay) as well as support of Asynchronous Transfer Mode (ATM) for different traffic types.

Remote Access Services

Remote access is the ability to connect and gain access to internal network resources that are physically disbursed. Typically, this means that a workstation equipped with remote access software will give authorized users at the remote site access to read email, troubleshoot problems, run applications, and transfer files to and from the corporate computers.

Remote users can either connect through their Internet service provider or dial into their corporate networks to gain access to all applications.

Several remote access methods are available today. The predominant methods are terminal servers, application specific, remote control, remote node, and a combination of several of these methods. Each of these methods differs significantly from the others and offers certain advantages that lend themselves to certain applications.

There are three areas that need to be secured when implementing remote access security: (1) positively authenticate the users to ensure that only authorized users get access to the network; (2) protect communication links from eavesdroppers to preserve the integrity and confidentiality of transmitted data; and (3) protect the network resources from unauthorized access by restricting users to access the resources that they are authorized to access.

Dial-In Access. PCs can make dial-up or remote access connections to a network. This is accomplished through a Remote Access Server (RAS) and a modem. The RAS may be a computer with a modem or specialized equipment providing these services. The remote PC requires a modem, communication software, and appropriate telephone network connectivity.

Remote access requires a user to log on to the network by providing a username and password. The RAS authenticates the logon credentials and the user is allowed or denied access. However, users with desktop PCs and modems can bypass the organization's remote access infrastructure, thus allowing access to their information and systems to anyone, potentially without a password. Consequently, dial-in capabilities can increase the risk of unauthorized access.

Virtual Private Networks (VPNs) can also be used to provide remote connectivity to the LAN, and are discussed later in this chapter.

Network Protocols

A communications protocol is a set of rules governing the transmission of information across communication lines. These rules control transmission speed, the number of data bits that each character comprises, what parity (if any) is used, which control characters are used, and when the various control characters are used. To communicate, both the sending and receiving devices must observe the same protocol, either directly through compatible systems software and hardware or indirectly through auxiliary protocol converters. This section discusses the Open Systems Interconnect (OSI) Model and the Transmission Control Protocol/Internet Protocol (TCP/IP).

Whenever two devices must pass information back and forth, they must observe a common protocol. For example, when a Central Processing Unit (CPU) and an I/O controller communicate, both observe a common channel protocol. Likewise, all devices attached to a local area network (LAN) would observe the LAN Media protocol. Although all devices require protocols to communicate with each other and the system processor may be forced to deal with several different types of protocols at any one time, each protocol is unique and accommodates a unique environment.

Communications protocols designed for LAN operations significantly differ in two key areas from protocols designed to transport information over WAN transmission facilities. LAN protocol designers rightly assumed that the error rate of the LAN transmission medium is many orders of magnitude lower than the error rate occurring when data is transmitted on a wide area network. Therefore, most LAN protocols are connectionless, which means that the protocol transmits information without requiring an acknowledgment that the packet of data transported was received at its destination. In comparison, almost all WAN protocols are connection oriented and require a response from the destination before the transmitting device can send subsequent packets.

A second major difference between LAN and WAN protocols concerns error detection and correction. Most LAN protocols assume that data is reliably transmitted on the LAN and do not perform error detection and correction. If error detection and correction is required, it must be performed at a higher level in the International Standards Institute (ISO) Open Systems Interconnect (OSI) Reference Model.

A wide variety of communication protocols exist, including LAN, WAN, network, and routing protocols. LAN protocols operate at the physical and data-link layers of the OSI Reference Model and define communication over the various LAN media. WAN protocols operate at the lowest three layers of the OSI Reference Model and define communication over the various wide area media. Routing protocols are network layer protocols that are responsible for exchanging information between routers to select the best path for network traffic. Finally, network protocols are the various upper-layer protocols that exist in a given protocol suite. Many protocols rely on others for operation. For example, many routing protocols use network protocols to exchange information between routers. This concept of building upon the layers already in existence is the foundation of the OSI Reference Model.

OSI Model and Communication between Systems

ISO Standard 7498 describes the OSI Reference Model (Exhibit 8), the security services that are available, and where they fit within the layered model. These services include encipherment, digital signatures, access

Application
Presentation
Session
Transport
Network
Data Link
Physical

Exhibit 8. The Open Systems Interconnection (OSI) Model

control, data integrity, authentication exchange, traffic padding, routing control, and notarization.

Information being transferred using OSI from a software application in one computer system to a software application in another must pass through the OSI layers. For example, if a software application in System A has information to transmit to a software application in System B, the application program in System A will pass its information to the application layer (layer 7) of System A. The application layer then passes the information to the presentation layer (layer 6), which relays the data to the session layer (layer 5), and so on down to the physical layer (layer 1). At the physical layer, the information is placed on the physical network medium and is sent across the medium to System B. The physical layer of System B removes the information from the physical medium, and then its physical layer passes the information up to the data-link layer (layer 2), which passes it to the network layer (layer 3), and so on, until it reaches the application layer (layer 7) of System B. Finally, the application layer of System B passes the information to the recipient application program to complete the communication process.

A given layer in the OSI Reference Model generally communicates with three other OSI layers: the layer directly above it, the layer directly below it, and its peer layer in other networked computer systems. The data-link layer in System A, for example, communicates with the network layer of System A, the physical layer of System A, and the data-link layer in System B.

Each layer has a defined interface with the layer above and below. This interface provides designers with the flexibility to implement various communications protocols with security features and still follow the standard.

The seven OSI layers use various forms of control information to communicate with their peer layers in other computer systems. This control

553

information consists of specific requests and instructions exchanged between the peer OSI layers.

Control information typically takes one of two forms: headers or trailers. Headers are prepended to data passed down from upper layers. Trailers are appended to data passed down from upper layers. An OSI layer is not required to attach a header or a trailer to data from upper layers.

Headers, trailers, and data are relative concepts, depending on the layer analyzing the information unit. At the network layer, for example, an information unit consists of a layer 3 header and data. At the data-link layer, however, all the information passed down by the network layer (the layer 3 header and the data) is treated as data.

In other words, the data portion of an information unit at a given OSI layer potentially contains headers, trailers, and data from all the higher layers. This is known as encapsulation.

The information exchange process occurs between peer OSI layers. Each layer in the source system adds control information to data, and each layer in the destination system analyzes and removes the control information from that data.

If System A has data from a software application to send to System B, the data is passed to the application layer. The application layer in System A then adds any control information required by the application layer in System B by prepending a header to the data. The resulting information unit (a header and the data) is passed to the presentation layer, which adds its own header containing control information intended for the presentation layer in System B. The information unit grows in size as each layer adds its own header (and, in some cases, a trailer) containing control information for the peer layer in System B. At the physical layer, the entire information unit is placed onto the network medium.

The physical layer in System B receives the information unit and passes it to the data-link layer. The data-link layer in System B then reads the control information contained in the header added by the data-link layer in System A. The header is then removed, and the remainder of the information unit is passed to the network layer. Each layer performs the same actions: the layer reads the header, or trailer, from its peer layer, strips it off, and passes the remaining information unit to the next highest layer. After the application layer performs these actions, the data is passed to the recipient software application in System B, in exactly the form in which it was transmitted by the application in System A.

Below is a summary of the layers, as depicted in the OSI Reference Model.

The *physical layer* defines the electrical, mechanical, procedural, and functional specifications for activating, maintaining, and deactivating the physical link between communicating network systems. Physical layer specifications define characteristics such as voltage levels, timing of voltage changes, physical data rates, maximum transmission distances, and physical connectors. Physical layer implementations can be categorized as either LAN or WAN specifications.

The *data-link layer* provides reliable transit of data across a physical network link. Different data-link layer specifications define different network and protocol characteristics, including physical addressing, network topology, error notification, sequencing of frames, and flow control. Physical addressing (as opposed to network addressing) defines how devices are addressed at the data-link layer. Network topology consists of the data-link layer specifications defining how devices are to be physically connected, such as in a bus or a ring topology. Error notification alerts upper-layer protocols of transmission errors, and the sequencing of data frames reorders frames that are transmitted out of sequence.

The Institute of Electrical and Electronics Engineers (IEEE) has subdivided the data-link layer into two sub-layers: Logical Link Control (LLC) and Media Access Control (MAC).

The Logical Link Control (LLC) sub-layer of the data-link layer manages communications between devices over a single link of a network. LLC is defined in the IEEE 802.2 specification and supports both connectionless and connection-oriented services used by higher-layer protocols. IEEE 802.2 defines a number of fields in data-link layer frames enabling multiple higher-layer protocols to share a single physical data link. The Media Access Control (MAC) sub-layer of the data-link layer manages protocol access to the physical network medium. The IEEE MAC specification defines MAC addresses, which enable multiple devices to uniquely identify one another at the data-link layer.

The *network layer* defines the network address, which differs from the MAC address described above. Some network layer implementations, such as the Internet Protocol (IP), define network addresses in a way such that route selection can be determined systematically by comparing the source network address with the destination network address and applying the subnet mask. Because this layer defines the logical network layout, routers can use this layer to determine how to forward packets. Because of this, much of the design and configuration work for internetworks happens at layer 3, the network layer.

The *transport layer* accepts data from the session layer and segments the data for transport across the network. Generally, the transport layer is responsible for making sure that the data is delivered error-free and in the proper sequence. Flow control generally occurs at the transport layer.

Flow control manages data transmission between devices so the transmitting device does not send more data than the receiving device can process. Multiplexing enables data from several applications to be transmitted onto a single physical link. Virtual circuits are established, maintained, and terminated by the transport layer. Error checking involves creating various mechanisms for detecting transmission errors, while error recovery involves actions, such as requesting that data be retransmitted, to resolve any errors in the data. The transport layer protocols used on the Internet are TCP and UDP.

The *session layer* establishes, manages, and terminates communication sessions. Communication sessions consist of service requests and service responses occurring between applications located in different network devices. These requests and responses are coordinated by protocols implemented at the session layer.

The *presentation layer* provides a variety of coding and conversion functions applied to application layer data. These functions ensure that the information sent from the application layer of one system will be readable by the application layer of another system. Some examples of presentation layer coding and conversion schemes include common data representation formats, conversion of character representation formats, common data compression schemes, and common data encryption schemes.

The *application layer* is the OSI layer closest to the end user, meaning that both the OSI application layer and the user interact directly with the software application.

This layer interacts with software applications implementing a communications component. Such application programs fall outside the scope of the OSI Reference Model. Application layer functions typically include identifying communication partners, determining resource availability, and synchronizing communication.

When identifying communication partners, the application layer determines the identity and availability of communication partners for an application with data to transmit. When determining resource availability, the application layer must decide whether sufficient network resources for the requested communication exist. In synchronizing communication, all communication between applications requires cooperation that is managed by the application layer.

Some examples of application layer implementations include Telnet, File Transfer Protocol (FTP), and Simple Mail Transfer Protocol (SMTP).

To summarize:

- The *application* layer is the highest level. It interfaces with users, gets information from databases, and transfers entire files. Email would be an example of an application at this level.
- The *presentation* layer defines how applications can enter the network.
- The *session* layer makes the initial contact with other computers and sets up the lines of communication. This layer allows devices to be referenced by name rather than by network address.
- The *transport* layer defines how to address the physical locations/devices on the network, how to make connections between nodes, and handles the internetworking of messages.
- The *network* layer defines how the small packets of data are routed and relayed between end systems on the same network or on interconnected networks.
- The *data-link* layer defines the protocols that computers must follow to access the network for transmitting and receiving messages. Token Ring and Ethernet operate within this layer and the physical layer, as defined below.
- The *physical* layer defines the physical connection between the computer and the network and, for example, converts the bits into voltages or light impulses for transmission.

Security is of fundamental importance to the acceptance and use of open systems in a LAN/WAN environment. Part 2 of the OSI Reference Model (Security Architecture) is now an international standard. The standard describes a general architecture for security in OSI, defines a set of security services that may be supported within the OSI Reference Model, and outlines a number of mechanisms that can be used in providing the services. However, no protocols, formats, or minimum requirements are contained in the standard.

An organization desiring security in a product being purchased in accordance with the Security Architecture profile must specify the security services required, the placement of the services within the OSI architecture, the mechanisms to provide the services, and the management features required. Security services may be provided at one or more of the layers. The primary security services defined in the OSI security architecture include (1) data confidentially services to protect against unauthorized disclosure; (2) data integrity services to protect against unauthorized modification, insertion, and deletion; (3) authentication services to verify the identity of communication peer entities and the source of data; and (4) access control services to allow only authorized communication and system access.

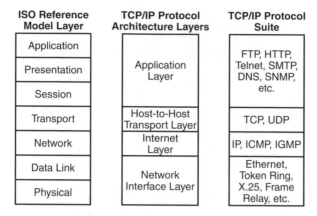

ISO Reference Model Layer	TCP/IP Protocol Architecture Layers	TCP/IP Protocol Suite
Application	Application Layer	FTP, HTTP, Telnet, SMTP, DNS, SNMP, etc.
Presentation		
Session		
Transport	Host-to-Host Transport Layer	TCP, UDP
Network	Internet Layer	IP, ICMP, IGMP
Data Link	Network Interface Layer	Ethernet, Token Ring, X.25, Frame Relay, etc.
Physical		

Exhibit 9. The TCP/IP Model

TCP/IP (Transmission Control Protocol/Internet Protocol)

TCP/IP is a set of protocols developed to allow cooperating computers to share resources across a network. It was developed by a community of researchers centered around the ARPANET, which really was the beginning of the global Internet of today. TCP/IP was actually developed before the OSI model discussed above; but in developing the OSI model, researchers made TCP/IP fit the specifications in such a way as to allow, and to maintain, TCP/IP's dominance in networking.

The most accurate name for the set of protocols we are describing is the Internet protocol "suite." This is because TCP/IP is actually a "family" of protocols. TCP and IP are two of the protocols in this suite. Because TCP and IP are the best known of the protocols, it has become common to use the term "TCP/IP" to refer to the entire family. A few of the protocols provide the low-level functions needed for many applications. Others are protocols for performing very specific tasks; for example, transferring files between computers, sending mail, or finding out who is logged in on another computer.

Before examining each layer of TCP/IP, we should cover a few basic concepts. At its most basic level, a computer network is simply a series of connections between computers allowing them to communicate. The content, scope, size, speed, and reliability of the network varies, depending on its protocols and implementation. Protocols are preestablished rules for communication. Exhibit 9 contains the standard "stack" diagram of TCP/IP. Although this exhibit shows a four-layer architecture, TCP/IP also includes the all-important physical layer, which sits below the data-link layer. Exhibit 9 also compares TCP/IP with the OSI model. Rather than make protocols monolithic (which would mean that FTP, Telnet, and SMTP would each have a full network protocol implementation, including separate copies of kernel code for the devices each protocol uses), the designers of TCP/IP broke down the job of a full network protocol suite into a number of components. Each layer corresponds to a different facet of communication. Conceptually, it is useful to envision TCP/IP as a stack. In implementations, programmers often blur the layers for increased performance.

TCP/IP protocols historically were only designed with network availability in mind. The ARPANET (the original Internet) was originally designed to withstand a nuclear strike, which might destroy routing nodes. The architects of the ARPANET never envisioned what the Internet has become today, so security was generally not designed into the protocols. Therefore, most IP networks are inherently insecure. Confidentiality and integrity controls, and more general availability controls, have only recently started being retrofitted into TCP/IP through the Internet Engineering Task Force (IETF) Request for Comment (RFC) process.

The *application layer* sits at the top of the protocol stack and provides the all-important interface to the user. In many ways, the application layer's job is the easiest in the protocol suite. Simply put, the application layer pushes data down to the transport layer and receives data the transport layer returns. For example, a Web browser requests a new URL to view by sending an instruction to the computer to access the document at a specific URL location. As the network layer receives the information from the URL, it passes the information up to the transport layer. The application layer retrieves the data that is coming from the transport layer and converts the data into a usable, viewable form that the application understands and can portray to the user.

Although the OSI Reference Model excludes the application process from the application layer, in TCP/IP we usually do not make that distinction.

The *transport layer's* role is to transfer data between applications. Just as the network layer controls the transmission of data between computers, the transport layer controls the transmission of data through the network layer. It constructs data in one of two ways using the TCP or UDP protocols. TCP is a connection-oriented protocol using a reliable byte stream to send and receive data, keyword here being "reliable." A reliable byte stream is any series of data whose transmission the receiving machine verifies. It can be equated to making a phone call; the individual who answers the phone confirms the connection by answering the telephone call. In contrast, UDP is an unreliable, connectionless protocol that uses datagrams to send and receive data. Unlike TCP, the receiving computer does not verify the UDP transmission. The UDP transmission then is like sending a letter through the mail and never knowing whether it reached its destination. In other words, UDP is considered an unreliable, "I'll try my best," type of protocol.

The *Internet (network) layer* defines how information the transport layer receives is sent over networks, and how the network addresses, or references, other hosts. The network layer contains the Internet Protocol (IP), the Internet Control Message Protocol (ICMP), and the Internet Group Management Protocol (IGMP). Because it contains the IP module, the network layer is considered the heart of any TCP/IP-based network. Within the network layer, the IP module performs most of the work. ICMP and IGMP are IP-support protocols helping the IP handle special network messages such as error messages and multicast messages (messages sent to two or more nodes). The network layer handles the delivery of information from one computer to the other computers across networks.

The *Network Interface (data-link layer)* defines how the physical layer, which resides below it, transmits the network layer packets between computers. The data-link layer resolves information into bits using protocols to control the construction and exchange of the packets (also referred to as data frames, or simply frames) over the transmission wire. Essentially, the data-link layer connects the physical layer to the network layer. Usually, the data-link layer corresponds to the network card residing inside your computer.

Sometimes you also see the term "Media Access Control" (MAC) referencing this layer, and "Network Interface" as in Network Interface Card (NIC).

The *physical layer* (not shown in Exhibit 9) defines electrical signaling on the transmission channel. An example of a network device operating at this layer would be a repeater. A repeater is an electronic device that regenerates the bits that it receives and passes them along the wire toward their destination. Repeaters are common in networks where transmissions may weaken between the client computer and the host computer.

The physical layer specifies the characteristics of the wire connecting the machines in a network. The physical layer also specifies how the network card or other converter will encode the bits it transmits across a network. For example, a network with a physical layer consisting of coaxial cable will be encoded differently from a network consisting of twisted pair cable. The physical layer includes the transmission medium carrying the network data, usually some type of twisted pair or coaxial cable. In a regular office LAN, the most common example of the physical layer is a wire running within the walls connecting the networked computers.

The TCP/IP Protocol Suite. As previously mentioned, TCP/IP is actually a "family" of protocols. We now discuss some of the major protocols comprising the TCP/IP protocol suite.

IP (Internet Protocol). IP is the Internet's most basic protocol. To function in a TCP/IP network, a network segment's only requirement is to forward IP packets. In fact, a TCP/IP network is sometimes defined as a communication medium capable of transporting IP packets. Almost all other TCP/IP functions are constructed by layering atop IP. IP is documented in RFC 791, and IP broadcasting procedures are discussed in RFC 919.

IP is a datagram-oriented protocol, treating each packet independently. This means that each packet must contain complete addressing information. Also, IP makes no attempt to determine if packets reach their destination or to take corrective action if they do not. Nor does IP checksum the contents of a packet, only the IP header.

IP provides several services, including:

- *Addressing.* IP headers contain 32-bit addresses (in IP version 4) identifying the sending and receiving hosts. Routers use these addresses to select a path through the network for the packet.
- *Fragmentation.* IP packets may be split, or fragmented, into smaller packets. This permits a large packet to travel across a network only handling smaller packets. IP fragments and reassembles packets transparently.
- *Packet timeouts.* Each IP packet contains a Time to Live (TTL) field, which is decremented every time a router handles the packet. If TTL reaches zero, the packet is discarded, preventing packets from running in circles forever and flooding a network.
- *Type of service.* IP supports traffic prioritization by allowing packets to be labeled with an abstract type of service.
- *Options.* IP provides several optional features, allowing a packet's sender to set requirements on the path it takes through the network (source routing), trace the route a packet takes (record route), and label packets with security features.

IP is the primary layer 3 (network) protocol in the TCP/IP suite. In addition to internetwork routing, IP provides error reporting, fragmentation, and reassembly of information units called datagrams for transmission over networks with different maximum data unit sizes. IP, therefore, represents the heart of the TCP/IP protocol suite.

For proper routing of datagrams, IP addresses must be globally unique. Presently, they are 32-bit numbers that permit IP networks anywhere in the world to communicate with each other. The current addressing scheme in popular use is IP version 4 (IPv4), although many devices also support the 128-bit addressing scheme used in IP version 6 (IPv6). At the time of this writing however, IPv6 is not in widespread use.

An IP address is divided into two parts. The first part designates the network address and the second part designates the host address, which can sometimes also include a subnet address if the network is subdivided.

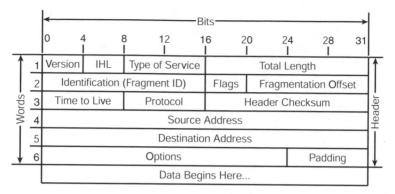

Exhibit 10. The IP Header Structure

IP addressing supports three different types of network classes. Class A networks are intended mainly for use with a few very large networks, because they typically allocate only 8 bits for the network address field. Class B networks allocate 16 bits, and Class C networks allocate 24 bits for the network address field. Class C networks typically allocate 8 bits for the host field, so the number of hosts per network may be a limiting factor. In all three cases, the leftmost bit(s) indicate the network class. IP addresses are written in dotted decimal format; for example, 48.0.0.1.

As discussed, Class A, Class B, and Class C networks historically demanded 8-bit, 16-bit, or 24-bit network prefixes, but with the advent of Classless Inter-Domain Routing (CIDR), the network prefix length can be arbitrary. Every network route gets advertised with the network prefix and a length indicator specifying where the network prefix ends and the host portion begins.

In summary, the Internet Protocol (IP) is the routing layer datagram service of the TCP/IP suite. All other protocols within the TCP/IP suite, except ARP and RARP, use IP to route frames from host to host. The IP frame header (Exhibit 10) contains routing information and control information associated with datagram delivery. Exhibit 11 describes each sector.

IPv6. IP version 6 (IPv6) is a new version of the Internet Protocol based on IPv4. IPv6 increases the IP address size from 32 to 128 bits, to support a larger addressing hierarchy, a much greater number of addressable nodes and simpler auto-configuration of addresses. Scalability of multicast addresses is introduced. A new type of address called an "anycast" address is also defined, to send a packet to any one of a group of nodes.

IPv6 also provides improved support for extensions and options. IPv6 options are placed in separate headers located between the IPv6 header and the transport layer header. Changes in the way IP header options are

Exhibit 11. Sectors of the IP Header

Version: Version field indicates the format of the Internet header.

IHL: Internet header length is the length of the Internet header in 32-bit words. This points to the beginning of the data. The minimum value for a correct header is 5.

Type of Service: Indicates the quality of service desired. Networks may offer service precedence, meaning that they accept traffic only above a certain precedence at times of high load. There is a three-way trade-off between low delay, high reliability, and high throughput.

- Bits 0–2: Precedence
  - 111 Network control.
  - 110 Internetwork control.
  - 101 CRITIC/ECP.
  - 100 Flash override.
  - 011 Flash.
  - 010 Immediate.
  - 001 Priority.
  - 000 Routine.
- Bit 3: Delay
  - 0 Normal delay.
  - 1 Low delay.
- Bit 4: Throughput
  - 0 Normal throughput.
  - 1 High throughput.
- Bit 5: Reliability
  - 0 Normal reliability.
  - 1 High reliability.
- Bits 6–7: Reserved for future use

Total Length: The length of the datagram in bytes, including the Internet header and data. The length of a datagram can be up to 65,535 bytes, although such long datagrams are impractical for most hosts and networks. All hosts must be prepared to accept datagrams of up to 576 bytes, regardless of whether they arrive whole or in fragments. It is recommended hosts send datagrams larger than 576 bytes only if the destination is prepared to accept the larger datagrams.

Identification: An identifying value assigned by the sender to aid in assembling the fragments of a datagram.

Flags: 3 bits. Control flags:

- Bit 0 is reserved and must be zero.
- Bit 1: Don't fragment bit:
  - 0 May fragment.
  - 1 Don't fragment.
- Bit 2: More fragments bit:
  - 0 Last fragment.
  - 1 More fragments.

Fragment Offset: 13 bits. Indicates where this fragment belongs in the datagram. The fragment offset is measured in units of 8 bytes (64 bits). The first fragment has offset zero.

(continued)

Exhibit 11. Sectors of the IP Header (Continued)

Time to Live (TTL): Indicates the maximum time the datagram is allowed to remain in the Internet system. If this field contains the value zero, the datagram must be destroyed. This field is modified in Internet header processing. The time is measured in units of seconds. However, because every module that processes a datagram must decrease the TTL by at least one (even if it processes the datagram in less than one second), the TTL must be thought of only as an upper limit on the time a datagram may exist. The intention is to cause undeliverable datagrams to be discarded and to bound the maximum datagram lifetime.

Protocol: Indicates the next level protocol used in the data portion of the Internet datagram.

Header Checksum: A checksum calculated on the header only. Because some header fields change (e.g., Time to Live), this is recomputed and verified at each point that the Internet header is processed.

Source Address/Destination Address: 32 bits each. A distinction is made between names, addresses, and routes. A name indicates an object to be sought. An address indicates the location of the object. A route indicates how to arrive at the object. The Internet protocol deals primarily with addresses. It is the task of higher-level protocols (such as host-to-host or application) to make the mapping from names to addresses. The Internet module maps Internet addresses to local network addresses. It is the task of lower-level procedures (such as local net or gateways) to make the mapping from local net addresses to routes.

Options: Options may or may not appear in datagrams. They must be implemented by all IP modules (host and gateways). What is optional is their transmission in any particular datagram, not their implementation. In some environments, the security option may be required in all datagrams.

The option field is variable in length. There may be zero or more options. There are two possible formats for an option:

- A single octet of option type
- An option type octet, an option length octet, and the actual option data octets

The length octet includes the option type octet and the actual option data octets.

The option type octet has three fields:

- 1 bit: Copied flag. Indicates that this option is copied into all fragments during fragmentation:
  - 0 Copied.
  - 1 Not copied.
- 2 bits: Option class:
  - 0 Control.
  - 1 Reserved for future use.
  - 2 Debugging and measurement.
  - 3 Reserved for future use.
- 5 bits: Option number.

Data: IP data or higher-layer protocol header.

encoded allow more efficient forwarding, less stringent limits on the length of options, and greater flexibility for introducing new options in the future. The extension headers include Hop-by-Hop Option, Routing (Type 0), Fragment, Destination Option, Authentication, and Encapsulation Payload.

IPv6 also supports a new flow labeling capability, allowing packets belonging to particular traffic flows for which the sender requests special handling, such as non-default Quality-of-Service or real-time service. These benefits make it easier to implement new services and technologies such as Voice-over-IP.

The IPv6 header has the structure shown in Exhibit 12.

Exhibit 12. Structure of the IPv6 Header

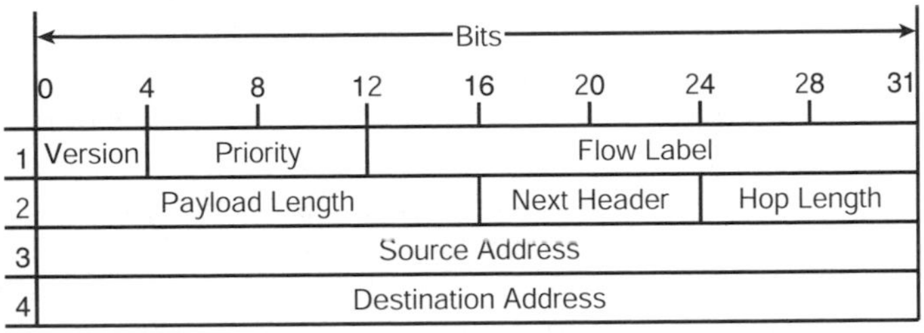

Version: Internet Protocol Version number (IPv6 is 6).

Priority: Enables a source to identify the desired delivery priority of the datagrama. Priority values are divided into ranges: traffic where the source provides congestion control and non-congestion control traffic.

Flow label: Used by a source to label those products for which it requests special handling by the IPv6 router. The flow is uniquely identified by the combination of a source address and a non-zero flow label.

Payload length: Length of payload (in octets).

Next header: Identifies the type of header immediately following the IPv6 header.

Hop limit: An 8-bit integer decremented by one by each node that forwards the datagram. The datagram is discarded if the Hop Limit is decremented to zero.

Source address: A 128-bit address designating the originator of the datagram.

Destination address: A 128-bit address designating the intended recipient of the datagram.

TCP (Transmission Control Protocol). The Transmission Control Protocol (TCP), documented in RFC 793, tries to make up for IP's deficiencies by providing reliable, stream-oriented connections to hide most of IP's shortcomings. The protocol suite gets its name because most TCP/IP protocols are based on TCP, which is in turn based on IP. TCP and IP are the twin pillars of TCP/IP.

TCP adds a great deal of functionality to the IP service over which it is layered:

- *Streams.* TCP data is organized as a stream of bytes, much like a file. The datagram nature of the network is concealed. A mechanism (the Urgent Pointer) exists to let out-of-band data be specially flagged.
- *Reliable delivery.* Sequence numbers are used to coordinate which data has been transmitted and received. TCP will arrange for retransmission if it determines that data has been lost.
- *Network adaptation.* TCP will dynamically learn the delay characteristics of a network and adjust its operation to maximize throughput without overloading the network.
- *Flow control.* TCP manages data buffers and coordinates traffic so that its buffers will never overflow. Fast senders will be stopped periodically to keep up with slower receivers.
- *Full-duplex operation.* No matter what the particular application, TCP almost always operates in full-duplex mode. Full-duplex mode means that transmission of data can happen in both directions, in an almost completely independent manner. It is sometimes useful to think of a TCP session as two independent byte streams, traveling in opposite directions. No TCP mechanism exists to associate data in the forward and reverse byte streams. Only during connection start and close sequences can TCP exhibit asymmetric behavior (i.e., data transfer in the forward direction but not in the reverse direction, or vice versa).
- *Sequence numbers.* TCP uses a 32-bit sequence number to count bytes in the data stream. Each TCP packet contains the starting sequence number of the data in that packet, and the sequence number (called the acknowledgment number) of the last byte received from the remote peer. With this information, a sliding-window protocol is implemented. Forward and reverse sequence numbers are completely independent, and each TCP peer must track both its own sequence numbering and the numbering used by the remote peer.

TCP uses a number of control flags to manage the connection. Some of these flags pertain to a single packet (such as the URG flag indicating valid data in the Urgent Pointer field), but two flags (SYN and FIN) require reliable delivery as they mark the beginning and end of the data stream. To ensure reliable delivery of these two flags, they are assigned spots in the sequence number space. Each flag occupies a single byte.

Window Size and Buffering. Each endpoint of a TCP connection has a buffer for storing transmitted data before the application is ready to read the data. This permits network transfers to occur while applications are busy with other processing, improving overall performance.

To avoid overflowing the buffer, TCP sets a Window Size field in each packet it transmits. This field contains the amount of data placed into the buffer. If this number falls to zero, the remote TCP can send no more data. It must wait until buffer space becomes available and it receives a packet announcing a non-zero window size.

Sometimes, the buffer space is too small. This happens when the network's bandwidth-delay product exceeds the buffer size. The simplest solution is to increase the buffer, but for extreme cases the protocol itself becomes the bottleneck (because it does not support a large enough Window Size). Under these conditions, the network is termed an LFN (Long Fat Network, pronounced elephant). RFC 1072 discusses LFNs.

Round-Trip Time Estimation. When a host transmits a TCP packet to its peer, it must wait a period of time for an acknowledgment. If the reply does not come within the expected period, the packet is assumed to have been lost and the data is retransmitted. The obvious question — How long do we wait? — lacks a simple answer. Over an Ethernet, no more than a few microseconds should be needed for a reply. If the traffic must flow over the wide-area Internet, a second or two might be reasonable during peak utilization times. All modern TCP implementations seek to answer this question by monitoring the normal exchange of data packets and developing an estimate of how long is "too long." This process is called Round-Trip Time (RTT) estimation. RTT estimates are one of the most important performance parameters in a TCP exchange, especially when you consider that on an indefinitely large transfer, all TCP implementations eventually drop packets and retransmit them, no matter how good the quality of the link. If the RTT estimate is too low, packets are retransmitted unnecessarily; if too high, the connection can sit idle while the host waits to time-out.

In summary, TCP provides a reliable stream delivery and virtual connection service to applications through the use of sequenced acknowledgment with retransmission of packets when necessary. Exhibit 13 shows the TCP header structure. Exhibit 14 describes the sectors of the TCP header.

UDP (User Datagram Protocol). UDP, documented in RFC 768, provides users with access to IP-like services. UDP packets are delivered just like IP packets — connectionless datagrams that can be discarded before reaching their targets. UDP is useful when TCP would be too complex, too slow, or just unnecessary. UDP is often used when the application layer wants to keep control over specific services. The Unix Network File System (NFS) is often implemented over UDP, although TCP implementations are now common.

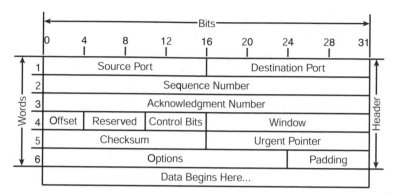

Exhibit 13. The TCP Header

UDP provides a few functions beyond that of IP, including:

- Port numbers. UDP provides 16-bit port numbers to let multiple processes use UDP services on the same host. A UDP address is the combination of a 32-bit IP address and the 16-bit port number.
- Checksumming. Unlike IP, UDP does checksum its data, ensuring data integrity. A packet failing checksum is simply discarded, with no further action taken.

The User Datagram Protocol (UDP), therefore, provides a simple but unreliable message service for transaction-oriented services. Each UDP header (Exhibit 15) carries both a source port identifier and destination port identifier, allowing high-level protocols to target specific applications and services among hosts. Exhibit 16 describes the fields in the UDP header.

ICMP (Internet Control Message Protocol). The Internet Control Message Protocol (ICMP), documented in RFC 792, is a required protocol tightly integrated with IP. ICMP messages, delivered in IP packets, are used for messaging aspects of networks, such as out-of-band messages related to network operation or mis-operation. Of course, because ICMP uses IP, ICMP packet delivery is unreliable, so hosts cannot count on receiving ICMP packets for any network problem. Some of ICMP's functions are to:

- *Announce network errors,* such as a host or entire portion of the network being unreachable, due to some type of failure. A TCP or UDP packet directed at a port number with no receiver attached is also reported via ICMP.
- *Announce network congestion.* When a router begins buffering too many packets, due to an inability to transmit them as fast as they are being received, it will generate ICMP Source Quench messages. Directed at the sender, these messages should cause the rate of packet transmission to be slowed. Of course, generating too many

Exhibit 14. Sectors of the TCP Header

Source port: Source port number.

Destination port: Destination port number.

Sequence number: The sequence number of the first data octet in this segment (except when SYN is present). If SYN is present, the sequence number is the initial sequence number (ISN) and the first data octet is ISN+1.

Acknowledgment number: If the ACK control bit is set, this field contains the value of the next sequence number the sender of the segment is expecting to receive from the receiver. Once a connection is established, this value is always sent.

Data offset: 4 bits. The number of 32-bit words in the TCP header, indicating where the data begins. The TCP header (even one including options) has a length, which is an integral number of 32 bits.

Reserved: 6 bits. Reserved for future use. Must be zero.

Control bits: 6 bits. The control bits may be (from right to left):

- U (URG) Urgent pointer field significant.
- A (ACK) Acknowledgment field significant.
- P (PSH) Push function.
- R (RST) Reset the connection.
- S (SYN) Synchronize sequence numbers.
- F (FIN) No more data from sender.

Window: 16 bits. The number of data octets the sender of this segment is willing to accept, beginning with the octet indicated in the acknowledgment field.

Checksum: 16 bits. The checksum field represents a numeric representation of the 16-bit words in the header and text. If a segment contains an odd number of header and text octets to be checksummed, the last octet is padded on the right with zeros to form a 16-bit word for checksum purposes. The pad is not transmitted as part of the segment. While computing the checksum, the checksum field itself is replaced with zeros.

Urgent Pointer: 16 bits. This field communicates the current value of the urgent pointer as a positive offset from the sequence number in this segment. The urgent pointer points to the sequence number of the octet following the urgent data. This field can only be interpreted in segments for which the URG control bit has been set.

Options: Options may be transmitted at the end of the TCP header and always have a length that is a multiple of 8 bits. All options are included in the checksum. An option may begin on any octet boundary. There are two possible formats for an option:

- A single octet of option type.
- An octet of option type, an octet of option length, and the actual option data octets.

The option length includes the option type and option length, as well as the option data octets. The list of options may be shorter than that designated by the data offset field because the contents of the header beyond the End-of-Option option must be header padding, i.e., zero. A TCP must implement all options.

Data: TCP data or higher-layer protocol.

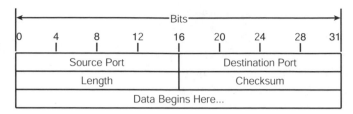

Exhibit 15. The UDP Header

Exhibit 16. Fields in the UDP Header

Source Port: Source port is an optional field. When used, it indicates the port of the sending process and may be assumed to be the port to which a reply should be addressed in the absence of any other information. If not used, a value of zero is inserted.

Destination Port: Destination port has a meaning within the context of a particular Internet destination address.

Length: The length in octets of this user datagram, including this header and the data. The minimum value of the length is 8.

Checksum: The 16-bit numeric representation of a pseudo header of information from the IP header, the UDP header, and the data, padded with zero octets at the end (if necessary) to make a multiple of two octets.

Data: The UDP data field.

Source Quench messages would cause even more network congestion, so they are used sparingly.

- *Assist troubleshooting.* ICMP supports an Echo function, which just sends a packet on a round-trip between two hosts. Ping, a common network management tool, is based on this feature. Ping will transmit a series of packets, measuring average round-trip times and computing loss percentages.

- *Announce timeouts.* If an IP packet's TTL field drops to zero, the router discarding the packet will often generate an ICMP packet announcing this fact. Traceroute is a tool that maps network routes by sending packets with small TTL values and watching the ICMP timeout announcements.

ICMP messages generally contain information about routing difficulties with IP datagrams or simple exchanges such as timestamp or echo transactions.

IGMP (Internet Group Management Protocol). The Internet Group Management Protocol (IGMP), documented in Appendix I of RFC 1112, allows

Internet hosts to participate in multicasting. RFC 1112 describes the basics of multicasting IP traffic, including the format of multicast IP addresses, multicast Ethernet encapsulation, and the concept of a host group.

A host group is the set of hosts interested in traffic for a particular multicast address. Important multicast addresses are documented in the most recent Assigned Numbers RFC, currently RFC 1700. IGMP allows a router to determine which host groups have members on a given network segment. The exchange of multicast packets between routers is not addressed by IGMP.

PPP (Point-to-Point Protocol). The Point-to-Point Protocol (PPP), documented in RFC 1661, is considered one of the best solutions for dial-up Internet connections, including ISDN.

The Point-to-Point Protocol (PPP) originally emerged as an encapsulation protocol for transporting IP traffic over point-to-point links. PPP also established a standard for the assignment and management of IP addresses, asynchronous (start/stop) and bit-oriented synchronous encapsulation, network protocol multiplexing, link configuration, link quality testing, error detection, and option negotiation for such capabilities as network layer address negotiation and data-compression negotiation. PPP supports these functions by providing an extensible Link Control Protocol (LCP) and a family of Network Control Protocols (NCPs) to negotiate optional configuration parameters and facilities. In addition to IP, PPP supports other protocols, including Novell's Internetwork Packet Exchange (IPX) and DECnet.

PPP is a complete specification for transmitting datagrams between data communications equipment from different manufacturers over dial-up and dedicated serial point-to-point links. It is a recommended standard of the Internet Architecture Board (IAB) and is represented by a number of RFCs (Request for Comments) produced by the Point-to-Point Protocol Working Group.

Traditionally, interoperability across serial links was restricted to equipment supplied by the same manufacturer. Now, PPP allows for multi-vendor interoperability. PPP was first proposed as a standard in 1990 to replace an older *de facto* standard known as SLIP (Serial Line Internet Protocol) that requires links to be established and torn down manually. However, unlike SLIP, which only supports IP, PPP is not limited in protocol support. PPP provides the flexibility to add support for other protocols through software upgrades. PPP can also simultaneously transmit multiple protocols across a single serial link, eliminating the need to set up a separate link for each protocol. PPP is also ideal for interconnecting dissimilar devices such as hosts, bridges, and routers over serial links. For example, a stand-alone TCP/IP host can communicate with a router across a serial PPP link.

Here are some key PPP features, all of which are lacking in SLIP:

- *Address notification* allows a server to inform a dial-up client of its IP address for the link, but the mechanism is powerful enough for clients to request IP addresses and supports fallback configurations. SLIP required the user to configure this information manually. PPP options have also been specified (RFC 1877) for notification of name server addresses, both Internet and NetBIOS.
- *Authentication* is available as an option, either with the Password Authentication Protocol (PAP), the Challenge Handshake Authentication Protocol (CHAP), or Extensible Authentication Protocol (EAP). Both are documented in RFC 1334.
- *Multiple protocols can interoperate* on the same link, simply by running additional NCPs. For example, both IP and IPX traffic can share a PPP link.
- *Link monitoring* facilities include a link-level echo facility that can periodically check link operation.

DNS (Domain Name System). The Internet Protocol address is a 32-bit integer. If somebody wants to send a message, it is necessary to include the destination address; however, people prefer to assign machines pronounceable, easily remembered names (host names). For this reason, the Domain Name System (DNS) is used. These logical names also allow independence from knowing the physical location of a host. A host can be moved to a different network, while the users continue to use the same logical name.

The DNS is a distributed database used by TCP/IP applications to map between hostnames and IP addresses, and to provide electronic-mail routing information. Each site (university department, campus, company, or department within a company, for example) maintains its own database of information and runs a server program that other systems across the Internet can query. The DNS provides the protocol, allowing clients and servers to communicate with each other.

The system accesses the DNS through a resolver. The resolver takes the hostname and returns the IP address or takes an IP address and looks up a hostname. The resolver returns the IP address before asking the TCP to open a connection or sending a datagram using UDP.

The DNS uses a hierarchical naming scheme known as domain names, similar to the Unix file system tree. The root of the DNS tree is a special node with a null label. The name of each node (except root) can be a maximum of 63 characters.

The domain name of any node in the tree is the list of labels, starting at that node and working up to the root, using a period ("dot") to separate the labels (individual sections of a name might represent sites or a group, but the domain system simply calls each section a label). The difference between the Unix file system and the tree of the DNS is that in the DNS we start on the ground and "go up" until the root. Writing them in this order makes it possible to compress messages containing multiple domain names. Thus, the domain name "hydro.mb.ca" contains three labels: "hydro," "mb," and "ca." Any suffix of a label in a domain name is also called a domain. In the above example, the lowest level domain is "hydro.mb.ca" (the domain name for a hydro company in the province of Manitoba, in Canada); the second level domain is "mb.ca" (the domain name for Manitoba organizations of Canada); and the top level domain (for this name) is "ca" (the domain name for Canada). The node "ca" is the second level node (after root).

A fundamental property of the DNS is caching. That is, when a name server receives information about a mapping, it caches that information. Thus, a later query for the same mapping can use the cached result and not result in additional queries to other servers.

Every server has a cache for recently used names, as well as a record of where the mapping information for that name was obtained. When a client asks the server to resolve a certain name, the server proceeds as follows:

- The server checks to see if it has authority for the name. If yes, the server does not need caching information.
- If not, the server checks its cache to see whether the name has been resolved recently. If yes, the server reports the caching information to its clients.
- If not, the server locates the authoritative DNS server for that domain and retrieves the requested information, which is then added to the cache.

ARP (Address Resolution Protocol). The Address Resolution Protocol (ARP) is a protocol for mapping an Internet Protocol address (IP address) to a physical machine address that is recognized in the local network. For example, in IPv4, the most common level of IP in use today, an address is 32 bits long. In an Ethernet local area network, however, addresses for attached devices are 48 bits long. (The physical machine address is also known as a Media Access Control [MAC] address.) A table, usually called the ARP cache, is used to maintain a correlation between each MAC address and its corresponding IP address. ARP provides the protocol rules for making this correlation and providing address conversion in both directions.

When an incoming packet destined for a host machine on a particular local area network arrives at a gateway, the gateway asks the ARP program to find a physical host or MAC address that matches the IP address. The

ARP program looks in the ARP cache and, if it finds the address, provides it so that the packet can be converted to the right packet length and format and sent to the machine. If no entry is found for the IP address, ARP broadcasts a request packet in a special format to all the machines on the LAN to see if one machine knows that it has that IP address associated with it. A machine recognizing the IP address as its own returns a reply indicating so. ARP updates the ARP cache for future reference and then sends the packet to the replying MAC address.

Because protocol details differ for each type of local area network, there are separate ARP Requests for Ethernet, ATM, Fiber Distributed-Data Interface, and other protocols.

RARP (Reverse ARP). RARP (Reverse Address Resolution Protocol) does the opposite of ARP. It is a protocol through which a diskless physical machine in a local area network can request to learn its IP address from a gateway server's Address Resolution Protocol (ARP) table or cache. A network administrator creates a table in a local area network's gateway router mapping the physical machine (or MAC address) addresses to corresponding Internet Protocol addresses. When a new machine is set up, its RARP client program requests from the RARP server on the router to be sent its IP address. Assuming that an entry has been set up in the router table, the RARP server will return the IP address to the machine, which can store it for future use.

SNMP (Simple Network Management Protocol). The Simple Network Management Protocol (SNMP) is the protocol governing network management and the monitoring of network devices and their functions. It is not necessarily limited to TCP/IP networks. The Internet community developed SNMP to allow diverse network objects to participate in a global network management architecture. Network management systems can poll network entities implementing SNMP for information relevant to a particular network management implementation. Network management systems learn of problems by receiving change notices from network devices implementing SNMP.

Routing Protocols. Routing is the process of directing data around networks. This is simple in LAN broadcast topologies (e.g., Bus, Ring, Star) but becomes more difficult in the WAN mesh topologies. At each router in the network, the datagrams are examined and the destination address is mapped to a routing table kept in memory. The table tells the router on which outgoing link to send out the datagram. Routers use the various routing protocols to determine the best route the data should travel.

Routers within the Internet are organized hierarchically. Some routers are used to move information through one particular group of networks under the same administrative authority and control. (Such an entity is called an *autonomous* system.) Routers used for information exchange within autonomous systems are called interior routers, and they use a variety of Interior Gateway Protocols (IGPs) to accomplish this. Routers moving information between autonomous systems are called exterior routers; they use the Exterior Gateway Protocol (EGP) or Border Gateway Protocol (BGP).

Routing protocols used with IP are dynamic in nature. Dynamic routing requires the software in the routing devices to calculate routes. Dynamic routing algorithms adapt to changes in the network and automatically select the best routes. In contrast with dynamic routing, static routing calls for routes to be established by the network administrator. Static routes do not change until the network administrator changes them. Consequently, if a device fails and the target network is no longer available, data for that network will never reach its destination, even if there is another network route to the target network.

IP routing tables consist of destination address/next hop pairs. As we have seen, IP routing specifies that IP datagrams travel through an internetwork one router hop at a time. The entire route is not known at the outset of the journey. Instead, at each stop, the next router hop is determined by matching the destination address within the datagram with an entry in the current node's routing table. Each node's involvement in the routing process consists only of forwarding packets based on internal information. IP does not provide for error reporting back to the source when routing anomalies occur. This task, as we learned earlier, is left to another Internet protocol: the Internet Control Message Protocol (ICMP.)

ICMP performs a number of tasks within an IP internetwork. In addition to the principal reason for which it was created (reporting routing failures back to the source), ICMP provides a method for testing node reachability across an internet (the ICMP Echo and Reply messages), a method for increasing routing efficiency (the ICMP Redirect message), a method for informing sources that a datagram has exceeded its allocated time to exist within an internet (the ICMP Time Exceeded message), and other helpful messages. All in all, ICMP is an integral part of any IP implementation, particularly those that run in routers.

Routing protocols generally are designed to be resistant to simple node or link failures, but not to a strategically placed intruder. Hierarchical routing architectures have the security advantage that a compromised router can only damage the routing tables it has access to, either inside the area or between areas. If attackers can compromise a router, they could alter the routing table to destroy availability, or reroute traffic out of a secure network to a compromised network for disclosure, or integrity attacks.

Proposed solutions use cryptography (shared secret key known only by the trusted routers), but this only protects against outsider attacks, not insider attacks where a router is compromised and the key is now no longer a secret. A compromised router can have other implications if the router is doing double duty as an IPSec encryption device, a VPN termination point, an intrusion detection sensor, or a firewall.

Interior Routing Protocols. Interior Routing Protocols or IGPs (Interior Gateway Protocols) operate within autonomous systems. The following sections provide brief descriptions of several IGPs that are currently popular in TCP/IP networks.

RIP. A discussion of routing protocols within an IP environment must begin with the Routing Information Protocol (RIP). RIP was developed by Xerox Corporation in the early 1980s for use in Xerox Network Systems (XNS) networks. Today, many PC networks use routing protocols based on RIP.

RIP works well in small environments but has serious limitations when used in larger internetworks. For example, RIP limits the number of router hops between any two hosts in a network to 16. RIP is also slow to converge, meaning that it takes a relatively long time for network changes to become known to all routers. Finally, RIP determines the best path through a network by looking only at the number of hops between the two end nodes. This technique ignores differences in line speed, line utilization, and all other metrics, many of which can be important factors in choosing the best path between two nodes. For this reason, many companies with large networks are migrating away from RIP to more sophisticated routing protocols.

IGRP. With the creation of the Interior Gateway Routing Protocol (IGRP) in the early 1980s, this protocol was the first to solve the problems associated with using RIP to route datagrams between interior routers. IGRP determines the best path through a network by examining the bandwidth and delay of the networks between routers. IGRP converges faster than RIP, thereby avoiding the routing loops caused by disagreement over the next routing hop to be taken. Further, IGRP does not share RIP's hop count limitation. As a result of these and other improvements over RIP, IGRP enabled many large, complex, topologically diverse internetworks to be deployed.

IGRP has been enhanced to handle the increasingly large, mission-critical networks being designed today. The new version of IGRP is called Enhanced IGRP. Enhanced IGRP combines the ease of use of traditional distance vector routing protocols with the fast rerouting capabilities of the newer link state routing protocols.

Enhanced IGRP consumes significantly less bandwidth than IGRP because it is able to limit the exchange of routing information to include only the changed information. In addition, Enhanced IGRP is capable of handling AppleTalk and Novell IPX routing information, as well as IP routing information.

OSPF. OSPF (Open Shortest Path First) was developed by the Internet Engineering Task Force (IETF) as a replacement for RIP. Almost every major IP routing vendor supports OSPF.

OSPF is an intra-domain, link state, hierarchical routing protocol. It supports hierarchical routing within an autonomous system. Autonomous systems can be divided into routing areas. A routing area is typically a collection of one or more closely related subnets. All areas must connect to the backbone area. It provides fast rerouting and supports variable-length subnet masks.

Integrated IS-IS. ISO 10589 IS-IS (intermediate system to intermediate system) is an intra-domain, link state, hierarchical routing protocol used as the DECnet Phase V routing algorithm. It is similar in many ways to OSPF. IS-IS can operate over a variety of subnetworks, including broadcast LANs, WANs, and point-to-point links.

Integrated IS-IS is an implementation of IS-IS for more than just OSI protocols. Today, Integrated IS-IS supports both OSI protocols and IPs. Like all integrated routing protocols, Integrated IS-IS calls for all routers to run a single routing algorithm. Link state advertisements sent by routers running Integrated IS-IS include all destinations running either IP or OSI network layer protocols.

Exterior Routing Protocols. EGPs (Exterior Gateway Protocols) provide routing between autonomous systems. The two most popular EGPs in the TCP/IP community are discussed below.

EGP. The first widespread exterior routing protocol was the Exterior Gateway Protocol. EGP provides dynamic connectivity but assumes that all autonomous systems are connected in a tree topology. This was mostly true in the early Internet but is no longer being followed.

Although EGP is a dynamic routing protocol, it uses a very simple design. It does not use metrics and therefore cannot make true intelligent routing decisions. EGP routing updates contain network reachability information. That is, the routing updates identify which routers provide connectivity to which networks. Because of its limitations with regard to today's complex internetworks, EGP is being phased out in favor of routing protocols such as BGP.

BGP. Border Gateway Protocol (BGP) represents an attempt to address the most serious of EGP's problems. Like EGP, BGP is an inter-domain routing protocol created for use in the Internet core routers. Unlike EGP, BGP was designed to prevent routing loops in arbitrary topologies and to allow policy-based route selection. The latest revisions of BGP are designed to handle the scaling problems of the growing Internet.

Network Threats and Attacks

Network threats and attacks grow on a daily basis. Computer security has become so pervasive as to see computer security issues and threats published in the popular media. The number of new hacker tools, and their relative ease of use, have led industry analysts to call today "the golden era of hacking."

Traditionally, the term "hacker" was a benign word, indicating someone who is focused on determining how something works and devising innovative approaches to computer problems. Malicious attackers are now coined as "crackers." A cracker may be a hacker, but with different motives. Hackers are trying to find ways to improve upon existing technologies or solutions, while crackers are trying to find ways to defeat existing technologies for gain or profit.

Many network security tools can be used for good and bad. It all comes down to the intent behind the person using the tool. For example, a packet sniffer can be used by a network engineer to isolate a network performance problem. However, in the hands of the malicious user, it can be used to find passwords and other information to gain unauthorized access to systems and information.

General Trends in the Computer Underground

There is a vast amount of research done on a daily basis to probe systems, understand their intricacies, and find new vulnerabilities or attack methods. This research is conducted by intelligent attackers and security practitioners alike and typically implemented into a program or script later on. The end result is that a less informed or experienced attacker, commonly referred to as a "script kiddie," can now launch comprehensive and detailed attacks without understanding the intricacies of how the attack works.

Consequently, security practitioners must not underestimate the abilities of their attackers. While it is most commonly a script kiddie attacking your network, the assumption that it is *always* a script kiddie ignores the likelihood that it could be someone else: organized crime, terrorists, foreign governments, even the competition.

Wide Distribution of High-Quality Tools. The widespread development of high-quality attack tools and diverse information sharing makes the attackers' jobs easier. While the security community tends not to talk about its concerns and weaknesses, we ignore the fact that the attackers do. At one time, information and tools were limited to a core group of elite attackers. With the predominance of the World Wide Web, any person interested in launching an attack can find the tools and information on how to do it. Addressing this threat by the security practitioner means knowing the tools and techniques used by the attackers in order to develop methods of defending against them.

Network Mapping and Port Scanning

Effective network attacks require information about network addressing and topology. This is easily obtained using tools called network mappers, which identify the systems connected to the target network. The network mapper uses Internet Control Message Protocol (ICMP) packets to identify the operational systems. For those networks that block incoming ICMP packets, or when an operational system is found, a SYN request can be sent to a port. If the port is open and there is a network listener, the network mapper will receive an ACK packet. If there is no network listener, the network mapper receives a "Port Unreachable" response. With the list of operational systems, the attackers can perform further refinements to narrow the list of actual systems they wish to attack.

A port scanner, often combined with a network mapper, identifies the listening ports on a target system. There are 65,535 TCP and 65,535 UDP ports on a system, with listener active on some ports, depending on the services active on that system. Most ports will be closed. Some services use specific ports. For example, a Web server uses port 80 and Telnet uses port 23. These are called well-known ports. By conducting a port scan, an attacker can identify the services running on your system and then determine how best to attack it.

TCP fingerprinting, a feature available in some tools, uses the unique response from a given system to identify with some degree of certainty what it is. TCP fingerprinting is based on how a system reacts to illegal packets. While the IETF has defined standards for TCP, many implementations do not handle illegal packets in a defined manner. Using combinations of illegal packets, the fingerprinting tools can decide the type of system being examined.

Through network mappers and port scanners, the attacker can determine a lot of information about the target system. In many cases, the attacker now has enough information to launch very specific and targeted attacks because the attacker generally knows enough about the operating system used, patch levels, and even services on the host. The attacker uses this information to find vulnerabilities that allow access to the target system.

Network Mapping and Port Scanning Defenses. Defending against network mapping and port scans involves disabling all unnecessary services and closing unused ports. Additional defenses include filtering at your organization's external router to allow only desired services into the network. Regardless, only those services with a defined business requirement should be operational. Periodic scanning by a security administrator should also be performed to ensure that the systems are configured as expected. Any ports found open that are not required for business operations should be closed.

Vulnerability Scanning

When attackers have identified a potential target, they research what vulnerabilities are likely for that system. There is a large number of vulnerabilities for most software components today, with more being discovered on a daily basis. Some of these vulnerabilities will allow a remote attacker to take total control of a system. The attacker will try each of these vulnerabilities using individual commands, but exhaustive vulnerability testing can take extraordinary amounts of time. However, it is unlikely an attacker will need to test every vulnerability before finding a weakness.

Attackers use automated scanning tools to speed up the process and provide probable sources of weakness in the target system. Automated vulnerability analysis tools use extensive databases with well-known vulnerabilities. The level of success of the scanning tool depends on the completeness of its vulnerability database and the ability to create new checks using a scripting language.

A variety of scanning tools are available, ranging from those that are freely available or open source to high-quality commercial tools. Attackers and security professionals use both types alike to assess the vulnerabilities on a given system. These tools typically offer scripting languages to create new checks and can identify vulnerabilities on remote systems. Consequently, both the attacker and the security professional can customize these tools to suit their own environments.

Some scanners are general purpose, capable of analyzing a variety of vulnerabilities on a platform, while others assess only specific components such as CGUI scripts or HTML code.

Vulnerability Scanning Defenses. As mentioned previously, the first line of defense against vulnerability scanning is to close open ports. Second, system patches must be applied in a timely fashion to ensure that the potential vulnerabilities are closed. Finally, every organization should have defined change control procedures indicating how and when systems will be patched.

Periodic vulnerability scanning should also be performed across the enterprise to find potential and real vulnerabilities before the attackers do. Scans should be conducted on a quarterly or even monthly basis, depending on the system and its proximity to potentially hostile networks such as the Internet. Any vulnerability found should be closed off as quickly as possible.

Wardialing

Prior to the widespread use of the Internet, the most common method of remote network access was the modem. Attackers used tools called wardialers to find modems connected to systems using the telephone network. Organizations often spend large amounts of money securing their Internet and network infrastructure, while ignoring the other avenue of network access. Attackers, on the other hand, will try all means of access into your network, which will not ignore modems and other network access points.

Wardialers, or "demon dialers," dial telephone numbers in a defined block of numbers looking for computer modem tones. The better software can determine when a fax answers and when a computer answers. If a computer answers, the dialer will try to get a prompt from the remote system. It logs the prompt and terminates the call. The telephone numbers are often guessed from information available on Web sites, telephone contacts, employee postings to newsgroups, and even the telephone company.

Once the attacker has a range of numbers, he simply enters the range into the dialer, and it automatically dials each number. Once the list of potential numbers has been received, the attacker can then connect to each one, looking for an interesting system on which to concentrate. The attacker uses a terminal program or other client to call each number in turn. Once connected, the attacker can identify the system using the banner information provided by the system and see if a password is required.

In some situations, the modem will not require a password to connect and the attacker will have access to the system. If a password is required, the attacker will attempt to guess passwords based on the company's products, business, or known default passwords for the platform.

In addition to detecting modem tones, some wardialing software can detect a second dial tone. This repeat dial tone can indicate unrestricted dialing within the organization's Private Branch Exchange (PBX). In some cases, the PBX is misconfigured, allowing unrestricted dialing to anywhere in the world through this scenario, with all costs being paid by the PBX owner.

Wardialing Defenses. Protecting your organization against wardialing consists of a strong policy against modems, including a definition of where and when a modem can be used, who has ownership of it, and configuration requirements. The authorized modems should be cataloged in a database for quick recall when needed. Second, periodic wardialing to find and investigate phone numbers is essential. When a phone number is found with a modem that is not in the database, appropriate action can be taken by the security professional to find the modem and remove it before the attacker uses it to gain access to your network.

Network Exploits: Sniffing, Spoofing, and Session Hijacking

Due to the assumptions made by the original designers, TCP/IP was not created with any underlying security services. Consequently, most TCP/IP-related protocols are inherently insecure. This lack of security has resulted in a whole series of attacks against the various protocols, with the most potentially damaging attacks being sniffing, spoofing, denial-of-service, and session hijacking.

Sniffing. Packet sniffers, commonly referred to as sniffers, are useful tools for both the network manager and the attacker. The network manager uses them to assist in network troubleshooting, while the attacker uses them for more nefarious intent.

Sniffers take advantage of the exploit characteristics of Token Ring and Ethernet networks. They can be used on other network technologies but these are, by far, the most common. Ethernet is a broadcast technology, as discussed previously. The packet is transmitted on the wire and all systems in the collision domain can see it. It is up to the receiving station to determine if the packet is intended for it.

A sniffer is a hardware device, or software running on a computer, that monitors and accepts all packets received on the network interface. When a network interface operates in this manner, it is configured for "promiscuous mode." Therefore, any machine can monitor the data flowing on the network and retrieve usernames, passwords, and other sensitive data simply by capturing the packets and performing an analysis on the data captured.

Many applications used by users every day transmit their authentication data in cleartext on the network. This means that anyone with a sniffer can intercept passwords for Telnet, Post Office Protocol (POP), FTP, Web, and many other applications. When attackers compromise a system, they will often install sniffer software so they can capture other information on the network. The sniffer acts as a "spy" for the attacker, storing captured passwords for later retrieval by the attacker or transmitting them to the attacker as they are captured.

The attackers then use the newly acquired authentication information to gain access to the system and the stored data, as well as using the compromised system to launch attacks against other systems. The process of compromising a system, installing a sniffer, and then using captured data to compromise other systems is referred to as an *island hopping attack*.

Sniffing Defenses. Unfortunately, the best defense against sniffing is to encrypt the data being transmitted, either by encrypting only the sensitive data or by encrypting all data on the network. Tools such as SSH, secure Telnet, and SSL provide good mechanisms for encrypting the data.

A second defense is to eliminate the broadcast nature of Ethernet using switch models. Switches reduce the size of both the broadcast and collision domains. With a switch, the effect and damage of a sniffer is reduced, although not eliminated. (Tools such as dsniff can still be used against a switched network.) Switches can be configured so that only the required source and destination ports carry the data. Consequently, none of the other ports can see the data on the switch because the traffic is not destined for them. Consequently, if an attacker compromises a system and installs a sniffer, he will only see the traffic destined for the compromised system. (It goes without saying that the sniffer will also see the broadcast packets; however, those packets do not carry passwords.)

Therefore, switches can help improve network level security in addition to overall network performance.

IP Spoofing. IP spoofing is a process to alter the source destination of a packet to make it appear that the packet originated at another system. IP spoofing is typically used to exploit weak authentication systems and initiate denial-of-service attacks. If the target system relies only on IP authentication, an attacker can spoof the source IP and gain access to the system. Furthermore, IP spoofing makes it difficult to identify the real attacker because the connection appears to have originated at an allowed system. Identification is difficult because all connection logs will refer to the authorized host making the connection.

Spoofing Defenses. The best defense is to prevent the use of IP addresses as an authentication technique. Applications and functions using IP address authentication, including the Unix "r-commands" (e.g., rlogin, rcp, rsh, and rexec), should be replaced because they are subject to IP spoofing attacks. Similarly, these commands can use a trust relationship through the .rhosts file and are frequently used by system administrators. IP spoofing with these services exposes root level accounts to unauthorized access.

The use of replacement tools such as Secure Shell (SSH) is strongly encouraged to eliminate the use of the r-commands. Additionally, any other function relying on IP address authentication should be replaced.

Furthermore, the use of anti-spoofing configurations on routers, particularly at the network perimeter, is highly encouraged. Anti-spoofing filters drop packets appearing on the public side of the router when they have a source address of the private network. This capability strengthens the perimeter defenses and can prevent some types of spoofing attacks.

Session Hijacking. Sniffing allows an attacker to view data on the network associated with a network connection. Session hijacking allows the attacker to assume control over a network connection while kicking off the legitimate user, or sharing the user's login credentials. Session hijacking tools are used against applications with persistent connections, such as Telnet, rlogin, or FTP. With a hijacked session, an attacker can cause a great deal of damage.

For session hijacking to be successful, the attacker must be located on a LAN segment between the two communicating systems. Observing an integrated sniffer, the hijacking tool monitors the connection examining the TCP sequence numbers on each half of the connection. Recall from our previous discussion that each packet has a sequence number so the receiving station can verify it has received all the data. The hijacking tool monitors the connection to determine the sequence numbers in use. To take over the session through either command insertion or session stealing, the hijacking tool spoofs the appropriate address and, using the correct sequence numbers, assumes control of the communication stream.

Session Hijacking Defenses. Avoiding insecure protocols is the best defense against session hijacking. For example, the easy-to-sniff, easy-to-hijack Telnet application should be avoided, using SSH instead. Because the attacker will not have the session key used to encrypt the session data, the encrypted session cannot be hijacked.

Other alternatives to solutions such as SSH are available, including the use of a virtual private network between the source and destination systems.

Denial-of-Service Attacks

One of the most common exploits seen today is the Denial of Service. A denial-of-service (DoS) attack is an attack against the availability of a service, because it prevents legitimate users from being able to access the service. The service can be an application, a system, or a network. With the vast number of e-commerce applications on the Internet today, a well-timed and well-planned DoS attack could put a company out of business. Aside from nuisance attacks, a DoS attack against a critical system such as power management, medical systems, or other critical components could cause significant damage and potentially loss of life.

The attacker uses several methods to flood the target system with bogus traffic and fake requests. The more common attack methods are the malformed packet and packet flood.

Malformed Packet Attacks. Proper operation of a complex system like TCP/IP depends on protocols. However, not all vendors implement the protocols correctly, or implement all the features of the protocol. The malformed packet attack involves a few packets that are formatted in an unexpected manner. If the software implementation does not handle unexpected packet or protocol options, the operating system may crash when a specific type of packet is received.

One common implementation of the malformed packet attack is sending overlapping IP fragments. If the Windows or Linux system has not been patched, it will likely crash when it receives a packet of this type. Other attacks exploit other weaknesses in vendor implementations of TCP/IP, including the WinNuke, Land, LaTierra, NewTear, Bonk, and Boink attacks. These are all examples of malformed packet attacks.

Packet Flood Attacks. The other major attack method is the packet flood attack. The packet flood attack is a DoS attack that sends a large number of packets to the remote host until it cannot respond to requests any longer. There are many packet flood attacks, with the most common being SYN floods, directed broadcast attacks, and distributed denial-of-service (DDoS) utilities.

SYN floods operate by initiating connections to the target system but never actually completing the TCP three-way handshake. To establish a TCP connection, a client and server must participate in a three-way handshake (SYN-SYN+ACK–ACK), which is used to establish the initial sequence numbers of the connection. First the client system sends a packet with the SYN (synchronize) flag set to the server. Then, the server acknowledges the client by sending a packet back with the SYN and ACK (acknowledge) flags set. Finally, the client completes the connection by sending a packet with the ACK flag set. The connection between the client and the server is then open, and the service-specific data can be exchanged between the client and the server. In this attack, the attacking system sends a SYN packet to the target requesting a connection and establishing the sequence number of TCP packets. The target host responds with a SYN-ACK packet to acknowledge the sequence number. By sending spoofed SYN packets and never acknowledging the SYN-ACK, the attacker exhausts a server's ability to respond to session requests.

In most system configurations, a server's ability to handle SYN requests is lower than the available bandwidth. This makes sense; otherwise, there could be many more connections than the available bandwidth will support. Consequently, SYN floods are the most popular type of packet flood attack.

The second packet flood is the directed broadcast. In this method, the attackers use another network to amplify their bandwidth. This attack method is commonly called a smurf attack and requires the attacker to find a network that responds to ICMP messages to the network's broadcast address. If the network is configured to allow requests and responses on the broadcast address, all machines on the network will send a response to the ping. By spoofing the source address, all the hosts on the amplified network send their ICMP responses to the spoofed address, the intended victim.

This type of attack can be dramatic. If a network has 200 hosts and they all send their ICMP responses to a single victim, the intended victim gets 200 packets. If the attacker sends multiple packets to the hosts on the amplified network, they send the same number of packets to the victim. It is easy to envision that even a small amount of bandwidth at the attacker's site can be translated into a very large number of packets at the victim's end. Other directed broadcast attack tools include Fraggle and Papasmurf.

The third major type of packet flood attack is the distributed denial-of-service (DDoS) attack. This attack method has seen a lot of attention in the popular media over the past several years. For a successful distributed attack, the attacker must find a group of vulnerable systems, typically on the Internet. The number of systems compromised for a distributed attack is quite large, numbering from hundreds to thousands of systems.

The vulnerable systems are compromised and simple processes, called zombies, are installed. The attacker then uses a control program to communicate with the zombies and instruct them to execute a specific action simultaneously. The typical action is launching a packet flood attack against a specific victim. Traditional SYN flood attacks send connection requests from a single system to a single host. With the distributed attack model, the compromised systems can easily flood the victim's available bandwidth, preventing any type of legitimate traffic.

DDoS tools support various attack methods, including SYN, UDP, and ICMP flooding attacks, as well as smurf and malformed packet attacks. Any or all of these options can be used by the attacker when initiating the attack.

Denial-of-Service Attack Defenses. Defending against denial-of-service attacks is mostly about patching. Vendors frequently provide patches to address new denial-of-service issues as new attacks are announced. Consequently, good patch management programs are a must for every organization.

Packet flood attacks require more effort because they involve network architecture designs capable of withstanding the attack. The architecture must include redundant paths to eliminate a single point of failure. Additionally, adequate bandwidth is required, as well as using routers and firewalls with capabilities to combat SYN flood attacks.

Appropriate network design for Internet-accessible systems can reduce an organization's susceptibility to DoS attacks and being used to launch smurf and DoS attacks against other networks. Preventing network devices from participating in smurf and similar attacks involves configuring the device to drop all directed broadcast requests from the public network, and likely from the private network as well.

Lowering the chance of involvement in a DoS attack means configuring the network devices with anti-spoofing filters and verifying that all outgoing packets from the private network have a source address that belongs to the organization. All other packets should be dropped by the network devices. Using egress filtering rules like these prevent a zombie or other denial-of-service program from sending spoofed packets from your network.

Stack-Based Buffer Overflows

Stack-based buffer overflows exploit how the operating system involved uses the stack, which is an internal data structure where programs temporarily store data. Manipulation of the stack through a buffer overflow can result in system crashes, elevation of privileges, and execution of arbitrary code. Worse yet, remote and local users, depending on the application with the overflow, can exploit buffer overflows.

The stack is used for temporary value storage during program execution. When the program executes a function call, the current program state and any variables to be passed to the function are put onto the stack. Space on the stack is also allocated for variables used by the function. Finally, the stack also stores the memory address to return to when the function is complete. Once the function call is complete, the return address is retrieved from the stack and program execution is resumed.

Most modern Unix systems and all Windows systems use a stack capable of storing both data and executable code. Because the stack is used to store local variables, poor program code can result in the stack being overrun. For example, if the data entered by a user is not checked for length, it may exceed the amount of storage space allocated on the stack. This overwrites program code, other variables, and possibly the return address where execution should resume. This is called "smashing" the stack and allows an attacker to insert executable code and another return address on the stack.

The attacker requires additional knowledge of the architecture under attack. The attacker must craft machine-specific bytecodes to execute a set of commands, followed by a return pointer to execute the inserted code. Consequently, with very carefully constructed code the attacker can enter information into a program, overflowing the stack and executing the inserted code. Performing these attacks allows the attacker to break out of the application and access any system components or data and start programs or gain administrator privileges.

However, exploiting the buffer overflow requires extensive knowledge of the hardware architecture being exploited to develop the initial commands. Once developed, they can be shared and executed without subsequent attackers understanding the complexities of the exploit.

Stack-Based Buffer Overflow Defenses. Because most buffer overflows exist as a result of bad programming or programming errors, the best defense is to thoroughly test code and software to prevent stack smashing. Code reviews and code audits are also good ways to find programming errors leading to buffer overflows. Every program should perform validation of user input to ensure that it will not exceed the allocated storage. Every variable should be checked, especially user input, to ensure it contains appropriate data. Unfortunately, verifying the actual program code is available only to the code developers and those specific individuals with access to the program source code.

Additionally, system administrators should monitor what programs are executed with elevated privileges, such as the SUID (set user ID bit) permissions within the Unix operating system. Only SUID programs with a specific business requirement should be installed on production systems.

Finally, if the system supports it, the stack should be configured to prevent execution of code from the stack. In particular, Linux and Solaris offer this option. If execution of code from the stack is disabled, programs doing so will crash. However, some programs legitimately require the need to execute code from the stack, and disabling this functionality affects those programs as well. Consequently, the purpose of the system may dictate the availability of executable code on the stack.

The Art and Science of Password Cracking

Most systems and applications in use authenticate the user using a static password. When the user requests access, the system collects a password, which is then checked by the system against a password database. If the password matches the value stored in the database, the user is granted access. Most operating systems provide a method of storing the passwords in an encrypted (hashed) form, making it more difficult for an attacker to simply acquire the database and obtain the passwords. The same is not true for all applications because it is up to the individual application developer to establish how authentication is performed.

The attacker uses password-cracking tools in an attempt to guess a password, encrypt it with the appropriate password encryption scheme, and compare the encrypted values to determine if there is a match. Consequently, successfully guessing a password is based on three things:

- Acquisition of the password database
- Knowledge of the password encryption algorithm
- Having a program that can encrypt and compare the passwords

Attackers will use whatever means are available, including buffer overflows, to gain access to a system and acquire the password database. Password-cracking tools can use either a dictionary of passwords to attempt to find a valid one or can brute-force the password by attempting every possible value for the password. Obviously, brute-force cracking requires a lot of time and computer horsepower to try all possible password values. Dozens of dictionaries are available, including specialized words, names, cities, and in different languages. Additionally, there are many different password-cracking tools available to the attacker.

Password-Cracking Defenses. Minimizing the exposure of the encrypted password database is the first line of defense in reducing the risk of password cracking. On Unix systems, the shadow password file can be used to accomplish this, as only the superuser should be able to access the shadow file. On Windows NT and 2000 systems, the SYSKEY feature should be enabled. Furthermore, all backups and system recovery disks should be stored in physically secured locations and possibly even encrypted.

Second, the organization should have a strong password policy defining password lifetimes, strength, and complexity. For example, passwords should be eight characters or more and contain upper- and lowercase letters, numbers, and special characters. Users must also be made aware of password management responsibilities through an awareness program.

Security practitioners should also use the same password-cracking tools as the attackers to periodically evaluate the strength of the passwords in their environment. When a weak password is discovered, the security group should use a defined procedure to interact with the user or to reset the password.

Finally, if possible, the system's controls should be implemented to prevent users from selecting weak passwords. If there are no controls in the system, there are several available tools to implement password controls. These programs check the user's password against defined rules for complexity and strength. These tools can enforce the organization's password policy. However, for these programs to be truly effective, they must be installed on every system in the organization, including servers, workstations, and password database systems such as Unix Network Information Service (NIS) and Windows domain controllers.

Backdoors

Traditional security checks can be bypassed through a backdoor. Backdoors are used by attackers to gain access to a system by bypassing the usual security checks. Unfortunately, backdoors are often installed by programmers for the same function during program development and are sometimes not removed.

Once installed by an attacker, the backdoor is activated and allows connections on special network ports. When a connection is received, the backdoor grants access to the system without any security checks or authentication, or through a special password known only to the backdoor.

Backdoor Defenses. System administrators and security practitioners should monitor the programs installed and running on their systems, especially high transaction volume or critical/sensitive systems. Thorough system monitoring is the best defense against backdoor programs. Backdoor programs running on specific network ports can be found through network vulnerability analysis tools and using operating system commands such as netstat – n.

Furthermore, many backdoor programs are also discovered by anti-virus programs, which should be installed on all servers and desktops within the enterprise. Coupled with a program to keep virus definitions updated on a regular basis, anti-virus software provides an effective defense.

Trojan Horses and Rootkits

Trojan horse programs are another component in the attacker's set of tools. The Trojan horse is similar to the Trojan horse in ancient Greece. The program appears to serve some useful purpose, yet it is really just disguising the malicious operation. Trojan horse programs rely on deceiving the user into performing one action, while surreptitiously performing another. Trojan horses commonly install backdoor programs on the user's system.

Rootkits. A Rootkit is a more powerful Trojan horse. Despite the name, a rootkit does not allow the attacker to gain root, or super-user privileges on a system. The attacker must already have root access and then use the rootkit to keep that access by preventing an administrator from finding the access. Rootkits typically contain a large number of Trojan horse programs that replace or patch critical system programs.

Typically, a rootkit will contain a Trojan horse version of the Unix/bin/login program. While the attacker has access to the system, he replaces the real/bin/login with the Trojan horse. The Trojan horse/bin/login contains a username and password that the attacker can use for later access. Likewise, the rootkit also contains a sniffer and a way to hide it from detection. Typically, analysis of the network interface will show the administrator that a sniffer is running because the network interface is in promiscuous mode. The rootkit contains a modified version of the *ifconfig* command to hide the promiscuous flag.

Programs, including *ps* and *du,* are also replaced by Unix-based rootkits. These programs are regularly used by system administrators to manage the system. The *ps* program, which lists all the processes running on the system, would list the attacker and any processes left running from the rootkit. The modified *ps* program hides these processes so that the administrator cannot detect them. Additionally, the *du* command, which shows disk utilization, is altered to hide the disk space consumed by the rootkit and any other programs installed by the attacker.

Replacing these programs makes them part of the operating system. Therefore, rootkits blind the administrators and convince them that nothing is out of the ordinary. However, the attacker actually has full access to the system and is actively using it to compromise and attack other systems.

Kernel-level rootkits have been recently developed to provide very low-level access to the system. The rootkit patches the kernel rather than replacing individual commands within the system. Many Unix commands rely on kernel-level features, including the operation of loadable kernel modules and dynamic libraries. By patching the kernel and installing the rootkit, the attacker can remap system functions and affect the operation of a wider range of programs.

By remapping system functions, the attacker can execute code without having to modify any system program. When a user, such as the system administrator, executes a program, the Trojan elements of the kernel execute the attacker's code. Trojan kernels are difficult to detect. With no system programs affected, an analysis of the system using file integrity tools will reveal nothing unusual to the administrator. However, when the program is executed, the malicious program is substituted by the kernel.

Trojan Horses and Rootkit Defenses. User awareness is key to protecting against Trojan horses. Users should understand the risks of executing programs from people they do not know as well as the importance of keeping their anti-virus software up-to-date. Every desktop and server system within the organization must have anti-virus defenses installed and virus definitions kept up-to-date. Additionally, organizations may wish to install and use programs that detect potentially malicious programs attached to email and remove or disable them from being executed.

Defending against rootkits means establishing programs that evaluate the system programs and to periodically check their integrity against a trusted source. Numerous tools are available to analyze a system and establish an integrity database of checksums for system programs that will not match against an altered program. Integrity checking must be performed on a frequency commensurate with the nature of the system and its criticality to the organization. The system or security administrators must reconcile any differences to establish if there has been a compromise of the system. If a rootkit or other malicious software is detected, the most expedient method of removal is to rebuild the operating system from trusted sources, followed by reinstalling applications and, finally, restoring system and application data.

Kernel-level rootkits cannot be detected using integrity check programs because the integrity checker is relying on the kernel to operate correctly. If the kernel produces incorrect results or hides information from the integrity checks, the analysis cannot be trusted. The only manageable defense against kernel-level rootkits is the use of a monolithic kernel with all device support compiled in and no reliance upon loadable kernel modules.

Monolithic kernels are highly recommended for systems such as firewalls, Web servers, DNS, and mail servers due to their proximity to hostile networks such as the Internet. A kernel that does not support loadable kernel modules is ultimately more difficult for the attacker to compromise.

Overall Defenses: Intrusion Detection and Incident Response Procedures

Building a strong defense requires a proactive effort to reduce vulnerabilities and patch systems, in addition to understanding the attacker's tools and methods. However, a truly effective defense requires the ability to detect when an attack is under way and having a method to respond to the attack. Detection and response are managed through intrusion detection systems and incident response procedures.

Basically, the Intrusion Detection System (IDS) acts like a burglar alarm. As events happen on the network meeting the alarm's criteria, the alarm sounds to alert an administrator so that further analysis and investigation are performed. In this manner, the IDS can provide early warning of a possible attack so the organization can be ready for it, thereby minimizing the damage caused.

Even more important than the early warning is incident response. Every organization should have an incident response procedure to quickly identify, contain, eradicate, and recover from incidents. Even with the latest protective technology, an attacker can still penetrate a network. Consequently, the incident response team must be skilled in a variety of technologies and applications to gauge the effect of the attack and recommend response methods.

The incident response team requires documented procedures to describe what should be done in a given situation, establish consistent processes, and provide contact information. Finally, the procedure must also provide the detail to determine when escalation to management is required. Trying to create the response process, contact lists, or escalation criteria during the incident leads to bad decisions.

With the impact of attacks potentially covering many aspects of the organization, multidisciplinary teams are required. Not just Information Technology, but Legal, Human Resources, Public Relations, and Security teams should all be involved. Specific people should be identified as the core Incident Response Team. While it is unlikely to be able to build a team that is all encompassing, it may be that this team is focused on Computer Security incidents while there is another team with different training to handle physical disasters such as chemical spills, fires, etc.

Many corporations are outsourcing some aspect of their Information Technology operations or business processes. Any IDS or incident response procedures must be developed to capture detecting and response capabilities from those organizations so they can understand what their role is in the event of an incident. Furthermore, the contract should clearly stipulate the outsource provider's responsibilities for detection, prevention, and correction of attacks against their systems.

8.3 Security Technology and Tools

Comprehensive security policy and awareness training is key to protecting the organization's key information and maintaining competitive advantage. This section reviews these and other security issues and options for distributed and remote environments.

Problems Addressed

Although distributed data networks improve productivity by making information, applications, processing power, and mass storage readily available to a large and growing user population, they also make those resources more vulnerable to abuse and misuse.

The situation is even more pronounced when dealing with such services as public key infrastructure (PKI), electronic funds transfer (EFT), electronic mail, and other data networking environments in which unauthorized usage, information theft, and malicious file tampering can result in immediate financial loss and long-term damage to a competitive position.

Sending email over the Internet is less secure than sending a postcard through regular mail. As messages pass through various servers on the

Internet on the way to their destination, they are exposed to virtually anyone who wants to read them. All a system administrator or technician needs to do is collect the packets that pass through the site's equipment (such as a router) by attaching a traffic analyzer. This device, which is designed for troubleshooting problems on the network, has the capability to record and decode packets all the way up to the application layer, meaning that the text of email messages can be easily played back and read.

Various protective measures can be taken to safeguard information in transit as well as information stored at various points on the network, including servers and desktop computers.

Physical Security

When protecting information, the first response is to make it difficult, if not impossible, for people to gain unauthorized access to your premises. This includes the external entrances, garage doors, wiring closets, air conditioning and heating plant, and offices. Physical protection typically starts with fences and guards where they implement access control through ID verification. Alternatively, automated access control systems can augment the guard services.

Security awareness is again important in the overall protection of the company. This would include training management and staff on the importance of securing information left on workstations and computers or in an unlocked office. Many people are shocked to see what information can be retrieved without opening a desk drawer. Simple measures such as disk drive, computer, and keyboard locks provide enough deterrence for the typical attacker.

Workstation security is also very important, especially if it contains key information on network topologies, access to wiring closets and various network devices. Finding network access passwords on an unsecured workstation is an attacker's dream. Likewise, users appropriately make backups or copies of information, yet they often leave them unlocked. All removable media, software, data, and original distribution media should be locked up to prevent theft, copyright infringement, and loss of intellectual property.

Controlling Data Access

Offering network access to information implies the requirement for controlling that access. Access to the network and stored data can be controlled through several means, including a password to access the network itself and a password to access the application. Two-factor authentication is preferred for sensitive/critical systems. Access to data must be restricted to only the information that users require to perform their jobs and the ability to copy the information to alternate sources must be a carefully controlled privilege.

Logon Security

Most systems and applications require a user to authenticate before access is granted. The authentication process is used to identify the user and validate his identity through a password or some other information only he knows or has. Operating systems and applications, wherever a user is authenticated, should be configured to suspend user accounts after a defined number of incorrect passwords have been entered. Doing so is a defense against trial-and-error password guessing.

Furthermore, periodic password changes with strong password complexity and length enhance the overall security of the environment. As the most common method of system access control, passwords are used to access most services. User awareness is critical to password protection — the user must understand why he must protect the password, and a policy specifying employees are responsible for actions taken using his account can assist in overall system security.

Other authentication methods are available to the security administrator, including biometrics, tokens, and smart cards. All of these devices and specific access control issues are discussed in Chapter 3, "Access Control Systems and Methodology."

Securing Network Traffic

Data Encryption. Protecting the data through encryption can be accomplished at several levels. The data can be encrypted at the application layer, which provides the most protection as it moves through the stack. It could be added lower down in the stack, and even done on the physical media itself.

Encryption provides two benefits: it hides the information from unauthorized access and it alerts us when the integrity of the message has been corrupted. Message integrity is important to validate the sender, receiver, and actual message content. Encryption systems, design, and implementation are discussed more fully in the Cryptography chapter (see Chapter 6).

Firewalls. A firewall is a method of protecting one network from another untrusted network. The method used varies, but a firewall consists of two components: one to block traffic and another to allow authorized traffic through. Firewalls can be packet filters, proxies, or a combination of the two.

Packet filtering focuses on analyzing the packets and comparing them to a set of rules to determine if the packet should be allowed through or blocked. Rules include time of day, source and destination address, the port being accessed and, if used, the authentication of the user, and simultaneous network connections. Packet filtering is available on firewalls and on many routers. It is appropriate to use all devices capable of packet filtering to provide multiple layers of control within the network architecture.

A proxy acts as a middleman in the connection process. The user's session establishes a connection to the proxy, which in turn establishes a connection to the external system. The advantage of the proxy is that it prevents a connection from being made directly from the user's workstation to the external system. The disadvantage is that you need a proxy for each type of protocol you want to use.

Typically proxies contain additional logging and authentication capabilities. However, because the proxy must understand the application and protocol being used, there may not be a proxy for the application or protocol desired. Most modern proxy firewalls contain proxies for the common applications and a generic proxy for supporting other applications.

Firewalls help reduce network penetrations; however, errors in firewall configuration or a very sophisticated attacker can result in penetrations through the firewall into the protected network. Consequently, firewalls are only one component in the network defense architecture.

Remote Access Security. The decentralized and increasingly mobile workforce places new demands on remote access to the organizational network. Sales forces, executives, and road warriors all want high speed, and reliable and secure access to their data, email, and applications.

Remote access technologies consist of any technology and application that allow a user access to the organizational network when he does not have a physical LAN connection. Remote access can consist of modems, virtual private networks, and encryption methods, depending on the size and complexity of the organization.

Regardless of organizational complexity and how the remote access services are acquired, the following security elements should be considered:

- *Authentication:* verification of the user's login credentials and allowing only those who have authorization access to the network.
- *Access restrictions:* to define what resources the user can access.
- *Time restrictions:* restricting when a user can connect and for what duration of time the connection is allowed.
- *Connection restrictions:* impose limits of simultaneous connections per user, consecutive failed login attempts, and hours of use.
- *Protocol restrictions:* restrict what protocols and services are available through the dial-up.

Additionally, remote access users should have personal firewalls and anti-virus software on their workstations to prevent another system from accessing them while connected to the remote access service.

Callback Systems. When there is a requirement for a modem to be directly attached to a system or for higher security remote access requirements, a callback system is recommended. However, for traditional, bulk user remote access, this can be difficult and expensive.

With callback security, the answering modem accepts the incoming call and authenticates the user. Once the user is authenticated, the modem disconnects the call and then places a callback to the user using a telephone number in a predefined database. The implementation assists in preventing unauthorized access or use of stolen credentials. It is, however, susceptible to compromise by call forwarding.

Callback security is especially beneficial when communication is permitted only between a small number of remote systems and a central host. Given the requirement for callback systems to have the authorized user's phone number in its database, this is not an acceptable solution for mobile users, support personnel, or any user who does not always call from the same phone number.

Link-Level Security. Remote access services must include the ability to authenticate a user and establish a reliable connection. Modern systems principally use the Point-to-Point Protocol (PPP) for establishing the connection, and either the Password Authentication Protocol (PAP), Challenge Handshake Protocol (CHAP), or Extensible Authentication Protocol (EAP) for authentication.

PPP was designed as a replacement for the Serial Line Internet Protocol (SLIP) and provides more robust and improved features. PPP is intended as a wide area network protocol allowing any system to contact another through a serial link including direct serial connections or through modems. PPP is a multi-protocol service, with support for additional protocols added through Network Control Programs (NCPs). This feature allows PPP to carry IP and IPX traffic for the same connection.

Authentication of the user for the purposes of allowing the connection is done using one of several methods, with PAP and CHAP being the most predominant. PAP uses a handshake when establishing the initial connection between the client and server. The user ID and password are transmitted repeatedly until the authentication is verified or the connection is terminated. The user ID and password are transmitted over the link in cleartext, offering no protection for the authentication information.

CHAP provides a higher degree of security for the authentication process. CHAP uses a three-way handshake. Upon connection, the server sends the connecting system a random challenge. The receiving system encrypts the challenge with the user's password. Once the server receives the encrypted value, it can look up the user's password, encrypt the random challenge, and determine if the values match. If the encrypted values match, the authentication credentials are accepted.

Each time the user connects to the server, a different token is used, meaning even if the handshake was observed and the credentials stolen, they cannot be reused. Most network device vendors support both PAP and CHAP. However, lower-end products tend to support only PAP, which is the less desirable of the two. EAP, which uses certificate-based authentication, has recently been developed and will likely be added as a more secure authentication method, especially for PPP use over public networks where the point-to-point connection is over a shared circuit.

Providing Security Awareness Training. Despite the often low level of effort applied to security awareness, it is a critical method of protecting your systems and intellectual property. The complexity of today's computing systems make awareness more important. Ensuring that users use the technology correctly, or apply good security practices, is essential. Without the training, the users do not know they are doing anything wrong.

Additionally, security awareness training explains to the users what their obligations are to protect company information and how both technology implementations and the users contribute to the overall security posture of the organization. The awareness program must cover all aspects of the security program, with an emphasis on what the users will actually interact with, and be described in a manner understandable by even the least technical individual.

The security awareness program should include:

- A review of the organization's security policy, including the roles of management and the employee
- Explanation of physical access controls, including badges, parking, and guest sign-in procedures
- Definition of information classifications and how to protect confidential data
- Viruses and handling information from unknown sources
- Social engineering techniques
- Corporate ethics
- Reporting security incidents

This is by no means an exhaustive list, but it provides the basis for generating awareness at the employee level of their responsibilities.

An effective awareness program consists of multiple information sources, initial training, and periodic follow-up training. Follow-up training ensures that everyone is still aware of their obligations and allows for updating information due to changing technology, policies, and legislation.

Centralized Authentication and Administration Servers: RADIUS, TACACS, DIAMETER

Centralized authentication systems provide significant benefits to the security administrators. They permit easier user administration for adding, modifying, and deleting users, because the account management process can be done in one place, which all other systems then use for authentication.

There are three principle authentication, authorization, and accounting (AAA) servers, as defined by the Internet Engineering Task Force (IETF). RADIUS, TACACS, and DIAMETER are these three AAA implementations.

Remote Authentication Dial-in User Service, or RADIUS, was originally developed by Livingston Enterprises for its Network Access Service devices. The protocol provided time-share and Internet service providers with account management, billing information, and connection configuration services. RADIUS was based on the IETF distributed security model. The client/server nature of RADIUS was intended to be open and easily adapted to other third-party products.

The exact origin of the Terminal Access Controller Access Control System, or TACACS, is unknown. Originally used in the early days of the ARPANET, TACACS was later adopted by Cisco Systems for AAA support in its products. Cisco then extended the protocol to support additional authentication types and request/response codes. The extended version of TACACS is now known as TACACS+. The IETF Network Working Group proposed RFC 1492 as the new TACACS standard and it was developed with the assistance of Cisco Systems.

In 1998, Pat Calhoun (Sun Laboratories) and Allan Rubens (Ascend Communications) proposed the DIAMETER AAA framework as a draft standard to the IETF. The name is not an acronym, but a play on the RADIUS name. DIAMETER was completely designed to support roaming applications and overcome the limitations of the TACACS and RADIUS protocols. It supports AAA extensions for NAS, mobile-IP, host, application, and Web-based requirements. DIAMETER has wide support, including involvement from Sun, Microsoft, Cisco, Nortel, and others.

Key Features of an AAA Service. AAA systems must support the following features:

- A distributed (client/server) security model
- Authenticated transactions
- Flexible authentication mechanisms
- An extensible protocol

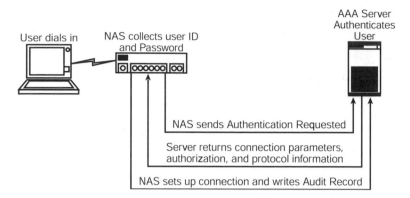

Exhibit 17. Key Features of a Centralized AAA Service
(From Bill Stackpole, "Centralized Authentication Services (RADIUS, TACACS, DIAMETER)," in *Information Security Management Handbook*, 4th ed., Vol. 2, Harold F. Tipton and Micki Krause, Eds. © 2001 CRC Press LLC.)

In a distributed security model, the communications and authentication elements are separated. This makes it possible for centralization of the user authentication data into a single database. Network access devices are the clients to the database. The Network Access Server (NAS) submits authentication credentials to the authentication server, which in turn validates or denies the credentials.

The information returned to the NAS device can include transport and protocol information, additional authentication requirements including callback and SecurID, authorization directives such as the allowed services, and accounting information (Exhibit 17).

Communications with the AAA server use a secret key known to the NAS device and the AAA server. This encrypts and protects the authentication credentials for the user. This is especially important when the authentication credentials are carried over public carrier services.

AAA servers must be capable of supporting multiple authentication protocols, including Password Authentication Protocol (PAP), Challenge Handshake Authentication Protocol (CHAP), the standard Unix login, and extensible authentication methods. Other authentication methods the AAA server must support include SecurID, Novell NDS, and Microsoft domain authentication systems.

Some AAA servers support additional security features, including calling number identification (Caller ID) and callback, to further increase the security of the connection. AAA technology changes very rapidly and consequently must provide extensible protocols to support new features as they become available.

AAA servers provide significant management benefits, including:

- Reduced setup and maintenance time because all user authentication information is stored on a central host
- Fewer configuration errors due to similar formats across heterogeneous devices
- Reduced security administrator training
- Improved auditing because all authentication is done through a single system
- Reduced help desk calls because the user interface is consistent across all access methods
- Improved access information dissemination because there are fewer systems on which to store the data

RADIUS: Remote Authentication Dial-In User Service. The most popular AAA service in use today is RADIUS, primarily due to Livingston's decision to make the source available to the public. Users were quick to port the software to various platforms and add customized features, many of which Livingston incorporated into the base code. Current RADIUS implementations exist for most major platforms as both freeware and commercial implementations.

A RADIUS server requires two configurations — one specifying client configurations and one for users. The client configuration file contains the IP addresses of the clients and the shared secret used to authenticate the connections. The user file contains the user ID, password, and authorization parameters. Parameters are passed between the client and the server using a five-field format encapsulated into a single UDP packet. The compact message, combined with the UDP protocol, means the RADIUS server can efficiently handle very large numbers of connections. However, the simple format does not scale well in some of today's very complex environments and retransmissions are frequent due to lost packets in heavily loaded networks.

There are eight standard RADIUS transactions:

- Access-request
- Access-accept
- Access-reject
- Accounting-request
- Accounting-response
- Access-challenge
- Status-server
- Status-client

When a user logs in to the NAS device, an access-request packet is sent to the RADIUS server and is encrypted using the shared secret. When the

RADIUS server receives the request, it authenticates the client by decrypting the packet using the shared secret for the client as configured in the client configuration file. If the packet cannot be decrypted, it is discarded as invalid.

If the packet can be decrypted, the user information is validated against the user configuration and a response returned to the NAS. There are three valid responses to the access-request packet:

- Access-accept
- Access-reject
- Access-challenge

If the user credentials match those stored in the RADIUS database, the server responds with an access-accept packet. A failed authentication results in an access-reject. If the user is configured to provide a callback identifier or additional information, such as from a token card, the access-challenge response is returned to the NAS.

Within RADIUS, authorization is part of the authentication response. When the RADIUS server validates the access request, all connection authorizations are returned to the NAS client as part of the authentication reply. Authorization components can include data-link types and network specifications. Additionally, the authorization field may also contain vendor-specific authorization parameters.

RADIUS accounting is a separate element as not all RADIUS clients support accounting. If the client is configured for RADIUS accounting, a RADIUS accounting-start packet is sent to the server once authenticated and an accounting-stop packet is sent when the session has ended. The accounting-start packet identifies the type of service, the port used, and the user ID. The accounting-stop packet adds session information, including elapsed time, bytes, and disconnect messages.

Because RADIUS is open and extensible, there can be variations in how the AAA, proxy, and database functionality is implemented between vendors. Consequently, when planning to implement RADIUS, it is best to focus on the functional requirements first and then choose NAS vendors based on those requirements. Some factors to consider in the functional implementation include:

- *What device types will be authenticated?* Modem pools and VPN servers are typical, although routers, firewalls, and other network devices can also be authenticated through RADIUS and should be considered.
- *What protocol support is required?* RADIUS provides information regarding the link types, network, and transport levels in the authentication response.

- *What services are required?* Is support for services such as Telnet, rlogin, and third-party authentication required? These often require additional components and expertise.
- *Are proxy support or redundant RADIUS servers required?* Both proxy support and redundant servers are provided differently by vendors and not all clients support these features. The use of proxies is required if an NAS device will support different management or security domains.

Client setup for RADIUS is straightforward. The client must be configured with the IP address of the server(s), the shared secret (encryption key), and the IP port numbers of the authentication and accounting services (the defaults are 1645 and 1646, respectively). Additional settings may be required by the vendor.

In environments where a single NAS type is used or a different RADIUS server is used for each type, the server configuration files become fairly uncomplicated. However, when there are a multitude of NAS devices, different access types, and a large number of users, the configuration can become quite complicated. This adds complexity to the configuration of the RADIUS server and to its administration.

Stumbling Blocks, Complexities, and Other RADIUS Limitations. While RADIUS works well for remote access authentication, it is not well suited for host or application authentication because it includes neither group membership primitives nor restrictions for time-of-day access, password management, or expiring a user's account. RADIUS also provides no support for monitoring nailed-up connections or system events. These are limitations of the RADIUS service and not an implementation deficiency. Using RADIUS to provide these services requires a secondary authentication service.

Despite these deficiencies, RADIUS is efficient, flexible, and well supported. It works best when utilized with an additional authentication service, such as Windows domain authentication used to provide additional account restrictions. Regardless, it is currently the most widely used AAA service.

TACACS: Terminal Access Controller Access Control System. Cisco Systems adopted the TACACS protocol to provide AAA service for its products and then further enhanced the protocol by separating the authentication, authorization, and accounting features. Cisco also added encryption to all TACACS transmissions, improving overall security of the service. Despite Cisco naming its enhanced implementation TACACS+, it has no compatible features with the earlier versions of the protocol. However, some newer implementations provide support for both versions. Unlike RADIUS, TACACS+ uses a single file to store all server options and user authentication information. The configuration file specifies the shared secret key and accounting information.

When a TACACS client requests authentication of user information, it sends a request to the server using a TCP session, including a series of attribute/value pairs with the data. The request type can be authentication, authorization, or accounting and is sent in the clear. However, the parameter data is encrypted using the shared secret. The variable-length parameter data is customizable to support site-specific extensions, while the use of TCP ensures reliable delivery. While the data is protected and reliable delivery is assured, these changes from RADIUS incur higher communications overhead, which can impact server performance during peak authentication cycles.

TACACS Authentication. The authentication element contains Start, Continue, and Reply packet types. The client authentication is initiated with the Start packet, describing the authentication to be performed. When simple authentication services such as PAP are used, the Start packet also contains the user ID and password.

Once the server validates the user data, a Reply packet is returned to the client. If additional information for the authentication is required, the client sends Continue packets until the process is complete and the authentication is granted or denied. The authentication transactions include login based upon privilege level and support multiple authentication protocols, including CHAP, PAP, PPP, etc. In a manner similar to RADIUS, the TACACS server provides attribute/value pairs upon successful authentication, which may include authorization information. If not specified, the authorization details can be requested separately from the TACACS server.

TACACS Authorization. The authorization component, which can be used separately from authentication, supports multiple requests to provide authorization for specific functions and services. The attribute/value pairs can be used to:

- Permit or deny access to certain commands, addresses, services, or protocols.
- Establish a user privilege level.
- Configure input or output packet filters.
- Implement Access Control Lists (ACLs).
- Invoke callback actions.
- Assign specific network configuration details, including the network address.

As mentioned previously, the authorization information can be delivered separately or as part of an authentication request.

TACACS Accounting. The accounting features in TACACS use a format similar to the authorization elements. The accounting functions include Start, Stop, More, and Watchdog. The Watchdog feature is used to validate sessions that have been inactive for extended periods of time. In addition to the standard RADIUS accounting data, TACACS also supports event logging capable of recording changes in the system level and access rights or privilege. Additional information regarding the reason for the event and traffic totals are also recorded in the accounting component.

Like RADIUS, TACACS can accommodate redundant servers and is capable of detecting failed nodes. Unlike RADIUS, however, TACACS does not support authentication proxies, thereby limiting its capabilities in large-scale operations.

Like RADIUS, the TACACS source code is available, making implementations vendor specific. There are servers available for several operating systems, including Windows NT, Unix, and Netware. However, the client implementations are principally on Cisco hardware. Once again, decide what functionality you require before choosing an implementation. If your organization uses Cisco network equipment heavily, TACACS may be the solution. If you do not use Cisco at all, then RADIUS is your best option. In a mixed environment, it could be well to choose a server that supports both RADIUS and TACACS protocols.

TACACS Limitations. The lack of use of TACACS is likely its principal limitation. Although a versatile and robust protocol, there are few server implementations and few NAS devices that support its feature set. Additionally, TACACS scalability and performance can be a concern in some environments.

RADIUS uses a single UDP packet design, which improves speed and server performance. On very busy networks, the UDP packet may not arrive, thus delaying the authentication process. TACACS, on the other hand, uses a TCP connection and incurs the cost of establishing the TCP connection and transmitting the data. The overhead of making the short-lived TCP connection can affect the overall performance of the client and the server. However, the lack of NAS vendor adoption outside Cisco affects the overall usage and acceptance of TACACS.

DIAMETER. The DIAMETER protocol is capable of supporting any number of authentication, authorization, account systems, and connection types. The protocol consists of the Base protocol and a set of extensions. The DIAMETER Base protocol defines the message format, transport, error reporting, and security services. The extensions are modules used to perform specific types of authentication, authorization, and accounting transactions. For example, DIAMETER supports NAS, Mobile-IP, ROAMOPS, and EAP. The current IETF draft also contains definitions for secure proxy, strong security, and accounting. Additionally, the protocol design makes any number of extensions possible.

DIAMETER is built upon RADIUS, with design improvements to overcome the latter's deficiencies. Although the two protocols do not share a common data unit, RADIUS environments will be able to make the switch to DIAMETER without much inconvenience. DIAMETER operates in a peer-to-peer operation rather than client/server. This allows a server to initiate a request as well as handle transmission errors locally. Despite being UDP based like RADIUS, DIAMETER includes transport extensions to reduce retransmissions, improve failed node detection, and reduce congestion. These enhancements to DIAMETER improve server performance and reduce overall latency.

Other enhancements include:

- Roaming support
- Cross-domain and broker-based authentication
- Full support for the Extensible Authentication Protocol (EAP)
- Vendor-defined attribute/value pairs
- Enhanced security functionality with replay attack protection and confidentiality

DIAMETER provides support for the two RADIUS proxy models and two additional Broker models. In the hierarchical mode, a request from a user is forwarded to the user's Home DIAMETER server for authentication. Because the proxy transmission is handled independently of the client, there are improved failed node and packet retransmissions. Additionally, the proxy connection can be protected with additional security, including IPSec. Despite the changes in the DIAMETER proxy model, it is still not capable of supporting all roaming applications.

The DIAMETER proxy Broker provides support across multiple management domains and reduces the amount of configuration information shared among ISPs and service providers. The Broker can forward the authentication request to the Home server as a proxy, or it can provide the keys necessary to communicate directly with the Home server.

DIAMETER Authorization. The DIAMETER authorization transactions can be combined with authentication or requested separately. The specific extension being used provides the detail for the specific transaction. Authorization requests occur over an existing session. An authorization request without an authentication is not permitted.

Accounting for Everything. The improvements in DIAMETER over RADIUS and TACACS include logging and accounting as well as event monitoring, periodic reporting, real-time record transfer, and ROAMOPS Accounting Data Interchange Format. The instructions regarding accounting are provided to the client during the authorization requests. Additionally, DIAMETER can force the client to provide accounting records, which become useful for troubleshooting connections.

Accounting records are typically batch transferred, but DIAMETER also supports real-time transfers for credit card transactions and fraud detection. Further improvements in usage accounting are available due to periodic reporting, which is useful for monitoring nailed-up circuits.

Security and Standards. The security improvements in DIAMETER are embedded into the Base protocol. Because many applications require sensitive connection information, hop-by-hop security is inadequate. The Strong Proxy extension overcomes the problem by encrypting the data in S/MIME objects and encapsulating them in standard attribute/value pairs.

Securing Network Services and Network User Authentication. Sun Microsystems developed the Network Information Service (NIS), Network File Systems (NFS), and Remote Procedure Call (RPC) network protocols in the 1980s, allowing networked workstations to operate as if they were a single system. While providing real benefits for users and simplifying network operation, NFS and RPC had virtually no security features. The lack of security meant these features were available to any network user and allowed them to access data on any system. With the increase in Unix workstation usage, HP, DEC, and IBM licensed or adopted some of the software and implemented NIS, NFS, and RPC on their Unix implementations.

Sun corrected some of the security deficiencies in FNS and RPC over time, while competing complementary systems, notably Kerberos and Distributed Computing Environment (DCE), were being developed to solve similar problems. Consequently, today's system manager has many options to solve similar problems for remote procedure calls and configuration management. However, each option has issues with performance, ease of administration, and security.

Securing Network Services. Systems providing network services must have several capabilities:

- Elements to store information on a network server
- Mechanisms to update stored information
- Protocols to distribute information to other systems on the network

In a potentially hostile environment, security over these functions becomes a greater concern. Even within an organization, security should be a focus due to business partners, contractors, service providers, and many other non-employees connected to the organization's network.

Providing security for network functions requires the following improvements:

- *Server authentication,* allowing the clients to verify the server they are connecting to
- *Client authentication,* allowing server to validate the client systems
- *User authentication,* to validate the user is, in fact, authenticated and authorized to perform the requested function
- *Data integrity,* ensuring the data has not been modified in transmission and no unauthorized modification has occurred while in storage
- *Data confidentiality,* to protect information from unauthorized disclosure while in storage or on the network

The capabilities identified are independent of one another. Both client and server authentication can be provided on a system and be designed so clients implicitly trust that the server is a legitimate server. A system can require and enforce authentication for systems and users, but still send all information unencrypted. For the best possible security, a system and network should provide all requirements.

Remote Procedure Call (RPC). The Remote Procedure Call (RPC) mechanisms provide the ability to execute a function on another computer in a reasonably transparent fashion. RPC allows for distributed programs, meaning a computationally expensive algorithm can be executed on a high-speed system while other functions are executed on other systems and the graphical interface executed on the system where the user is located.

RPC Authentication. Client programs must be able to authenticate themselves to an RPC server before the server executes the requested function. When no authentication method is available, any client on the network can send a packet to the RPC server and access any function. No authentication means any piece of data accessible on the server could be accessed through a remote function. There are, in fact, several different RPC authentication mechanisms available, but not in all RPC versions and implementations:

- AUTH_NONE. No authentication. Anonymous access.
- AUTH_UNIX. The RPC clients send the Unix UID and GID to the server. The server implicitly trusts the user is who he claims to be.
- AUTH_DES. Authentication based on public key cryptography and DES, although not widely available except in Sun Microsystems implementations.
- AUTH_KERB. Authentication based on Kerberos, but depends on a Kerberos server being available in the network.
- AUTH_UNIX is called AUTH_SYS in at least one version of Sun Solaris.

Secure RPC. Sun Microsystems later developed Secure RPC to address the security weaknesses in the RPC implementations. Secure RPC employs a combination of symmetric and asymmetric cryptography. Sun's implementation uses the Diffie-Hellman key exchange mechanism and DES for encrypting information sent over the network. DES is also used to protect the user's secret key stored on a central network server.

Secure RPC addresses most of the problems associated with the AUTH_UNIX authentication method. Because both users and computers must be authenticated, it also resolved many spoofing problems to which these protocols are susceptible. When coupled with higher-level protocols like NFS, Secure RPC can create a very secure network.

Secure RPC Authentication. Secure RPC implementations use the Diffie-Hellman key exchange protocol where each Secure RPC entity has a public and private key, both of which are stored on the Secure RPC server. The public key is stored unencrypted; the secret key is stored encrypted with the entity's password. Both keys are typically hexadecimal numbers of several hundred digits. Secure RPC principals are users who have Secure RPC passwords and computers that are configured to use Secure RPC.

A Secure RPC entity proves his, her, or its identity by being able to decrypt the stored secret key and participating in the Diffie-Hellman key exchange. Each entity combines its secret key with the other's public key, allowing both to arrive independently at a common mutually known key. This key is then used to exchange a session key.

Proving Your Identity. Proving your identity with a public key system is accomplished by providing the correct secret key. Unfortunately, most people are not good at remembering very large numbers, and deriving a good pair of numbers for a public and private key pair from a Unix password is relatively difficult.

Sun solves these problems by distributing a database consisting of usernames, public keys, and encrypted secret keys using the Sun NIS or NIS+ network database system. The secret key is encrypted using the user's Unix password as the key and the DES encryption algorithm. If the user knows his Unix password, his workstation software can get his secret key and decrypt it.

When the user logs in to a computer running Secure RPC, the computer obtains a copy of the user's encrypted secret key. The computer then attempts to decrypt the secret key using the user's provided password. The secret key must now be stored for use in communication with the Secure RPC server. In Version 4.1 and above, the unencrypted key is kept in the memory of the key server process.

Next, the software on the workstation uses the user's secret key and the server's public key to generate a session key. (The server meanwhile has done the same thing using its secret key and the user's public key.) The workstation then generates a random 56-bit conversation key and sends it to the server, encrypted with the session key. The conversation key is used for the duration of the login and is stored in the key server process.

The file server knows that the user is who he claims to be because:

- The packet the user sent was encrypted using a conversation key.
- The only way the user could know the conversation key would be by generating it using the server's public key and the user's secret key.
- To know the user's secret key, the workstation had to look up the secret key using NIS and decrypt it.
- To decrypt the encrypted secret key, the user had to have known the key it was encrypted with — which is, in fact, the user's password.

Some of the security features of the above process include:

- The user's password is never transmitted over the network.
- The only time the secret key is transmitted over the network is when it is encrypted using the user's password as the key.
- There is no "secret" information on the file server that must be protected from attackers.

Using Secure RPC Services. After the workstation and the server have agreed upon a session key, Secure RPC authenticates all RPC requests. The session key has a defined lifetime and when it expires, the workstation and the server automatically renegotiate a new session key.

When the workstation communicates with a server, the user provides a netname that the server automatically translates into a local UID and GID. Ideally, this means the user's UID on the server does not have to be the same as the user's UID on the workstation. In practice, most organizations insist its users have a single UID throughout the organization, so the ability of Secure RPC to map UIDs from one computer to another is not terribly important.

Setting the Window. A timestamp is included in every Secure RPC packet to prevent an attacker from capturing the packets and replaying them at a later time. Consequently, Secure RPC is not highly susceptible to replay attacks.

For a timestamp-based system to operate properly, it is necessary for both the client and the server to agree on what time it is. Unfortunately, the real-time clocks on computers are sometimes difficult to synchronize. This can present a serious problem to the user of Secure RPC: if the clock on the workstation and the clock on the file server drift too far apart, the server will not accept any more requests from the client. The client and server will then have to re-authenticate each other. Consequently, the use of network time protocol servers on the network is extremely important.

Because re-authenticating takes time, Secure RPC allows the workstation system administrator to set a "window" the server uses to determine how far the client's clock can drift and remain acceptable. Obviously, using a large window reduces the danger of drift. Unfortunately, large windows similarly increase the chance of a playback attack. In the playback attack, the attacker sniffs a packet from the network, and then uses the authenticated credentials for his or her own purposes. Larger windows increase the possibility of a playback attack because any intercepted packet is valid for a longer period of time.

Limitations of Secure RPC. The Secure RPC implementation presents a performance penalty. Secure RPC penalizes every RPC transaction because the RPC authenticator must be decrypted using DES to verify each transmission. Fortunately, the performance penalty is small: on a Sun-4, only 1.5 milliseconds is required for the decryption. In comparison, the time to complete an average NFS transaction is about 20 milliseconds, making the performance penalty about 8%.

Secure RPC does not provide for data integrity or confidentiality. Secure RPC authenticates the user but does not protect the transmitted data with either encryption or digital signatures. It is the responsibility of programs using Secure RPC to encrypt using a suitable key and algorithm.

It may be possible to break the public key. Any piece of information encrypted with the Diffie-Hellman public key encryption system used in Secure RPC can be decrypted if an attacker can calculate the discrete logarithm of the public key. In 1989, Brian LaMacchia and Andrew Odlyzko at AT&T's Bell Laboratories in New Jersey discovered a significant performance improvement for the computation of discrete logarithms. Since then, numerous other advances in this field of mathematics have taken place. Secure RPC makes the public key and the encrypted secret key available to RPC client computers on the network. Thus, keys that are secure today may be broken tomorrow.

Similarly, it may be possible to break the secret key. The Secure RPC secret key is encrypted with a 56-bit DES key and is made publicly available on the network server. As computers become faster, the possibility of a brute-force attack against the user's encrypted secret key may become a reality.

In the final analysis, using Secure RPC appears to provide much better protection than many other approaches, especially with multi-user machines. Secure RPC is clearly better than plain RPC. Unfortunately, because Secure RPC requires the use of either NIS or NIS+, some multi-vendor sites have chosen not to use it. These sites should consider DCE, which provides a workable solution for a heterogeneous environment.

Network Information Service (NIS). Network Information Service (NIS) is a distributed database system allowing network users the capability to share password files, group files, host tables, and other files over the network. Although the files appear to be available on every computer, they are actually stored on only a single computer, called the NIS server. The other computers on the network, NIS clients, can use the databases stored on the master server as if they were stored locally. These databases are called NIS maps.

With NIS, a large network can be managed more easily because all of the account and configuration information needs to be stored on only a single machine.

Limitations with NIS. NIS has been used by hackers as the starting point for many successful penetrations into Unix networks. Because NIS controls user accounts, if you can convince an NIS server to broadcast that you have an account, then you can use that fictitious account to break into a client on the network. NIS can also make confidential information, such as encrypted password entries, widely available.

Additionally, NIS stores the encrypted password values in the passwd map, which can be downloaded by any user. Such a configuration makes it possible for an attacker to obtain the encrypted password hashes and launch brute-force password-cracking tools to guess passwords.

Spoofing NIS. There are design flaws in the code of the NIS implementations of several vendors that allow a user to reconfigure and spoof the NIS system. This spoofing can be done in two ways: by spoofing the underlying RPC system and by spoofing NIS.

NIS clients get information from a NIS server through RPC calls. A local daemon, ypbind, caches contact information for the appropriate NIS server daemon, ypserv. The ypserv daemon may be local or remote.

Under early SunOS versions of the NIS service (and current versions by some vendors), it was possible to instantiate a program acting like ypserv and responding to ypbind requests. The local ypbind daemon could then be instructed to use that program instead of the real ypserv daemon. As a result, an attacker could supply his or her own version of the password file to a login request, therefore allowing access to the system.

Unintended Disclosure of Site Information with NIS. Because NIS has relatively weak security, it can unintentionally disclose information about your site to attackers. In particular, NIS can disclose encrypted passwords, usernames, hostnames and their IP addresses, and mail aliases.

Unless you protect your NIS server with a firewall or with a modified portmap process, anyone on the outside of your system can obtain copies of the databases exported by your NIS server. To do this, all the outsider needs to do is guess the name of your NIS domain, bind to your NIS server using the ypset command, and request the databases. This can result in the disclosure of your distributed password file, and all the other information contained in your NIS databases.

The simplest method of restricting access to your NIS database is to protect your site with a firewall, or at least a smart router, and not allow RPC UDP packets to cross between your internal network and the outside world. Unfortunately, because RPC is based on the portmapper, the actual UDP port that is used is not fixed. In practice, the only safe strategy is to block all UDP packets except those that you specifically wish to let cross.

Another approach is to use freely available portmapper programs, which will allow you to specify a list of computers by hostname or IP address that should be allowed or denied access to specific RPC servers.

NIS+. NIS was designed for a small, friendly computing environment. As network managers began to build networks with thousands or tens of thousands of workstations, NIS started to show its weaknesses, including:

- NIS maps could only be updated by logging onto the server and editing files.
- NIS servers could only be updated in a single batch operation. Updates could take many minutes, or even hours, to complete.
- All information transmitted by NIS was transmitted without encryption, making it subject to eavesdropping.
- NIS updates themselves were authenticated with AUTH_UNIX RPC authentication, making them subject to spoofing.

To respond to these complaints, NIS+ was released and today it has become a more reliable system for secure network management and control, simply because it provides increased security.

Functions of NIS+. NIS+ creates network databases used to store information about computers and users within an organization. NIS+ calls these databases tables and they are functionally similar to NIS maps. Unlike NIS, NIS+ allows for incremental updates of the information stored on replicated database servers throughout the network.

Each NIS+ domain has one and only one NIS+ root domain server. The root domain server contains the master copy of the information stored in the NIS+ root domain. The information stored on this server can be replicated, allowing the network to remain usable even when the root server is down or unavailable. There may also be NIS+ servers for sub-domains.

Entities that communicate using NIS+ are called NIS+ principals. An NIS+ principal may be a host or an authenticated user. Each NIS+ principal has a public key and a secret key that are stored on an NIS+ server in the domain. (As this is Secure RPC, the secret key is stored encrypted.)

All communications between NIS+ servers and NIS+ principals use Secure RPC. This makes the communication resistant to both eavesdropping and spoofing attacks. NIS+ also oversees the creation and management of Secure RPC keys; by virtue of using NIS+, every member of the organization is enabled to use Secure RPC.

Using NIS+. For users, using an NIS+ domain can be very easy. When a user logs in to a workstation, the /bin/login command automatically acquires the user's NIS+ security credentials and attempts to decrypt them with the user's login password.

If the account password and the NIS+ credentials password are the same, the NIS+ keyserv process will cache the user's secret key and the user will have transparent access to all Secure RPC services. If the account password and the NIS+ credentials password are not the same, then the user will need to manually log in to the NIS+ domain using the keylogin command.

NIS+ Limitations. If properly configured, NIS+ can be a very secure system for network management and authentication. However, like all security systems, if the implementation of the configuration is not done properly or the management of NIS+ is not taken care of properly, then the overall security might be less than adequate.

NIS+ has an NIS compatibility mode that allows the NIS+ server to interoperate with NIS clients. If you run NIS+ in this mode, then any NIS server on your network (and possibly other networks as well) will have the ability to access any piece of information stored within your NIS+ server. Typically, NIS access is used by attackers to obtain a copy of your domain's encrypted password file, which is then used to probe for weaknesses. Consequently, if you have invested the time to configure NIS+, do not use compatibility mode.

To ensure the integrity of the objects in your NIS+ database, they should be periodically inspected and any old or invalid entries removed.

Your NIS+ server is only as secure as the computer on which it is running. If attackers can obtain root access on your NIS+ server, they can make any change they wish to your NIS+ domain, including creating new users, changing user passwords, and even changing your NIS+ server's master password.

NIS+ servers operate at one of three security levels, which are described below. Make sure that your server is operating at level 2, which is the default level. The NIS+ security levels are:

- 0 — NIS+ server runs with all security options turned off. Any NIS+ principal can make any change to any NIS+ object. This level is designed for testing and initially setting up the NIS+ namespace.
- 1 — NIS+ server runs with security turned on, but with DES authentication turned off. That is, the server will respond to any request in which LOCAL or DES authentication is specified, opening it up to a wide variety of attacks. Security level 1 is designed for testing and debugging.
- 2 — NIS+ server runs with full security authentication and access checking enabled. Only run NIS+ servers at security level 2.

Kerberos. Kerberos is a distributed security system providing a wide range of security services for distributed environments. Those services include authentication and message protection, as well as the ability to securely carry authorization information needed by applications, operating systems, and networks. Kerberos also provides the facilities necessary for delegation, where limited-trust intermediaries perform operations on behalf of a client.

Kerberos uses DES cryptography to protect sensitive information such as passwords on an open network. When the user logs in to a workstation running Kerberos, the user is issued a ticket from the Kerberos Server. The user's ticket can only be decrypted with the user's password; it contains information necessary to obtain additional tickets. From that point on, whenever the user wishes to access a network service, an appropriate ticket for the desired service must be presented. As all of the information in the Kerberos tickets is encrypted before it is sent over the network, the information is not susceptible to eavesdropping or misappropriation.

Kerberos Authentication. Kerberos authentication is based entirely on the knowledge of passwords stored on the Kerberos Server. Unlike Unix passwords, which are encrypted with a one-way algorithm, Kerberos passwords are stored on the server encrypted with a conventional encryption algorithm — in this case, DES — so they can be decrypted by the server when needed. A user proves his or her identity to the Kerberos Server by demonstrating knowledge of the proper key.

The fact that the Kerberos Server has access to the user's decrypted password is because Kerberos does not use public key cryptography. This is a serious disadvantage of the Kerberos system. It means that the Kerberos Server must be both physically secure and "computationally secure." The server must be physically secure to prevent an attacker from stealing the Kerberos Server and learning all of the users' passwords. The server must also be immune to login attacks: if an attacker could log onto the server and become root, that attacker could, once again, steal all of the passwords.

Kerberos was designed to be stateless. The Kerberos Server simply answers requests from users and issues tickets (when appropriate). This design makes it relatively simple to create replicated, secondary servers to handle authentication requests when the primary server is down or otherwise unavailable. Unfortunately, these secondary servers need complete copies of the entire Kerberos database, meaning they must also be physically and computationally secure.

Authentication, Data Integrity, and Secrecy. Kerberos is a general-purpose system for sharing secret keys between entities on the network. Normally, Kerberos is used solely for authentication. However, the ability to exchange keys can also be used to ensure data integrity and secrecy.

If eavesdropping is an ongoing concern, all information transmitted between the workstation and the service can be encrypted using a key exchanged between the two principals. Unfortunately, encryption carries a performance penalty.

Limitations of Kerberos. Every network service must be individually modified for use with Kerberos. Because of the Kerberos design, every program using the Kerberos system must be modified, or "Kerberized." The amount of work involved depends entirely on the application program. Of course, to Kerberize an application, you must have the application's source code.

Kerberos does not work well in a time-sharing environment. Kerberos is designed for an environment in which there is one user per workstation. Because of the difficulty in sharing data between different processes running on the same Unix computer, Kerberos keeps tickets in cache. If a user is sharing the computer with several other people, it is possible that the user's tickets can be stolen, that is, copied by an attacker. Stolen tickets can then be used to obtain resources.

Kerberos requires a secure Kerberos Server. By design, Kerberos requires a secure central server maintaining the master password database. To ensure security, a site should use the Kerberos Server for absolutely nothing beyond running the Kerberos Server program. The Kerberos Server must be kept in a physically secure area. In some environments, maintaining such a server is an administrative or financial burden.

Kerberos requires a continuously available Kerberos Server. If the Kerberos Server goes down, the Kerberos network is unusable.

The Kerberos Server stores all passwords encrypted with the server's master key, located on the same hard disk as the encrypted passwords. In the event the Kerberos Server is compromised, all user passwords must be changed.

Kerberos does not protect against modifications to system software (Trojan horses). Kerberos does not have the computer authenticate itself to the user. Consequently, there is no way for a user sitting at a computer to determine whether or not the computer has been compromised. This failing is easily exploited by a knowledgeable attacker.

Kerberos may result in a cascading loss of trust. If a server or a user password is broken or otherwise disclosed, it is possible for an eavesdropper to use the password to decrypt other tickets and spoof servers and users.

Other Network Authentication Systems. Besides those mentioned above, there are a variety of other systems for providing authentication and encryption services over an unprotected network.

DCE. DCE is the Distributed Computing Environment developed by the Open Software Foundation. DCE is an integrated computing environment providing many services, including user authentication, remote procedure call, distributed file sharing, and configuration management. DCE's authentication is very similar to Kerberos.

DCE's security is also based on a Security Server. The Security Server maintains an access control list for various operations and decides whether clients have the right to request operations. DCE clients communicate with DCE servers using DCE Authenticated RPC. To use Authenticated RPC, each DCE entity must have a secret key known only to itself and the Security Server.

SESAME. SESAME is the Secure European System for Applications in a Multi-vendor Environment. It is a single sign-on authentication system similar to Kerberos. SESAME incorporates many features of Kerberos, but adds heterogeneity, access control features, scalability of public key systems, improved manageability, and an audit system.

The primary difference between SESAME and Kerberos is SESAME's use of public key and single key cryptography. Using both public and shared secret key cryptography allows SESAME to overcome some of the design deficiencies in the Kerberos system.

Firewalls and Perimeter Security

The term "firewall" was first officially used in the early 1990s, although firewall-like devices have been used since the late 1980s. It was during the initial rush of commercial connectivity to the Internet when firewall development took some gigantic leaps forward. Since the early firewall days, many changes and improvements have been developed and new firewall architecture and models have evolved.

There are several major types of firewall implementation, each with pros and cons. However, today's firewalls usually contain all four elements.

Packet Filters. Packet filter firewalls operate at layer 3 (network layer) of the OSI Reference Model. Decisions on whether to allow or deny the packet are made by examining the packet header for the following information:

- Source address
- Destination address
- Source port (UDP, TCP, or ICMP)
- Destination port (UDP, TCP, or ICMP)
- Acknowledgment bit (TCP)

Packet filtering is quite fast due to the relatively simple process of reading the packet header and comparing it against a set of rules. However, packet filters are prone to spoofing of source and destination addresses and ports. The packet filter cannot make any decisions regarding the connection above the network layer. The inability to work above the network layer means a packet filter cannot offer additional protection to upper layer protocols.

Packet filtering has been implemented in many devices, including network switches, routers, and within operating systems including Unix and Windows NT/2000. Packet filtering is widely used and an essential part of the network infrastructure.

Not to be confused with Stateful Inspection, packet filters are stateless, meaning that they store no information about the state of the session, or the requests and response. Packet filter systems have typically been difficult to administer and have problems logging information.

Application Proxy Servers. Application proxy firewalls operate at layer 7 (application layer) of the OSI Reference Model. Fitting the definition of the term "proxy," the application proxy firewall acts as a relay between the source and destination systems. The proxy accepts the connection and data from the sender, and then forwards it on to the receiver. Unlike other models, there is no direct routing or connectivity between the sender and receiver, thus providing a protective wall between the devices.

Application proxies support authentication very well and are often combined with caching services to reduce network congestion. Because the application proxy makes the decision about the packet at layer 7, the packet must travel up the stack and be examined by the proxy. Consequently, the proxy must be fully aware and understand the intricacies of the specific protocol. This means there must be a specific proxy for each type of traffic that will be examined. For example, a Telnet proxy cannot be used for FTP traffic.

While many systems provide a generic proxy for handling non-supported services, this somewhat defeats the purpose of the application proxy. Using the generic proxy is like putting big locks on your front door, and then leaving the window unlocked. Additionally, the application proxy adds a performance cost to the network connection, as two connections are required. The first connection is between the originator and the proxy. Once allowed, the second connection is between the proxy and the destination. It takes time to authenticate and establish the connections. Consequently, some protocols, such as HTTP, are not well suited for application proxies.

Circuit-Level Gateway. Circuit-level gateways operate at layer 5 (session layer) of the OSI Reference Model. The gateway establishes connections between trusted hosts and clients. Similar to the proxy, there is no direct connection between the systems. Additionally, the application must support the relay mechanism. One example of compatible relay mechanisms is SOCKS-compliant applications.

SOCKS, defined in RFC 1928, is a protocol for handling TCP traffic through a proxy server. It can be used with virtually any TCP application, including Web browsers and FTP clients. SOCKS includes two components: the SOCKS server and the SOCKS client. The SOCKS server is implemented at the application layer, while the SOCKS client is implemented between the application and transport layers. The basic purpose of the protocol is to enable hosts on one side of a SOCKS server to gain access to hosts on the other side of a SOCKS server, without requiring direct IP-reachability. It provides a simple firewall because it checks incoming and outgoing packets and hides the IP addresses of client applications.

Stateful Inspection. The stateful inspection firewall is capable of working at all seven layers of the OSI Reference Model as shown in Exhibit 18, making this a very versatile firewall technology.

Despite its multi-layer ability, most stateful inspection firewalls are operated at layers 3 and 4. And despite the typical operation model, the application and communications state are derived from all seven layers and used to build a state table. The state table is consulted and used to make decisions to allow or reject a given packet. If a response packet is received at the firewall, there must be an entry in the state table or the packet is rejected.

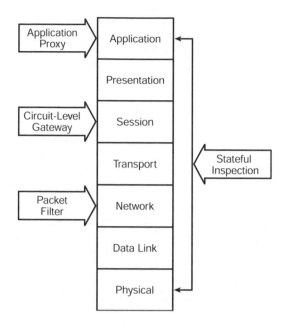

Exhibit 18. Firewall Model's Place in the OSI Model
(From Thomas DeFelice, "Designing and Implementing Firewalls," in *Data Communications Management,* 27(3), 3, June 2002. © CRC Press LLC.)

It is safe to consider the stateful inspection firewall as the *de facto* standard because most modern firewalls are based on this model. Reliance upon this model comes from its performance and reduced vulnerability to spoofing.

Firewall Platforms. There are a variety of ways to deploy a firewall, including host-based gateways, appliances, and personal or desktop firewalls.

Host-Based Gateway. Most commonly used, the host-based gateway uses an operating system platform such as Unix, Linux, and Windows NT to provide the underlying operating resources. Use of a traditional operating system to provide the firewall host requires the operating system to undergo a hardening process to remove security problems affecting the firewall operation.

Performing the hardening activity requires in-depth knowledge of the operating system in question and a thorough understanding of the interaction of the firewall software and the operating system components. The hardening process can lengthen the time to deploy the firewall and increase maintenance due to patch evaluation and application.

However, these general-purpose firewalls offer additional capabilities because they can provide more services than just a firewall. More importantly, for the smaller organization, the host-based solution tends to have a lower start-up cost than other implementations.

Appliance. Firewall appliances use specialized hardware, often running some form of proprietary operating system. Because these are not general-purpose computer systems, they are not exploited by an attacker as easily because the traditional operating system vulnerabilities do not apply. For the same reason, the general operating system hardening associated with the host-based firewall is not applicable.

Because these devices are designed and built to be only firewalls, their additional capabilities and functionality are limited. However, it also means the firewall appliance tends to have better throughput and performance than host-based firewalls. Consequently, many firewall vendors are moving to the firewall appliance exclusively, or as an additional product offering to the traditional host-based firewall.

Desktop Firewalls. Desktop firewalls operate on the specific host where the connection is received. While most firewalls provide a gateway service between two networks, the desktop firewall resides on the user's workstation and provides firewall services between the host and the network. Some desktop firewalls also provide application-level protection between the various applications on the host itself.

The services and features offered in the available desktop firewalls vary greatly, from providing simple network access controls, to buffer overflow and complex application-layer protections. Desktop firewalls can act in a stand-alone configuration and in an agent configuration, where the policy is centrally managed. The available modes of operation are implementation dependent.

Deploying Network Topologies. Network design is made more complex with the reduction in available address space. As the pool of available registered addresses is used up, more and more companies are turning to private, non-routable address usage as defined in RFC 1918. As more and more companies may be using the same pool of network addresses, Network Address Translation (NAT) must occur to avoid collisions. Most current router and firewall services provide NAT functionality.

NAT supports both static and dynamic modes. When using static mode, a specific host is given a public and private address, forming a one-to-one relationship. When the NAT device receives a packet destined for the public address, it is converted to the private address and forwarded to the device. Dynamic NAT is a many-to-one relationship, where all private IP addresses are converted to a single public address. The NAT device keeps track of the connections and sends response packets to the correct device on the private network.

However, not all protocols handle NAT in a particularly good fashion, especially IPSec, which is used in both VPN sessions and secure IP. Consequently, implementing NAT requires some consideration of application implementation and support.

There are several security models available that have different benefits to companies that provide public Internet access or connectivity to an external partner's extranet. There can be many different variations of these models, depending on specific implementation considerations. Consequently, the diversity in their design and implementation reflects the importance of proper placement of specific firewall functions.

Single-Tier Configuration. The single-tier configuration uses a firewall with a public and private network interface. Through this configuration, support can be provided to accept inbound connections and direct them to other public systems, thereby protecting private systems. Exhibit 19 shows the configuration discussed below.

This model is fairly simple to implement, and has little or no complexity associated with it for routing. However, publicly accessible systems are often configured with open access to the internal network. Consequently, compromising any of the public systems means an attacker could gain unlimited access to the enterprise network and all associated data.

Two-Tier Configuration. An alternate and more secure solution uses a single firewall with three or more interfaces, or several two-interface firewalls. The configuration provides for public, private, and demilitarized (DMZ) segments. The DMZ is separate from both the public and private networks and can use either public or private addressing. If private addressing is used on the DMZ, all the applications must support the use of NAT at the firewall.

Using this model provides a higher degree of security and control over the back-end systems hosted on the private network. However, the overall configuration can be more difficult to create and maintain due to routing and rule complexities.

Three-Tier Configuration. A third and even more secure design uses at least two firewalls, with security controls on each firewall in the network. The initial firewall connects the public network and the DMZ, where any publicly accessible systems are connected. A second firewall connects the DMZ to a middle network, where other supporting systems are placed outside the corporate network. The firewall between the DMZ and the middle tier is configured to allow only traffic for the middle-tier servers and any traffic for internally originated sessions to be passed through.

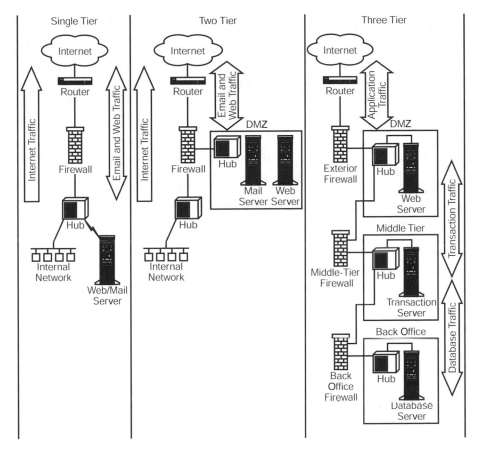

Exhibit 19. Firewall Deployment Models
(From Thomas DeFelice, "Designing and Implementing Firewalls," in *Data Communications Management,* 27(3), 8, June 2002. © CRC Press LLC.)

A third firewall is established to provide connectivity from the middle-tier systems to the corporate office and allows only connections from the middle-tier systems and any other valid traffic through to the enterprise private network. Consequently, information that must be available to customers can be stored or processed outside the enterprise network, while highly sensitive information is maintained in the private network.

This model provides a higher degree of security by providing another layer between the public and private networks. Now an attacker must compromise the public system and the middle-tier system to gain access to the corporate network. This is, however, the most expensive of the three models due to the complexity of the hardware involved. Routing configurations and security policies on multiple devices must be maintained and are more difficult to manage than the previous configurations.

High Availability and Load Balancing. As use of the Internet as a business tool has increased, so too have the requirements for performance, availability, and confidentiality. As a result, many organizations have implemented load-balancing systems to maximize system availability and increase overall capacity to meet those performance requirements. Just as improvements in redundancy at the system and network infrastructure have occurred, so too are security controls being adjusted to meet the same overall requirements.

Differences between High Availability and Load Balancing. Although the terms "high availability" and "load balancing" are often used in a synonymous context, they are distinctly different. High availability systems mean that the connection or service is maintained through a single or multiple failure. High availability systems maintain policy implementation and enforcement during the failure and ensure no reduction in performance, availability, or security controls.

Using firewalls to implement a high availability model requires more than one device, with an automatic switchover to the alternate device should one system fail. For this to be effective, both firewalls must be fully aware of the state information on both devices and be able to assume control over the connections from both devices. One significant drawback of high availability environments is the reliance upon a "hot" spare — an operational device with full knowledge of the environment, but is not used until needed.

High availability solutions maintain a heartbeat, indicating the systems are operating in state synchronization. Communications between the devices are often chatty, and usually occur on a dedicated link to prevent interference with the actual data traffic. Consequently, a firewall using two interfaces will require a third for the high availability operation.

Load balancing is different in operation and design, as the connections are aggregated across multiple devices to provide high performance and fault tolerance. Load balancers do not necessarily manage state information, which is vendor and implementation dependent. If state information is not maintained by the load balancing device, the connection must be reestablished, causing user frustration.

Load balancing systems focus on dividing the user load across the connected systems to meet the performance requirements and take advantage of lesser utilized systems to maximize performance. Consequently, in architectures where high performance is required, load balancing is a solution. Some load balancing implementations make such good use of the hardware that it is possible to reduce the overall number of systems needed to support and operate an application.

Deployment Strategies. Proper planning and requirements gathering is required prior to making technology decisions and product/vendor selections.

Policy Support. When selecting a technology and implementation, a thorough understanding of the organization's security policy is required. There should be no reason why an organization cannot define a security policy; however, if technology decisions must be made without one, the following should be considered:

- Is there an organization that is tasked with managing the firewalls?
- Is there a network security organization?
- What change control process will be used for network security devices (prior testing, code review, contingency planning, formal reviews, change control software)?
- Is there a basic acceptable use policy for email, Internet access, etc.?
- What auditing, logging, and reporting requirements does the organization have or desire?
- Is there a data classification model to assist in security control placement and protection levels?

Use of these concepts when a security policy is not available can assist in selecting the appropriate technology and implementation.

Application Requirements. Understanding the applications to control, especially those accessible outside the enterprise network, is critical to technology selection and implementation. Construction of a matrix of applications and requirements identifies those intolerant to specific configurations such as Network Address Translation or proxies. Consequently, specific implementations may be required to make certain applications available to non-enterprise network users.

Additionally, applications available over the Internet may require additional controls, including VPN access or SSL services to maintain data confidentiality.

Determining Feature Requirements. Unfortunately for the security professional, there are many different firewalls, each with specific features to distinguish itself from other implementations. Consequently, product selection is driven by the features required and the network architecture in which the devices will operate. Specific issues affecting the firewall or security control devices include:

- How many network interfaces do we need today, and how many will the device support for future expansion?
- What is the total network capacity and throughput of the device?
- How is the device managed, and how easy is it to manage?

- What are the requirements to train existing management staff?
- How easy is it to maintain and upgrade?
- What reporting capabilities are required? Is a third-party reporting tool required?
- What are the high availability and load balancing requirements?
- Do we have server redundancy concerns?
- What are the bandwidth requirements for the networks connecting to the device?
- Will the device also serve as a VPN endpoint?
- Will we require additional hardware to provide encryption services?
- What is the vendor support availability? What is the vendor's history and likelihood of continued operation?
- What is the initial cost of ownership? Sometimes, the cheapest solution is not the best solution.

Content Filtering and Inspection

The Internet provides many benefits to the user and to the corporation, including information sharing, email, knowledge retrieval, support, and business opportunities. However, the Internet is also rife with unscrupulous organizations promoting pornography, pyramid schemes, spam, and other corporately unwanted or undesirable content. Content filtering products implement controls to prevent employee access to unwanted and undesirable materials. Typically, content filtering must be considered in both the inbound and outbound directions.

Inbound content filtering is focused at SPAM and unsolicited commercial email (UCE). Email and SPAM content filters can remove attachments, filter on keywords, known spam mailers, and other controls to prevent this unwanted material from entering your organization. Content inspection can remove viruses while leaving the attachment intact, or can completely remove the attachment as with executable files, preventing unwary employees from creating an exposure in your network.

Outbound content filtering can be done with email to prevent unwanted messages from being sent from your network, but is typically more associated with content filtering of Web sites. Web content filtering can include blocking specific domain names but is more often driven by keyword matches in the HTML.

Content filtering technology is available in commercial and open source forms, each with their own advantages. However, the technology changes rapidly, offering improvements on a frequent basis. While the technology can be effective, it is not perfect and should not be used as the sole method of controlling employee behavior. Controlling behavior is best done through policy and awareness, with the technology providing a method of determining when users are not behaving as they should.

Intrusion Detection

Unlike the past, when the security professional could just sit around and wait for an event, real proactive response is the important mitigation factor today. Waiting for the event to occur and then doing something is the fast track to disaster. Many network security devices include some basic form of intrusion detection capability. However, the flimsy capability in the network security device is no replacement for a full-blown intrusion detection system.

By implementing an intrusion detection system (IDS) and integrating it with other devices in your network, such as firewalls, it is possible to limit the amount of damage an attacker can cause. Most full-scale intrusion detection systems and firewalls support some level of integration, allowing the IDS to inform the firewall of suspicious activity and to make rule changes in the firewall. From time to time this automatic rule insertion can block legitimate traffic, but should still be considered in the overall network security architecture.

Remote Access Security

Establishing and controlling remote access to the corporate network is a daunting challenge in today's environment. The sheer number of methods for a remote user to access the network is staggering, whether it be through SSL or IPSec VPNs, partner networks, cable and DSL services, the Internet, ISDN, or plain old modems. The number of users who work in hotel rooms and their homes has increased many times over, pushing the boundary of the corporate network to their desktops. People are as effective doing their jobs at home on Saturday night in their family rooms as they are when sitting in their offices. The "mobile" workforce has changed the corporation and the network.

Today's users expect the speed and ease of use brought through Internet connectivity, regardless of their location. They want both wired and wireless access, with high availability and high performance. Consequently, more demands are placed on network and security managers to provide efficient, reliable, and cost-effective access to the corporate network without compromising the company's intellectual property and information.

Users within a private network include not only the organization's employees, but also customers, business partners, and telecommuters. The wide array of users makes remote access design tougher. LAN users typically have unrestricted access to all information in the LAN. On some occasions, more granular access control is implemented, restricting access to systems or applications, depending on the user's functional requirements. Isolating network resources through mechanisms including

627

router filters or firewalls imposes the access restrictions. For example, it is possible to allow a user access to a system or application when connected to the LAN, but otherwise deny access.

Consequently, the remote access implementation must be geared to the organizational security requirements to minimize the risks of allowing remote access. Without a remote access security policy, it is possible for connectivity to be misconfigured, allowing the compromise of data.

Security Goals for Remote Access. The purpose of remote access is to provide legitimate users access to system resources and applications that are not connected to their primary location or the corporate LAN. Protection of the corporate resources is critical, with data confidentiality, integrity, and availability forming the fundamental basis of this protection. A secure remote access system provides the following features:

- Reliable user and system authentication
- Granular access control for systems, files, users, and other network resources
- Protection of confidential data
- System utilization logging and auditing
- Access logging, including successful and unsuccessful authentication
- Transparent access to resources
- Connectivity to the network regardless of location
- Connectivity for all remote users when required
- Minimal network connectivity and support costs

Reliable Authentication of Remote Users/Hosts. The primary difference in authenticating remote users is their lack of physical presence at the organization's offices. Even small organizations perform periodic authentication checks through visual recognition and knowing who is allowed to be where in the office. When organizations require high security controls, additional technological controls are implemented, such as badge access, photographic ID, security guards, and other tools.

However, when the user is not present, it is much more difficult to verify his identification, thus making authentication even more important. The network user's identity is used as the basis for access to the requested resources. Regardless of who the user is, if he has authorization to access the network, reliable authentication is the only method to grant access. If an attacker finds a way to provide an identity that seems authentic, the user is allowed access.

Remote access systems should be capable of supporting multiple authentication methods, including passwords, secure tokens, and digital certificates.

Granular Access Control. Access control systems must be able to provide granular control — down to the application on a system if necessary. Working with the assumption that a remote access user can access only the components he has been authorized for, the security manager must approve the configured access.

The remote access authentication system must be flexible enough to support multiple authentication methods and scalable enough to provide for growth in users, systems, and access points. There must also be a strong interface for administration and management of the approved users, systems, etc. A poor interface makes it more difficult to add, modify, or delete new users and systems. The administration system must also have very granular authorization features to control access, authorizations, and trust relationships.

There are numerous methods for controlling access and authorization for remote access systems. They can be access control lists, static routes, secure token cards, authentication and authorization systems such as RADIUS, and host or application filters. Many systems support user groups, machine and network policies, to make it easier to group systems or users together for authorization purposes, or to apply a common set of restrictions. Indeed, the access control rules are most commonly implemented on technology, including firewalls, routers, remote access servers, and AAA servers.

The remote access systems must be complementary to the existing security infrastructure and access control. For example, if Windows NT domain controllers are used to provide authentication, the remote access system must interact with the domain controller. Implementing and using these interactions can benefit the administrators and simplify user experience.

Protection of Confidential Data. Unless your organization owns the physical wire itself, remote access services depend upon a service provider to provide connectivity from the user to the organization. This is often done through the Internet, but can also include other data network services, including Frame Relay and ISDN. Additionally, users still use modem dial-up services on a regular basis. Regardless of the connection method, due care and consideration must be utilized to protect the data while in transit.

It is generally accepted that the public switched telephone network (PSTN) is a public network and is supposed to be secured by the carrier providing the local service. However, data network connectivity is often delivered over common or shared network connections, including Frame Relay and the Internet. Shared data network services can easily be used to sniff and acquire data. Sniffers are used by telecommunications providers to troubleshoot and analyze network connections over the data networks they provide. The sniffer, as discussed earlier, can allow for unauthorized retrieval of information.

The principal countermeasure over data circuits is encryption of the data by a network device prior to transmission over a public network, or by an application prior to even being placed on the network.

Logging and Auditing of System Utilization. Logging and auditing are essential to record system events, authorized actions, unauthorized actions, and errors. Sooner or later they are invaluable to finding out what happened, what went wrong, and how to fix it. When analyzing the cause of the problem, it often becomes evident that the problem is deliberately caused. The security professional can then turn to the application or system audit logs to determine what did what and when.

However, if the system does not record, or cannot tell who is performing the action, then nothing can be done to correct the problem. Many remote access servers provide only rudimentary logging. However, in many cases, the problem is at the application level. Many applications and systems perform no logging at all. In some cases, the logging is there in the application but never enabled, or is deliberately turned off due to "performance or disk space" issues. Consequently, logging at the remote access server is an essential element of the network.

Transparent Reproduction of the Workplace Environment. A critical goal of the remote access service is allowing remote users the same levels of access, functionality, connectivity, and overall experience as they would have at their office desk. If the internal network is generally accessible to every employee, the same expectation applies when using the remote access service. Similarly, if there are access restraints within the internal network, the remote access service must ensure that those restrictions are enforced.

Transparent connectivity is a challenge in today's multi-function, multi-system environment. All functionality must be available to the users with no additional configuration or configuration changes because they are accessing the network remotely. Any configuration changes required to access the network and use the resources and services, beyond possibly changing the phone number to dial, means that the goal of transparency has not been reached.

Connectivity to Remote Users and Locations. Connectivity for remote users means having enough dial-up access points or Internet VPN capacity to meet the demand from the user community. As changes to the overall network architecture are made, similar changes to the remote access infrastructure may be needed to take maximum advantage of the network changes.

As support for different types of connectivity are offered — wireless LAN, wireless/cellular, VPN, Internet, traditional dial-up — more users can access the organization's systems. Multiple connectivity options means that users can access the organization's network from wherever they are: hotels, homes, customers, partners, airports, etc.

Minimize Costs. When remote access solutions are deployed effectively, they can minimize the need for additional hardware, network components, people, and support costs. To achieve this cost savings, however, appropriate budgets, equipment acquisition, and training must have occurred. Additionally, the cost savings depend on each organization and its sensitivity to various factors, including the loss of resources, corporate expertise in network design, security design, and possibly regulatory issues.

In most remote access designs, the highest costs are associated with telephone capacity, private network connections, and the Internet. The individual organization must determine what access type is most prevalent and pay the associated costs to provide that access type. Remember that there are initial start-up charges for software licenses, hardware, and installation, although these are rarely differentiators from one remote access solution to another.

To fairly estimate costs and future growth, the following areas should be considered:

- One-time hardware and software costs
- Initial setup fees if buying services from a provider
- Installation charges for equipment and circuits
- Maintenance and upgrade costs
- Network and telephone circuits
- Installation and administration personnel

Most organizations are turning to Internet VPNs as their primary remote access source due to the low cost of connectivity when compared to dial-up services and ISDN. Most consumer cable or DSL Internet access methods are paid on a flat-rate basis. As long as this charging philosophy remains in place, Internet VPNs will be the preferred solution.

From the organization's Internet access strategy perspective, it may be cost-effective to use Internet VPN connections from small and branch offices to the corporate network. This eliminates expensive leased lines, which are often not effectively utilized. However, if the organization does not have trained staff to make the transition and support the new environment, the cost savings from implementing the VPN environment are reduced dramatically.

Well-designed remote access implementations have scalability, cost, and supportability as part of the design requirements. The solution must be scalable because remote access requirements will increase over time. This means that network capacity from the Internet or service provider must be capable of growth, and a plan to implement the changes must be ready. Additional considerations are the remote access servers, firewalls, and authentication systems, all of which must also meet the increased demand.

Well-trained people are critical to the success of the remote access infrastructure. These people must be trained to understand security controls for their environment and how those controls can contribute to effectively reducing risk, or how they can be misused to illegally obtain the organization's information.

If the remote access infrastructure is providing mission-critical access, then backup and redundant methods of remote access connectivity must be provided. Backup methods will vary from location to location, and each site requiring access to the mission-critical applications must have backup connectivity.

Remote Access Mechanisms. There are three principle technologies used in remote access connectivity. These are:

- Access via analog modems using the public switched telephone network
- Access via dedicated network connections, either persistent or on-demand
- Access via public networks, such as the Internet

Telephones. The modem has been the ubiquitous symbol of remote access computing for decades. The user connects the computer to a modem, and then to the local telephone service using a standard telephone outlet. Using remote access software on the computer, the user dials a phone number through the modem, and the call is routed through the public switched telephone network, where a modem on the dialed number receives the call.

The network access server on the receiving end provides authentication, authorization, access control, and accounting functions to determine if the user is permitted access to the network. While access speeds are limited, there is a high degree of familiarity with this access method and the cost of implementation is usually quite low.

Modems are good remote access devices in any place where there is an abundance of telephone lines. However, location often limits availability due to outdated equipment or lack of support from the public carrier. Additionally, business will often not allow modem use by a vendor while on site, if nothing else but to safeguard the organization's information.

Even worse, phone lines and phone systems can be part of the problem. Excessive noise on a line can interfere with call setup, authentication with the network access server, or even result in dropped calls. Additionally, telephone systems (PBXs) operate differently. Some systems require that a key be pressed to access lines, while others use digital phone sets, making analog modem use impossible.

Once the connection is established, use of some applications is difficult using the lower speeds associated with modems. Highly graphical or multimedia-oriented services do not operate well at slower speeds. Finally, modem technology changes frequently, forcing upgrades and changes to equipment. The network access server is also a good attack target because configuration errors are likely and it provides a single point of access into the network.

Dedicated Network Connections. Dedicated network connections are used to provide connectivity between corporate offices, suppliers, customers, and other business partners as agreements and services require. The dedicated circuit is a point-to-point circuit provided by the telecommunications carrier. These circuits are generally considered the safest for carrying enterprise data because the only data on the circuit belongs to the organization. Just as their name implies, dedicated circuits provide physical isolation from other users because the circuit is dedicated to the subscriber.

Attacks against dedicated circuits are launched at the telecommunications provider. While this can offer some protection, attacks against the telephone companies are older than some of the attackers. This is primarily because the infrastructure provided by one carrier is the same as another, due primarily to the low number of vendors providing the equipment and the commonalities in service design, provisioning, and device configurations.

The alternative to a dedicated circuit is the use of a shared facility such as Frame Relay or Asynchronous Transport Mode (ATM). Both of these services are provided by the telecommunications carrier and are considered shared because the network contains data from multiple organizations. As explained earlier in this chapter, a virtual connection is established from one entity to another based on service availability and bandwidth.

However, dedicated and shared subscription services can be very expensive. They are typically priced based upon speed, availability, and if the service is shared. The more speed, availability, and dedicated access, the higher the cost. However, dedicated access offers a great deal of flexibility to the organization. Bear in mind, however, that the location of the organization or the other office determines what dedicated or shared services are actually available from the carrier.

Internet-Based Remote Access. Using the Internet as the remote access vehicle is the most cost-effective solution if the organization can take advantage of it. The Internet allows for shared services and relatively low-cost, easy-to-use capabilities. However, there are important reliability and security issues to address.

Implementing Internet-based remote access is less expensive than internally managed modem pools and dedicated circuits. Cost savings are driven by lower access costs, and support and equipment maintenance is less expensive.

Of paramount importance is securing the Internet access to prevent unauthorized disclosure of the organization's data. Because most TCP/IP protocols carry data in cleartext, they are vulnerable to eavesdropping attacks. When an insecure protocol is used over an insecure network, the risk of disclosure is heightened. Additionally, Internet-based systems are more likely to suffer attacks and affect service availability.

Additionally, the Internet as a whole suffers from reliability and quality-of-service issues. Determining the cause of a problem when it is Internet related can be a source of frustration because most of the equipment will be outside the control of the in-house support teams. Because the Internet is a collection of managed networks, there is no centralized authority for resolving service and performance issues. Consequently, loss of connections, lost packets, and higher latency can affect overall operations of the Internet-based remote access service.

Selecting a Remote Access System. When selecting a remote access system, the size and configuration of the organization has an impact on service selection. For example, a smaller organization may see limited benefits from using a VPN over traditional access methods. Larger, more complex organizations with significant security controls will likely see a greater benefit from VPNs due to the speed at which they can be deployed to business partners, customers, and branch offices. Other benefits that VPNs can provide include:

- Enabling the traveling employee to access the corporate network through the Internet or other means, including local Internet service providers
- Allowing employees to work at home, customer sites, business partners, hotels, and other untrusted locations
- Allowing an organization to provide customer support using the Internet, while minimizing risks to the client's computer networks
- Facilitating highly controlled access to the corporate network for consultants, support technicians, and other users

Most VPNs interoperate with firewalls and other security devices, creating a complex security environment. The VPN technologies can support multiple authentication systems, thereby simplifying remote access user configuration and management.

Despite the benefits described and seen from VPNs, they are not appropriate in all situations. Here are some situations where a VPN may not be appropriate:

- The remote user or entity does not have adequate Internet connectivity. If there is limited or no Internet access, a VPN is not an option.
- The application uses non-IP technology such as SNA or IPX. These solutions are much more complex, although possible. The VPN client, server, or gateway must be capable of supporting or translating the non-IP packets for routing over the VPN.
- The use of the Internet is forbidden by security policy or industry regulation. For example, healthcare providers cannot use the Internet to transmit patient data. There are some cases where a cryptographic VPN must be used even within the private network.

Remote Access Policy. While all the discussion of the various remote access technologies is important, no decisions on the technologies and methodologies should be made until there is a formal security policy covering remote access connectivity. The remote access policy is a subset of the overall organizational security policy. From the remote access policy, it becomes possible to make decisions on the specific requirements that the remote access solution must meet. With the requirements established, technology selection and design decisions are made to get to an actual implementation.

The remote access policy should clearly define the employees and other personnel permitted to use the remote access services. Some organizations may choose to allow every trusted user access; however, it may be advisable to require users to justify their access requirements.

Additionally, end-user awareness and education regarding the issues of remote access, including connectivity to the corporate network from their homes, hotels, and customer locations, is necessary. Through this awareness program, the users can better understand the specific risks of unauthorized information disclosure when using remote access services.

Virtual Private Networks (VPNs)

Wide area networking is commonly achieved through Frame Relay, ATM, or other leased line services. Typically, these capabilities are used to build private networks for organizations to transfer their private data. While these network facilities are capable of providing a high degree of privacy, they are typically expensive for the organization to acquire and manage. Consequently, only reasonably large organizations build networks in this manner.

With the availability of high-speed Internet access, more and more individuals and business are turning to the Internet for their communications needs. Businesses use it as an alternative to the higher-priced services. These changes have brought the Internet into direct competition with the traditional network solution as the Internet spans the globe and provides connectivity over copper wire, fiber-optic, and wireless links. All Internet connectivity is accomplished using the IP suite and any device supporting IP can connect to any other device.

The Internet as a publicly shared network has several disadvantages. First, the shared nature and openness of the protocols make eavesdropping, packet manipulation, and spoofing a major security concern. Using a virtual private network (VPN) addresses these concerns by implementing encryption, data integrity, and authentication. Second, there is no quality of service on the Internet, meaning that packets arrive when they arrive, if they arrive at all. No protocol has specific service privileges and cannot request that a device give a protocol preferred treatment over other traffic.

The VPN standards define methods of encapsulating the data at the source, tunneling through the protocols, and un-encapsulation at the destination. Encryption, error checking, and authentication are also defined in the standards. Layer 2 protocols are highly flexible, offering protocol support for typically non-routable protocols, including NetBEUI and IPX/SPX. The traditional layer 3 VPN is IP-based and can be transparently implemented on any IP-based network without interfering with existing network traffic.

Internet connections are vulnerable to traffic congestion, node or link failures, and unresponsive hosts. Several programs are under way to review Quality of Service (QoS), addressing how traffic is handled on the Internet. Protocols such as the Resource Reservation Setup Protocol (RSVP) and Multi-Protocol Label Switching (MPLS) use the Type-of-Service flag to assist in giving specific protocols preferred treatment.

However, the changes in implementing QoS are still not widely deployed in the Internet and may not be for some time to come. While the IP VPN does not address QoS issues, it could run transparently on a QoS-enabled solution.

The international trade association for VPN manufacturers, the VPN Consortium, supports three major standards:

- Point-to-Point Tunneling Protocol (PPTP)
- IPSec
- Layer 2 Tunneling Protocol (L2TP) over IPSec

At the current time, IPSec is expected to become the dominant VPN standard because it utilizes IP and is supported in the IPv6 addressing standard. Changes to L2TP now allow support over IPSec, and it has the advantage that it is not restricted to VPN sessions between endpoints. PPTP is a Microsoft protocol and widely supported by VPN manufacturers.

PPTP. PPTP encapsulates datagrams into an IP packet, allowing PPTP to route many network protocols across an IP network. PPTP is based on Microsoft's Remote Access Services (RAS), first included in Windows NT. PPTP is a layer 2 protocol, also containing data-link information. PPP (Point-to-Point Protocol) is often used over PPTP.

With PPTP, authentication is done using PPP with MS-CHAP, CHAP, PAP, EAP, or the Shiva Passwords Authentication Protocol. The authentication is validated by a dial-up network user account on the RAS server, or through a Microsoft domain controller. With PPTP, the security of the service relies solely upon the user's password. Once the connection is authenticated, the RAS server handles the PPP connection as a regular dial-up connection.

PPTP transparently uses the Microsoft Domain authentication infrastructure and user validation, and PPTP is fairly easy and inexpensive to implement. Because PPTP supports tunneling NetBEUI and IPX protocols, small companies can enjoy the value of a VPN using PPTP.

IPSec. IPSec is a collection of protocols forming an extension to the Internet Protocol (IP). IPSec provides authentication and encryption services, operating at layer 3 (transport layer) of the OSI Reference Model. As IPSec has been included in the IETF's specification of IP version 6 (IPv6), any IPv6 implementation will seamlessly support IPSec.

Three protocols are used to provide the IPSec services. Specifically, these are the Authentication Header (AH), the Encapsulating Security Payload (ESP), and Internet Key Exchange (IKE), and can be implemented to be completely transparent to the end user. Because IPSec gateways can be configured to require no end-user action, users are likely not aware that they are using IPSec to transfer their data on the network.

The Authentication Header (AH) is normally 96 bits long and forms a hash or digest of the authentication token, which is a shared secret. The secret is commonly hashed using the MD5 algorithm or the Secure Hash Algorithm (SHA). These authentication methods are used because use of digital certificates or cryptographic keys is too slow and would delay authentication. IPSec itself does not specify how encryption and authentication are performed; rather, it provides an open framework supporting the industry standard algorithms. AH itself is not used for encryption.

Because it is only used for authentication, all AH does is verify who the sender says he is.

The Encapsulating Security Payload (ESP) can provide both authentication and encryption. ESP can be used with or without the AH. While the tunnel is configured with authentication and encryption, it is still vulnerable to attacks against the block cipher. The encryption uses a symmetric or shared key cipher operating on fixed blocks of plaintext. Triple-DES (3DES) is the most common encryption algorithm used, although RFCs have been issued providing support for Blowfish, IDEA, and RC4. The keys used in the encryption process are exchanged using the IKE protocol.

The IKE protocol is responsible for negotiating the connection parameters, including the initialization, handling, and renewal of encryption keys. The authentication of the two parties is accomplished using a shared secret key, such as a passphrase, which uniquely identifies the two parties. Implementations using X.509 certificates and the Diffie-Hellman method for exchanging cryptographic keys are also supported.

IKE renegotiates the regeneration of the encryption keys at specific times for added security, while MD5 and SHA provide authentication for each packet. IPSec is capable of securing communications between subnets, points, or a point to a subnet. IPSec supports transport and tunnel modes.

In transport mode, IPSec provides only source-to-destination protection of the datagram. IPSec encrypts and protects the IP data but leaves the IP transport headers intact. Consequently, transport mode is generally used to authenticate host-to-host-based tunnels. Tunnel mode encapsulates the entire packet, hiding the original header information.

Tunnel mode is commonly used to protect data between private subnets, where Network Address Translation (NAT) is used. The original packet becomes the payload for a new IP packet, allowing IPSec data to traverse any IP network. The principle reason for IPSec popularity is because IPv4 networks can carry the IPSec traffic with no modification to the network.

A major benefit of IPSec is its implementation in both hardware and software. All major network vendors support IPSec, as do most current operating systems, as well as open source implementations. While there are many IPSec implementations, they may not interoperate with each other. Consequently, before buying different IPSec implementations, be sure to test them and verify correct operation.

Some network configurations negatively affect IPSec operation. This is especially true for NAT. Because the packet header is modified by NAT, the IPSec packet integrity checks fail. Consequently, IPSec packets must be routed through gateways capable of performing the header translation. Additionally, un-encapsulation must be performed prior to the header translation.

Scalability issues arise when many IPSec tunnels must be managed. As the number of connections increases, so does the level of manual labor involved in managing them. Current proposed solutions include using BIND extensions to create a Secure DNS server. When a packet leaves the network interface, DNS is used to find the public key associated with the packet destination. If a public key is available, IKE negotiates the key exchange with the remote system and the packet is delivered fully encrypted. Using DNS in this manner is being discussed within the IETF, although there are several Internet drafts on the subject.

While IPSec is highly popular, it is restricted to carrying IP traffic. This means networks that do not support IP cannot use IPSec. Cisco Systems and Microsoft have resolved this problem with the L2TP.

L2TP. Microsoft and Cisco co-developed L2TP as an open standard for secure multi-protocol routing. This could include support for IPX, DECNet, NetBIOS, and AppleTalk, although support for legacy networking protocols is often nonexistent. Consequently, many operating systems only support one, such as Windows 2000, which supports only IP. Like PPTP, L2TP is a layer 2 protocol with stringent authentication, including the use of certificates. This is an improvement over PPTP, which uses only a user-supplied password. However, unlike PPTP, L2TP is affected by packet header modification and cannot cope with firewalls and network devices that perform NAT.

L2TP connections are initiated through PPP and are, in turn, encapsulated with the L2TP header. The resulting L2TP encapsulated packet is again encapsulated with UDP and transmitted. Microsoft uses TCP reliability checks using Next-Received and Next-Send fields in the L2TP messages, which are similar to the TCP acknowledgment numbers. L2TP uses UDP port 1701 as the source and destination port.

Typically, the L2TP packet is then encapsulated with IPSec ESP and AH, followed by another PPP encapsulation for transmission over the data-link layer. The reverse occurs at the receiving end where the data is then delivered to the receiving station. Host-level authentication is performed using IPSec and, once verified, user authentication is then performed using one of the supported user authentication methods. Specifically, the supported authentication methods are EAP, CHAP, MS-CHAP, and PAP.

VPNs and the Future of Secure Communication Environments. VPNs allow the remote user to function in a network as secure as the local user. VPNs provide transparent transport services without requiring that applications be rewritten or redesigned. This is a benefit over Secure Sockets Layer

(SSL) and Transport Layer Security (TLS), which require that the application be rewritten and compiled with the support in the application. Likewise, SSH, while effective, requires that users be properly trained to use it. It is important to remember that SSL, TLS, and SSH secure an individual port, while VPNs are capable of securing all data regardless of the protocol and port.

Correctly implemented VPNs are generally insensitive to traditional network attacks, including password sniffing, replay attacks, and identity spoofing. However, the VPN offers no protection from user error and carelessness. Any individual who can obtain your identity can masquerade as you, and the VPN cannot distinguish between you and the attacker.

Network Availability and Network Disaster Recovery Planning

There has been a lot of attention paid to protecting the computing resources over the past several years. However, the network itself has not been adequately examined to properly understand the risks and recovery strategies necessary. Networks are susceptible to many of the same problems as computer systems; however, we are extremely dependent upon information arriving over the network properly. When information does not arrive or is not intact, the receiving computer may accept the erroneous information, thus affecting service operation, decisions, and safety.

There are many more network links than computers because of network design and redundancy considerations. This makes the network a bigger target for attack and more likely to suffer from failures. In some cases, organizations establish their entire disaster recovery plans around the applications and implementation within a hot or cold site, yet they completely ignore network connectivity.

Network Reliability. Networks are reliable when critical components fail and data still travels over the network. The critical elements are different for each topology, as presented in the following sections.

Star Topology. The star topology is highly reliable because a failure of a single link between a host and the hub affects only the single host. All other nodes continue to have network connectivity. However, the hub is the weak link in this configuration, and the reliability of the network is dependent upon the reliability of the hub.

Improving the reliability of the hub is accomplished through redundant power supplies, backplane, and control logic. If one of these critical components fails, the redundant unit will ensure that the hub continues operating. If the central hub supports active monitoring, reliability can be increased through management of the critical components.

Ring Topology. Typically, the ring topology offers poor reliability because each node is connected to two others to form the ring. If a link failure occurs, the entire network stops functioning. The same is true for a node failure, because each node is actively involved in the transmissions of all other nodes through token passing. If a node fails and the electrical connection is lost, the network stops functioning. The only method to address these weaknesses is to add redundant links to each node and include bypass circuitry. These changes, however, make implementation of the ring more expensive.

Bus Topology. The bus topology provides poor reliability because a link failure results in the entire network being inoperative. However, if a node fails, the network continues to function. Like the ring topology, redundant network segments address the link failure issue, but at a much higher cost.

Network Availability. Network availability is concerned with the network's ability to provide service and support all users wishing to access it. High availability networks provide immediate access to the user. Conversely, low availability, which may be suffering from excessive traffic or other problems, forces users to wait for access or response from systems.

Component Availability. Network load, access points, protocols, and the length of the bus affect the bus topology. When there is light network load, availability is high. However, as network load increases, so do collisions, and availability decreases.

Mesh Topology. The mesh topology provides the highest level of availability due to the multiple links between each hop on the mesh. Consequently, hosts in the mesh topology are always available, subject to the host being operational. When a link fails, the mesh topology provides alternate paths to the desired host. If a host fails, only the host is affected, as the links are maintained.

Methods of Protection. Today's computing environment requires appropriate protection methods to maintain network and system availability and reduce the risk of data loss. Protection methods include redundant wide area network links, bandwidth on-demand using Integrated Services Digital Network (ISDN), and dial backup. LAN controls include fault-tolerant servers and wiring, and implementation of Redundant Arrays of Inexpensive (or Independent) Disks (RAID).

- *Tariffed redundancy and protection.* Most carriers offer tariffed backup and recovery protection services for wide area network links. The most common backup method is redundant network links, although it may be more expensive than some companies can afford. Telecommunications providers generally implement special redundant routing methods for digital and analog services, both providing diversity and avoidance of failures.

- *Diversity.* Diversity is implemented through designated groups of interoffice channels over physically separate routes. This is a feature provided by the telecommunications carriers.
- *Avoidance.* Avoidance is selected by customers who wish to specify a channel avoid a specific geographic area. This allows the customer to minimize potential outages, congestion, and delay, which can be made worse through long routes. Specifically, the customer can specify circuits that bypass or are not routed through high-risk areas prone to earthquakes, floods, or hurricanes.
- *Automatic protection capability.* Automatic protection is a telecommunication carrier service protecting the customer against failure of a local channel or similar access service. The protection capability is implemented through switching configurations, which automatically switches to alternate circuits when the primary fails. While this is a service provided by the carrier, the customer must order the alternate switching circuits and install the switching equipment at its premises.
- *Network protection capability.* This can be an expensive solution, providing protection against the failure of a carrier's interoffice channel. When the primary circuit fails, it is switched over to a high-speed alternate. Purchasing this option means the customer incurs an installation charge. However, most carriers already use network protection — when they lose a circuit, connectivity is automatically rerouted.
- *Dial backup.* Dial backup uses an alternate modem card in a router or similar device or stand-alone unit to provide traditional dial capabilities over the public switched telephone network. When the primary circuit fails, a network manager can initiate the dial backup; and when answered by the receiving station, data flow between the networks resumes. Once the primary circuit is recovered, the dial circuit is terminated, with all network traffic restored to the primary circuit.
- *Rerouting on T1 lines.* When a customer requires full T1 or higher services, dial backup is commonly available from the telecommunications carrier. However, the carrier can bring a dedicated T1 facility back online after a phone call from the customer. There is an associated delay of one to several hours. Despite the delay period, this may be an acceptable alternative to having an outage of indefinite duration.
- *Customer-controlled reconfiguration.* Another option is user-configured circuit rerouting, where the customer specifies the route reconfiguration and gives it to the carrier. The carrier installs a user management terminal at the customer premises, where the selected

reconfiguration is performed and delivered to the carrier over dial-up services. This can incur a delay while the carrier performs the reconfiguration to match the user's requirements. Because the recovery delay can be significant when using this option, these types of services from the carriers are typically used to address long-term rather than short-term outages.

- *ISDN facilities.* The instantaneous reconfiguration and recovery of high-speed services requires a T1 or similar multiplexer with an advanced management transport system. One example is an ISDN equipped multiplexer, providing a cost-effective alternate method of backing up T1 and fractional T1 services. ISDN call setup times range from three to ten seconds. The short call setup means the failing T1 can be switched over to ISDN services in seconds rather than hours or days. The use of ISDN services is generally more cost-effective than installing a fully redundant circuit. With the fully redundant circuit, the customer pays for the circuit whether it is used or not. With ISDN services, the customer pays for the local channels and only pays for the interoffice channels when the service is used, because ISDN call charges are distance and time sensitive. The T1 multiplexer's intelligent routing capabilities allow the customer to purchase less expensive ISDN services rather than a T1 circuit that may not be used until there is a network failure.
- *DDS dial backup.* Digital Data Services offer a high degree of reliability. However, there is still room for annual downtime. The downtime can be especially costly for an organization that requires no downtime for maintenance of business operations, such as a financial institution.

Organizations that require no downtime can use a digital data set with intelligent failover to a dial service, which is implemented when the primary communications channel fails. The backup service routes the call over the public switched telephone network when the digital data senses a loss of signal on the primary circuit.

When the backup mode is operating, the digital data sent continues to monitor the failed facility and resumes normal operation once the primary circuit is restored.

Recovery Options for LANs. The organization depends on the LAN for carrying data when required by users. The critical or sensitive nature of the LAN means it too requires special considerations for protecting its operation. Of specific concern is the protection of the information on the LAN to prevent data loss through manual or automated means. Minimizing the information loss requires redundant circuitry and subsystems capable of activation upon failure of a device. This maintains network availability and minimizes data loss.

Recovery and Reconfiguration. LAN recovery is the process of restoring stable service to the LAN after a failure. Reconfigurations involve the process of how to restore the network. Reconfigurations may involve replacement of a link or network interface card. Recovering the network implies the organization has the ability and means to recognize a failure has occurred and determine what actions are required to minimize data loss and the adverse effect on the system's performance.

Typically, the available mechanisms are:

- Performance monitoring
- Fault location
- Network management
- System availability management
- Configuration management

Using these techniques, the network and security managers can detect errors, minimize impact, and restore service with minimal impact to the network and minimal data loss.

Reconfiguration is the process of bypassing major failures of network components. The process involves detecting a failure not correctable by the usual methods. Once the failure has occurred, the network impact is assessed to choose an appropriate reconfiguration. Once the reconfiguration is implemented, normal operations can resume.

Restoration Capabilities of LAN Servers. The network provides connectivity to critical systems and applications. While the network can be designed with fault tolerance and high availability, systems must also be analyzed for their recovery methods. A high availability without systems redundancy means the network may be available but the application is not.

The server provides the application and computing facilities that the users access via the network. Servers provide many different resources, including printers, faxes, databases, data storage, applications, and communications facilities. The nature and criticality of the application determines the backup systems and methodologies applied to maintain its operation and availability. By distributing applications across multiple servers, the failure of a single host makes some applications unavailable, while others remain in service.

Software failures, programming errors, user errors, and operating system problems can all contribute to system failures and lost data. Additionally, power surges, power outages, and hardware failures can often be more catastrophic, especially when involving mass storage devices like disk drives. Many of these conditions, at minimum, affect the data not yet written to the storage medium, resulting in data loss. Establishing sound maintenance procedures for hardware, establishing strong security procedures for facilities, and implementing good data backup processes can reduce the risk of hardware failure and data loss.

Backup Procedures. Traditional data backup procedures can be implemented for the servers on the LAN to minimize the risk of data loss. Some procedures include full or incremental daily backups and archival backups done weekly and monthly. Additionally, copies of the backups must be maintained off-site. Backup and recovery issues and strategies are fully covered in Chapter 5, "Operations Security."

Quality of Service (QoS)

As discussed throughout this chapter, more and more organizations are relying on the Internet for some form of their business communications. This has reduced their carrier costs and allowed the benefits of the public Internet to expand their opportunities. However, the public Internet is a shared resource, with no single organization or type of packet having superiority over any other.

Emerging Quality-of-Service (QoS) technologies can be used to establish preferences for specific types of data packets. For example, data traffic is unaware of lost or delayed packets, while Voice-over-IP and media services are less tolerant of lost packets, typically interrupting service in one way or another. QoS implementations, therefore, do not treat the packets equally, but establish prioritization of delay-sensitive or higher-priority traffic ahead of other traffic. Every network at one time or another will experience congestion, resulting in lost packets, degraded service, and possible business impacts.

Properly implemented QoS functionality means improvements in network operations without requiring changes to the existing infrastructure. Additionally, a network can handle more traffic without significant bandwidth increases and ensure that end-user response times are met.

QoS Levels. There are three QoS levels available for traffic on a network (Exhibit 20). These are best-effort, differentiated, and guaranteed service.

Best-Effort Service. There is no guarantee of delivery, throughput, or delay when using the best-effort service. The packets are delivered after all guaranteed and differentiated service level packets have been processed. Consequently, best-effort traffic has the longest delays and, if congestion is severe, is the first to be discarded. For the most part, the current Internet uses best-effort service.

Differentiated Service. Differentiated service is a step above best effort and provides a higher level of preference for designated traffic. The differentiated service can mean that there is a higher percentage of the overall

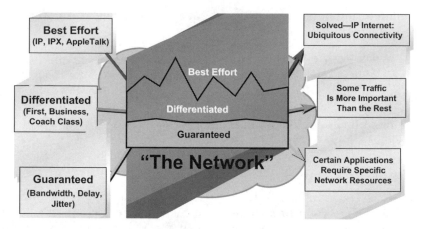

Exhibit 20. Quality of Service Levels
(From Donna Kidder, "Enabling the Future with Quality of Service," in *Data Communications Management*, June 2000. © CRC Press LLC.)

bandwidth available, less delay, or fewer packet drops during periods of network congestion. Differentiated service is appropriate for corporate mission-critical applications.

Guaranteed Service. Guaranteed service is the highest level of service in QoS implementations. It ensures a specific maximum delay or minimum available throughput for this traffic. The service is managed by reserving resources for the connection. If the reservation criteria cannot be met, the connection is established. Guaranteed service is optimal for delay-sensitive traffic, including voice and video. Through this service, critical data can be delivered in a timely manner, such as large data volumes necessary to meet operational or production deadlines.

Improved utilization of bandwidth, buffers, and processing capacity ensures that the network resources required for guaranteed delivery are never exceeded. However, all remaining resources are allocated to differentiated services first and finally to best-effort traffic.

QoS Components. QoS technologies include several components:

- Classification, related to priority and network policy
- Signaling, to labeling the traffic to identify the classification
- Congestion management, to prioritize and schedule the traffic
- Congestion avoidance, to optimize network performance and avoid congestion
- Traffic shaping and policing, to control the amount of data entering a network
- Link utilization, to minimize delay and maximize link utilization

- Monitoring and reporting, to identify and report on potential problems

Each of the above components is examined in more detail below.

Classification. Every packet must be classified as to priority and delay, such as high priority, low delay or low priority, moderate delay. A human at some point must make the actual classification decision, which is then implemented by a network device, the application, or a server.

Classification can be determined by the application by setting the precedence bits in the packets when they are transmitted. Alternatively, a policy manager on the server can set the appropriate precedence bit for each application on that server, although ideally, the policy manager should propagate the policy decisions to the network devices.

If the network devices have the policy, they can quickly process traffic based on that policy. The network device can also modify the classification or base policy depending upon congestion, multi-service requirements, or other parameters defined by the network or security managers.

Signaling. Once the packet is classified, the packet is marked or signaled, preventing another network node from having to reassess the classification. Signaling improves network performance by eliminating further classification decisions, which would slow down traffic and cause congestion — exactly what QoS is trying to prevent. Signaling is best done at layer 3 or IP, because many diverse systems may process a packet and therefore require a standard signaling protocol.

Both in-band and out-of-band signaling is available to QoS. In-band signaling is accomplished with the IP precedence bits in the IP header, establishing eight different service classes. Additionally, differentiated service bits identify another 64 service classes. By using either of these techniques, intermediate nodes can easily determine how the packet is to be processed. Aside from layer 3 signaling, packets can also be marked in the layer 2 header, although this may not be implemented unless the intermediate devices properly distinguish between service classes at this level.

Out-of-band signaling is supported using the Resource Reservation Protocol (RSVP). Using RVSP, every node in the data path is advised of the resource requirements before the connection is established. If all nodes in the path meet the criteria, the connection is made; otherwise, the connection is not established. Using RSVP, the user or application is assured that the required resources are available. The nodes in the network identify traffic from flow and reservation information by examining the source and destination address and port numbers.

Congestion Management. The prioritization and scheduling involved in congestion management are applied if there is congestion and queuing of network traffic. Consequently, when congestion occurs, it is necessary to prioritize the traffic and provide service to the higher-priority traffic. Prioritization can be absolute, class-based queuing, and fair queuing.

Absolute prioritization specifies that one traffic type has precedence over all others, ensuring that high-priority traffic has the highest performance and lowest delay. However, absolute priority works best with lower bandwidth services, because high-bandwidth service can significantly affect other network traffic. The second prioritization method is class-based queuing, which is also known as bandwidth reservation. This technique allocates bandwidth to queues of differing classes, attempting to divide the available bandwidth appropriately. Bandwidth reservation is affected by the granularity of the classification and the effectiveness of the technique for matching bandwidth allocation with configured amounts. Granularity of control is important to ensure that traffic is placed in the correct queue. Additionally, the prioritization software must ensure that any allocated bandwidth not used by a given protocol is allocated elsewhere, thereby utilizing all available bandwidth. Bandwidth reservation works most effectively when multiple traffic types, all requiring a guaranteed service level, are involved.

Fair queuing ensures that large file transfers do not adversely affect interactive traffic, such as Telnet. Traffic flow is classified in this technique by analyzing parameters including TCP and UDP ports, MAC source and destination pairs, or IPX address pairs. Fair queuing creates a queue for each individual data flow, and allocated bandwidth to isolate low-bandwidth users from high-bandwidth users. While processing data, the lower bandwidth users receive better service levels, and the network appears to adjust operations based upon traffic patterns.

If there is the possibility that a particular flow will become bandwidth-starved, the flows are classified to ensure that bandwidth allocation is corrected. A variation is to implement the IP precedence settings in the header to influence how much bandwidth each flow receives.

Congestion Avoidance. Typically, a congested network suffers from reduced performance and poor bandwidth efficiency. TCP constantly attempts to measure bandwidth with round-trip times and packet drops. When packet drops occur, TCP reduces the data being sent before waiting for an acknowledgment. If a link is completely congested, all subsequent frames are dropped. Consequently, all TCP connections experiencing drops on congested links slow down their transmissions and then rebuild. This has the effect of creating waves of congestion with underutilized links between each wave. Known as global synchronization, the problem is avoided by discarding the packets prior to severe congestion.

Randomly dropping packets, thereby dispersing the buildup and avoiding the wave, resolves the global synchronization problem. Using signaling techniques with the IP Header or RSVP, high-priority, mission-critical traffic is less affected by congestion. Normal-priority traffic experiences improved performance due to more efficient utilization of the network links.

Policing and Traffic Shaping. Limiting the amount of traffic admitted to a network is called *policing*. This prevents network congestion and maintains the integrity of the network. In this model, traffic exceeding allowable maximums is dropped, marked for discard, or set to a low IP precedence. Implementing granular policing can limit some types of traffic while continuing to allow other types. For example, a network manager can limit the amount of Internet Web traffic without restricting mission-critical traffic on the corporate network.

Traffic shaping involves controlling traffic so that it fits into a smaller pipe and limits the data bursts. Implementing traffic shaping involves queuing at specific points in the network. In networks where over-subscription is common, such as Frame Relay and ATM, traffic shaping addresses speed mismatches on either side of the network.

Link Efficiency. Prioritization is not enough when dealing with highly delay-sensitive traffic such as voice. A 200-millisecond delay is enough to impact the voice connection, making queuing only one component in the QoS equation. Thus far, our discussion has focused on queuing to address the issue of delay. Once a large data packet has started transmission on an interface, a more delay-sensitive packet must wait until it can be transmitted. Called serialization delay, it can significantly affect delay-sensitive packets such as voice.

Serialization delay is greatly affected by the speed of the transmission link — if a 1514-byte packet takes 214 milliseconds to transmit on a 56K link, the quality of the voice connection is degraded. Addressing this situation requires the larger data packets be fragmented into much smaller packets, making it less likely that any packet will be transmitted beyond its delay threshold. However, once the network speeds reach 512K, packet fragmentation is no longer required.

Overall network performance is also achievable through header and payload compression, which increases link utilization and minimizes delay.

Policy Management, Measurement, and Monitoring. Policy management is a means to define, distribute, and enforce QoS rules. For greater effectiveness, policies should be established at a central system and "pushed" out to the various devices, either automatically or manually when required. Monitoring requires a feedback mechanism to detect changes in network utilization and respond to those changes in real-time.

Capacity and network planning are best done in advance so that appropriate measurements and growth estimates can be made. Once this information is gathered, changes are made to devices or network links prior to a problem actually occurring. Monitoring service levels and link utilization provides a sure indication of potential problems.

Measuring response time from device to device through the entire network is especially important. Monitoring tools can alert network operations staff of impending congestion, device problems, or possible link failures, thus allowing immediate corrective action. Reporting tools must also be capable of identifying when designated thresholds have been reached, as this is a sign that changes are required.

Implementing QoS technologies is no replacement for good network design, monitoring, and management. It is not possible for any technology, even QoS, to create additional bandwidth when there is none available. Consequently, if the monitoring tools consistently report bandwidth over utilization and congestion, the network manager must increase it before the network becomes unstable or, worse, unavailable.

8.4 Assurance, Trust, and Confidence Mechanisms

The implementation of confidence mechanisms providing assurance and trust that a company's network is secure is very important. There are many such mechanisms that companies can implement, but a good combination of all of them provides indication of an adequate security posture. The following are such examples.

Audit Trails

An audit trail is a series of records of computer events, about an operating system, an application, or user activities. It is generated by an auditing system that monitors system activity. Audit trails have many uses in the realm of computer security, to include:

- *Individual accountability.* An individual's actions are tracked in an audit trail, allowing users to be personally accountable for their actions. This deters users from circumventing security policies. Even if they do, they can be held accountable.
- *Reconstruction of events.* Audit trails can also be used to reconstruct events after a problem has occurred. Reviewing the system audit trails can identify what, when, how, and why an event has occurred.

This information is beneficial in determining the amount of damage actually incurred.

- *Problem monitoring.* Audit trails can also be used as online tools to help monitor problems as they occur. Such real-time monitoring helps in the detection of problems like disk failures, overutilization of system resources, or network outages.
- *Intrusion detection.* Intrusion detection is the process of identifying attempts to penetrate a system and gain unauthorized access. Audit trails can help in intrusion detection if they record appropriate events. Determining what events to audit for effective audit trails is one of the present research issues being looked into by the research community.

Security Reviews

The IT security professional must do more than review parameters to understand the level of security in effect. As every security professional learns, things appearing on paper or on screen do not always work as they should. No audit would be complete without a thorough test of the access privilege rules to make sure they are working properly.

The security professional should obtain access rules and draw an organization chart of the security rules. Security rules are usually written in a structured fashion along divisional or department lines. The organization chart will help the security professional quickly visualize the structure of the rules file.

A review of the rules may identify multiple rules created for the same reason. These redundant rules make maintenance difficult for the security administrator because the removal of an obsolete rule may require the location and deletion of several independent rules. As the rule file grows, extraneous rules begin to hamper a thorough review of the file. The security professional should ensure that rules applied across the board are implemented only in one place.

One possible test is simulating resource access. Simulating resource access involves accessing the rules file — but not the resource — in a way that the security package still permits or denies access. This is the safest audit technique because the security professional can prevent the accidental destruction or disclosure of information and the security package can identify which rule allowed or denied access to the source. This is extremely useful for large files, which make organized reviews difficult and time-consuming. In addition, this technique allows the security professional to perform "what-if" tests to determine whether a particular access would be permitted or denied under a specific set of circumstances.

The security professional should attempt to update a production program or file to determine whether the controls are effective. If the security professional's understanding of the rules file is correct, the access will be permitted or denied in accordance with the predetermined analysis.

Another testing technique is attempting unauthorized access. Unless properly executed, an unauthorized access attempt could be the most risky of the auditing techniques. It is important for the security professional to obtain approval before attempting unauthorized access to a resource. If the access is successful, the security professional may have a difficult time explaining the access obtained was only part of a test. If the access results in the generation of a live monetary transaction or the destruction of a production file, the rapport built with the auditee may be destroyed. IT security professionals are in the position to learn many weaknesses in the security system and should not use this privileged knowledge without notifying the appropriate individuals.

Most packages give selected user IDs exceptional authority to override any security rules and parameters in place. The security professional should conduct a review of the individuals provided this exceptional authority and the reason for these exceptions.

One of the most basic reviews for the security professional to perform is identifying the user IDs permitted to bypass security checks. Although this authority is necessary, the IT security professional should determine whether the practice is prevalent and uncontrolled.

A listing of all user IDs authorized to bypass security controls should be generated by any utility program or report writer that can read the rules file. Although some system tasks may require security bypass capabilities, users or programmers do not usually need it. Sometimes, the capability is permitted while the security package is being installed and, because of oversight, it is not removed when the installation process has concluded.

The security professional should ensure that activities exempt from security rules are automatically logged to a file. Because some activities can bypass security checking, a complete log of exempted activity is needed to ascertain how much of this activity has occurred in the past. The current level of exempted activity may not be indicative of past levels.

The security professional should determine the prevalence of exempt activity. A large number of user IDs exempt from security rules or checking indicates ineffective rules enforcement.

Certain security packages allow protection on a terminal basis. Critical applications should be restricted to selected terminals on a need basis. Of particular concern is the usage of the system console.

The ability to make system changes is not always limited to the master console in the computer room. Permission to make console changes should usually be limited to the operations personnel. Any requests by the applications development staff or by the systems programmer should be carefully reviewed. If changes are permitted outside the computer room, the identification of the command issuer should be logged by the system. The identification method should be active, rather than passive, to prohibit an unauthorized individual from issuing a command without proper identification. The only type of console commands to be issued should be restricted to those that require a job function to be performed.

The security professional should review the appropriateness of the authority given to each individual and recommend removal of those functions not needed.

Vulnerability Assessments

To thrive — or even survive — in this era of global business interconnectivity and cyber threats, organizations are quickly realizing the need to conduct frequent and thorough vulnerability assessments of every entry point to their sensitive information — the Internet, internal networks, applications, remote access, and wireless implementations.

The purpose of vulnerability assessments is to discover as many vulnerabilities as possible, decide how risky they are to your environment, and then reduce the risk they pose. Vulnerability assessment is one method of helping you find and plug the holes, before others get through those holes first with evil intent. We must remember, however, that it is not always possible to reduce the risk to none, only to an acceptable level.

Penetration Testing. Penetration testing is defined as security testing in which evaluators attempt to circumvent the security features of a system based on their understanding of the system design and implementation.

Penetration testing is a part of computer system security testing in which the test team collects information on the security features inherent in a target system and then attempts to circumvent the security features in order to gain access to the system. Except by agreement with the target system management, penetration testing is essentially unconstrained and may make use of automated tools, live penetration attempts by a test team member posing as a hacker, and any other combination of conventional or unconventional access methods. A penetration test team can be expected to use any information it can gather to gain access to the system, including code listings, documentation, manuals, diagrams, or interviews with system personnel. Running an automated tool against a target system for the purpose of collecting information on the target's security features is included in this definition of penetration testing, although no logon to the target system has occurred.

Penetration testing is essentially computer hacking covered by a pre-coordinated set of rules under which the test will be conducted, a pre-established boundary within which the test will be contained, and by an appropriate authorization to proceed with the test. A penetration test ends with a report to the affected line management on the vulnerabilities uncovered by the test, including recommendations to resolve or mitigate these vulnerabilities.

Sound Network Design. Networks offer users unprecedented capabilities for sharing resources and information. However, to make sure of an adequate security posture utilizing advanced network technologies, significant resources are required to plan their proper implementation and installation. Companies need to involve the right people, expertise, and programs required to effectively plan, implement, and support today's complex distributed computing environments with the proper security built in. The solutions implemented should be built around proven methodologies that maximize network performance, streamline business functions, and, at the same time, provide efficient and effective network security.

8.5 Information Protection and Management Services

The development of security policies, standards, procedures, and guidelines is only the beginning of an effective information security program. A strong network security architecture will be less effective if there is no process in place to make sure that the employees are aware of their rights and responsibilities. All too often, security professionals implement the "perfect" security program and then forget to factor the employee into the formula.

For the product to be as successful as possible, the information security professional must find a way to sell this product to the employees. An effective security awareness program could be the most cost-effective action that management can take to protect its critical information assets. Implementing an effective security awareness program will help all employees understand why they need to take information security seriously, what they will gain from its implementation, and how it will assist them in completing their assigned tasks. The process should begin at new-employee orientation and continue on a regular basis for all employees at all levels of the organization.

Summary

The Telecommunications, Network, and Internet Security Domain is by far the most technical and challenging (for those not working in telecommunications). It involves the understanding and use of many protocols to enable systems to communicate securely. For the information security person, it is necessary to understand the TCP/IP suite of protocols to be able to respond to the multitude of network attack types present in the environment. It is also necessary to be familiar with the OSI layers to understand where in the hierarchy various mechanisms operate. There are many choices from an array of security solutions to be made, so a thorough understanding of their pros and cons is a must. Many if not most organizations support their data processing operations through a network of networks structure, usually including connections to the Internet. This is an inherently dangerous arrangement. Accordingly, we spend a larger amount of our text on the telecommunications and network security topics.

8.6 Common Body of Knowledge (CBK)

The current CBK for the Telecommunications, Network, and Internet Security Domain is listed below to assist in determining topics for further review. Although this Study Guide is very detailed in many areas, it is not possible to thoroughly discuss every CBK topic in a single book. Therefore, additional study of items from the bibliography may be advisable.

The professional can meet the expectations defined in the introduction by understanding such Telecommunications, Network, and Internet Security topics and methodologies as:

- Email security
- Facsimile security
- Internet/Intranet/Extranet
- Firewalls
- Proxies
- Network Address Translation (NAT)
- Transparency
- Gateways and Routers
- Transmission Control Protocol/Internet Protocol (TCP/IP)
- IPSec authentication and confidentiality
- ISO OSI Layers and Characteristics
- Network Layer Security Protocols (e.g., IPSec, SKIP, SWIPE)
- Transport Layer Security (e.g., SSL)
- Application Layer Security Protocols
  - Secure Electronic Transactions (SET)
  - Privacy Enhanced Mail (PEM)

- – Secure Hypertext Transfer Protocol (S-HTTP/HTTPS)
- – S/MIME
- – Secure Remote Procedure Call (S-RPC)
- Local Area Network (LAN)
- Wide Area Network (WAN)
- Virtual Private Network (VPN)
- Network Attacks and Countermeasures
- Network Monitors and Packet Sniffers
- PBX Fraud and Abuse
- Physical Media Characteristics
  - – Fiber Optics/Coaxial/Twisted Pair
- Network Topologies
  - – Star/Bus/Ring
- Remote Access/Telecommuting Techniques
  - – SLIP/PPP/CHAP/PAP/EAP
- Secure Voice Communications
- TCP/IP Protocol Characteristics and Vulnerabilities
- Transmission Protocols and Services
  - – X.25
  - – Frame Relay
  - – HDLC
  - – SDLC
  - – ISDN

Examples of Knowledgeability

- Compare and contrast the management and administrative functions concerned with network security management, remote access, or voice/facsimile/video.
- Identify examples of misuse and abuse of systems, data, processes, etc.
- Define network authentication services.
- Compare and contrast remote access security architectures.
- Compare and contrast the strengths and weaknesses of static password mechanisms, two-factor authentication tokens, and the use of smart cards.
- Define RADIUS/TACACS/TACACS+.
- Describe the concept of filtering (screening) by communications protocol/services.
- Identify encapsulation (HDLC, SDLC, Frame Relay).
- Describe remote access control.
- Describe node authentication.
- Define network segment/sub-domain isolation.
- Define the concept of proxy services.
- Identify policies and procedures to limit virus attacks.

- Describe the concept of virtual private networks (VPNs)/tunneling.
- Compare and contrast methods of intrusion detection and access control.
- Identify and define vulnerabilities relating to physical security.
- Compare and contrast LANs and WANs.
- Define the concepts of extranets and intranets.
- Define the characteristics of VPNs/tunneling.
- Define network operating system (NOS).
- Describe the use of bridges and switches.
- Compare and contrast the capabilities of "smart" and "dumb" hubs, concentrators, and repeaters.
- Compare and contrast bridges, routers, and switches.
- Identify and define various types of data network services.
- Identify and define network management services.
- Define trusted network interpretation (TNI).
- Describe differences between Subjects and Objects as they pertain to TNI.
- Compare and contrast the differences within and between TNI evaluation classes.
- Define mandatory protection evaluation classification.
- Compare and contrast differences between "B" classification levels.
- Compare and contrast TCP/IP and OSI.
- Describe TCP/IP characteristics and operations.
- Describe OSI characteristics and operations.
- Define the seven levels of OSI protocol layers.
- Compare and contrast asynchronous and synchronous communications.
- Compare and contrast the "client/server" and "thin client" concepts.
- Identify and distinguish between normal client and normal server tasks.
- Define client/server controls.
- Identify and define client/server limitations.
- Identify and define client/server security and control limitations.
- Distinguish between types of remote access.
- Describe vulnerabilities of remote access.
- Explain why remote access is a favorite target of hackers.
- Define general remote access security safeguards.
- Describe the operation of VPNs.
- Compare and contrast the methods of securing VPNs.
- Compare and contrast tape backup and CD backup.
- Describe the terms "file mirroring" and "clustering."
- Compare and contrast the differences between Internet and Web security.
- Identify methods of securing network/subnetwork perimeters.
- Describe operational capabilities of firewalls.

- Identify types of firewalls.
- Describe what is meant by the term "IPSec."
- Compare and contrast SKIP and SSL.
- Describe what is meant by the term "application layer security protocols."
- Describe and contrast "Secure Electronic Transactions" and "Privacy Enhanced Mail."
- Identify well-known network attack methods.
- Describe well-known network threats.
- Define types of network attacks and methods.
- Describe multimedia (data/voice/facsimile) security.
- Explain the mission of and how to utilize a Computer Emergency Response Team (CERT).

8.7 Sample Questions for the CISSP Exam

1. What is a network protocol?
   a. A defined set of rules of behavior
   b. An early version of a new product
   c. The maximum bandwidth of a transmission medium
   d. Rules of communication
2. A datagram will often contain the message itself plus several other headers and trailers. This is called:
   a. Encryption
   b. Transport adjacency
   c. Encapsulation
   d. Attenuation
3. The Media Access Control (MAC) layer operates as a subset of the:
   a. Physical layer
   b. Data-link layer
   c. Internet layer
   d. Transport layer
4. Flow control is usually coordinated by which layer of the OSI stack?
   a. Data-link layer
   b. Network layer
   c. Application layer
   d. Transport layer
5. Sending several communications simultaneously over the same physical medium is facilitated by:
   a. Asynchronous communication
   b. Digital communications
   c. Multiplexing
   d. Baseband technology
6. The two portions of an IP address are:

    a. Network and subnet
    c. Host and network
    c. Host and subnet
    d. Class A and Class C

7. Full-duplex transmission means that:
    a. A site can either send or receive but not at the same time.
    b. A site can either send or receive but not both.
    c. A site can multiplex several sending channels.
    d. A site can send and receive at the same time.

8. What is the purpose of a sequence number in a TCP transmission?
    a. Ensuring all messages are received
    b. Putting message fragments back into their correct order
    c. Controlling the distribution of several multiplexed channels
    d. Identifying network congestion

9. The Internet Group Management Protocol (IGMP) is used primarily in IPv4 for:
    a. Broadcast traffic
    b. Peer-to-peer communications
    c. Multicast transmissions
    d. Administration of remote Internet groups

10. Poisoning the Domain Name Server system may result in:
    a. A user's IP address being deleted
    b. A user being unable to reach an organization via its IP address
    c. A user being routed to the wrong organization
    d. A user being denied access to a remote server

11. What would you find in an ARP cache?
    a. History of sites visited by a user
    b. Configuration tables for a firewall
    c. Domain registry information
    d. Cross-reference of IP and MAC addresses

12. Which of the following is not a function of the ICMP (Internet Control Message Protocol)?
    a. Reporting packet failure
    b. Testing node reachability
    c. Increasing routing efficiency
    d. Reporting network failures

13. Which of the following applies to the Routing Information Protocol (RIP)?
    a. It is best for use in large autonomous networks.
    b. It determines routing by number of hops rather than line speeds.
    c. It is relatively fast at identifying network changes.
    d. It considers line utilization as a metric for determining the best route.

14. An autonomous network is one that is:
    a. Isolated from other systems for greater security

b. Designed to be robust enough to resist internal attacks
c. Under one point of authority or control
d. Enhanced for maximized speed and error correction

15. Which method of setting up a WAN is considered most private?
   a. Microwave link
   b. Leased line
   c. Internet
   d. Wireless infrared

16. Which of the following are not normally associated with wireless technologies?
   a. Noise
   b. Interception
   c. Access points
   d. Direct sequence frequency hopping

17. What is the best defense against "wardialing"?
   a. Strong modem policies
   b. Restrictions on lines with outgoing dial tone
   c. Justify all remote users
   d. Having all internal numbers unlisted

18. A good measure to prevent sniffing is:
   a. The NIC is in promiscuous mode.
   b. All transmitted data is encrypted.
   c. Password files are kept protected.
   d. Exclusive use of coaxial cable for networks.

19. What is the best defense against session hijacking?
   a. Rigorous physical security
   b. Closing unneeded ports
   c. Strong user authentication policies
   d. Choosing strong protocols

20. Denial-of-service attacks are usually the result of all of the following EXCEPT:
   a. Malformed packets
   b. Software not handling errors properly
   c. Duplicate MAC addresses
   d. Packet floods

21. An organization can prevent most buffer overflows by all of the following EXCEPT:
   a. Properly code and test the software.
   b. Expand memory allocation.
   c. Validate all user inputs.
   d. Control inputs from other programs.

22. A rootkit can perform all of the following EXCEPT:
   a. Grant super-user access to the attacker.
   b. Hide sniffers.
   c. Replace critical system files.

    d. Contain a backdoor account for the hacker.

23. One of the MOST critical parts of an information security program is:
    a. Having an IDS (intrusion detection system)
    b. Having a routine to install system patches
    c. Strong authentication methods
    d. Documented incident response procedures

24. A remote access system may limit user activity through all of the following EXCEPT:
    a. Access restrictions to certain drives or servers
    b. Login restrictions based on time of day
    c. Restrictions to protocols accepted
    d. Restrictions on bandwidth allocated to users

25. Which of the following is NOT a valid type of firewall?
    a. Desktop
    b. Packet filtering
    c. Statistical inspection
    d. Application proxy

26. A circuit-level gateway operates at which level of the OSI stack?
    a. Transport
    b. Application
    c. Network
    d. Session

27. Which of the following is NOT a protocol used in IPSec?
    a. Point-to-Point Tunneling (PPTP)
    b. Authentication Header (AH)
    c. Internet Key Exchange (IKE)
    d. Encapsulated Security Payload (ESP)

References

Christina Bird, "An Introduction to Secure Remote Access," in *Information Security Management Handbook,* 4th ed., Vol. 2, Harold F. Tipton and Micki Krause (eds.), Boca Raton, FL: Auerbach Publications, 2001.

Steven F. Blanding, "An Introduction to LAN/WAN Security," in *Handbook of Information Security Management,* Harold F. Tipton and Micki Krause (eds.), Boca Raton, FL: Auerbach Publications, 1998.

Cisco Systems, Inc., *Internetworking Technology Handbook*, 3rd ed., Indianapolis, IN: Cisco Press, 2000.

Thomas DeFelice, "Designing and Implementing Firewalls," *Data Communications Management,* 27(3), June 2002.

Frederick Gallegos, "Wireless LANs: Technology and Security," *Enterprise Operations Management,* 25(5), October 2001.

Gilbert Held, "Overcoming Wireless LAN Security Vulnerabilities," in *Information Security Management Handbook*, 4th ed., Vol. 4, Harold F. Tipton and Micki Krause (eds.), Boca Raton, FL: Auerbach Publications, 2003.

Donna Kidder, "Enabling the Future with Quality of Service," *Data Communications Management,* 25(6), June 2000.

Joe Kovara and Ray Kaplan, "Implementing Kerberos in Distributed Systems," in *Handbook of Information Security Management*, Harold F. Tipton and Micki Krause (eds.), Boca Raton, FL: Auerbach Publications, 1998.

Nathan Muller, "Protecting Information in Distributed Environments," *Information Management: Strategy, Systems, and Technology*.

Nathan Muller, "Network Disaster Recovery Planning," *Enterprise Operations Management*.

Duncan Napier, "Security of Virtual Private Networks," *Enterprise Operations Management*, 26(4), August 2002.

Ed Skoudis, "Hacker Tools and Techniques," in *Information Security Management Handbook*, 4th ed., Vol. 2, Harold F. Tipton and Micki Krause (eds.), Boca Raton, FL: Auerbach Publications, 2001.

Bill Stackpole, "Centralized Authentication Services (RADIUS, TACACS, and DIAMETER)," in *Information Security Management Handbook*, 4th ed., Vol. 2, Harold F. Tipton and Micki Krause (eds.), Boca Raton, FL: Auerbach Publications, 2001.

Chapter 9
Business Continuity Planning (BCP)

The Business Continuity Planning (BCP) Domain addresses the capability to process critical business systems in the event of disruption to normal business data processing operations. The formulation of the BCP involves the preparation, testing, and maintenance of specific actions to protect critical business processes from the effect of extended data processing service outages.

The CISSP should have an understanding of the preparation of specific actions required to preserve continuity of critical data processing activities in the event of a major disruption to normal data processing operations. This knowledge should be from the perspective of creating, documenting, implementing, testing, and updating a business continuity plan.

Organizations write several types of plans, such as the Contingency Plan, Business Continuity Plan (BCP), Business Resumption Plan (BRP), or Disaster Recovery Plan (DRP), to ensure the availability of critical information system resources in the event of an expected network interruption or a disaster. Because the procedures for developing any of these types of plans are essentially the same, throughout this chapter we have used the term "BCP" to refer to any of these plans.

This chapter begins by defining some of the key terms of Business Continuity Planning. The next topic describes the traditional phases of designing and developing a BCP, including specific details for each phase. The final section provides information on the BPC testing and maintenance steps.

Introduction

For the past several years, commonly accepted definitions for continuity planning and the related planning documents have not been available. This lack of clear definitions can sometimes lead to confusion regarding the actual scope and purpose of the various types of plans. In this introduction section, several other types of plans are identified and described in

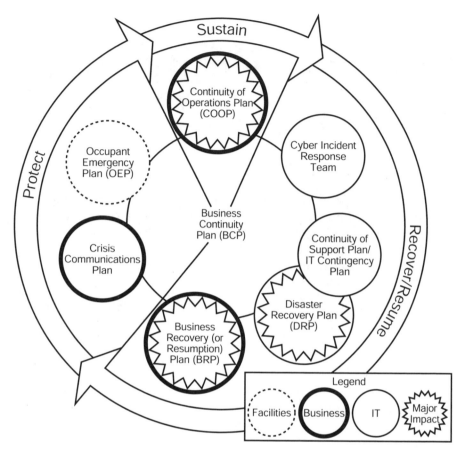

Exhibit 1. NIST SP800-34 Interrelationship of Emergency Action Plans

attempt to help provide a common understanding of the many types of recovery plans.

Exhibit 1 is from the U.S. National Institute of Standards and Technology (NIST) Special Publication 800-34 and provides one example of how the various types of plans revolve around the BCP.

Business Continuity Plan (BCP). A document describing how an organization responds to an event to ensure critical business functions continue without unacceptable delay or change.

Business Continuity Planning. Business continuity is the ability to maintain the constant availability of critical systems, applications, and information across the enterprise. Business continuity planning will help organizations:

- Identify the impacts of potential data processing operational disruptions and data loss.
- Formulate and implement viable recovery plans to ensure the availability of data processing support for critical applications, data, and services.
- Develop, implement, and administer a comprehensive BCP training, testing, and maintenance program.

Business Impact Analysis. The process of analyzing all business functions within the organization to determine the impact a data processing outage will have. The impact should be measured in terms of accumulated financial loss by periods of time to determine how long each business function can tolerate an absence of data processing support.

Business Resumption Planning. Business Resumption Planning develops procedures to initiate the recovery of business operations immediately following an outage or disaster. It can also outline the procedures for returning critical business functions to the normal processing site following the interruption.

Contingency Plan. The IT contingency plan is a document providing the procedures for recovering a major application or local information system network in the event of an outage or disaster.

Continuity of Operations Plan (COOP). A COOP is a document describing the procedures and capabilities to sustain an organization's essential, strategic functions at an alternate site for up to 30 days.

Crisis Communication Plan. A document that outlines the procedures for disseminating status reports to personnel and the public in the event of an outage or disaster.

Critical System. The hardware and software necessary to ensure the viability of a business unit or organization during an interruption in normal data processing support.

Critical Business Functions. In the event of an outage, it is the business and support functions that must be restored to ensure that the organization's assets are protected, the organizational goals are met, and the organization is in compliance with government or industry regulations.

Cyber Incident Response Plan. This document provides the strategies to detect, respond to, and limit consequences of malicious cyber incidents. The focus is on information security responses to incidents affecting systems and/or networks.

Disaster Recovery Plan. A documented plan that provides detailed procedures to facilitate recovery of capabilities at an alternate site. It is usually limited to major disruptions with long-term effects.

Disaster Recovery Planning. Disaster recovery refers to the immediate and temporary restoration of critical computing and network operations after a natural or man-made disaster within defined timeframes. An organization documents how it will respond to a disaster and resume the critical business functions within a predetermined period of time; minimize the amount of loss; and repair (or replace) the primary facility to resume data processing support.

Infrastructure. The infrastructure refers to the basic installations and facilities on which the continuance and growth of a community or an organization are reliant, such as power plants and transportation systems.

Network Contingency Planning. Network contingency planning develops the procedures to initiate in case of an unexpected network interruption. It enables an organization to respond effectively to an interruption and minimize the business impact.

Occupant Emergency Plan (OEP). The OEP is a document providing coordinated procedures for minimizing loss of life or injury and protecting property damage in response to a physical threat. It does not necessarily deal with business systems or IT system functionality, but rather focuses on personnel and property at a specific facility.

Defining a Disaster

A disaster is any sudden, unplanned calamitous event that brings about great damage or loss. In the business environment, it is any event creating an inability for the organization to support critical business functions for some predetermined period of time. The key element in determining if an event is a disaster is based on the time period that the organization is without its critical business functions. For example, an electronic retail store may define an eight-hour outage of their Web site as a disaster, while a traditional retail store would define an eight-hour Web site outage as an inconvenience. Thus, every organization will define a disaster based on an individualized definition of their specific critical business functions.

Organizations must look at disasters in a realistic fashion. Initially, the large variety of potential disasters can seem overwhelming. Although most organizations will not experience a disaster that will completely disable the facility and network processing, it is wise to be prepared, just in case. It may be helpful to look at disasters in terms of an outage of any kind, for example, loss of information, loss of access, loss of facility, or loss of personnel. A preliminary step is to review the likelihood of a disaster

Exhibit 2. Causes of Disasters

Natural	Earthquakes, floods, storms (i.e., thunder, hail, lightning, electrical, snow, winter ice), tornadoes, hurricanes, volcanic eruptions, natural fires
System/technical	Hardware/software outages, programming/system errors
Supply systems	Communication outages, power distribution (i.e., blackouts), burst pipes
Man-made	Bombings, explosions, disgruntled employees, fires, purposeful destruction, aircraft crashes, hazardous/toxic spills, chemical contamination, malicious code
Political events	Terrorist attacks, espionage, riots or civil disturbances, strikes

occurring that will produce total loss. This determination can be used to justify the expense of preparing a BCP. Organizations perform risk assessments to determine this type of information. Exhibit 2 provides examples of possible disasters.

A disaster can be characterized as an (1) unplanned service interruption, (2) extended service interruption, (3) interruption that cannot be handled through the typical problem management procedures, and (4) event that causes great or severe damage or loss. Defining a disaster also depends on how the organization identifies its critical information processing systems. In addition, once the organization has identified its critical systems, it must determine how long these critical information processing systems can be unavailable before declaring a disaster.

9.1 Information Protection Requirements

BCP Objectives

Regardless of what an organization defines as a disaster or a critical business function, the reason why a BCP is needed is to meet the organization's information system security goals. The A-I-C Triad reminds us to assure the *availability* of information and system resources to support business functions, provide *integrity* for data and processes, and protect the *confidentiality* of sensitive information.

IT systems are susceptible to many types of outages, from those with minimal consequences (e.g., power outages) to those with critical consequences (e.g., total destruction from a fire). While vulnerabilities can be minimized or eliminated through management, operational, or /technical countermeasures as part of the risk management effort, not all risks can be eliminated. For example, the organization may not have control over its

667

resources, such as controlling the power or other support services. Remember that continuity planning is just one part of an overall system security plan that can provide availability of the organization's information in the event that an outage occurs.

Other objectives for the BCP include:

- Provide an immediate, accurate, and measured response to emergency situations.
- Facilitate the recovery of business operations to reduce the overall impact of an event, while at the same time resume the critical business function within a predetermined period of time.
- Minimize the amount of loss.
- Provide procedures and a listing of resources to assist in the recovery process of critical data processing support for business functions and IT applications.
- Document the procedures in clear terms so that knowledgeable persons can execute them.
- Identify vendors that may be needed in the recovery process and put agreements in place with those vendors.
- Avoid the confusion experienced during a crisis by documenting and testing plan procedures and training personnel in their use.
- Document storage, safeguarding, and retrieval procedures for critical records and information, documents, and supplies.
- Provide the necessary direction and procedures to serve as guidance during an outage to ensure the timely resumption of critical services.
- Describe the actions, resources, and materials to restore critical operations at an alternate site in the event that the primary site has suffered a prolonged outage.
- Repair or replace the damaged facilities as soon as possible.

Another critical objective of a BCP is to fulfill the legal and regulatory reasons for having the plans. This includes following the required auditing standards and specific industry compliance requirements and fulfilling standards of due care.

9.2 Information Protection Environment

The environment for BCPs includes all aspects of an organization, such as personnel, facilities, infrastructure, support systems (air conditioning, heating), and information systems. Traditionally, plans focused on the recovery of critical computer systems running at data centers. Today, plans must also focus on the critical computer systems operating in a distributed environment involving items such as personal computers, LANs, and telecommunications equipment. Essentially, plans should address every critical business function of an enterprise.

The history of continuity and recovery plans can be charted as:

- 1970s: Focused on the data center recovery where processing occurred. Manual operations were predominant and mainframes performed high-level data processing.
- 1980s: Began utilizing alternative mainframe processing sites.
- 1990s: Saw widespread implementation of distributed data processing and network connections. End users processed data directly at workstations and data was sent to the data center electronically. Planning was expanded to include recovery of network systems.
- 2000+: Comprehensive enterprisewide approach to contingency planning:
  - Continuity of critical business functions
  - Increasing dependence on Internet and World Wide Web capabilities
  - Outage timeframes decreasing due to redundancy of operations and recovery options
  - Addresses every critical data processing function at an enterprisewide level
  - Decreasing maximum acceptable outage timeframes

9.3 Security Technology and Tools

Creating the BCP

The BCP provides a detailed description of actions to be taken in response to an unacceptable interruption in the use of a facility and/or availability of the data processing systems supporting the critical business functions. It is a comprehensive document that describes the actions that must be taken to reestablish the critical business operations within an acceptable timeframe. The plan should also document how to minimize the disruption of operations and ensure an orderly recovery after an outage.

Preparing a full-scale BCP can take a long time. For some people, it may seem to be a lot of time and money spent for something that may never produce any direct payback. Thus, it is sometimes compared to home insurance — hopefully, you will never need it but, if you do, it is priceless.

Although there are distinct phases that have traditionally been identified for developing a BCP, it is important to understand that continuity planning is not a single project with a specified ending (i.e., the written plan). Once you have developed the plan, the process does not end; rather, it is a continuous process that includes testing, maintaining, and updating the plan as needed. Also, the plan must be designed to be sufficiently flexible to allow for change as the organization's critical business processes evolve.

The traditional phases involved in preparing a BCP include:

I. *Project Management and Initiation:* establishes a project team and a supporting project management approach to develop the plan.
II. *Business Impact Analysis (BIA):* identifies time-critical aspects of the critical business processes, and determines their maximum tolerable downtime.
III. *Recovery Strategies:* identifies and selects the appropriate recovery alternatives that meet the recovery time requirements outlined in the BIA.
IV. *Plan Design and Development:* documents the results of the BIA findings and recovery strategies in a written plan.
V. *Testing, Maintenance, Awareness, and Training:* establishes the processes for testing the recovery strategies, maintaining the BCP, and ensuring that those involved are aware of and trained in the recovery strategies.

Although there are new paradigms for developing the BCP that focus on the client/server and enterprise environments, the traditional phases remain as essential elements for developing the plan. Therefore, the CISSP should be familiar with these basic phases. It is expected that each organization will develop its own methodology to create a BCP that matches its specific needs. For example, government agencies must follow specific regulatory guidelines, while private-sector organizations may follow industry-specific standards.

Phase I: Project Management and Initiation

The Project Management and Initiation phase involves the following items:

- Establish the need for a BCP. This can include performing a focused risk analysis to identify potential outages to critical systems.
- Obtain management support.
- Identify strategic internal and external resources to ensure that the BCP matches overall business and technology plans.
- Establish members of the BCP team, including functional (i.e., business function representatives) and technical specialists (i.e., system experts).
- Establish the project management work plan, including the project scope, identification of objectives, determination of methods for organizing and managing the BCP, identification of related tasks and responsibilities, and scheduling of task completion dates.

- Determine the need for automated data collection tools, including installation of the software and, if necessary, plans to provide training on how to use the software.
- Prepare and present an initial report to management on how the BCP will meet its objectives.
- Establish members of the BCP team, both technical and functional representatives.
- Develop formal meeting schedules.
- Prepare and present status reports.

A project is defined as a series of tasks performed in a certain sequence to achieve a goal or objective. The management of a project involves planning, organizing, and managing the project's tasks and resources to accomplish the goal, usually with time and/or cost restrictions. Unfortunately, the project management role is often overlooked when developing plans. However, as with any project, a successfully designed and developed BCP is based on applying proven project management techniques and methods.

An important element of the beginning phase is to ensure the support of senior-level management. In some organizations, it may be necessary for the security or audit team to educate management on why the BCP is important. Of particular importance to executives may be the legal liability of NOT having a BCP. For example, in recent legal actions, executives have been held legally responsible for not taking appropriate care in safeguarding information. In the United States, some of the regulatory reasons include the Banking Regulation Act, the Privacy and Security Act, and the Foreign Corrupt Practices Act. In addition, executives could face civil suits from stockholders and clients because they did not take the necessary precautions to protect the information system resources. All of these factors should help convince management to support the BCP development, test, and maintenance activities.

Once the goals and objectives of the BCP have been defined, the next step is to identify who will be responsible for developing and maintaining the plan. The key player is the *business continuity planner/coordinator.* This individual must ensure that all elements of the plan are addressed and an appropriate level of planning, preparation, and training has been accomplished for everyone involved in the BCP process.

The business continuity coordinator serves as the leader for the development team. Because this person will be responsible for the successful development of the BCP, it is important that care is taken when assigning this role.

671

The job requirements for a business continuity coordinator include:

- To serve as the liaison between the planning development team and management
- Have direct access and authority to interact with all employees necessary to complete the planning
- Possess a thorough knowledge of the business to understand how an outage can affect the organization
- Be familiar with the entire organization and in a position within the organization to balance the overall needs of the organization with the needs of individual business units that would be affected
- Have easy access to executive management
- Understand the charter, mission statement, and executive viewpoint
- Have the credibility and ability to influence senior management when decisions need to be made

Once the coordinator role has been established, the next step is to develop the BCP design and development team. Exhibit 3 lists the people who should be involved in the process and the roles they would fulfill as members of the BCP development team.

If possible, the preparation of the BCP should involve the same people who would be responsible for executing the plan. By doing so, it is possible for the key individuals to recognize errors and better plan for most eventualities. Because they understand the plan, the key players would be able to extrapolate the correct course of action based on the goals of the plan. Note that the plan should also be written with enough detail so that it can be executed by anyone with the appropriate expertise.

Once the business continuity coordinator has established the plan development team, the next step is to delineate the phases to begin managing the project. Establish BCP project characteristics such as goals/objectives, tasks, resources (personnel, financial), time schedules, budget estimates, and critical success factors. Financial resources include costs such as those associated with project initiation, planning team time, consulting fees, additional equipment, awareness and training programs, buying and implementing automated tools, disaster mitigation items, insurance, and plan maintenance. The BCP phases are similar to traditional project plan phases such as problem definition, feasibility study, systems description, implementation, installation, and evaluation. Once the project plan is established and approved by management, the next phase begins.

Phase II: Business Impact Analysis (BIA)

Keep in mind that business continuity planning is a business issue, not a technical one. Although each business unit of an organization partici-

Exhibit 3. BCP Roles

Team Members	Roles
Senior management	Demonstrate commitment and support to the program. Participation from senior management is critical because it establishes the authority level necessary to obtain resources and cooperation.
BCP planner/ coordinator	The business continuity coordinator, in a joint effort with the recovery team leaders, must ensure that all elements of the plan are thoroughly addressed and that an appropriate level of planning, preparation, and training has been accomplished for specific business functions. In most cases, this person serves as the project manager, with the responsibility for budget and administrative duties.
Recovery teams (leaders and team members)	Recovery teams are a structured group of individuals ready to take control of the recovery operations if a disaster should occur. The recovery teams are required to: • Respond to the disaster and determine the need to activate the BCP/DRP. • Recover critical data processing functions and applications at the designated alternate site(s). • Resume non-critical data processing functions and applications at the designated alternate site(s). • Restore the primary site. • Return to the primary site.
Business unit representatives	Functional representatives from business units have the knowledge of the business operation and any related systems. Thus, they are key to identifying critical business functions. Representatives define how each business unit operates, define what operations are critical, assist in the development of recovery strategies, and ensure the recovery plan identifies those critical business units that need to be recovered within the proper priority and respective recovery time.
Crisis management team	The crisis management team has the responsibility to provide executive-level decisions in the period following a disaster and the authority to declare a disaster and mobilize teams to recover at an alternate site. This decision will be made after input from the damage assessment process.
User community	Users need to receive awareness and training on their role in the event of a loss of services.
Systems and network experts	Individuals who can provide guidance on operating system environments and the interconnection requirements are essential when assessing critical system recovery options.
Information security department	This department provides guidance and security expertise when analyzing recovery options.
Legal representatives	A legal expert is needed to provide guidance on issues related to potential organization liabilities and make sure such issues are addressed in the BCP.

pates to varying degrees during the development, testing, and maintenance of a BCP, it is during the *business impact analysis* (BIA) process that the first widespread interaction between business areas and security managers occurs.

During the creation of the BCP, an important consideration is the potential impact of an outage to the business operation. It is necessary to understand the underlying risks that could cause an outage, as these are the foundations upon which contingency plans that can prevent an incident from becoming a disaster should be built. The BIA element of the BCP process sets the stage for shaping a business-oriented judgment concerning the appropriation of resources for planning efforts.

Business Impact Analysis (BIA)

The BIA is a management-level analysis that identifies the impact should a potential data processing outage occur. Impact is measured by the maximum allowable time the data processing services can be interrupted before causing irreparable harm to the business operations and how well the business can recover from the operational and financial impact of the interruption.

The goal of performing a BIA is to obtain a formal agreement with executive-level management as to the Maximum Tolerable Downtime (MTD) for each time-critical business support resource. MTD is also referred to as Maximum Allowable Outage (MAO). The formalized MTDs must then be communicated to business units, their support services organizations (i.e., IT/network management, facilities, etc.), and the BCP team so that realistic, cost-effective, recovery alternatives can be acquired and/or developed. When executive management makes a formalized decision to accept the MTD for each critical system, the BIA is completed.

The BIA must quantify, to the extent possible, the loss impact from a business interruption (number of days) in terms of a financial cost standpoint. A BIA does not consider what types of incidents cause a disruption to business operations; it is concerned only with identifying consequences in terms of financial loss, additional expense, and embarrassment due to the expected duration of the interruption.

The purpose of the BIA is to:

- Provide written documentation to assist the organization's management in understanding the impact associated with possible outages.
- Identify an organization's business functions and associated systems, applications, and technology to determine how critical those functions are to the organization.
- Identify any concerns that staff or management may have regarding the ability to function in less than optimal modes.

- Prioritize critical systems.
- Analyze the impact of an outage, such as lost revenue, additional operating expenses, delay of income, and loss of competitive advantage and public confidence.
- Determine recovery windows for each business function, such as determining how long the organization may be able to perform critical functions manually or through some other alternative methods.

The steps involved in conducting a BIA include:

1. Determine information gathering techniques, such as surveys or interviews.
2. Select interviewees.
3. Customize the questionnaire to gather economic and operational impact information.
4. Analyze information.
5. Determine time-critical business functions.
6. Determine maximum tolerable downtimes (MTDs).
7. Prioritize the restoration of critical business functions based on MTDs.
8. Document, prepare, and report recommendations.

Step 1: Determine Information Gathering Techniques. There are several methodologies available for gathering BIA information. These include electronic or paper-based surveys and questionnaires, one-on-one interviews, group interviews or workshops, technology-based media such as videoconference meetings, and automated software BIA tools.

Step 2: Select Interviewees. Management and staff individuals within each business unit are identified, as well as those in supporting service units, to determine critical business processes. Because it is usually not feasible to ask every employee, a sample must be selected based on who will provide the best information in the time period required.

For example, a technical systems expert would be asked to provide information on high-volume users and the various applications the organization is using. Financial representatives can provide the financial contributions of each group. This can help identify critical business functions based on a potential financial loss. Business unit representatives assist in identifying expenses associated with an interruption, such as cost of additional personnel.

Step 3: Customize Questionnaire. There is no "standard" set of BIA questions applicable to each organization. Although many questions may overlap across various organizations, it is important that the questions are based on the organization's customs and culture. They should be appropriate for the intended audience and relevant to the BCP. In addition, the questions should be based on identifying time-critical business processes and their support services.

There are two types of questions that will be included in the BIA: quantitative and qualitative. Quantitative questions ask the interviewee to describe the financial impacts (monetary terms) of a potential disaster or disruption. They deal with loss of sales, late payments, fines, wages, emergency purchases, etc. Qualitative questions ask the interviewee to estimate the emotional impacts from a loss, such as customer service capabilities or loss of customer confidence. Exhibit 4 outlines sample BIA question topics.

The questions should provide assistance in determining the impact of an interruption on business functions, the loss of revenue, any additional expenses, and intangible losses, such as losing customer confidence.

Step 4: Analyze Information. The information gathered during Step 3 must be organized, correlated, and analyzed. To begin, the results are document based on each business unit. The results can then be summarized into a BIA summary sheet containing the information collected during the interview process. These summary sheets should subsequently be sent to each business unit for review and, if necessary, a formal approval signature.

The following items should be included in the analysis of questionnaire data:

- Identify work functions that are most critical to the success of the business and identify the information systems that support those functions. Determine what economic and operational impact these functions would have on the business if it were not able to operate.
- Use the qualitative and quantitative assessment tools to help identify the impact on the business if data processing support is interrupted.
- Identify the business function interdependencies, and likewise identify the information system interdependencies of the critical systems.
- Validate the findings by verifying with those knowledgeable in each business unit.

Step 5: Determine Time-Critical Business Functions. Based on the analysis of the collected data, the time-critical business functions are identified. These are the work processes requiring recovery within an MTD. This will

Exhibit 4. Sample BIA Question Topics

Item	Description
Business function	• Name of the business function • Size • Hours of operation • Number of employees • Number of customers • Identify most critical timeframes • Heaviest volumes and legal obligations • Interdependencies with other business units that either receive or give the function support
Date of interview	Notates the day the questions were answered
Contact name	Provides information on who answered the questions and who can be called for follow-up questions or comments
Business process	Briefly describes the overall business function and critical business processes, applications, networks, etc.
Financial impacts	Estimates of revenue loss, including additional expenses that would occur as a result of the outage (i.e., rental equipment, temporary help, etc.)
Operational impacts	Loss due to business interruptions (i.e., loss of customer service capabilities or loss of confidence)
Legal obligations	Qualitative analysis: at what time would the business unit be in violation of legal commitments?
Damage to reputation	Qualitative analysis: at what time would there be a loss of confidence by clients; loss of clients to competitors?
Technological dependence	Identify reliance on each system, such as hardware, software, applications, data, networks, etc.
Interdependencies	Identify interdependence with other business processes, between departments, applications, and systems
Existing BCP measures	Identify any current documented plans
Alternate processing options	Identify other options for processing and associated costs
Customized questions	Narrative questions identifying the: • Financial impact • Operational impact • Legal obligation • Damage to reputation

help establish the order in which the applications and services are restored.

> *For example, an order department might list the following tasks and recovery time periods:*
>
> *Receive orders electronically via e-commerce Web site — Critical/Essential*
>
> *Receive orders by facsimile machine — Critical/Essential*
>
> *Receive orders by phone system — Critical/Essential*
>
> *Input orders into ordering system — Important*
>
> *Process orders — Important*
>
> *Issue and mail invoices — Important*

While identifying the critical business functions, remember to identify any additional business units or functions that might depend on the business process. The interdependencies among business units for the same resources may necessitate assigning a higher criticality to the operation.

A related aspect of identifying the critical business functions is also identifying the resources needed to support the critical processes. Resource requirement planning is the process of identifying the resources a business unit needs to reestablish its operational functions at an alternate location. While not an essential part of the BIA, resource requirement planning enables the BCP to identify the resources used in a typical working environment that would be needed in establishing an alternate site. These include the computer system, network, telecommunication links, facilities, electricity/HVAC, other equipment and supplies, and personnel.

Step 6: Determine Maximum Tolerable Downtimes (MTDs). The MTD is the period of time a business function or process can remain interrupted before its ability to recover becomes questionable. The business processes requiring shorter time periods are considered more time-critical. For example, in a travel agency, having access to the reservation system is most likely a very time-critical function (one- to four-hour outage acceptable), while having access to the payroll system may be considered important (72 hours outage acceptable) or normal (seven-day outage acceptable).

Step 7: Prioritize Critical Business Functions Based on MTDs. Once the key business processes are identified — those that would have a significant impact on the organization if not completed — they are ranked to determine those that are most critical. Typically, the shorter the period of recovery, the higher the business function will be on the priority list. In addition,

Exhibit 5. Critical Business Function Categories: Sample 1

Item	Required Recovery Time Following an Outage
Nonessential	30 days
Normal	7 days
Important	72 hours
Urgent	24 hours
Critical/Essential	1–4 hours

Exhibit 6. Critical Business Function Categories: Sample 2

Priority Rating	Required Recovery Time Following an Outage
Very High (1)	0–12 hours
High (2)	12–24 hours
Moderate (3)	24–72 hours
Low (4)	72+ hours

the shorter recovery period usually requires a more expensive recovery strategy. Exhibit 5 and Exhibit 6 are examples of how critical business functions can be categorized/prioritized.

Step 8: Document and Prepare Report for Recovery Recommendations. The results of the BIA are prepared for executive-level management review and approval BEFORE continuing to the next phase (Recovery Strategies). It is important that the information is clear, concise, and matches the organization's culture for preparing and submitting reports. In many organizations, a verbal presentation is made to highlight the key points, as well as distributing a more detailed final written report.

The next step is to identify effective recovery alternatives. Once the alternatives have been identified, plans can be developed and implemented to ensure that critical business functions and processes will not be unacceptably impacted in the event of an outage.

Phase III: Recovery Strategies

In this phase, the alternative business recovery strategies are identified. Recovery strategies consist of a set of predefined and management-approved actions implemented in response to an unacceptable business interruption. The focus is on recovery methods to meet the predetermined recovery timeframes established for the operation and functioning of the critical business functions. Developing the recovery strategies includes compiling the resource requirements and identifying the alternatives available during recovery. Resource requirements include personnel, systems, computer equipment, communication support, funding, etc. When all information is available, a strategy is then developed and documented for the recovery efforts and submitted to management for approval.

The type of strategy to implement will most likely be based on the results of the BIA process, monetary costs, insurance analysis, etc. A key point that should be stressed is that the recovery time for mission-critical business functions and/or applications identified in the BIA is the driving force to determine what type of technical recovery is to be used.

The steps involved in developing recovery strategies include:

1. Document all costs with each alternative.
2. Obtain costs for any outside services, such as developing a Request for Proposal (RFP) from outside vendors. The RFP should include the recovery objectives and requirements, costs, request for references, the technical approach for the objectives, payment terms, and the deadline response date.
3. Develop written agreements, including definitions, terms, responsibilities, recovery requirements, costs, and testing options.
4. Evaluate risk reduction and resumption strategies based on a full loss of the facility.
5. Identify risk reduction measures and revise resumption priorities and timeframes.
6. Document recovery strategies and present them to management for comments and approval.

When determining recovery strategies, consider the following:

- Business recovery
- Facility and supply recovery
- User recovery
- Technical recovery
- Data recovery

Business Recovery Strategies

Business recovery strategies focus on critical resources and the MTD for each business function. Remember that the MTD is determined during the BIA analysis.

The business unit priorities are taken directly from the BIA. The length of the recovery window for each business unit dictates the priority for recovery. Exhibit 7 provides an example of business units that could be prioritized based on Exhibit 6 categories.

Exhibit 7. Sample of Business Unit Priorities

Business Unit	Recovery Window (hrs)	IT Platforms	Priority
IT Security	2	Mainframe, LAN, WAN	1
Facilities	2	LAN, WAN	1
Legal	36	LAN, WAN	3
Administrative	18	LAN, WAN	2
Accounting	48	LAN, WAN	3
Human Resources	48	LAN, WAN	3

The strategies involved in business recovery consist of identifying the following:

- Critical business units and their associated business functions.
- Critical IT system requirements for each business function, such as hardware, software (i.e., operating system and application), and telecommunication needs.
- Procedures for connectivity to IT infrastructures (e.g., mainframe, mini, LAN, WAN).
- Critical equipment and supply requirements for each business function (to include the number of workstations, servers, peripheral equipment, and telephone lines).
- Essential office space requirements of each business unit. Each business unit identifies the minimal amount of space needed and the number of employees needing the space.
- Key personnel for each business unit. From each business function, the number of staff members required based on specific timeframes. For example, the first day at the recovery sites requires five staff members to complete setup and establish critical operations.
- Redirection of postal service mail, voice telecommunications, and data networks to the recovery site.
- Business unit interdependencies with other units.
- Off-site storage (procedures, media, documents).
- Vendor services.

Facility and Supply Recovery Strategies

Facility recovery involves identifying recovery procedures for the alternate facility, including space, security, fire protection, infrastructure, utility, supply, and environmental requirements. This includes the following:

- Determine minimum space for recovery of critical business units such as work areas and conference rooms.
- Determine space needs for less critical resources.

- Determine security needs at recovery sites. Examples include guard station or gate, security patrols, control over physical access to facility, intrusion alarms, restricted access floors, windows connected to security system, limited number of entry doors, secure loading dock, mantrap area at entrance, closed-circuit television (CCTV), detectors connected to security entrance, and emergency lights. More information on physical security requirements is provided in the Physical Security chapter (Chapter 7).
- Determine fire protection needs. For example, fire-suppression systems, smoke and fire detection, fireproof vaults, and fire extinguishers may be needed.
- Determine critical furnishings and office equipment.
- Determine infrastructure requirements, such as construction needs, underground telephone lines, and underground electrical lines.
- Determine utility and environmental needs. This includes heat, ventilation, and air conditioning (HVAC); power; water supplies; and whether emergency generators or uninterruptible power supplies (UPSs) are needed.
- Determine what office/business supplies are needed, such as forms, notepads, pens, etc.

User Recovery Strategies

The recovery strategies involved with personnel requirements focus on manual procedures, vital records, and restoration procedures. This involves identifying processes performed using manual procedures during a system outage. A critical component is establishing methods to implement the process *and* maintain the records so that information can be easily and accurately updated to the electronic format when service is restored. Items to consider include:

- Could critical processes be accomplished manually? For example, instead of processing and printing checks via the network, could the process be performed manually?
- If manual processes can be implemented, how will the business unit address lost data or transactions? What type of record or paper trail will be established?
- What are the vital record storage requirements? This includes retrieval of off-site storage materials, such as manuals and documentation, in-house policies and procedures, forms, media, etc.
- What are the special needs for employees, such as transportation and any necessary logistics, such as housing, meals, and incidentals?
- Notification procedures.

The user group recovery plans should specify the following:

- Manual procedures

- Vital record storage (i.e., medical, personnel)
- Employee notification procedures
- Employee transportation arrangements
- Employee accommodations

Technical Recovery Strategies

Technical recovery strategies define alternate recovery strategies for the data center and network infrastructure components. This is especially important if the primary business location is unavailable and an alternate processing capability is needed.

Data Center Recovery. The data center recovery plan is designed to respond to a disaster that will affect the data center located at the primary facility. It documents the data center responsibilities, procedures, checklists, and any forms needed to manage and control the recovery of critical computer operations following a disaster. It does not address recovery strategies for networks or computers installed at other locations outside of the primary facility — that is, those that do not depend on the main data center capabilities for business operations.

The first step is to determine if and when the data center at the primary facility can be reoccupied after an incident. An initial damage assessment is conducted to determine the extent of damage to the facility and estimate the time needed to resume normal operations. After the preliminary damage estimate is completed, management is notified of the situation and the condition of the facility. If the time estimated to resume operations exceeds the maximum amount of allowable downtime for mission-critical business functions, then management should consider implementing the BCP recovery plan.

Network and Data Communication Recovery Planning. This involves the recovery of network systems that are separate from a main data center, such as local area networks (LANs) at individual business units or other locations. The first step is to determine the network support requirements, such as the hardware requirements. This includes computers and other LAN equipment (peripherals, cabling, etc.). Data communication requirements involve listing hardware requirements for connecting input and output devices to the recovery systems, such as channel extenders, switching equipment, routers, bridges, gateways, etc.

The next step is to identify what types of links exist to local company offices by identifying the locations and types of telephone and network services. In addition, wide area network services must be outlined.

Telecommunications Recovery. In this age of dependence on telecommunications, special care should be taken to ensure that communication capabilities are recoverable. A sample communication inventory checklist might contain the following items:

- Telephone systems:
  - Key telephone lines
  - Private branch exchange (PBX)
  - Voice-mail systems
  - Fax machines
  - Paging systems
  - Radio and cell phone
- LAN components:
  - Computer hardware
  - Cable distribution system
  - Power supplies
  - Modems
  - Switches, routers
  - Personal computers
  - Teleconferencing equipment
  - Test and measurement equipment
- Physical security systems:
  - Close-circuit television (CCTV)
  - Motion detectors
  - Lighting controls

There are four primary technical recovery strategies: subscription services, reciprocal or mutual aid agreements, multiple processing centers, and service bureaus.

Subscription Services. Subscription services provide an alternate facility or "site" for recovery. They are characterized as hot, warm, cold, mirror, and mobile sites.

A *hot site* is defined as a fully configured site with complete customer-required hardware and software provided by the service.

- Advantages include:
  - Subscription service is generally available in hours and is preferable because processing can be operational in a very short period of time.
  - The subscription service assures exclusive use of the facility and supports both short- and long-term outages.
  - The contract for the hot site includes annual test time to ensure that everything is compatible and can be made operational as expected.
  - Typically, a subscription service will have multiple sites available so you can go to an alternate site if your assigned site is not available.

- Disadvantages include:
  - It is the most expensive to maintain.
  - If there is a regional disaster and someone else uses the same subscription service, there is the possibility of contention for the hot site between one or more companies.
  - If an organization has special or unusual hardware, there are limited choices available to provide support.

A **warm site** is similar to a hot site, although the expensive equipment (i.e., mainframe) is not available on-site. The site is ready in hours after the needed equipment arrives.

- Advantages include:
  - The availability is usually assured for longer timeframes.
  - An organization can use various convenient locations.
  - The site is available for exclusive use by the organization.
  - Less expensive than a hot site.
  - Practical for less-popular hardware configurations.
- Disadvantages include:
  - Operational testing is not possible.
  - Required resources may not be immediately available.
  - More expensive than cold site or in-house recovery sites.

A **cold site** does not include any technical equipment or resources, except environmental support such as air conditioning, power, telecommunication links, raised floors, etc. Equipment and other resources must be installed in a cold site facility to support the critical business functions. Various support resources may also be necessary, depending on requirements for communication facilities, UPS systems, etc.

- Advantages include:
  - Available for longer periods of time.
  - Site can be in various locations.
  - Organizations have exclusive use.
  - Less expensive than other options.
  - Practical for less-popular hardware configurations.
- Disadvantages include:
  - Operational testing is not possible.
  - Required resources are not immediately available.
  - Costs are more expensive than in-house facilities.

A **mirror site** is a computer service facility equipped with utilities, communication lines, and appropriate hardware that is fully operational and processes each transaction along with the primary site. Typically, a high-speed network exists between the facilities to support the mirroring operations. This can also be referred to as full redundancy, where the resources and equipment used in the day-to-day operations are duplicated at an alternate site. This includes symmetrical mirroring. As data is written to storage platforms in the primary location, it is also written to identical storage platforms at the backup site.

- Advantages include:
  - There is no loss of data if a disaster occurs to the primary site.
  - Site is instantly available for processing.
- Disadvantages include:
  - It is expensive to maintain.

A *mobile site* is a computer-ready trailer that can be set up in a subscriber's parking lot and linked by a trailer sleeve to create a space to suit the subscriber's recovery needs.

- Advantages include:
  - Travel is minimized for employees who may be reluctant to leave their homes and families after a disaster.
  - Allows a decentralized organization to engage one vendor to service its entire organization.
- Disadvantages include:
  - Operational testing may not be possible.
  - Required resources are not immediately available.
  - Costs are more expensive than in-house facilities.

Reciprocal or Mutual Aid Agreements. Another technical facility recovery option is to establish reciprocal or mutual aid agreements. These types of agreements are arrangements between two (or more) companies to provide facilities to the other in the event of a disaster. Reciprocal agreements require the companies to have similar hardware and software computing environments.

- Advantages include:
  - It is free of charge or of low cost to both organizations.
  - It is good if there is an unusual hardware or software configuration shared by both companies.
- Disadvantages include:
  - Informal agreements are often not legally binding.
  - It is unlikely that there will be enough excess capacity to handle the processing requirements for both organizations.
  - Operational testing is usually not possible; however, without testing there is no guarantee of capability.
  - Required resources may not be immediately available.
  - Short-term outages are all that can be handled.
  - Mixed operations between the organizations can create security problems.
  - There is little or no technical, administrative, and logistical support.

Typically, reciprocal agreements are dismissed in practice because few information system facilities have the extra capacity needed to run both their own and another organization's needs for any extended period of time.

Multiple Processing Centers. These centers involve the capability to distribute the work requirements over two or more compatible in-house centers.

- Advantages include:
  - The organization has more control to ensure availability and compatibility of both centers.
  - Technical, administrative, and logistical support are available.
- Disadvantages include:
  - Need a formalized agreement to "share the disaster."
  - Critical workload could be a high percentage of the total processing and it cannot be guaranteed that the other in-house facility can accommodate the critical processing for both facilities within the predetermined recovery timeframe.
  - Maintenance of excess capacity can be expensive.
  - Can lead to configuration management problems, such as version control issues for operating system and applications.

Service Bureaus. Service bureaus offer data processing services to many organizations. Their normal processing load is close to their maximum capability; so if they accept a load of critical systems that is not part of their normal load, existing clients must share the disaster with the one that needs the service. Thus, it is necessary to obtain disaster-sharing agreements with other service bureau clients (not an easy sell, by the way).

- Advantages include:
  - Quick response and availability for those that are already clients.
  - Testing is possible.
- Disadvantages include:
  - Few, if any, service bureaus can offer this support, except for small organizations with limited requirements.
  - Costs are similar to maintaining a hot site.
  - Configuration management problems can occur for those not already a client of the service bureau.

Data Recovery Strategies

Because data processing capability is essential and critical to most users on a daily basis, data recovery strategies are critical to the recovery process. The objectives are to back up critical software and data, store the backups at an off-site location, and retrieve the backups quickly during a recovery operation. Included in backups are operating system software and utilities, application software, production data, and databases with their associated transaction logs or journal files. Note that off-site storage of backup tapes is the most common type of data recovery strategy.

Backup and off-site storage is the process of backing up data and applications, and securing the backup media. The initial questions to answer include:

- How often should a backup be performed?
- How fully backed up should the backups be?

The answers will depend on several factors, such as the total amount of data, the volatility of the data, the time available to make backups (sometimes called the backup window), and the length of time needed to recover files (sometimes called the data horizon). The types of backups include:

- *Full complete backup.* A full backup includes an entire drive — both the system and data files. Although this is the preferred backup type, it requires space to store the backed up files. An advantage is that restoring from a full backup requires only the full backup file. When possible, doing a complete, full backup every day is easiest and gives the most data redundancy. The full complete would be the type to use to be able to start up processing at an alternate site unless electronic vaulting or mirroring is used.
- *Incremental backup.* An incremental backup includes all the files that have changed since the previous backup. Often, the term "incremental" is used to describe differential; however, a differential backup will have everything that has changed since the previous *complete* backup, whereas an incremental backup will only have files that have changed since the previous *incremental* backup. Following a full backup, incremental and differential backups would be exactly the same; subsequent backups would probably contain different files. A disadvantage is that incremental backups require additional storage media because the last full or incremental backup and any additional incremental backups will be required to restore data (remember that only the files changed since the last backup will be copied). Also, restoring from incremental backups can take time, require a series of incremental backups, and may also require a good understanding of backups.
- *Differential backup.* A differential backup includes only those files changed since the previous full backup; thus, any changed file appears only on one differential backup. A disadvantage is that differential backups do not mark files as having been backed up. Because differential backups store the files that have been created or changed since the previous full or incremental backup, in order to restore data, both the previous full *and* the previous differential backup are needed.

- *Continuous backup.* Some backup applications perform continuous (or progressive) backups that keep a database of the files that exist on each system and their locations on the backup media. After an initial full backup, these systems perform incremental backups on a regular basis. If it is necessary to restore the data, the applications provide the ability to perform a full, or point-in-time, restore by building a list of files to be restored from the database and restoring the files from the backup media. These types of backups minimize the server time and bandwidth required for a comprehensive backup regime and the media or storage space needed.

Once a backup schedule is completed, the next step is to develop a storage retention and location plan. This can include a complete records retention worksheet for records produced or used by each business unit by indicating the following information: respective class (e.g., accounting, personnel records), media type, volume, and special requirements.

Where backup media is stored has a significant impact on the time and effort involved in restoring data. For minimal outages or user errors, having backups tapes located locally, such as in a library, makes it easy to restore the data quickly. However, having backup tapes on-site can be detrimental if a disaster (e.g., fire) occurs. Thus, most organizations will store a separate set of backups off-site. Off-site storage requirements include:

- Facilities must have the following features:
  - Security controls (access control systems connected to local police station)
  - Environmental controls (appropriate humidity and temperature levels)
  - Fire and water protection (fire-resistant construction, fire detection, alarm, and suppression connections to local fire department)
  - Location sufficiently distant from the organization's primary facility as not to be affected by the same disaster that impacts the organization's primary operation
- Transportation issues include:
  - Secure transportation of the backup media to alternate recovery sites
  - Delivery vehicles that are secure (e.g., bonded) and provide the appropriate environment to protect your media/records
  - Delivery personnel aware of the appropriate security procedures and the appropriate way to handle magnetic media and vital records
  - Procedures to allow access to the organization's media/records 24/7 in case of an emergency
- Administrative and personnel requirements include:

- Knowledgeable personnel with appropriate security clearances, background checks, etc.
- Testing of off-site procedures to ensure that they are up-to-date and adequate
- Procedures to store, segregate, retrieve, and dispose of media/records that meet all expectations

Electronic vaulting is the electronic bulk transfer of backup data to an alternate site. It includes three types:

- *Online tape vaulting:* the electronic transmission of data to a storage or recovery location. The primary data processing center executes the tape backups; but instead of writing to a local tape drive, a channel is established over telecommunication links to a tape drive off-site.
- *Remote journaling:* the transmission of journal/transaction log data to an off-site location. Both an on-site and off-site journal are created. This allows the off-site location to recover the files to the point of interruption, which reduces the time required to reconstruct the files and limits the loss of data.
- *Database shadowing:* the system creates an update to the production database, journals it, and transfers it to an off-site computer. At the production site, the journal record is applied to a copy of the production database.

Standby services represent the operation of critical operating systems and applications at an alternate site when called upon.

Software escrow is when a vendor places a copy of critical source code with a trusted third party so that it can be obtained in the event that the vendor goes out of business.

Hardcopy Records. Hardcopy records and data tapes should be protected against fire and water damage. Records stored off-site should receive protection similar to those at the primary facility. For example, fire-resistant cabinets should be considered for the storage of hardcopy records that are mission-critical to the organization.

Recovery Management. An important consideration in the recovery strategy is providing an outline of how to handle the disaster. This is sometimes referred to as Crisis Management. Essentially, it is the overall coordination of the organization's response to a crisis. This goal is to deal with the issues in an effective and timely manner and avoid or minimize damage to the organization's profitability, reputation, and ability to operate. Because the flow of accurate information is a key ingredient to effective crisis management, the information and information delivery systems can become the most valuable components of the organization's infrastructure. Therefore, the effective management of information can serve as the first line of defense against a crisis and can also be the most effective mechanism in the process of restoring both the business functions and public confidence.

Keep in mind that the selection of the recovery strategy depends on the extent to which the functions of the organization depend on its computer systems. For example, if the organization will experience significant impacts, then it should plan for an immediate recovery at a hot site. If, on the other hand, the computer system operations can be delayed for a week or two without causing a significant impact, it might elect a cold site strategy.

Phase IV: Plan Development and Implementation

In this phase, the BCP team prepares and *documents* a detailed plan for recovery of critical business functions. The recovery strategies must be documented according to the organization's documentation format. The end products of this phase include business and service recovery plans, plan maintenance programs, employee awareness and training programs, test method descriptions, and restoration plans.

The steps involved in this phase include:

1. Determine management concerns and priorities.
2. Determine planning scope such as geographical concerns, organizational issues, and the various recovery functions to be covered in the plan (critical business units, facilities, IT support, and additional security needs).
3. Establish outage assumptions.
4. Define prevention strategies for risk management, physical security, information security, insurance coverage, and how to mitigate the emergency.
5. Identify resumption strategies for mission-critical applications and systems at alternate sites.
6. Identify recovery strategies for non-mission-critical applications and systems at alternate sites and for relocating the emergency operations center/command center to the recovery site. An important element of the final plan development is preparing for where the plan implementation and recovery will be located. If the primary location is not available, an alternate site must be available from which recovery operations can occur. Essentially, the BCP must outline what type of command center is needed for managing outages that may affect the company's operations.
7. Develop service function recovery plans, including information processing, telecommunications, etc.
8. Develop business function recovery plans and procedures.

9. Develop facility recovery plans.
10. Identify the response procedures, including:
    - Evacuation and safety of personnel
    - Notification of disaster
    - Notifying alternate site(s)
    - Initial damage assessment
    - Securing home site
    - Activating teams
    - Activating emergency operations center/command center
    - Relocating to alternate site(s)
11. Gather data required for plan completion. This includes information about personnel, vendor services, equipment, software, forms, supplies, vital records, technical information, and office space requirements.
12. Review and outline how the organization will interface with external groups.
13. Review and outline how the organization will cope with other complications beyond the actual disaster.

Although there are several formats for documenting a BCP, Exhibit 8 provides a simple outline of the items that should be covered in the final documented BCP.

Additional factors that should be documented include how to respond to the disaster, resume critical business function, and deal with external groups. The following provides some sample procedures that may be included in the documented plan.

- Responding to the disaster:
    - Determine procedures for how to contact recovery team members to participate in the initial damage assessment.
    - Determine the extent of damage to the primary site facility, including the building structure, damage to utilities, and building access locations, and whether the building can be secured. If the outage time from the initial damage assessment is greater than the MTD for any of the critical business operations, then the recommendation must be made to management to invoke the BCP.
    - Calculate the time required to resume critical business operations. Because this should already be identified in the plan, it should just be a matter of verifying estimates noted in the plan.
    - Notify management of the results.
    - Declare a disaster and begin implementation of the continuity and recovery plans.
- Resume critical business functions:

Exhibit 8. Sample BCP Outline

Item	Description	Elements
General Introduction and Overview	Provides an introduction to the plan	Introduction; Mission Statement; Goal; Objectives; Brief Summary of BIA
Policy Statement	The top management statement that the organization has critical systems that must be run for the organization to survive, thereby requiring creation of a BCP/DRP	Policy statement signed by top management
Functional Areas	Defines the critical functional areas	Critical business functions
Priorities	Designates which critical systems have priority over others for implementation at the alternate site	List of critical systems by priority
Critical Resources	Outline of the critical resources required by each critical business unit	Critical Business Unit Functions; Critical Equipment and Software; Critical Forms and Supplies; Critical Office Space; Critical Vital Data; Critical Vendors
Non-Critical Resources	Outline of the non-critical resources required by each critical business unit	Non-Critical Business Unit Functions; Equipment and Software; Forms and Supplies; Office Space; Vital Resources; Vendors
Procedural Considerations	Important procedures for the organization's employees to follow during and after the disaster	When and where to report for work; how to communicate with other employees; etc.
Emergency and Evacuation Procedures	Includes the plans for what to do in the event of an emergency	Notification Procedures; Emergency Management Team/Crisis Response Team; Disaster Declaration Procedures; Mobilization Procedures; Damage Assessment Concepts
Recovery Teams	Written recovery procedures for each of the recovery teams	Emergency Operations Team; Crises Management Team; Administrative Team (i.e., insurance, transport, security, legal, public relations, etc.)

(continued)

Exhibit 8. Sample BCP Outline (Continued)

Item	Description	Elements
Recovery Processes	Outlines the recovery processes	Business Recovery; Facility Recovery; User Recovery; Technical Recovery; Data Recovery
Emergency Operations Center/Command Center	Command center for managing major incidents that may affect the company's operations	Identification of location and teams
Facility Considerations	Defines the characteristics of the primary and any off-site locations; protection requirements for the off-site storage facility should also be specified	Main building; remote facilities, including off-site storage and backup site(s)
Inventory Considerations	Outlines the current inventory for the network; includes the operations, technical, and support needs	Hardware, mainframe, tape, print, communications, applications, operating systems and subsystems, supplies and equipment, paper/forms
Equipment Considerations	Defines the equipment needs for recovery procedures	The main computer system (more important in a mainframe or centralized computing environment); the availability of microcomputers and networks; data and voice communication issues and any other critical equipment that has been identified in the vulnerability assessment
Communication Considerations	Defines the telecommunications needs the business functions have and will need	The organization must have information on the circuits in use, phone configurations and locations, modems and test equipment to support the communications network

Documentation Considerations	The organization must have documentation available in off-site storage to support it during the disaster	The available documents must include operations run materials, application documentation, technical documentation, and the BCP; documentation should be available in cases where information systems are not, and available in multiple sites where communication is not available
Data/Software Considerations	Identifying the data and software that is and will need to be available to work with	In addition to the primary application data files, supporting files, tables, and parameter files must be available; it is essential to have procedures to recover backup data from the off-site storage location
Transportation Considerations	There may be the need to move personnel from one location to another very quickly during the disaster	Suitable transportation arrangements should be made (e.g., how employees get access to a car, truck, or aircraft after a disaster must be included in the plan)
Supporting Equipment	Outlines the need for support services	Arrangement for adequate air conditioning, water, power, UPSs, safety and security equipment, and services

- Establish the command center to provide management control, administrative, logistic, and communications support.
- Contact the recovery site to confirm the availability of the space needs, security needs, fire protection, and any infrastructure requirements.
- Notify off-site storage to move tapes and materials to recovery site.
- Allocate the required office space and recovery resources to the recovery team.
- Verify equipment at site.
- Activate operating systems for mainframes, servers, and workstations.
- Configure voice communications systems.
- Install software backups and restore data.
- Test voice communications to other sites, as appropriate.
- Log on to equipment and test applications and connectivity.
- Notify users of schedule and alternate site location.
- Test the system and certify that it is ready for operation.
- Begin critical application processing.

Resume Non-Critical Business Functions. Follow similar procedures for critical business function recovery. Review procedures for crisis management, logistics and supplies, and documentation.

Planning for Return to the Primary Site (Restoration Operations).

- Complete a detailed assessment of all damage at the primary site.
- Contact restoration service vendors to salvage equipment and water-soaked documents, as necessary.
- Initiate cleanup of the primary site.
- If necessary, dispose of damaged equipment and procure new equipment.
- Review insurance policies and document information, as needed.
- Coordinate activities to have repairs made to the damaged areas within the primary site, including:
  - Facility structure: walls, floors, ceilings, etc.
  - Equipment
  - Support systems: HVAC, plumbing, etc.
- Reactivate fire protection and other alarm systems.
- Restore the primary site to normal operating conditions (planning is different from recovery plan — least critical work should be returned first from alternate site).
- Implement and test the network system.
- Certify the system is ready for operations.
- Initiate normal processing.

Interfacing with External Groups. An important aspect in dealing with a disaster includes reviewing how you will interface with external groups, such as customers, shareholders, civic officials, community, region, and state emergency services groups, utility providers, industry group coalitions, and the media. Some helpful hints for dealing with external groups include:

- Establish a unified organizational response to media.
- Have the public relations officer as the focal point for distributing information. This alleviates the problem of getting misleading information from various sources.
- Report your own bad news. It is better to report all news (whether good or bad) to the press and the public before someone demands an explanation after something has become fact. If it is not reported, it may appear that the organization is trying to cover up the event and this leads to mistrust.
- Determine in advance the appropriate approval and clearance processes for information that is to be conveyed to the public.
- Maintain a mailing list for larger audiences. This allows for quick information transfer to customers, suppliers, and shareholders regarding the disaster and how it is being handled. If appropriate, prepare background releases on the company for the media to avoid having to create these during the disaster.
- Identify emergency press conference sites in advance. This provides the public relations officer with the opportunity to hold press conferences at the organization's preferred location. It can also give the appearance that the situation is under control.
- Record events as the crisis evolves. This includes using photographs, video, etc., as a method of recording what happened and how things were handled. This type of information may be useful in the event of a civil or criminal trial, as well as in reviewing lessons learned for use in developing future plans.

In the event of a true disaster, additional factors may complicate the recovery procedures. Thus, it may be necessary to consider and make plans for how to deal with possible events. Because every organization will face different issues, it is difficult to have a cookie-cutter approach to all BCPs. Thus, the BCP coordinator/team should review how some of the following might affect the organization:

- Police coordination
- Responsibility to families
- Coordination with human resources
- Fraud opportunities
- Looting and vandalism

697

- Ensuring that the primary site is protected during disaster
- Safety and legal problems
- Coordination with legal departments
- Coordination with health and safety committee
- Expenses exceeding emergency manager authority

The final aspect of the plan development phase is to combine all the various steps into the organization's BCP. This plan should then be integrated into the organization's other emergency plans. Thus, in the event of a disaster, all information will be readily available.

Phase V: Testing, Maintenance, Awareness, and Training

Information for this phase is contained in the next section, Assurance, Trust, and Confidence Mechanisms.

9.4 Assurance, Trust, and Confidence Mechanisms

Testing and Maintenance

In this phase, plans for testing and maintaining the BCP are implemented, and awareness and training procedures are conducted.

Plan Testing

An appropriate testing strategy for the recovery plan is developed and implemented during this phase. Testing of the recovery plan ensures that the business continuity capability remains effective. There is no demonstrated capability until the plan is tested. Testing plans generally include the testing objectives, measurement criteria, test schedules, post-test reviews, and test reporting to management.

The goals of plan testing are to:

- Ensure the understanding and workability of documented recovery procedures.
- Acquaint test participants and recovery teams with their roles in the event of a disaster.
- Verify that recovery strategies are viable.
- Train team leaders and members in the procedures of executing the continuity plan.
- Identify flaws and oversights in plan procedures and strategies.
- Obtain information about recovery strategy implementation.
- Demonstrate that output performance of backup systems and networks are consistent with production systems and networks.
- Adapt and update existing plans to encompass new requirements resulting from business, systems, networks, or personnel changes.

- Test all components of the plan, including hardware, software, personnel, data and voice communications, procedures, supplies and forms, documentation, transportation, utilities, alternate site processing, etc.

Before conducting the test, document the test goals/objectives and the scenario. This includes outlining the purpose of the test, test objectives, type of test, test timing, scheduling, duration, test participants, assignments, constraints, assumptions, and test steps. The five main types of BCP testing strategies are Structured Walk-Through, Checklist, Simulation, Parallel, and Full Interruption.

Types of Tests.

- Structured walk-through:
    - Functional representatives meet to review the plan in detail.
    - Strategy involves a thorough look at each of the plan steps and the procedures that are invoked at that point in the plan.
    - This ensures that the actual planned activities are accurately described in the plan.
- Checklist test:
    - Distribute copies to each of the functional areas.
    - Each area reviews the plan and checks off the points that are listed to ensure that the plan addresses all concerns and activities.
- Simulation:
    - All operational and support functions meet to practice execution of the BCP based on a scenario played out to test the reaction of all functions to that situation.
    - Only those materials and information available in a real disaster are allowed to be used during the simulation.
    - Simulation continues up to the point of actual relocation to the alternate site and shipment of replacement equipment.
- Parallel test:
    - This is an operational test of the BCP.
    - Critical systems are placed into operation at the alternate site to verify correct operation.
    - The results can be compared with the real operational output and the differences noted.
- Full interruption test:
    - This is a full test of the BCP.
    - Normal operations are completely shut down and processing is conducted at the alternate site using the materials that are available at the off-site storage location and personnel assigned to the recovery teams. This test is not recommended for large or-

ganizations because of the danger of precipitating an actual disaster.

Plan Maintenance

As the organization and its businesses change, so must the plan. Maintaining the currency of continuity capabilities and the BCP document in accordance with the organization's strategic direction is of vital importance to a successful recovery.

Maintenance Techniques.

- Change management procedures need to be outlined to provide a method for regularly updating plan procedures.
- Resolve all problems/deficiencies found during testing.
- Auditors report findings after evaluating the effectiveness of the overall recovery plan.
- Build maintenance procedures into the organization operation. For example, include plan maintenance responsibility into job descriptions and personnel evaluations. Maintenance should also be built into annual audit/review procedures.
- Centralize responsibility for updates.
- Report updates regularly to team members and, if necessary, to senior management.

Plan Maintenance Functions.

- Receive and monitor input on needed revisions:
  - Keep a distribution list for copies of the plan, control circulation of copies, and distribute updates as necessary.
  - Maintain the revision history of the plan.
  - Ensure that the review and revisions are carried out on schedule.
  - Coordinate the review and revision cycle with testing and training schedules.
- Plan maintenance reviews:
  - At a minimum, review the BCP annually or whenever major changes occur within the organization or to the information system.
  - During the review, the entire plan should be reviewed with all members of the recovery teams. This type of information should be contained in the plan maintenance history form.
- Section reviews:
  - The sections to be reviewed and the review frequency depend on the practices and conditions of the business unit.
  - Frequent upgrades to the systems and software will require more frequent reviews of the plan.
- Plan maintenance distribution:

- Compile a distribution list of specific persons who will receive a copy of the plan and subsequent updates.
- Keep a record of plan maintenance history that identifies dates of tests, changes to the documentation, etc.
- Ensure that obsolete editions of the plan are collected and destroyed.

9.5   Information Protection and Management Services

One of the most important items that management can do is to support the design and development of the BCP. This includes providing adequate financial and personnel resources to develop a sound plan.

BCP Awareness and Training

Another key management task is to support an awareness and training program. All staff should be trained in the business recovery process. This is particularly important when the procedures are significantly different from those pertaining to normal operations.

The goals of BCP awareness and training are to design and develop a program to create corporate awareness and enhance the skills required to develop, implement, maintain, and execute the BCP. Keep in mind that many problems can be avoided if employees have been trained to be pro-active — to look for conditions that could result in an outage.

The overall objectives for BCP training should cover a range of outcomes, from simple awareness of the major provisions of the plan to the ability to carry out specific procedures. The BCP training plan should:

- Describe the recovery organization (teams and functions).
- Explain the flow of recovery events and activities following a disaster.
- State team members' responsibilities in recovery activities.
- Provide an opportunity for each recovery team to meet to develop in-depth knowledge of their responsibilities and procedures.
- Require teams to conduct drills using the actual checklists and procedures in their section of the recovery plan.
- If possible, include a plan for cross-training teams so those individuals are familiar with a variety of recovery roles and responsibilities.

Awareness Training

Awareness training should ensure that personnel know what to look for, how to detect potential safety and outage situations and conditions, and how to react when they encounter such conditions in order to prevent, if possible, an incident from becoming a disaster. Having a recovery plan is good — preventing an outage or disaster is even better. This training includes:

- Develop a good security and safety awareness program.
- Conduct exercises where employees identify potential safety hazards and other conditions that could lead to an emergency.
- Host awareness seminars and consider having an awareness day with seminars on the appropriate topics.
- Invite community service representatives (e.g., fire department, law enforcement agencies, and security companies) to speak to employees at awareness sessions.
- Provide employees with copies of emergency procedures such as fire, evacuation, or how to respond to a bomb threat.
- Include with the employee orientation program an awareness session that addresses safety, emergency, security, and other related procedures.
- Acquire safety videos and use them during awareness sessions.
- Post safety and security posters on bulletin boards throughout the organization.
- Write articles for internal/external publications that identify the priority of security awareness and to announce any new programs, procedures, safety and emergency equipment installations, etc.
- Participate in local/regional/national safety, emergency, and other programs.

Summary

Every organization can experience a serious incident that can prevent it from continuing normal business operations, and it can happen at any time. The type of outage might be from an external environmental condition such as flood or power outage, or from a serious computer malfunction or information security incident. To minimize the impact of an outage, it is important to have a plan that documents how the organization will continue to operate. This includes identifying the critical business functions and the resources needed to keep those business functions operating.

The plan procedures should include all the aspects that would need to be implemented in the event of an outage. This includes the response team's ability to react to the outage, contact the appropriate personnel and external service providers, and respond appropriately to get the critical business functions operating within a predetermined timeframe. Finally, the plan is an ongoing program that needs to be reviewed and tested to ensure that it meets the requirements of current business operations and information system components.

9.6 Common Body of Knowledge (CBK)

The current CBK for the Business Continuity Planning Domain is listed below to assist in determining topics for further review. Although this Study Guide is very detailed in many areas, it is not possible to thoroughly discuss every CBK topic in a single book; therefore, additional study of items may be advisable.

The professional should fully understand:

* Business Continuity Planning (plan development, plan implementation, resumption strategies, etc.)
* Business Impact Assessment
* Emergency Plans

Components

* Business Continuity Planning
* Project Scoping and Planning: Business Organization Analysis and Resource Requirements
* Business Impact Assessment: Emergency Assessment, Business Success Factors, Critical Business Functions, Establishment of Priorities
* Recovery Strategy: Business Unit Priorities; Crisis Management; Work Group Recovery; Alternatives such as Cold/Warm/Hot/Mobile Sites, Electronic Vaulting, and Selection Criteria; Processing Agreements such as Reciprocal/Mutual
* Recovery Plan Development
* Emergency Response: how to develop emergency response teams and procedures
* Personnel Notification: how to handle personnel notification and communications to management
* Backups and Off-Site Storage: how to determine what to back up (data, software, parameters, tables, formulas, documentation, etc.) and how often (cost of backups versus cost to recreate or process to bring up-to-date) and how to determine a proper storage facility for backups
* Software Escrow Arrangements
* External Communications
* Utilities: how to determine proper applications of UPSs
* Logistics and Supplies
* Fire and Water Protection
* Documentation

- Implementation
- Work Group Recovery
- Recovery Techniques
- How to develop a containment strategy
- How to determine provisions to stock and where to store them
- How to develop recovery processes for Facilities, Telecommunications, Software, Data
- How to develop a recovery strategy: Networks, Systems, Applications
- Training/Testing/Maintenance: how to develop a training strategy, how to test the plans and how often, and how to keep the plans up-to-date
- Disaster Recovery Planning
- Recovery Plan Development
- System Software, Application Software, and Data Reconstruction from Backups: movement of files from off-site storage, loading all software and installation of applicable updates, loading of data, parameter, and supporting files
- Crisis Management
- Restoration: Cleaning, Procurement, Data Recovery, Software Recovery
- Relocation to Primary Site

Examples

- Define Business Continuity Planning (BCP).
- Compare and contrast BCP and DRP.
- Define what disasters must be prepared for in a BCP.
- Define information security goals and their relationship to BCP and DRP.
- Describe how to promote security awareness for BCP.
- Compare and contrast possible organizational placement of the BCP planner.
- Define what is involved in BCP.
- Define who is involved in BCP.
- Define and describe the role of senior management in BCP.
- Define BCP organization guidelines.
- Define and describe legal and regulatory reasons for BCP.
- Describe methodology for identifying critical business units.
- Describe methodology for identifying critical support units.
- Identify the steps to be taken in performance of a criticality survey.
- Identify objectives, major activities, and end products of a vulnerability assessment.
- Define areas of end-user BCP.
- Describe how to determine what is backed up, how often, and where the backups are stored.

- Compare and contrast strategies for backup.
- Identify the advantages and disadvantages of mutual aid agreements.
- Compare and contrast the advantages and disadvantages of hot sites and cold sites.
- Compare and contrast the advantages and disadvantages of using service bureaus.
- Identify BCP events.
- Define and describe required steps to perform a Business Impact Analysis (BIA) to determine critical applications.
- Identify areas that must be considered when writing a BCP.
- Define roles for maintaining the BCP.
- Define the characteristics of an effective test of a BCP.
- Describe how to formulate a recovery strategy.

9.7 Sample Questions for the CISSP Exam

1. Business continuity primarily addresses:
   a. Availability
   b. Integrity
   c. Confidentiality
   d. Accountability
2. Preparing a full-scale BCP can:
   a. Be quickly achieved
   b. Take a long time
   c. Ensure a separation of responsibilities
   d. Not involve vendors
3. Which is NOT a traditional phase in preparing a BCP?
   a. Testing, Maintenance, Awareness, and Training
   b. Business Impact Analysis
   c. Project Management and Initiation
   d. Quantitative Risk Analysis
4. The BCP Project Management and Initiation Phase does NOT involve:
   a. Establishing members of the BCP team
   b. Determining the need for automated data collection tools
   c. Performing a Business Impact Analysis
   d. Preparing and presenting status reports
5. The purposes of a BIA include:
   a. Identifying additional countermeasures
   b. Prioritizing critical systems
   c. Completing a cost/benefit analysis
   d. Naming the recovery team
6. Recovery strategies consider all EXCEPT:
   a. User recovery
   b. Expense recovery

   c. Data recovery
   d. Facility recovery
 7. Advantages of a cold site include:
   a. Availability in hours
   b. Operational testing is available
   c. Costs less than in-house facility
   d. Practical for less-popular hardware
 8. Electronic vaulting includes all EXCEPT:
   a. Online tape vaulting
   b. Off-site storage facility
   c. Remote journaling
   d. Database shadowing
 9. Resuming critical business functions includes:
   a. Determining the extent of damage
   b. Declaring a disaster
   c. Establishing the command center
   d. Contacting recovery team members
10. Types of tests include:
   a. Simulation
   b. All out
   c. Evacuation
   d. Operational

References

Arnell, Alvin, 1990. *Handbook of Effective Disaster Recovery Planning: A Seminar-Workshop Approach*. McGraw Hill, New York.

Devlin, Edward S., Cole Emerson, and Leo Wrobel, Jr., 1998. *Business Resumption Planning*. Auerbach Publications, Boca Raton, FL.

Dorf, John and Marty Johnson, 2000. "Restoration Component of Business Continuity Planning," in the *Handbook of Information Security Management, 2000 edition*. Hal Tipton and Micki Krause, Eds. CRC Press, Boca Raton, FL.

Doughty, Ken, 2001. *Business Continuity Planning: Protecting Your Organization's Life*. Auerbach Publications, Boca Raton, FL.

Fortson, Judith, 1992. *Disaster Planning and Recovery*. Neal-Schuman Publishers, Inc., New York.

Hiatt, Charlotte, 2000. *A Primer for Disaster Recovery Planning in an IT Environment*. Idea Group Publisher, Hershey, PA.

Jackson, Carl B., 2000. "Reengineering the Business Continuity Planning Process," in the *Handbook of Information Security Management, 2000 edition*. Hal Tipton and Micki Krause, Eds. CRC Press, Boca Raton, FL.

Jackson, Carl B., 2001. "The Business Impact Assessment Process," in the *Handbook of Information Security Management, 2001 edition*. Hal Tipton and Micki Krause, Eds. CRC Press, Boca Raton, FL.

National Institute of Standards and Technology (NIST), Special Publication 800-34, June 2002. "Contingency Planning Guide for Information Technology Systems." http://csrc.nist.gov/publications/nistpubs/index.html

Toigo, John, 1996. *Disaster Recovery Planning for Computers and Communication Resources*. John Wiley & Sons, New York.

Toigo, John, 2000. *Disaster Recovery Planning — Strategies for Protecting Critical Information Assets.* Prentice Hall, Upper Saddle River, NJ.

Wold, Geoffrey and Tina Vick, 2000. "An Efficient Approach for Organizing and Developing a Comprehensive Business Continuity Plan." Presentation at the 12th International Disaster Recovery Symposium and Exhibition, September 2000, Orlando, FL.

Web Sites

Business Continuity Institute (BCI) URL: http://www.bci.com

Disaster Recovery Institute International (DRII) URL: http://www.dr.org

Disaster Recovery Journal (DRJ) URL: http://www.drj.com

Disaster Recovery Planning URL: http://www.drplanning.org

Disaster Resource Guide URL: http://www.disaster-resource.com

Chapter 10
Law, Investigations and Ethics

The Law, Investigations and Ethics Domain addresses computer crime laws and regulations, the investigative measures and techniques that can be used to determine if a crime has been committed, methods to gather evidence if it has, as well as the ethical issues and code of conduct for the security professional. Incident-handling capabilities provide the ability to react quickly and efficiently to malicious technical threats or incidents.

The CISSP candidate should be able to understand the following:

- Laws:
  - How to determine what laws are applicable to computer crime
  - How to determine if a computer crime has occurred
  - Ways to gather and preserve evidence and investigate computer crimes
- Security incidents:
  - What constitutes a security incident, including:
    - Viruses and other malicious code
    - Human error
    - Terrorist attack
    - Unauthorized acts by privileged and non-privileged employees
    - Natural disasters
    - Hardware and software malfunctions
    - Utility outages
  - Common system/network attacks, including:
    - Spam attacks
    - Email attacks
    - Firewall breaches
    - Social engineering
    - Redirects
    - Hacker and cracker attacks
    - Unauthorized use of sniffers
    - Emanation interception

- Recognition skills, including:
  - Pattern recognition
  - Abnormal activities
  - Suspicious activities
  - Alarms
  - Virus activities
- Response skills, including:
  - The key components and items necessary to properly identify the security event
  - The ability to contain and repair the damage
  - The generally accepted guidelines for data integrity, retention, and preservation
  - The generally accepted guidelines for reporting incidents
  - The escalation procedures used after a security incident is discovered:
    - The generally accepted guidelines for confiscating equipment, software, and data
    - The ability to prevent future damage
- Technical skills, including:
  - Gathering and protecting evidence
  - Maintaining incident logs and related documentation
  - Appropriate countermeasures or corrective measures
- How the (ISC)² Code of Ethics applies to CISSPs

The professional can meet the expectations defined above by understanding such Law, Investigations, and Ethics topics and methodologies as:

- Laws:
  - Licensing
  - Intellectual properties
  - Import/export
  - Liability
  - Transborder data flow
- Investigations:
  - Evidence:
    - Types of admissible evidence
    - Collection and preservation of evidence
    - Chain of evidence
  - Investigation processes and techniques:
    - Target
    - Object/subject
    - Team composition
    - Forensics
    - Privacy
    - Interrogation
    - Internal/external confidentiality

- Incident handling:
  - Common types of incidents
  - Abnormal and suspicious activity
  - Generally accepted guidelines for confiscating equipment, software, and data
  - Generally accepted guidelines for incident data integrity and retention
  - Generally accepted guidelines for reporting incidents
- Ethics:
  - (ISC)² Code of Ethics
  - Request for Comment 1087 — Internet Activity Board "Ethics and the Internet"

This Law, Investigation and Ethics chapter is divided into the three topics: (1) Law, (2) Investigation, and (3) Ethics. Within each topic the material is separated into the five sections of the CBK: Information Protection Requirements, Information Protection Environment, Security Technology and Tools, Assurance and Confidence Mechanisms, and Information Management Services.

10.1 Law

The topic of law is addressed from an international perspective. Although examples are provided from U.S. and U.K. laws, it is assumed that these are similar to those enacted in other nations throughout the world to some extent. From an Information Security Professional's point of view, it is important to understand and provide organizational guidance with respect to the computer crime laws that relate to your operation. These can, of course, be only the laws of your country or, if your organization operates in a multinational environment, can include the laws of other countries.

Information Protection Requirements

Many information security requirements stem directly from legislation enacted by governments throughout the world. It is incumbent upon information security professionals to be familiar with the laws pertaining to information system operations that affect their organizations. An important part of the information security job consists of interpreting law for top management and instituting policy and procedures designed to keep the organization and its employees from violating the law.

In the United States, for example, many private-sector information security functions were initiated as a result of the Foreign Corrupt Practices Act of 1977, which made top management of publicly held corporations personally responsible for the security of financial information. A more recent example is the Health Insurance Portability and Accountability Act (HIPAA) of 1996, which establishes a process that regulates the electronic transfer of health information among health plans, healthcare providers, and clearing houses while protecting the security and privacy of the transmitted information.

Similar legislation has been enacted in other countries, some as a result of the expanded availability of the Internet. A particular concern has been the rampant pirating of software. And in the European Union (EU), there is a focus on the protection of the privacy of personal information and the transmission of it to locations where adequate protection is not generally provided.

The bottom line is that, globally, laws have established specific security requirements that need to be understood and complied with in the information processing field — read that as a responsibility of the information security functions both in the public and private sectors.

A concerted effort by national governments and the international community as a whole is required to address the challenges facing the international community and the private sector. The need for universality and for a forum in which all countries can participate in drawing up policies, legal reforms, and technical solutions suggests that the United Nations may play an important role.

Aggressive strategies are needed to protect the technology itself from such things as "hacking," invasions of privacy, and the propagation of harmful programs such as computer viruses. New methods of creating, transmitting, and storing information also raise issues. Copying data has led to pressures to prosecute copyright infringement. The lack of control has exacerbated the transmission of "offensive content" such as hate propaganda or content considered blasphemous, subversive, pornographic, or as inciting or assisting in the committing of crimes. Religious and cultural differences will also play a role in developing international policies against crime.

A strategy for combating computer crime would have to incorporate investigative powers that could be used to obtain evidence from anywhere on a computer network — regardless of national jurisdiction — more quickly than offenders can either move or erase evidence. At the same time there should be national and international requirements for the protection of privacy, freedom of expression, and other basic human rights. This will be particularly difficult because, at present, the most effective human rights protections in criminal cases are codified in national laws and constitutions and enforced by national courts ill-equipped to deal with transnational cases.

Most security and crime control measures on the Internet today consist of technical standards set by the industry itself, irrespective of political pressures or basic human rights protection. The private sector also tends to generate effective crime controls where they are needed for commercial reasons, but not where the controls would interfere with easy customer access or would increase operating costs. There is a risk that developing countries may be excluded by the industry itself because they are not able to effectively control domestic computer crime or because they cannot meet technical security requirements for communications or electronic commerce.

Perhaps the greatest challenge in developing an effective global strategy is to train skilled investigators and prosecutors and keep them up-to-date on the latest technological and criminal developments. This effort strains even wealthy and technically advanced countries, and expertise will be needed to avoid the legal loopholes that electronic offenders can exploit.

Information Protection Environment

Incidents of computer-related crime and telecommunications fraud have increased dramatically over the past decade. However, because of the esoteric nature of this crime, there have been very few prosecutions and even fewer convictions. The new technology allowing the advancement and automation of many business processes has also opened the door to many new forms of computer abuse. Although some of these system attacks merely use contemporary methods to commit older, more familiar types of crime, others involve the use of completely new forms of criminal activity that evolved along with the technology.

Computer crime investigation and computer forensics are also evolving sciences affected by many external factors, such as continued advancements in technology, societal issues, and legal issues. Many gray areas need to be sorted out and tested through the courts so that the necessary precedents can be established. Until then, the system attackers will have an advantage and computer abuse will continue to increase. Computer security professionals must be aware of the myriad of technological and legal issues that affect systems and users, including issues dealing with investigations and enforcement.

Some of the major categories of computer crime include:

- *Computer assisted crime.* Criminal activities that are not unique to computers but merely use computers as tools to assist the criminal endeavor (e.g., fraud, child pornography).
- *Computer specific or targeted crime.* Crimes directed at computers, networks, and the information stored on these systems (e.g., denial of service, sniffers, attacking passwords).

- *Computer is incidental.* The computer is incidental to the criminal activity (e.g., customer lists for traffickers).

Communications security includes the protection of mail, fax, telephone, and voice-mail communications, as well as the transmission of data from one computer to another across a network connection. Communications security breaches can be defined as any loss, unauthorized disclosure, or manipulation of information through voice, fax, or digital communications that is caused by an individual intending to use this information for unlawful purposes or to cause willful damage to one or more of the authorized recipients or the sender of the information.

Information security has three major computer crime-related components:

- Increasing awareness among potential victims of possible computer crimes
- Keeping computer criminals from actually committing a computer crime
- Investigating the occurrence of a computer crime.

Criminals do not need to have access to a computer to collect information. They can take advantage of breaches of operational security that include user activities such as choosing poor passwords, writing them down in an open space, disposing of classified or sensitive business or government material in the trash, or through social engineering. Many of these undesirable user activities can be corrected through awareness training and insisting on good business practices.

Some leading historical examples of computer crime include:

- *Equity Funding.* The Equity Funding Corporation is considered by some to be one of the first large computer crimes. Corporate management used its computer to create false policies and other instruments to increase the corporation's value. The auditors, who worked around the computer (checking transactions as they went into the computer and after they came out of the computer) rather than auditing transactions during processing in the computer, missed the manipulations. As a result of the fraud becoming known, serious questions arose as to why the financial auditors missed the evidence. As a result, the field of EDP auditing was developed.
- *414 Gang.* A teenage group of hackers that called itself the 414 Gang (after the area code of their location) gained national attention in the United States by breaking into the computer databanks at Sloan-Kettering Cancer Center and the Los Alamos, New Mexico, military computers in 1982.

- *Kevin Mitnick.* Mitnick is likely the most recognized hacker of all time. He mastered the art of social engineering, and used it extensively to obtain unauthorized access to many computer systems.
- *The Cuckoo's Egg.* Cliff Stoll tracked down a German hacker (from the Chaos Computer Club) through an amazing trail after a 75-cent computer usage accounting discrepancy turned up at Lawrence Livermore Labs. The hacker was trying to obtain Star Wars defense information from U.S. Government and aerospace industry databases. His experiences have been documented in the book entitled *The Cuckoo's Egg.*
- *Chaos Computer Club.* This club is a hacker community of people of all ages, genders, races, and social positions. Their principal belief is to demand unlimited freedom and flow of information without censorship. For more than a decade, the Chaos Computer Club has been a voice for all hackers around the world.
- *International Economic Espionage.* The following are some U.S. examples (brief) of situations in which industrial espionage techniques, up to and including illegal or covert means, resulted in lost or misdirected technology:

  - One foreign-government-controlled corporation targeted U.S. proprietary business documents and information from U.S. telecommunications competitors.
  - Another foreign competitor acquired technical specifications from a U.S. automotive manufacturer.
  - In violation of U.S. export laws, a foreign company attempted to acquire a U.S. company's restricted radar technology.
  - Several U.S. companies reported the targeting and acquisition of proprietary biotechnology information.
  - One U.S. company reported the foreign theft of its manufacturing technology regarding its microprocessors.

Jerry Kovacich (1999) defines information warfare as actions taken to achieve information superiority in support of national military strategy by corrupting adversary information and information systems while protecting your own systems.

The statistics and extent of computer crime are largely guesstimates. No one really knows the extent of computer crime because not all of it is found, and much of it is not reported. Relatively few criminals are caught and punished, and both high- and low-tech attacks are used, making it very difficult for professionals to deal with the crimes. High-tech attacks are those utilizing the latest technology and technological tools. Low-tech attacks do not rely on technology in order for the success of the attack, but rather on techniques such as social engineering.

Dealing with computer crime is still a significant problem because the legal systems around the world are lagging behind the available technology. This impacts both the justice systems (laws) and law enforcement agencies. We have also witnessed changes in the perpetrators themselves. With today's technology, it is not necessary to be technologically skilled to launch effective attacks. The high-tech hackers have built tools that less-experienced and less-knowledgeable people can use to attack and break into systems in a very efficient manner.

In addition, organizations often lack the basic protection mechanisms to prevent successful attacks. Inadequate information security safeguards, add-on rather than built-in protection mechanisms, and insufficient staff and resources all lead to problems in preventing, detecting, and reacting to attacks.

The Anglo-American system of jurisprudence developed out of what is called the Common Law, that is, the general law of private property known in the United Kingdom. Common Law was designed through the centuries to secure the rights of individuals to property and to make it difficult for property to be taken away by a government or governmental structure (bureaucracy) without due process of law. The Common Law was expounded over the years in hundreds of thousands of case decisions as a result of trials in which the Common Law jury acted as the judges, and in which they exercised the authority to hear and decide questions of both law and fact. Common Law deals with legal relationships, powers and liabilities, and types of actions, rather than theoretical definitions of abstract legal concepts.

Major Categories and Types of Common Law

Criminal Law. Criminal law is defined as individual conduct violating government laws enacted for the protection of the public. Criminal law identifies a crime as being a wrong against society. Even if an individual is victimized, under the law, society is considered the victim. A conviction under criminal law normally results in a jail term or probation for the defendant. It could also result in a financial award to the victim as restitution for the crime. The main purpose of prosecuting under criminal law is punishment for the offender. This punishment is also meant to serve as a deterrent against future crime. The deterrent aspect of punishment only works if the punishment is severe enough to discourage further criminal activity. This is certainly not the case for computer crime in the United States, where very few computer criminals ever go to jail. In other areas of the world, very strong deterrents exist. For example, in China in 1995, a computer hacker was executed after being found guilty of embezzling

$200,000 from a national bank. This certainly should act as a deterrent to other hackers in China.

To be found guilty of a criminal offense under criminal law, the jury must believe, beyond a reasonable doubt, that the offender is guilty of the offense. The lack of technical expertise, combined with the many confusing questions posed by the defense attorney, may cause doubt for many jury members, thus rendering a not guilty decision. The only short-term solution to this problem is to provide simple testimony in laymen's terms and to use demonstrative evidence whenever possible. Even with this, it will be difficult for many juries to return a guilty verdict in computer crime cases.

Criminal conduct in the United States is broken down into two classifications: felony and misdemeanor, depending on severity. A felony is the more serious of the two, normally resulting in a jail term of more than one year. Misdemeanors are normally punishable by a fine or a jail sentence of less than a year. It is important to understand that to deter future attacks, stricter sentencing must be sought, which only occurs under the felonious classification. The type of attack or the total dollar loss relates directly to the crime classification. Some of the computer-related crimes that can be addressed by criminal law include:

- Unauthorized access
- Exceeding authorized access
- Intellectual property theft or misuse of information
- Pornography
- Theft of computing services
- Forgery using a computer
- Property theft (e.g., computer hardware and chips)
- Invasion of privacy
- Denial-of-services
- Computer fraud
- Releasing viruses and other malicious code
- Sabotage (i.e., data alteration or malicious destruction)
- Extortion by computer
- Embezzlement using a computer
- Espionage involving computers
- Terrorism involving computers
- Identity theft

Although new laws have been adopted for use in the prosecution of a computer-related offense, some of the older, proven federal laws may offer a simpler case to present to judges and juries. These existing laws are usually used by prosecutors, instead of the new computer crime laws, simply because parties involved feel more comfortable with those older type laws and it is easier to prosecute when previous courts have ruled (established precedents). Precedents have not been well established for many of the computer crime laws. These older laws include:

- Wire fraud
- Mail fraud
- Interstate transportation of stolen property
- Racketeer influenced and corrupt organizations

Civil Law. Civil law (or tort law) identifies a tort as a wrong against an individual or business, typically resulting in damage or loss to that individual or business. The major differences between criminal and civil law are the type of punishment and the level of proof required to obtain a guilty verdict. There is no jail sentence under the civil law system. Victims may receive financial or injunctive relief as restitution for their loss. An injunction against the offender will attempt to thwart any further loss to the victim. In addition, a violation of the injunction may result in a contempt of court order, which places the offender in jeopardy of going to jail. The main purpose of seeking civil remedy is for financial restitution, which can be awarded as follows:

- Compensatory damages
- Punitive damages
- Statutory damages

In a civil action, if there is no fault on the part of the victim, the victim may be entitled to compensatory (i.e., restitution) and punitive damages. Compensatory damages are actual damages to the victim and include attorney fees, lost profits, and investigation costs. Punitive damages are damages set by the jury with the intent to punish the offender. Even if the victim is partially at fault, an award may be made on the victim's behalf, but may be lessened due to the victim's culpable negligence.

Statutory damages are determined by law. Mere violation of the law entitles the victim to a statutory award. Civil cases are much easier to convict under because the burden of proof required for the conviction is much less. To be found guilty of a civil wrong, the jury must believe, based only on the preponderance of the evidence, that the offender is guilty of the offense. It is much easier to show that the majority (i.e., 51% or more) of the evidence points to the defendant's guilt.

Administrative Law. Administrative law is also known as *regulatory law* and establishes the standards of performance and conduct for organizations conducting business in various industries. Violations of these laws can result in financial penalties or imprisonment.

Intellectual Property and Privacy Laws

There are other categories of law under the Common Law systems that are directly related to information. These are referred to as Intellectual Property and Privacy Laws.

A *patent* is an invention that has been sufficiently documented and explained as to allow the federal patent office of your country to verify its originality and to grant a patent. This patent limits the development and use of that design to the patent holder for some period of time. The patent holder may then grant a license to others to use the design information, typically for a fee.

A *trademark* is any distinguishing name, character, logo, or other symbol that establishes an identity for a product, service, or organization. Trademarks can be registered, meaning they have been filed in the appropriate jurisdiction. This prevents others from being legally able to use that trademark.

While a patent protects the process of how to build the product of the idea (the invention), a *copyright* allows an author to protect how the idea is expressed. An author does not generally have to file for copyright protection, as the law states the copyright comes into force as soon as the idea is expressed in a tangible form. Many people will register their copyright through either a federal copyright registry or by mailing themselves a copy of their work through registered mail. Computer programs are automatically copyrighted as soon as they are written.

According to Boni, a *trade secret* is proprietary information; that is, information that is used, made, or marketed by one having the exclusive legal rights. This means that the company has ownership rights to its exclusive use of the information. A trade secret is specific proprietary information that meets specific criteria under the law. Thus, to qualify as a trade secret under U.S. law, the information must conform to all three of the following requirements:

- The information must be a genuine, but not absolute or exclusive, "secret." This means that an organization does not need to enforce "ridiculous" security measures to protect that information, although elements of the secret, and maybe the secret itself, may become discoverable. The owner can license the secret to others; and as long as reasonable operational and legal protections are in place, it remains a protected asset.
- The trade secret must provide the owner with competitive or economic advantages. This means that the secret must have real business value to the owner. If there is no real business value other than to protect it from the public, the information cannot be classified as a trade secret.

- The owner must take "reasonable" steps to protect that information. However, there is no checklist of what "reasonable" might be. The court will itself apply the issue of "reasonable" to the specific situation and arrive at the conclusion. It should be noted, however, that many plaintiffs have lost their claims to trade secret status due to the lack of a specific safeguard.

Trans-Border Computer Crime

One of the most significant forms of transnational crime facing the entire international community is computer-related, or *cybercrime.*

The Internet is used by hackers and criminals to transmit computer viruses, invade privacy, steal or corrupt valuable information, perpetrate frauds, and manipulate stock markets. It has been exploited by pedophiles to create and distribute child pornography and, in some cases, to befriend and abduct children.

Because electronic crimes can simultaneously be committed across borders, questions of national sovereignty are an issue. Today's technologies and the proliferation of computer networks have removed barriers for criminals. Investigators, judges, and prosecutors, and indeed the entire legal community, are struggling to catch up. In some cases, countries are requesting the extradition of computer hackers who have never physically entered the country whose laws they have allegedly broken. Law enforcement officials are contending with new computer-based evidence that to use, they must convince a court of its authenticity and show that it has not been electronically altered.

Internet communications can easily be routed through many different jurisdictions, thus making tracing and the assignment of jurisdiction difficult. Electronic evidence or proceeds from electronic transactions can easily be moved to locations where a lack of effective laws or technical expertise puts them beyond legal recourse. Data can be encrypted to make it difficult for law enforcement agencies to read.

The spread of networks in the developing world is proceeding at a slower pace. Many developing countries are caught in between the need to go "online" to spur economic development and the desire to prevent cybercrime. The lack of effective legal frameworks creates greater opportunities for offenders to commit economic crimes beyond the borders of their home countries.

Nations typically have different views regarding the seriousness of computer crime and how they interpret technology and crime issues. This sometimes leads to problems with regard to consistency in treating computer crimes effectively. What is illegal in one country may not be illegal in another.

Additionally, evidence rules generally differ in various legal systems, which poses other problems in the evidence collection approach. Add to this the problem associated with different technical capabilities of the various law enforcement units and dealing with computer crimes becomes very complicated. Finally, some governments may not wish to cooperate and assist one another in international cases. This means that the computer criminal may be, and often is, "untouchable" by the country where the offence has occurred.

The Future of Cybercrime

Preventive measures should focus on the following key trends:

- The rapid evolution of cybercrime will continue. Driven by technology and the creativity of offenders, new schemes will spread rapidly over the Internet. This poses challenges for domestic and international law enforcement bodies and for the development of international legal standards.
- Traditional crime patterns will change. Some crimes, such as fraud and child pornography, which are currently limited by language barriers, will expand in scope as language translation software becomes available. As the use of networks gradually shifts from purely informational to electronic commercial activities, crime patterns will follow suit. New opportunities for fraud and money-laundering offenses will be created.
- Transnational crime will increase. Networks make cross-border crimes easier to commit and bring them within reach of individual offenders. There will be an increase in minor transnational offenses committed by unsophisticated offenders. This will put a serious strain on traditional frameworks for extradition and mutual legal assistance, which are not equipped to handle the caseloads.
- Organized crime will take advantage of the changes. Trans-national organized crime uses networks, because they provide relatively secure media for communication, the concealment of evidence, and the electronic movement of money of illegal origin. Data can be encrypted and used to thwart law enforcement.
- Not all trans-national computer crime is "organized crime." Computer networks open up opportunities that allow individual offenders to commit sophisticated crimes, which were once associated with organized crime. Networks may also support entirely new forms of criminal organizations that do not fit within existing legal definitions or approaches.

U.S.-Specific Computer Crime Laws

Acts considered felonies under 18 U.S.C. 1030 include:

- Unauthorized access to a computer that stores classified information
- Unauthorized access to a computer
- Obtaining classified information
- Injuring the United States or giving advantage to a foreign nation
- Using the computer to defraud others
- Unauthorized access to a "federal interest computer"
- Intending to defraud
- Illegally obtaining something of value
- Extortion
- Using a computer in interstate commerce or communications intending that the transmission will damage the computer system or prevent its use
- Damaging a computer system
- Withholding or denying authorized use
- Causing a loss greater than $1000
- Unauthorized modification of medical information

The Electronic Communications Privacy Act of 1986

Exhibit 1 is an excerpt from the Electronic Communications Privacy Act of 1986. Essentially, this means that unless you have the permission of either party involved in a communication in any form, or you are a law enforcement officer with the expressed permission from an authorized court (this means a court order to search warrant), you are not permitted to intercept any communication regardless of how it was transmitted.

The Computer Security Act of 1987

The act states that the security and privacy of federal computer systems are in the public interest. It gives to NIST the computer security mission, including the development of standards. The Act requires that each U.S. federal agency provide its employees with training in computer security awareness and practice and to set up a security plan for each of its systems.

The U.S. Federal Privacy Act of 1974

This act was amended in 1980. Exhibit 2 lists excerpts taken from the act.

The Privacy Act means that is it illegal for any U.S. Government agency to release information that it has acquired about you:

- Without your express consent
- Unless it is required directly for their job and will not be disclosed publicly
- Unless requested officially by a court of the jurisdiction

Exhibit 1. The Electronic Communications Privacy Act of 1986

On the basis of its own investigations and of published studies, the Congress makes the following findings:

(a) Wire communications are normally conducted through the use of facilities which form part of an interstate network. The same facilities are used for interstate and intrastate communications. There has been extensive wiretapping carried on without legal sanctions, and without the consent of any of the parties to the conversation. Electronic, mechanical, and other intercepting devices are being used to overhear oral conversations made in private, without the consent of any of the parties to such communications. The contents of these communications and evidence derived there from are being used by public and private parties as evidence in court and administrative proceedings and by persons whose activities affect interstate commerce. The possession, manufacture, distribution, advertising, and use of these devices are facilitated by interstate commerce.

(b) In order to protect effectively the privacy of wire and oral communications, to protect the integrity of court and administrative proceedings, and to prevent the obstruction of interstate commerce, it is necessary for Congress to define on a uniform basis the circumstances and conditions under which the interception of wire and oral communications may be authorized, to prohibit any unauthorized interception of such communications, and the use of the contents thereof in evidence in courts and administrative proceedings.

(c) Organized criminals make extensive use of wire and oral communications in their criminal activities. The interception of such communications to obtain evidence of the commission of crimes or to prevent their commission is an indispensable aid to law enforcement and the administration of justice.

(d) To safeguard the privacy of innocent persons, the interception of wire or oral communications where none of the parties to the communication has consented to the interception should be allowed only when authorized by a court of competent jurisdiction and should remain under the control and supervision of the authorizing court. Interception of wire and oral communications should further be limited to certain major types of offenses and specific categories of crime with assurances that the interception is justified and that the information obtained thereby will not be misused.

The U.S. Computer Fraud and Abuse Act of 1986 (amended 1996)

The original act was very narrow in defining what was a computer crime. The act covered only:

- Classified defense or foreign relations information
- Records of financial institutions or credit reporting agencies
- Government computers
- Unauthorized access or access in excess of authorization became a felony on classified information and a misdemeanor for financial information; it also became a misdemeanor to access a government computer with or without authorization should the government's use of the computer be affected

Exhibit 2. The U.S. Federal Privacy Act of 1974

b) Conditions of Disclosure. — No agency shall disclose any record that is contained in a system of records by any means of communication to any person, or to another agency, except pursuant to a written request by, or with the prior written consent of, the individual to whom the record pertains, unless disclosure of the record would be

1. to those officers and employees of the agency which maintains the record who have a need for the record in the performance of their duties;
2. required under section 552 of this title;
3. for a routine use as defined in subsection (a)(7) of this section and described under subsection (e)(4)(D) of this section;
4. to the Bureau of the Census for purposes of planning or carrying out a census or survey or related activity pursuant to the provisions of title 13;
5. to a recipient who has provided the agency with advance adequate written assurance that the record will be used solely as a statistical research or reporting record, and the record is to be transferred in a form that is not individually identifiable;
6. to the National Archives and Records Administration as a record which has sufficient historical or other value to warrant its continued preservation by the United States Government, or for evaluation by the Archivist of the United States or the designee of the Archivist to determine whether the record has such value;
7. to another agency or to an instrumentality of any governmental jurisdiction within or under the control of the United States for a civil or criminal law enforcement activity if the activity is authorized by law, and if the head of the agency or instrumentality has made a written request to the agency which maintains the record specifying the particular portion desired and the law enforcement activity for which the record is sought;
8. to a person pursuant to a showing of compelling circumstances affecting the health or safety of an individual if upon such disclosure, notification is transmitted to the last known address of such individual;
9. to either House of Congress, or, to the extent of matter within its jurisdiction, any committee or subcommittee thereof, any joint committee of Congress or subcommittee of any such joint committee;
10. to the Comptroller General, or any of his authorized representatives, in the course of the performance of the duties of the General Accounting Office;
11. pursuant to the order of a court of competent jurisdiction; or
12. to a consumer reporting agency in accordance with section 3711(e) of title 31.

Note: This law applies only to government computer systems. Private-sector systems are all covered by state law.

The amendments in 1986 clarified the law and added three new crimes:

- Where use of a "federal interest computer" furthers an intended fraud
- Altering, damaging, or destroying information in a federal interest computer preventing the use of the computer or information when this causes a loss of $1000 or more or could impair medical treatment

- Trafficking in computer passwords if it affects interstate or foreign commerce or permits unauthorized access to government computers

Characteristics of Due Care. The officers and directors of the company are expected to act carefully in fulfilling their tasks of monitoring and directing the activities of corporate management. A director shall discharge his or her duties:

- In good faith
- With the care an ordinarily prudent person in a like position would exercise under similar circumstances
- In a manner he or she reasonably believes is in the best interest of the enterprise

Surveys. Patterns and statistics of computer crime from various reputable sources such as the CSI/FBI Computer Crime Survey are inconclusive, in that only a small percentage of people return them. Consequently, it is difficult to extrapolate them to the entire picture. However, the trends include:

- Decreasing sophistication of the attack
- Increasing sophistication of the tools
- Increasing industrial espionage activity
- Increasing number of external penetrations

Privacy

Many people have an intuitive idea of what "privacy" means, yet different people interpret the term in different ways. According to Agranoff, the right of privacy is often variously expressed as:

- The right to be left alone
- The right to be free from unreasonable personal intrusion
- An individual's right to determine what personal information can be communicated, and to whom

People are often surprised to learn that privacy is not traditionally stated as a constitutional right. Rather, privacy rights have largely developed in the 20th century as a mixture of state common law, federal and state statutes, and constitutional law.

An organization wishing to develop policies for secure personal data could quickly become bogged down trying to decide exactly what kind of information should be protected. Budget constraints may make it appear pointless to spend money to protect an interest that is not judged to be of importance. The organization must clarify for itself exactly what interests it wishes to protect. It is important to understand that when computers are involved, two major issues must be addressed: unreasonable intrusion and due process.

Protection against Unreasonable Intrusion

Permitting others to intrude on their private affairs is one price individuals pay for being members of a highly mobile, commercial society. For example, if individuals wish to have health insurance, they must allow insurers to review their medical and hospital records. To obtain commercial or mortgage credit, consumers must allow others to have access to records that indicate their credit history and spending habits.

Most people would agree that these are reasonable intrusions. When, then, do they become unreasonable? It seems, at the very least, that individuals should know what kind of data is being gathered about them and give their consent (which may be implied from the individual's applying for employment or credit). Individuals should be able to trust that the organization gathering such data will not release it to unauthorized persons and will take active steps to ensure all employees are properly trained and supervised in this regard. Privacy policy and procedures should address the issues of data collection and confidentiality, emphasizing the personal responsibility of those who deal with computerized data to safeguard personal information. This responsibility should not be avoided on the grounds that "the computer did it."

Protection against Lack of Due Process

Most individuals have a fundamental belief in the idea of fair play and justice. This notion of due process revolves around letting individuals know precisely what is charged against them and giving them a fair opportunity to defend themselves against the charge.

People have the right to demand that accurate information about them is collected and maintained. Otherwise, adverse decisions may be made against them without the opportunity to state their side of the story. Indeed, individuals might not even know there has been a charge made against them. It is, of course, possible that an innocent mistake has been made; if so, it should be corrected. It is also possible that a legitimate dispute exists between the data gatherer and the subject, in which case the subject should at least have his or her say. To store erroneous data on individuals without their knowledge, and without offering them the opportunity to correct the data, offends traditional ideas of fundamental fair play and justice.

Privacy codes should, therefore, emphasize the personal responsibility of managers dealing with computerized data. Management might consider itself responsible for fairness in the gathering, storage, and dissemination of personal data. This responsibility should not be avoided on the grounds that it is someone else's problem. It is possible that the organization could be held liable if personal data was disclosed to an unauthorized person; however, without formal standards, the law is unclear in this regard.

Email Privacy

As a general rule, the courts do not like to get involved in workplace privacy issues. Traditionally, employers, whether public or private, have been allowed great leeway to protect their business and financial interests by almost any means not clearly illegal. Various cases presented to the courts have upheld the right of employers to search desks, lockers, file cabinets, and interoffice mail without a search warrant. There are limits if conduct is truly outrageous, but clearly the courts do not have time to get involved in the management decision process.

Questions may arise as to whether employers should be able to read the electronic mail sent by employees. Because email uses company-owned facilities to transmit business matters, it cannot have the same degree of protection as, for example, normal "snail mail." Furthermore, companies have traditionally had legitimate reasons to read email, such as finding lost messages, studying system effectiveness, protecting against fraud and misuse, and recovery. Nonetheless, most employees do not give up all privacy expectations simply by coming to work.

What is needed is a well-written, communicated email policy. Privacy policies regarding email should, therefore, emphasize that business resources are not intended for personal use. Employees should be informed to expect no privacy when using the corporate email system, and any message or mailbox may be examined. One can hardly have an expectation of privacy in an email letter that could have numerous recipients. Finally, managers and email system administrators must also be told, through policy, not to abuse their authority; they have no right to rifle through employee items without just cause.

Trans-Border Data Flows

Privacy is also a concern with what is commonly known as *trans-border data flows*. If privacy is not ensured here, it could result in a potential barrier to the free flow of information between nations. Some European countries require an export license for the transfer of personal data because these countries believe that if personal information is violated in another country, it is an infringement on the basic rights of the citizens and a violation of the nation's sovereignty.

The 1981 Guidelines of the Organization for Economic Cooperation and Development (OECD) stated that its European member countries should take all reasonable steps to ensure uninterrupted and secure transit for the trans-border flow of personal data, but should not develop policies creating severe obstacles to such flow.

Successful Privacy Codes

The following are examples of organizations that have set up their own successful security codes for protecting personal information. Although this type of specific information will not be included on the CISSP exam, it may be helpful to the CISSP candidate to get an understanding of what type of privacy guidelines have been enacted. All of them can be used as guidelines in the treatment of private personal information.

The Canadian Independent Computing Services Association. The Canadian Independent Computing Services Association has developed the *Privacy Principles for Data Processors*, which has been passed by management and recommended to its members for implementation within its individual companies. This code can act as a guide for corporations that are considering implementing their own internal privacy codes. It reads as follows:

The following principles guide data processing firms in handling client information. Information received from a client:

- Remains the property of the client
- Will be used only for the purpose for which it was intended
- Will not be disposed of, transferred, sold, or made available to any other party or parties without the specific permission of the client
- Will be retained only for the limited time necessary for the performance of its functions

The management of the data processing firm will:

- Have all employees sign a written agreement to use client information only in accordance with the principles outlined above
- Secure all data in all reasonable ways against theft or abuse of any kind
- Restrict the use of client data to those employees who require it to fulfill their obligations to the client

The OECD Guidelines. The European Organization for Economic Cooperation and Development (OECD) has promulgated guidelines for privacy protection and trans-border personal data flow. The OECD specified that these are minimum standards and should be supplemented by additional security measures. These guidelines include the following provisions:

- Personal data should be collected in limited amounts only, and (where appropriate) with the knowledge or consent of the person concerned.
- Data should be obtained by lawful and fair means.
- Data should be accurate, complete, and up-to-date to ensure its relevance to the purpose for which it was collected.
- Data should be collected only for legitimate purposes, and then not used for other purposes.
- Data should not be disclosed to others, except by consent or in accordance with law enforcement.
- Reasonable security safeguards should exist to ensure protection of data against unauthorized modification, disclosure, or destruction.
- A data controller should be accountable for complying with the preceding principles.

Conferees at a privacy and data protection conference sponsored by the International Chamber of Commerce upheld these basic principles and further specified that any data subject should be entitled to the following protection:

- To be informed if an organization is holding data on the individual
- To examine such data on request
- To be able to correct or delete the data, if appropriate

The European Council of Ministers. The Council of Ministers of the Committee of Experts on Human Rights of the Council of Europe adopted the following principles for protection of individual privacy in the private sector. Although nearly 20 years old, these principles seem remarkably apt today:

- The information stored should be accurate and should be kept up-to-date. In general, information relating to the intimate private life of persons or information that might lead to unfair discrimination should not be recorded or, if recorded, should not be disseminated.
- The information should be appropriate and relevant with regard to the purpose for which it has been stored.
- The information should not be obtained by fraudulent or unfair means.
- Rules should be laid down to specify the periods beyond which certain categories of information should no longer be kept or used.
- Without proper authorization, information should not be used for purposes other than those for which it has been stored, nor communicated to third parties.
- As a general rule, the people concerned should have the right to know the information stored about them, the purpose for which it

has been recorded, and particulars of each release of this information.

- Every care should be taken to correct inaccurate information and to erase obsolete information.
- Precautions should be taken against any abuse or misuse of information, and data banks should be protected from unauthorized access.
- Access to the information stored should be confined to persons who have a valid reason to know it.
- Statistical data should be released only in aggregate form and in such a way that it is impossible to link the information to a particular person.

Policies for Secure Personal Data. Policies for secure personal data require, at minimum, two elements:

- *Commitment to internal privacy code principles.* An organization should not develop policies until it knows precisely what it is trying to protect and to what principles it will adhere. Otherwise, the policies will tend to be ignored when they come up against organizational realities. Privacy code principles, based on protection against unreasonable intrusion and due process principles, may be a good starting point; it should be remembered, however, that each organization is different and must adopt its own principles.
- *Commitment to meaningful data security.* It is useless for an organization to develop policies, however sound, if technology cannot support those policies. Laws against bank robbery and theft would be meaningless if banks left money in the open with no guards, vaults, or alarms to protect it. A commitment to data privacy unsupported by necessary technological and administrative methods is just as foolish and deceives the public, senior management, and the board of directors. Independent information security management is a must.

Recommended Course of Action

Most organizations believe they must take responsibility for the computer systems they create, and this responsibility includes taking reasonable measures to secure the personal data stored in such systems. The problem is in deciding what measures are reasonable. Organizations should consider this problem in two steps. First, they must determine privacy code principles by defining major goals and the personal responsibilities of those involved. Second, they must determine what technical and administrative measures are reasonably required to meet these goals.

Password, authorization, and administrative schemes that merely look good on paper are not the answer. Choices are inevitably made on the basis of cost considerations, but organizations must implement internal privacy codes if they believe voluntary compliance is better than government mandate. In all cases, the assignment of specific individual responsibility for information privacy and security is essential for success in a large organization.

Security Technology and Tools

In the new global age, borders have opened up, trade barriers have fallen, and information speeds around the world at the touch of a button. Business is booming — and so is trans-national computer crime. Because of this, there are international groups that are trying to address the problems related to computer crime on a global scale. Some of the international efforts being used to address the challenges of worldwide computer crime include:

- *The G8 nations.* The most economically advanced nations, these nations have developed a number of recent agreements to fight computer crime.
- *Mutual Legal Assistance Treaties (MLAT).* MLAT involves U.S. law enforcement agents who are working with law enforcement agents in other nations to fight computer crime, terrorism, fraud, money laundering, etc.
- *European Union border controls (Interpol).* Interpol is the international police organization involved in cooperative relationships with national police forces.
- *United Nations (UN) Agreements.* The UN has also addressed various issues among the member nations in dealing with computer crime.

Information Security Related Issues: Tracking of Computer Crime

There are various organizations that are attempting to track and help with the extent of the computer crime problem on a global scale. These organizations include:

- CERT — Computer Emergency Response Team, Carnegie Mellon University
- CERIAS — Center for Education and Research in Information Assurance and Security, Purdue University
- BugTraq — full-disclosure, moderated mailing list for discussions and notifications of security vulnerabilities
- CIAC — Computer Incident Advisory Capability, U.S. Department of Energy

Assurance, Trust, and Confidence Mechanisms

Reviews of laws and regulations that pertain to the security of the organization's data processing operations can provide the basis for an audit of current practices to ensure that appropriate measures are being followed. On the basis of this audit, management can be assured of compliance or advised of the need for additional policies and procedures.

Information Protection and Management Services

The information security role is to be aware of legal issues as they arise and study new legislation or regulations to determine those that have a significant impact on the security of data processing operations. They need to keep management aware of legal liabilities in time to take appropriate action to avoid breaking the law. Completed staff work is very important here because presenting management with a problem, but without a solution, is not enough. If possible, potential solutions should be investigated, perhaps in conjunction with a cost/benefit analysis, to provide management with a best recommendation. Included in this process could be an investigation of what similar organizations are doing to resolve the same issue. This enables management to exercise its "due care" role.

10.2 Investigation

Information Protection Requirements

Although many information system security professionals in the private or public sector will never lead or even participate in the investigation of computer crimes, it is important that they become familiar with the process so that when called upon they will be ready to contribute effectively. This is an area where errors made in the investigation process can seriously damage the ability to successfully prosecute a computer crime case. Also, because of other commitments, federal and local police agencies may not be able to participate.

The basic need is to be able to conduct reliable investigations that will stand up to scrutiny and cross-examination in a courtroom environment. This includes ensuring that evidence is properly obtained and carefully protected throughout the chain-of-custody. Also, it is important to ensure that incidents are properly reported, both within the organization in accordance with policy and to external agencies as required by regulations.

All investigations must be conducted thoroughly and equitably, so as not to further complicate or damage an already dangerous and potentially explosive situation.

Information Protection Environment

Incident Response and Handling

Currently, there is no one definitive method for dealing with the investigations of IT incidents. However, there have been some coordinated efforts to arrive at generally accepted guidelines and a formal methodology based on a consensus approach. These efforts have been under way since at least 1989. The Internet Engineering Task Force (IETF), CERT/Coordination Center at Carnegie Mellon Software Engineering Institute (CERT/CC), U.S. Department of Energy (DoE), Forum of Incident Response and Security Teams (FIRST), and the Center for Education and Research in Information Security and Assurance (CERIAS) at Purdue University have all contributed to the effort. The consensus approach to incident response, response escalation, and computer forensics has become the *de facto* standard.

The term "incident" has become commonplace; but what exactly is a security incident? A security incident is an adverse event or series of events that adversely impacts the security or ability of an organization to conduct normal business. The definition introduces yet another term: *event*. An event is simply an observable occurrence; an aspect that can be documented, verified, and analyzed.

A security incident includes, but is certainly not limited to:

- Virus and other malicious code attacks
- Hacker attack
- Terrorist attack
- Insider attack
- Competitive intelligence gathering (unethically)
- Unauthorized acts by employees
- Employee error
- Hardware or software malfunction

Motives for Committing Computer and Internet Offenses

Although many computer criminals claim they have altruistic intent, the motives for committing computer-related offenses are the same as the motives for general crimes. These include but are not limited to:

- Ego, i.e., bragging rights
- Revenge
- Profit or financial need
- Attention

During the course of an investigation, it is important to examine the *modus operandi* (method of operation; MO). A suspect's MO normally has three main purposes:

- To protect the attacker's identity (terrorists, however, often identify themselves or their organization intentionally)
- To ensure success of the crime
- To assist in the attacker's escape

Examining the MO of a suspect can provide key information about who might be responsible for the crime. The field of criminal profiling looks at the MO as part of the process of narrowing down the field of potential suspects. This process can be extended to computer crime as well. The characteristics contained in a suspect's MO can paint a picture of their skills, experience, etc. In particular, an investigator should focus on:

- Amount of prior planning that would have been necessary
- Materials used by the suspect
- Any indication of pre-surveillance or intelligence gathering
- Offense location selection
- Method used to conduct the "attack" (e.g., DDoS, Trojans attached to email)
- Any precautionary acts (e.g., using zombied systems as a base)

Developing an understanding or at least a partial picture of the suspect can greatly reduce the time and effort required to complete an investigation. Investigating a computer crime incident consumes precious time and resources and can be expensive; any advantage should be used to increase the efficiency and effectiveness of this process.

Security Technology and Tools

Investigative Techniques and Concepts

One of the impacts of computer crime has been the shift from physical to the less tangible electronic environment. This means that the computer criminals and the method of investigation used to catch them are no longer subject to traditional rules and constraints. For example, the ability to steal something was previously bound by the size of the physical object and the limitations of the thief, including physical access and the amount that could be carried away. That is no longer true. Now, a thief can electronically download an entire file cabinet full of information without obtaining physical access or lifting anything. Second, in many countries, law enforcement may have a problem obtaining search warrants. For example, in the United States, the law specifies that a search warrant must be obtained by law enforcement officers, and only after they have demonstrated sufficient cause to search the suspect's office or home.

As another example, in the United States, computer-generated evidence is considered hearsay because it is not consistent with the best evidence rule, discussed later. We will also discuss *hearsay evidence* in more detail later, but it is that which is not gathered from the personal knowledge of the witness, but through other indirect sources. The value of the evidence depends on the veracity (i.e., truthfulness) and competence of the source. Business records are generally considered hearsay because there is no way to prove that they, in and of themselves, are accurate, reliable, and trustworthy in general.

However, should the business documents be used regularly in business activity and presented by an individual who is involved in their formation and use, it may be possible to submit *business documents as evidence.*

Rules of Evidence

Before delving into the investigative process and computer forensics, it is essential that the investigator have a thorough understanding of the *Rules of Evidence.* The submission of evidence in any type of legal proceeding generally amounts to a significant challenge; but when computers are involved, the problems are intensified. Special knowledge is needed to locate and collect evidence, and special care is required to preserve and transport the evidence. Evidence in a computer crime case may differ from traditional forms of evidence inasmuch as most computer-related evidence is intangible — in the form of an electronic pulse or magnetic charge.

Before evidence can be presented in a case, it must be competent, relevant, and material to the issue, and it must be presented in compliance with the rules of evidence. Anything legally obtained that tends to prove, directly or indirectly, that a person may be responsible for the commission of a criminal offense can be legally presented. Proof may include the oral testimony of witnesses or the introduction of physical or documentary evidence.

By definition, *evidence* is any species of proof or probative matter, legally presented at the trial of an issue, by the act of the parties and through the medium of witnesses, records, documents, objects, etc., for the purpose of inducing belief in the minds of the court and jurors as to their contention. In short, evidence is anything offered in court to prove the truth or falsity of a fact at issue. This section discusses each of the Rules of Evidence as they relate to computer crime investigations.

Types of Evidence

Many types of evidence can be offered in court to prove the truth or falsity of a given fact. The most common forms of evidence are direct, real, documentary, and demonstrative. Direct evidence is oral testimony, whereby the knowledge is obtained from any of the witness's five senses and is, in itself, proof or disproof of a fact in issue. Direct evidence is called to prove a specific act (i.e., Eye Witness Statement). Real evidence, also known as associative or physical evidence, is made up of tangible objects that prove or disprove guilt.

Physical evidence includes such things as tools used in the crime, fruits of the crime, perishable evidence capable of reproduction, etc. The purpose of the physical evidence is to link the suspect to the scene of the crime. It is this evidence that has material existence and can be presented to the view of the court and jury for consideration. Documentary evidence is presented to the court in the form of business records, manuals, printouts, etc. Much of the evidence submitted in a computer crime case is documentary evidence. Finally, demonstrative evidence is evidence used to aid the jury. It may be in the form of a model, experiment, chart, or an illustration offered as proof.

When seizing evidence from a computer-related crime, the investigator should collect any and all physical evidence, such as the computer, peripherals, notepads, documentation, etc., in addition to computer-generated evidence. There are four types of computer-generated evidence. They are:

- Visual output on the monitor
- Printed evidence on a printer
- Printed evidence on a plotter
- Film recorder, including magnetic representation on disk, tape, or cartridge, and optical representation on CD

Best Evidence Rule

The Best Evidence Rule, which was established to deter any alteration of evidence, either intentionally or unintentionally, states that the court prefers the original evidence at the trial, rather than a copy, but will accept a duplicate under the following conditions:

- Original is lost or destroyed by fire, flood, or other acts of God. This has included such things as destruction by careless employees or cleaning staff.
- Original is destroyed during the normal course of business.
- Original is in possession of a third party who is beyond the court's subpoena power.

This rule has been relaxed to now allow duplicates unless there is a genuine question as to the original's authenticity, or admission of the duplicate would under the circumstances be unfair.

Exclusionary Rule

In the United States, evidence must be gathered by law enforcement in accordance with court guidelines governing search and seizure or it will be excluded (Fourth Amendment). Any evidence collected in violation of the

Fourth Amendment is considered to be "Fruit of the Poisonous Tree" and will not be admissible. Furthermore, any evidence identified and gathered as a result of the initial inadmissible evidence will also be held to be inadmissible. Evidence may also be excluded for other reasons, such as violations of the Electronic Communications Privacy Act (ECPA) or violations related to provisions of Chapters 2500 and 2700 of Title 18 of the United States Penal Code.

Private citizens are not subject to the Fourth Amendment's guidelines on search and seizure, but are exposed to potential exclusions for violations of the ECPA or Privacy Act. Therefore, internal investigators, private investigators, and Computer Emergency Response Team (CERT) team members should take caution when conducting any internal search, even on company computers. For example, if there were no policy in place explicitly stating the company's right to electronically monitor network traffic on company systems, then internal investigators would be well advised not to set up a sniffer on the network to monitor such traffic. To do so may be a violation of the ECPA.

Hearsay Rule

In the United States and some other countries, a legal factor of computer-generated evidence is that it is considered hearsay. Hearsay is second-hand evidence: evidence that is not gathered from the personal knowledge of the witness but from another source. Its value depends on the veracity and competence of the source. The magnetic charge of the disk or the electronic bit value in memory, which represents the data, is the actual original evidence. The computer-generated evidence is merely a representation of the original evidence.

Under the U.S. Federal Rules of Evidence, all business records, including computer records, are considered "hearsay" because there is no firsthand proof that they are accurate, reliable, and trustworthy. In general, hearsay evidence is not admissible in court. However, there are some well-established exceptions (Rule 803) to the hearsay rule for business records. In *Rosenberg v. Collins,* the court held that if the computer output is used in the regular course of business, then the evidence shall be admitted.

Business Record Exemption to the Hearsay Rule

U.S. Federal Rules of Evidence 803(6) allows a court to admit a report or other business document made at or near the time by, or from information transmitted by, a person with knowledge, if kept in the course of regularly conducted business activity, and if it was the regular practice of that business activity to make the [report or document], all as shown by testimony of the custodian or other qualified witness, unless the source of information or the method or circumstances of preparation indicate lack of trustworthiness.

To meet Rule 803(6), the witness must:

- Have custody of the records in question on a regular basis
- Rely on those records in the regular course of business
- Know that they were prepared in the regular course of business

Audit trails would meet the criteria if they were produced in the normal course of business. The process to produce the output will have to be proven reliable. If computer-generated evidence is used and admissible, the court may order disclosure of the details of the computer, logs, maintenance records, etc., related to the system generating the printout, and then the defense may use that material to attack the reliability of the evidence. If the audit trails are not used or reviewed (at least the exceptions — i.e., failed logon attempts) in the regular course of business, then they may not meet the criteria for admissibility.

U.S. Federal Rules of Evidence 1001(3) provides another exception to the Hearsay Rule. This rule allows a memory or disk dump to be admitted as evidence, although it is not done in the regular course of business. This dump merely acts as statement of fact. System dumps (in binary or hexadecimal) would not be hearsay because they are not being offered to prove the truth of the contents, but only the state of the computer at that time.

Chain of Evidence (Custody)

Once evidence is seized, the next step is to provide for its accountability and to protect its integrity. The Chain of Evidence, which provides a means of accountability, must be adhered to by law enforcement or other investigators when conducting any type of criminal investigation, including a computer crime investigation. The Chain of Evidence is intended to minimize the possibility of tampering with the evidence. The Chain of Evidence must account for all persons who handled or who had access to the evidence. The Chain of Evidence shows:

- Who obtained the evidence
- What was the evidence
- Where and when the evidence was obtained
- Who secured the evidence
- Who had control or possession of the evidence

It may be necessary to have anyone associated with the evidence testify at trial. Private citizens are not required to maintain the same level of control of the evidence as law enforcement, although they would be well advised to do so. Should an internal investigation result in the discovery and collection of computer-related evidence, the investigation team should follow the same, detailed chain of evidence as required by law enforcement. This will help to dispel any objection by the defense, that the evidence is unreliable, should the case go to court.

Admissibility of Evidence

The admissibility of computer-generated evidence is, at best, a moving target. Computer-generated evidence is always suspect because of the ease with which it can be tampered — usually without a trace! Precautionary measures must be taken to ensure that computer-generated evidence has not been tampered with, erased, or added to.

To ensure that only relevant and reliable evidence is entered into the proceedings, the judicial system has adopted the concept of admissibility.

- *Relevancy of evidence:* evidence tending to prove or disprove a material fact. All evidence in court must be relevant and material to the case.
- *Reliability of evidence:* the evidence and the process to produce the evidence must be proven to be reliable. This is one of the most critical aspects of computer-generated evidence.

Once computer-generated evidence meets the Business Record Exemption to the Hearsay Rule, is not excluded for some technicality or violation, follows the Chain of Custody, and is found to be both relevant and reliable, then it is held to be admissible. The defense will attack both the relevancy and reliability of the evidence, so great care should be taken to protect both.

Evidence Life Cycle

The Evidence Life Cycle starts with the discovery and collection of the evidence. It progresses through the following series of states until it is finally returned to the victim or owner:

- Acquisition collection and identification
- Analysis
- Storage, preservation, and transportation
- Presented in court
- Returned to victim (owner)

Collection and Identification. As the evidence is obtained or collected, it must be properly marked to identify it as being the particular piece of evidence gathered at the scene. The collection must be recorded in a logbook identifying the particular piece of evidence, the person who discovered it, and the date, time, and location discovered. The location should be specific enough for later recollection in court. All other types of identifying marks, such as make, model, or serial number, should also be logged. It is of paramount importance to list any type of damage to the particular piece of evidence. This is not only for identification purposes, but will also limit any potential liability should a claim be made later on that you damaged the evidence. When marking evidence, the following guidelines should be followed:

- Mark the actual piece of evidence, if it will not damage the evidence, by writing or scribing your initials, the date, and the case number if known. Seal this evidence in the appropriate container and, again, mark the container by writing or scribing your initials, the date, and the case number, if known.
- If the actual piece of evidence cannot be marked, then seal the evidence in an appropriate container, and mark the container by writing or scribing your initials, the date, and the case number, if known.
- The container should be sealed with evidence tape and your marking should write over the tape, so that if the seal is broken it can be noticed.
- Be extremely careful not to damage the evidence while engraving or marking the piece.

When marking glass or metal, a diamond scriber should be used. For all other objects, a felt-tip pen with indelible ink is recommended. Depending on the nature of the crime, the investigator may wish to preserve latent fingerprints. If so, static-free gloves should be used if working with computer components, instead of standard latex gloves.

Try to always mark evidence the same way, because you will be asked to testify to the fact that you are the person identified by the evidence markings. Keep in mind that the defense is going to try to discredit you as a witness or try some way to keep the evidence out of court, so something as simple as quick, positive identification of your mark is greatly beneficial to the case.

Analysis. This is the stage where comprehensive examination of the evidence itself takes place. Often, this is a very time-consuming exercise, but when done properly, it can yield quality evidence that will be considered reliable in a court of law.

Storage, Preservation, and Transportation. All evidence must be packed and preserved to prevent contamination. It should be protected against heat, extreme cold, humidity, water, magnetic fields, and vibration. The evidence must be protected for future use in court and for return to the original owner. If the evidence is not properly protected, the person or agency responsible for the collection and storage of the evidence may be held liable for damages. Therefore, the proper packing materials should be used whenever possible. Documents and disks (hard, floppy, optical, tapes, etc.)

should be seized and stored in appropriate containers to prevent their destruction. For example, hard disks should be packed in a sealed, static-free bag, within a cardboard box with a foam container. The box should be sealed with evidence tape and an electromagnetic field (EMF) warning label should be affixed to the box. It may be wise to defer to the system administrator or a technical advisor on how to best protect a particular type of system, especially minicomputer systems or mainframes.

Finally, evidence should be transported to a location where it can be stored and locked. Sometimes, the systems are too large to transport; thus, the forensic examination of the system may need to take place on-site.

Presented in Court. Each piece of evidence that is used to prove or disprove a material fact needs to be presented in court. After the initial seizure, the evidence is stored until needed for trial. Each time the evidence is transported to and from the courthouse for the trial, it needs to be handled with the same care as with the original seizure. Additionally, the Chain of Custody must continue to be followed. This process will continue until all testimony related to the evidence is completed. Once the trail is over, the evidence can be returned to the victim (owner).

Returned to Victim (Owner). The final destination of most types of evidence is back with its original owner. Some types of evidence, such as drugs or drug paraphernalia (i.e., contraband), are destroyed after the trial. Any evidence gathered during a search, although maintained by law enforcement, is legally under the control of the courts. And although a seized item may be yours and may even have your name on it, it might not be returned to you unless the suspect signs a release or after a hearing by the court. Unfortunately, many victims do not want to go to trial; they just want to get their property back.

Many investigations merely need the information on a disk to prove or disprove a fact in question; thus, there is no need to seize the entire system. Once a schematic of the system is drawn or photographed, the hard disk can be removed and then transported to a forensic lab for copying. Mirror copies of the suspect disk are obtained using forensic software and then one of those copies can be returned to the victim so that business operations can resume.

Summary

The concept of admissibility is based on the following:

- *Relevancy of evidence.* This means that the evidence must prove or disprove a material fact. That is, the evidence proves or disproves that a crime occurred. It documents the timeframe of the crime, identifies how it was committed, links in suspects through acts or methods, and demonstrates motives for the crime.

- *Reliability of evidence.* The evidence and the process to produce the evidence must be proven reliable.
- *Foundation of admissibility.* Witnesses show that evidence is trustworthy through the identification of the custodian of the information, and the familiarity of the custodian with the information and with EDP procedures in general. They must also document how the evidence is collected, and illustrate how errors are prevented and corrected if they occur. If necessary, the custodian must be able to explain why media is erased, how the information is regularly used in the operation of the business, and how unnecessary operations are eliminated.
- *Legally permissible.* The evidence must have been collected using legal means. For example, information/evidence that is collected using unconstitutional means, unlawful search and seizure, secret recordings (except where authorized by a court), questionable privacy violations, or forced confessions/statements will be inadmissable in court.
- *Evidence identification.* Mark (scribe) correctly.
- *Preservation of evidence.* All evidence must be properly handled and prepared for storage. This has several purposes, including:
  - To protect the evidence from being damaged during transportation and storage prior to court
  - To protect the evidence for its return to the owner
- *Evidence storage.* Once the evidence is properly preserved, it should be transported to a storage facility where it can be locked up and guarded until needed for a trial, or its return to its owner.

Surveillance generally falls into two categories: physical and computer.

- *Physical surveillance* is done at the time of the abuse, through either closed-circuit television (CCTV) or after the fact through undercover operations.
- *Computer surveillance* is accomplished passively through the use of audit logs or actively using electronic monitoring tools, including keyboard and line monitoring. To do this, you must have either a warrant or a statement in your security policy that informs users that they are being monitored or that the corporation has assumed the right to monitor.

Obtaining a *search warrant* is required before an investigator can visit and search for information at a suspect's home or office (only required for law enforcement). Before a warrant can be issued to a law enforcement officer, he or she must demonstrate probable cause, what is to be searched, where, and why.

Entrapment: a person is "entrapped" when he is induced or persuaded to commit a crime that he had no previous intent to commit; and the law as a matter of policy forbids conviction in such a case.

However, there is no entrapment where a person is ready and willing to break the law (or is already breaking the law by unauthorized access) and is merely provided with what appears to be a favorable opportunity to commit the crime. This is usually referred to as *enticement.* For example, it is not entrapment for a police agent to pretend to be someone else and to offer, either directly or through an informer or other decoy, to engage in an unlawful transaction with the person. So, a person would not be a victim of entrapment if the person was ready, willing, and able to commit the crime charged in the indictment whenever opportunity was afforded, and that the police officer(s) or their agent(s) did no more than offer an opportunity.

Search and seizure of computer evidence is often done quickly due to the nature of the evidence. The fact that it is online and electronic usually means that it can be easily erased without any trace and without any proof of it ever existing.

In any case, evidence can be obtained by several means:

- Voluntarily provided or by consent to obtain
- Subpoena from a court
- Search warrant from a court

A court issues the *subpoena* to an individual with the instructions to bring the evidence to court. A *search warrant* is issued to a law enforcement officer or other investigator, allowing them to take the equipment or other evidence, such as telephone logs, email, memos, etc. After seizing the equipment or other materials, it is necessary to preserve the evidence. The evidence must be preserved by maintaining the chain of custody. This includes proper labeling and preservation of the evidence, and a log entry to show where it was taken from, who took it, and who has had contact with it since it was seized.

Dealing with Incidents

Incident response involves actions taken to deal with an incident during and after it occurs. The actions are usually designed to mitigate the impact of the incident. The primary goals of incident response include:

- Provide an effective and efficient means of dealing with the situation in a manner that reduces the potential impact on the organization.
- Provide management with sufficient information to decide on an appropriate course of action.

- Maintain or restore business continuity.
- Defend against future attacks.
- Deter future attacks through investigation and prosecution.

Effective incident response requires not only some type of formal methodology, but also a diverse skill set on the part of the people involved in the process. To meet the listed goals, the members of any incident response team should have recognition, technical, and response skills.

Recognition Skills

Being able to recognize that a computer crime incident has actually occurred is a vital skill. Although there are various automated systems that can be used as part of an incident detection capability, it usually comes down to a person making the final decision as to whether an incident has actually occurred or it was a false-positive. Crucial skills include the ability to recognize:

- Abnormal activities
- Suspicious activities
- Malicious code activities
- Pattern recognition
- Alarms

Abnormal activities are different from suspicious activities. An event is abnormal relative to the environment. A relatively neutral activity that alone might not seem to be a problem may be considered "abnormal," assuming that normal network activity patterns are known (e.g., excessive CPU usage during off-peak times). Suspicious activities are more obvious and easier to notice (e.g., port scanning, brute-force password guessing). Pattern recognition, on the other hand, refers to identifying particular patterns throughout the network environment that indicate the presence or remnants of a potential attack or incident.

Technical Skills

Once an incident has been recognized, special skills are required to begin dealing with the various pieces of technology involved and correctly handling the incident itself. These skills involve proper training related to:

- Audit trails and event logs
- Incident logs
- Forensic evidence collection and protection
- Counter or corrective measures

The proper collection of evidence from the log files is paramount, as usually there is only one chance to collect the data in a manner that does not "taint" the evidence. If the log file evidence is handled incorrectly, it may be inadmissible in a court of law or labor hearing, despite being the proverbial "smoking gun."

Response Skills

Once the decision has been made to initiate the response escalation process, the knowledge and training of the team is tested to proficiently execute the phases of the escalation process. These skills can be obtained from various organizations such as the Carnegie Mellon CERT Coordination Center (CERT/CC), or the Forum for Incident Response and Security Teams (FIRST).

Guidelines for Incident Response

Incident response is linked to the primary goals of information system security. Incident response can be used to restore confidentiality, integrity, and availability. Following a formal methodology for incident response provides several advantages to the organization. A methodology assists in providing a structured logical approach during a chaotic situation. A formal methodology or process also increases the efficiency of dealing with the incident, which can greatly reduce the impact on the organization, both financially and from a resources perspective. A formal methodology breaks the incident into more manageable, smaller phases or stages that can be tackled in a logical fashion. Following a formal methodology also provides evidence of due diligence and forethought, which may become considerations if liability issues arise in the aftermath of an incident.

Policies, Procedures, and Guidelines. Policies, procedures, and guidelines are the foundation for any good process or methodology. This is true with incident response as well. Incident response policy and procedures need to be developed before an incident occurs. Although incident response appears to be a reactive process, it is really the reactive execution of a proactive plan.

A formal incident response policy and related procedures are required for successful response to an incident. The policy and procedures must have the approval and support of senior management to ensure that appropriate resources are available when required. Additionally, each member of the incident response team must be informed and knowledgeable of the plan, as well as their specific responsibilities. Communication and enforcement of the organization's policies aid in ensuring that potential incidents are reported in a timely fashion for proper investigation and response. During the follow-up phase of response escalation, the policies and procedures are reviewed to ensure that they are adequate.

Incident Response Team

The formation of an incident response team is a critical step in being proactive. The incident response team should be made up of individuals from the various business units who would be affected by an incident, or be required to provide necessary skills or knowledge. These individuals should have clearly defined roles and responsibilities. The following list, while not exhaustive, does represent some of the more common functions that should be represented on a team:

- Information Security
- Legal
- Human Resources
- Public Relations
- Communications
- Physical Security
- Network Security
- Network and System Administrators
- Internal Audit

Response Escalation Process

The response escalation process assumes that sufficient preparation activities have taken place. This includes having management-sanctioned policies, procedures, and a clearly defined incident response team with clearly defined roles and responsibilities. The escalation process consists of three major functional categories or stages. These are further broken down into six phases. The phases are:

- Triage
- Notification and Identification
- Action/Reaction
- Containment, Analysis, Tracing
- Follow-up
- Repair and Recovery, Prevention

Information, observations, and recommendations from the all the phases are "fed back" into the system in order to mature the escalation process.

Triage. The term *triage* is borrowed from the medical community and refers to the process of receiving, initially sorting, and prioritizing information to facilitate its appropriate handling. The initial act of detecting when an incident has occurred is vital to the triage process.

Detection includes:

- Notification of an event
- Identifying that an event has become an incident
- Determining if an incident has violated any policies or laws

Notification and Identification. Notification and identification is one of the key steps in effectively dealing with an incident. Before one can respond to an incident, the appropriate team must be alerted to a possible incident. Reports may be received manually; however, they should be as automated as possible. Automated alert systems increase the speed at which alerts are processed and may assist in the triage process. Although the process should be automated, a person should still make the final judgment as to the validity of the alerts. One of the downfalls of automated systems continues to be the high rate of false-positives.

The notification and identification process covers:

- Being alerted to the fact that something has happened
- Monitoring systems:
  - Intrusion detection systems
  - Firewall logs
  - Event logs
- Alert function
  - Preferably automated
- Human decision
  - False-positives

Action/Reaction. Having identified a potential incident and organized the relevant facts, the Incident Response Team is notified and everyone plays their respective roles. One of the main goals of incident response is to mitigate the damage that an incident may cause to the organization. It is bad enough that something got through the defenses; now we have to deal with it, both as effectively and as efficiently as possible.

Once an event becomes an incident, it must be addressed quickly, efficiently, and within the appropriate legal boundaries. Blindly reacting will not necessarily reduce the impact; in fact, in some cases it may compound things. The Incident Response Team needs to decide how to react appropriately to the incident, what actions need to be taken, and in what order. Action/Reaction encompasses the phases of:

- Containment
- Analysis
- Tracking

Containment. Containment limits the extent of the attack. This may involve unplugging systems from the network, or from the Internet. The decision of when or how to contain a system(s) may be a simple decision, as with viruses (i.e., isolating the affected or infected systems), or it may be more complicated, especially if the system is vital to the organization, such as the Website for online banking. It is important to keep in mind that there are some attacks that cannot be easily contained, such as distributed denial-of-service attacks, network scans, and some of the newer viruses and malicious applets.

In some cases, the decision to track down the attacker may take precedence and the decision is made not to contain the incident but to keep it "alive" in the hopes of discovering the source of the attack. Keeping the incident alive carries with it the risk of exposing other systems to the attack, or the attackers realize they are being watched and either erase the evidence or use the system to jump from, resulting in an attack against a third party. It is therefore necessary for organizations to determine their level of acceptable risk regarding incidents as part of their preparation process.

The containment strategy should also address controlling what information is given to the press or media. The public relations fallout from an attack can be just as damaging as the loss of any data or proprietary information (e.g., negative consumer confidence, negative shareholder confidence, lowered stock price). Only those team members trained and authorized to talk with the press should be allowed to do so.

Analysis. During the early stages of an incident, we may not completely understand the ramifications of the attack. Careful analysis of logs, audit trails, videotapes, etc., will increase the amount of information available to the team. The more information the team can collect, the better will be its understanding of the scope, extent, and impact of the incident. Some decisions during the incident require executive management or corporate counsel involvement. Consequently, the incident response team must be capable of presenting accurate and concise information to senior management. Management needs to make informed decisions during a crisis, as opposed to merely being reflexive.

During the analysis phase, proper documentation must be maintained, and any potential evidence must be handled in a forensic-friendly manner. "Forensic friendly" refers to maintaining the chain of custody, documenting all the steps taken, ensuring the integrity of the logs, files, etc. Integrity can be maintained by making copies of all important logs, files, and data. These copies should be made to a write-once media, and both the original and the copies should be mathematically signed. Hash signatures used in the signing should be documented.

Depending on what is discovered during the analysis phase, a proper forensic examination of the system(s) may be required. A forensic examination should only be carried out by someone properly trained in computer forensics. Some general guidelines are covered in the forensic section of the guide.

Ultimately, the analysis should provide information related to:

- Who
- What
- When
- Where
- Why
- How

Tracing. Tracing attacks in the context of response escalation refers to attempting to discover the origin of the attack. This may include finding the source IP address, domain name, MAC address, or hostname.

There are a number of different methods available to trace the source of an incident. The method chosen depends on whether there is any initial indication the attack origin was internal or external. Information relating to the apparent source can often be obtained from examining router, intrusion detection system, or firewall logs.

Tracing an attack back to its source usually depends on the cross-correlation of the various log file information from several different systems. Many of the logs may belong to systems owned by outside agencies or third parties (e.g., Internet service providers or telecommunications carriers). Time is a critical factor here, as the period of log file retentions both internally and externally is often left to the discretion of the system administrators. If the system generates a large amount of log information or it is not used for billing purposes in the case of third parties, the data related to the incident may have been overwritten or unavailable. The sooner requests for log file information are made internally and to outside third parties, the better the chance that this information will still be available.

There are two primary types of tracing. Tracing can be done using either a direct trace or indirect trace method. In the direct method, the tracing is done in real-time — while the attack is still occurring. This allows the investigator to have the most up-to-date information. The direct method often requires the cooperation of outside administrators whose systems have been used to perpetrate the attack or as "gateways" for the attack. The direct tracing method attempts to work the source back, often through several parties. It continues until the apparent source of the attack is obtained. It is important to remember that source addresses can be "spoofed," and not every third party or outside agency may be willing or able to cooperate.

The indirect tracing method does not occur in "real-time." The investigator constructs an attack path from various log and system files. This path indicates the times and dates, as well as the source of various connections made during the attack. The indirect method allows for a more thorough examination, as there is not as much emphasis on reacting quickly. However, by not reacting quickly, the "trail" may go cold and result in the inability to trace beyond a certain point.

Again, evidence collection cannot be stressed enough. Investigators must make detailed notes outlining their activities, who had access to the data, how it was collected, what integrity controls were used, and where the data was stored.

Follow-Up. There are actually two kinds of follow-up (repair and recovery, and prevention) in the response escalation methodology. The broader area deals with events and procedures occurring after the tracking phase and the actual identification of lessons learned from dealing with a particular attack.

Follow-up is one of the most important stages in incident response. This stage enables the organization to mature its response escalation process and learn what worked well and what needs to be fixed. The follow-up phase usually includes a "post-mortem" analysis of sorts, but is not intended to be a blame-laying exercise. The focus is on improving the response capability and must be constructive.

Once the incident has been dealt with, a debriefing to determine what went well and what did not is highly recommended. The debriefing should include a walk-through of the process, how and why decisions were made, and an evaluation of the conclusions and the process used. The findings from the post-incident debriefing should be adapted into a formal document and presented to management. The report should emphasize any recommendations and an action plan for implementation. As previously indicated, the findings must be "fed" back into the Incident Response process, forming a "feedback" loop.

Incident response is a dynamic process and the procedures are living documents providing the necessary framework. However, the team's process must continue to develop as deficiencies are identified or as new technology and techniques are learned and available.

The phases that are after the tracking phase focus on activities required to bring systems back online and functioning securely again. These phases include:

- Repair and Recovery
- Prevention

Upon successful evaluation and containment of the incident, affected systems may require restoration to return them to full service. The Repair and Recovery process ensures the systems are returned to a known state for continued operations. Finally, further evaluation is required to determine how the incident could have been prevented.

Repair and Recovery. Systems affected by the incident or attack may need to be restored from known clean sources to ensure that any artifacts and residue from the attack have been completely cleaned from the systems. In most cases, the organization will want to restore normal or near-normal service as soon as possible. Care must be taken to ensure that the need to resume business is balanced against the danger of placing systems back online before they have been completely repaired or recovered. Depending on the nature and effect of the incident, the organization may choose to implement its disaster recovery plan to manage the service restoration process. As indicated in the previous phases, concerns over the preservation of evidence must also be considered.

The repair/recovery phase's goals can be summarized as:

- Reduce the damage:
  - Reputation
  - Contractual obligations
  - Financial
- Protect the environment while recovering:
  - Limit services and functions
- Repair systems and environment

Prevention. Despite the controls in place, unless reviewed and possibly strengthened, the attacked system may be vulnerable to additional attacks without further countermeasures. Preventative strategies should include detailed plans for system patches and upgrades, additional security controls and safeguards such as new firewalls, intrusion detection systems, active monitoring, anti-virus systems, and, in some cases, additional education and training for administrators and users. It is common to see these preventative strategies highlighted in the Recommendations section of the executive management document submitted as part of the overall follow-up process.

Sanctions. Successfully dealing with an incident does not necessarily end when the response escalation phases are complete; there are still other issues that management will need to address. These decisions often include deciding whether or not to proceed with sanctions against the party(ies) responsible for the incident. Management should be arriving at this decision after reviewing all the relevant information collected and analyzed by the incident response team during the course of the response process. This information may include details from a forensic analysis of compromised systems. The decision to proceed with sanctions should be made in consultation with the appropriate legal and human resource advisors, and should weigh the impact of the incident with the impact that any publicity arising from the sanctions might generate.

The types of sanctions that can be considered following an incident include:

- Criminal
- Civil
- Job sanctions
  - Termination
  - Suspension
  - Permanent file entry

Information Sharing. A key component of a mature incident response methodology is the ability to share information both internally within the business units or departments, and with external agencies. It is vital that the incident response policy and procedures clearly indicate how internal information sharing is conducted. Regardless of the attack source, the age-old adage that "loose lips sink ships" is very pertinent. This is especially true if the source of the attack is internal. Management-approved procedures should clearly specify how and who is authorized to deal with:

- Internal reporting teams
- External reporting agencies
- Law enforcement

Most organizations that suffer an attack never share this fact with anyone else. This lack of sharing of information allows attackers to spread their respective attacks to a much larger victim base. The attackers themselves readily share information about their attacks or conquests and exchange intelligence as to the vulnerabilities, etc. There have been efforts to establish centralized bodies to collect and disseminate information regarding attacks and vulnerabilities, although the lack of attack reporting has limited the success of these efforts. This lack of information sharing has left security professionals in the unenviable position of playing a game of catch-up with the attackers.

External Reporting. Businesses and organizations need encouragement to contact external agencies, including law enforcement. Many industries (e.g., automotive, healthcare, education, government, etc.) have started to form ad hoc security groups sharing limited amounts of information regarding attempts, attacks, discovered vulnerabilities, and in some cases generally accepted security practices. The goal is to help their respective industries become harder targets and be more proactive.

When dealing with external agencies, providing the appropriate amount of information relating to the incident and specifying exactly what information you expect/require is extremely important. CERT/CC has several excellent online documents dealing with the reporting of incidents, and even what to report. Generally, the following provides a good starting point for information to include when contacting an outside agency:

- Any assigned incident reference numbers
- Contact information
- Disclosure information
- Summary of hosts involved
- Description of activity
- Log extracts showing the activity
- Time zone and accuracy of your clock
- Clarification of what you would like from the recipient

It is highly recommended to report time zones as an offset from Greenwich Mean Time (GMT) (e.g., +6 GMT). This establishes a common reference point and can avoid confusion when dealing with agencies or organizations in different time zones.

According to the CERT/CC, the types of violations organizations and businesses should report include:

- Any violations of security policy
- Attempted violations
- Denial-of-service
- Unauthorized use of a system
- Unauthorized changes to hardware, software, or firmware

Reporting to Law Enforcement. Although the decision to liaise or report an incident to law enforcement is generally made by corporate counsel or management, the actual relationship will often be handled by an information system security professional. Therefore, it is prudent to establish a relationship with local law enforcement prior to an incident, as part of the incident response preparation process.

Obtaining a clear understanding of who exactly to contact, what information they require, the specifics of the media that they prefer to have data and potential evidence stored on, and whether they have the technical capability and preference to conduct a forensic analysis can greatly smooth the entire process and eliminate unnecessary delays.

Some general rules of thumb when dealing with law enforcement include:

- Obtain management permission.
- Use a single point of contact (e.g., information security officer, legal department).
- Provide a detailed chronology of the incident.
- Provide all documentation, logs, data, videotapes, etc.
- Develop a formal contact procedure with the assistance of the local agency.

Assurance, Trust, and Confidence Mechanisms

Although the incident response methodology is presented in a serial manner, most incidents are not so kind. Members of the incident response team need to be flexible and be ready to have phases occur in parallel. Generally, there is no clear transition between one phase and the next and, as in the case of internal attacks, there may be no clear phases whatsoever.

When developing an incident response capability, it is important to remember the following points:

- It takes time to use a methodology; there is a learning curve.
- Practice scenarios should be part of the training process.
- Methodologies need tailor-made customization for the organization.
- The follow-up stage is critical to mature the process and methodology.
- Using a methodology brings some control to the chaos of dealing with incidents.

An indication of the success of the investigation process is available through use of a follow-up procedure. In the form of an audit of investigations, it can be determined if there was a timely resolution of the situation. This will also enable a determination of whether there was a thorough and comprehensive investigation and a feel for the effectiveness of interaction with other departments or outside agencies during the investigation. Finally, an effort should be made to assess the impact on morale within the organization as a result of the investigation. If it is conducted with appropriate discretion, the morale impact should be minimal, if not even positive.

Information Protection and Management Services

The information security function should be prepared to assist in the creation of policy and procedures related to incident investigation. This should include helping with the selection and training of members for the computer incident response team.

Also, completed investigations can be used as a training tool in security awareness training classes to create an awareness of policy, risks, and threats to the organization because they provide recognizable situations that employees can relate to. They can be used to show lessons learned — see, it can happen here. It is a useful way to explain the risk to sensitive/critical information. However, care should be taken to ensure that people's reputations are not harmed and that the information used is accurate and meaningful, not just inflammatory.

10.3 Ethics

Ethics is the field of study concerned with questions of value, that is, judgments about what type of human behavior is "good" or "bad" in any given situation. Ethics are the standards, values, morals, principles, etc., on which to base one's decisions or actions; often, there is no clear "right" or "wrong" answer.

Information Protection Requirements

Certified professionals, including those holding the CISSP, are held morally, and sometimes legally, to a higher standard of ethical behavior. In promoting proper computing behavior within the industry and the confines of our corporate boundaries, professionals should incorporate ethics into their organizational policies and awareness programs. Several organizations have addressed the issue of ethical behavior through ethics guidelines. These include organizations such as the Computer Ethics Institute, the Internet Activities Board, the International Computer Security Association, the Information Systems Security Association, and of most importance to the CISSP, (ISC)^2.

In many instances, there is a fine line between ethical and unethical activities. What may be unethical does not even have to be illegal, depending on the company and its line of business. However, in general, any user who intentionally uses a computer to remove or disrupt services to other users, impact privacy, or conduct Internet-wide experiments is considered unethical.

As far as the information security field is concerned, there is an ongoing need to encourage adoption of ethical guidelines and standards. There is also a seemingly ever-growing need to inform users through security awareness training activities about their ethical responsibilities.

Summarized in the following list are the ethical responsibilities of certain user groups to others.

- *Data collectors to data subjects:* accuracy and privacy
- *Data custodians to data owner:* availability, integrity, and confidentiality
- *Data users to owners/subjects:* confidentiality and integrity
- *System users to system owner:* availability and software integrity
- *System managers to users:* availability, integrity
- *Users to other users:* availability

Computer Ethics

The computer security professional needs to both understand and influence the behavior of everyday computer users. Traditionally, security managers have concentrated on building security into the system hardware and software, on developing procedures, and on educating end users about procedures and acceptable behavior. Now, the computer professional must also help develop the meaning of ethical computing and help influence computer end users to adopt notions of ethical computing into their everyday behavior.

Fundamental Changes to Society

Computer technology has changed the practical meaning of many important, even fundamental, human and societal concepts. Although most computer professionals would agree that computers change nothing about human ethics, computer and information technologies have caused and will pose many new problems. Indeed, computers have changed the nature and scope of accessing and manipulating information and communications. As a result, computers and computer communications have significantly changed many of the concepts most basic to society. There is little doubt that the digital age is causing significant changes in ways that are not yet fully appreciated.

Some of those changes are bad. For example, combining the known costs of the apparent unethical and illegal uses of computer and information technology — factors such as telephone and PBX fraud, computer viruses, and digital piracy — amounts to several billion dollars annually. When these obvious problems are combined with the kinds of computing behavior that society does not yet fully comprehend as unethical and that society has not yet labeled illegal or antisocial, it is clear that a great computer ethics void exists.

Computer security professionals must lead the way in educating the digital society about policies and procedures and behavior that clearly can be discerned as right or wrong. The education process involves defining those issues that will become gut feelings, common sense, and acceptable etiquette of the whole society of end users. Computer professionals need to help develop and disseminate the rituals, celebrations, habits, and beliefs for users.

In other words, they are the pivotal people responsible for both defining computer ethics and disseminating their understanding to the computer-using public.

Information Protection Environment

Common Fallacies of the Computer Generation

The lack of early, computer-oriented childhood rearing and conditioning has led to several pervasive fallacies that generally (and loosely) apply to nearly all computer and digital information users. The generation of computer users includes those from 7 to 70 years old who use computing and other information technologies. Like all fallacies, some people are heavily influenced by them, and some are less so. There are clearly more fallacies than those described here, but these are probably the most important. Most ethical problems that surface in discussions show roots in one or more of these fallacies.

The Computer Game Fallacy

Most computer games are structured in such a way that they do not generally let the user cheat. So it is hardly surprising for computer users to think, at least subliminally, that computers in general will prevent them from cheating and, by extension, from otherwise doing wrong.

This fallacy also probably has roots in the very binary nature of computers. Programmers in particular are used to the precise nature that all instructions must have before a program will work. An error in syntax, a misplaced comma, improper capitalization, and transposed characters in a program will almost certainly prevent it from compiling or running correctly once compiled. Even nonprogramming computer users are introduced to the powerful message that everything about computers is exact and that the computer will not allow even the tiniest transgression. DOS commands, batch file commands, configuration parameters, macro commands, spreadsheet formulas, and even file names used for word processing must have precisely the right format and syntax, or they will not work. To most users, computers seem entirely black and white — sometimes frustratingly so. By extension, what people do with computers seems to take on a black-and-white quality. But what users often misunderstand while using computers is that although the computer operates with a very strict set of inviolable rules, most of what people do with computers is just as gray as all other human interactions.

It is a common defense for malicious hackers to say something like, "If they didn't want people to break into their computer, they should have used better security." Many hackers think that they are providing a service to computer and telecommunication system professionals when they explore computer systems, find faults and weaknesses in the security systems, and then publish how to break into these systems.

Some hackers are effectively saying, "If you don't want me to break in, make it impossible to do so. If there is a way to get around your security, then I should get around it in order to expose the problem." These malicious hackers would never consider jumping over a fence into their neighbor's backyard, entering the kitchen through an open kitchen window, sitting in the living room, reading the mail, making a few phone calls, watching television, and leaving. They would not brag or publish that their neighbor's home was not secure enough, that they found a problem or loophole, or that it was permissible to go in because it was possible to do so. However, using a computer to perform analogous activities makes perfect sense to them.

The computer game fallacy also affects the rest of the members of the computer-user generation in ways that are a good deal more subtle. The computer provides a powerful one-way mirror behind which people can hide. Computer users can be voyeurs without being caught. And if what is being done is not permissible, the thinking is that the system would somehow prevent them from doing it.

The Law-Abiding Citizen Fallacy

Recognizing that computers cannot prevent everything that might be wrong, many users understand that laws will provide some guidance. But many (perhaps most) users sometimes confuse what is legal, which defines the minimum standard about which all can be justly judged, with what is reasonable behavior, which clearly calls for individual judgment.

Similarly, people confuse things that they have a right to do with things that are right to do. Computer virus writers do this all the time. They say, "The First Amendment (of the United States) gives me the constitutional right to write anything I want, including computer viruses. Because computer viruses are an expression, and a form of writing, the Constitution also protects the distribution of them, the talking about them, and the promotion of them as free speech."

Nearly anyone living in the civilized world would agree that people have the right to write almost anything they want. However, they also have the responsibility to consider the ramifications of their actions and to behave accordingly.

The Shatterproof Fallacy

How many times have computer novices been told, "Don't worry, the worst you can do with your computer is accidentally erase or mess up a file — and even if you do that, you can probably get it back. You can't really hurt anything."

Although computers are tools, they are tools that can harm. Yet most users are totally oblivious to the fact that they have actually hurt someone else through actions on their computer. Using electronic mail on the Internet to denigrate someone constitutes malicious chastisement of someone in public. In the non-digital world, people can be sued for libel for these kinds of actions; but on the Internet, users find it convenient to not be held responsible for their words.

Forwarding email without at least the implied permission of all of its authors often leads to harm or embarrassment of participants who thought they were conferring privately. Using email to stalk someone, to send unwanted mail or junk mail, and to send sexual innuendoes or other material that is not appreciated by the recipient all constitute harmful use of computers.

Software piracy is another way in which computer users can hurt people. Those people are not only programmers and struggling software companies, but also end users who must pay artificially high prices for the software and systems they buy and the stockholders and owners of successful companies who deserve a fair return on their investment.

It is astonishing that a computer user would defend the writing of computer viruses. Typically, the user says, "My virus is not a malicious one. It does not cause any harm. It is a benign virus. The only reason I wrote it was to satisfy my intellectual curiosity and to see how it would spread." Such users truly miss out on the ramifications of their actions. Viruses, by definition, travel from computer to computer without the knowledge or permission of the computer's owner or operator.

Viruses are just like other kinds of contaminants (e.g., contaminants in a lake) except that they grow (replicate) much like a cancer. Computer users cannot know they have a virus unless they specifically test their computers or diskettes for it. If the neighbor of a user discovers a virus, then the user is obliged to test his or her system for it and so are the thousand or so other neighbors that the user and the user's neighbors have collectively.

759

The hidden costs of computer viruses are enormous. Even if an experienced person with the right tools needs only ten minutes to get rid of a virus — and even if the virus infects only four or five computers in a site, then the people at the site are obliged to check all 1000 computers to find out just which five computers are infected.

The shatterproof fallacy is the pervasive feeling that what a person does with a computer could hurt at most a few files on the machine. It stems from the computer generation's frequent inability to consider the ramifications of the things we do with computers before we do them.

The Candy-from-a-Baby Fallacy

Guns and poison make killing easy (i.e., it can be done from a distance with no strength or fight), but not necessarily right. Poisoning the water supply is quite easy, but it is beyond the gut-level acceptability of even the most bizarre schizophrenic.

Software piracy and plagiarism are incredibly easy using a computer. Computers excel at copying things, and nearly every computer user is guilty of software piracy. But just because it is easy does not mean that it is right.

Studies by the Software Publisher's Association (SPA) and Business Software Alliance (BSA) show that software piracy is a multi-billion dollar problem in the world today — clearly a huge problem.

By law and by any semblance of intellectual property rights held both in Western societies and most of the rest of the world, copying a program for use without paying for it is theft. It is no different than shoplifting or being a stowaway on an airliner, and an average user would never consider stealing a box of software from a computer store's display case or stowing away on a flight because the plane had empty seats.

The Hacker's Fallacy

The single most widely held piece of The Hacker's Ethic is: "As long as the motivation for doing something is to learn and not to otherwise gain or make a profit, then doing it is acceptable." This is actually quite a strong, respected, and widely held belief among people who call themselves non-malicious hackers.

To be a hacker, a person's primary goal must be to learn for the sake of learning — just to find out what happens if one does a certain thing at a particular time under a specific condition.

The Free Information Fallacy

There is a common notion that information wants to be free, as though it had a mind of its own. The fallacy probably stems from the fact that once created in digital form, information is very easy to copy and tends to get distributed widely. The fallacy totally misses the point that the wide distribution is at the whim of people who copy and disseminate data and people who allow this to happen.

The field of ethics, also called moral philosophy, involves systematizing, defending, and recommending concepts of right and wrong behavior. Philosophers today usually divide ethical theories into three general subject areas: metaethics, normative ethics, and applied ethics.

Metaethics investigates where our ethical principles come from and what they mean. Are they merely social inventions? Do they involve more than expressions of our individual emotions? Metaethical answers to these questions focus on the issues of universal truths, the will of God, the role of reason in ethical judgments, and the meaning of ethical terms themselves.

Normative ethics involves a more practical task, which is to arrive at moral standards that regulate right and wrong conduct. Should I borrow my roommate's car without first asking him? Should I steal food to support my starving family? Ideally, these moral questions could be immediately answered by consulting the moral guidelines provided by normative theories.

Finally, applied ethics involves examining specific controversial issues, such as abortion, infanticide, animal rights, environmental concerns, homosexuality, capital punishment, or nuclear war. By using the conceptual tools of metaethics and normative ethics, discussions in applied ethics try to resolve these controversial issues. The lines of distinction between metaethics, normative ethics, and applied ethics are often blurry. For example, the issue of abortion is an applied ethical topic because it involves a specific type of controversial behavior. But it also depends on more general normative principles, such as the right of self-rule and the right to life, which are litmus tests for determining the morality of that procedure. The issue also rests on metaethical issues such as, "where do rights come from?" and "what kind of beings have rights?"

Computer ethics are normally associated with normative ethics. Moral guidelines are usually what dictate "normal" ethical behavior for computer users, but even "normal ethical behavior" tends to be different for most people. The reason for this is that normative ethics are shaped by a number of different elements, which may include:

- Common good/interest
- National interest

761

- Religion
- Individual rights
- Enlightened self-interest
- Law professional ethics/practices
- Standards of good practice
- Tradition/culture
- Family values
- Educational experiences
- Work experiences
- Personal relationships
- Etc.

The environment for ethics includes all aspects of an organization — the culture, market, government interface, policies, and procedures that govern employees behavior and interactions with outside vendors, customers, regulatory agencies, and law enforcement.

Professional Codes of Ethics

Relevant professional codes of ethics for the security professional include the (ISC)² and the ISSA codes of ethics, which follow below. The sources for these are the respective Web sites, www.ISC2.org and www.issa.org. Also included below are the ethical statements made by the Internet Architecture Board (IAB) (www.iab.org) in relation to Internet usage. Exhibit 3 is an excerpt from the (ISC)² Code of Ethics.

The Internet Architecture Board

The IAB is now known as the Internet Architecture Board. Established in 1983, the IAB was originally called the Internet Activities Board when the Internet was still largely a research activity of the U.S. Government. Today, the IAB consists of 13 voting members; and one of its goals is to offer ethics-related statements concerning the use of the Internet. Some issues discussed in IAB meetings include:

- The future of Internet addressing
- Architectural principles of the Internet
- Future goals and directions for the IETF
- Management of top-level domains in the Domain Name System
- Registration of MIME types
- International character sets
- Charging for addresses
- Tools needed for renumbering

Ethics and the Internet (RFC 1087) state that access to and use of the Internet is a privilege and should be treated as such by all users.

Exhibit 3. (ISC)² Code of Ethics

All information systems security professionals who are certified by (ISC)² recognize that such certification is a privilege that must be both earned and maintained. In support of this principle, all Certified Information Systems Security Professionals (CISSPs) commit to fully support this Code of Ethics. CISSPs who intentionally or knowingly violate any provision of the Code will be subject to action by a peer review panel, which may result in the revocation of certification.

There are only four mandatory canons in the code. By necessity such high-level guidance is not intended to substitute for the ethical judgment of the professional.

Additional guidance is provided for each of the canons. While this guidance may be considered by the Board in judging behavior, it is advisory rather than mandatory. It is intended to help the professional in identifying and resolving the inevitable ethical dilemmas that will confront him/her.

Code of Ethics Preamble:

- Safety of the commonwealth, duty to our principals, and to each other requires that we adhere, and be seen to adhere, to the highest ethical standards of behavior.
- Therefore, strict adherence to this code is a condition of certification.

Code of Ethics Canons:

- Protect society, the commonwealth, and the infrastructure.
- Act honorably, honestly, justly, responsibly, and legally.
- Provide diligent and competent service to principals.
- Advance and protect the profession.

The following additional guidance is given in furtherance of these goals.

Objectives for Guidance

In arriving at the following guidance, the committee is mindful of its responsibility to:

- Give guidance for resolving good v. good and bad v. bad dilemmas.
- To encourage right behavior such as:
  - Research
  - Teaching
  - Identifying, mentoring, and sponsoring candidates for the profession
  - Valuing the certificate
- To discourage such behavior as:
  - Raising unnecessary alarm, fear, uncertainty, or doubt
  - Giving unwarranted comfort or reassurance
  - Consenting to bad practice
  - Attaching weak systems to the public net
  - Professional association with non-professionals
  - Professional recognition of or association with amateurs
  - Associating or appearing to associate with criminals or criminal behavior

However, these objectives are provided for information only; the professional is not required or expected to agree with them

In resolving the choices that confront him, the professional should keep in mind that the following guidance is advisory only. Compliance with the guidance is neither necessary nor sufficient for ethical conduct.

(continued)

Exhibit 3. (ISC)² Code of Ethics (Continued)

Protect society, the commonwealth, and the infrastructure

- Promote and preserve public trust and confidence in information and systems.
- Promote the understanding and acceptance of prudent information security measures.
- Preserve and strengthen the integrity of the public infrastructure.
- Discourage unsafe practice.

Act honorably, honestly, justly, responsibly, and legally

- Tell the truth; make all stakeholders aware of your actions on a timely basis.
- Observe all contracts and agreements, express or implied.
- Treat all constituents fairly. In resolving conflicts, consider public safety and duties to principals, individuals, and the profession in that order.
- Give prudent advice; avoid raising unnecessary alarm or giving unwarranted comfort. Take care to be truthful, objective, cautious, and within your competence.
- When resolving differing laws in different jurisdictions, give preference to the laws of the jurisdiction in which you render your service.

Provide diligent and competent service to principals

- Preserve the value of their systems, applications, and information.
- Respect their trust and the privileges that they grant you.
- Avoid conflicts of interest or the appearance thereof.
- Render only those services for which you are fully competent and qualified.

Advance and protect the profession

- Sponsor for professional advancement those best qualified. All other things equal, prefer those who are certified and who adhere to these canons. Avoid professional association with those whose practices or reputation might diminish the profession.
- Take care not to injure the reputation of other professionals through malice or indifference.
- Maintain your competence; keep your skills and knowledge current. Give generously of your time and knowledge in training others.

ISSA Code of Ethics

The Information Systems Security Association, Inc. (ISSA) promotes management practices ensuring the availability, integrity and confidentiality of organizational information resources. To achieve this goal, members of the association must reflect the highest standards of ethical conduct and technical competence. Therefore, ISSA has established the following Code of Ethics and requires its observance as a prerequisite and continuation of membership and affiliation with the association.

As an applicant for membership and as a member of ISSA, I have in the past and will in the future:

- Perform all professional activities and duties in accordance with the law and the highest of ethical principles;
- Promote good information security concepts and practices;
- Maintain the confidentiality of all proprietary or otherwise sensitive information encountered in the course of professional activities;

(continued)

Exhibit 3. (ISC)² Code of Ethics (Continued)

- Discharge professional responsibilities with diligence and honesty;
- Refrain from any activities that might constitute a conflict of interest or otherwise damage the reputation of employers, the information security profession, or the association; and
- Not intentionally injure or impugn the professional reputation or practice of colleagues, clients, or employers.

As far as ethical usage of the Internet is concerned, the IAB strongly characterizes as unethical and unacceptable any activity that purposely:

- Seeks to gain unauthorized access to the resources of the Internet
- Disrupts the intended use of the Internet
- Wastes resources (people, capacity, computer) through such actions
- Destroys the integrity of computer-based information
- Compromises the privacy of users

As a general ethical guideline, the IAB publishes the following statement:

The Internet exists in the general research milieu. Portions of it continue to be used to support research and experimentation on networking. Because experimentation on the Internet has the potential to affect all of its components and users, researchers have the responsibility to exercise great caution in the conduct of their work. Negligence in the conduct of Internet-wide experiments is both irresponsible and unacceptable.

Security Technology and Tools

There are some organizations sponsoring and addressing good ethical practices and codes in the professional community. These include the:

- Computer Ethics Institute
- Association for Computing Machinery
- Canadian Information Processing Society
- Information Systems Security Association
- The National Computer Ethics and Responsibilities Campaign (NCERC)
- International Computer Security Association

The following activities can help security managers encourage ethical use of computers within their organizations:

- Develop a corporate guide to computer ethics for the organization.
- Develop a computer ethics policy to supplement the computer security policy.
- Add information about computer ethics to the employee handbook.
- Find out whether the organization has a business ethics policy, and expand it to include computer ethics.

- Learn more about computer ethics and spread what is learned.

Assurance, Trust, and Confidence Mechanisms

Confidence in the computing ethics program can be obtained from periodic security reviews that consist of monitoring employee's performance. The use of violation reporting mechanisms can be useful inputs for such reviews. Employees consistently attempting to access resources for which they are not authorized or to exceed their assigned privileges may be suspect of not following ethical standards established by the organization. Often, complaints from customers, vendors, and employees can lead to uncovering unethical behavior. These should always be thoroughly investigated. Other criteria that bear investigation include the number of complaints being received and an unusually high rate of employee turnover in a certain area.

An independent review of the corporate culture might reveal fraudulent practices and provide an important awareness of this problem. The most likely candidates would be sales practices and purchasing procedures. Another area where unethical practices often appear is in the collection of competitive intelligence. Although these may not be specifically related to the data processing environment, unethical practices in one part of an organization have a way of migrating into other functions. The goal, obviously, should be achieving a solid ethical culture throughout the organization.

Information Protection and Management Services

The management services that can be performed to help ensure ethical operations involve some of those already discussed in other chapters, but for a different purpose. In the case of ethics, regular training programs that utilize the workshop technique to pose ethical issues and discuss possible resolutions have been an excellent way to bring good ethics to the attention of employees.

Poster cartoons depicting ethical questions and answers can be an interesting way of keeping employees thinking about proper ethics, and statements both aural and written by top management can reinforce the organization's ethics posture. Finally, the observation of good ethics practices by employees can result in simple rewards to sort of catch the attention of other employees.

Summary

In this chapter we have discussed three major topics. In Law discussion stressed the need for international cooperation in the battle against computer crime. Privacy issues seem to require a large amount of time to resolve. Understandably, countries that have a high respect for the protection of an individual's right to privacy have a problem in allowing personal information to be transmitted to a country with apparently less concern for privacy rights. This and other issues must be resolved so that multinational companies can effectively conduct e-business.

The Investigation discussion provided an understanding of how to conduct an investigation. This is inherent in the duties of an information security professional. Sooner or later, this knowledge will be required and there is no excuse for not being prepared. The number of reported computer incidents is more than doubling every year — far faster than the professional investigator resources.

The Ethics discussion focused on why ethics is such a difficult issue to resolve. Ethics means something different to everyone and obtaining a general consensus, particularly worldwide, is probably impossible. However, specific ethical behavior is described in the ethics statements of professional organizations and, coupled with training sessions focused on specific scenarios, a limited consensus can and should be obtainable.

10.4 Common Body of Knowledge (CBK)

The current CBK for the Law, Investigations and Ethics Domain is listed below to assist in determining topics for further review. Although this Study Guide is very detailed in many areas, it is not possible to thoroughly discuss every CBK topic in a single book; therefore, additional study of items from the bibliography may be advisable.

Examples of Knowledgeability

- Identify the types and categories of computer crimes.
- Distinguish between breaches of communications/data security and operations security.
- Describe some leading examples of computer crime.
- Define and distinguish characteristics and statistics on computer crime.
- Define basic protections against computer crime.
- Compare and contrast common law systems (U.S.) and civil law systems (Europe).
- Define the major categories and types of laws.
- Compare and contrast penalties of criminal law versus civil law.
- Distinguish between patent, trademark, and copyright.
- Define the term "trade secret."
- Identify information security-related laws.
- Identify and define privacy-related laws.

- Compare and contrast differences in international computer crime-related laws.
- Define the U.S. Federal Privacy Act of 1974.
- Define the U.S. Federal Comprehensive Crime Control Act of 1984.
- Define the U.S. Medical Computer Crime Act of 1984.
- Define the U.S. Computer Fraud and Abuse Act of 1986 (as amended in 1996).
- Define the National Infrastructure Protection Act of 1996 and its relationship to the Computer Fraud and Abuse Act of 1986.
- Identify acts considered felonies under 18 U.S.C. 1030.
- Identify mitigating circumstances to the above felonies that limit them to being misdemeanors.
- Define the term "federal interest computer."
- Describe the Electronic Communications Privacy Act of 1986.
- Define and describe the Computer Security Act of 1987.
- Distinguish between NIST and NSA/DoD controls.
- Identify the one state that has not enacted computer crime-related laws.
- Identify and define international computer crime-related laws such as Canadian Criminal Code: Section 342.1-section 430 (1.1)-section 326, the Copyright Act: Section 42, and Bill C-17, 1997.
- Identify and define European Union computer crime-related laws such as the Appendix to Recommendations No. R. (95) 13.
- Distinguish between common legal definition differences between countries.
- Define liabilities of corporate officers for violations of law, violations of due care, and violations of privacy.
- Define and describe the Foreign Corrupt Practices Act of 1977.
- Define the characteristics of due care.
- Define and describe the elements of negligence in performing due care.
- Identify patterns and statistics of computer crime from various reputable sources such as the CSI/FBI Computer Crime Survey.
- Identify and define the impacts of computer crime.
- Define the Hearsay Rule.
- Define witness requirements.
- Describe the evidence life cycle.
- Define the steps in conducting computer crime investigations.
- Identify when and how to contact law enforcement of suspected computer crimes.
- Define characteristics of "admissible" evidence.
- Describe methods of ensuring evidence identification and preservation.
- Define two types of surveillance.
- Define and describe the warrant process in the United States.

- Compare and contrast enticement versus entrapment.
- Define and describe search and seizure rules and procedures.
- Define what constitutes a security incident.
- Describe what might constitute abnormal or suspicious activities.
- Describe the generally accepted guidelines for incident data integrity and retention.
- Describe the generally accepted guidelines for confiscating equipment, software, and data.
- Describe the generally accepted guidelines for reporting incidents.
- Distinguish between *ethical* and *unethical* computer-related practices.
- Define relevant professional codes of ethics.
- Identify common ethical fallacies.
- Define the activities of the Internet Activities Board (IAB).
- Compare and contrast competitive intelligence versus industrial espionage.

10.5 Sample Questions for the CISSP Exam

1. What form of law can also be referred to as "tort" law?
   a. Criminal
   b. Administrative
   c. Napoleonic
   d. Civil
2. An organization suspects that it has suffered loss due to an employee's malfeasance. What should be the first step in pursuing this scenario?
   a. Call law enforcement
   b. Terminate the employee
   c. Set up awareness training
   d. Review organizational policy
3. A unique packaging method or symbol is probably reason to register a:
   a. Trade secret
   b. Patent
   c. Trademark
   d. Copyright
4. One problem NOT associated with investigating Internet-based computer crime is:
   a. Jurisdiction
   b. Data diddling
   c. Evidence rules
   d. Skill of investigators
5. Privacy issues deal with all of the following EXCEPT:
   a. Gathering information
   b. Dissemination of information

    c. Accuracy of information

    d. Proliferation of information

6. Before evidence can be accepted, it must be all of the following EXCEPT:

    a. Tangible

    b. Relevant

    c. Material

    d. Competent

7. Which is NOT a common form of evidence?

    a. Direct

    b. Conclusive

    c. Real

    d. Documentary

8. The Best Evidence Rule is designed to:

    a. Ensure only relevant material is presented in court

    b. Rank the importance of evidence according to veracity

    c. Deter any alteration of evidence

    d. Require expert testimony to present electronic evidence

9. Which of the following is NOT a step in the Evidence Life Cycle?

    a. Discovery

    b. Presentation in court

    c. Storage, preservation, and transportation

    d. Return to owner

10. The basic skills necessary to handle an incident are all of the following EXCEPT:

    a. Recognition

    b. Technical

    c. Response

    d. Presentation

11. One of the largest problems facing an organization is understanding when to pursue an investigation. Usually this is a failure to correctly identify an incident or lack of:

    a. Technical skills

    b. Knowing baseline activity

    c. Senior management involvement

    d. Reactionary skills

12. The procedures established to handle an incident must be:

    a. Supported by senior management

    b. Prepared in advance

    c. Trustworthy

    d. Communicated

13. Which of the following is NOT a section of the Action/Reaction phase of incident handling?

    a. Identification

    b. Containment

    c. Tracking
    d. Analysis
14. Ethics is often dependent on written standards of ethical behavior. These often include:
    a. Diligence to security concepts and practices
    b. Looking out for number one
    c. Protecting principals from prosecution
    d. Keeping security knowledge secret

References

Michael H. Agranoff, "Policies for Secure Personal Data," *EDP Auditing.*

William C. Boni, "Protecting High-Tech Trade Secrets," in *Information Security Management Handbook,* 4th ed., Vol. 1, Harold F. Tipton and Micki Krause (eds.), Boca Raton, FL: Auerbach Publications, 2000.

Gerald Kovacich, "Information Warfare and the Information Systems Security Professional," in *Handbook of Information Security Management*, Harold F. Tipton and Micki Krause (eds). Boca Raton, FL: Auerbach Publications, 1999.

Marcus Rogers, "Incident Response Escalation," unpublished paper, University of Manitoba, 2002.

Summary Paper, "Transnational Computer Crime: The Crimes of Tomorrow Are on Our Doorstep," United Nations Convention against Transnational Organized Crime, Palermo, Italy, 2001.

Peter S. Tippett, "Computer Ethics," in *Handbook of Information Security Management,* Harold F. Tipton and Micki Krause (eds.), Boca Raton, FL: Auerbach Publications, 1999.

Thomas Welch, "Computer Crime Investigations and Computer Forensics," in *Information Security Management Handbook*, 4th ed., Vol. 1., Harold F. Tipton and Micki Krause (eds). Boca Raton, FL: Auerbach Publications, 2000.

Appendix A
Glossary

Abend: The abnormal termination of a computer application or job because of a non-system condition or failure that causes a program to halt.

Abstraction: The process of identifying the characteristics that distinguish a collection of similar objects; the result of the process of abstraction is a type.

Acceptable Use Policy (AUP): A definition of what is acceptable online behavior, and what is not.

Acceptance Testing: The formal testing conducted to determine whether a software system satisfies its acceptance criteria, enabling the customer to determine whether to accept the system.

Access: The ability of a subject to view, change, or communicate with an object. Typically, access involves a flow of information between the subject and the object.

Access Control: The process of allowing only authorized users, programs, or other computer system (i.e., networks) to access the resources of a computer system.

Access Control List (ACL): Most network security systems operate by allowing selective use of service. An Access Control List is the usual means by which access to, and denial of, service is controlled. It is simply a list of the services available, each with a list of the hosts permitted to use the services.

Access Control Mechanisms: Hardware, software, or firmware features and operating and management procedures in various combinations designed to detect and prevent unauthorized access and to permit authorized access to a computer system.

Access Period: A segment of time, generally expressed on a daily or weekly basis, during which access rights prevail.

Access Type: The nature of access granted to a particular device, program, or file (e.g., read, write, execute, append, modify, delete, or create).

Accountability: A security principle stating that individuals must be able to be identified. With accountability, violations or attempted violations can be traced to individuals who can be held responsible for their actions.

Accreditation: A program whereby a laboratory demonstrates that something is operating under accepted standards to ensure quality assurance.

Acknowledgment (ACK): A type of message sent to indicate that a block of data arrived at its destination without error. A negative acknowledgment is called a "NAK."

Active Object: An object that has its own process; the process must be ongoing while the active object exists.

Active Wiretapping: The attachment of an unauthorized device (e.g., a computer terminal) to a communications circuit to gain access to data by generating false messages or control signals or by altering the communications of legitimate users.

ActiveX: Microsoft's Windows-specific non-Java technique for writing applets. ActiveX applets take considerably longer to download than the equivalent Java applets; however, they more fully exploit the features of Windows. ActiveX is sometimes said to be a "superset of Java."

Ada: A programming language that allows use of structured techniques for program design; concise but powerful language designed to fill government requirements for real-time applications.

Add-On Security: The retrofitting of protection mechanisms, implemented by hardware, firmware, or software, on a computer system that has become operational.

Address: (1) A sequence of bits or characters that identifies the destination and sometimes the source of a transmission. (2) An identification (e.g., number, name, or label) for a location in which data is stored.

Address Mapping: The process by which an alphabetic Internet address is converted into a numeric IP address, and vice versa.

Address Mask: A bit mask used to identify which bits in an IP address correspond to the network address and subnet portions of the address. This mask is often referred to as the subnet mask because the network portion of the address can be determined by the class inherent in an IP address. The address mask has ones in positions corresponding to the network and subnet numbers and zeros in the host number positions.

Address Resolution: A means for mapping network layer addresses onto media-specific addresses.

Address Resolution Protocol (ARP): The Internet protocol used to dynamically map Internet addresses to physical (hardware) addresses on the local area network. Limited to networks that support hardware broadcast.

Administrative Security: The management constraints, operational procedures, accountability procedures, and supplemental controls established to provide an acceptable level of protection for sensitive data.

Agent: In the client/server model, the part of the system that performs information preparation and exchange on behalf of a client or server application.

Aggregation: A relation, such as CONSISTS OF or CONTAINS between types that defines the composition of a type from other types.

Aging: The identification, by date, of unprocessed or retained items in a file. This is usually done by date of transaction, classifying items according to ranges of data.

Algorithm: A computing procedure designed to perform a task such as encryption, compressing, or hashing.

Aliases: Used to reroute browser requests from one URL to another.

American National Standards Institute (ANSI): The agency that recommends standards for computer hardware, software, and firmware design and use.

American Registry for Internet Numbers (ARIN): A nonprofit organization established for the purpose of administration and registration of Internet Protocol (IP) numbers to the geographical areas currently managed by Network Solutions (InterNIC). Those areas include, but are not limited to North America, South America, South Africa, and the Caribbean.

American Standard Code for Information Interchange (ASCII): A byte-oriented coding system based on an 8-bit code and used primarily to format information for transfer in a data communications environment.

Amplitude Modulation (AM): The technique of varying the amplitude or wavelength of a carrier wave in direct proportion to the strength of the input signal while maintaining a constant frequency and phase.

Analog: A voice transmission mode that is not digital in which information is transmitted in its original form by converting it to a continuously variable electrical signal.

Analysis and Design Phase: The phase of the systems development life cycle in which an existing system is studied in detail and its functional specifications are generated.

Annual Loss Expectancy (ALE): In risk assessment, the average monetary value of losses per year.

Anonymous FTP: A type of FTP that allows a user to log on to a remote host, which the user would otherwise not have access to, to download files.

ANSI: *See* American National Standards Institute.

Applet: A small Java program embedded in an HTML document.

Application: Computer software used to perform a distinct function. Also used to describe the function itself.

Application Layer: The top-most layer in the OSI Reference Model providing such communication service is invoked through a software package.

Application Objects: Applications and their components that are managed within an object-oriented system. Example operations on such objects are OPEN, INSTALL, MOVE, and REMOVE.

Application Program Interface (API): A set of calling conventions defining how a service is invoked through a software package.

Architecture: The structure or ordering of components in a computational or other system. The classes and the interrelation of the classes define the architecture of a particular application. At another level, the architecture of a system is determined by the arrangement of the hardware and software components. The terms "logical architecture" and "physical architecture" are often used to emphasize this distinction.

Array: Consecutive storage areas in memory that are identified by the same name. The elements (or groups) within these storage areas are accessed through subscripts.

Artificial Intelligence (AI): A field of study involving techniques and methods under which computers can simulate such human intellectual activities as learning.

Assembler Language: A computer programming language in which alphanumeric symbols represent computer operations and memory addresses. Each assembler instruction translates into a single machine language instruction.

Assembler Program: A program language translator that converts assembler language into machine code.

Asynchronous: A variable or random time interval between successive characters, blocks, operations, or events. Asynchronous data transmission provides variable intercharacter time but fixed interbit time within characters.

Asynchronous Transfer Mode (ATM): A transfer mode in which data is transmitted in the form of 53-byte units called cells. Each cell consists of a 5-byte header and a 48-byte payload. The term "asynchronous" in this context refers to the fact that cells from any one particular source need not be periodically spaced within the overall cell stream. That is, users are not assigned a set position in a recurring frame as is common in circuit switching.

Atomicity: The assurance that an operation either changes the state of all participating objects consistent with the semantics of the operation or changes none at all.

Attribute: A characteristic defined for a class. Attributes are used to maintain the state of the object of a class. Values can be connected to objects via the attributes of the class. Typically, the connected value is determined by an operation with a single parameter identifying the object. Attributes implement the properties of a type.

Audit: An independent review and examination of system records and activities that test for the adequacy of system controls, ensure compliance with established policy and operational procedures, and recommend any indicated changes in controls, policy, and procedures.

Audit trail: A chronological record of system activities that is sufficient to enable the reconstruction, review, and examination of each event in a transaction from inception to output of final results.

Authentication: The act of identifying or verifying the eligibility of a station, originator, or individual to access specific categories of information. Typically, a measure designed to protect against fraudulent transmissions by establishing the validity of a transmission, message, station, or originator.

Authorization: The granting of right of access to a user, program, or process.

Backbone: The primary connectivity mechanism of a hierarchical distributed system. All systems that have connectivity to an intermediate system on the backbone are assured of connectivity to each other.

Backoff: The (usually random) retransmission delay enforced by contentious MAC protocols after a network node with data to transmit determines that the physical medium is already in use.

Backup and Recovery: The ability to recreate current master files using appropriate prior master records and transactions.

Backup Procedures: Provisions make for the recovery of data files and program libraries and for the restart or replacement of computer equipment after the occurrence of a system failure or disaster.

Bandwidth: Difference between the highest and lowest frequencies available for network signals. The term is also used to describe the rated throughput capacity of a given network medium or protocol.

Baseband: Characteristic of any network technology that uses a single carrier frequency and requires all stations attached to the network to participate in every transmission. *See* broadband.

BCP: The newest subseries of RFCs that are written to describe Best Current Practices in the Internet. Rather than specify the best ways to use the protocols and the best ways to configure options to ensure interoperability between various vendors' products, BCPs carry the endorsement of the IESG.

Between-the-Lines Entry: Access obtained through the use of active wiretapping by an unauthorized user to a momentarily inactive terminal of a legitimate user assigned to a communications channel.

BIOS: The BIOS is built-in software that determines what a computer can do without accessing programs from a disk. On PCs, the BIOS contains all the code required to control the keyboard, display screen, disk drives, serial communications, and a number of miscellaneous functions.

Bit: A binary value represented by an electronic component that has a value of 0 or 1.

Bit Error Rate (BER): The probability that a particular bit will have the wrong value.

Bit Map: A specialized form of an index indicating the existence or non-existence of a condition for a group of blocks or records. Although they are expensive to build and maintain, they provide very fast comparison and access facilities.

Bit Mask: A pattern of binary values that is combined with some value using bitwise AND with the result that bits in the value in positions where the mask is zero are also set to zero.

Bit Rate: This is the speed at which bits are transmitted on a circuit, usually expressed in bits per second.

Block Cipher: A method of encrypting text to produce ciphertext in which a cryptographic key and algorithm are applied to a block of data as a group instead of one bit at a time.

Body: One of four possible components of a message. Other components are the headings, attachment, and the envelope.

Bounds Checking: The testing of computer program results for access to storage outside of its authorized limits.

Bridge: A device that connects two or more physical networks and forwards packets between them. Bridges can usually be made to filter packets, that is, to forward only certain traffic.

Broadband: Characteristic of any network that multiplexes multiple, independent network carriers onto a single cable. Broadband technology allows several networks to coexist on one single cable; traffic from one network does not interfere with traffic from another because the conversations happen on different frequencies in the "ether," rather like the commercial radio system.

Broadcast: A packet delivery system where a copy of a given packet is given to all hosts attached to the network. Example: Ethernet.

Broadcast Storm: A condition that can occur on broadcast type networks such as Ethernet. This can happen for a number of reasons, ranging from hardware malfunction to configuration error and bandwidth saturation.

Brouter: A concatenation of "bridge" and "router." Used to refer to devices that perform both bridging and routing.

Browser: Short for *Web browser,* a software application used to locate and display Web pages. The two most popular browsers are Netscape Navigator and Microsoft Internet Explorer. Both of these are *graphical browsers,* which means that they can display graphics as well as text. In addition, most modern browsers can present multimedia information, including sound and video, although they require plug-ins for some formats.

Browsing: The searching of computer storage to locate or acquire information, without necessarily knowing whether it exists or in what format.

Buffer *(n)*: A temporary storage area, usually in RAM. The purpose of most buffers is to act as a holding area, enabling the CPU to manipulate data before transferring it to a device. Because the processes of reading and writing data to a disk are relatively slow, many programs keep track of data changes in a buffer and then copy the buffer to a disk. For example, word processors employ a buffer to keep track of changes to files. Then when you *save* the file, the word processor updates the disk file with the contents of the buffer. This is much more efficient than accessing the file on the disk each time you make a change to the file. Note that because your changes are initially stored in a buffer, not on the disk, all of them will be lost if the computer fails during an editing session. For this reason, it is a good idea to save your file periodically. Most word processors automatically save files at regular intervals. Another common use of buffers is for printing documents. When you enter a PRINT command, the operating system copies your document to a print buffer (a free area in memory or on a disk) from which the printer can draw characters at its own pace. This frees the computer to perform other tasks while the printer is running in the background. Print buffering is called *spooling*. Most keyboard drivers also contain a buffer so that you can edit typing mistakes before sending your command to a program. Many operating systems, including DOS, also use a *disk buffer* to temporarily hold data that they have read from a disk. The disk buffer is really a cache.

Bug: A coded program statement containing a logical or syntactical error.

Bulletin Board Service (BBS): A computer that allows you to log on and post messages to other subscribers to the service.

Burn Box: A device used to destroy computer data. Usually a box with magnets or electrical current that will degauss disks and tapes.

Bus: A data path that connects the CPU, input, output, and storage devices.

Business Continuity Plan (BCP): A documented and tested plan for responding to an emergency.

Byte: The basic unit of storage for many computers; typically, one configuration consists of 8 bits used to represent data plus a parity bit for checking the accuracy of representation.

C: A third-generation computer language used for programming on microcomputers. Most microcomputer software products such as spreadsheets and DBMS programs are written in C.

Cable: Transmission medium of copper wire or optical fiber wrapped in a protective cover.

Cache: Pronounced *cash*, a special high-speed storage mechanism. It can be either a reserved section of main memory or an independent high-speed storage device. Two types of caching are commonly used in personal computers: *memory caching* and *disk caching*. A memory cache, sometimes called a *cache store* or *RAM cache*, is a portion of memory made of high-speed static RAM (SRAM) instead of the slower and cheaper dynamic RAM (DRAM) used for main memory. Memory caching is effective because most programs access the same data or instructions over and over. Disk caching works under the same principle as memory caching, but instead of using high-speed SRAM, a disk cache uses conventional main memory. When data is found in the cache, it is called a *cache hit,* and the effectiveness of a cache is judged by its *hit rate.*

Callback: A procedure that identifies a terminal dialing into a computer system or network by disconnecting the calling terminal, verifying the authorized terminal against the automated control table, and then, if authorized, reestablishing the connection by having the computer system dial the telephone number of the calling terminal.

Carrier Sense, Multiple Access (CSMA): A multiple-station access scheme for avoiding contention in packet networks in which each station can sense the presence of carrier signals from other stations and thus avoid transmitting a packet that would result in a collision. *See also* collision detection.

Central Processing Unit (CPU): The part of the computer system containing the control and arithmetic logic units.

CERN: European Laboratory for Particle Physics. Birthplace of the World Wide Web.

Certification: The acceptance of software by an authorized agent, usually after the software has been validated by the agent or its validity has been demonstrated to the agent.

Chain of Custody: The identity of persons who handle evidence between the time of commission of the alleged offense and the ultimate disposition of the case. It is the responsibility of each transferee to ensure that the items are accounted for during the time that it is in their possession, that it is properly protected, and that there is a record of the names of the persons from whom they received it and to whom they delivered it, together with the time and date of such receipt and delivery.

Chain of Evidence: The "sequencing" of the chain of evidence follows this order:
> Collection and identification
> Analysis
> Storage
> Preservation
> Presentation in court
> Return to owner

Chain of evidence shows:
> Who obtained the evidence
> Where and when the evidence was obtained

Who secured the evidence

Who had control or possession of the evidence

CHAP (Challenge Handshake Authentication Protocol): Applies a three-way handshaking procedure. After the link is established, the server sends a "challenge" message to the originator. The originator responds with a value calculated using a one-way hash function. The server checks the response against its own calculation of the expected hash value. If the values match, the authentication is acknowledged; otherwise, the connection is usually terminated.

Chat Room: An area of a Web chat service that people can "enter" with their Web browsers where the conversations are devoted to a specific topic; equivalent to a channel in IRC.

Check Digit: One digit, usually the last, of an identifying field is a mathematical function of all of the other digits in the field. This value can be calculated from the other digits in the field and compared with the check digit to verify validity of the whole field.

Checksum: A computed value that depends on the contents of a packet. This value is sent along with the packet when it is transmitted. The receiving system computes a new checksum based on receiving data and compares this value with the one sent with the packet. If the two values are the same, the receiver has a high degree of confidence that the data was received correctly.

Ciphertext: Information that has been encrypted, making it unreadable without knowledge of the key.

Circuit Switching: A communications paradigm in which a dedicated communication path is established between two hosts and on which all packets travel. The telephone system is an example of a circuit-switched network.

Class: An implementation of an abstract data type. A definition of the data structures, methods, and interface of software objects. A template for the instantiation (creation) of software objects.

Client: A workstation in a network that is set up to use the resources of a server.

Client/Server: In networking, a network in which several PC-type systems (clients) are connected to one or more powerful, central computers (servers). In databases, refers to a model in which a client system runs a database application (front end) that accesses information in a database management system situated on a server (back end).

Client/Server Architecture: A local area network in which microcomputers, called servers, provide specialized service on behalf of the user's computers, which are called clients.

Cloning: The term given to the operation of creating an exact duplicate of one medium on another like medium. This is also referred to as a Mirror Image or Physical Sector Copy.

Coaxial Cable: A medium used for telecommunications. It is similar to the type of cable used for carrying television signals.

Code Division Multiple Access (CDMA): A technique permitting the use of a single frequency band by a number of users. Users are allocated a sequence that uniquely identifies them.

Collision: This is a condition that is present when two or more terminals are in contention during simultaneous network access attempts.

Collision Detection: An avoidance method for communications channel contention that depends on two stations detecting the simultaneous start of each other's transmission, stopping, and waiting a random period of time before beginning again. *See also* carrier sense, multiple access.

Commit: A condition implemented by the programmer signaling to the DBMS that all update activity that the program conducts be executed against a database. Before the commit, all update activity can be rolled back or canceled without negative impact on the database contents.

Commit Protocol: An algorithm to ensure that a transaction is successfully completed.

Common Business Oriented Language (COBOL): A high-level programming language for business computer applications.

Common Carrier: An organization or company that provides data or other electronic communication services for a fee.

Common Object Request Broker Architecture (CORBA): CORBA is the Object Management Group's (OMG) answer to the need for interoperability among the rapidly proliferating number of hardware and software products available today. Simply stated, CORBA allows applications to communicate with one another no matter where they are located or who has designed them.

Communications Security: The protection that ensures the authenticity of telecommunications and that results from the application of measures taken to deny unauthorized persons access to valuable information that might be derived from the acquisition of telecommunications.

Compartmentalization: The isolation of the operating system, user programs, and data files from one another in main storage to protect them against unauthorized or concurrent access by other users or programs. Also, the division of sensitive data into small, isolated blocks to reduce risk to the data.

Compiler: A program that translates high-level computer language instructions into machine code.

Compromise: Unauthorized disclosure or loss of sensitive information.

Compromising Emanations: Electromagnetic emanations that convey data and that, if intercepted and analyzed, could compromise sensitive information being processed by a computer system.

Computer Emergency Response Team (CERT): The CERT is chartered to work with the Internet community to facilitate its response to computer security events involving Internet hosts, to take proactive steps to raise the community's awareness of computer security issues, and to conduct research targeted at improving the security of existing systems. The U.S. CERT is based at Carnegie Mellon University in Pittsburgh; regional CERTs are like NICs, springing up in different parts of the world.

Computer Evidence: Computer evidence is a copy of a document stored in a computer file that is identical to the original. The legal "best evidence" rules change when it comes to the processing of computer evidence. Another unique aspect of computer evidence is the potential for unauthorized copies to be made of important computer files without leaving behind a trace that the copy was made. This situation creates problems concerning the investigation of the theft of trade secrets (e.g., client lists, research materials, computer-aided design files, formulas, and proprietary software).

Computer Forensics: The term "computer forensics" was coined in 1991 in the first training session held by the International Association of Computer Specialists (IACIS) in Portland, Oregon. Since then, computer forensics has become a popular topic in computer security circles and in the legal community. Like any other forensic science, computer forensics deals with the application of law to a science. In this case, the science involved is computer science and some refer to it as Forensic Computer Science. Computer forensics has also been described as the autopsy of a computer hard disk drive because specialized software tools and techniques are required to analyze the various levels at which computer data is stored after the fact. Computer forensics deals with the preservation, identification, extraction, and documentation of computer evidence. The field is relatively new to the private sector, but it has been the mainstay of technology-related investigations and intelligence gathering in law enforcement and military agencies since the mid-1980s. Like any other forensic science, computer forensics involves the use of sophisticated technology tools and procedures that must be followed to guarantee the accuracy of the preservation of evidence and the accuracy of results concerning computer evidence processing. Typically, computer forensic tools exist in the form of computer software.

Computer Fraud and Abuse Act PL 99-474: Computer Fraud and Abuse Act of 1986. Strengthens and expands the 1984 Federal Computer Crime Legislation. Law extended to computer crimes in private enterprise and anyone who willfully disseminates information for the purpose of committing a computer crime (i.e., distribute phone numbers to hackers from a BBS).

Computer Matching Act Public Law (PL) 100-53: Computer Matching and Privacy Act of 1988. Ensures privacy, integrity, and verification of data disclosed for computer matching; establishes Data Integrity Boards within federal agencies.

Computer Security: The practice of protecting a computer system against internal failures, human error, attacks, and natural catastrophes that might cause improper disclosure, modification, destruction, or denial-of-service.

Computer Security Act PL 100-235: Computer Security Act of 1987 directs the National Bureau of Standards (now the National Institute of Standards and Technology [NIST]) to establish a computer security standards program for federal computer systems.

Computer System: An interacting assembly of elements, including at least computer hardware and usually software, data procedures, and people.

Computer System Security: All of the technological safeguards and managerial procedures established and applied to computers and their networks (including related hardware, firmware, software, and data) to protect organizational assets and individual privacy.

Computer-Aided Software Engineering (CASE): Tools that automate the design, development, operation, and maintenance of software.

Concealment Systems: A method of keeping sensitive information confidential by embedding it in irrelevant data.

Concurrent Processing: The capability of a computer to share memory with several programs and simultaneously execute the instructions provided by each.

Condensation: The process of reducing the volume of data managed without reducing the logical consistency of data. It is essentially different than compaction in that condensation is done at the record level whereas compaction is done at the system level.

Confidentiality: A concept that applies to data that must be held in confidence and describes that status or degree of protection that must be provided for such data about individuals as well as organizations.

Configuration Management: The use of procedures appropriate for controlling changes to a system's hardware, software, or firmware structure to ensure that such changes will not lead to a weakness or fault in the system.

Connection-Oriented: The model of interconnection in which communication proceeds through three well-defined phases: connection establishment, data transfer, and connection release. Examples: X.25, Internet TCP and OSI TP4, ordinary telephone calls.

Connectionless: The model of interconnection in which communication takes place without first establishing a connection. Sometimes (imprecisely) called datagram. Examples: Internet IP and OSI CLNP, UDP, ordinary postcards.

Console Operator: Someone who works at a computer console to monitor operations and initiate instructions for efficient use of computer resources.

Construct: An object; especially a concept that is constructed or synthesized from simple elements.

Contention: Occurs during multiple access to a network in which the network capacity is allocated on a "first come, first served" basis.

Contingency Plans: Plans for emergency response, backup operations, and post-disaster recovery maintained by a computer information processing facility as a part of its security program.

Control: Any protective action, device, procedure, technique, or other measure that reduces exposures.

Control Break: A point during program processing at which some special processing event takes place. A change in the value of a control field within a data record is characteristic of a control break.

Control Totals: Accumulations of numeric data fields that are used to check the accuracy of the input, processing, or output data.

Control Zone: The space surrounding equipment that is used to process sensitive information and that is under sufficient physical and technical control to preclude an unauthorized entry or compromise.

Cookie: A small file stored on your computer by a Web browser that tracks your surfing activity.

Cooperative Processing: The ability to distribute resources (i.e., programs, files, and databases) across the network.

Copy: An accurate reproduction of information contained on an original physical item, independent of the original physical item.

Copyright: The author or artist's right to control the copying of his or her work.

CORBA: Common Object Request Broker Architecture, introduced in 1991 by the OMG, defined the Interface Definition Language (IDL) and the Application Programming Interfaces (APIs) that enable client/server object interaction within a specific implementation of an Object Request Broker (ORB).

Corrective Action: The practice and procedure for reporting, tracking, and resolving identified problems, in both the software product and the development process. Their resolution provides a final solution to the identified problem.

Corrective Maintenance: The identification and removal of code defects.

Cost/Benefit Analysis: Determination of the economic feasibility of developing a system on the basis of a comparison of the projected costs of a proposed system and the expected benefits from its operation.

Cost-Risk Analysis: The assessment of the cost of potential risk of loss or compromise of data in a computer system without data protection versus the cost of providing data protection.

CPU: The central processing unit; the brains of the computer.

Critical Path: A tool used in project management techniques and is the duration based on the sum of the individual tasks and their dependencies. The critical path is the shortest period in which a project can be accomplished.

Crossover Error Rate (CER): A comparison metric for different biometric devices and technologies; the error rate at which FAR equals FRR. The lower the CER, the more accurate and reliable the biometric device.

Cryptanalysis: The study of techniques for attempting to defeat cryptographic techniques and, more generally, information security services.

Cryptanalyst: Someone who engages in cryptanalysis.

Cryptography: The study of mathematical techniques related to aspects of information security such as confidentiality, data integrity, entity authentication, and data origin authentication. Cryptography is not the only means of providing information security services, but rather one set of techniques. The word itself comes from the Greek word *kryptos,* which means "hidden" or "covered." Cryptography is a way to hide writing ("-graphy") but yet retain a way to uncover it again.

Cryptology: The field of study that encompasses both cryptography and cryptanalysis.

Cryptosystem: A general term referring to a set of cryptographic primitives used to provide information security services.

Cyberspace: A term coined to denote the online world of the Internet.

Cyclic Redundancy Check (CRC): A number derived from a set of data that will be transmitted.

Data: Raw facts and figures that are meaningless by themselves. Data can be expressed in characters, digits, and symbols, which can represent people, things, and events.

Data Communications: The transmission of data between more than one site through the use of public and private communications channels or lines.

Data Contamination: A deliberate or accidental process or act that compromises the integrity of the original data.

Data Definition Language (DDL): A set of instructions or commands used to define data for the data dictionary. A data definition language (DDL) is used to describe the structure of a database.

Data Dictionary: A document or listing defining all items or processes represented in a data flow diagram or used in a system.

Data Element: The smallest unit of data accessible to a database management system or a field of data within a file processing system.

Data Encryption Standard (DES): A data encryption standard developed by the U.S. National Bureau of Standards (NBS). DES is a symmetric block cipher with a block length of 64 bits and an effective key length of 56 bits.

Data Integrity: The state that exists when automated information or data is the same as that in the source documents and has not been exposed to accidental or malicious modification, alteration, or destruction.

Data Item: A discrete representation having the properties that define the data element to which it belongs. *See also* data element.

Data Link: A serial communications path between nodes or devices without any intermediate switching nodes. Also, the physical two-way connection between such devices.

Data Manipulation Language (DML): A data manipulation language (DML) provides the necessary commands for all database operations, including storing, retrieving, updating, and deleting database records.

Data Objects: Objects or information of potential probative value that are associated with physical items. Data objects may occur in different formats without altering the original information.

Data Record: An identifiable set of data values treated as a unit, an occurrence of a schema in a database, or collection of atomic data items describing a specific object, event, or tuple (e.g., row of a table).

Data Security: The protection of data from accidental or malicious modification, destruction, or disclosure.

Data Set: A named collection of logically related data items, arranged in a prescribed manner and described by control information to which the programming system has access.

Data Warehouse: A collection of integrated subject-oriented databases designed to support the Decision Support function, where each unit of data is relevant to some moment in time. The data warehouse contains atomic data and summarized data.

Database: An integrated aggregation of data usually organized to reflect logical or functional relationships among data elements.

Database Administrator (DBA): (1) A person who is in charge of defining and managing the contents of a database. (2) The individual in an organization who is responsible for the daily monitoring and maintenance of the databases. The database administrator's function is more closely associated with physical database design than the data administrator's function is.

Database Management System (DBMS): The software that directs and controls data resources.

Datagram: Logical grouping of information sent as a network layer unit over a transmission medium without prior establishment of a virtual circuit. IP datagrams are the primary information units in the Internet. The terms "cell," "frame," "message," "packet," and "segment" are also used to describe logical information groupings at various layers of the OSI Reference Model and in various technology circles.

Data-Link Control Layer: Layer 2 in the SNA architectural model. Responsible for the transmission of data over a particular physical link. Corresponds roughly to the data-link layer of the OSI model.

Data-Link Layer: Layer 2 of the OSI reference model. Provides reliable transit of data across a physical link. The data-link layer is concerned with physical addressing, network topology, line discipline, error notification, ordered delivery of frames, and flow control. The IEEE divided this layer into two sublayers: the MAC sublayer and the LLC sublayer. Sometimes simply called the link layer. Roughly corresponds to the data-link control layer of the SNA model.

Deadlock: A condition that occurs when two users invoke conflicting locks in trying to gain access to a specific record or records.

Decipher: The ability to convert, by use of the appropriate key, enciphered text into its equivalent plaintext.

Decrypt: Synonymous with decipher.

Decrypt/Decipher/Decode: Decryption is the opposite of encryption. It is the transformation of encrypted information back into a legible form. Essentially, decryption is about removing disguise and reclaiming the meaning of information.

Decryption: The conversion through mechanisms or procedures of encrypted data into its original form.

Dedicated Lines: Private circuits between two or more stations, switches, or subscribers.

Dedicated Mode: The operation of a computer system such that the central computer facility, connected peripheral devices, communications facilities, and all remote terminals are used and controlled exclusively by the users or groups of users for the processing of particular types and categories of information.

Degauss: To erase or demagnetize magnetic recording media (usually tapes) by applying a variable, alternating current (AC) field.

Degree (of a relation): The number of attributes or columns of a relation.

Delegation: The notation that an object can issue a request to another object in response to a request. The first object therefore delegates the responsibility to the second object. Delegation can be used as an alternative to inheritance.

Delphi: A forecasting method where several knowledgeable individuals make forecasts and a forecast is derived by a trained analyst from a weighted average.

Demodulation: The reconstruction of an original signal from the modulated signal received at a destination device.

Denial-of-Service (DoS): Attacks on systems written to deny users legitimate access to system resources. These attacks take many forms, but are primarily applications or malicious applets that take more processes or memory allocation area than they should use, such as filling up a file system or allocating all of a system's memory.

Denial-of-service (DoS) attacks are among the most commonly encountered Java security concerns and, unfortunately, Java has a weak defense against it.

Design: The aspect of the specification process that involves the prior consideration of the implementation. Design is the process that extends and modifies an analysis specification. It accommodates certain qualities including extensibility, reusability, testability, and maintainability. Design also includes the specification of implementation requirements such as user interface and data persistence.

Design and Implementation: A phase of the systems development life cycle in which a set of functional specifications produced during systems analysis is transformed into an operational system for hardware, software, and firmware.

Design Review: The quality assurance process in which all aspects of a system are reviewed publicly.

Dial-Up: Access to switched network, usually through a dial or push-button telephone.

Digital: A mode of transmission where information is coded in binary form for transmission on the network.

Digital Audio Tape (DAT): A magnetic tape technology. DAT uses 4-mm cassettes capable of backing up anywhere between 26 and 126 bytes of information.

Digital Signature: The act of electronically affixing an encrypted message digest to a computer file or message in which the originator is then authenticated to the recipient.

Digital Signature Standard (DSS): The National Security Administration's standard for verifying an electronic message.

Direct Access: The method of reading and writing specific records without having to process all preceding records in a file.

Direct Access Storage Device (DASD): A data storage unit on which data can be accessed directly without having to progress through a serial file such as a magnetic tape file. A disk unit is a direct access storage device.

Directory: A table specifying the relationships between items of data. Sometimes a table (index) giving the addresses of data.

Discrepancy Reports: A listing of items that have violated some detective control and require further investigation.

Disk Duplexing: This refers to the use of two controllers to drive a disk subsystem. Should one of the controllers fail, the other is still available for disk I/O. Software applications can take advantage of both controllers to simultaneously read and write to different drives.

Disk Mirroring: Disk mirroring protects data against hardware failure. In its simplest form, a two-disk subsystem would be attached to a host controller. One disk serves as the mirror image of the other. When data is written to it, it is also written to the other disk. Both disks will contain exactly the same information. If one fails, the other can supply the user data without problem.

Disk Operating System (DOS): Software that controls the execution of programs and may provide system services as resource allocation.

Diskette: A flexible disk storage medium most often used with microcomputers; also called a floppy disk.

Distributed Component Object Model (DCOM): A protocol that enables software components to communicate directly over a network. Developed by Microsoft and previously called "Network OLE," DCOM is designed for use across multiple network transports including Internet Protocols such as HTTP.

Distributed Computing: The distribution of processes among computing components that are within the same computer or different computers on a shared network.

Distributed Database: A database management system with the ability to effectively manage data that is distributed across multiple computers on a network.

Distributed Environment: A set of related data processing systems in which each system has its own capacity to operate autonomously but has some applications that are executed at multiple sites. Some of the systems may be connected with teleprocessing links into a network with each system serving as a node.

Domain Name: The name used to identify an Internet host.

Domain Name Server: An Internet host that checks the addresses of incoming and outgoing Internet messages.

Domain Name System (DNS): The distributed name and address mechanism used in the Internet.

Dumb Terminal: A device used to interact directly with the end user where all data is processed on a remote computer. A dumb terminal only gathers and displays data; it has no processing capability.

Dump: The contents of a file or memory that are output as listings. These listing can be formatted.

Duplex: Communications systems or equipment that can simultaneously carry information in both directions between two points. Also used to describe redundant equipment configurations (e.g., duplexed processors).

Early Token Release: Technique used in Token Ring networks that allows a station to release a new token onto the ring immediately after transmitting, instead of waiting for the first frame to return. This feature can increase the total bandwidth on the ring. *See also* Token Ring.

Earth Stations: Ground terminals that use antennas and other related electronic equipment designed to transmit, receive, and process satellite communications.

Eavesdropping: The unauthorized interception of information-bearing emanations through methods other than wiretapping.

Echo: The display of characters on a terminal output device as they are entered into the system.

Edit: The process of inspecting a data field or element to verify the correctness of its content.

Electromagnetic Emanations: Signals transmitted as radiation through the air or conductors.

Electromagnetic Interference (EMI): Electromagnetic waves emitted by a device.

Electronic Code Book (ECB): A basic encryption method that provides privacy but not authentication.

Electronic Communications Privacy Act of 1986 PL 99-508 (ECPA): Electronic Communications Privacy Act of 1986; extends the Privacy Act of 1974 to all forms of electronic communication, including email.

Electronic Data Interchange (EDI): A process whereby such specially formatted documents as an invoice can be transmitted from one organization to another.

Electronic Data Vaulting: Electronic vaulting protects information from loss by providing automatic and transparent backup of valuable data over high-speed phone lines to a secure facility.

Electronic Frontier Foundation: A foundation established to address social and legal issues arising from the impact on society of the increasingly pervasive use of computers as the means of communication and information distribution.

Electronic Funds Transfer (EFT): The process of moving money between accounts via computer.

Electronic Journal: A computerized log file summarizing, in chronological sequence, the processing activities and events performed by a system. The log file is usually maintained on magnetic storage media.

Emanation Security: The protection that results from all measures designed to deny unauthorized persons access to valuable information that might be derived from interception and analysis of compromising emanations.

Encrypt/Encipher/Encode: Encryption is the transformation of information into a form that is impossible to read unless you have a specific piece of information, which is usually referred to as the "key." The purpose is to keep information private from those who are not intended to have access to it. To encrypt is essentially about making information confusing and hiding the meaning of it.

Encryption: The use of algorithms to encode data in order to render a message or other file readable only for the intended recipient.

Encryption Algorithm: A set of mathematically expressed rules for encoding information, thereby rendering it unintelligible to those who do not have the algorithm decoding key.

Encryption Key: A special mathematical code that allows encryption hardware/software to encode and then decipher an encrypted message.

End System: An OSI system that contains application processes capable of communication through all seven layers of OSI protocols. Equivalent to Internet host.

End-to-End Encryption: The encryption of information at the point of origin within the communications network and postponing of decryption to the final destination point.

Enrollment: The initial process of collecting biometric data from a user and then storing it in a template for later comparison.

Entrapment: The deliberate planting of apparent flows in a system to invite penetrations.

Error: A discrepancy between actual values or conditions and those expected.

Error Rate: A measure of the quality of circuits or equipment. The ratio of erroneously transmitted information to the total sent (generally computed per million characters sent).

Espionage: The practice or employment of spies; the practice of watching the words and conduct of others, to make discoveries, as spies or secret emissaries; secret watching. This category of computer crime includes international spies and their contractors who steal secrets from defense, academic, and laboratory research facility computer systems. It includes criminals who steal information and intelligence from law enforcement computers, and industrial espionage agents who operate for competitive companies or for foreign governments who are willing to pay for the information. What has generally been known as industrial espionage is now being called competitive intelligence. A lot of information can be gained through "open source" collection and analysis without ever having to break into a competitor's computer. This information gathering is also competitive intelligence, although it is not as ethically questionable as other techniques.

Ethernet: A 10-Mbps standard for LANs, initially developed by Xerox and later refined by Digital, Intel, and Xerox (DIX). All hosts are connected to a coaxial cable where they contend for network access using a Carrier Sense Multiple Access with Collision Detection (CSMA/CD) paradigm.

Exception Report: A manager report that highlights abnormal business conditions. Usually, such reports prompt management action or inquiry.

Expert System: The application of computer-based artificial intelligence in areas of specialized knowledge.

Extensibility: A property of software such that new kinds of object or functionality can be added to it with little or no effect to the existing system.

eXtensible Markup Language (XML): Designed to enable the use of SGML on the World Wide Web, XML is a regular markup language that defines what you can do (or what you have done) in the way of describing information for a fixed class of documents (like HTML). XML goes beyond this and allows you to define your own customized markup language. It can do this because it is an application profile of SGML. XML is a metalanguage, a language for describing languages.

Fail Safe: The automatic termination and protection of programs or other processing operations when a hardware, software, or firmware failure is detected in a computer system.

Fail Soft: The selective termination of nonessential processing affected by a hardware, software, or firmware failure in a computer system.

Fallback Procedures: Predefined operations (manual or automatic) invoked when a fault or failure is detected in a system.

False Acceptance Rate (FAR): The percentage of imposters incorrectly matched to a valid user's biometric. False rejection rate (FRR) is the percentage of incorrectly rejected valid users.

Fast Ethernet: Any of a number of 100-Mbps Ethernet specifications. Fast Ethernet offers a speed increase ten times that of the 10BaseT Ethernet specification, while preserving such qualities as frame format, MAC mechanisms, and MTU. Such similarities allow the use of existing 10BaseT applications and network management tools on Fast Ethernet networks. Based on an extension to the IEEE 802.3 specification. *Compare with* Ethernet.

Fetch Protection: A system-provided restriction to prevent a program from accessing data in another user's segment of storage.

Fiber Distributed Data Interface (FDDI): LAN standard, defined by ANSI X3T9.5, specifying a 100-Mbps token-passing network using fiber-optic cable, with transmission distances of up to 2 km. FDDI uses a dual-ring architecture to provide redundancy.

Field Definition Record (FDR): A record of field definition. A list of the attributes that define the type of information that can be entered into a data field.

File Protection: The aggregate of all processes and procedures established in a computer system and designed to inhibit unauthorized access, contamination, or elimination of a file.

File Transfer: The process of copying a file from one computer to another over a network.

File Transfer Protocol (FTP): The Internet protocol (and program) used to transfer files between hosts.

Filter: A process or device that screens incoming information for definite characteristics and allows a subset of that information to pass through.

Finger: A program (and a protocol) that displays information about a particular user, or all users, logged on a local system or on a remote system. It typically shows full-time name, last login time, idle time, terminal line, and terminal location (where applicable). It may also display plan and project files left by the user.

Firewall: A system designed to prevent unauthorized access to or from a private network. Firewalls can be implemented in both hardware and software, or a combination of both. Firewalls are frequently used to prevent unauthorized Internet users from accessing private networks connected to the Internet, especially *intranets*. All messages entering or leaving the intranet pass through the firewall, which examines each message and blocks those that do not meet the specified security criteria. There are several types of firewall techniques:

- *Packet filter:* Looks at each packet entering or leaving the network and accepts or rejects it based on user-defined rules. Packet filtering is fairly effective and transparent to users, but it is difficult to configure. In addition, it is susceptible to IP spoofing.
- *Application gateway:* Applies security mechanisms to specific applications, such as FTP and Telnet servers. This is very effective, but can impose performance degradation.
- *Circuit-level gateway:* Applies security mechanisms when a TCP or UDP connection is established. Once the connection has been made, packets can flow between the hosts without further checking.
- *Proxy server:* Intercepts all messages entering and leaving the network. The proxy server effectively hides the true network addresses.

Firmware: Software or computer instructions that have been permanently encoded into the circuits of semiconductor chips.

Flame: To express strong opinion or criticism of something, usually as a frank inflammatory statement in an electronic message.

Flat File: A collection of records containing no data aggregates, nested, or repeated data items, or groups of data items.

Foreign Corrupt Practices Act: The act covers an organization's system of internal accounting control and requires public companies to make and keep books, records, and accounts that, in reasonable detail, accurately and fairly reflect the transactions and disposition of company assets and to devise and maintain a system of sufficient internal accounting controls. This act was amended in 1988.

Formal Review: A type of review typically scheduled at the end of each activity or stage of development to review a component of a deliverable or, in some cases, a complete deliverable or the software product and its supporting documentation.

Format: The physical arrangement of data characters, fields, records, and files.

Forum of Incident Response and Security Teams (FIRST): A unit of the Internet Society that coordinates the activities of worldwide Computer Emergency Response Teams, regarding security-related incidents and information sharing on Internet security risks.

Fragment: A piece of a packet. When a router is forwarding an IP packet to a network with a Maximum Transmission Unit smaller than the packet size, it is forced to break up that packet into multiple fragments. These fragments will be reassembled by the IP layer at the destination host.

Fragmentation: The process in which an IP datagram is broken into smaller pieces to fit the requirements of a given physical network. The reverse process is termed "reassembly."

Frame Relay: A switching interface that operates in packet mode. Generally regarded as the replacement for X.25.

Front-End Computer: A computer that offloads input and output activities from the central computer so it can operate primarily in a processing mode; sometimes called a front-end processor.

Front-End Processor (FEP): (1) A communications computer associated with a host computer can perform line control, message handling, code conversion, error control, and application functions. (2) A teleprocessing concentrator and router, as opposed to a back-end processor or a database machine.

Front Porch: The access point to a secure network environment; also known as a firewall.

Full-Duplex (FDX): An asynchronous communications protocol that allows the communications channel to transmit and receive signals simultaneously.

Fully Qualified Domain Name (FQDN): A complete Internet address, including the complete host and domain name.

Function: In computer programming, a processing activity that performs a single identifiable task.

Functional Specification: The main product of systems analysis, which presents a detailed logical description of the new system. It contains sets of input, processing, storage, and output requirements specifying what the new system can do.

Garbage Collection: A language mechanism that automatically deallocates memory for objects that are not accessible or referenced.

Gateway: A product that enables two dissimilar networks to communicate or interface with each other. In the IP community, an older term referring to a routing device. Today, the term "router" is used to describe nodes that perform this function, and "gateway" refers to a special-purpose device that performs an application layer conversion of information from one protocol stack to another. *Compare with* router.

General-Purpose Computer: A computer that can be programmed to perform a wide variety of processing tests.

Government OSI Profile (GOSIP): A U.S. Government procurement specification for OSI protocols.

Granularity: The level of detail contained in a unit of data. The more there is, the lower the level of granularity; the less detail, the higher the level of granularity.

Graphical User Interface (GUI): An interface in which the user can manipulate icons, windows, pop-down menus, or other related constructs. A graphical user interface uses graphics such as a window, box, and menu to allow the user to communicate with the system. Allows users to move in and out of programs and manipulate their commands using a pointing device (usually a mouse). *Synonymous with* user interface.

Groupware: Software designed to function over a network to allow several people to work together on documents and files.

Hacker: A person who attempts to break into computers that he or she is not authorized to use.

Hacking: A computer crime in which a person breaks into an information system simply for the challenge of doing so.

Half-Duplex: Capability for data transmission in only one direction at a time between a sending station and a receiving station.

Handprint Character Recognition (HCR): One of several pattern recognition technologies used by digital imaging systems to interpret handprinted characters.

Handshake: Sequence of messages exchanged between two or more network devices to ensure transmission synchronization.

Handshaking Procedure: Dialogue between a user and a computer, two computers, or two programs to identify a user and authenticate his or her identity. This is done through a sequence of questions and answers that are based on information either previously stored in the computer or supplied to the computer by the initiator of the dialogue.

Hard Disk: A fixed or removable disk mass storage system permitting rapid direct access to data, programs, or information.

Hash Total: A total of the values on one or more fields, used for the purpose of auditability and control.

HDLC (High-Level Data-Link Control): Bit-oriented synchronous data-link layer protocol developed by ISO. Derived from SDLC, HDLC specifies a data encapsulation method on synchronous serial links using frame characters and checksums.

HDSL: High-data-rate digital subscriber line. One of four DSL technologies. HDSL delivers 1.544 Mbps of bandwidth each way over two copper twisted pairs. Because HDSL provides T1 speed, telephone companies have been using HDSL to provision local access to T1 services whenever possible. The operating range of HDSL is limited to 12,000 feet (3658.5 meters), so signal repeaters are installed to extend the service. HDSL requires two twisted pairs, so it is deployed primarily for PBX network connections, digital loop carrier systems, interexchange POPs, Internet servers, and private data networks. *Compare with* ADSL, SDSL, and VDSL.

Header: The beginning of a message sent over the Internet; typically contains addressing information to route the message or packet to its destination.

Hertz (Hz): One cycle per second.

Heuristics The mode of analysis in which the next step is determined by the results of the current step of analysis. Used for decision support processing.

Hexadecimal: A number system with a base of 16.

Hierarchical Database: In a hierarchical database, data is organized like a family tree or organization chart with branches of parent records and child records.

High-Level Data-Link Control (HDLC): A protocol used at the data-link layer that provides point-to-point communications over a physical transmission medium by creating and recognizing frame boundaries.

High-Level Language: The class of procedure-oriented language.

Home Page: The initial screen of information displayed to the user when initiating the client or browser software or when connecting to a remote computer. The home page resides at the top of the directory tree.

Hop: A term used in routing. A hop is one data link. A path from source to destination in a network is a series of hops.

Host: A remote computer that provides a variety of services, typically to multiple users concurrently.

Host Address: The IP address of the host computer.

Host Computer: A computer that, in addition to providing a local service, acts as a central processor for a communications network.

Hostname: The name of the user computer on the network.

HTML: *See* HyperText Markup Language.

HTTP: *See* HyperText Transport Protocol.

Hub: A device connected to several other devices. In ARCnet, a hub is used to connect several computers together. In a message-handling service, a hub is used for transfer of messages across the network. An Ethernet hub is basically a "collapsed network-in-a-box" with a number of ports for the connected devices.

Hypertext: Text that is held in frames and authors develop or define the linkage between frames.

HyperText Markup Language (HTML): The specialized language used to insert formatting commands and links in a hypertext document.

HyperText Transfer Protocol (HTTP): The protocol used to transport hypertext files across the Internet.

IAB: Internet Architecture Board. Board of internetwork researchers who discuss issues pertinent to Internet architecture. Responsible for appointing a variety of Internet-related groups such as the IANA, IESG, and IRSG. The IAB is appointed by the trustees of the ISOC.

ICMP: Internet Control Message Protocol. Network layer Internet protocol that reports errors and provides other information relevant to IP packet processing. Documented in RFC 792.

Icon: A pictorial symbol used to represent data, information, or a program on a GUI screen.

Identification: The process, generally employing unique machine-readable names, that enables recognition of users or resources as identical to those previously described to the computer system.

Impersonation: An attempt to gain access to a system by posing as an authorized user.

Implementation: The specific activities within the systems development life cycle through which the software portion of the system is developed, coded, debugged, tested, and integrated with existing or new software.

Incident: An event that has actual or potentially adverse effects on an information system. A computer security incident can result from a computer virus, other malicious code, intruder, terrorist, unauthorized insider act, malfunction, etc.

Incomplete Parameter Checking: A system fault that exists when all parameters have not been fully checked for correctness and consistency by the operating system, thus leaving the system vulnerable to penetration.

Inference Engine: A system of computer programs in an expert systems application that uses expert experience as a basis for conclusions.

Infobots: Software agents that perform specified tasks for a user or application.

Information Security Service: A method to provide some specific aspect of security. For example, integrity of transmitted data is a security objective, and a method that would achieve that is considered an information security service.

Inheritance: The language mechanism that allows the definition of a class to include the attributes and methods for another more general class. Inheritance is an implementation construct for the specialization relation. The general class is the superclass and the specific class is the subclass in the inheritance relation. Inheritance is a relation between classes that enables the reuse of code and the definition of generalized interface to one or more subclasses.

Input Controls: Techniques and methods for verifying, validating, and editing data to ensure that only correct data enters a system.

Instance: A set of values representing a specific entity belonging to a particular entity type. A single value is also the instance of a data item.

Integrated Data Dictionary (IDD): A database technology that facilitates functional communication among system components.

Integrated Services Digital Network (ISDN): An emerging technology that is beginning to be offered by the telephone carriers of the world. ISDN combines voice and digital network services in a single medium, making it possible to offer customers digital data services as well as voice connections through a single wire. The standards that define ISDN are specified by ITU-TSS.

Integrity: *See also* data integrity. A security service that allows verification that an unauthorized modification (including changes, insertions, deletions and duplications) has not occurred either maliciously or accidentally.

Integrity Checking: The testing of programs to verify the soundness of a software product at each phase of development.

Interactive: A mode of processing that combines some aspects of online processing and some aspects of batch processing. In interactive processing, the user can directly interact with data over which he or she has exclusive control. In addition, the user can cause sequential activity to initiate background activity to be run against the data.

Interface: A shared boundary between devices, equipment, or software components defined by common interconnection characteristics.

Interleaving: The alternating execution of programs residing in the memory of a multiprogramming environment.

Internal Control: The method of safeguarding business assets, including verifying the accuracy and reliability of accounting data, promoting operational efficiency, and encouraging adherence to prescribed organizational policies and procedures.

Internet: The Internet consists of large national backbone networks (such as MILNET, NSFNET, and CREN) and a myriad of regional and local campus networks all over the world. The Internet uses the Internet Protocol suite. To be on the Internet, you must have IP connectivity (i.e., be able to Telnet to — or ping — other systems). Networks with only email connectivity are not actually classified as being on the Internet.

Internet Address: A 32-bit address assigned to hosts using TCP/IP.

Internet Architecture Board (IAB): Formally called the Internet Activities Board. The technical body that oversees the development of the Internet suite of protocols (commonly referred to as "TCP/IP"). It has two task forces (the IRTF and the IETF), each charged with investigating a particular area.

799

Internet Assigned Numbers Authority (IANA): A largely government-funded overseer of IP allocations chartered by the FNC and the ISOC.

Internet Control Message Protocol (ICMP): The protocol used to handle errors and control messages at the IP layer. ICMP is actually part of the IP.

Internet Engineering Task Force (IETF): An open international community of network designers, operators, vendors, and researchers concerned with the evolution of the Internet's architecture; established by the IAB.

Internet Layer: The stack in the TCP/IP protocols that addresses a packet and sends the packets to the network access layer.

Internet Message Access Protocol (IMAP): A method of accessing electronic mail or bulletin board messages that are kept on a (possibly shared) mail server. IMAP permits a "client" email program to access remote message stores as if they were local. For example, email stored on an IMAP server can be manipulated from a desktop computer at home, a workstation at the office, and a notebook computer while traveling, without the need to transfer messages of files back and forth between these computers. IMAP can be regarded as the next-generation POP.

Internet Protocol (IP, IPv4): The Internet Protocol (version 4), defined in RFC 791, is the network layer for the TCP/IP suite. It is a connectionless, best-effort, packet-switching protocol.

Internet Protocol (Ping, IPv6): IPv6 is a new version of the Internet Protocol that is designed to be evolutionary.

Internet Service Provider (ISP): An organization that provides direct access to the Internet, such as the provider that links your college or university to the Net.

Interoperability: The ability to exchange requests between entities. Objects interoperate if the methods that apply to one object can request services of another object.

Investigation: The phase of the systems development life cycle in which the problem or need is identified and a decision is made on whether to proceed with a full-scale study.

IP Address: A unique number assigned to each computer on the Internet, consisting of four numbers, each less than 256, and each separated by a period, such as 129.16.255.0.

IP Datagram: The fundamental unit of information passed across the Internet. Contains source and destination addresses, along with data and a number of fields that define such things as the length of the datagram, the header checksum, and flags to say whether the datagram can be (or has been) fragmented.

ISO 9000: A certification program that demonstrates an organization adheres to steps that ensure quality of goods and services. A quality series that comprises a set of five documents and was developed in 1987 by the International Standards Organization (ISO).

Isolation: The separation of users and processes in a computer system from one another, as well as from the protection controls of the operating system.

Iterative Development Life Cycle: A strategy for developing systems that allows for the controlled reworking of parts of a system to remove mistakes or to make improvements based on feedback.

Java: Object-oriented programming language developed at Sun Microsystems to solve a number of problems in modern programming practice. The Java language is used extensively on the World Wide Web, particularly for applets.

Join: An operation that takes two relations as operand and produces a new relation by concealing the tuples and matching the corresponding columns when a stated condition holds between the two.

Jukebox: Hardware that houses, reads, and writes to many optical disks using a variety of mechanical methods for operation.

Kerberos: Developing standard for authenticating network users. Kerberos offers two key benefits: it functions in a multi-vendor network, and it does not transmit passwords over the network.

Key: In cryptography, a sequence of symbols that controls encryption and decryption.

Key/Cryptovariable: Encryption and decryption generally require the use of some secret information, referred to as a *key*. For some encryption mechanisms, the same key is used for both encryption and decryption; for other mechanisms, the keys used for encryption and decryption are different.

Key Generation: The origination of a key or set of distinct keys.

Key, Primary: A unique attribute used to identify a class of records in a database.

Knowledge Base: The part of an expert system that contains specific information and facts about the expert area. Rules that the expert system uses to make decisions are derived from this source.

L2F Protocol: Layer 2 Forwarding Protocol. Protocol that supports the creation of secure virtual private dial-up networks over the Internet.

Label: A set of symbols used to identify or describe an item, record, message, or file.

LAN: Local Area Network. High-speed, low-error data network covering a relatively small geographic area (up to a few thousand meters). LANs connect workstations, peripherals, terminals, and other devices in a single building or other geographically limited area. LAN standards specify cabling and signaling at the physical and data-link layers of the OSI model. Ethernet, FDDI, and Token Ring are widely used LAN technologies. *Compare with* MAN and WAN.

LAN Switch: High-speed switch that forwards packets between data-link segments. Most LAN switches forward traffic based on MAC addresses. This variety of LAN switch is sometimes called a frame switch. LAN switches are often categorized according to the method they use to forward traffic: cut-through packet switching or store-and-forward packet switching. Multi-layer switches are an intelligent subset of LAN switches. *Compare with* multi-layer switch. *See also* cut-through packet switching and store-and-forward packet switching.

Language Translator: Systems software that converts programs written in assembler or a higher-level language into machine code.

Laser: Light Amplification by Stimulated Emission of Radiation. Analog transmission device in which a suitable active material is excited by an external stimulus to produce a narrow beam of coherent light that can be modulated into pulses to carry data. Networks based on laser technology are sometimes run over SONET.

Laser Printer: An output unit that uses intensified light beams to form an image on an electrically charged drum and then transfers the image to paper.

Latency: In local networking, the time (measured in bits at the transmission rate) for a signal to propagate around or throughput the network. The time taken by a DASD device to position a storage location to reach the read arm over the physical storage medium. For general purposes, average latency time is used. Delay between the time a device requests access to a network and the time it is granted permission to transmit.

Layer 3 Switching: The emerging layer 3 switching technology integrates routing with switching to yield very high routing throughput rates in the millions-of-packets-per-second range. The movement to layer 3 switching is designed to address the downsides of the current generation of layer 2 switches, which are functionally equivalent to bridges. These downsides for a large, flat network include being subject to broadcast storms, spanning tree loops, and address limitations that drove the injection of routers into bridged networks in the late 1980s. Currently, layer 3 switching is represented by a number of approaches in the industry.

LDAP: Lightweight Directory Access Protocol. Protocol that provides access for management and browser applications that provide read/write interactive access to the X.500 Directory.

Leased Line: An un-switched telecommunications channel leased to an organization for its exclusive use.

Least Recently Used (LRU): A replacement strategy in which new data must replace existing data in an area of storage; the least recently used items are replaced.

Lightweight Directory Access Protocol (LDAP): This protocol provides access for management and browser application that provide read/write interactive access to the X.500 Directory.

Limit Check: An input control text that assesses the value of a data field to determine whether values fall within set limits.

Line Conditioning: A service offered by common carriers to reduce delay, noise, and amplitude distortion to produce transmission of higher data speeds.

Line Printer: An output unit that prints alphanumeric characters one line at a time.

Line Speed: The transmission rate of signals over a circuit, usually expressed in bits per second.

Load Sharing: A multiple-computer system that shares the load during peak hours. During non-peak periods or standard operation, one system can handle the entire load with the others acting as fallback units.

Logging: The automatic recording of data for the purpose of accessing and updating it.

MAC (Media Access Control): Lower of the two sub-layers of the data-link layer defined by the IEEE. The MAC sub-layer handles access to shared media, such as whether token passing or contention will be used.

MAC Address: Standardized data-link layer address that is required for every port or device that connects to a LAN. Other devices in the network use these addresses to locate specific ports in the network and to create and update routing tables and data structures. MAC addresses are 6 bytes long and are controlled by the IEEE. Also known as a hardware address, MAC-layer address, and physical address. *Compare with* network address.

Machine Language: Computer instructions or code representing computer operations and memory addresses in a numeric form that is executable by the computer without translation.

Maintenance: Tasks associated with the modification or enhancement of production software.

Maintenance Programmer: An applications programmer responsible for making authorized changes to one or more computer programs and ensuring that the changes are tested, documented, and verified.

Masquerade: A type of security threat that occurs when an entity successfully pretends to be a different entity.

Media: The various physical forms (e.g., disk, tape, and diskette) on which data is recorded in machine-readable formats.

Media Access Control (MAC): A local network control protocol that governs station access to a shared transmission medium. Examples are token passing and CSMA. *See* carrier sense, multiple access.

Megabyte (Mbyte, MB): The equivalent of 1,048,576 bytes.

Memory: The area in a computer that serves as temporary storage for programs and data during program execution.

Memory Address: The location of a byte or word of storage in computer memory.

Memory Bounds: The limits in the range of storage addresses for a protected region in memory.

Memory Chips: A small integrated circuit chip with a semiconductor matrix used as computer memory.

Menu: A section of the computer program — usually the top-level module — that controls the order of execution of other program modules. Also, online options displayed to a user, prompting the user for specific input.

Message: The data input by the user in the online environment that is used to drive a transaction. The output of transaction.

Message Address: The information contained in the message header that indicates the destination of the message.

Metadata: The description of such things as the structure, content, keys, and indexes of data.

Metalanguage: A language used to specify other languages.

Metropolitan Area Network (MAN): A data network intended to serve an area approximating that of a large city. Such networks are being implemented by innovative techniques, such as running fiber cables through subway tunnels.

Microprocessor: A single small chip containing circuitry and components for arithmetic, logical, and control operations.

Middleware: The distributed software needed to support interactions between client and servers.

Minicomputer: Typically, a word-oriented computer whose memory size and processing speed falls between that of a microcomputer and a medium-sized computer.

Mirror Image Backup: Mirror image backups (also referred to as bitstream backups) involve the backup of all areas of a computer hard disk drive or another type of storage media (e.g., Zip disks, floppy disks, Jazz disks, etc.). Such mirror image backups exactly replicate all sectors on a given storage device. Thus, all files and ambient data storage areas are copied. Such backups are sometimes referred to as "evidence-grade" backups and they differ substantially from standard file backups and network server backups. The making of a mirror image backup is simple in theory, but the accuracy of the backup must meet evidence standards. Accuracy is essential and to guarantee accuracy, mirror image backup programs typically rely on mathematical CRC computations in the validation process. These mathematical validation processes compare the original source data with the restored data. When computer evidence is involved, accuracy is extremely important, and the making of a mirror image backup is typically described as the preservation of the "electronic crime scene."

Mode of Operation: A classification for systems that execute in a similar fashion and share distinctive operational characteristics (e.g., Production, DSS, online, and Interactive).

Model: A representation of a problem or subject area that uses abstraction to express concepts.

Modem (Modulator/Demodulator): A device that converts the digital language of the PC to a series of high- and low-pitched tones for transmission over analog telephone lines.

Modification: A type of security threat that occurs when its content is modified in an unanticipated manner by a non-authorized entity.

Multiple Inheritance: The language mechanism that allows the definition of a class to include the attributes and methods defined for more than one superclass.

Multiprocessing: A computer operating method in which two or more processors are linked and execute multiple programs simultaneously.

Multiprogramming: A computer operating environment in which several programs can be placed in memory and executed concurrently.

Multi-purpose Internet Mail Extension (MIME): The standard for multimedia mail contents in the Internet suite of protocols.

NAK: Negative acknowledgment. Response sent from a receiving device to a sending device indicating that the information received contained errors. *Compare with* acknowledgment.

NAK Attack: A penetration technique that capitalizes on an operating system's inability to properly handle asynchronous interrupts.

Name Resolution: The process of mapping a name into the corresponding address.

NAT (Network Address Translation): Mechanism for reducing the need for globally unique IP addresses. NAT allows an organization with addresses that are not globally unique to connect to the Internet by translating those addresses into globally routable address space. *Also known as* Network Address Translator.

Need-to-Know: A security principle stating that an individual should have access only to that needed to perform a particular function.

Negative Acknowledgment (NAK): A response sent by the receiver to indicate that the previous block was unacceptable and the receiver is ready to accept a retransmission.

Network: An integrated, communicating aggregation of computers and peripherals linked through communications facilities.

Network Access Layer: The layer of the TCP/IP stack that sends the message out through the physical network onto the Internet.

Network Access Points (NAPs): (1) Nodes providing entry to the high-speed Internet backbone system. (2) Another name for an Internet Exchange Point.

Network Address: The network portion of an IP address. For a class A network, the network address is the first byte of the IP address. For a class B network, the network address is the first two bytes of the IP address. For a class C network, the network address is the first three bytes of the IP address. In the Internet, assigned network addresses are globally unique.

Network Administrator: The person who maintains user accounts, password files, and system software on your campus network.

Network Information Center (NIC): Originally, there was only one, located at SRI International and tasked to serve the ARPANET (and later DDN) community. Today, there are many NICs, operated by local, regional, and national networks all over the world. Such centers provided user assistance, document service, training, and much more.

Network Layer: The OSI layer that is responsible for routing, switching, and subnetwork access across the entire OSI environment.

Neural Network: A type of system developed by artificial intelligence researchers used for processing logic.

Node: A device attached to a network.

Noise: Random electrical signals introduced by circuit components or natural disturbances that tend to degrade the performance of a communications channel.

Object-Oriented: Any method, language, or system that supports object identity, classification, and encapsulation and specialization. C++, Smalltalk, Objective-C, and Eiffel are examples of object-oriented implementation languages.

Object-Oriented Analysis (OOA): The specification of requirements in terms of objects with identity that encapsulate properties and operations, messaging, inheritance, polymorphism, and binding.

Object-Oriented Database Management System (OODBMS): A database that stores, retrieves, and updates objects using transaction control, queries, locking, and versioning.

Object-Oriented Design (OOD): The development activity that specifies the implementation of a system using the conceptual model defined during the analysis phase.

Object-Oriented Language: A language that supports objects, method resolution, specialization, encapsulation, polymorphism, and inheritance.

Object Program: A program that has been translated from a higher-level source code into machine language.

Object Request Broker (ORB): A software mechanism by which objects make and receive requests and responses.

OLE: Microsoft's Object Linking and Embedding technology designed to let applications share functionality through live data exchange and embedded data. Embedded objects are packaged statically within the source application, called the "client;" linked objects launch the "server" applications when instructed by the client application. Linking is the capability to call a program, embedding places data in a foreign program.

Online System: Applications that allow direct interaction of the user with the computer (CPU) via a CRT, thus enabling the user to receive back an immediate response to data entered (i.e., an airline reservation system). Only one root node can be used at the beginning of the hierarchical structure.

Open System: A system whose architecture permits components developed by independent organizations or vendors to be combined.

Open Systems Interconnection (OSI): An international standardization program to facilitate communications among computers from different manufactures. *See* ISO.

Operating System: The various sets of computer programs and other software that monitor and operate the computer hardware and the firmware to facilitate use of the hardware.

Optical Disk: A disk that is written to or read from by optical means.

Optical Fiber: A form of transmission medium that uses light to encode signals and has the highest transmission rate of any medium.

Optical Storage: A medium requiring lasers to permanently alter the physical media to create a permanent record. The storage also requires lasers to read stored information from this medium.

OSI Reference Model: The seven-layer architecture designed by OSI for open data communications network.

Overwriting: The obliteration of recorded data by recording different data on the same surface.

PABX: Private Automatic Branch Exchange. Telephone switch for use inside a corporation. PABX is the preferred term in Europe, while PBX is used in the United States.

Packet: Logical grouping of information that includes a header containing control information and (usually) user data. Packets are most often used to refer to network layer units of data. The terms "datagram," "frame," "message," and "segment" are also used to describe logical information groupings at various layers of the OSI Reference Model and in various technology circles.

Packet Internet Grouper (PING): A program used to test reachability of destinations by sending them an ICMP echo request and waiting for a reply. The term is used as a verb: "Ping host X to see if it is up."

Packet Switch: WAN device that routes packets along the most efficient path and allows a communications channel to be shared by multiple connections. Formerly called an Interface Message Processor (IMP).

Packet Switching: A switching procedure that breaks up messages into fixed-length units (called packets) at the message source. These units may travel along different routes before reaching their intended destination.

Padding: A technique used to fill a field, record, or block with default information (e.g., blanks or zeros).

Page: A basic unit of storage in main memory.

Page Fault: A program interruption that occurs when a page that is referred to is not in main memory and must be read from external storage.

Paging: A method of dividing a program into parts called pages and introducing a given page into memory as the processing on the page is required for program execution.

PAP (Password Authentication Protocol): Authentication protocol that allows PPP peers to authenticate one another. The remote router attempting to connect to the local router is required to send an authentication request. Unlike CHAP, PAP passes the password and hostname or username in the clear (unencrypted). PAP does not itself prevent unauthorized access, but merely identifies the remote end. The router or access server then determines if that user is allowed access. PAP is supported only on PPP lines. *Compare with* CHAP.

Parallel Port: The computer's printer port, which in a pinch, allows user access to notebooks and computers that cannot be opened.

Parent: A unit of data in a 1:n relationship with another unit of data called a child, where the parent can exist independently but the child cannot.

Parity: A bit or series of bits appended to a character or block of characters to ensure that the information received is the same as the information that was sent. Parity is used for error detection.

Parity Bit: A bit attached to a byte that is used to check the accuracy of data storage.

Partition: A memory area assigned to a computer program during its execution.

Passive Wiretapping: The monitoring or recording of data while it is being transmitted over a communications link.

Password: A word or string of characters that authenticates a user, a specific resource, or an access type.

Patent: Exclusive right granted to an inventor to produce, sell, and distribute the invention for a specified number of years.

Penetration: A successful unauthorized access to a computer system.

Penetration Testing: The use of special programmer or analyst teams to attempt to penetrate a system to identify security weaknesses.

Persistent Object: An object that can survive the process that created it. A persistent object exists until it is explicitly deleted.

Physical Layer: The OSI layer that provides the means to activate and use physical connections for bit transmission. In plain terms, the physical layer provides the procedures for transferring a single bit across a physical medium.

Piggyback Entry: Unauthorized access to a computer system that is gained through another user's legitimate connection.

Plain Old Telephone System (POTS): What we consider to be the "normal" phone system used with modems. Does not include leased lines or digital lines.

Plaintext: Intelligible text or signals that have meaning and can be read or acted on without being decrypted.

Platform: Foundation upon which processes and systems are built and which can include hardware, software, firmware, etc.

Point-of-Presence (POP): A site where there exists a collection of telecommunications equipment, usually digital leased lines and multi-protocol routers.

Point-to-Point: A network configuration interconnecting only two points. The connection can be dedicated or switched.

Point-to-Point Protocol (PPP): The successor to SLIP, PPP provides router-to-router and host-to-network connections over both synchronous and asynchronous circuits.

Pointer: The address of a record (or other data grouping) contained in another record so that a program may access the former record when it has retrieved the latter record. The address can be absolute, relative, or symbolic, and hence the pointer is referred to as absolute, relative, or symbolic.

Polling: A procedure by which a computer controller unit asks terminals and other peripheral devices in a serial fashion if they have any messages to send.

Polymorphism: A request-handling mechanism that selects a method based on the type of target object. This allows the specification of one request that can result in invocation of different methods depending on the type of the target object. Most object-oriented languages support the selection of the appropriate method based on the class of the object (classical polymorphism). A few languages or systems support characteristics of the object, including values and user-defined defaults (generalized polymorphism).

Port: An outlet, usually on the exterior of a computer system, that enables peripheral devices to be connected and interfaced with the computer.

Portability: The ability to implement and execute software in one type of computing space and have it execute in a different computing space with little or no changes.

Presentation Layer: The OSI layer that determines how application information is represented (i.e., encoded) while in transit between two end systems.

Pretty Good Privacy (PGP): PGP provides confidentiality and authentication services for electronic mail and file storage applications. Developed by Phil Zimmerman and distributed for free on the Internet. Widely used by the Internet technical community.

Primary Key: An attribute that contains values that uniquely identifies the record in which the key exists.

Principle of Least Privilege: A security procedure under which users are granted only the minimum access authorization they need to perform required tasks.

Privacy: The prevention of unauthorized access and manipulation of data.

Privacy Act of 1974: The federal law that allows individuals to know what information about them is on file and how it is used by all government agencies and their contractors. The 1986 Electronic Communication Act is an extension of the Privacy Act.

Privacy Enhanced Mail (PEM): Internet email standard that provides confidentiality, authentication, and message integrity using various encryption methods. Not widely deployed in the Internet.

Privacy Protection: The establishment of appropriate administrative, technical, and physical safeguards to protect the security and confidentiality of data records against anticipated threats or hazards that could result in substantial harm, embarrassment, inconvenience, or unfairness to any individual about whom such information is maintained.

Private Network: A network established and operated by a private organization for the benefit of members of the organization.

Privilege: A right granted to an individual, a program, or a process.

Privileged Instructions: A set of instructions generally executable only when the computer system is operating in the executive state (e.g., while handling interrupts). These special instructions are typically designed to control such protection features as the storage protection features.

Problem: Any deviation from predefined standards.

Problem Reporting: The method of identifying, tracking, and assigning attributes to problems detected within the software product, deliverables, or within the development processes.

Procedure: Required "how-to" instructions that support some part of a policy or standard.

Processor: The hardware unit containing the functions of memory and the central processing unit.

Program Development Process: The activities involved in developing computer programs, including problem analysis, program design, process design, program coding, debugging, and testing.

Program Maintenance: The process of altering program code or instructions to meet new or changing requirements.

Programmable Read-Only Memory (PROM): Computer memory chips that can be programmed permanently to carry out a defined process.

Programmer: The individual who designs and develops computer programs.

Programmer/Analyst: The individual who analyzes processing requirements and then designs and develops computer programs to direct processing.

Programming Language: A language with special syntax and style conventions for coding computer programs.

Programming Specifications: The complete description of input, processing, output, and storage requirements necessary to code a computer program.

Protection Ring: A hierarchy of access modes through which a computer system enforces the access rights granted to each user, program, and process, ensuring that each operates only within its authorized access mode.

Protocol: A set of instructions required to initiate and maintain communication between sender and receiver devices.

Protocol Analyzer: A data communications testing unit set that enables a network engineer to observe bit patterns and simulate network elements.

Prototype: A usable system or subcomponent that is built inexpensively or quickly with the intention of modifying or replacing it.

Public Key Encryption: An encryption scheme where two pairs of algorithmic keys (one private and one public) are used to encrypt and decrypt messages, files, etc.

Purging: The orderly review of storage and removal of inactive or obsolete data files.

Quality: The totality of features and characteristics of a product or service that bear on its ability to meet stated or implied needs.

Quality Assurance: An overview process that entails planning and systematic actions to ensure that a project is following good quality management practices.

Quality Control: Process by which product quality is compared with standards.

Quality of Service (QoS): The service level defined by a service agreement between a network user and a network provider, which guarantees a certain level of bandwidth and data flow rates.

Query Language: A language that enables a user to interact indirectly with a DBMS to retrieve and possibly modify data held under the DBMS.

RADIUS (Remote Dial-In User Service): Database for authenticating modem and ISDN connections and for tracking connection time.

RAID (Redundant Arrays of Inexpensive Disks): Instead of using one large disk to store data, you use many smaller disks (because they are cheaper). *See* disk mirroring and duplexing. An approach to using many low-cost drives as a group to improve performance, yet also provides a degree of redundancy that makes the chance of data loss remote.

RAM: A type of computer memory that can be accessed randomly; that is, any byte of memory can be accessed without touching the preceding bytes. RAM is the most common type of memory found in computers and other devices, such as printers. There are two basic types of RAM: dynamic RAM (DRAM) and static RAM (SRAM).

RARP (Reverse Address Resolution Protocol): Protocol in the TCP/IP stack that provides a method for finding IP addresses based on MAC addresses. *Compare with* Address Resolution Protocol (ARP).

Read-Only Memory (ROM): Computer memory chips with preprogrammed circuits for storing such software as word processors and spreadsheets.

Reassembly: The process by which an IP datagram is "put back together" at the receiving hosts after having been fragmented in transit.

Recovery: The restoration of the information processing facility or other related assets following physical destruction or damage.

Recovery Procedures: The action necessary to restore a system's computational capability and data files after system failure or penetration.

Recursion: The definition of something in terms of itself. For example, a bill of material is usually defined in terms of itself.

Referential Integrity: The assurance that an object handle identifies a single object. The facility of a DBMS that ensures the validity of predefined relationships.

Regression Testing: The rerunning of test cases that a program has previously executed correctly to detect errors created during software correction or modification. Tests used to verify a previously tested system whenever it is modified.

Relational Database: In a relational database, data is organized in two-dimensional tables or relations.

Remanence: The residual magnetism that remains on magnetic storage media after degaussing.

Remote Access: The ability to dial into a computer over a local telephone number using a number of digital access techniques.

Remote Authentication Dial-In User Service (RADIUS): A security and authentication mechanism for remote access.

Remote Procedure Call (RPC): An easy and popular paradigm for implementing the client/server model of distributed computing. A request is sent to a remote system to execute a designated procedure, using arguments supplied, and the result returned to the caller.

Replay: A type of security threat that occurs when an exchange is captured and resent at a later time to confuse the original recipients

Replication: The process of keeping a copy of data through either shadowing or caching.

Report: Printed or displayed output that communicates the content of files and other activities. The output is typically organized and easily read.

Request for Comments (RFC): The document series, begun in 1969, that describes the Internet suite of protocols and related experiments. Not all (in fact, very few) RFCs describe Internet standards, but all Internet standards are written up as RFCs.

Residue: Data left in storage after processing operations and before degaussing or rewriting has occurred.

Resource: In a computer system, any function, device, or data collection that can be allocated to users or programs.

Risk: The probability that a particular security threat will exploit a particular vulnerability.

Risk Analysis: An analysis that examines an organization's information resources, its existing controls, and its remaining organization and computer system vulnerabilities. It combines the loss potential for each resource or combination of resources with an estimated rate of occurrence to establish a potential level of damage in dollars or other assets.

Risk Assessment: Synonymous with risk analysis.

Role: A job type defined in terms of a set of responsibilities.

Rollback: (1) Restoration of a system to its former condition after it has switched to a fallback mode of operation when the cause of the fallback has been removed. (2) The restoration of the database to an original position or condition often after major damage to the physical medium. (3) The restoration of the information processing facility or other related assets following physical destruction or damage.

Router: A system responsible for making decisions about which of several paths network (or Internet) traffic will follow. To do this, it uses a routing protocol to gain information about the network, and algorithms to choose the best route based on several criteria known as "routing metrics."

RSA: A public-key cryptographic system that may be used for encryption and authentication. It was invented in 1977 and named for its inventors: Ron Rivest, Adi Shamir, and Leonard Adleman.

Safeguard: Synonymous with control.

Sanitizing: The degaussing or overwriting of sensitive information in magnetic or other storage media.

Scalability: The likelihood that an artifact can be extended to provide additional functionality with little or no additional effort.

Scavenging: The searching of residue for the purpose of unauthorized data acquisition.

Scripts: Executable programs used to perform specified tasks for servers and clients.

Search Engine: A program written to allow users to search the Web for documents that match user-specified parameters.

Secrecy: A security principle that keeps information from being disclosed to anyone not authorized to access it.

Secure Electronic Transaction (SET): The SET specification has been developed to allow for secure credit card and offline debit card (check card) transactions over the World Wide Web.

Secure Operating System: An operating system that effectively controls hardware, software, and firmware functions to provide the level of protection appropriate to the value of the data resources managed by this operating system.

Secure Socket Layer (SSL): An encryption technology for the Web used to secure transactions such as the transmission of credit card numbers for e-commerce.

Security Audit: An examination of data security procedures and measures to evaluate their adequacy and compliance with established policy.

Security Controls: Techniques and methods to ensure that only authorized users can access the computer information system and its resources.

Security Filter: A set of software or firmware routines and techniques employed in a computer system to prevent automatic forwarding of specified data over unprotected links or to unauthorized persons.

Security Kernel: The central part of a computer system (hardware, software, or firmware) that implements the fundamental security procedures for controlling access to system resources.

Security Program: A systems program that controls access to data in files and permits only authorized use of terminals and other related equipment. Control is usually exercised through various levels of safeguards assigned on the basis of the user's need-to-know.

Seepage: The accidental flow, to unauthorized individuals, of data or information that is presumed to be protected by computer security safeguards.

Sensitive Data: Data that is considered confidential or proprietary. The kind of data that, if disclosed to a competitor, might give away an advantage.

Sensitive Information: Any information that requires protection and that should not be made generally available.

Serial Line Internet Protocol (SLIP): An Internet protocol used to run IP over serial lines such as telephone circuits or RS-232 cables interconnecting two systems. SLIP is now being replaced by Point-to-Point Protocol. *See* Point-to-Point Protocol.

Server: A computer that provides a service to another computer, such as a mail server, a file server, or a news server.

Session: A completed connection to an Internet service, and the ensuing connect time.

Session Layer: The OSI layer that provides means for dialogue control between end systems.

Shareware: Software available on the Internet that may be downloaded to your machine for evaluation and for which you are generally expected to pay a fee to the originator of the software if you decide to keep it.

Simple Network Management Protocol (SNMP): Provides remote administration of network device; "simple" because the agent requires minimal software.

Simulation: The use of an executable model to represent the behavior of an object. During testing, the computational hardware, the external environment, and even the coding segments may be simulated.

Simultaneous Processing: The execution of two or more computer program instructions at the same time in a multiprocessing environment.

Single Inheritance: The language mechanism that allows the definition of a class to include the attributes and methods defined for, at most, one superclass.

Social Engineering: An attack based on deceiving users or administrators at the target site.

Socket: A paring of an IP address and a port number. *See* port.

Softlifting: Illegal copying of licensed software for personal use.

Software: Computer programs, procedures, rules, and possibly documentation and data pertaining to the operation of the computer system.

Software Life Cycle: The period of time beginning when a software product is conceived and ending when the product is no longer available for use. The software life cycle is typically broken into phases (e.g., requirements, design, programming, testing, conversion, operations, and maintenance).

Software Maintenance: All changes, corrections, and enhancements that occur after an application has been placed into production.

Software Piracy: To illegally copy software.

Source Document: The form that is used for the initial recording of data prior to system input.

Source Program: The computer program that is coded in an assembler or higher-level programming language.

Spam: The act of posting the same information repeatedly on inappropriate places or too many places so as to overburden the network.

Specification: A description of a problem or subject that will be implemented in a computational or other system. The specification includes both a description of the subject and aspects of the implementation that affect its representation. Also, the process and analysis and design that results in a description of a problem or subject that can be implemented in a computation or other system.

Spoofing: The deliberate inducement of a user or resource to take incorrect action.

Spooling: A technique that maximizes processing speed through the temporary use of high-speed storage devices. Input files are transferred from slower, permanent storage and queued in the high-speed devices to await processing, or output files are queued in high-speed devices to await transfer to slower storage devices.

Standard: Mandatory statement of minimum requirements that support some part of a policy.

Standard Generalized Markup Language (SGML): An international standard for encoding textual information that specifies particular ways to annotate text documents separating the structure of the document from the information content. HTML is a generalized form of SGML.

State Transition: A change of state for an object; something that can be signaled by an event.

State Variable: A property or type that is part of an identified state of a given type.

Static Data: Data that, once established, remains constant.

Stream Cipher: An encryption method in which a cryptographic key and an algorithm are applied to each bit in a datastream, one bit at a time.

Structured Design: A methodology for designing systems and programs through a top-down, hierarchical segmentation.

Structured Programming: The process of writing computer programs using logical, hierarchical control structures to carry out processing.

Structured Query Language (SQL): The international standard language for defining and accessing a relational database.

Subnet: A portion of a network, which may be a physically independent network segment, that shares a network address with other portions of the network and is distinguished by a subnet number. A subnet is to a network what a network is to the Internet.

Subnet Address: The subnet portion of an IP address. In a subnetted network, the host portion of an IP address is split into a subnet and a host portion using an address (subnet) mask.

Subroutine: A segment of code that can be called up by a program and executed at any time from any point.

Superclass: A class from which another class inherits attributes and methods.

Swapping: A method of computer processing in which programs not actively being processed are held on special storage devices and alternated in and out of memory with other programs according to priority.

Synchronous: A protocol of transmitting data over a network where the sending and receiving terminals are kept in synchronization with each other by a clock signal embedded in the data.

Synchronous Optical NETwork (SONET): SONET is an international standard for high-speed data communications over fiber-optic media. The transmission rates range from 51.84 Mbps to 2.5 Gbps.

System: A series of related procedures designed to perform a specific task.

System Analysis: The process of studying information requirements and preparing a set of functional specifications that identify what a new or replacement system should accomplish.

System Design: The development of a plan for implementing a set of functional requirements as an operational system.

System Integrity Procedures: Procedures established to ensure that hardware, software, firmware, and data in a computer system maintain their state of original integrity and are not tampered with by unauthorized personnel.

System Log: An audit trail of relevant system happenings (e.g., transaction entries, database changes).

Systems Analysis: The process of studying information requirements and preparing a set of functional specifications that identify what a new or replacement system should accomplish.

Systems Design: The development of a plan for implementing a set of functional requirements as an operational system.

Systems Development Life Cycle (SDLC): (1) The classical operational development methodology that typically includes the phases of requirements gathering, analysis, design, programming, testing, integration, and implementation. (2) The systematic systems building process consisting of specific phases; for example, preliminary investigation, requirements determination, systems analysis, systems design, systems development, and systems implementation.

TACACS (Terminal Access Controller Access Control System): Authentication protocol, developed by the DDN community, that provides remote access authentication and related services, such as event logging. User passwords are administered in a central database rather than in individual routers, providing an easily scalable network security solution.

Technological Attack: An attack that can be perpetrated by circumventing or nullifying hardware, software, and firmware access control mechanisms rather than by subverting system personnel or other users.

Telecommunications: Any transmission, emission, or reception of signs, signals, writing, images, sounds, or other information by wire, radio, visual, satellite, or electromagnetic systems.

Teleprocessing: Information processing and transmission performed by an integrated system of telecommunications, computers, and person-to-machine interface equipment.

Teleprocessing Security: The protection that results from all measures designed to prevent deliberate, inadvertent, or unauthorized disclosure or acquisition of information stored in or transmitted by a teleprocessing system.

TEMPEST: The study and control of spurious electronic signals emitted from electronic equipment. TEMPEST is a classification of technology designed to minimize the electromagnetic emanations generated by computing devices. TEMPEST technology makes it difficult, if not impossible, to compromise confidentiality by capturing emanated information.

Test Data: Data that simulates actual data to form and content and is used to evaluate a system or program before it is put into operation.

Threat Monitoring: The analysis assessment and review of audit trails and other data collected to search out system events that may constitute violations or precipitate incidents involving data privacy.

Three-Way Handshake: The process whereby two protocol entities synchronize during connection establishment.

Throughput: The process of measuring the amount of work a computer system can handle within a specified timeframe.

Timestamping: The practice of tagging each record with some moment in time, usually when the record was created or when the record was passed from one environment to another.

Time-Dependent Password: A password that is valid only at a certain time of day or during a specified timeframe.

Token Passing: A network access method that uses a distinctive character sequence as a symbol (token), which is passed from node to node, indicating when to begin transmission. Any node can remove the token, begin transmission, and replace the token when it is finished.

Token Ring: A type of area network in which the devices are arranged in a virtual ring in which the devices use a particular type of message called a token to communicate with one another.

Traceroute: A program available on many systems that traces the path a packet takes to a destination. It is mostly used to debug routing problems between hosts. There is also a traceroute protocol defined in RFC 1393.

Trademark: A registered word, letter, or device granting the owner exclusive rights to sell/distribute the goods to which it is applied.

Traffic Analysis: A type of security threat that occurs when an outside entity is able to monitor and analyze traffic patterns on a network.

Traffic Flow Security: The protection that results from those features in some cryptography equipment that conceal the presence of valid messages on a communications circuit, usually by causing the circuit to appear busy at all times or by encrypting the source and destination addresses of valid messages.

Transaction: A transaction is an activity or request to a computer. Purchase orders, changes, additions, and deletions are examples of transactions that are recorded in a business information environment.

Transmission Control Protocol (TCP): The major transport protocol in the Internet suite of protocols providing reliable, connection-oriented, full-duplex streams.

Transport Layer: The OSI layer that is responsible for reliable end-to-end data transfer between end systems.

Trojan Horse: A computer program that is apparently or actually useful and contains a trapdoor or unexpected code.

Trust: Reliance on the ability of a system or process to meet its specifications.

Trusted Computer Security Evaluation Criteria (TCSEC): A security development standard for system manufacturers and a basis for comparing and evaluating different computer systems. Also known as the *Orange Book*.

Tunneling: Tunneling refers to encapsulation of protocol A with protocol B, such that A treats B as though it were a data-link layer. Tunneling is used to get data between administrative domains, which use a protocol that is not supported by the internet connecting those domains.

Twisted Pair: A type of network physical medium made of copper wires twisted around each other. Example: Ordinary telephone cable.

UDP: User Datagram Protocol. Connectionless transport layer protocol in the TCP/IP stack. UDP is a simple protocol that exchanges datagrams without acknowledgments or guaranteed delivery, requiring that error processing and retransmission be handled by other protocols. UDP is defined in RFC 768.

Uniform Resource Locator (URL): The primary means of navigating the web; consists of the means of access, the Web site, the path, and the document name of a Web resource, such as http://www.auerbach-publications.com.

Unshielded Twisted Pair (UTP): A generic term for "telephone" wire used to carry data such as 10Base-T and 100Base-T. Various categories (qualities) of cable exist that are certified for different kinds of networking technologies.

Update: The file processing activity in which master records are altered to reflect the current business activity contained in transactional files.

USENET: A facility of the Internet, also called "the news," that allows users to read and post messages to thousands of discussion groups on various topics.

User Datagram Protocol (UDP): A transport protocol in the Internet suite of protocols. UDP, like TCP, uses IP for delivery; however, unlike TCP, UDP provides for exchange of datagrams without acknowledgments or guaranteed delivery.

Validation: The determination of the correctness, with respect to the user needs and requirements, of the final program or software produced from a development project.

Validation, Verification, and Testing: Used as an entity to define a procedure of review, analysis, and testing throughout the software life cycle to discover errors; the process of validation, verification, and testing determines that functions operate as specified and ensures the production of quality software.

Value-Added Network (VAN): A communications network using existing common carrier networks and providing such additional features as message switching and protocol handling.

Verification: (1) The authentication process by which the biometric system matches a captured biometric against the person's stored template. (2) The demonstration of consistency, completeness, and correctness of the software at and between each stage of the development life cycle.

Virtual Circuit: A network service that provides connection-oriented service, regardless of the underlying network structure.

Virtual Memory: A method of extending computer memory using secondary storage devices to store program pages that are not being executed at the time.

Virtual Private Network (VPN): A VPN allows IP traffic to travel securely over public TCP/IP network by encrypting all traffic from one network to another. A VPN uses "tunneling" to encrypt all information at the IP level.

Virus: A type of malicious software that can destroy the computer's hard drive, files, and programs in memory, and that replicates itself to other disks.

WAN (Wide Area Network): Data communications network that serves users across a broad geographic area and often uses transmission devices provided by common carriers. Frame Relay, SMDS, and X.25 are examples of WANs. *Compare with* LAN and MAN.

Waterfall Life Cycle: A software development process that structures the analysis, design, programming, and testing. Each step is completed before the next step begins.

Web Crawler: A software program that searches the Web for specified purposes such as to find a list of all URLs within a particular site.

Whois: An Internet resource that permits users to initiate queries to a database containing information on users, hosts, networks, and domains.

Wiring Closet: Specially designed room used for wiring a data or voice network. Wiring closets serve as a central junction point for the wiring and wiring equipment that is used for interconnecting devices.

Work Factor: The effort and time required to break a protective measure.

X.400: ITU-T recommendation specifying a standard for email transfer.

X.500: The CITT and ISO standard for electronic directory services.

XDSL: A group term used to refer to ADSL (Asymmetrical Digital Subscriber Line), HDSL (High data rate Digital Subscriber Line), and SDSL (Symmetrical Digital Subscriber Line). All are digital technologies using the existing copper infrastructure provided by the telephone companies. XDSL is a high-speed alternative to ISDN.

Appendix B
Annotated Bibliography
(Prepared by Rob Slade)

The various chapters in this book have provided a number of references for your further study. However, looking at the total length of those lists might be a bit daunting. Therefore, this will be an attempt to provide you with a bit more information about select, recommended texts.

This material may have been updated on the "by domain" page maintained at:

- http://victoria.tc.ca/techrev/mnbksccd.htm or
- http://sun.soci.niu.edu/~rslade/mnbksccd.htm

Please do not panic at the size of this list. It is not intended to say that you need to read all these books. This list is provided as a reference, and it is divided by the CBK domains so that you can get help with specific topics where you feel you need more information.

First off, some general resources.

There are some guides that are written with the intent of helping you pass the exam, addressing all the domains. Reviews for these can be found listed on a separate page at:

- http://victoria.tc.ca/techrev/mnbkscci.htm or
- http://sun.soci.niu.edu/~rslade/mnbkscci.htm

In terms of general textbooks for the CBK review course and the CISSP exam, the best is probably:

- Harold F. Tipton and Micki Krause, Eds., *Information Security Management Handbook,* (Auerbach Publications, 1999–2003) ISBN: 0-8493-9829-0, 0-8493-0800-3, 0-8493-1127-6, 0-8493-1518-2

This work has come out in different versions over the years. If your company or library has old versions, they are still worth studying, although you should look for more current versions as well. The handbook is

823

a collection of papers focusing on various aspects of security. Each volume of the book is structured by the CBK domains, so you can look to the table of contents and find out what particular issues are addressed for the domain you are interested in. The specific topics, papers, and authors may change with each edition. Possibly the most useful, for the current exam, is the third (1998) edition, which is actually fully available online at http://secinf.net/info/misc/handbook/ewtoc.html. The current version is the fourth edition, which may be referred to by various dates, since the four existing volumes were published in different years.

As an overview for the CISSP (Certified Information Systems Security Professional) CBK (Common Body of Knowledge), this work covers a vast range of topics. The text provides some excellent articles, some of which are general but detailed overviews, and others that address particular problems or new technologies. However, even with all these articles and pages, there are gaps, some surprisingly basic.

The quality of the articles can vary widely, but most are written and researched very well: much better than in other, similar compilation works.

It should be noted that there is a significant difference in character between the volumes. The first volume deals with topics that are closer to the heart of security, and the essays are generally more valuable to the practitioner. Later volumes contain papers covering a wider range of subjects, many of which have little or no relevance to security beyond fundamental concerns that are well covered elsewhere. Book 1 will be useful to the CISSP candidate and any specialty security worker: the other volumes may be of interest to a narrower group of senior security executives and theorists, and, ironically, a wider audience of those interested in newer technologies in general.

An absolutely excellent text is Ross Anderson's *Security Engineering* (John Wiley & Sons, 2001). If you are involved with security and you have not read it, you should. This work is particularly good in regard to security architecture and models. But it also covers a lot of material that can help you in crypto, access control, database security, law, privacy, and a number of other areas. Although the material is presented in a very formal way, the writing is usually quite readable, and the exceptional stilted passages are still accessible to the determined reader. On occasion, one could hope for additional explanations of some items that are mentioned briefly and passed over, but, by and large, one has to agree with Bruce Schneier's assessment, reprinted on the book jacket, that this is one of the most comprehensive works on security concepts available. The constant emphasis on how security protections have failed can be depressing, but the examination of the errors of others does provide the basis for better designs in the future.

A reasonable text is Dieter Gollmann's *Computer Security* (John Wiley & Sons, 1999). Gollmann is fairly explicit in stating the intention and audience of the book. It is to be a text for a course, rather than a handbook, encyclopedia, or history. It is about computer security rather than information security in general, although there are sections on computer network security and database security. The objective of the course for which it was prepared is to give students a sufficient background to evaluate security products, rather than to address issues of policy or risk analysis. Thus, the emphasis is on technical rather than managerial aspects.

In terms of readability, Gollmann's writing is not always fluid, but it is always clear. While intended as a class text, the book is, in most parts, accessible to any intelligent reader. The exercises provided at the end of each chapter are not mere buzzword tests, although most are more suitable for discussion starters rather than checks for understanding.

The bibliography is not annotated, but the "Further Reading" section at the end of each chapter helps make up for this shortcoming. Having to flip between two sections to find the referenced work is a bit awkward, but not unduly so.

It has frequently been noted that a security dictionary or glossary would be extremely helpful to CBK students or candidates for the CISSP exam. A brief one, aimed at the necessary basics, is maintained at http://victoria.tc.ca/techrev/secgloss.htm and http://sun.soci.niu.edu/~rslade/secgloss.htm, and this document also points to a number of other such resources on the Net, such as the much larger work at http://security.isu.edu/pdf/NIATECV30d.pdf.

There is one published security dictionary: Vir V. Phoha, *Internet Security Dictionary* (Springer-Verlag, 2002). Overall, despite a number of problems, this is a useful reference. Primarily, of course, this is because it is the first of its type. However, it does cover a reasonable range of the security field, and is, for the most part, reliable within limits. However, I would hope that the content is updated, expanded, and improved relatively soon, and regularly thereafter.

I should also note a very frequently cited resource, the excellent CISSP and SSCP Open Study Guide at http://www.cccure.org/. This site is particularly useful for its set of "example" exam questions. Many people want to have a try at a set of questions before they sit the actual CISSP exam, and understandably so. The exam sets in the various CISSP guides (and the set that you have to buy, from Boson) are generally too simple to give you a real feeling for the exam. The questions at "C-C-Cure," as it is called, are much closer to the real thing. (I do have to note that a number of questions added recently, and referring to recent books, are of much lower standard than those done previously.)

And now, on to the domains.

Information Security Management

Information Security Management Handbook is one of the major texts, particularly the online (1998) version.

Donn B. Parker, *Fighting Computer Crime* (John Wiley & Sons, 1998) may not always be completely reliable, but is an interesting alternative voice in the field. It is probably important to have the contrarian view.

A number of very useful papers, most related to security management in some form or other, are available in the NIST Special Publications at the Computer Security Resource Center (CSRC) of the National Institute of Standards and Technology (http://csrc.nist.gov/publications/nist-pubs/index.html). The 800 series papers have a number of interesting documents, including a "Risk Management Guide for Information Technology Systems" and the "Security Self-Assessment Guide for Information Technology Systems," which is handy for audit and "control objectives" outlines. You may have to translate from governmentese to corporatese, but the concepts are there.

Policy creation is an important topic. The "classic" in the field is *Information Security Policies Made Easy* by Charles Cresson-Wood, although it tends to be used as a "cut-and-paste" tool, which is not appropriate in many cases.

A more recent, and more general, guide is Scott Barman's *Writing Information Security Policies* (New Riders Press, 2002). While still aimed at the non-technical manager responsible for producing the policy, it uses minimal examples, concentrating on the process of policy formation. Although not a panacea, this book is clear, well written, and helpful. There is valuable advice packed into few enough pages that a manager should be able to read it on a cross-country plane trip.

A big part of the security management domain is risk management. One resource is the RISKS — Forum Digest. Moderated by Peter G. Neumann (aka PGN), RISKS (or RISKS-L, as it is known to the old-time crowd) is not only an exemplar of how moderated mailing lists should be run, but is a prime resource for all topics related to security. Probably the easiest way to get at it is via the Usenet newsgroup comp.risks, which should also be accessible via the Usenet connection and archives at Yahoo and Google. You can also subscribe to the mailing list once you get instructions from any issue, and there is an archive of back issues at http://catless.ncl.ac.uk/Risks, and now an Illustrative Risks compendium at http://www.csl.sri.com/users/neumann/illustrative.html.

Security Architecture and Models

The *Information Security Management Handbook,* again. And this time I think I have to say that the online version is "better" than the current hardcopy one. *Security Engineering* will definitely help you in this domain.

Access Control Systems and Methodology

The *Information Security Management Handbook* and *Security Engineering.*

Simson Garfinkel and Gene Spafford, *Practical UNIX and Internet Security* (O'Reilly & Associates, 1996), is definitely practical; and if your job involves system security, at whatever level, this book belongs on your desk. The expansion of the title is no mere attempt to gain market share: this edition is twice the size of the old one. The book is well planned and comprehensive. While the emphasis and examples are from the Unix operating system and Internet protocols, background information is given on related (and important) topics such as modems and physical security. The writing and examples are clear and understandable, and should present no problems to the intelligent novice, but the additional material ensures that there is value here even for the Unix guru.

After a slow (but interesting) start, Richard F. Smith, *Authentication: From Passwords to Public Keys* (Addison-Wesley, 2002), does have a good deal of useful material in the later chapters. Long on verbiage and a bit short on focus, this text does have enough to recommend it to security practitioners serious about the authentication problem.

Applications and Systems Development

If you have a background in applications development, you have an advantage over most candidates. The *Information Security Management Handbook* and the *Software Engineering Body of Knowledge* (SWEBOK, http://www.swebok.org/) are useful references. There is also a good chapter in Barman's *Writing Information Security Policies. Security Engineering* really applies to any kind of systems design work.

A great resource is Ian Sommerville, *Software Engineering* (Addison-Wesley, 2001). The book is written as a textbook, with a summary of key points and a very decent set of exercises at the end of every chapter. It certainly stands above the other systems development texts that I have experienced. However, this work also has value beyond the classroom.

Information security officers need to know the operations, procedures, and concepts of software engineering without necessarily being programmers themselves. For these people, this volume makes a clear and excellent reference.

More directly, there is John Viega and Gary McGraw, *Building Secure Software* (Addison-Wesley, 2002). The preface states that the book is concerned with broad principles of systems development, and so does not cover specialized topics such as code authentication and sandboxing. A bit heavy on code in the latter part of the book, but a number of important points are made.

Viruses come under this domain. The two texts listed on the (ISC)² reference page (https://www.isc2.org/cgi-bin/content.cgi?page = 36) happen to be Robert M. Slade, David Harley, and Urs Gattiker, *Viruses Revealed* (McGraw-Hill, 2001), and Robert M. Slade, *Robert Slade's Guide to Computer Viruses, second edition* (Springer-Verlag, 1996).

However, I feel it only fair to say that I found some of the virus-related questions on the exam to be a bit odd.

Operations Security

The *Information Security Management Handbook* and *Practical UNIX*. Deborah Russell and G.T. Gangemi, Sr., *Computer Security Basics* (O'Reilly and Associates, 1991), is a pretty accurate name. The book is an overview of many aspects that go into the security of computers and data systems. While not exhaustive, it at least provides a starting point from which to pursue specific topics that require more detailed study. A thorough reading of the book will ensure that those charged with security will not miss certain aspects of the field in a single-minded pursuit of one particular threat.

Cryptography

Cryptography is an area that most candidates are concerned about. The (ISC)² course, and this book, cover almost all of what you need for the exam.

The classic text is Bruce Schneier, *Applied Cryptography, second edition* (John Wiley & Sons, 1996). Another particularly good book on the history is F.L. Bauer, *Decrypted Secrets* (Springer-Verlag, 2002). Most of the "easy" books on cryptography are so simplistic that they will actually get you into trouble on a number of exam questions. Two, however, Richard E. Smith,

Internet Cryptography (Addison-Wesley, 1997), and H.X. Mel and Doris Baker, *Cryptography Decrypted* (Addison-Wesley Publishing, 2001), provide — almost — enough to get you through.

Physical Security

Physical security tends to be the domain that almost all candidates do poorly in.

Lawrence J. Fennelly, *Effective Physical Security* (Butterworth-Heinemann, 1997), is an excellent review of everything except fire protection and personnel safety.

Neil Cumming, *Security* (Butterworth-Heinemann, 1992), has good information on evaluating equipment.

Joel Konicek and Karen Little, *Security, ID Systems and Locks* (Butterworth-Heinemann, 1997), is an easy-to-read, illustrated, quick guide to a lot (not all) of physical security. While limited to electronic systems, the book is a very reasonable guide to a lot of physical security technology.

A number of excellent resources for physical security (and also for investigations) are available in the free, downloadable publications from the RCMP Technical Security Branch (http://www.rcmp-grc.gc.ca/tsb/pubs/phys_sec/index.htm).

Telecommunications and Networking

This domain is a bit odd because you are expected to know a fair bit about communications technology as well as the security aspects, so you will need to cover a wider range. *Practical Unix and Internet* is helpful, and *Security Engineering* in places, plus the classic communications security text, Charlie Kaufman, Radia Perlman, and Mike Speciner, *Network Security* (Prentice Hall, 2002). The explanations are thorough and well written, with a humor that illuminates the material rather than obscuring it. The organization of the book may be a bit odd at times (the explanation of number theory comes only after the discussion of encryption that it supports), but generally makes sense. (It is sometimes evident that later text has created chapters that are slightly out of place.) The end of chapter "homework" problems are well thought out, and much better than the usual reading completion test. If there is a major weakness in the book, it is that the level of detail seems to vary arbitrarily, and readers may find this frustrating. Overall, however, this work provides a solid introduction and reference for network security-related topics and technologies.

A great general reference, with a solid awareness of security issues, is Andrew S. Tanenbaum, *Computer Networks, fourth edition* (Prentice Hall, 2003).

There are a great many good references for a variety of topics within telecommunications. A number are listed in the online version of this bibliography. Virtual private networks are, however, not well served, and a book that really is good at explaining VPNs is Oleg Kolesnikov and Brian Hatch, *Building Linux Virtual Private Networks* (New Riders, 2002).

Business Continuity Planning and Disaster Recovery Planning

Information Security Management Handbook, again. Some good reminders in RISKS.

It ends weaker than it starts, but the best that I have found thus far is Jon Toigo, *Disaster Recovery Planning* (John Wiley & Sons, 1996).

Law, Investigation and Ethics

Roy J. Girasa, *Cyberlaw: National and International Perspectives* (Prentice Hall, 2002), is a very comprehensive review of U.S., and some international, law related to computers, and particularly the Internet. However, it is definitely written for law students and can be extremely frustrating for people without a legal background.

Johnson, *Computer Ethics* (Prentice Hall, 1994), is the basic work in the field, thorough coverage and a good discussion starter.

Glee Harrah Cady and Pat McGregor, *Protect Your Digital Privacy* (Macmillan Computer Publishing, 2002), has some rough spots, but does a good job in many areas.

Warren G. Kruse II and Jay G. Heiser, *Computer Forensics* (Addison-Wesley, 2001), concentrates on data recovery and chain of evidence, but is not bad in those areas.

Appendix C
Answers to Sample Test Questions

Domain 1: Information Security Management

1. In addition to protecting important assets, security rules and procedures should:
   a. Be cost effective
   b. Justified by risk analysis
   c. Support the organizational mission
   d. Apply to everyone in the organization

Answer c: Information security rules and procedures should not exist for their own sake — they are put in place to protect important assets and, thereby, support the overall organizational mission.

All of the answers are good, but the best answer is *c*. It brings into focus additional requirements beyond those mentioned in the other answers. The other answers are really subsets of the "protecting important assets" as listed in the question.

2. Masquerading is:
   a. Attempting to hack a system through backdoors to an operating system or application
   b. Pretending to be an authorized user
   c. Always done through IP spoofing
   d. Applying a subnet mask to an internal IP range

Answer b: Pretending to be the authorized user.

3. Integrity is protection of data from all of the following EXCEPT:
   a. Unauthorized changes
   b. Accidental changes
   c. Data analysis
   d. Intentional manipulation

Answer c: Integrity is the protection of system information or processes from intentional or accidental unauthorized changes. Data analysis would usually be associated with confidentiality.

4. A security program cannot address which of the following business goals?
   a. Accuracy of information
   b. Change control
   c. User expectations
   d. Prevention of fraud

Answer a: The security program cannot improve the accuracy of data that is put into the system by users, but it can help ensure that any changes are intended and correctly applied.

5. In most cases, integrity is enforced through:
   a. Physical security
   b. Logical security
   c. Confidentiality
   d. Access controls

Answer d: Integrity depends on access controls; therefore, it is necessary to positively and uniquely identify and authorize all persons who attempt access.

Answers a and b are good but not thorough enough on their own — they are portions of a complete access control system.

6. A "well-formed transaction" is one that:
   a. Has all the necessary paperwork to substantiate the transaction.
   b. Is based on clear business objectives.
   c. Ensures that data can be manipulated only by a specific set of programs.
   d. Is subject to duplicate processing.

Answer c: Well-formed transactions must ensure that data can be manipulated only by a specific set of programs.

7. In an accounting department, several people are required to complete a financial process. This is most likely an example of:
   a. Segregation of duties
   b. Rotation of duties
   c. Need-to-know
   d. Collusion

Answer a: No single employee has control of a transaction from beginning to end; two or more people should be responsible for performing it.

8. Risk Management is commonly understood as all of the following EXCEPT:
   a. Analyzing and assessing risk
   b. Identifying risk
   c. Accepting or mitigation of risk
   d. Likelihood of a risk occurring

Answer d: The processes of identifying, analyzing, and assessing, mitigating, or transferring risk is generally characterized as risk management.

9. The percentage or degree of damage inflicted on an asset used in the calculation of single loss expectancy can be referred to as:
   a. Exposure Factor (EF)
   b. Annualized Rate of Occurrence (ARO)
   c. Vulnerability
   d. Likelihood

Answer a: This factor represents a measure of the magnitude of loss or impact on the value of an asset. It is expressed as a percent, ranging from 0% to 100%, of asset value loss arising from a threat event. This factor is used in the calculation of single loss expectancy (SLE).

10. The absence of a fire-suppression system would be best characterized as a(n):
    a. Exposure
    b. Threat
    c. Vulnerability
    d. Risk

Answer c: This term characterizes the absence or weakness of a risk-reducing safeguard.

11. Risk Assessment includes all of the following EXCEPT:
    a. Implementation of effective countermeasures
    b. Ensuring that risk is managed
    c. Analysis of the current state of security in the target environment
    d. Strategic analysis of risk

Answer a: Fundamental applications of risk assessment to be addressed include (1) determining the current status of information security in the target environment(s) and ensuring that associated risk is managed (accepted, mitigated, or transferred) according to policy, and (2) assessing risk strategically.

12. A risk management project may be subject to overlooking certain types of threats. What can assist the risk management team to prevent that?
    a. Automated tools
    b. Adoption of qualitative risk assessment processes
    c. Increased reliance on internal experts for risk assessment
    d. Recalculation of the work factor

Answer a: The best automated tools currently available include a well-researched threat population and associated statistics. Using one of these tools virtually assures that no relevant threat is overlooked.

13. Data classification can assist an organization in:
    a. Eliminating regulatory mandates

    b. Lowering accountability of data classifiers

    c. Reducing costs for protecting data

    d. Normalization of databases

Answer c: Data classification is intended to lower the cost of overprotecting all data.

14. Who "owns" an organization's data?

    a. Information technology group

    b. Users

    c. Data custodians

    d. Business units

Answer d: The business units, not IT (information technology), own the data. Decisions regarding who has what access, what classification the data should be assigned, etc., are decisions that rest solely with the business data owner and based on organization policy.

15. An information security policy does NOT usually include:

    a. Authority for information security department

    b. Guidelines for how to implement policy

    c. Basis for data classification

    d. Recognition of information as an asset of the organization

Answer b: Policy is written at a very high level and is intended to describe the "whats" of information security. Procedures, standards, baselines, and guidelines are the "hows" for implementation of the policy.

16. The role of an information custodian should NOT include:

    a. Restoration of lost or corrupted data

    b. Regular backups of data

    c. Establishing retention periods for data

    d. Ensuring the availability of data

Answer c: Ensure record retention requirements are met based on the information owner's analysis.

17. A main objective of awareness training is:

    a. Provide understanding of responsibilities

    b. Entertaining the users through creative programs

    c. Overcoming all resistance to security procedures

    d. To be repetitive to ensure accountability

Answer a: All employees must understand their basic security responsibilities.

18. What is a primary target of a person employing social engineering?

    a. An individual

    b. A policy

    c. Government agencies

    d. An information system

Answer a: Social engineering deals with individual dynamics as opposed to group dynamics, as the primary targets are help desks and/or administrative or technical support people.

19. Social engineering can take many forms EXCEPT:
    a. Dumpster diving
    b. Coercion or intimidation
    c. Sympathy
    d. Eavesdropping

Answer d: An effective countermeasure is to have very good, established information security policies that are communicated across your organization.

20. Incident response planning can be instrumental in:
    a. Meeting regulatory requirements
    b. Creating customer loyalty
    c. Reducing the impact of an adverse event on the organization
    d. Ensuring management makes the correct decisions in a crisis

Answer c: The goals of a well-prepared incident response team are to detect potential information security breaches and provide an effective and efficient means of dealing with the situation in a manner that reduces the potential impact to the corporation.

Domain 2: Security Architecture and Models

1. Why should security elements be located in a lower layer of the system architecture?
    a. They are easier to adjust according to user requirements.
    b. This may increase system performance.
    c. This allows for multitasking.
    d. It is simpler to install system security bypasses.

Answer b: The reason for putting security mechanisms in a lower layer is to increase the performance of the system.

2. In pre-emptive multitasking mode, who controls the use of system resources?
    a. The user
    b. The application program
    c. Input-output devices
    d. The operating system

Answer d: A pre-emptive system relies on the operating system to manage the time intervals, or slices, an application or task is allocated within the CPU.

3. In cooperative mode, who controls the use of system resources?
    a. The user

    b. The application program
    c. Input/output devices
    d. The operating system

Answer b: In cooperative mode, the application manages the resources of the CPU.

4. What is a vulnerability of a multiprocessing system?
    a. Different levels of users operating simultaneously
    b. Synchronous data attacks
    c. Object reuse
    d. Insufficient random memory

Answer c: A vulnerability associated with multiprogramming systems is object reuse.

5. Which of the following is NOT usually referred to as a maintenance hook?
    a. Privileged program
    b. Backdoor program
    c. Wormhole
    d. Trojan horse

Answer d: Maintenance hooks and privileged programs.

6. Which of the following is considered a general protection feature of a trusted operating system?
    a. Mandatory access controls and discretionary access controls
    b. Anti-virus controls
    c. Authentication of users to the system
    d. Audit logs cannot be modified after creation

Answer b: Anti-virus controls are not typically a protection feature of an OS, but rather additional software that must be added.

7. What is the security risk with virtual storage?
    a. The data is volatile and may be lost when powering down.
    b. The data may be read by other processes running simultaneously.
    c. The temporary files may not delete after use.
    d. System performance may be impacted.

Answer c: The data stored in virtual memory remains on the hard drive when the computer is turned off and may be recovered from these temporary files.

8. What security risk can be associated with interrupt processing?
    a. An interrupted process may assume the priority of the higher-level process.
    b. An interrupted process may lose data integrity.
    c. A higher-level process may not receive sufficient CPU cycles.
    d. A low-level process may time-out before completion.

Answer a: If interrupt handling is not handled securely, a breach may occur allowing a previous process to gain the supervisor status of an operating system call.

9. In dedicated security mode, the system must have all of the following EXCEPT:
   a. One classification of data running for a set time
   b. Access approval clearance for all users or nondisclosure agreements
   c. Need-to-know for all information within the system
   d. Direct access only to the system

Answer d: Indirect access is also permitted *Dedicated Security Mode.*

10. A subject most commonly has:
    a. Authentication
    b. Clearance
    c. Classification
    d. Collusion

Answer b: And people, also referred to as the *"subject,"* possess a clearance.

11. Biba's invocation property is intended to prevent:
    a. A subject requesting a service of an object at a lower classification
    b. An administrator granting an increased level of clearance to a authorized user
    c. A process from gaining elevated access through a higher-level process
    d. The deferring of processing until resources are available

Answer c: The *invocation property* states that the subject cannot send messages (logical request for service) to subjects of higher integrity. Subjects are only allowed to invoke utilities or tools at the same or lower level.

12. Which of the following is NOT a rule of integrity?
    a. All users must be subject to need-to-know.
    b. Unauthorized users should make no changes.
    c. The system should maintain internal and external consistency.
    d. Authorized users should make no unauthorized changes.

Answer a: Clark-Wilson model.

13. Which is commonly associated with the Clark-Wilson security model?
    a. The access tuple
    b. Read down/write up
    c. Subject/program binding
    d. Lattice-based model

Answer c: Binding is established between the user and the program.

14. A capability listing is based on which primary item?
    a. A subject
    b. A program
    c. A system
    d. An object

Answer a: A capability list specifies authorized objects and operations for a user. Note answers b and c may be correct in certain situations but answer a is a more thorough answer.

15. State machine models are concerned with each of the following EXCEPT:
    a. Initial state
    b. State transition functions
    c. State variables
    d. State classification

Answer d: The steps involved in developing a state machine model include a, b, and c.

16. The Chinese Wall model was associated with the work of:
    a. Harrison and Ullman
    b. Brewer and Nash
    c. Glasser
    c. El Gamal

Answer b: Brewer and Nash proposed the Chinese Wall model in 1989.

17. Certification refers to:
    a. The technical review of a product
    b. Management's approval for an implementation
    c. A stringent evaluation of a system in a test environment
    d. Formal acceptance of risk

Answer a: Certification is the technical evaluation of compliance with security requirements for the purpose of accreditation.

18. What is the Common Criteria (CC) supposed to do?
    a. Provide a forum for Europeans, Canadians, and Americans to discuss privacy laws.
    b. Document the international information warfare threats and create international cooperation to counter those threats.
    c. Provide an international center to track the outbreak of viruses across the globe in order to reduce infections.
    d. Document the international standards for evaluating trust in information systems and products.

Answer d: The CC is an international criterion for evaluating trust of a system.

19. A class of a system containing various levels of sensitive information that also permits users with different security clearances best describes:
    a. a multi-level security system
    b. a trusted computer based with security kernels
    c. a system using a state machine model to control subjects and objects
    d. a system using an information flow model to control subjects and objects

Answer a: A multi-level security system is a class of system containing information with different sensitivities that simultaneously permits access by users with different security clearances and needs-to-know, but prevents users from obtaining access to information for which they lack authorization.

20. A trusted computing base is defined as:
    a. The totality of protection mechanisms within a computer system
    b. The ability to prevent and detect unauthorized use of an object
    c. Containing a security kernel and reference monitor with the ability to encrypt its processes
    d. A logical access control concept where the security kernel mediates all accesses to objects by subjects

Answer a: A TCB is defined as the totality of protection mechanisms within a computer system, including hardware, firmware, software, processes, and some inter-process communications; and when combined are responsible for ensuring a security policy.

Domain 3: Access Control Systems and Methodology

1. Two types of covert channels are storage based or:
   a. Accidental
   b. Timing
   c. Cooperative
   d. Malicious

Answer b: Timing channel — using timing of occurrences of an activity to transfer information in an unintended manner. Saturating or not saturating a communications path in a timed fashion can transfer information to a receiver observing the communication path in synchronism with the sender.

2. Data remanence is:
   a. When residual data remains on a storage medium following degaussing
   b. The permanence of the data resisting accidental deletion

    c. Data that exceeds the boundaries of its memory buffers

    d. The process of overwriting data

Answer a: When some data, after the magnetic media is written over or degaussed, still remains on the magnetic media.

3. Internal intruders are NOT usually defined as:
   a. Authorized users exceeding their authority
   b. Persons who have defeated the physical access controls of a facility
   c. Employees gaining access to controlled areas
   d. Users who access unintended areas of the network

Answer b: Authorized users trying to gain access to data or resources beyond their need-to-know or access limitations. Authorized users trying to gain unauthorized physical access to network connections, server equipment, etc.

4. How might an attacker with little systems experience gain privileged systems access?
   a. Dictionary attack
   b. Brute-force attack
   c. Birthday attack
   d. Shoulder-surfing attack

Answer d: Shoulder-surfing, the process of direct visual observation of monitor displays to obtain access to sensitive information.

5. Which of the following is NOT a characteristic of a virus?
   a. Its primary effect is to consume system resources.
   b. It may or may not carry a malicious payload.
   c. It spreads through user action.
   d. It attaches itself to executable code.

Answer a: Worms usually do not cause damage to data; instead, the worm absorbs the network's resources causing the damage.

6. Requiring approval before granting system access would be:
   a. A physical control
   b. A logical control
   c. A compensating control
   d. An administrative control

Answer d: Administrative controls consist of management activities such as organizational policies and procedures.

7. Granting of access privileges to certain files is:
   a. Authentication
   b. Identification
   c. Authorization
   d. Accountability

Answer c: Be careful not to confuse authentication with authorization. Authentication is the process of verifying the identity of the sender and/or receiver of information. Authorization establishes what the user is allowed to do once the user has been identified and authenticated by the system. Another "A" term sometimes misinterpreted is accountability, which is the ability to track actions to users.

8. What is the best method of reducing a brute-force denial-of-service attack against a password file?
   a. Setting a higher clipping level
   b. Locking out a user for a set time period
   c. Establishing a lockout that requires administrator intervention
   d. Using a stronger cryptographic algorithm

Answer b: Denial-of-service attack, whereby the perpetrator is able to lock out many users by discovering their user identifications and entering a specified number of invalid passwords, is minimized.

Note that answer *a* could also be correct but is not the best answer from a security perspective.

9. Which of the following is a characteristic of a synchronous token?
   a. Challenge–response based
   b. Counter based
   c. Random number based
   d. Nonce based

Answer b: Counter-based token that combines the base secret with a synchronized counter to generate the OTP.

10. Which of the following is NOT a common attack performed against smart cards?
    a. Etching
    b. Microprobing
    c. Fault generation
    d. Eavesdropping

Answer a: There are several weaknesses and types of attacks against smart cards, including answers b, c, and d.

11. Important elements in choosing a biometric system include all of the following EXCEPT:
    a. User acceptance
    b. Accuracy
    c. Productivity
    d. Processing speed

Answer c: Important elements of biometric devices are accuracy, processing speed, and user acceptability.

12. TACACS+ has a "watchdog" function to prevent what kind of attacks?
    a. Synchronous

841

b. Side channel
c. Fault
d. TOCTOU

Answer d: The watchdog function is used to validate TCP sessions when data is not sent for extended periods of time. This functionality is often referred to as TOC/TOU (Time of Check versus Time of Use) validation.

13. What is a security benefit related to thin-client architecture?
    a. Reduced total cost of ownership of desktops
    b. Standardized access control
    c. Easier training for users
    d. Wider availability of applications

Answer b: Access controls can be centrally located on the server.

14. Discretionary access control (DAC) involves:
    a. Review of the classification of the object
    b. The data owner granting permission to access a file
    c. The system authorizing access based on labels
    d. Sensitive programs only running during specific time periods

Answer b: DACs permit resource owners to specify who has access and what privileges other users will have.

15. Mandatory access control (MAC) requires all of the following EXCEPT:
    a. Data owners' permission
    b. Enforcement of security policy
    c. Sensitivity labels on all critical files
    d. Need-to-know authorization

Answer d: Access decisions are based on the owner's authorization, the subject's label, the object's label, and the security policy.

16. What is the most secure method for controlling privileged access to a system available for use in a public area?
    a. Mandatory Access Control (MAC)
    b. Role-Based Access Control (RBAC)
    c. Database views
    d. Constrained user interfaces

Answer d: Constrained user interfaces restrict user access to specific system resources by not allowing them to request the function, information, or access to specific system resources.

17. What is NOT a basic component of an IDS?
    a. Analyzer
    b. Notifier
    c. Sensor
    d. User interface

Answer b: There are three basic components of an IDS: a sensor, analyzer, and user (security administrator) interface.

18. What does a host-based IDS use for analysis?
    a. Audit logs
    b. Traffic patterns
    c. Packet structure
    d. Promiscuous mode

Answer a: The agent scrutinizes event logs, critical system files, and other auditable resources.

19. An IDS does NOT use which of the following techniques for detecting intrusions?
    a. Model based
    b. Statistical based
    c. Authorization based
    d. State based

Answer c: Rule-based IDSs are characterized by their expert system properties that create rules to detect system status information.

20. Audit logs should record all of the following EXCEPT:
    a. Successful access attempts
    b. System performance measurements
    c. Failed access attempts
    d. Changes to user permissions

Answer b: The audit data will reveal that a specific user accessed the file, the time of access, and the type of access.

21. Clipping levels helps prevent:
    a. Unnecessary investigation by administrators
    b. Denial-of-service attacks
    c. Unauthorized users from logging on
    d. "Fat finger" attacks

Answer a: Anything that occurs beyond the baseline would be considered worth reviewing in more detail.

22. Audit logs should be protected for all of the reasons EXCEPT:
    a. Modification may impede an investigation.
    b. An attacker may try to alter them.
    c. They may contain confidential information.
    d. Standard format is critical for automated processing.

Answer d: The audit trail data should be protected at the most sensitive system level.

23. A penetration test is NOT designed to:
    a. Find vulnerabilities in a network
    b. Test incident response capabilities

c. Alter system access permissions

d. Exploit social engineering opportunities

Answer c: In addition to finding holes in the security measures, a penetration test can be initiated to test an intrusion detection system and intrusion response capability.

24. Access control systems should consider all of the following EXCEPT:
    a. Technical controls
    b. Legal requirements
    c. Sensitivity of information on the system
    d. Availability of trained staff

Answer d: It is important to balance the goals of the organization's access control policy with the technical mechanisms. This includes reviewing the legal requirements that are necessary to protect access; conducting a risk analysis that identifies the typical threats to the system; reviewing accepted industry practices; identifying users who need access and what type of access they need; and identifying the sensitivity of the information stored and processed on the system.

Domain 4: Applications and Systems Development

1. What is the correct definition of "transaction persistence"?
   a. A transaction that repeats until all affected records are changed
   b. A timing-based transaction that executes on a regular basis
   c. A transaction that requires user intervention to complete
   d. A transaction that preserves the state of the database

Answer d: Transaction persistence, the state of the database is the same after a transaction (process) has occurred as it was prior to the transaction.

2. Shadow recovery of a database is accomplished through:
   a. Applying journalized transactions to an earlier copy of a database
   b. Having a mirror copy of the database in case of interruption
   c. Doing hourly backups of the database to prevent failure
   d. Having all transactions recorded in a transaction file and updated in batch mode at a later time

Answer a: Shadow recovery occurs when transactions are reapplied to a previous version of the database. Shadow recovery requires the use of transaction logging to identify the last good transaction.

3. When designing a database, what is LEAST important?
   a. Knowing the quantity of data
   b. Knowing the sensitivity of the data
   c. Knowing the hardware platform
   d. Knowing user access requirements

Answer c: When an organization is designing a database, the first step is to understand the requirements for the database and then design a system that meets those requirements. This includes what information will be stored, who is allowed access, and estimating how many people will need to access the data at the same time.

4. In database terminology, "atomic" refers to:
   a. Each field can be changed dynamically by any user.
   b. All relational items are linked through keys and indexes.
   c. The database is a single independent unit.
   d. All fields can contain only one value.

Answer d: Atomic values mean that at every row/column position in every table there is always exactly one data value and never a set of values.

5. A database "view" is:
   a. A logical subset of a database
   b. The layout of the database
   c. The relationship between the records and the key
   d. A method of disguising data by creating duplicate records

Answer a: Views define what information a user can view in the tables — the view can be customized so that an entire table may be visible or a user may be limited to only being able to see just a row or a column. Views are created dynamically by the system for each user and provide access control granularity. Answer b relates to a schema, answer c to normalization, answer d to polymorphism.

6. One of the greatest risks with many driver programs is:
   a. The drivers are not standard across vendors.
   b. Use of a driver may grant high-level access to the calling program.
   c. A driver may execute unwanted actions.
   d. The drivers may contain backdoors or maintenance hooks.

Answer b: Calling applications must be checked to ensure they do not attempt to exploit the ODBC drivers and gain elevated system access.

7. One method of protecting confidential corporate data accessed through an Internet-based application is:
   a. Refusing remote access to all users
   b. Placing stringent security policies on the data storage system
   c. Having tiers of applications and storage
   d. Storing the data on an isolated Web server

Answer c: One approach for Internet access is to create a "tiered" application approach that manages data in layers. There can be any number of layers; however, the most typical architecture is to use a three-tier approach: presentation layer, business logic layer, and the data layer. This is sometimes referred to as the Internet Computing Model because the browser is used to connect to an application server that then connects to a database.

8. Which of the following is NOT true of a data warehouse?
   a. It contains data from many sources and databases.
   b. It is used for operational data storage.
   c. It provides analysis and management support.
   d. It can increase the risk of privacy violations.

Answer b: Data warehouses do not contain operational data, which is their distinguishing characteristic. That is, the data stored in a data warehouse is not used for operational tasks, but rather for analytical purposes. The data warehouse combines all of the data from various databases into one large data container.

9. What is one of the differences between a virus and a worm?
   a. Only the virus is distributed through email attachments.
   b. Only the worm is capable of executing without user interaction.
   c. Only the worm is capable of attaching to an application and creating it's own macro programming infections.
   d. Only the virus is a stand-alone file that can be executed by an interpreter.

Answer b: The term worm has evolved to distinguish between programs that involve the user in some way, such as a virus, and programs that do not involve the user but directly probe network-attached computers trying to exploit a specific weakness.

10. Which of the following best describes a remote access Trojan considered to be malware?
   a. Software is installed on a remote target computer that allows the target computer and its information to be accessed via remote connection, without the target's knowledge.
   b. Software is executed on a remote target computer and is activated when a specific event occurs, such as Friday the 13th.
   c. The user at the target machine downloads software from the Internet and in addition to the legitimate software; malware is also wrapped into the software and installed on the machine.
   d. Software in executed on a remote target machine and immediately installs itself into the boot sector of the machine and allows the attacker to take control over the machine.

Answer a: A remote access Trojan is best characterized as software that is installed on a target computer allowing the controlling computer to obtain information about the target computer, upload or download information, etc.

11. What is a security risk of allowing mobile code to execute on a target machine?
   a. The time delay from when it is downloaded and executed could initiate an asynchronous attack.

   b. Malware may be included in the downloaded code and infect the target machine.

   c. It will move or overwrite the original boot process so that every time the machine is powered on, the code will be activated.

   d. It will contaminate files that contain computer code, especially .exe and .com files.

Answer b: Malware may be wrapped inside the downloaded code and when the code is executed on the machine, the malware will also be executed.

12. The ability to combine nonsensitive data from separate sources to create sensitive information is referred to as _____.

   a. Concurrency

   b. Inference

   c. Polyinstantiation

   d. Aggregation

Answer d: Concurrency is when actions or processes run at the same time; inference is the ability to deduce (infer) information from observing available information; polyinstantiation is when information is stored in more than one location in the database; and aggregation is the ability to combine nonsensitive data to create sensitive data.

13. Which of the following best describes data contamination in a database?

   a. Occurs when two users try to access the information at the same time and the original information becomes corrupted.

   b. Occurs when two users try to access the information at the same time and the original information is deleted.

   c. Occurs when data entry personnel corrupt the data integrity by input data errors or erroneous processing.

   d. Occurs when users bypass the front end controls and manipulate the backend database information.

Answer c: The definition of data contamination is the corruption of data integrity by input data errors or erroneous processing. This can occur in a file, a report, or a database.

14. Company XYZ has decided to develop its own travel manager software that will allow employees to expense travel reports electronically. It is important for several of the employees who travel a lot to have input into the design and development. Based on this scenario, which software development model may be best suited for this project?

   a. Ad-hoc model

   b. Prototype model

   c. Exploratory model

   d. Cleanroom

Answer b: The ad-hoc model would not provide enough team input; the prototype model would allow for an initial review by employees before final development; exploratory is used to allow for expansion because all requirements are not currently known; and cleanroom is based on writing clean code the first time, not necessarily involving outside input.

15. During which phase of the software project will the team conduct a comprehensive analysis of current and possible future security requirements?
    a. Project initiation and planning
    b. Functional requirements definition
    c. System design specifications
    d. System development specifications

Answer b: During the functional requirements definition is when the security requirements should also be documented.

16. What is the process of conducting an independent evaluation of the software to determine whether the planned security standards or features have been implemented?
    a. Certification
    b. Accreditation
    c. Authorization
    d. Acceptance

Answer a: Certification is the process of evaluating the security stance of the software against a predetermined set of security standards.

17. Which of the following would be the best method for a software developer to limit the vulnerability of buffer overflows in software?
    a. Reduce the number of backdoor entry points.
    b. Ensure that the software runs only in Level 0 of the processor ring.
    c. Budget more time into production to allow for more bounds checking in the software.
    d. Ensure that the software is certified and accredited before allowing full-scale entry of production data.

Answer b: A buffer overflow is caused by improper or lack of bounds checking in a program. The best way to ensure that buffer overflow vulnerabilities are reduced is to have programmers test the bounds checking.

18. What is defined as an information flow that is not controlled by a security control?
    a. TOC/TOU
    b. Incomplete parameter check
    c. Buffer overflow
    d. Covert channel

Answer d: A covert channel, also called a confinement problem, is an information flow that is not controlled by a security control. It is a communication channel that allows two cooperating processes to transfer information in such a way that violates the system's security policy.

19. Which type of the following password controls, if added, would NOT provide adequate security to the software?
    a. Password complexity requirements
    b. Encryption of the password file
    c. Overstrike or password masking feature
    d. Reference monitor authorization

Answer d: The key word here is authorization instead of authentication. All of the other three would provide additional authentication mechanisms.

20. If following the concept of separation of duties during software production, which of the following would NOT occur?
    a. Separation between programmers.
    b. Separation between programmers and system administrators.
    c. Separation between programmers and quality assurance personnel.
    d. Separation between programmers and production personnel.

Answer a: During development it would not make sense to separate the programmers; however, to ensure separate and independent evaluations it is best to provide the other types of separation.

Domain 5: Operations Security

1. Critical data is:
   a. Subject to classification by regulatory bodies or legislation
   b. Data of high integrity
   c. Always protected at the highest level
   d. Instrumental for business operations

Answer d: Critical information is that which must be available to authorized users for the organization to remain in business. Sensitive information is that which must be protected by classification procedures to prevent it being seen by unauthorized persons.

2. When an organization is determining which data is sensitive, it must consider all of the following EXCEPT:
   a. Expectations of customers
   b. Legislation or regulations
   c. Quantity of data
   d. Age of the data

Answer c: Age (answer d) is important because declassifying of data must be considered as part of the classification process.

3. All of the following are examples of a preventative control EXCEPT:
   a. Intrusion detection system

b. Human resources policies
c. Anti-virus software
d. Fences

Answer a: Included in preventive controls are physical, administrative, and technical measures intended to preclude actions violating policy or increasing risk to system resources.

4. Recovery controls attempt to:
   a. Establish countermeasures to prevent further incidents
   b. Return to normal operations
   c. Compensate for vulnerabilities in other controls
   d. Ensure that audit logs are reviewed regularly

Answer b: Recovery controls are necessary to restore the system or operation to a normal operating state. Answer a is more correctly a corrective control.

5. Privileged access permissions should:
   a. Never be granted
   b. Be subject to recertification
   c. Only be granted on an emergency basis
   d. Be provided to all trusted personnel

Answer b: Privileged users must be subject to periodic recertification to maintain the broad level of privileges that have been assigned to them.

6. Transparency of controls does all of the following EXCEPT:
   a. Allow authorized access without hindering business operations.
   b. Deny unauthorized access without revealing system knowledge to attackers.
   c. Log all important activity without identifying monitoring techniques.
   d. Ensure that security activity does not impact system performance.

Answer d: Ideally, controls must be transparent to users within the resource protection schema.

7. The ISF proscribes that change management must include all of the following EXCEPT:
   a. Be reviewed by security
   b. Be a formal process
   c. Be ready to handle unexpected events
   d. Be subject to acceptance

Answer a: The area of "change management" consists of four objectives:

- To ensure changes to the computer installation are made in conformance with sound disciplines.
- Changes affecting the computer installation should be made in accordance with a formal process.

- To ensure rigorous acceptance criteria are met before new systems and significant changes are made to the computer installation.
- To enable unforeseen problems to be addressed in a timely yet disciplined manner.

8. Which of the following is NOT a class of failures identified in the Trusted Recovery Guide by the National Computer Security Center?
   a. State transition
   b. Trusted computing base (TCB)
   c. Buffer overflow
   d. Discontinuity of operation

Answer c: The classes of failures that have been identified in the Trusted Recovery Guide by the National Computer Security Center include: state-transition (action) failures, trusted computing base failures, media failures, and discontinuity of operation. Note that a buffer overflow may be a state transition type of failure, but the reader should know these terms and what they apply to.

9. Separation of duties controls can be defeated through:
   a. Mutual exclusivity
   b. Collusion
   c. Dual control
   d. Accreditation

Answer b: With an effective separation of responsibilities, fraudulent use of a system can only be accomplished by collusion between all of those participating in its operation.

10. The best technique for preventing and detecting abuse by a user with privileged access is:
    a. Good policy
    b. Review by management
    c. Strong authentication
    d. Audit logs

Answer b: Certainly, this whole environment presents many opportunities for wrongdoing and calls for close monitoring by supervisors. Answer a would not detect abuse, answer c is only a preventative measure, and answer d would not be effective if no one ever checks the logs.

11. Fault tolerance can be defined as:
    a. The ability to detect and attempt recovery from failure
    b. A robust system that resists failure
    c. A system that is backed up to prevent data loss
    d. Preparing alternate processing in case of loss of primary system

Answer a: A fault-tolerance system must identify that a failure has occurred and then take corrective action to ensure the continuity of operations is maintained with the least possible delay.

12. To speed up disk access, an organization can:
    a. Use larger hard drives
    b. Stripe the data across several drives
    c. Mirror critical drives
    d. Disallow ad hoc queries

Answer b: Striping is the process of writing data across multiple disks rather than just one, as is done in mirroring, to maximize efficiency.

13. The Common Criteria define the term "fail secure" as:
    a. A system that is tolerant of component failure
    b. The ability of a system to fail in a controlled manner
    c. A system failure does not affect normal business operations
    d. The preservation of a secure state in the event of a failure

Answer d: Fail secure means that the failure occurs with the preservation of a secure state.

14. If a report contains no data, should it be printed anyway?
    a. No, save paper and be environmentally conscious.
    b. No, there is no need to print an empty report.
    c. Yes, so that the owner knows the report is empty — not just lost.
    d. Yes, in order to preserve the regular job flow and prevent errors.

Answer c: When a report is processed but contains no information, there should be printed a "no output" message so that the recipient will not be concerned about lost data.

15. When contracting a vendor for software or hardware provisioning, care must be taken to:
    a. Ensure all changes are kept up-to-date.
    b. Ensure all changes go through a change management process.
    c. Ensure that in-house technical staff learn the system.
    d. Ensure that all activity on the system is monitored.

Answer b: Non-employee (vendor) personnel performing maintenance should be supervised by a knowledgeable employee or other trusted person who can understand the implications of actions being taken.

16. System documentation must contain all of the following EXCEPT:
    a. A description of the system functionality
    b. A record of all changes to a system
    c. The identity of the person or position responsible for the system
    d. The volume of transactions processed by the system

Answer d.

17. When an employee transfers within an organization:
    a. They must undergo a new security review.
    b. All old system IDs must be disabled.
    c. All access permissions should be reviewed.
    d. The employee must turn in all remote access devices.

Answer c: Employee transfers or terminations must be addressed in organization policy. Answer a is not correct if the employee is not going to a job of greater responsibility; answer b is not correct — they may still need several of their old email, voice-mail accesses, etc.; and answer d is not correct because they may still need these devices.

18. Emergency fixes to a system must:
    a. Be implemented as rapidly as possible
    b. Be scrutinized subsequently to ensure they were performed correctly
    c. Be performed only by following normal change control procedures
    d. Be made permanent within 72 hours

Answer b: Emergency fixes should then be documented, subjected to normal change management disciplines, and reviewed by the installation owner.

Domain 6: Cryptography

1. The act of scrambling data to make it difficult for an unauthorized person from seeing it is called all of the following EXCEPT:
    a. Encode
    b. Emboss
    c. Encrypt
    d. Encipher

Answer b: Encrypt/encipher/encode are synonymous.

2. The key used in a cryptographic operation is also called:
    a. Cryptovariable
    b. Cryptosequence
    c. Cryptoform
    d. Cryptolock

Answer a: Key/cryptovariable are synonymous.

3. What determines the correct choice of cryptographic algorithm?
    a. Cost
    b. Availability
    c. Business risk
    d. Government regulations

Answer c: Probably no one is going to try and crack your current financial budget; but if your company's livelihood depends on e-business and multi-million dollar deals, DES may not be strong enough.

4. Most cryptographic algorithms operate in either block mode or:
    a. Cipher mode
    b. Logical mode

    c. Stream mode

    d. Decryption mode

Answer c: There are two ways that encryption algorithms will apply their methods on information. These are "block" and "stream."

5. Work factor is defined as:
    a. The time taken by a system to perform a ciphering operation
    b. The computer resources required to compute a cryptographic algorithm
    c. The problem of finding the two prime numbers used in RSA
    d. The time and effort required to break a security function

Answer d: Work factor is simply the effort and time required to break a protective measure.

6. A one-time pad operates as a(an):
    a. Stream
    b. Linear
    c. S-box
    d. Differential

Answer a: Current interests in stream ciphers are most commonly equated to what is referred to as a one-time pad.

7. Which of the following is NOT one of the four primary objectives of cryptography?
    a. Non-repudiation
    b. Authentication
    c. Data integrity
    d. Authorization

Answer d: A fundamental goal of cryptography is to adequately address four areas in both theory and practice. Confidentiality is normally achieved by encrypting the message content, data integrity is achieved through cryptographic hashing functions, authentication is achieved through the use of asymmetric cryptography, and non-repudiation is normally achieved through the use of cryptographic digital signatures.

8. Another name for symmetric key cryptography is:
    a. Shared
    b. Public
    c. Elliptic curve
    d. Key clustering

Answer a: Secret key or symmetric key cryptography is the technology in which encryption and decryption use the same key, a *secret key*. Users share a secret key, keeping the key to themselves.

9. One of the greatest disadvantages of symmetric key cryptography is:
    a. Scalability
    b. Availability

    c. Computing resource requirements

    d. Confidentiality

Answer a: Disadvantages include:

Key management and implementation

Key distribution

Scalability

Limited security (provides only limited information security services)

10. Encrypting a message with a private key in an asymmetric system provides:

    a. Proof of receipt

    b. Confidentiality

    c. Proof of origin

    d. Message availability

Answer c: Because the message was encrypted using the sender's private key, it offers a way to prove that it was actually encrypted by the sender.

11. How many keys would need to be managed for a public key system with 500 users (n)?

    a. N(n–1)/2

    b. N×2

    c. N

    d. N/2

Answer b: If 1000 people need to communicate securely with each other, a total of 2000 keys (1000 matched pairs) is needed.

12. A hybrid system uses:

    a. Symmetric algorithms for key distribution

    b. Asymmetric algorithms for message confidentiality

    c. Symmetric algorithms for proof of origin

    d. Symmetric algorithms for fast encryption

Answer d: Normally, these hybrid systems will use asymmetric key cryptography to do the key management, and symmetric key cryptography to do the bulk encryption/decryption.

13. Which of the following techniques is NOT commonly used by encryption systems?

    a. Transposition

    b. Diffusion

    c. Substitution

    d. Transformation

Answer d: Substitution and transposition ciphers do not disguise the linguistic patterns of letters and word frequency in the encrypted message, so they are easily cracked using frequency analysis but are used together in DES in multiple cycles, thereby avoiding the frequency analysis problem. Diffusion is created using variable block sizes and key lengths as in RC5 (integer multiplication is used to increase the diffusion achieved per round).

14. Which mode of DES is best suited for communication between a terminal and a server?
    a. Output feedback
    b. Electronic Code Book
    c. Cipher block chaining
    d. Cipher feedback

Answer d: CFB is best for encrypting a stream of data one character at a time (e.g., between a terminal and a host).

15. How many keys are required to operate Triple-DES?
    a. 1, 2, or 3
    b. 2 or 3
    c. 2
    d. 3

Answer b: With Triple-DES (3-DES), you use three DES encryptions with either three or two different and separate keys.

16. Which of the following does NOT support variable block sizes?
    a. Rijndael
    b. RC5
    c. Triple-DES
    d. Rivest Cipher 6

Answer c: RC5 is a parameterized algorithm with a variable block size; Rijndael has a variable block size of 128, 192, or 256 bits; RC6 is a block cipher based on RC5 and just like its predecessor, it is a parameterized algorithm where the block size, the key size, and the number of rounds are variable.

17. Message integrity codes are especially useful for:
    a. Detecting changes to a message
    b. Authenticating the source of a message
    c. Verifying the confidentiality of a message
    d. Ensuring that the message was sent from a reputable source

Answer a: If the independently calculated message fingerprint is exactly equal to the message fingerprint received from the sender, the receiver is assured that the message has not been changed in transit.

18. Birthday attacks are used against:
    a. Digital signatures
    b. Message integrity codes
    c. Asymmetric algorithms
    d. Brute-force attacks

Answer b: It is important to note that MD5 is more susceptible to Birthday attacks (an attack that is very pertinent to hashing algorithms).

19. Hashed MACing using SHA-1 is:
    a. RFC 1087
    b. X.509
    c. RFC 2104
    d. ANSI 9.9

Answer c: HMAC-SHA-1 is defined as a keyed version of SHA-1, specified in IETF RFC 2104.

20. Digital signatures do not allow for:
    a. Unauthorized modifications to a message
    b. Authentication of the signatory
    c. Third-party verification of a sender
    d. Confidentiality of a document

Answer d: Digital signatures are used to detect unauthorized modifications to data and to authenticate the identity of the signatory or the creator of the document. In addition, the recipient of signed data can use a digital signature in proving to a third party that the signature was in fact generated by the signatory.

21. What does a certificate issued by a trusted third party indicate?
    a. It binds a public key to a person or organization.
    b. It proves the authenticity of a message.
    c. It allows for secure e-commerce transactions.
    d. It prevents ciphertext attacks.

Answer a: Some convincing strategy is necessary to reliably associate a particular person or entity to the key pair.

22. Who "signs" the certificate?
    a. The registration authority
    b. The subscriber to the certificate
    c. The certificate authority
    d. The recipient of the message

Answer c: To assure both message and identity authenticity of the certificate, the certification authority digitally signs it.

23. When a certificate is invalidated, what is the proper process to follow?
    a. The certificate authority must issue a new key-pair.
    b. The user must re-issue all documents produced under the old certificate.
    c. The recipient must re-authenticate all documents received from that individual.
    d. The certificate authority must place the certificate on a CRL.

Answer d: A CA must have an efficient way of alerting the rest of the user population that it is no longer acceptable to use a specific public key for an individual. Answer a is incorrect because the key may be invalidated by an employee leaving the organization and a new key-pair is not needed.

Answer b is incorrect because the timestamp on the documents will indicate that they were issued during the effective life of the key.

24. What is a common error in key management?
    a. Keys are too long for the algorithm to compute effectively.
    b. Keys are stored in secure areas and are not recoverable.
    c. Keys are chosen from a small or predictable portion of the key space.
    d. Key lifetimes are not long enough to be cost-effective.

Answer c: For example, years ago students found that a release of Netscape's SSL implementation chose the key from a recognizable subspace of the total key space.

Domain 7: Physical Security

1. Physical security often follows which of the following models?
    a. High-security defense model
    b. Deterrent-based security model
    c. Layered defense model
    d. Trusted systems security model

Answer c: An easy method of viewing the physical security environment is to think of it as a layered defense model.

2. Physical crime prevention is often a combination of all of the following EXCEPT:
    a. Disposition
    b. Psychology
    c. Hardware
    d. Site design

Answer a: By combining security hardware, psychology, and site design, a physical environment can be created that would, by its very nature, discourage crime.

3. Crime prevention through *environmental design* builds on the strategies of access control, natural surveillance, and:
    a. Possession
    b. Territoriality
    c. Isolation
    d. Obscurity

Answer b: CPTED builds on several key strategies: territoriality, natural surveillance, and access control.

4. Site location should consider all of the following EXCEPT:
    a. Lighting
    b. Crime

    c. Natural disaster

    d. Emergency response facilities

Answer a: Physical security should begin with a detailed site selection process; however, lighting is not related to site selection.

5. A fault is a:

    a. Electrostatic discharge

    b. Momentary loss of power

    c. A spike in voltage

    d. Transient noise

Answer b: Fault is a momentary power outage.

6. Positive pressurization of a facility means:

    a. Positive ions in the air will prevent the adhesion of contaminants.

    b. Higher air pressure inside a building may reduce external contamination.

    c. Increased air pressure provides better working conditions.

    d. Opening a door may draw fresh air into a building.

Answer b: Positive pressurization would force the smoke to exit the building and external particles (or smoke) could not enter.

7. The greatest risk to most organizations through portable computing is:

    a. Loss of expensive hardware

    b. Vulnerability of remote access

    c. Loss of confidential data

    d. Tracking and inventory of equipment

Answer c: Because a large amount of information can be stored on a laptop, its loss can be devastating for both the user and the organization.

8. Standby lighting is:

    a. Operated only in hours of darkness

    b. Operated in the event of a power failure

    c. Operated to facilitate emergency evacuation

    d. Operated in response to suspicious activity

Answer d: Automatically or manually turned on when suspicious activity is suspected.

9. A microwave-based sensor provides which type of control?

    a. Deterrent

    b. Preventative

    c. Detective

    d. Compensating

Answer c: Sensors can be installed as perimeter and building ground devices to detect unauthorized access into an area.

10. A closed-circuit TV splitter is not effective for:

    a. Replaying individual camera scenes

859

b. Switching between camera inputs sequentially
c. Displaying many cameras at once
d. Recording several camera inputs concurrently

Answer b: A splitter (also called a multiplexer) enables multiple simultaneous camera shots (i.e., four, nine, or sixteen shots) to be viewed at the same time.

11. Intensified camera lenses are effective for:
    a. Low-light surveillance
    b. Using heat signatures to record activity
    c. Magnifying the detail of an incident
    d. Creating a stereoscopic image of the scene

Answer a: Intensified cameras amplify the reflected scene when used in low-light areas.

12. Which is the most secure form of window?
    a. Wired glass
    b. Tempered glass
    c. Glass-clad polycarbonate
    d. Acrylic glass

Answer c: Glass-clad polycarbonate combines the best qualities of glass and acrylics. They are high-security windows that are resistant to abrasion, chemicals, fires, and are even anti-ballistic. Because they are expensive, they are usually limited to high-security areas.

13. What method is NOT effective for mitigating damage from static?
    a. Static mats and wrist straps
    b. Reducing humidity
    c. Anti-static sprays
    d. Anti-static flooring materials

Answer b: Static is minimized by controlling humidity; low humidity can cause static.

14. What type of fire-suppression system does the insurance industry recommend for use in computer rooms?
    a. Carbon dioxide (CO_2)
    b. Water
    c. Halon 1211
    d. Dry powder

Answer b: The U.S. Fire Protection and Insurance Industries support the use of water as the primary fire-extinguishing agent for all business environments.

15. When determining the best physical security countermeasures to implement, which of the following should be the key factor?
    a. Initial financial costs
    b. Installation costs

    c. Maintenance costs

    d. Life safety concerns

Answer d: Life safety concerns will always override other security or financial issues.

16. Due to heightened security, your security officer has asked you for options that would control and monitor automobile traffic into the employee parking lot. Which of the following do you think would be a good option to recommend?

    a. Install trip lighting at the entrance area.

    b. Install vehicle barriers at the entrance area.

    c. Install a Class I vehicular gate.

    d. Install a Class II vehicular gate.

Answer d: Trip lighting would only display the vehicle, but does not provide any control mechanism. A vehicle barrier would prevent the vehicle from entering. A Class I vehicular gate is for residential gate operation. A Class II vehicular gate is designed for commercial use, such as a parking lot or garage.

17. To improve security in the employee parking lot, the security officer has asked to recommend some lighting options. Which of the following do you think would be a good option to recommend?

    a. Continuous lighting

    b. Trip lighting

    c. Standby lighting

    d. Emergency lighting

Answer a: Continuous lighting is a series of fixed luminaries arranged to flood an area continuously during hours of darkness; trip lighting is only activated by some trigger point, such as movement in front of a sensor; standby lighting is activated either automatically or manually when suspicious activity is suspected; and emergency lighting is used for limited times of power failures.

18. What is an emergency panic bar on a door designed to do?

    a. Eliminate the shrinkage or cracking of the doorframe due to excessive use.

    b. Indicate whether the door is open or closed.

    c. Allow instant exit, but controlled entrance.

    d. Reinforce the hinge frame, so the door cannot be kicked in or pried open.

Answer c: Panic bars are door-locking devices designed to allow instant exit by pressing on a cross bar that releases the locking bolt, thus allowing a safe exit.

19. Where would you likely to find a mantrap installed?

    a. Prison entranceway

    b. Public library entranceway

    c. Amusement park entranceway

    d. Bridge toll-gate

Answer a: A mantrap interlocks two controlled doors and routes individuals through the double-doored facility – a prison would be very likely to have a mantrap control.

20. The primary entrance door to the server room has a push-button lock for daytime control and a spin-dial lock for after hour access control. A secondary door to the server room should have what type of lock installed?

    a. Same as the primary entrance door

    b. Deadbolt on the inside, allowing no access from the outside

    c. Electronic combination lock on the outside

    d. Pushbutton lock on the outside for daytime control and spin-dial lock on the outside for after hour control.

Answer b: Entrance to the server room should be allowed only through the main primary door. Secondary doors should be secured from the inside so that outside entrance is not permitted.

Domain 8: Telecommunications, Network, and Internet Security

1. What is a network protocol?

    a. A defined set of rules of behavior

    b. An early version of a new product

    c. The maximum bandwidth of a transmission medium

    d. Rules of communication

Answer d: A protocol is a formal set of rules that computers use to control the flow of messages between them.

2. A datagram will often contain the message itself plus several other headers and trailers. This is called:

    a. Encryption

    b. Transport adjacency

    c. Encapsulation

    d. Attenuation

Answer c: The data portion of an information unit at a given OSI layer potentially can contain headers, trailers, and data from all the higher layers. This is known as encapsulation.

3. The Media Access Control (MAC) layer operates as a subset of the:

    a. Physical layer

    b. Data-link layer

    c. Internet layer

    d. Transport layer

Answer b: The Media Access Control (MAC) sub-layer of the data-link layer manages protocol access to the physical network medium.

4. Flow control is usually coordinated by which layer of the OSI stack?
    a. Data-link layer
    b. Network layer
    c. Application layer
    d. Transport layer

Answer d: Flow control generally occurs at the transport layer. Flow control manages data transmission between devices so that the transmitting device does not send more data than the receiving device can process.

5. Sending several communications simultaneously over the same physical medium is facilitated by:
    a. Asynchronous communication
    b. Digital communications
    c. Multiplexing
    d. Baseband technology

Answer c: Multiplexing enables data from several applications to be transmitted onto a single physical link.

6. The two portions of an IP address are:
    a. Network and subnet
    b. Host and network
    c. Host and subnet
    d. Class A and Class C

Answer b.

7. Full-duplex transmission means that:
    a. A site can either send or receive but not at the same time.
    b. A site can either send or receive but not both
    c. A site can multiplex several sending channels.
    d. A site can send and receive at the same time.

Answer d: Full-duplex mode means that transmission of data can happen in both directions, in an almost completely independent manner.

8. What is the purpose of a sequence number in a TCP transmission?
    a. Ensuring all messages are received
    b. Putting message fragments back into their correct order
    c. Controlling the distribution of several multiplexed channels
    d. Identifying network congestion

Answer a: Each TCP packet contains the starting sequence number of the data in that packet, and the sequence number (called the acknowledgment number) of the last byte received from the remote peer.

9. Internet Group Management Protocol (IGMP) is used primarily in IPv4 for:
    a. Broadcast traffic

    b. Peer-to-peer communications

    c. Multicast transmissions

    d. Administration of remote Internet groups

Answer c: Internet Group Management Protocol (IGMP), documented in Appendix I of RFC 1112, allows Internet hosts to participate in multicasting. RFC 1112 describes the basics of multicasting IP traffic.

10. Poisoning the Domain Name Server system may result in:

    a. A user's IP address being deleted

    b. A user unable to reach an organization via its IP address

    c. A user being routed to the wrong organization

    d. A user being denied access to a remote server

Answer c: The resolver takes the hostname and returns the IP address or takes an IP address and looks up a hostname.

11. What would you find in an ARP cache?

    a. History of sites visited by a user

    b. Configuration tables for a firewall

    c. Domain registry information

    d. Cross-reference of IP and MAC addresses

Answer d: Address Resolution Protocol (ARP) is a protocol for mapping an Internet Protocol address (IP address) to a physical machine address that is recognized in the local network. For example, in IP version 4, the most common level of IP in use today, an address is 32 bits long. In an Ethernet local area network, however, addresses for attached devices are 48 bits long.

12. Which of the following is NOT a function of the ICMP (Internet Control Message Protocol)?

    a. Reporting packet failure

    b. Testing node reachability

    c. Increasing routing efficiency

    d. Reporting network failures

Answer a: In addition to the principal reason for which it was created (reporting routing failures back to the source), ICMP provides a method for testing node reachability across an internet (the ICMP Echo and Reply messages), a method for increasing routing efficiency (the ICMP Redirect message), a method for informing sources that a datagram has exceeded its allocated time to exist within an internet (the ICMP Time Exceeded message), and other helpful messages.

13. Which of the following applies to the Routing Information Protocol (RIP)?

    a. It is best for use in large autonomous networks.

    b. It determines routing by number of hops rather than line speeds.

    c. It is relatively fast at identifying network changes.

    d. It considers line utilization as a metric for determining best route.

Answer b: RIP limits the number of router hops between any two hosts in an internet to 16. RIP is also slow to converge, meaning that it takes a relatively long time for network changes to become known to all routers. Finally, RIP determines the best path through a network by looking only at the number of hops between the two end nodes. This technique ignores differences in line speed, line utilization, and all other metrics.

14. An autonomous network is one that:
    a. Is isolated from other systems for greater security
    b. Is designed to be robust enough to resist internal attacks
    c. Is under one point of authority or control
    d. Is enhanced for maximized speed and error correction

Answer c: Routers within the Internet are organized hierarchically. Some routers are used to move information through one particular group of networks under the same administrative authority and control. (Such an entity is called an autonomous system.)

15. Which method of setting up a WAN is considered most private?
    a. Microwave link
    b. Leased line
    c. Internet
    d. Wireless infrared

Answer b: Using private circuits such as leased lines and dedicated lines, or by using T1 or T3. For Frame Relay and ATM, a layer of privacy is established through the separation of various data channels with permanent virtual circuits (PVCs).

16. Which of the following are NOT normally associated with wireless technologies?
    a. Noise
    b. Interception
    c. Access points
    d. Direct sequence frequency hopping

Answer d: Detractor.

17. What is the best defense against "wardialing"?
    a. Strong modem policies
    b. Restrictions on lines with outgoing dial tone
    c. Justify all remote users
    d. Having all internal numbers unlisted

Answer a: The best defense against wardialing attacks is a strong modem policy that prohibits the use of modems and incoming lines without a defined business need.

18. A good measure to prevent sniffing is:
    a. The NIC card is in promiscuous mode.
    b. All transmitted data is encrypted.

    c. Password files are kept protected.

    d. Exclusive use of coaxial cable for networks.

Answer b: The best defense against sniffing attacks is to encrypt the data in transit.

19. What is the best defense against session hijacking?

    a. Rigorous physical security

    b. Closing unneeded ports

    c. Strong user authentication policies

    d. Choosing strong protocols

Answer d: The best defense against session hijacking is to avoid the use of insecure protocols and applications for sensitive sessions.

20. Denial-of-service attacks are usually the result of all of the following EXCEPT:

    a. Malformed packets

    b. Software not handling errors properly

    c. Duplicate MAC addresses

    d. Packet floods

Answer c: If the software handles such errors poorly, the system may crash when it receives such packets.

21. An organization can prevent most buffer overflows by all of the following means EXCEPT:

    a. Proper code and test software

    b. Expand memory allocation

    c. Validate all user inputs

    d. Control inputs from other programs

Answer b: The most thorough defenses against buffer overflow attacks are to properly code and test software so that it cannot be used to smash the stack. All programs should validate all input from users and other programs, ensuring that it fits into allocated memory structures.

22. A rootkit can perform all of the following EXCEPT:

    a. Grant super-user access to the attacker

    b. Hide sniffers

    c. Replace critical system files

    d. Contain a backdoor account for the hacker

Answer a: Rootkits do not allow an attacker to gain "root" (super-user) access to a system. Instead, rootkits allow an attacker who already has super-user access to keep that access by foiling all attempts of an administrator to detect the invasion. Rootkits consist of an entire suite of Trojan horse programs that replace or patch critical system programs.

23. One of the MOST critical parts of an information security program is:

    a. Having an IDS (intrusion detection system)

    b. Having a routine to install system patches

c. Strong authentication methods

d. Documented incident response procedures

Answer d: Perhaps even more important than IDSs, documented incident response procedures are among the most critical elements of an effective security program.

24. A remote access system may limit user activity through all of the following EXCEPT:
    a. Access restrictions to certain drives or servers
    b. Login restrictions based on time of day
    c. Restrictions to protocols accepted
    d. Restrictions on bandwidth allocated to users

Answer d: Depending on the size of the network and the sensitivity of the information that can be remotely accessed, one or more of the a, b, and c security methods can be employed.

25. Which of the following is not a valid type of firewall?
    a. Desktop
    b. Packet filtering
    c, Statistical inspection
    d. Application proxy

Answer c: See "A Brief Introduction of Firewalls."

26. A circuit-level gateway operates at which level of the OSI stack:
    a. Transport
    b. Application
    c. Network
    d. Session

Answer d: This model works at the session layer of the OSI model.

27. Which of the following is NOT a protocol used in IPSec?
    a. Point-to-Point Tunneling (PPTP)
    b. Authentication Header (AH)
    c. Internet Key Exchange (IKE)
    d. Encapsulated Security Payload (ESP)

Answer a: Three protocols are used to handle encapsulation, encryption, and authentication: AH (Authentication Header), ESP (Encapsulating Security Payload), and IKE (Internet Key Exchange).

Domain 9: Business Continuity Planning (BCP)

1. Business continuity addresses:
    a. Availability
    b. Integrity
    c. Confidentiality
    d. Accountability

Answer a: Business continuity addresses the availability leg of the security triad.

2. Preparing a full-scale BCP can:
   a. Be quickly achieved
   b. Take a long time
   c. Ensure a separation of responsibilities
   d. Not involve vendors

Answer b: Preparing a full-scale BCP can take a long time.

3. Which is NOT a traditional phase in preparing a BCP?
   a. Testing, Maintenance, Awareness, and Training
   b. Business Impact Analysis
   c. Project Management and Initiation
   d. Quantitative Risk Analysis

Answer d: Traditional BCP phases include Project Management and Initiation; Business Impact Analysis; Recovery Strategy; Plan Design and Development; and Testing, Maintenance, Awareness, and Training.

4. The BCP Project Management and Initiation Phase does NOT involve:
   a. Establishing members of the BCP team
   b. Determining the need for automated data collection tools
   c. Performing a Business Impact Analysis
   d. Preparing and presenting status reports

Answer c: The Project Management and Initiation Phase consists of:

- Establishing need for the BCP
- Obtaining management support
- Identifying strategic internal and external resources
- Establishing members of team
- Establishing project management work plan
- Determining need for automated data collection tools
- Preparing and presenting status reports

5. Purposes of a BIA include:
   a. Identifying additional countermeasures
   b. Prioritizing critical systems
   c. Completing a cost/benefit analysis
   d. Naming the recovery team

Answer b: Purposes of a BIA include:

- Document impact of outages.
- Identify organization critical business functions.
- Identify concerns if operation is degraded.
- Prioritize critical systems.
- Analyze outage impact.
- Determine recovery windows.

6. Recovery strategies consider all EXCEPT:
   a, User recovery
   b. Expense recovery
   c. Data recovery
   d. Facility recovery

Answer b: Recovery strategies consider:

- Business recovery
- Facility and supply recovery
- User recovery
- Technical recovery
- Data recovery

7. Advantages of a cold site include:
   a. Availability in hours
   b. Operational testing is available
   c. Costs less than in-house facility
   d. Practical for less-popular hardware

Answer d: Cold site advantages include:

- Available for a long time
- Various site locations
- Exclusive use by organization
- Less expensive than a hot site
- Practical for less-popular hardware configurations

8. Electronic vaulting includes all EXCEPT:
   a. Online tape vaulting
   b. Off-site storage facility
   c. Remote journaling
   d. Database shadowing

Answer b: Electronic vaulting includes three types: that is, answers a, c, and d.

9. Resuming critical business functions includes:
   a. Determining the extent of damage
   b. Declaring a disaster
   c. Establishing the command center
   d. Contacting recovery team members

Answer c: Resuming critical business functions includes establishing the command center to provide management control and administrative, logistic, and communications support.

10. Types of tests include:
    a. Simulation
    b. All out
    c. Evacuation
    d. Operational

Answer a: Types of tests include:

- Structured walk-through
- Checklist
- Simulation
- Parallel
- Full interruption

Domain 10: Law, Investigations, and Ethics

1. What form of law can also be referred to as "tort" law?
   a. Criminal
   b. Administrative
   c. Napoleonic
   d. Civil

Answer d: Civil law (or tort law) identifies a tort as a wrong against an individual or business.

2. An organization suspects that it has suffered loss due to an employee's malfeasance. What should be the first step in pursuing this scenario?
   a. Call law enforcement.
   b. Terminate the employee.
   c. Set up awareness training.
   d. Review organizational policy.

Answer d: If there were no policy in place explicitly stating the company's right to electronically monitor network traffic on company systems, then internal investigators would be well advised not to set up a sniffer on the network to monitor such traffic.

3. A unique packaging method or symbol is probably reason to register a:
   a. Trade secret
   b. Patent
   c. Trademark
   d. Copyright

Answer c: A *trademark* is any distinguishing name, character, logo, or other symbol that establishes an identity for a product, service, or organization.

4. One problem not associated with investigating Internet-based computer crime is:
   a. Jurisdiction
   b. Data diddling
   c. Evidence rules
   d. Skill of investigators

Answer b: Making tracing and the assignment of jurisdiction difficult; evidence rules generally differ in various legal systems, which poses problems in evidence collection. The problem is associated with different technical capabilities of the various law enforcement units.

5. Privacy issues deal with all of the following EXCEPT:
   a. Gathering information
   b. Dissemination of information
   c. Accuracy of information
   d. Proliferation of information

Answer d: Management might consider itself responsible for fairness in the gathering, storage, and dissemination of personal data.

6. Before evidence can be accepted, it must be all of the following EXCEPT:
   a. Tangible
   b. Relevant
   c. Material
   d. Competent

Answer a: Before evidence can be presented in a case, it must be competent, relevant, and material to the issue.

7. Which is NOT a common form of evidence?
   a. Direct
   b. Conclusive
   c. Real
   d. Documentary

Answer b: The most common forms of evidence are direct, real, documentary, and demonstrative.

8. The Best Evidence Rule is designed to:
   a. Ensure only relevant material is presented in court
   b. Rank the importance of evidence according to veracity
   c. Deter any alteration of evidence
   d. Require expert testimony to present electronic evidence

Answer c: Best Evidence Rule, which was established to deter any alteration of evidence.

9. Which of the following is NOT a step in the Evidence Life Cycle:
   a. Discovery
   b. Presentation in court
   c. Storage, preservation, and transportation
   d. Return to owner

Answer a: Discovery is the legal process of releasing evidence to the other party in a lawsuit. The correct steps are:

- Collection and identification
- Analysis

- Storage, preservation, and transportation
- Presentation in court
- Returned to victim (owner)

10. The basic skills necessary to handle an incident are all of the following EXCEPT:
    a. Recognition
    b. Technical
    c. Response
    d. Presentation

Answer d: To meet the listed goals, the members of any incident response team should have recognition, technical, and response skills.

11. One of the largest problems facing an organization is understanding when to pursue an investigation. Usually, this is a failure to correctly identify an incident or lack of:
    a. Technical skills
    b. Knowing baseline activity
    c. Senior management involvement
    d. Reactionary skills

Answer b: It usually comes down to a person making the final decision as to whether an incident has actually occurred or it was a false-positive. Crucial skills include the ability to recognize abnormal activities.

12. The procedures established to handle an incident must be:
    a. Supported by senior management
    b. Prepared in advance
    c. Trustworthy
    d. Communicated

Answer c: Policies, Procedures, and Guidelines.

13. Which of the following is not a section of the Action/Reaction phase of incident handling?
    a. Identification
    b. Containment
    c. Tracking
    d. Analysis

Answer a: Action/Reaction encompasses the phases of:

- Containment
- Analysis
- Tracking

14. Ethics often depends on written standards of ethical behavior. These often include:
    a. Diligence to security concepts and practices
    b. Looking out for number one
    c. Protecting principals from prosecution
    d. Keeping security knowledge secret

Answer a.

Index

A

AAA, *see* Authentication,
    authorization, and
    accounting
ABR, *see* Available Bit Rate
Access
    decisions, 201
    matrix, definition of, 306
    need-to-know, 6
    requests, 124
    unauthorized, 257
Access control(s), 352, 456
    administration, 217
    compromising database views for,
        255
    confidentiality aspects of, 104
    content-based, 204
    defining, 148
    discretionary, 120
    grant and revoke, 307
    granular, 629
    locking methods, 305
    matrix, sample, 109, 200
    methods, examples of, 165
    organizational policy, 149
    role-based, 202
    rule-based, 202
    security function activity for, 214
    techniques, 148
    testing of, 215
    view-based, 307
Access Control List (ACL), 109, 195,
    199, 200, 604
    example, 110
    shared memory objects and, 295
Access control systems and
    methodology, 147–223
    assurance, trust, and confidence
        mechanisms, 205–214
    analysis engine methods,
        207–214

    intrusion detection, 205–207
    common body of knowledge,
        216–219
    components, 217–218
    examples, 218–219
    information protection
        environment, 150–164
    malicious code threats, 161–163
    password threats, 163–164
    threats, 151–155
    transmission threats, 155–161
    information protection and
        management services,
        214–216
    information protection
        requirements, 148–150
    A-I-C triad, 149
    defining access controls, 148
    least privilege, 150
    separation of duties, 149–150
    sample questions for CISSP exam,
        219–222
    security technology and tools,
        164–205
    access to data, 199–205
    access to system, 165–172
    biometric devices, 181–184
    centralized access control
        methodologies, 184–190
    decentralized/distributed access
        control methodologies,
        190–198
    definition of controls, 164–165
    synchronous tokens, 172–181
Account lockout example, 171
Accreditation, 137, 72
ACID test, 305
ACL, *see* Access Control List
Active protection mechanism, 114
ActiveX, 285
    controls, 277
    Data Objects (ADO), 247, 249

875

Adaptive-chosen-ciphertext attack, 390
Adaptive-chosen-plaintext attack, 390
Address Resolution Protocol (ARP), 573
Ad-hoc software development, 259
Administrative security, Social Engineering and, 64
ADO, *see* ActiveX Data Objects
ADSL, *see* Asymmetric Digital Subscriber Line
Advanced Encryption Standard (AES), 390, 409, 412–413
AES, *see* Advanced Encryption Standard
Affirmative act, 428
AH, *see* Authentication Header
A-I-C triad, 81, 149, 227, 378, 452
Air traffic control systems, integrity and, 5
ALE, *see* Annualized loss expectancy
Algebraic attacks, 391
ALU, *see* Arithmetic Logic Unit
Amazon, 157
American National Standards Institute (ANSI), 246
Analog signal, 524
Analysis engine methods, 207
ANDF, *see* Architectural neural distribution format
ANN, *see* Artificial neural network
Annualized loss expectancy (ALE), 10, 16, 29
Annualized rate of occurrence (ARO), 10, 13
ANSI, *see* American National Standards Institute
Anthrax, 450
Anti-virus software, 301, 340
APIs, *see* Application programming interfaces
Applet(s)
  malicious, 748
  security, 303
Application
  development procedures, 227
  layer protection, 124
  -level privilege, 293
  owner, 41

programming interfaces (APIs), 247, 249
  Java Capabilities, 288
  Java Certification Path, 279
  proxy servers, 618
  security requirements for, 228
  software, 226
  support, 327
Applications and systems development, 225–324
  assurance, trust, and confidence mechanisms, 312–314
    evaluation/certification and accreditation, 314
    information accuracy, 313
    information auditing, 313
    information integrity, 313
  common body of knowledge, 315–318
    components, 316
    examples, 316–318
  information protection environment, 228–257
    database and data warehousing environment, 239
    database interface languages, 247–251
    database vulnerabilities, 255–257
    data warehousing, 251–255
    DBMS architecture, 239–247
    open source code and closed source code, 229
    Security Assertion Markup Language, 251
    software environment, 230–239
  information protection and management services, 314–315
  information protection requirements, 227–228
  sample questions for CISSP exam, 318–322
  security technology and tools, 257–312
    assemblers, compilers, and interpreters, 274–289
    DBMS controls, 304–312

including security in Systems Development Method, 265–273

programming languages, 273–274

programming language and security, 289–290

software protection mechanisms, 290–304

System Development Methods, 258–264

system life cycle and systems development, 257–258

Architectural neural distribution format (ANDF), 317

Archives, 332

Arithmetic Logic Unit (ALU), 88

ARO, *see* Annualized rate of occurrence

ARP, *see* Address Resolution Protocol

ARPANET, 558, 559

Artificial neural network (ANN), 317

AS, *see* Authentication Service

Assembler, definition of, 274

Asset(s)

identification and valuation, 15, 16, 25

intangible, 25

mapping, 27

tangible, 25

value, 21

Assurance, trust, and confidence mechanisms

access control systems and methodology

analysis engine methods, 207–214

intrusion detection, 205–207

applications and systems development

evaluation/certification and accreditation, 314

information accuracy, 313

information auditing, 313

information integrity, 313

Business Continuity Planning

plan maintenance, 700–701

plan testing, 698–700

testing and maintenance, 698

cryptography

digital signatures and certificate authorities, 426–431

Public Key Infrastructure, 431–434

information security management implementation (delivery) options, 69–70

information classification, 38–40

risk analysis and assessment, 29–30

law, investigations and ethics

ethics, 766

investigation, 754

law, 732

physical security

checklist creation, 505

drills/exercises/testing, 505

maintenance and service, 505–506

vulnerability/penetration tests, 505

security architecture and models

certification and accreditation, 136–137

Common Criteria, 134–136

Information Technology Security Evaluation Criteria, 131–134

Trusted Computer Security Evaluation Criteria, 129–130

Trusted Network Interpretation, 131

telecommunications, network, and Internet security

audit trails, 650–651

security reviews, 651–653

vulnerability assessments, 653–654

Asymmetric cryptography, 401, 402, 426

Asymmetric Digital Subscriber Line (ADSL), 544

Asymmetric key cryptography

algorithms, 414

bases and trapdoor functions, 415

elliptic curve cryptography, 419

one-way functions and trapdoor functions, 415

open, secure, and signed and secure messages using, 416

RSA algorithm, 419
Asynchronous tokens, 175
Asynchronous Transfer Mode (ATM),
    547, 549, 633
ATM, *see* Asynchronous Transfer Mode
Attack(s)
    adaptive-chosen-ciphertext, 390
    adaptive-chosen-plaintext, 390
    algebraic, 391
    brute-force, 154, 390, 412, 440
    buffer overflow, 228, 294
    categories, 389–390
    chosen-ciphertext, 390
    chosen-plaintext, 390
    ciphertext-only, 390, 440
    covert channel, 296
    denial-of-service, 155, 171, 331
    dictionary, 154
    distributed denial-of-service, 155,
        156, 748
    ego, 61
    gateways for, 749
    hash function, 392
    intimidation, 62
    known-plaintext, 390
    man-in-the-middle, 153, 393
    message authentication code, 392
    methods, 217, 371
    network, 709
    packet flood, 585
    Ping of Death, 155, 157
    public relations fallout from, 748
    query, 257
    simulated, 216
    smurfing, 158, 159
    social engineering, 60, 61, 65, 154
    stream cipher, 391
    symmetric block cipher, 391
    sympathy, 61
    tracing of, 749
    zero-knowledge, 215
Attribute value pairs (AVPs), 189
Audit
    events, 212
    logs, 120, 208, 216
    resolution standards, 2
    trail(s), 166, 650, 744
        corrupting, 339
        data volume and, 213

monitoring, 211
Authentication
    authorization, and accounting
        (AAA), 184, 522, 599
    definition of, 166
    factors, 168
    Header (AH), 637
    multi-factor, 167
    Service (AS), 193
    two-factor, 594
    types of, 167
Automatic key update, 432
Availability
    attack on, 151
    definition of, 3
    known threats to, 4
    loss of, 26
    value of, 26
Available Bit Rate (ABR), 547
AVPs, *see* Attribute value pairs

B

Backdoors, 238, 333, 345, 590
Background checks, 1
Backhoe transmission loss, 155
Backup(s), 348
    planning, 358
    types of, 688
Badge systems, 166
Bandwidth reservation, 648
Baselines, definition of, 51
Basic rate interface (BRI), 542
Basic Service Set (BSS), 537
Batch jobs, 86
BCP, *see* Business Continuity Planning
BEDO DRAM, *see* Burst Extended Data
        Output DRAM, 90
Behavior blockers, 301, 345
Bell-LaPadula model, 104, 105, 112
Benchmark testing, trusted system,
        116
Best Evidence Rule, 736
BGP, *see* Border Gateway Protocol
BIA, *see* Business Impact Analysis
Biba integrity model, 106, 107
Binding, 122
Biometric accuracy terms, 184

Biometric attributes, 182–183
Biometric devices, 166, 180
Biometric systems, 489
Birthday paradox, 392
Blended environments, 299
Block ciphers, stream ciphers versus, 397
Bluetooth, 534
Bollards, 470, 471
Bomb, definition of, 236
Boot sector infector, 233
Border Gateway Protocol (BGP), 575, 577
BRI, *see* Basic rate interface
Brooks's Law, 258
BRP, *see* Business Resumption Plan
Brute-force attack, 154, 390, 412, 440
BSA, *see* Business Software Alliance
BSS, *see* Basic Service Set
Buffer overflows, 151, 208, 228, 230
    security controls for, 294
    stack-based, 587
BugTraq, 731
Building, inside of, 489
    fire protection, 493
    supply system controls, 489
Building entry points, 481
    annunciation panels, 489
    card access control or biometric systems, 489
    doors, 481
    facility wall structures, 481
    guard stations, 488
    locks, 484
    vulnerability, 464
    windows, 483
Building grounds boundary protection, 466
    closed-circuit television, 473
    perimeter intrusion detection systems, 473
    protective barriers, 466
    surveillance devices, 473
Burst Extended Data Output DRAM (BEDO DRAM), 90
Business
    ethics, 68
    function(s)
        categories, critical, 679

non-critical, 696
        recovery plans, 691
        time-critical, 676
    Impact Analysis (BIA), 35, 670, 672, 674
    needs, security infrastructure meeting, 79
    recovery strategies, 680
    Reference Model, 102
    Resumption Plan (BRP), 663
    unit priorities, 681
Business Continuity Planning (BCP), 36, 663–707
    assurance, trust, and confidence mechanisms, 698–701
        plan maintenance, 700–701
        plan testing, 698–700
        testing and maintenance, 698
    common body of knowledge, 703–705
        components, 703–704
        examples, 704–705
    definition of disaster, 666–667
    information protection environment, 668–669
    information protection and management services, 701–703
        awareness training, 701–702
        BCP awareness and training, 701
    information protection requirements, 667–668
    outline, sample, 693–695
    roles, 673
    sample questions for CISSP exam, 705–706
    security technology and tools, 669–698
        BCP creation, 669–670
        business impact analysis, 672–679
        plan development and implementation, 691–698
        project management and initiation, 670–672
        recovery strategies, 679–691
        testing, maintenance, awareness, and training, 698

Business Software Alliance (BSA), 332, 760

C

Cable
    modems, 544, 545
    television (CATV), 545
Caching, 573
Callback systems, 597
Caller ID, 600
Calling number identification (CLID), 185
Canadian Independent Computing Services Association, 728
Candy-from-a-baby fallacy, 760
Capability Maturity Model for Software (SW-CMM), 263, 264
Capability tables, 203
Card access systems, 451
Carrier Sense Multiple Access with Collision Detection (CSMA/CD), 529, 530
CAs, see Certification Authorities
CASE, see Computer Aided Software Engineering
Cathode ray tube (CRT), 475
CATV, see Cable television
CBC, see Cipher block chaining
CBK, see Common body of knowledge
CBR, see Constant Bit Rate
CC, see Common Criteria
CCD camera, see Charge-coupled discharge camera
CCTV, see Closed-circuit television
CDIs, see Constrained Data Items
CDMA, see Code Division Multiple Access
CD-ROMs, audit data stored on, 213
CDSL, see Consumer Digital Subscriber Line
Cellular phones, 336
Cellular technology, 550
Center for Education and Research in Information Assurance and Security (CERIAS), 731, 733
Central Processing Unit (CPU), 82, 85, 228, 552
    failure, 126
    hardware interrupt, 94
    protection, 122
    resources, 86
    run state, 89
    states, 88
    supervisor state, 89
    user state, 89
    utilization, intruder detection and, 205
CER, see Crossover error rate
CERIAS, see Center for Education and Research in Information Assurance and Security
CERT, see Computer Emergency Response Team
CERT® Coordination Center, 364, 365
Certificate
    authorities, 426, 429, 430
    repository, 432
    revocation, 432
    Revocation List (CRL), 287
Certification, 271
    Authorities (CAs), 431
    vulnerabilities associated with, 137
Certification and Accreditation, 136
CFB, see Cipher feedback
CFCs, see Chlorofluorocarbons
CGEA, see Community General Export Authorization
Chain of Evidence, 738
Chain-link fencing, 467, 468
Challenge Handshake Authentication Protocol (CHAP), 185, 597, 600
Change
    analysis, 360
    cataloging of, 360
    control
        analyst, 42
        management, 359
    implementation, 361
    management, 327
    scheduling, 360
Channel service unit/digital service unit (CSU/DSU), 520, 549
Chaos Computer Club, 715
CHAP, see Challenge Handshake Authentication Protocol

Charge-coupled discharge (CCD)
    camera, 475
Chief Information Officer (CIO), 55
Child pornography, 721
Chinese Wall Model, 112
Chlorofluorocarbons (CFCs), 495
Chor Rivest Knapsack problem, 423
Chosen-ciphertext attack, 390
Chosen-plaintext attack, 390
CIAC, *see* Computer Incident Advisory
    Capability
CIO, *see* Chief Information Officer
Cipher(s)
    block chaining (CBC), 409, 411
    feedback (CFB), 409
    polyalphabetic, 406
    substitution, 403
    transposition, 404
    Vigenere, 406, 407
Ciphertext-only attack, 390, 440
CIR, *see* Committed Information Rate
Circuit
    -level gateways, 619
    switching, 524
CISSP exam sample questions
    access control systems and
        methodology, 219
    applications and systems
        development, 318
    Business Continuity Planning, 705
    cryptography, 444
    information security management,
        75
    law, investigations and ethics, 769
    operations security, 372
    physical security, 509
    security architecture and models,
        142
    telecommunications, network, and
        Internet security, 658
Citizen programmers, 230
Citrix Independent Computing
    Architecture, 198
Clark-Wilson model, 107, 109
Classification security schemes, 46
Classified information, 38
Cleanroom software development, 263
CLID, *see* Calling number identification
Client

machines, 98
/server, definition of, 98
software, 433
Clock-based token, 172–173
Closed-circuit television (CCTV), 473,
    474, 682, 742
    camera, light surrounding, 477, 480
    monitor, 478
    system
        components of, 475
        equipment included in, 479
Closed source, 229
Closed systems, 98
CM, *see* Configuration Management
CNN.com, 157
COCOM, *see* Coordinating Committee
        for Multilateral Export
        Controls
Code(s)
    science of cracking, 389
    -signing technique, 287
Codebook collection problems, 410
Code Division Multiple Access (CDMA),
        550
Code of ethics, 763–765
COFC, *see* Commercial Oriented
        Functionality Class
Cold site, 685
COM, *see* Component Object Model
Commercial off-the-shelf (COTS)
        products, 136
Commercial Oriented Functionality
        Class (COFC), 135
Committed Information Rate (CIR), 547
Common body of knowledge (CBK)
    Access Control Domain, 216
    Application Program Domain, 315
    Business Continuity Planning
        Domain, 703
    Computer, System, and Security
        Architecture Domain, 139
    Cryptography Domain, 441
    Law, Investigations and Ethics
        Domain, 767
    Operations Security Domain, 366
    Physical Security, 507
    Security Management Domain, 72

Telecommunications, Network, and Internet Security Domain, 655

Common Criteria (CC), 134, 291, 314, 346

Common Law, categories and types of, 716
administrative law, 718
civil law, 718
criminal law, 716

Common-mode noise, 461

Common Object Request Broker Architecture (CORBA), 281, 283, 285, 288, 317

Communication(s)
integrity, 131
security, 714

Community General Export Authorization (CGEA), 395

Compiler, definition of, 274

Compliance policies, 48

Component Object Model (COM), 249, 250, 286

Comprehensive PKI, 434

Computer
Aided Software Engineering (CASE), 260
architecture, management activities for, 137–138
crime
categories of, 713–714
investigation, 713
laws, U.S.-specific, 721
seizing evidence from, 736
statistics, 72
trans-border, 720
equipment protection, 500
ethics, 756, 761
federal interest, 724
forensics, 713
fraud, 717
game fallacy, 757
generation, common fallacies of, 757
Incident Advisory Capability (CIAC), 731
offenses, motives for committing, 733
system layered approach, 82
viruses, 4, 51

Computer Emergency Response Team (CERT), 658, 731, 733, 737, 745

Computer Ethics Institute, 755

Computer Security Act, 722

Confidentiality, 47
attack on, 151
definition of, 6
threats to, 7
value of, 26

Configuration Management (CM), 314, 327, 357

Conflict of interest, 47

Congestion management, 648

Constant Bit Rate (CBR), 547

Constrained Data Items (CDIs), 108

Consumer Digital Subscriber Line (CDSL), 545

Content filtering products, 626

Contingency
management, 358
plan, 358

Continuity of operations plan (COOP), 358, 665

Control(s)
access, 352
corrective, 341
data classification, 353
definition of, 164
detective, 341
directive, 340
easily sidestepped, 359
hardware, 342–343
input/output, 353
object reuse, 352
operation, 346
recovery, 341
software, 343

COOP, see Continuity of operations plan

Coordinating Committee for Multilateral Export Controls (COCOM, 393

CORBA, see Common Object Request Broker Architecture

Corporate memory, 310

Corporate opportunity, 47

Corrective controls, 341

COTS products, *see* Commercial off-
the-shelf products
Counter-based token, 172, 173–174
Covert channel, 230, 296
Covert storage channel, 231
Covert timing channel, 231
C programming language, 275
CPTED, *see* Crime Prevention through
Environmental Design
CPU, *see* Central Processing Unit
Cracker, 7, 152, 171, 578
Crash, definition of, 347
Crime Prevention through
Environmental Design
(CPTED), 455
construction impacts, 457
electrical power, 458
entry points, 457
facility impacts, 457
infrastructure support systems, 458
interference, 460
internal sensitive or
compartmentalized areas,
463
portable computing, 463
site location, 456
water/plumbing, 461
Crisis communication plan, 665
CRL, *see* Certificate Revocation List
Cross-certification, 432
Crossover error rate (CER), 181
CRT, *see* Cathode ray tube
Cryptanalysis, 389
differential, 391
linear, 391
Cryptography, 296, 377–447
assurance, trust, and confidence
mechanisms, 426–434
digital signatures and certificate
authorities, 426–431
Public Key Infrastructure,
431–434
asymmetric, 401, 402
common body of knowledge,
441–444
components, 441–442
examples, 442–444
data modification and, 131
history of, 380–389

information protection
environment, 379–396
cryptanalysis and attacks,
389–393
definitions, 379–389
import/export issues, 393–396
information protection and
management services,
434–441
change, 436–437
control, 437
disposal, 437
distribution, 435–436
installation, 436
key generation, 435
key management, 434–435
modern key management,
437–439
principles of key management,
439–441
storage, 436
information protection
requirements, 378–379
sample questions for CISSP exam,
444–447
security technology and tools,
396–426
asymmetric key cryptography
algorithms, 414–423
basic concepts of cryptography,
396–403
encryption systems, 403–408
message integrity controls,
423–426
symmetric key cryptography
algorithms, 408–414
symmetric key, 400
CSI/FBI Computer Crime and Security
Survey, 449
CSMA/CD, *see* Carrier Sense Multiple
Access with Collision
Detection
CSU/DSU, *see* Channel service
unit/digital service unit
Cybercrime, 720, 721
Cyber incident response plan, 665

D

DAC, *see* Discretionary access control
DASDs, *see* Direct Access Storage
      Devices
Data
  access, control of, 594
  accuracy, 45
  analyst, 42
  center
    recovery, 683
    security, good security practices
      for, 501–502
  Circuit-terminating Equipment, 546
  classification
    controls, 353
    definition, 37
    importance of, 1
    program, methodology for
      developing, 32
    regulatory requirements and, 33
  communications system,
      components of, 519
  confidentiality, 31
  contamination, 256, 309
  corruption, 351
  diddler, 236
  disposal, 335, 352
  encryption, 351, 595
  Encryption Standard (DES), 192,
      408, 437, 615
  flows, trans-border, 727
  hiding, 117, 280
  integrity, 398
  interception of, 256
  loss, 644
  Management Policy, 34
  marts, 251
  mining, 254
  modeling, 280
  modification, cryptography and,
      131
  networks, 516
    components, 519
    structures, 517
    technologies, 523
    wireless security, 537
  ownership, 33
  policies for secure personal, 730

  recovery strategies, 687
  scroungers, 231
  securing of, 351
  Terminal Equipment (DTE), 546
  transfer, 525
  transmission controls, 125
  warehouse
    definition of, 251
    environment, 239
    process of building, 252
Database(s)
  access controls associated with, 203
  architecture models for, 241
  interface languages, 247
  model, 240
  object-oriented, 307
  object-relational, 247
  relational, 244
  security requirements for, 228
  shadowing, 348, 349
  vulnerabilities, 255
Database Management System (DBMS),
      239, 240
  architecture, 239
  controls, 304
    access controls, 306
    data contamination controls, 309
    knowledge management, 310
    lock controls, 305
    metadata controls, 309
    online transaction processing,
      309
    ORION, 308
    security for OO databases, 307
    SODA, 308
    SORION MACs, 308
  elements, 240
  threats to, 255
DBMS, *see* Database Management
      System
DCE, *see* Distributed Computing
      Environment
DCMI, *see* Dublin Core Metadata
      Initiative
DCOM, *see* Distributed Component
      Object Model
DDoS attack, *see* Distributed Denial-of-
      Service attack
DDR, *see* Dial-on-demand routing

DDR SDRAM, *see* Double Data Rate SDRAM
DDS, *see* Digital Data Services
Deadlocking, 256
Decompilers, 276
Decryption, 397
Demon dialers, 581
Denial-of-Service (DoS) attacks, 4, 155, 171, 331
DES, *see* Data Encryption Standard
Desktop firewalls, 621
Detective controls, 341
Development environment, 299
Dial backup, 542
Dial-on-demand routing (DDR), 542
DIAMETER, 188, 599, 605
    Accounting, 189
    Authentication, 189
    Authorization, 189
Dictionary attacks, 154
Diffie-Hellman algorithm, 416, 418, 421
Digital Data Services (DDS), 643
Digital signal, 524
Digital signature, 418, 426
    creation, 427
    timestamped, 430
    verification, 427, 428
Digital Subscriber Line (DSL), 544
Direct Access Storage Devices (DASDs), 348, 349
Directive controls, 340
Direct sequence spread spectrum (DSSS), 533, 540
Disassemblers, 276
Disaster(s)
    causes of, 667
    definition of, 666
    Recovery Plan (DRP), 451, 663, 666
    response to, 692
    Tolerant Disk Systems (DTDSs), 350
Discrete Logarithm Problem, 420
Discretionary access control (DAC), 199, 217, 306
    file structure and, 199
    resource ownership and, 199
Disk
    dump, 738
    error, 126

Distributed Component Object Model (DCOM), 283, 285
Distributed computing characteristics, 285
Distributed Computing Environment (DCE), 607, 617
Distributed Denial-of-Service (DDoS) attack, 155, 156, 748
Distributed systems, advent of, 449
DNS, *see* Domain Name System
Documents, sensitive, 67
DoD, *see* U.S. Department of Defense
Domain Name System (DNS), 161, 572
    fundamental property of, 573
    server, 573
DoS attacks, *see* Denial-of-Service attacks
Double Data Rate SDRAM (DDR SDRAM), 90
Downloading, confidential information and, 7
DRAM, *see* Dynamic Random Access Memory
DRP, *see* Disaster Recovery Plan
DSL, *see* Digital Subscriber Line
DSSS, *see* Direct sequence spread spectrum
DTDSs, *see* Disaster Tolerant Disk Systems
DTE, *see* Data Terminal Equipment
Dublin Core Metadata Initiative (DCMI), 253
Due diligence, 47
Due process, protection against lack of, 726
Dumb terminals, 546
Dumpster driving, 152
Duty of fairness, 47
Duty of loyalty, 47
Dynamic Random Access Memory (DRAM), 90

E

EAP, *see* Extensible Authentication Protocol
Eavesdropping, 152, 179
ECB, *see* Electronic code book

ECC, *see* Elliptic curve cryptography

ECMA, *see* European Computer Manufacturers Association

E-commerce, 516

ECPA, *see* Electronic Communications Privacy Act

EDAP, *see* Extended Data Availability and Protection

EDI, *see* Electronic data interchange

EDO RAM, *see* Extended Data Output RAM

EDP auditing, 363

EF, *see* Exposure factor

EFT, *see* Electronic funds transfer

Ego attacks, 61

EGP, *see* Exterior Gateway Protocol

Eiffel, 262

EJB, *see* Enterprise JavaBeans

Electrically Erasable Programmable Read-Only Memory (EEPROM)

Electric power controls, 489

Electric Power Research Institute (EPRI), 459

Electromagnetic interference (EMI), 460, 508

Electronic burglar tools, 231

Electronic code book (ECB), 411

Electronic commerce, 429

Electronic Communications Privacy Act (ECPA), 722, 723, 737

Electronic data interchange (EDI), 429

Electronic funds transfer (EFT), 593

Electronic vaulting, 349, 690

El Gamal algorithm, 416, 418, 422

Elliptic curve cryptography (ECC), 419, 421

Email

   policy, sample, 51

   privacy, 727

   unsolicited, 626

   virus, 233

Emanation interception, 709

Emergency Power Off (EPO) switch, 491

Emergency system restart, 346

EMI, *see* Electromagnetic interference

Employee(s)

awareness program objectives for, 55

   information provided to, 49

   information systems security and, 56

   sabotage, 371

   security deficiencies reported by, 507

   termination, 41

Encapsulating Security Payload (ESP), 637, 638

Encapsulation, 280, 281

Encryption, 38

   memory and, 93

   requirements, 45

   software, 125, 503

   systems, 403

      polyalphabetic ciphers, 406

      problems with substitution and transposition ciphers, 405

      smart cards and, 178

      substitution ciphers, 403

      transposition ciphers, 404

      Vigenere cipher, 406, 407

End user, 43

Enterprise

   architecture, 101

   Resource Program (ERP), 196

Enterprise JavaBeans (EJB), 283, 289

Entity integrity rule, 245

Entrapment, 468

Entrepreneurial culture, 19

EPO switch, *see* Emergency Power Off switch

EPRI, *see* Electric Power Research Institute

Erasable and Programmable Read-Only Memory (EPROM)

ERP, *see* Enterprise Resource Program

ESP, *see* Encapsulating Security Payload

Ethernet, 529, 530

Ethics, *see also* Law, investigations and ethics

   definition of, 755

   elements shaping, 761–762

   professional codes of, 762

EU, *see* European Union

European Computer Manufacturers Association (ECMA), 135, 195
European Council of Ministers, 729
European Union (EU), 395, 712
Event logs, 744, 747
Evidence
  admissibility of, 739
  business documents and, 735
  forensic-friendly, 748
  identification, 742
  life cycle, 739
  physical, 736
  protection of, 732
  relevancy of, 739, 741
  reliability of, 739, 742
  Rules of, 735
  search and seizure of, 743
  types of, 735
Execution domain switching, 115
Exploratory model, 261
Exposure factor (EF), 11, 13
Extended Data Availability and Protection (EDAP), 350
Extended Data Output RAM (EDO RAM), 90
Extensible Authentication Protocol (EAP), 597, 606
eXtensible Markup Language (XML), 247, 250
Exterior Gateway Protocol (EGP), 575, 577
Extranets, 516, 517, 519
Extreme programming, 262
Eye Witness Statement, 735

F

Failure Tolerant Disk Systems (FTDSs), 350
Fault
  generation techniques, 179
  tolerance, 4, 348, 349
FDDI, *see* Fiber Distributed Data Interface
FEAF, *see* Federal Enterprise Architecture Framework

Federal Communications Commission, 532
Federal Enterprise Architecture Framework (FEAF), 102
Federal interest computer, 724
FHSS, *see* Frequency hopping spread spectrum
Fiber Distributed Data Interface (FDDI), 531
Field locking, 305
File(s)
  infector, 232
  permissions, 199
  protection, 138
  redundant, 239
  Transfer Protocol (FTP), 556
Fire
  classes, 495
  detection, 494
  prevention, 493
  -safety regulations, 454
  suppression, 451, 494
  zones of coverage, 496
Firewall(s), 336, 595, 613
  breaches, 709
  deployment models, 623
  desktop, 621
  logs, 747
  packet filter, 618
  perimeter security and, 617
  platforms, 620
  stateful inspection, 619
FIRST, *see* Forum of Incident Response and Security Teams
Flash Memory security, 93
Foreign Corrupt Practices Act, 711
Foreign key, 243
Forum of Incident Response and Security Teams (FIRST), 733, 745
Fourth Amendment, 736
Frame check sequence, 525
Frame Relay, 545, 546, 635, 656
Fraud, 371
  computer, 717
  mail, 718
  opportunities, 697
Free information fallacy, 761

Frequency hopping spread spectrum (FHSS), 533, 535, 540
FTDs, *see* Failure Tolerant Disk Systems
FTP, *see* File Transfer Protocol
Function recovery, 347

G

Gas lines, 493
General packet radio services (GPRS), 550
General Software Note (GSN), 394
German Enigma machine, 436
GIV, *see* Guideline for Information Valuation
Global synchronization, 649
Global System for Mobile Communications (GSM), 550
GMT, *see* Greenwich Mean Time
Government
  -classified work, 355
  security clearance, 337
GPRS, *see* General packet radio services
Graphical user interface (GUI), 83
Greenwich Mean Time (GMT), 753
GSM, *see* Global System for Mobile Communications
GSN, *see* General Software Note
Guards, automated, 119
GUI, *see* Graphical user interface
Guideline for Information Valuation (GIV), 26
Guidelines, definition of, 52

H

Hacker(s), 578
  definition of, 7, 152
  fallacy, 760
  malicious, 152
  most recognized, 715
  NIS used by, 612
  white-hat, 152
Halon systems, 495
Hand geometry, 166
Hardcopy records, 690

Hardening, operating system, 120
Hard problems, 416
Hardware
  controls, 328, 342–343
  equipment, 331
  segmentation, 122
Hash
  function, 392, 425
  totals, 126
Hashed algorithms, 426
HDTV, *see* High-Definition Television
Health Insurance Portability and Accountability Act (HIPAA), 328, 712
Hearsay rule, 737
Heating, ventilation, and air conditioning (HVAC), 458, 461, 682
  controls, 492
  systems vulnerability, 462
HIDS, *see* Host-based IDS
Hierarchical database management model, 241
High-Definition Television (HDTV), 478
HIPAA, *see* Health Insurance Portability and Accountability Act
Hoaxes, 162, 236
Host-based IDS (HIDS), 207
HTML, *see* Hypertext Markup Language
Human nature, Social Engineering attack and, 59
Human rights protection, 713
HVAC, *see* Heating, ventilation, and air conditioning
Hypertext Markup Language (HTML), 248, 250, 276, 626

I

I&A, *see* Identify and authenticate
IAB, *see* Internet Architecture Board
IBM Systems Journal, 437
ICMP, *see* Internet Control Message Protocol
ICSA, *see* International Computer Security Association
IDEA, *see* International Data Encryption Algorithm

Identification, types of, 166
Identify and authenticate (I&A), 149
IDSs, *see* Intrusion detection systems
IEEE, *see* Institute of Electrical and
    Electronics Engineers
IETF, *see* Internet Engineering Task
    Force
IGMP, *see* Internet Group Management
    Protocol
IGRP, *see* Interior Gateway Routing
    Protocol
IIS, *see* Microsoft Internet Information
    Server
IKE, *see* Internet Key Exchange
Impersonation, 152
Incident
    handling, 711, 733
    reporting, 364
    response, 733
        guidelines for, 745
        plan, 665
        procedures, 592
        team, 66, 746
Industrial espionage, 371
Industry guidelines, compliance with,
    328
Information
    asset, 11
    classification, 31, 44
    classified, 38
    custodian, 41, 52
    diode, 415
    flow model, 110, 111
    improper modification of, 256
    integrity, 313
    ownership, 40, 44
    processing, ISF, 329
    Risk Management (IRM), 9
        methodology, 14
        performance, monitoring of, 17
        policy, 14, 15
    secret, 150
    security
        crime-related components, 714
        encryption and, 398
        officer, 32, 33
        program, objective of, 46
        purpose of, 3
    security policy

characteristics of, 53
    sample, 34
    sharing, 752
    technology (IT), 10
        daily life and, 56
        environment, risks associated
            with, 28
        security awareness materials and
            techniques, examples of, 68
    value of expressed in monetary
        terms, 23
Information protection environment
    access control systems and
        methodology
        malicious code threats, 161–163
        password threats, 163–164
        threats, 151–155
        transmission threats, 155–161
    applications and systems
        development
        database and data warehousing
            environment, 239
        database interface languages,
            247–251
        database vulnerabilities, 255–257
        data warehousing, 251–255
        DBMS architecture, 239–247
        open source code and closed
            source code, 229
        Security Assertion Markup
            Language, 251
        software environment, 230–239
    Business Continuity Planning,
        668–669
    cryptography, cryptanalysis and
        attacks, 389–393
        definitions, 379–389
        import/export issues, 393–396
    information security management
        goal setting, 56–57
        information classification, 32–33
        policies, procedures, standards,
            baselines, guidelines, 47–48
        risk analysis and assessment,
            15–20
    law, investigations and ethics
        ethics, 757–765
        investigation, 733–734
        law, 713–725

operations security
  data and media, 334–336
  hardware equipment, 331
  operations, 333–334
  personnel, 336–340
  software, 331–333
  support systems, 336
  telecommunications equipment, 336
physical security, 454–463
security architecture and models
  enterprise architecture, 101–103
  network environment, 97–100
  platform architecture, 82–97
  security models, 103–114
telecommunications, network, and Internet security
  data networks, 516–550
  network protocols, 551–578
  network threats and attacks, 578–593
  remote access services, 550–551
Information protection and management services
access control systems and methodology, 214–216
applications and systems development, 314–315
Business Continuity Planning, awareness training, 701–702
cryptography
  change, 436–437
  control, 437
  disposal, 437
  distribution, 435–436
  installation, 436
  key generation, 435
  key management, 434–435
  modern key management, 437–439
  principles of key management, 439–441
  storage, 436
information security management
  implementation (delivery) options, 70–72
  information classification, 40–46
  risk analysis and assessment, 30–31

law, investigations and ethics
  ethics, 766
  investigation, 754–755
  law, 732
operations security
  incident reporting, 364–365
  problem management, 365–366
  security reviews, 364
physical security, 506–507
security architecture and models, 137–139
telecommunications, network, and Internet security, 654–655
Information protection requirements
access control systems and methodology
  A-I-C triad, 149
  defining access controls, 148
  least privilege, 150
  separation of duties, 149–150
applications and systems development, 227–228
Business Continuity Planning, 667–668
cryptography, 378–379
information security management
  information classification, 32–33
  policies, procedures, standards, baselines, guidelines, 46–47
  risk analysis and assessment, 8–15
law, investigations and ethics
  ethics, 755–756
  investigation, 732
  law, 711–713
operations security, 326–329
physical security, 452–454
security architecture and models, 81
telecommunications, network, and Internet security, 516
Information Security Forum (ISF), 329
Information security management, 1–77
common body of knowledge, 72–75
  components, 72–73
  examples, 73–75
goal setting, 55–57

awareness program objectives,
55
deciding on content, 55–56
information protection
environment, 56–57
implementation (delivery) options,
68–72
assurance, trust, and confidence
mechanisms, 69–70
information protection and
management services, 70–72
security technology and tools,
68–69
information classification, 31–46
assurance, trust, and confidence
mechanisms, 38–40
information protection
environment, 32–33
information protection and
management services, 40–46
information protection
requirements, 31
security technology and tools,
33–37
policies, procedures, standards,
baselines, guidelines, 46–55
information protection
environment, 47–48
information protection
requirements, 46–47
security technology and tools,
48–54
purposes, 3–8
availability, 3–5
confidentiality, 6–7
integrity, 5–6
threats to confidentiality, 7–8
risk analysis and assessment, 8–31
assurance, trust, and confidence
mechanisms, 29–30
information protection
environment, 15–20
information protection and
management services, 30–31
information protection
requirements, 8–15
security technology and tools,
20–29

sample questions for CISSP exam,
75–77
social engineering, 57–68
coverage, 65
definition, 58–59
immediate notification to
targeted groups, 67–68
preparedness of incident
response teams, 66
protection against, 63–64
readiness testing, 66–67
reason for success of, 59–63
recognition of good catches, 66
securing against attacks, 65–66
Information Systems Security
Association, 755
Information Technology Security
Evaluation Criteria (ITSEC),
74, 131, 132, 133
Initialization vector (IV), 411
Initial program load (IPL), 83, 337
Input checking, 124
Input/output (I/O), 85
controls, 353
devices, 94, 122
fully-mapped, 124
instructions, 343–344
operations, monitoring of, 116
premapped, 123
programmed, 123
requests, 85, 91, 228
unmapped, 123
Institute of Electrical and Electronics
Engineers (IEEE), 179, 555
Intangible assets, 25
Integer Factorization Problem, 420
Integrated services digital network
(ISDN), 542, 631, 641
facilities, 643
objective of, 542
Integrity
attack on, 151
components, corruption potential
and, 106
controls, principles used to
establish, 6
data, 398
definition of, 5
mechanisms for enforcing, 108

rules of, 107
threats to, 5
value of, 26
Verification Procedures (IVPs), 108
Intel
co-founder of, 409
platform, 232
Intellectual property and privacy laws, 719
Intelligence gathering, Social Engineering and, 60
Interior Gateway Routing Protocol (IGRP), 576
Internal Audit Department, 45
International Computer Security Association (ICSA), 136, 755
International Data Encryption Algorithm (IDEA), 391, 413
International Standards Organization (ISO), 246, 264
Open Systems Interconnection model, 97
software development, 264
International Telecommunication Union-Telecommunication Standardization Sector (ITU-T), 546
Internet
accessing databases through, 249
-based remote access, 634
downloading of shareware from, 72
security, see Telecommunications, network, and Internet security
Service Providers (ISPs), 186
Internet Architecture Board (IAB), 571, 762
Internet Engineering Task Force (IETF), 185
AAA Working Group, 185, 190
IPSec, 139
Request for Comment, 559
Internet Protocol (IP), 158, 555, 560
Control Message Protocol (ICMP), 156, 560, 568, 575, 579
Group Management Protocol (IGMP), 570
header
sectors, 563–564

structure, 562
Key Exchange (IKE), 637
Relay Chat (IRC), 235, 236
routing tables, 575
specification for, 158
-spoofed packets, 159
Internetwork Packet Exchange (IPX), 571
Interpol, 731
Interpreter program, 275
Interrupt, 94, 95
Intimidation attacks, 62
Intranets, 516, 517, 518
Intrusion
alarms and signals, 210
detection, 120
network availability and network disaster recovery planning, 640
Quality-of-Service, 645
remote access security, 627
rule-based, 207
virtual private networks, 635
protection against unreasonable, 726
response, 210
Intrusion detection systems (IDSs), 205, 211, 361, 496, 592, 627
compartmentalized areas, 499
computer equipment protection, 500
data center or server room security, 500
host-based, 207
microwave systems, 499
network-based, 206
object protection, 504
rule-based, 208
signature-based, 209
statistical-based, 208, 209
types of, 206
ultrasonic systems, 498
Investigations, see Law, investigations and ethics
Invocation property, 107
I/O, see Input/output
IP, see Internet Protocol
IPL, see Initial program load
IPX, see Internetwork Packet Exchange

IRC, *see* Internet Relay Chat
Iris pattern, 180
IRM, *see* Information Risk Management
ISDN, *see* Integrated services digital
    network
ISF, *see* Information Security Forum
ISO, *see* International Standards
    Organization
ISPs, *see* Internet Service Providers
IT, *see* Information technology
ITSEC, *see* Information Technology
    Security Evaluation Criteria
ITU-T, *see* International
    Telecommunication Union-
    Telecommunication
    Standardization Sector
IV, *see* Initialization vector
IVPs, *see* Integrity Verification
    Procedures

J

JAAS, *see* Java Authentication and
    Authorization Service
JAD, *see* Joint Analysis Development
Java, 250, 262, 275
    applets, 303
    Authentication and Authorization
        Service (JAAS), 279
    bytecode, 276
    Capabilities API, 288
    Cryptography Extension (JCE), 279
    Database Connectivity (JDBC), 247,
        249, 250
    GSS-API, 279
    Remote Method Invocation (JRMI),
        283, 289
    Secure Socket Extension (JSSE), 279
    security, 277
    verifier, criticism of, 278
    Virtual Machine (JVM), 276
    Web code development using, 226
JCE, *see* Java Cryptography Extension
JDBC, *see* Java Database Connectivity
Joint Analysis Development (JAD), 261
JRMI, *see* Java Remote Method
    Invocation
JSSE, *see* Java Secure Socket Extension

Junkie, 233
JVM, *see* Java Virtual Machine

K

KBSs, *see* Knowledge-based systems
KDC, *see* Key distribution center
KDD, *see* Knowledge Discovery in
    Databases
Kerberos, 187, 192, 377, 607, 615
    client software, 194
    data structures, 195
    limitations of, 616
    primary use of, 193
    requirements, 193
    Server, 615, 616
    trust and, 195
Key
    backup and recovery, 432
    change, 436
    control, 437
    disposal, 437
    distribution, 435
    distribution center (KDC), 193
    generation, 435
    history, 432
    installation, 436
    key-encrypting, 439, 440
    management, 434
        fully automated, 439
        functions, 435
        modern, 437
        principles of, 439
    storage mechanism, 436
    update, automatic, 432
    WEP, 539
Keystroke
    loggers, 231
    monitoring, 213
KM, *see* Knowledge management
Knowledge
    -based systems (KBSs), 311
    Discovery in Databases (KDD), 253,
        311
    management (KM), 310
Knowledgeability, examples of, 73–75,
    656
Known-plaintext attack, 390

L

LAN, *see* Local area network
Landscaping, security and, 467
Language, safe, 304
Laptop
  anti-virus software updated on, 503
  computers, 125
  users, 503
Lattice model, 113
Law-abiding citizen fallacy, 758
Law enforcement, reporting to, 753
Law, investigations and ethics, 709–771
  common body of knowledge,
    767–769
  ethics, 755–767
    assurance, trust, and confidence
      mechanisms, 766
    computer ethics, 756–757
    information protection
      environment, 757–765
    information protection and
      management services, 766
    information protection
      requirements, 755–756
    security technology and tools,
      765
  investigation, 732–755
    assurance, trust, and confidence
      mechanisms, 754
    information protection
      environment, 733–734
    information protection and
      management services,
      754–755
    information protection
      requirements, 732
    security technology and tools,
      734–754
  law, 711–732
    assurance, trust, and confidence
      mechanisms, 732
    information protection
      environment, 713–725
    information protection and
      management services, 732
    information protection
      requirements, 711–713
    privacy, 725–730
    recommended course of action,
      730–731
    security technology and tools,
      731
  sample questions for CISSP exam,
    769–771
LCP, *see* Link Control Protocol
Least privilege, 6, 371
  definition of, 150
  enforcement of, 119
  implementing, 298
Legislative requirements, compliance
  with, 328
Lehigh virus, 233
LEO satellite, *see* Low Earth orbit
  satellite
Lighting systems, protective, 471–472
Link Control Protocol (LCP), 571
Linux, 93, 303
LLC, *see* Logical Link Control
Local area network (LAN), 517
  Ethernet, 531
  implementations, 530
  media access methods, 529
  recovery options for, 643, 644
  transmission methods, 528
Lock
  raking of, 485
  security measures, 487
Locked memory, 91
Locking devices, types of, 485
Logical Link Control (LLC), 555
Logical security, Social Engineering
  and, 64
Logic bombs, 4, 161, 162
Logon security, 595
Looting, 697
Loveletter, 233
Low Earth orbit (LEO) satellite, 548
LUC, 423

M

MAC, *see* Media Access Control
Machine-language program, 275, 276
Macro virus, 234
Mail fraud, 718

Mainframe facility, restart procedures in, 347
Maintenance hooks, 88, 333
Malicious code threats, 161
Malicious hacker, 152
Malware, 231
   controls, 301
   definition of, 231
MAN, *see* Metropolitan Area Network
Man-in-the-middle attacks, 153, 393
MAO, *see* Maximum Allowable Outage
Masquerader, definition of, 7
Maximum Allowable Outage (MAO), 674
Maximum Tolerable Downtime (MTD), 674, 675, 678
MC-ES, *see* Mobile Commerce Extension Specification
MDCs, *see* Modification Detection Codes
Mechanical combination locks, 451
Media
   failures, 348
   label, 351
   protection of in operations environment, 334
   storage, 351
   tracking of, 351
Media Access Control (MAC), 199, 217, 306, 555, 560
   address checking, 539
   hashed, 425
Melissa, 233, 234
Memory, 228
   built-in, 90
   cards, 176
   corporate, 310
   dump, 738
   encryption and, 93
   example, 85
   locked, 91
   management, 89, 91
   protection, 116, 121, 138
   reuse, 237
   virtual, 92
Merkle-Hellman Knapsack cryptosystem, 423
Message(s)
   authentication code, 392, 424

digests, non-keyed, 423, 425
fingerprint, 424
integrity controls, 423
   hashed MAC, 425
   Message Authentication Codes, 424
   MICs/MDCs, 425
open, 417
sender identity, verification of, 418
Messaging, out-of-band, 400
Metadata, 253
Metaethics, 761
Metropolitan Area Network (MAN), 517
Microsoft
   Authenticode, 286, 287
   client applications, 286
   domain authentication, 600
   Exchange, 286
   Internet Explorer, 286
   Internet Information Server (IIS), 216
   Office suite, 230
   Outlook, 286
   Outlook Express, 286
Military
   fire control systems, integrity and, 5
   security policy, 103
Mirror site, 685
Misdemeanors, 717
Misuse detections, 209
MLAT, *see* Mutual Legal Assistance Treaties
Mobile code, 153, 302
Mobile Commerce Extension Specification (MC-ES), 93
Mobile computing, 125
Mobile site, 686
Model(s)
   Bell-LaPadula, 104, 105, 112
   Biba integrity, 106, 107
   Business Reference, 102
   Chinese Wall, 112
   Clark-Wilson, 107, 109
   Component Object, 250, 286
   database, 240
   Data and Information Reference, 102
   dial-up, WAN, 542
   exploratory, 261
   firewall deployment, 623

hierarchical database management, 241
information flow, 110, 111
Java security, 277
lattice, 113
network database management, 242
object-oriented database, 246
OSI, 97, 139, 551, 553, 618
Performance Reference, 102
relational database management, 242
Secure Object-Oriented Database, 308
security, 81, 103
Service Component Reference, 102
spiral, 262
state machine, 110
Technical Reference, 102
threat risk, 30
waterfall life cycle, 259
Modem(s)
cable, 544, 545
error, 126
Modification Detection Codes (MDCs), 423
Modified Prototype Model (MPM), 261
Monolithic operating system, 293
Moral philosophy, 761
MPLS, *see* Multi-Protocol Label Switching
MPM, *see* Modified Prototype Model
MS-DOS operating system, 121
MTD, *see* Maximum Tolerable Downtime
Multi-factor authentication, 167
Multi-level security system, purpose of, 103
Multipartite virus, 233
Multiprocessing, 87
Multiprogramming system, vulnerability associated with, 87
Multi-Protocol Label Switching (MPLS), 636
Multitasking systems, 86
Multithreading, 86
Mutual Legal Assistance Treaties (MLAT), 731

N

NAS, *see* Network Access Server
NAT, *see* Network Address Translation
National Computer Security Center (NCSC), 129
National Institute of Standards and Technology (NIST), 408, 412, 664
National Security Agency (NSA), 170
National Television Systems Committee (NTSC), 478
NATO, 113
NCPs, *see* Network Control Protocols
NCs, *see* Network Computers
NCSC, *see* National Computer Security Center
Need-to-know, 6, 150
Netscape, 435
Network(s)
Access Server (NAS), 186, 600, 602
Address Translation (NAT), 621, 638, 655
attacks, 709
availability, 640, 641
-based IDS (NIDS), 206
cabling, 342
Computers (NCs), 198
confidentiality and, 7
congestion, 568
connections, redundant, 349
contingency planning, 666
Control Protocols (NCPs), 571, 597
database management model, 242
data mirroring, 348, 349
definition of, 97
disaster recovery planning, 640
File System (NFS), 567, 607
Information Service (NIS), 589, 607, 612
interface cards (NICs), 336, 521, 560
name, 537
operating system (NOS), 657
packet-switched, 525
protection, 125
protocols, 551
OSI mode and communication between systems, 552
TCP/IP, 558

scans, 748
security, *see* Telecommunications, network, and Internet security
systems, shared, 97
topologies, 526, 621
traffic security, 595
Xerox Network Systems, 576
Network threats and attacks, 578
  backdoors, 590
  denial-of-service attacks, 584
  general trends in computer underground, 578
  intrusion detection and incident response procedures, 592
  network mapping and port scanning, 579
  password cracking, 588
  sniffing, spoofing, and session hijacking, 582–584
  stack-based buffer overflows, 587
  Trojan horses and rootkits, 590
  vulnerability scanning, 580
  wardialing, 581
NFS, *see* Network File System
NICs, *see* Network interface cards
NIDS, *see* Network-based IDS
NIS, *see* Network Information Service
NIST, *see* National Institute of Standards and Technology
Noise, 461
Non-repudiation, 377, 426, 433
Nonvolatile storage, 96
Normalization, 246
NOS, *see* Network operating system
Novell
  Internetwork Packet Exchange, 571
  NDS, 600
NSA, *see* National Security Agency
NTSC, *see* National Television Systems Committee
Number Field Sieve, 421

O

Object
  code, 274

Linkage and Embedding (OLE), 284, 317
Linking and Embedding Database (OLE DB), 247, 248
Management Group (OMG), 285
Request Broker (ORB), 285, 288, 317
reuse, 153, 237, 336, 352
Object-oriented (OO) database, 246, 307
Object-oriented design (OOD), 317
Object-oriented languages
  building blocks of, 250
  examples of, 262
Object-oriented programming (OOP), 262, 281, 317
Object-oriented technology, 280
  encapsulation, 280
  inheritance, 280, 283
  polymorphism, 280, 282
  predefined types, 280
Object-relational database, 247
Occupant emergency plan (OEP), 666
ODBC, *see* Open DataBase Connectivity
OECD, *see* Organization for Economic Cooperation and Development
OEP, *see* Occupant emergency plan
OFB, *see* Output feedback
Office doors, vulnerability of secured, 465
OLAP, *see* Online Analytical Processing
OLE, *see* Object Linking and Embedding
OLE DB, *see* Object Linking and Embedding Database
OLTP, *see* Online transaction processing
OMG, *see* Object Management Group
One Half, 233
One-Time Pad, 398
One-time passwords (OTPs), 172
One-Way Function, 415
One-way hash function, 427
Online Analytical Processing (OLAP), 253
Online banking, 748
Online transaction processing (OLTP), 309, 318

OOD, *see* Object-oriented design
OO database, *see* Object-oriented
    database
OOP, *see* Object-oriented programming
Open DataBase Connectivity (ODBC),
    247
Open Shortest Path First (OSPF), 577
Open source, 229, 396
Open systems, 99
Open Systems Interconnection (OSI)
    model, 97, 139, 551, 553, 618
Operating system (OS), 83, 84
    COTS, 225
    design, layering, 117, 118
    fingerprinting attempts, 208
    hardening, 120
    layering, 83
    monolithic, 293
    MS-DOS, 121
    primary objectives of, 83
    protection, 115, 120
    responsibility of, 86
    software, 83
    Windows NT 4.0, 137
Operation(s)
    controls, 346
    management, 327, 364
    security personnel, 336–337
Operations security, 325–375
    assurance, trust, and confidence
        mechanisms, 357–363
    backup planning, 358
    change control management,
        359–361
    configuration management,
        357–358
    contingency management, 358
    contingency plan, 358
    continuity of operations plan,
        358
    intrusion detection systems, 361
    penetration testing, 363
    system events/audit reports,
        361–363
    common body of knowledge,
        366–372
    information protection
        environment, 330–340
    data and media, 334–336

hardware equipment, 331
    operations, 333–334
    personnel, 336–340
    software, 331–333
    support systems, 336
    telecommunications equipment,
        336
information protection and
        management services,
        363–366
    incident reporting, 364–365
    problem management, 365–366
    security reviews, 364
information protection
        requirements, 326–329
sample questions for CISSP exam,
    372–374
security technology and tools,
    340–357
    data and media, 348–353
    hardware controls, 342–343
    operation controls, 346–348
    personnel, 355–357
    physical areas, 355
    software controls, 343–345
    support systems, 354
    telecommunications equipment,
        353–354
Orange Book, evaluation classes, 129,
    130
ORB, *see* Object Request Broker
Organizational memory, 310
Organization for Economic
        Cooperation and
        Development (OECD), 727,
        728
Organizations, increased security
        exposure of, 516
Organized crime, 721
ORION system, 308
OS, *see* Operating system
OSI model, *see* Open Systems
        Interconnection model
OSPF, *see* Open Shortest Path First
OTPs, *see* One-time passwords
Out-of-band messaging, 400
Out-of-the-box thinking, 198
Output feedback (OFB), 409

P

PAC, *see* Privileged Attribute
    Certificate
Packet
  filter firewalls, 618
  flood attacks, 585
  -switched networks (PSNs), 546
  switching, 525
Page locking, 305
Paging, 92
PAL, *see* Phase Alternative Line
Palm organizer, 175–176
Palm Pilots, 534
Palm print, 180
PAP, *see* Password Authentication
    Protocol
Partial ordering rules, 113
Passive protection mechanism, 114
Passphrase, 168, 169
Password(s)
  Authentication Protocol (PAP), 185,
    597, 600
  confidentiality of logon, 43
  crackers, 154, 171, 231
  cracking, 70, 170, 588
  creation of weak, 72
  definition of, 168
  guessing, 612, 744
  history of, 169
  lifetime, 169
  management privileges, 356
  NSA recommendation, 170
  one-time, 172, 218
  protection, 171, 297
  sharing, 72
  threats, 163
  Unix, 615
  weak, 164
Patent, 719
PBX, *see* Private branch exchange
PC connectivity, 535
PDAs, *see* Personal digital assistants
PDNs, *see* Public data networks
Pedophiles, 720
PEM, *see* Privacy Enhanced Mail
Penetration testing, 215, 363, 505, 653
Performance Reference Model, 102
Perl, 262, 275, 315

Permanent virtual circuits (PVCs), 525
Personal digital assistants (PDAs), 93,
    251, 500
Personnel
  security controls for, 355
  vendor, 354, 357
  vulnerability of, 339
Phase Alternative Line (PAL), 478
Physical environment, security
    challenges associated with,
    450
Physical evidence, 736
Physical security, 449–513
  assurance, trust, and confidence
    mechanisms, 505–506
    checklist creation, 505
    drills/exercises/testing, 505
    maintenance and service,
     505–506
    vulnerability/penetration tests,
     505
  common body of knowledge,
    507–509
    components, 508
    examples, 508–509
  information protection
    environment, 454–463
  information protection and
    management services,
    506–507
  information protection
    requirements, 452–454
  sample questions for CISSP exam,
    509–512
  security technology and tools,
    464–504
    building entry points, 481–489
    building floors, office suites,
     offices, 489–496
    layered defense, 464–466
    penetration (intrusion) detection
     systems, 496–504
    perimeter and building grounds
     boundary protection,
     466–481
  Social Engineering and, 64
PICS, *see* Platform for Internet Content
    Selection
Ping of Death, 155, 157

Ping request, 159
PKI, see Public key infrastructure
Platform for Internet Content Selection (PICS), 204
Platform protection, 114
Point-to-Point Protocol (PPP), 571, 597
Point-to-Point Tunneling Protocol (PPTP), 636, 637
Police coordination, 697
Policing, 649
Policy(ies)
 chart, 50
 definition of, 50
 least privilege, 150
 organizational, access control, 149
 remote access, 635
 sample email, 51
 secure personal data, 730
 security
  definition of, 82
  military, 103
  multi-level, 202
 system high, 202
Polyinstantiation, 256
Polymorphism, 280, 282
Portable device security, 500
Portable digital assistants (PDAs), 463
Port scanning, 579
Power degradation, 459
PPP, see Point-to-Point Protocol
PPTP, see Point-to-Point Tunneling Protocol
Pranks, 152, 237
Preventive controls, 341
PRI, see Primary rate interface
Primary key, 243
Primary rate interface (PRI), 542
Principle of irreversibility, 427
Privacy
 codes, successful, 728
 email, 727
 Enhanced Mail (PEM), 655
 interpretation of, 725
Private branch exchange (PBX), 684
Private key, 401, 431
Privilege(s)
 password management, 356
 restricted, 344
 state failure, 293

Privileged Attribute Certificate (PAC), 195
Privileged-entity controls, 328
Probability, 12
Problem(s)
 hard, 416
 management, 327, 365
Procedures, definition of, 52
Process
 activation, monitoring of, 115
 isolation, 119
 owner, 43
 states, CPU states vs., 89
Processing problems, 342–343
Processor privilege states, 291
Product(s)
 commercial off-the-shelf, 136
 factors involved in selecting, 127
 line manager, 43
 methods used for evaluating, 128
Production environment, 299
Programmable Read-Only Memory (PROM)
Programming language(s)
 choosing, 289, 315
 generations of, 273, 274
 support, 304
Project sizing, 15, 16, 23
Protection
 mechanisms, categories of, 114
 profile developments, 134
Prototyping, 261
PSNs, see Packet-switched networks
PSTN, see Public-switched telephone network
Public criticism, avoidance of, 48
Public data networks (PDNs), 546
Public key
 algorithms, 418
 certificates, 429, 432
 cryptography, 401, 414, 426
 infrastructure (PKI), 431, 593
  components, 433–434
  comprehensive, 434
  core services, 433
Public-switched telephone network (PSTN), 524, 629, 632
PVCs, see Permanent virtual circuits
Python, 262

Q

QoS, *see* Quality of Service
Qualitative risk analysis, 11
Quality assurance environment, 299
Quality of Service (QoS), 636, 645
   components, 646
   implementations, 645
   levels, 645
Quantitative risk analysis, 11
Query attacks, 257

R

RA, *see* Risk analysis
RAB, *see* RAID Advisory Board
RAD, *see* Rapid Application
   Development
Radio frequency interference (RFI),
   461, 508
RADIUS, 186, 599, 601
   Accounting, 187
   Authentication, 186
   Authorization, 187
RAID, *see* Redundant Arrays of
   Independent Disks
RAID Advisory Board (RAB), 350
RAM, *see* Random access memory
Random access memory (RAM), 83, 89,
   96, 121
Rapid Application Development (RAD),
   261
RARP, *see* Reverse Address Resolution
   Protocol
RAS, *see* Remote Access Server
RAT, *see* Remote Access Trojan
Read-Only Memory (ROM), 90
Recovery
   actions, categories, 346
   controls, 341
   plan
      maintenance, 700
      testing, 698
      types of, 346
Red Book, key features of, 131
Redirection of interrupts, 95

Redundant Arrays of Independent
   Disks (RAID), 301, 348, 350,
   641
Reference monitor concept, 115, 116
Referential integrity rule, 245
Regulatory law, 718
Relational database management
   model, 242
Relational model, elements, 243
Remote access
   Internet-based, 634
   policy, 635
   security, 596
Remote Access Server (RAS), 551
Remote Access Trojan (RAT), 231, 232,
   235
Remote journaling, 348, 349
Remote Method Invocation (RMI), 289
Remote Procedure Call (RPC), 607, 608
Request for Comment (RFC), 559, 571
Requested Privilege Level (RPL), 123
Request for Proposal (RFP), 680
Resource(s)
   access, simulating, 651
   protection, 327, 367
   theft of, 330
Resource Reservation Protocol (RSVP),
   636, 647
Response
   escalation process, 746
   skills, 710
Restart procedures, mainframe facility,
   347
Retail crypto, 396
Retransmission control, 126
Reverse Address Resolution Protocol
   (RARP), 574
RFC, *see* Request for Comment
RFI, *see* Radio frequency interference
RFP, *see* Request for Proposal
Rijndael algorithm, 412, 413
RIP, *see* Routing Information Protocol
Risk
   acceptance criteria, 16
   analysis (RA), 8, 12, 35, 40
      qualitative, 11
      quantitative, 11
   assessment, 12
      qualitative, 20, 22

quantitative, 20, 22
resistance to, 18, 19
tasks of, 23
evaluation, 16
management, 2, 13
measurement, 15
metrics, 21, 28
mitigation, 9
analysis, 16, 17, 28
expected, 28
Social Engineering, 62
modeling, 28
RMI, *see* Remote Method Invocation
Role-based capability table, 203
ROM, *see* Read-Only Memory
Rosenberg v. Collins, 737
Rotation of duties, 6
Round-Trip Time (RTT) estimation, 567
Routers, 336
Routing Information Protocol (RIP),
576
Row locking, 305
RPC, *see* Remote Procedure Call
RPL, *see* Requested Privilege Level
RSA algorithm, 416, 418
RSA DES Key Challenge, 440
RSVP, *see* Resource Reservation
Protocol
RTT estimation, *see* Round-Trip Time
estimation
Ruby, 262
Rules of Evidence, 735

S

Safeguard, 13
analysis, 28
cost/benefit analysis, 29
costing, 29
effectiveness, 13
selection, 17
Safe language, 304
Safes, security measures for, 504
SAML, *see* Security Assertion Markup
Language
Sandbox, 303
SCBA equipment, *see* Self-Contained
Breathing Apparatus

Screensaver software, illegal copies of,
72
Script viruses, 233, 234
SDLC, *see* Systems Development Life
Cycle
SDM, *see* System Development
Methods
SDRAM, *see* Synchronous DRAM
Search warrant, 742, 743
Secret key, 425
Secret words, shared, 147
Secure Electronic Transactions (SET),
655
Secure Hash Algorithm (SHA), 637
Secure Object-Oriented Database
(SODA) model, 308
Secure Socket Layer (SSL), 279, 435,
639–640, 655
SecurID, 600
Security
administrative, Social Engineering
and, 64
administrator, 42
analyst, 42
awareness
characteristics of, 71
evaluation of, 69
goal of, 54
obstacles, 71
training, importance of, 1
chain, 57
clearances, 355
domain, 196, 197
evaluation criteria, 127
exception, 279
functionality, 132
goals, 326–327
incidents, 709
kernel, 116, 117, 290, 291, 343
logical, Social Engineering and, 64
logon, 595
Management Practices, Topics, and
Methodologies, 72–73
models, 81, 103
multi-level, 103
network traffic, 595
objectives, 132
by obscurity, 229
perimeter, 117

physical, Social Engineering and, 64
policy
    definition of, 82
    multi-level, 202
    ratings, profiles for commercial, 135
    reviews, 364
    simple, 105
    target, 132
Security architecture and models,
    79–145
    assurance, trust, and confidence
        mechanisms, 127–137
    certification and accreditation,
        136–137
    Common Criteria, 134–136
    Information Technology Security
        Evaluation Criteria, 131–134
    Trusted Computer Security
        Evaluation Criteria, 129–130
    Trusted Network Interpretation,
        131
    common body of knowledge,
        139–142
    components, 139–140
    examples, 140–142
    expectation, 139
    defining security architecture, 80–81
    information protection
        environment, 81–114
    enterprise architecture, 101–103
    network environment, 97–100
    platform architecture, 82–97
    security models, 103–114
    information protection and
        management services,
        137–139
    information protection
        requirements, 81
    sample questions for CISSP exam,
        142–144
    security technology and tools,
        114–126
    application layer protection, 124
    CPU and input/output device
        protection, 122–124
    memory protection, 121–122
    network protection, 125–126
    operating system protection,
        115–120

    platform protection, 114
    storage device protection,
        124–125
Security Assertion Markup Language
    (SAML), 247, 251
Security environments, types of,
    99–100
    compartmentalized security mode,
        100
    controlled mode, 100
    dedicated security mode, 99
    multi-level security mode, 100
    system high-security mode, 99–100
Security Services Technical Committee
    (SSTC), 251
Security technology and tools
    access control systems and
        methodology
        access to data, 199–205
        access to system, 165–172
        biometric devices, 181–184
        centralized access control
            methodologies, 184–190
        decentralized/distributed access
            control methodologies,
            190–198
        definition of controls, 164–165
        synchronous tokens, 172–181
    applications and systems
        development
        assemblers, compilers, and
            interpreters, 274–289
        DBMS controls, 304–312
        including security in Systems
            Development Method,
            265–273
        programming languages,
            273–274, 289–290
        software protection
            mechanisms, 290–304
        System Development Methods,
            258–264
        system life cycle and systems
            development, 257–258
    Business Continuity Planning
        BCP creation, 669–670
        business impact analysis,
            672–679

plan development and
implementation, 691–698
project management and
initiation, 670–672
recovery strategies, 679–691
testing, maintenance, awareness,
and training, 698
cryptography
asymmetric key cryptography
algorithms, 414–423
basic concepts of cryptography,
396–403
encryption systems, 403–408
message integrity controls,
423–426
symmetric key cryptography
algorithms, 408–414
information security management
implementation (delivery)
options, 68–69
information classification, 33–37
policies, procedures, standards,
baselines, guidelines, 48–54
risk analysis and assessment,
20–29
law, investigations and ethics
ethics, 765
investigation, 734–754
law, 731
operations security
data and media, 348–353
hardware controls, 342
operation controls, 346–348
physical areas, 355
software controls, 343–345
support systems, 354
telecommunications equipment,
353–354
physical security
building entry points, 481–489
building floors, office suites,
offices, 489–496
layered defense, 464–466
penetration (intrusion) detection
systems, 496–504
perimeter and building grounds
boundary protection,
466–481
security architecture and models

application layer protection, 124
CPU and input/output device
protection, 122–124
memory protection, 121–122
network protection, 125–126
operating system protection,
115–120
platform protection, 114
storage device protection,
124–125
telecommunications, network, and
Internet security
centralized authentication and
administration servers,
599–617
content filtering and inspection,
626
controlling data access, 594–595
firewalls and perimeter security,
617–626
intrusion detection, 627–650
logon security, 595
physical security, 594
problems addressed, 593–594
securing network traffic, 595–599
Self-Contained Breathing Apparatus
(SCBA) equipment, 492
Separation of duties, 6, 38, 49, 438
definition of, 149
integrity and, 108
Sequence checking, recording of, 126
Server(s)
access, 257
application proxy, 618
bootup sequence, 367
centralized authentication, 599
DNS, 573
Kerberos, 615, 616
network address, hijacking of, 334
room security, 500
Service
bureaus, 687
Component Reference Model, 102
level management, 327
Set Identifier (SSID), 537
SESAME, 195, 196, 617
SET, see Secure Electronic
Transactions
Sexual harassment, 68

SGML, *see* Standard Generalized
    Markup Language
SHA, *see* Secure Hash Algorithm
Shared environments, threats to, 98
Shareware, downloading of from
    Internet, 72
Shatterproof fallacy, 759
Shoulder surfing, 154
Simple Mail Transfer Protocol (SMTP),
    556
Simple Network Management Protocol
    (SNMP), 574
Simple security, 105
Single loss expectancy (SLE), 10, 11, 13
Single Sign-On (SSO), 218
    advantages of, 190
    auditing capability, enterprisewide,
        192
    disadvantages of, 191
SirCam, 233
SLE, *see* Single loss expectancy
Smalltalk, 262
Smart card, 176
    microprocessor chips in, 177
    value of, 178
SMTP, *see* Simple Mail Transfer
    Protocol
Smurfing, 155, 158, 159
Snail mail, 727
Sniffers, 8, 154, 164, 354
SNMP, *see* Simple Network
    Management Protocol
Snort, 208
Social engineering, 8, 57, 154, 238
    attack(s), 60, 61
        human nature and, 59
        securing against, 65
    best method of preventing, 300
    business environment and, 59
    defining, 58
    intelligence gathering and, 60
    protection against, 63
    readiness testing, 66
    risk mitigation, 62
    success of, 59
    target selection, 60
Social Security, 5
SOCKS, 619

SODA model, *see* Secure Object-
    Oriented Database model
Soft tokens, 175
Software
    access control of, 39
    anti-virus, 301, 340
    application, 226
    attacks, 179
    classified information and, 39
    client, 433
    controls, 343
    criteria in secure, 313
    description of, 331
    development
        ad-hoc, 259
        cleanroom, 263
        iterative, 260
        methods, primary approaches,
            258
        waterfall method, 259
    encryption, 125, 503
    engineering, 258
    environment, threats to, 230
    isolation, 122
    Kerberos client, 194
    open source, 229, 396
    operating system, 83
    password-cracking, 172
    shared, 314
    signaling, 524
Software Engineering Institute
    Capability Maturity Model
    for Software, 263
Software protection mechanisms, 290
    backup controls, 300
    covert channel controls, 295
    cryptography, 296
    inadequate granularity of controls,
        297
    malicious code/malware controls,
        301
    memory protection, 294
    mobile code controls, 302
    password protection techniques,
        297
    processor privilege states, 291
    programming language support, 304
    sandbox, 303
    security kernels, 290, 291

social engineering, 300
TOC/TOU, 300
virus protection controls, 301
Software Publisher's Association (SPA), 760
Solution provider, 43
SPA, *see* Software Publisher's Association
SPAM, 626
Spiral model, 262
Spoofing, 154, 612
Spying, 154
SQL, *see* Structured Query Language
SSID, *see* Service Set Identifier
SSL, *see* Secure Socket Layer
SSO, *see* Single Sign-On
SSTC, *see* Security Services Technical Committee
Standard Generalized Markup Language (SGML), 276
Standard of Good Practices, 329
Standards, definition of, 51
Stateful inspection firewall, 619
State machine models, 110
Station authentication, 540
Storage
    channel, 152
    device(s)
        examples of common, 96–97
        protection, 124
        types of, 96
Stream cipher(s)
    attacks, 391
    block ciphers versus, 397
Structured Query Language (SQL), 245
Sun Microsystems Network Information Service, 607
Support systems, 336, 354
Surge suppressors, 489
Surveillance, 456
SVCs, *see* Switched virtual circuits
Swapping, 92
SW-CMM, *see* Capability Maturity Model for Software
Switched virtual circuits (SVCs), 525
Symmetric block cipher attacks, 391
Symmetric key cryptography
    algorithms, 408
    cipher block chaining, 411

cipher feedback, 410
DES, 408, 409
double-DES and triple-DES, 412
electronic code book, 411
IDEA, 413
output feedback, 410
RC5, 413
RC6, 414
Rijndael algorithm, 412
Sympathy attacks, 61
Synchronous DRAM (SDRAM), 90
Synchronous tokens, 172, 174
SYN flooding, 155, 160, 161
SysKey, 170
System
    administrator privileges, 338
    cold start, 346
    Development Methods (SDMs), 258, *see also* Systems development method, including security in
    events/audit reports, 361
    high policy, 202
    infector, 233
    reboot, 346
    shutdown, forcing of, 334
System Development Life Cycle (SDLC), 227, 259, 344
Systems development method, including security in, 265
    acceptance, 270
    build/development and documentation, 267
    documentation and common program controls, 269
    functional requirements definition, 266
    operations and maintenance support, 272
    project initiation, 265
    revisions and system replacement, 273
    system design specifications, 267
    testing and evaluation controls, 271
    transition to production, 272

T

Table locking, 305
TACACS, 187, 599, 603
   Accounting, 188
   Authentication, 188
   Authorization, 188
Tailgating, 470
Tangible assets, 25
Targeted data mining, 154
Target of Evaluation (TOE), 132
TCB, *see* Trusted computing base
TCP, *see* Transmission Control
   Protocol
TCP/IP, *see* Transmission Control
   Protocol/Internet Protocol
TCSEC, *see* Trusted Computer System
   Evaluation Criteria
TDMA, *see* Time Division Multiple
   Access
Technical Reference Model, 102
Telecommunications, network, and
   Internet security, 515–662
   assurance, trust, and confidence
      mechanisms, 650–654
      audit trails, 650–651
      security reviews, 651–653
      vulnerability assessments,
         653–654
   common body of knowledge,
      655–658
   information protection
      environment, 516–593
      data networks, 516–550
      network protocols, 551–578
      network threats and attacks,
         578–593
      remote access services, 550–551
   information protection and
      management services,
      654–655
   information protection
      requirements, 516
   sample questions for CISSP exam,
      658–661
   security technology and tools,
      593–650

      centralized authentication and
         administration servers,
         599–617
      content filtering and inspection,
         626
      controlling data access, 594–595
      firewalls and perimeter security,
         617–626
      intrusion detection, 627–650
      logon security, 595
      physical security, 594
      problems addressed, 593–594
      securing network traffic, 595–599
Telefonica, 233
Telnet proxy, 619
TEMPEST equipment, emanations and,
   152
Terminate and Stay Resident (TSR)
   programs, 95, 121
Terrorist
   attacks, 453
   countries, 396
TGS, *see* Ticket Granting Service
TGT, *see* Ticket Granting Ticket
Thin clients, 197
Threat(s), 13
   analysis, 15, 24
   buffer overflows, 151
   categories of, 151
   covert channel, 151
   data remanence, 152
   dumpster driving, 152
   eavesdropping, 152
   emanations, 152
   event, 9
   hackers, 152
   impersonation, 152
   internal intruders, 152
   malicious code, 161
   man-made, 453
   man-in-the-middle attacks, 153
   mobile code, 153
   natural, 453
   object reuse, 153
   password, 154, 163
   physical access, 154
   political events, 453
   risk models, 30
   shared environment, 98

shoulder surfing, 154
sniffers, 154
social engineering, 154
software environment, 230
spoofing, 154
spying, 154
supply systems, 453
targeted data mining, 154
transmission, 155
trapdoor, 154
tunneling, 155
types of, 151, 330
Ticket Granting Service (TGS), 193
Ticket Granting Ticket (TGT), 187, 193, 194
Time bombs, 161
Time of check/time of use (TOC/TOU), 87, 118, 238, 257
Time Division Multiple Access (TDMA), 550
Timestamping, 430, 433
Timing channels, 152, 231
T1 line, 543, 642
TLS, *see* Transport Layer Security
TNI, *see* Trusted network interpretation
TOC/TOU, *see* Time of check/time of use
TOE, *see* Target of Evaluation
Token(s)
    asynchronous, 175
    clock-based, 172–173
    counter-based, 172, 173–174
    passing, 529
    soft, 175
    synchronous, 172, 174
Token Ring, 531
TPs, *see* Transformation Procedures
Tracing calls, 67
Trademark, 719
Trade secret, 719
Traffic
    shaping, 649
    sniffers, 231
Transformation Procedures (TPs), 108, 109
Transmission
    error correction, 126
    integrity, 126

logging, 126
threats, 155
Transmission Control Protocol (TCP), 565
    connections, 648
    header, 568, 569
    session, persistence of, 438
Transmission Control Protocol/Internet Protocol (TCP/IP), 551, 558, 655
    applications, distributed database used by, 572
    header, 296
    traffic, 518
Transport Layer Security (TLS), 279, 640
Trapdoors, 154, 238, 333, 345, 401, 416
Traverse-mode noise, 461
Triage, 746
Trojan horse, 4, 156, 161, 590
    definition of, 162, 235
    programming of, 8
Trusted Computer System Evaluation Criteria (TCSEC), 73, 99, 129, 291
Trusted computing base (TCB), 115, 116, 135, 290
Trusted network interpretation (TNI), 131, 657
Trusted recovery, 329, 371
Trusted system, definition of, 116
TSR programs, *see* Terminate and Stay Resident programs
Tunneling, 155

U

UBR, *see* Unspecified Bit Rate
UCE, *see* Unsolicited commercial email
UDIs, *see* Unconstrained Data Items
UDP, *see* User Datagram Protocol
UID, *see* Universal ID
UL, *see* Underwriters Laboratory
Unauthorized access, attempting, 652
Unauthorized user activity, 7
Unconstrained Data Items (UDIs), 108
Underwriters Laboratory (UL), 504

UNEP, *see* United Nations Environment
    Programme
Uninterruptible power supply (UPS),
    342, 490, 682
United Nations, 712
    Agreements, 731
    Environment Programme (UNEP),
       495
United States controls, cryptography,
    395
Universal ID (UID), 300
Unix
    Network File System, 567
    Network Information Service, 589
    passwords, 615
    processor access modes, 292
Unprotected downloaded files, 7
Unrestricted crypto source code, 396
Unsolicited commercial email (UCE),
    626
Unspecified Bit Rate (UBR), 547
UPS, *see* Uninterruptible power supply
U.S. Computer Fraud and Abuse Act,
    723
U.S. Department of Defense (DoD), 129
    security policy for, 103
    Trusted Computer Security
       Evaluation Criteria, 129
User
    behavior, spot checks of, 69
    clearance, 115
    Datagram Protocol (UDP), 567, 568
    education, 50
    ID, 165, 652
       administrative, 42
       guidelines for, 167
       most common type of, 166
       security policy based on, 192
    interfaces, constrained, 204
    -known authentication, most
       common type of, 168
    -level privilege, 293
    manager, 41
    masquerading as authorized, 152
    -mode program, 292
    training, 351
U.S. Federal Criteria, 134
U.S. Federal Privacy Act, 722, 724
U.S. Federal Rules of Evidence, 738

U.S. Government mail, irradiated, 450
U.S. Office of Management and Budget
    Federal Enterprise
    Architecture Program
    Management Office, 102

V

Value-added networks (VANs), 517, 519
Vandalism, 697
VANs, *see* Value-added networks
Variable Bit Rate (VBR), 547
VBR, *see* Variable Bit Rate
Vehicular gates, 469, 470
Vendor service personnel, 357
Verifier, 278
VeriSign™, 287
Vigenere cipher, 406, 407
Violation(s)
    analysis, 367
    reports, 211
    tracking, 362
    types of, 362
Virtual circuits, 525
Virtual memory, 92
Virtual private network (VPN), 184,
    551, 635, 656
Virus(es), 161
    boot sector, 233
    checking, 40
    defense of writing computer, 759
    definition of, 232
    email, 233
    file-infecting, 232
    Lehigh, 233
    macro, 234
    methods for detecting, 301
    multipartite, 233
    protection controls, 301
    rumors of, 162
    script, 233, 234
    spreading of, 162
Visual Basic, 230, 250, 262
Visual programming languages, 280
Voice-over-Frame Relay, 550
Voice recognition systems, 166
Volume labels, human-readable, 352
VPN, *see* Virtual private network

Vulnerability(ies), 13
  analysis, 15, 27
  assessment, 653
  building entry points, 464
  certification, 137
  cryptographic functions, 378
  database, 255
  HVAC systems, 462
  multiprogramming system, 87
  personnel, 339
  qualitative statement of, 12
  scanning, 580
  test, 505
  write-down, 104

W

Wall structures, security and, 467
WAN, *see* Wide area network
WAP, *see* Wireless Application Protocol
Wardialing, 581
War driving, 533
Warm site, 685
Wassenaar Arrangement, 394
Waterfall life cycle model, 259
W3C, *see* World Wide Web Consortium
Weak keys, 391
Web
  browser, Java, 278, 279
  security, 257
  sites, poorly thought-out, 60
Welfare system, 5
WEP, *see* Wired Equivalent Privacy
What-if analysis, 20, 29
White-hat hacker, 152
Wide area network (WAN), 516, 517, 518
  devices, 548
  internetworking devices for, 541
  modem dial-up, 542
  point-to-point link through, 543
Windows 2000, processor access
      modes, 292

Windows NT operating system, 137,
      170
Wired Equivalent Privacy (WEP), 538
Wireless Application Protocol (WAP),
      549
Wireless LAN (WLAN), 522, 532
Wireless Markup Language (WML),
      251, 549
Wireless technologies, 516
WLAN, *see* Wireless LAN
WML, *see* Wireless Markup Language
Workstation security, 594
World Wide Web (WWW), 519, *see also*
      Web
World Wide Web Consortium (W3C),
      204, 250
WORM, *see* Write-Once Read Memory
Worm, definition of, 162, 234
Write-down
  controlling of, 105
  vulnerability, 104
Write-Once Read Memory (WORM), 96
WWW, *see* World Wide Web

X

Xerox Network Systems (XNS)
      networks, 576
XML, *see* eXtensible Markup Language
XNS networks, *see* Xerox Network
      Systems networks

Y

Yahoo!, 157

Z

Zachman Framework, 101
Zero-knowledge attack, 215
Zombie, 156